THE AMERICAN WEST

THE AMERICAN WEST

LARRY SCHWEIKART
AND
BRADLEY J. BIRZER

A Wiley Desk Reference

John Wiley & Sons, Inc.

Produced by New England Publishing Associates, Inc.
President: Elizabeth Frost-Knappman
Vice President: Edward W. Knappman
Staff: Ron Formica, Kristine Schiavi, Victoria Harlow

Design and Production: Ron Formica
Copy Editor: Phil Saltz
Proofreading: Elizabeth D. Crawford of Miccinello Associates

Schweikart, Larry.
   The Americn West / Larry Schweikart, Bradley J. Birzer.
    p.   cm.
   Includes bibliographical references.
   ISBN: 0-471-40138-2 (acid-free paper)
   1. West (U.S.)—Civilization—Encyclopedias. 2. West (U.S.)—History—Encyclopedias.
   I. Birzer, Bradley J., date– II. Title.
   F591.S38 2002
   978'.003—dc21   2002032395

Printed in the United States of America

10 9 8 7 6 5 4 3 2 1

Contents

PART III **From Lewis and Clark to the Pony Express (1803–1861)** **124**

Select Bibliography 519

Acknowledgments

W e take this opportunity to express our gratitude to many individuals who made this volume possible. Although most of the entries were written by Larry Schweikart, Bradley J. Birzer, and Dedra McDonald Birzer, several authors contributed material to many of the entries, and we gladly cite their assistance at the end of the acknowledgments. Cynthia King of the University of Dayton provided monumental word-processing support, and in many ways this is as much her volume as ours. Ron Acklin, map maker *extraordinaire* at the University of Dayton's Print and Design shop, drew marvelous maps that enhanced the volume. Several students performed research for the project, including Julia Cupples, Brian Rogan, and Nick Brown. The entire office staffs of the University of Dayton history department and the Hillsdale College Mossey Library rendered timely and important assistance, most notably Jennifer Dwyer, Linda Moore, and Judy Leising. Thanks also to Professor Janet Bednarek, the chair of UD's history department, Dean Paul Mormon, and Provost John Geiger (now retired), all of whom contributed funding assistance.

Leroy Eid, the "western" historian at the University of Dayton, graciously proofread early versions of many of the entries and saved us from innumerable errors. Likewise, Don Porrier, an antique gun enthusiast, helped us with important information on early western firearms and gave us photographs of frontier weapons. Thanks to Lynne Doti, professor of economics at Chapman University, for her picture of the Bodie, California, bank vault; Crystal Cathedral and Crenshaw Christian Center for the photos of their beautiful sanctuaries; and the staff members of the Library of Congress photo division for timely work despite terrorist acts of September 11, 2001, that virtually shut down their operations at about the time they received our orders. Our editing team of Chip Rossetti at John Wiley & Sons and Ed and Elizabeth Knappman and their fine associates at New England Publishing deserve praise for improving the prose, spotting the errors, and cleaning up our messes. Nevertheless, we alone bear responsibility for any errors of fact or interpretation that remain.

All entries were written by Larry Schweikart, Bradley J. Birzer, and Dedra McDonald Birzer, with the following exceptions, all of which were written by Larry Schweikart, with:

Rodney Carlisle (aerospace industry in the West, Alamogordo, George H. W. Bush, Lyndon Johnson, Lawrence Livermore National Laboratory, Richard Nixon, and Sandia)

Noel Holstein (the "western" on television)

Ron Irwin (commercial fishing in the West, cowboy poetry, Louis L'Amour, Lyndon B. Johnson Space Center, military base closures in the West, Larry McMurtry, New Age movement in the West, petroleum (oil) industry in the West)

Elizabeth Frost-Knappman (Barbara Charlene Jordan, Sandra Day O'Connor, Jeanette Pickering Rankin, Dixie Lee Ray, Patricia Scott Schroeder)

Rachel Kranz (Texas Instruments)

Dan Nesbitt (skiing, tourism development in the West)

Lisa Paddock (Amy Tan)

Carl Rollyson (Beats)

Tom Smith (Bakersfield Sound, chili cookoffs, John Denver, El Teatro Campesino, Japanese internment in World War II, Lubbock and the sound of west Texas, H. Ross Perot, Monty Roberts, Selena, surf music, western swing dancing, and Womens Professional Rodeo Association)

Orla Swift (Ansel Adams, Sundance Institute)

Larry Schweikart
Bradley J. Birzer

THE AMERICAN WEST

Introduction

C owboys, Indians, miners, trappers, farmers, ranchers, and "sodbusters"—these are images people normally associate with the American West, and rightly so. Likewise, the first names that come to mind generally might be "Buffalo Bill" Cody, Sitting Bull, Wyatt Earp, Annie Oakley, Geronimo, Davy Crockett, or maybe even John Wayne or Clint Eastwood. But as much as these are accurate symbols and figures that characterize the West, the true American frontier began with the arrival of Europeans to North America and Mexico in the 1500s and spread steadily toward the Pacific Ocean. Over the ensuing 500 years, the West indeed included such characters as Crazy Horse, Daniel Boone, and Jim Bowie, but it also included important individuals such as A. P. Giannini, Sam Walton, Walt Disney, and Samuel Colt in business; Lyndon Baines Johnson, Jeannette Pickering Rankin, Richard Nixon, William Jennings Bryan, and both George H. W. and George W. Bush in politics; and Albert Bierstadt, Frederick Remington, Larry McMurtry, Willa Cather, the Beach Boys, Los Lobos, and Johnny Cash in art, literature, and music.

For every famous western gunfighter, there was an equally important inventor, and for every well-known Indian battle, there was an important—but sometimes obscure—government agency. The natural tendency to associate earlier periods with "history" has thus tended to limit encyclopedias and general surveys of the West to the frontier period, or at least to mid-20th century. Yet as the 21st century is already well underway, it is time for the newer western monuments—the Crystal Cathedral and FaithDome in California, the Space Needle in Seattle, or the Astrodome to take their place among the revered images of earlier generations, such as Mount Rushmore and the Alamo.

This encyclopedia embraces and incorporates entries from the *whole* of "western" history, from the Spanish, French, and English explorers to the early land speculators and fur trappers, through the 19th century railroaders and miners, to the social activists and entertainment icons of modern times. It is divided into five sections (acknowledging that any separation of history into periods is problematic and risks misplacement of entries): Exploration, up to about 1700 when most of the European powers had established colonies in the New World; European Ascension, up to 1803 when the size of the young United States doubled through the Louisiana Purchase; American Expansion, up to the beginning of the American Civil War; The Far West Frontier, up to 1893 when Frederick Jackson Turner announced that the "frontier" was closed; and The Modern Era, from 1893 to the present. For the reader's convenience, cross-referenced entries will appear in bold the first time they appear in the text of an entry. If the bolded cross-reference refers to an entry from a different section of the book, its location will be identified with the section number in brackets; otherwise, the cross-reference will simply appear in bold.

Instead of entry references, we have included an extensive bibliography. But that by no means contains all the sources used in the research, which was greatly facilitated by the Internet. Numerous excellent western web sites exist at the click of a mouse—perhaps it is appropriate that even this contribution to technology came from some of the subjects of our entries, Apple Computers, Intel, and Microsoft, all of which are western-based companies.

Our purpose has been to present the entire panorama of the West, not just the caricature of the "cowboy" West captured on celluloid, or, perhaps, digital CDs. But those silver screen images and portraits of western life that are so prominent in American culture are another type of "West" and no less important in their own right. Thus, we have included popular western television stars and shows, well-known country and western musicians, and famous movies or big-screen personalities. Unlike other encyclopedias, however, we have also sought to include appropriate modern entries: religious movements and key individuals, such as the Azusa Street Revival and Aimee Semple McPherson; businesses that originated in the West, such as Amazon.com, Starbucks, and Douglas Aircraft; music, art, and literature of the 20th century, such as the Lubbock and Grunge sounds, western writers such as Louis L'Amour and Zane Grey, and a wide range of Native American authors and poets; and popular tourist sites or places of historic interest to the modern world, such as Los Alamos, Hoover Dam, Disneyland, and Yellowstone National Park. Such a broad definition of the West, we hope, will provide a more appropriate panorama of the cultural, political, and economic contributions of that nebulous and continually changing part of America called . . . the West.

PART I

From Prehistory to Early European Explorations (?–ca. 1700)

Just as the Supreme Court was famous for knowing what "pornography" was—but was hard pressed to define it—"westerners" know what "the West" is. Historians, however, seem to have difficulty determining what constitutes the West. Journals such as the *Journal of Southern History* and *Western Historical Quarterly* cannot agree on whether Texas is west or south. One of the difficulties in trying to define the West is that the line of demarcation has steadily moved . . . west.

Indeed, the West came from a strong push by Europeans to explore and establish commercial ties with the "East." Christopher Columbus—at least, according to most historians—thought he was en route to China and remained convinced for many years that he had found Cathay. So, somewhat quickly, "east" became "west," and the New World that Columbus encountered (discovered, as far as Europeans were concerned) immediately became a frontier. Spanish explorers spread out into Mexico, the southeastern corner of North America, and Central America, while French expeditions made their way into Canada and upper North America. English settlers soon followed on the Atlantic seaboard. Although most of those who arrived came for one of three reasons—"God, Glory, or Gold"— virtually all who crossed the ocean had multiple motivations. Certainly after the initial waves of *conquistadores* and missionaries, many arrived seeking little more than the liberty to pursue their own lives or religions with a minimum of interference from the state, or even to obtain land— something denied them in Europe.

After an initial wave of seafaring Spanish explorers, expeditions led by Hernán Cortés, Francisco Vásquez de Coronado, Francisco Alvarado, Hernando de Soto, Ponce de Leon, and others fanned out across the southern part of the new continent. Under Coronado, the Spanish established a base on the Rio Grande, then moved through the southwestern part of North America, while Juan Rodríguez Cabrillo sailed up the Pacific seaboard. These adventurers and those who followed engaged in exploration, planted cities, and conquered native tribes. In the process came tales of individual resilience, none better than Cabeza de Vaca, whose capture and escape made for a remarkable story. They were accompanied by missionaries, including Fray Marcos de Niza and Bartolomé de Las Casas, who took up the cause of the native peoples.

As the Spanish searched for cities of gold, Jacques Cartier, Samuel de Champlain, and other French explorers penetrated the northern tier of North America, establishing fur trading outposts. The French had a different strategy for conquest, hoping to make the Indians commercial partners and allies rather than subjugated peoples—although they had no compunction about crushing native opposition when they encountered it. By limiting their immigration to the New World, however, the French unwittingly ceded an important advantage to the British, who were latecomers in the exploration game.

Both the Spanish and the French utilized the Catholic Church to enhance their empires. Franciscans, Jesuits, and Dominicans accompanied the soldiers, and in some cases preceded them. Although the church and the state frequently intertwined and occasionally clashed, most of the time each benefited from the other: missionaries provided reports on geography, flora and fauna, and Indian tribes, while the state established bases of support and, eventually, trade that the church used to encourage Indians to adopt the ways of Christian Europeans. French missionaries, such as Father Jacques Marquette, reached as far as the Missouri River, extending French influence deep into the interior of North America. Spanish missionaries helped stabilize the system of *encomienda* and *repartimiento* that placed native workers in the hands of Spanish settlers as virtual serfs. This was an extraction economy (i.e., one that dug or mined silver and gold out of the ground) that did little to encourage entrepreneurship or participation by the "consumers" and it soon found itself struggling, despite the vast wealth of the Mexican gold and silver mines. The oppressive control of the Spanish also produced its share of revolts. The Pueblo Revolt in 1680 under a Pueblo chief named Popé followed the Church's attempts to eliminate Indian religious rituals. As a result of the revolt, the Spanish had to temporarily leave the province, only to return later in force to reoccupy Santa Fe. This time, they treated their subjects better, and even won the alliance of the Pueblos against other tribes.

English settlers were not far behind the French, arriving in the early 1600s all along the Atlantic coast. At Jamestown, Plymouth, and Massachusetts Bay, the English quickly discovered none of the precious metals that had rewarded the Spanish explorers, nor the rich fur trading areas that had benefitted the French. Instead—although few knew it at the time—they had found something more important: a rich, diverse land that could support not only almost every variety of agriculture but also excellent natural harbors that encouraged the development of trade and commerce. Where the French discouraged settlement, the English subsidized it. Where the Spanish held firm to mercantilist notions of wealth that discouraged innovation, British Americans embraced a new entrepreneurial spirit that fostered private property rights, competition, and the sanctity of contract.

Each group of Europeans dealt with the numerous Indian tribes they encountered in different ways. Spaniards enlisted other Indian allies to help defeat the powerful Aztecs, then organized their land-holding system around the subjugation of Native Americans. The French, encountering Iroquois, Mohawk, Huron, Fox, and other North American tribes, engaged in a thriving fur trade that viewed Indians as sources of supply. While this proved generally less intrusive on Indian culture than the Spanish strategy—even to the point that many tribes sided with the French well into the late 1700s—the reliance on the fur trade stifled settlement and farming, and really only postponed dealing with the natives to a later time. Meanwhile, the policy ensured that New France would soon be eclipsed by the English colonies just as New Spain was.

British America had both fought and negotiated with Indians. The mere contact with Europeans led to an exchange of diseases—particularly smallpox—that devastated many tribes. Of course, the reverse was also true: North American diseases struck the European settlers with a fury, such as at Jamestown, where only half the first group of settlers survived at the end of two seasons. Ultimately, the British concept of property rights, which was more developed than that of either Spain or France, proved to be the critical dividing line. Many tribes did not accept private property in the European sense, making treaties meaningless. Other difficulties occurred when the English mistakenly presumed that self-proclaimed native "leaders" indeed spoke for the entire tribe. Then there was old-fashioned greed, which led to no end of conflict.

Several wars, even when they resulted in temporary Native American victories, such as Popé's rebellion, produced massive retaliation that eventually led to the Indians' defeat. From the Aztecs to the Pamunkeys, the Indians demonstrated a consistent inability to organize the numerous tribes into effective units of resistance, and whites learned that Indians often viewed their worst enemies as other Indians. A steady string of treaties pushed back the line separating English from Native Americans, but even limiting new settlement past that demarcation proved no small challenge to royal authorities. In addition, British Americans constantly harbored concerns that both the French and the Spanish were engaged in fomenting rebellion on the frontier, adding to the distrust and suspicion.

Europeans had their own conflicts, which spilled over into the New World as well. Spanish settlement had constantly been hampered by pirate attacks from the "sea dogs" like Sir Francis Drake. English pirates were welcomed into British ports, where they could refit, so long as they directed their activities against Spanish vessels and towns. The impact of piracy on Spanish settlement—not to mention the horrific regular losses of ships and people to hurricanes—cannot be overstated and dampened the growth of New Spain.

By the time the European powers engaged in a truly worldwide struggle, England's settlements in the New World had become substantial but still remained disparate colonies, each with its own royal governor and laws. The diversification of the colonies included religions, languages, and

Southwestern badlands, known as the Bisti Badlands, are located in northwestern New Mexico on the Navajo Reservation. Today the Bureau of Land Management manages its 4,000 acres. *Bradley J. Birzer*

ethnic origin, as well as condition of servitude (African slaves were admitted to Virginia in 1619). Already, however, the frontier mentality had been established. Pioneers constantly prodded westward from British America, southwest from New France, and northwest from New Spain. The Mississippi was explored and mapped; expeditions traversed modern-day Kansas and Nebraska; and Spanish sailors on the Pacific Coast bumped into Russians near modern-day Oregon. The frontier mentality—explore, conquer, tame, build—had already characterized the West.

CHRONOLOGY   From Prehistory to Early European Explorations

1492–1504	*Columbus's four voyages*
1494	*Treaty of Tordesillas*
ca. 1500	*Final demise of Mississippian and Hopewellian Indian cultures*
1519–1521	*Cortés conquers Mexico*
1528–1536	*Cabeza de Vaca's journey*
1534	*Cartier's expedition to the St. Lawrence*
1540–1541	*Coronado expedition in northern Mexico, the North American Southwest*
1512–1539	*Spanish explorers de Léon, Nárvaez, and de Soto explore Florida and the southeastern part of North America*
1565	*St. Augustine (Florida) settled by Spanish*
1585–1587	*Roanoke Island (Carolinas) colony fails*
1598	*El Paso founded by Juan de Oñate*
1607	*Jamestown (Virginia) founded*
1607	*Pocahontas rescues John Smith*
1608–1701	*Mourning Wars*
1620	*Pilgrims found Plymouth (Massachusetts)*
1629	*Puritan migration to Massachusetts*
1635–1636	*Pequot Indian War (Massachusetts)*
1664	*English conquer New Netherlands (New York)*
1673	*Marquette and Jolliet lead an expedition down the Mississippi*
1675–1676	*King Phillip's (Metacomet's) War (Massachusetts)*
1676	*Bacon's Rebellion (Virginia)*

Ácoma

Ácoma, a Pueblo village west of Albuquerque, stands on top of a steep, 357-foot-high mesa and remains the longest occupied village in North America. Founded in 1100 by the *Anasazi* Indians, it maintains much of its traditional culture, having changed little in the past 900 years. Some scholars argue that it is as old as 1,400 years, dating back to A.D. 600. The coma *kiva* is one of the longest used in the American Southwest.

adobe

The absence of abundant wood and stone in parts of the West and Southwest led Indians and early settlers to use the earth to provide materials for shelter in the form of adobe. Made by mixing clay with water, grass, plant roots, straw, or almost any other bonding material, placed in a brick-sized mold, and baked to rock hardness in the sun, adobe proved strong enough for Indians and white settlers to construct an entire dwelling. Adobe brick structures range from small, boxlike abodes to large ceremonial houses with multiple stories. Europeans had also seen adobe construction brought to Spain by the Moors, and had some familiarity with the construction techniques.

Adobe Indian sites have been uncovered in New Mexico, Colorado, Utah, and Arizona, with a five-story adobe pueblo house in Taos, New Mexico, remaining as an example of the solid structure provided by this sun-baked clay brick. Some of the earliest European references to adobe come from the settlement by Don Juan de *Oñate* at Yunque in 1598, where Spanish settlers took possession of Indian huts. Those early houses lacked windows and doors; entry was made through a hole in the thatched roof. As a result, these pueblos were stifling and hot, and filled with smoke from cooking.

While Indians did not hesitate to put up multiple-story dwellings, Spanish settlers tended to build long, single-story houses around a courtyard. Adobe bricks were 10 inches by 18 inches by 5 inches, weighing 50 to 60 pounds, with walls constructed of adobe being about 2 feet thick. Walls were tapered so that the top of the walls would be thinner than the base. Ceilings were constructed of beams of juniper poles up to two inches in diameter, overlaid with a thatch of straw, adobe dirt, and hardened mud to make a thick surface. This roof was slightly tilted, allowing for water runoff into drainage pipes. The finished product was whitewashed, and a porch, or portal, made out of rounded posts covered by cloth or thatched skirts, ran around the outside walls to provide shade. Small windows covered with skin or sheets broke the monotony of the solid walls. Thick walls and small windows provided excellent protection during Indian or bandit raids.

Adobe style—though not materials—still dominates parts of the Southwest. Many cities in New Mexico and Arizona, using zoning ordinances, have adopted adobe-style motifs. Even where not controlled by zoning commissions, architects in the West have retained their affection for this effective and natural-looking material.

Alarcón, Hernando de (1500–?)

Born in Trujillo, Spain, Hernando de Alarcón joined the *Coronado* expedition of 1540 searching for the Seven Cities of Cibola, the mythological cities made out of gold that attracted the Spanish conquistadors. Alarcón commanded an expedition that sailed up the Gulf of California to the mouth of the Colorado River. Proceeding in two smaller boats from the main ships, Alarcón heard Indian rumors that Coronado's forces were nearby, but was unable to contact them, and Alarcón returned to his vessels.

Alarcón headed up the Colorado again, arriving at the Grand Canyon, where he erected a cross. He buried letters there, later found by Melchior *Diaz*, Coronado's lieutenant. Alarcón mapped much of the region, showing California was not an island.

Alvarado Expedition

Under the command of Francisco Vásquez de *Coronado*, Spanish forces in Mexico began to explore and conquer various parts of the American Southwest and northern Mexico. From 1540 to 1541 Coronado's lieutenants spread out to the Colorado River (under Garca Lopéz de *Cárdenas*) then, under Hernando de Alvarado, eastward toward *coma*, the "Sky City." Alvarado's expedition moved up the *Rio Grande* to Taos, New Mexico, and on its journey, the members of the expedition heard rumors of fabulous riches far to the northeast. In 1541, the expedition quartered at Tiguex, between Albuquerque and Bernalillo, New Mexico.

Anasazi

The Anasazi (meaning "the ancient ones") were one of the three most advanced pre-Columbian civilizations in North America, along with the Mesoamericans (Olmecs, Toltecs, and Aztecs) and Moundbuilders. Initial settlement of the four-corners region of what is now the American Southwest began roughly 8,000 years ago. Though originally a less advanced people, the Anasazi came into contact with more advanced civilizations from Mesoamerica, thereby transforming their entire culture. Most important for the Anasazi and their new dynamic culture was the introduction from Mexico of an early form of corn, allowing the society to increase its population and, consequently, its division of labor, leading to an increasingly complex economic, social, and cultural order. The Anasazi also mined and refined turquoise, a treasured commodity and form of currency among the ancient civilizations.

Anasazi tended to have nuclear families and live in permanent settlements. They were skilled in pottery as well as in cotton weaving, both of which would become fundamental aspects of Southwestern culture. To facilitate the immense population growth, which probably continued unabated between A.D. 300 and 1100, the Anasazi developed a complex irrigation system and canals. In addition, their most impressive creation was *Chaco Canyon*, a cultural and economic mecca.

The culture most likely reached its zenith between 1050 and 1275. In the 1270s, though, the culture began a swift collapse. Three things contributed to this downfall. First, several major droughts hit the region in the late 13th century. Already fragile ecologically, the desert had reached its breaking point. Canals and irrigation systems no longer worked as they once did in times of more precipitation. Second, nomads—the ancestors of the Apaches, Navajos, and Utes—entered the region, overrunning the higher civilization. Finally, the Mesoamericans, so closely related to Anasazi culturally and economically, entered a period of civil war, disrupting their allies to the north.

There is much speculation concerning the origins and culture of the Anasazi, and scholarship on both matters is currently in flux. Some scholars contend that the reign of the Anasazi was peaceful, based on free trade and liberal notions. Others argue equally well that it was based on terror and death cults. Recently uncovered evidence certainly suggests that the latter is true. The descendants of the Anasazi are the modern-day Pueblos.

Cabeza de Vaca, Álvar Núñez (1490–1557)

In one of the greatest tales of endurance in history, Cabeza de Vaca and three other survivors of a shipwreck in 1528 wandered the American Southwest for nearly eight years before reaching the Spanish Viceroy in 1536. Cabeza de Vaca's name literally meant "head of a cow," an honorary title handed down for service in a battle where a pass was marked with a cow's skull. He grew up not far from Cadiz, Spain, where he had doubtless seen both Magellan and Christopher Columbus come through the port.

While a teenager, Cabeza de Vaca became a soldier, and in 1527 he received an appointment as treasurer and second in command of the Pánfilo de Nárvaez expedition to Florida. The squadron in which Cabeza de Vaca sailed became separated from the Nárvaez ships and wrecked off the Texas coast, perhaps near Galveston Island. Although 80 survived the actual wreck, within a short time they were reduced to 15, then dispersed among the Indians as slaves.

Given latitude by his Indian captors, Cabeza de Vaca gained a reputation as a healer and medicine man. He also became a merchant trader, using his freedom to map the region and to plot his escape. By 1534 he and three other men, including a Moor or Arab slave, wandered near San Antonio, then headed west and southwest, crossing the Rio Grande, perhaps near modern-day New Mexico. On April 1, 1536, they reached Culiacan on the Mexican coast, having been the first to cross the North American continent. Cabeza de Vaca reported to the Viceroy, and later sent a detailed review of his long mission to the crown, called *La Relación* or, in later editions, *Los Naufragios* ("the Shipwrecked"). He remained convinced that there existed the "Seven Cities of Cibola" in Florida or southern North America, even though the appointment of Hernando **de Soto** to conduct an expedition there effectively ended his hopes of ever leading an expedition to the region. The king eventually gave Cabeza de Vaca an appointment to Rio de la Plata in 1540, but his personal tenacity in pushing his men, combined with his integrity in refusing to allow the Spanish soldiers to abuse and enslave the Indians, led to a coup by his men in 1543. Held prisoner by the Spanish government for some eight years, he was tried by the Council for the Indies, which sentenced him to exile in Africa. But the king annulled the sentence and awarded Cabeza de Vaca a pension and other honors. Cabeza de Vaca died in 1557.

IN THEIR OWN
Words

Cabeza de Vaca's *La Relación*

In 1542 Álvar Núñez Cabeza de Vaca published a narrative of his record kept during his explorations on the North American interior from 1528 to 1537. It was copied from his original letter to King Charles V of Spain and printed for the general public. After all but a handful of the members of his expedition were lost, Cabeza de Vaca became a slave of the Indians, who then considered him a healer and granted him greater liberty until his escape. Wandering from the eastern Texas coast to, ultimately, the Pacific coast of Mexico, Cabeza de Vaca, usually without bitterness, recounts the hardships he faced in the New World.

I had to stay with the Capoques [Indians] more than a year. Because of the hard work they put me to, and their harsh treatment, I resolved to flee to the people of Charruco in the forests of the main. My life had become unbearable. In addition to much other work, I had to grub roots in the water or from underground in the canebrakes. My fingers got so raw that if a straw touched them they would bleed. The broken canes often slashed my flesh; I had to work amidst them without benefit of clothes. So I set to contriving how I might transfer to the forest-dwellers, who looked more propitious. My solution was to turn to trade.

We set a time for our escape [from another tribe near San Antonio], but that same day the Indians dispersed to different locales of the cactus country. I told my comrades I would wait for them at a certain spot among the prickly pear plants until the full moon. This day I was speaking to them was the new moon, September 1. I said that if they did not appear by the time the moon was full, I would go on alone. So we parted, each going with his Indian group.

On the thirteenth day of the moon, Andres Dorantes came with Estevenico and told me

Cabrillo, Juan Rodriguez (ca. 1500–January 3, 1543)

Born in Portugal, Juan Rodriguez Cabrillo became a skilled sailor who went to Mexico in 1520 with Narvaez. He marched with *Cortés* to take Mexico City and then accompanied the expeditions south to Guatemala. After getting as far south as Panama, the sailors headed north along the

they had left Castillo with other Indians nearby, called Anagados; that they had encountered great obstacles and got lost; that tomorrow the Mariames were going to move to the place where Castillo was and unite in friendship with this tribe which held him, having heretofore been at war with them. In this way we would recover Castillo.

The thirst we had all the while we ate the pears, we quenched with their juice. We caught it in a hole we hollowed out in the ground. When the hole was full, we drank until slaked. The juice is sweet and must-colored. The Indians collect it like this for lack of vessels.

All the [Avavares and Arbadaos] Indians of this region are ignorant of time, either by the sun or moon; nor do they reckon by the month or year. They understand the seasons in terms of the ripening of fruits, the dying of fish, and the position of stars, in which dating they are adept.

The Avavares always treated us well. We lived as free agents, dug our own food, and lugged our loads of wood and water. The houses and our diet were like those of the nation we had just come from, but the Avavares suffer yet greater want, having no corn, acorns, or pecans. We always went naked like them and covered ourselves with deerskins.

Among them [the Arbadaos] we underwent fiercer hunger than among the Avavares. We ate not more than two handfuls of prickly pears a day, and they were still so green and milky they burned our mouths. In our lack of water, eating brought great thirst. At nearly the end of our endurance we bought two dogs for some nets, with other things, and a skin I used for cover.

When we saw for certain that we were drawing near the Christians, we gave thanks to God our Lord for choosing to bring us out of such a melancholy and wretched captivity. The joy we felt can only be conjectured in terms of the time, the suffering, and the peril we had endured in that land.

—SOURCE: CYCLONE COVEY, TRANSLATOR AND ANNOTATOR, *CABEZA DE VACA'S ADVENTURES IN THE UNKNOWN INTERIOR OF AMERICA [1542]* (ALBUQUERQUE, NEW MEXICO: UNIVERSITY OF NEW MEXICO PRESS, 1983 [1961]).

coast, and when *Cabeza de Vaca*'s reports came in, Cortés dispatched one of his subordinates, named Ulloa, through the peninsula of California. Cabrillo accompanied Pedro de *Alvarado* to sail northward from Guatemala in 1540. Viceroy Mendoza ordered Cabrillo to take two vessels and continue northward. Setting sail in June 1542, Cabrillo headed north, stopping at various spots along the way, discovering San Diego in September, along with Santa Catalina Island, San Pedro Bay, Santa Monica Bay, and the Santa Barbara Channel. He had injured himself in a fall at San Miguel Island, and after locating Monterey, returned to San Miguel, where illness related to his fall ended his life, on January 3, 1543. His chief pilot, Bartolemé Ferello, took over.

Canyon de Chelly

A national monument located near modern-day Chinle, Arizona, Canyon de Chelly covers 83,840 acres. The canyon itself has sheer red cliffs and its wall caves contain ruins of Indian villages built between A.D. 350 and 1300. Today *Navajo* Indians live and farm there. National monument status was authorized on April 1, 1931.

Cárdenas, García López de (1520–?)

Born to a noble family in Mexico, García López de Cárdenas migrated to Mexico, where he settled before joining the *Coronado* expedition to New Mexico as a captain from 1540 to 1542. During the expedition he displayed such bravery that he was promoted to camp master; then Coronado chose him to go with the advance guard to Cibola. There, during a battle with the Zuni Pueblo Indians, Cárdenas and Hernando *Alvarado* saved Coronado's life. Following up on reports of the Colorado River from Pedro de Tovar, Coronado dispatched Cárdenas to explore the river. Cárdenas and his party discovered the *Grand Canyon*, then spent three days searching for a trail to the river. However, even the smallest and lightest men were unable to climb to the bottom, and Cárdenas gave up the effort, returning to the *Rio Grande*, where he established a camp for the main army. During the winter, however, the Indians rose in revolt, and Cárdenas had to subdue them. The following year, Cárdenas again accompanied Coronado's expeditions, this time to Kansas. Cárdenas traveled back and forth between New Mexico and Coronado's expeditionary forces until both returned to Spain.

Cartier, Jacques (1491–September 1, 1557)

Jacques Cartier, a French explorer, launched three expeditions to North America, each of which laid France's imperial claim to significant sections of the continent. Cartier's first expedition was in 1534, funded by King Francis I. He discovered Newfoundland and the opening to the St. Lawrence River. The Frenchman explored the St. Lawrence down to the site of present-day Quebec the following year. Cartier returned to North America in 1541, but made few new discoveries. He experienced good relations with the Native Americans, most of whom, he observed, desired trade rather than war.

Chaco Canyon

Around A.D. 900, *Anasazi* leaders decided to make Chaco Canyon (in modern-day New Mexico) the economic and spiritual center of their world. They built more than 400 miles of roads leading into the canyon. Each had signal stations and police to guard against bandits. The political and economic leaders built "official" towns on the north side of the canyon, while poorer Anasazi built between 200 and 350 unplanned villages on the south side. Chaco Canyon remained an impressive monument to Anasazi ingenuity until the decline of their culture shortly before 1300.

Champlain, Samuel de (ca. 1567–December 25, 1635)

One of the earliest French explorers of the New World, Samuel de Champlain was born about 1567 in a small village near Rochefort, France. Little is known of his early life. Sailing to Spain with his uncle, he joined an expedition to the West Indies and two years later, after his return, formed an alliance with Francis Grave, Sieur du Pont (or Pontgrave), a fur trader and merchant. The two men embarked on a journey up the St. Lawrence River in 1603, although Champlain quickly separated from Pontgrave and explored up the river to modern-day Montreal.

Like other early explorers, Champlain sought a quicker and easier water route to the Far East and was convinced one lay to the south of the St. Lawrence, a land the French referred to as "Acadia" and which, by 1609, included parts of modern-day Maine. On several subsequent voyages, Champlain and other colonists resided in Acadia, where Champlain was the French agent for a trading company. In 1608 he again sailed up the St. Lawrence, founding Quebec, a French colony that would become the North American capital of New France. In addition to his own explorations, he dispatched teams westward, including one with Jean Nicolet. Sent by Champlain in 1634, Nicolet reached the Fox River and modern-day Green Bay, Wisconsin. Samuel de Champlain died on December 25, 1635, in Quebec.

chili peppers

A staple of Southwestern cooking and a mainstay of Mexican food, the chili pepper is a small, hot fruit of the *Capsaicum* species. Cooks generally use peppers in two forms, liquid and dried. Liquid peppers, such as *jalapenos*, range from 2 inches to 12 inches, are yellow or green, and can be eaten raw or squeezed for juice. Red peppers are usually mashed with tomatoes into *salsa* to provide a hot sauce for foods. Dried peppers usually are ground, then mixed into cooked dishes or sprinkled on top. Aficionados of chili peppers have developed the "Scoville Test" to determine the capsasinoid content, or the "hotness" of the pepper. The *habanero* pepper, the hottest of all peppers, has a rating of 300,000 units, while bell peppers have a rating of zero.

Columbus, Christopher (August 25 or October 31, 1451– May 20, 1506)

Christopher Columbus was an explorer, sailor, and navigator who earned the title "Admiral of the Ocean Sea." His birthplace remains in dispute. Most think he was born in 1451 in Genoa, Italy, to a weaver, Domenico Coloumbo. He learned weaving and worked in his father's wine and cheese shop, possibly studying mathematics and sciences, as well as the works of Aristotle and Duns Scotis. After his father began commercial voyages into the Mediterranean in 1474, Columbus soon went to sea with the merchant fleet, sailing in 1476 to Lisbon, then on to England. Shipwrecked following an attack by French vessels, Columbus managed to reach Portugal and learn mapmaking from his brother, Bartholomew. (Some historians believe he reached Iceland in 1477.)

Settling in Lisbon, Portugal, Columbus and Bartholomew established a reputation as map makers. In 1479 he married Doña Filipa Perestrello e Moniz, whose family lived on the island of Madeira, where he moved and entered the sugar trade. His sugar purchases took him on several voyages along the African coast as far south as Ghana. There, he heard tales of lands lying westward across the Atlantic (then known only as the "Ocean Sea"), accounts that reinforced earlier reports by Norsemen. Already, Columbus had started to conceive of a water route to the Indies, based on the travels of Marco Polo and Ptolemy. However, a number of inaccuracies had crept into his calculations for a westward voyage to Cathay (or China). Relying on Marco Polo's estimates, Columbus thought the earth smaller than it really was and had placed Japan some 1,500 miles east of Cathay. This calculation gave him a voyage of approximately 3,000—a distance that ships of the day were covering as they sailed around Africa. Columbus also thought Asia much larger than it was, putting its shoreline even closer to Europe.

Seeking financial support for a voyage, Columbus offered his plan to King John II of Portugal in 1484, but the royal cartographers found his distance estimates wildly optimistic, suggesting that the distance from Europe to Asia was 10,000 miles or more. The following year his wife died, and Columbus moved to Spain, presenting his plan to the Spanish monarchs, Ferdinand and Isabella, and again he was rejected. For several years Columbus approached several monarchs, including the Spanish a second time, for help.

Finally, in 1492, Queen Isabella of Castile, concerned that Muslims had closed off Turkish trade routes and convinced by her finance minister that the return on a small investment might be great, agreed to support Columbus with three ships. He would receive 10 percent of any profits, would be granted governorship of any uncharted islands he found, and would gain the title "Admiral of the Ocean Sea." Columbus sought riches, no doubt, but he also acted out of a deep commitment to the Christian faith and the spreading of the Gospel. A pair of mariner brothers, Martin Alonzo Pinzon and Vincente Yanez Pinzon, plus a group of Genoese merchants, contributed additional support for the voyage. The Pinzons provided three ships that would be immortalized: the *Nina*, the *Pinta*, and Columbus's flagship, the *Santa Maria*. On August 3, 1492, Columbus's expedition left Palos en route to the Canary Islands, then on September 6 sailed westward across the Atlantic.

As the trade winds pushed the small fleet along westward, Columbus navigated by "dead reckoning." Using the ship's last known position, the location of the sun (fixed by a compass), and computing speed, Columbus could estimate a location accurately. Aware that he was engaged in a daring undertaking that would probably cause some of his men to wilt as the voyage dragged on, Columbus deliberately understated the number of miles covered in his log. His suspicions about the crew proved accurate; in October, after five weeks at sea, the crew of the *Santa Maria* mutinied. Columbus prevailed upon them to be patient, and turning the fleet southwest, he sighted land on October 12, 1492. Columbus named the territory San Salvador (it was Watling Island in the Bahamas). Convinced he had made it to Asia, Columbus reasoned that the dark-skinned natives, of the Arawak tribe, were from India; hence he called them "Indians." The expedition soon sailed further south, to Cuba, which Columbus took to be China. There, he sent messengers to look, unsuccessfully, for the Great Khan.

The *Pinta* had sailed off in search of gold, and while it was away, on Christmas Eve, 1492, the *Santa Maria* was swept ashore and smashed during a storm. The crew, with the help of the Indians, rescued much of the cargo and made a fort of the wood, but Columbus's men now had only one ship left of the three that started the voyage. Columbus had failed to find precious metals but did encounter new animals and an odd leaf that Indians "smoked." Leaving some sailors in the land he called Hispaniola (today's Haiti and Dominican Republic), Columbus set sail in the *Nina* for Spain, meeting the *Pinta* en route. Finally Columbus reached Palos de Frontera in March 1493. King Ferdinand and Queen Isabella welcomed him with celebrations and bestowed upon him the title "Admiral of the Ocean Sea." The queen then commanded him to return to Hispaniola— still unaware that he had not found Asia, but an entirely new continent. He did so, in 1493, with 17 ships and 1,200 colonists, only to learn that the small party he left the previous year had been killed by Indians.

Founding a new settlement, Isabella, Columbus sailed through the Caribbean, still under the impression he was in Asia. In 1496 Bartholomew Columbus arrived in the New World and was put in charge of constructing a city on Hispaniola (present-day Santo Domingo). By then many of the colonists and Columbus himself had concluded there was no gold on the islands. Columbus tried to make profits by enslaving the Indians, a practice that the queen did not support. This delayed his next voyage for two years. Following discovery of Trinidad, then the Venezuelan coast, Columbus returned to Santo Domingo to find that his brother was under sharp criticism for mismanagement of the colony. In 1500 Columbus lost his title of governor to Francisco de Bobadilla, who had the Columbus brothers arrested and returned to Spain in irons. Isabella released him, but the admiral never regained his former position.

From 1502 to 1504 Columbus made one last voyage to what he still considered Asia, encountering the coast of Honduras and the Mayan Indians. He named the area "Costa Rica," then sailed south to Panama, before leaving for Spain again. A serious storm wrecked the ships at Jamaica, where the group held out for more than a year. When Columbus finally returned to Spain, Isabella was dead, and his titles gone. Although not poor, Columbus had lost favor with the new Royal Court, and was not feted in Spain.

Whether he died thinking he had reached Asia is a matter of speculation. Some historians now conclude that Columbus knew all along he would encounter new lands, but that only the lure of Oriental riches would keep the crews focused on the task. Others claim he remained deluded until his death in Valladolid, Spain, on May 20, 1506, that he had found China. But the impact of Columbus's discovery opened the Americas to European exploration and conquest. From a Native American perspective Columbus's arrival marked a disastrous turning point, although new studies suggest that the Indian population of the Americas was far smaller than originally thought, and that rampant diseases may have swept North and Central America long before Columbus arrived. In seeking to show that the world was smaller than it really was, Columbus demonstrated that it was larger than anyone dreamed.

Coronado, Francisco Vásquez de (1510–1554)

Coronado was born in Salamanca, Spain, in 1510. He was governor of New Galicia (near Nayarit, Mexico), when he was informed by Fray Marcos *de Niza*, whom he had sent north to explore, that vast wealth existed in the

"Seven Cities of Cibola." In 1540 Coronado led an expedition of more than 1,000 Spanish, Indian allies, and slaves up the coast of Gulf of California across the Sonora desert, then to modern-day New Mexico. Instead of a golden city, Coronado found a pueblo of Zuni Indians, which he proceeded to conquer. None of the remaining six pueblos had any gold. Coronado sent Melchior *Díaz* to the Colorado River to rendezvous with Hernando de *Alarcón*, who was bringing supplies, while Hernando de *Alvarado* headed east.

Coronado returned to Mexico in 1542, having failed to find any gold in the "Seven Cities." He remained governor of New Galicia until he retired in 1544 and died in Mexico City 10 years later.

Cortés, Hernán (1485–October 12, 1547)

Hernán Cortés was born in Medellín, Spain, and studied law at the University of Salamanca. He quit law school after two years to join the command of Alonso Quintero bound for Hispaniola. He advanced through the ranks, becoming the secretary to the governor of Cuba. In 1519 Cortés was appointed to command an expedition to the Yucatan in Mexico. The party, including more than 500 soldiers along with horses and artillery, landed on the Mexican coast near Veracruz, where the Aztecs at first sought to placate the invaders with gifts, including slaves. One of the slave girls, "la Malinche," became Cortés's interpreter and lover. Cortés discovered that the Aztec king Montezuma lived in a magnificent city of great wealth. In August 1519, Cortés led his column toward Mexico City (Tenochtitlan), along the way finding numerous other Indian tribes who champed at the bit to revolt against the oppressive Aztecs. Cortés wisely befriended as many of them as he could.

Montezuma welcomed Cortés and his men (although there is considerable debate over whether by that time the Aztecs still thought the Spaniards were "gods"). Once Cortés got inside the city, however, the Spaniards held Montezuma hostage, until the Aztecs rose up to attack the Spanish. In July 1520, against vastly overwhelming odds, Cortés successfully backed his troops out of Tenochtitlan and back to Veracruz, where he outfitted and reinforced his troops. The Spaniards returned to Tenochtitlan in 1521. Again, volley fire from Spanish muskets and cannons, an assault by ships that the Spaniards built and carried overland, and solid discipline overcame the 10-to-1 odds in favor of the Aztecs. By defeating the single, most important Indian power in central or North America, Hernan Cortés thus truly claimed Mexico for Spain.

de Benavides, Fray Alonso (ca. 1600s)

Franciscan father Alonso de Benavides oversaw the New Mexico missions from 1626 to 1629. In 1630 he penned a *Memorial* to the Spanish crown, depicting a successful mission field along the **Rio Grande** in New Mexico and requesting additional funds and personnel to continue the spiritual labor in the colony. He reported to the king that Franciscans had baptized 86,000 New Mexican Indians (Pueblos, *Navajos*, and Apaches). He left New Mexico in 1629 with the annual trade caravan, traveling to Mexico City and then to Spain, where he published his *Memorial* and met with a Franciscan nun, Maria de Jesus de Agreda, who had apparently bilocated from her convent, making visits to Apache and Jumano tribes on the Plains and telling them to seek the Franciscans. Tales of the "lady in blue" circulated among Southwestern tribes for centuries. Benavides never returned to New Mexico.

de Niza, Fray Marcos (d. ca. 1550)

A Franciscan mendicant from Nice, France, Fray Marcos de Niza arrived in Spanish America in 1531. He participated in the conquests of Guatemala and Peru but was best known for his exaggerated account of the Pueblo Indian civilizations in New Spain's far northwest.

Fray Marcos arrived in Mexico City in 1537, where he quickly gained favor with Viceroy Antonio Mendoza. When none of the three Spanish survivors of Pnfilo de Narváez's expedition to Florida would agree to lead an expedition to the Northern Mystery (the northern trading center at the northern edge of New Spain, Cibola), Mendoza chose Fray Marcos, with the Moorish slave *Esteban* at his side. The expedition departed from Culiacán in 1539.

Esteban traveled several days' journey ahead of Fray Marcos, sending back word of his findings in the form of crosses of varying sizes. The news that Zuni Indians had killed Esteban frightened Fray Marcos. Eager to return to Mexico City, the Franciscan friar caught a glimpse of the Zuni village from afar. Mistakenly declaring it the long sought after Cibola, Fray Marcos renamed the pueblo Nuevo Reino de San Francisco and returned to Mexico City. His glowing tales of untold riches prompted Viceroy Mendoza to send Francisco Vsquez de *Coronado* on an expedition to the north. Fray Marcos's seemingly successful expedition also led him to be named Father Provincial of the Franciscan Holy Gospel province.

The Coronado expedition set out for Cibola in April 1540. Upon reaching the Zuni villages that Fray Marcos had identified as the legendary Seven Cities of Cibola, a rival to the wealth and size of Mexico City, Coronado and his forces discovered an adobe pueblo of some 100 families. Disgusted with the friar's apparent lies, Coronado wrote the provincial about the friar and sent him back to Mexico City. Upon his return to Mexico City, Fray Marcos served out his term as Father Provincial and died in the late 1550s.

de Soto, Hernando (1500–May 21, 1542)

Hernando de Soto, born in Barcarrota, Spain, attended the University of Salamanca thanks to a benefactor, Pedrarias Davila. De Soto followed Davilla to the New World, and married Davilla's daughter. In 1532 De Soto served with Francisco Pizarro in Peru, and returning to Spain with much gold, de Soto in 1537 was named governor of Cuba. Leading one thousand men, de Soto arrived in Cuba, then, according to the King's orders, was to conquer Florida. He arrived at Tampa Bay in May 1539.

De Soto battled Indians constantly, marching northward, through Florida and the Carolinas, then westward. De Soto found no gold, but in 1541 his party encountered the Mississippi River. De Soto was significant for his exploration of the Southeastern United States and part of Texas. His expedition led to renewed interest in settling in New Spain and Mexico.

Díaz, Melchior (ca. 1500–1540)

Born in Estremadura, Spain, Melchior Díaz, a Spanish explorer, served as civilian lieutenant under Francisco Vásquez de *Coronado* in his search for the "Seven Cities of Cibola." A commoner who had migrated to New Spain in 1527, he was made *alcalde* and Military Commander of the Mexican city of Culiacn in 1536, where he welcomed Álvar Núñez *Cabeza de Vaca* and *Esteban* after they had wandered across the American Southwest. In 1539 Díaz led a cavalry squadron northward to search for the "Seven Cities," covering 1,500 miles, much of it ground already traveled by Marcos *de Niza*. Díaz prepared a detailed report on the region's geography, but informed the authorities that no golden cities existed.

Along with de Niza, Díaz joined Coronado in an expedition to New Mexico. Díaz carried dispatches from Coronado to the Spanish Viceroy of Mexico, Antonio de Mendoza, again confirming the news that the expedition had found no golden cities. Díaz was assigned to take a unit to meet Hernando de *Alarcón*'s supply ships, scheduled to arrive at the Gulf of California. In September 1540 Díaz and 25 troops left to rendezvous with the ships, which never arrived: Alarcn had already waited for Coronado, then departed. Díaz crossed the Colorado River and explored the peninsula of Baja California, but did not locate Alarcón.

On his return to Mexico City, Daz found a stone cross on the banks of the Colorado River, underneath which Alarcón had buried several letters. Díaz then resumed his march, whereupon the detachment encountered Indians. During the battle, Díaz hurled his lance, which stuck in the ground with the point facing up. Díaz's horse reared up, throwing him onto the lance, killing him.

Drake, Francis (ca.1540–January 28, 1596)

Francis Drake, the son of a Protestant lay minister, was born in Devon, England. He served as one of the most important anti–Roman Catholic and pro-Reformation men of the 16th century. At the age of 13, Drake became the apprentice of a captain who sailed the hazardous and volatile North Sea. This experience also shaped Drake, bestowing upon him expert navigational and piloting knowledge and skill. After working for several years as a commercial pilot, Drake joined John Hawkins's military and mercantilist-oriented fleet. On his second voyage to the West Indies, the Spanish attacked and Drake barely survived. Returning to England, Drake found himself the admiration of the Court.

A devout Calvinist, Drake began working for Queen Elizabeth and the English as a privateer (a government-sponsored pirate) in 1572. Known as the "Elizabethan Sea-Dogge," Drake ruthlessly pursued the Spanish, self-proclaimed to be the most Roman Catholic of nations.

Drake performed brilliantly under Queen Elizabeth's rule. More than any other ship's captain, Drake paved the way for the English colonization of North America and created insecurity among the Spanish. He explored the Pacific and the Atlantic oceans, discovered a number of usable harbors, and developed good relations with several Indian tribes. In September 1578 Drake and his men sailed around the Straits of Magellan, entered the Pacific, and raided almost every Spanish port on the Pacific coast of South America, much to the surprise of the unwary Spaniards. Upon reaching northern California, Drake declared it "New Albion," turned west, and circumnavigated the earth. Upon his return to England in September 1580, Elizabeth knighted him on the deck of his famous ship, the *Golden Hind*, formerly known as the *Pelican*. He preached to his men daily from the decks, but also rewarded them with profits of up to 5,000 percent. In 1585 Drake again raided Spanish possessions in North America. A year later, commanding 23 ships, Drake burned *St. Augustine*, Florida, Spain's oldest settlement in North America. Overall, Drake's mission was so successful that Spain lost much of its financial credit with Italian and German banks. For the Spanish, Drake represented their greatest threat, as he had penetrated an area they regarded as completely secure and as a part of their domain.

El Morro/Inscription Rock

Springs at the base of El Morro mesa, a 200-foot sandstone monolith in the northwest corner of modern New Mexico, have beckoned travelers for centuries. A soft, flat rock near the springs became a message board for the ages, with petroglyphs by early Indian groups mixing with carvings by Spanish conquistadors, U.S. Army regulars, and American pioneers. The earliest dated signature was carved in 1593 by a member of the *Espejo* expedition. Twelve years later, New Mexico colonizer Don Juan de *Oate* added his name and the phrase, *Paso por aqui* (passed by here), as he returned to New Mexico from an exploration trip to the Sea of California.

At this location Diego de *Vargas*, recolonizer of New Mexico, recorded his triumph over the rebellious Pueblos. The latest dated inscription in Spanish was made in 1774. In 1849 a U.S. Army lieutenant named Simpson recorded his presence at El Morro, as did other travelers throughout the 19th century. In 1906 Inscription Rock became a part of El Morro National Monument.

El Paso del Norte

Founded in 1598 by Juan de *Oñate*, "the pass to the North" became a leading town in New Mexico. Ciudad Juárez, as the town was first called, lies on the *Rio Grande* at the foot of the Franklin mountains. Franciscan *missionaries* established the Mission Nuestra Señora de Guadalupe there in 1659. After 1827 a village of El Paso was established on the river's north bank. In 1859 the town served as a stop on the *Butterfield Overland Mail [III]* route to California and was on the *Southern Pacific [IV]* rail line. By 1890 El Paso had a population of 10,000, and in the 20th century it grew rapidly.

Espejo, Antonio (ca. 1540)

Little is known of Espejo's early career, but in 1582 a group of Franciscans were under siege in the New Mexico region. Espejo, visiting at the time, joined the relief effort. In 1582 he left San Bartolomé for the *Rio Grande*, then into the region of the Pueblo Indians. Discovering that the Franciscans he sought to rescue were dead, his party began to engage in gold seeking. The explorers covered substantial territory, ranging across the Rio Grande to the Pecos, returning to San Bartolomé in 1583, and brought back stories of mineral wealth.

Esteban (d. 1539)

The North African (Moorish) slave of Spaniard Andrs Dorantes, Esteban was one of the four survivors of Pnfilo de Narváez's failed expedition to Florida in 1528. In 1534 Esteban, Dorantes, and Alonso del Castillo met up with *Cabeza de Vaca*. Together, the four survivors became itinerant healers, known as the "Sons of the Sun." Esteban had a knack for languages and was quite theatrical, playing into his role. Wandering about northwestern Mexico in 1536, the four ran across a group of Spaniards on an enslaving mission. Upon their return to Mexico City, the survivors were debriefed by the viceroy and Hernn *Corts*. They did not exaggerate tales of the north, but their report fired the imaginations and desires of their listeners, who hoped to find an "otro Mexico," a previously undiscovered city that offered riches parallel to those of the Aztec capital.

Viceroy Antonio de Mendoza purchased the slave Esteban, who was eager to return to the north, where natives had treated him with respect and he had exercised considerable freedom. A slave, however, could not lead an expedition. In 1539 the viceroy selected Fray Marcos *de Niza* to lead the expedition northward to verify the presence of wealthy northern cities, to be accompanied by the experienced Esteban. After departing from Culiacn, Esteban and his native retinue ranged ahead of Fray Marcos. In accordance with their plans, Esteban sent to Fray Marcos crosses of varying sizes, depending on his findings. When Esteban heard of Cibola, he sent a large cross to Fray Marcos. The friar instructed Esteban to wait, but to no avail. Esteban forged ahead, arriving at one of the Zuni pueblos, Hawikuh. Interestingly, Esteban, a black slave, was the first representative of Spanish culture to the Indians of what would become the American Southwest.

At Zuni, Esteban met his demise. The circumstances of his untimely death remain shrouded in mystery. Did Esteban make a dramatic entrance into the pueblo and interrupt a religious ceremony? Did the gourd rattle he carried offend the Zunis? Did he make too many demands for food and women? Whatever the circumstances, the Zunis seized and killed Esteban. Legend has it that his body was cut into pieces and distributed among the Zuni pueblos as proof of Esteban's mortality. Horrified at his companion's fate, Fray Marcos glimpsed the pueblo from afar and reported that it was bigger than Mexico City and that what he saw was indeed the fabled city of Cibola.

Ferrelo, Bartolomé (1542–1543)

Bartolomé Ferrelo served as the pilot for the Spanish expedition of Juan Rodriguez *Cabrillo*, which explored the coast of California from Mexico to Oregon. In 1542 the viceroy of New Spain ordered Cabrillo to take two vessels northward along the coast of California. The expedition stopped at various spots, including Santa Catalina Island, San Pedro Bay, and Santa Monica Bay. On San Miguel Island, Cabrillo fell, and died of his injuries in 1543. Ferrelo took over the expedition, completing the exploration and returning to Puerto de Navidad, near Manzanillo, in April 1543.

Folsom Point

In Folsom, New Mexico, in 1925 archaeologists discovered flint shaped by humans next to the remains of bison extinct for nearly 8,000 years. It remains one of the key finds to understanding Indian origins as well as the time and place of Indian migrations to North and South America. New finds, such as *Kennewick Man*, however, are challenging the supremacy and ultimate importance of the Folsom Point discovery.

Fox Indians

An agricultural people in Wisconsin and Illinois, the Fox called themselves "Mesquakies," meaning the "People of the Red Earth." At the time of contact with the French in the 17th century, they lived in semipermanent lodges, composed of elm bark and poles, which housed up to 30 persons. The Mesquakie divided their labor by the seasons. In the winter, they moved onto the prairies, where men hunted and trapped fur, and the women provided for the needs of children and the village. When warmer weather came, men continued to hunt and trap, but women did the agricultural work as well as child care.

Virtually nothing is known of the Fox prior to their contact with the French. With the signing of the Grand Settlement of 1701, ending the *Mourning Wars*, the *Iroquois* left the western Great Lakes region, and the Fox Indians took up residence at Green Bay and on the southern edge of Lake Superior.

Hoping to control the Indians of the Great Lakes, the French demanded that all Indians in the region move to the Detroit area. This put the Fox in close proximity to their traditional enemies, the Ottawas and Ojibwas. One-half of the Foxes settled in the Detroit area, at the urging of the French, only to be massacred by other Indians. France sided with the victors, a deception which left a bitter resentment in the mouths of the remaining Fox. They attacked French settlers whenever possible from Green Bay, and between 1711 and 1715, the Fox successfully disrupted French trade on the Mississippi River and throughout the Great Lakes.

Threatened by the tribe, the French made the destruction of the Fox official policy. In 1716 a French-Indian army of nearly 800 attacked the Fox at Green Bay, forcing them into a surrender, but the Fox never abided by the terms of agreement. Instead, between 1720 and 1727, the Fox continued their attacks against the French and their allies. In addition, they formed a trade and military alliance with the Iroquois in the east, their enemies the previous century, and the *Sioux* in the west. This massive chain of alliances from the Atlantic to the Great Plains terrified the French, who sent a force of more than 1,600 against the Fox. Knowing they would not survive such an assault, the Fox attempted to escape the Great Lakes in mass, heading for sanctuary with the Seneca, one of the five tribes of the Iroquois.

En route, an allied Franco-Indian army cornered the Fox, killing nearly 500 and enslaving another 500. The French and their allies spent much of 1731 to 1734 hunting down the remaining refugees, murdering the vast majority of the surviving Fox, in one of the rare instances of French genocide against North American Indians.

Grand Canyon

The Colorado River dug this astounding gorge over millions of years, resulting in an "open book of nature," containing millions of records regarding the natural and geological history of the American Southwest. Located in northwest Arizona, the Grand Canyon is nearly 300 miles long, up to 1 mile deep, and 18 miles wide. American John Wesley Powell surveyed and studied it extensively in the 1870s.

Hopi Indians

A tribe located in northern Arizona, the Hopi Indians are well known for their colorful religious dances and dramas. European contacts with the Hopi occurred when members of *Coronado*'s expeditions under Garcia

Cárdenas encountered them in the 1540s. Franciscan *missionaries* visited the Hopis frequently, establishing a church in Hopi territory in 1629, although the tribe strongly resisted Christianity. Hopi Indians remained isolated from Americans until the 1880s, but they were in constant conflict with the *Navajo*, who occupied the regions around them. In 1882 the U.S. government established the Hopi reservation, which, over time, was completely surrounded by Navajo lands, leading to a number of clashes in the 20th century.

horses

Contrary to the belief that Europeans brought the first horses to North America, wild horses were indigenous to the continent, roaming the prairies in huge herds. Indians apparently hunted them to extinction; then the horse was reintroduced by Christopher *Columbus* in 1493 and by Hernán *Cortés* in 1519. Spanish colonists utilized the grasslands by pasturing herds of cattle and supervising them by riders on horseback, called *vaqueros* or, in English, *"cowboys" [IV]*. By the 1770s Indians had acquired horses and their use spread to hunting buffalo on the plains.

    Shoshone [III], *Crow [III]*, and *Nez Perce [IV]* obtained horses by the end of the 1600s; all of the animals descended from the ponies brought by

These canyons and formations in Goosenecks State Park, Utah, were dug by the Colorado River, the same that created the Grand Canyon. Goosenecks is rarely visited but hauntingly beautiful. *Bradley J. Birzer*

the Spanish settlers and *conquistadores*. The horses stood from 56 inches high (14 hands) to 62 inches (15 hands) and weighed roughly 1,000 pounds, although the size and weight depended on the particular breed. Indian "ponies" were smaller, and lighter—owing to the fact that they received less food on the plains than was provided in the Europeans barns—while Europeans bred larger draft animals to pull wagons and plows. In addition to riding herd on cattle and farm work, horses soon were employed as pack animals for the *fur trade [II]*. During the Civil War large numbers of western horses were purchased for the Union Cavalry, artillery teams, and quartermasters' wagons.

Aside from the cavalry and basic transportation, the primary use of horses in the West was for handling cattle herds on the open grasslands. Cowboys developed an entire culture associated with "cow punching," including original clothing (*chaps [IV]*, *spurs [III]*, bandanas, *Stetson hats [IV]*), well-known roping techniques, specific methods of marking cattle and horses through *branding [III]*, and a romanticized rite of breaking horses, which became a staple of *rodeos [IV]*.

A variety of specialized horses appeared. The cutting horse was specifically trained to "cut" a cow from the rest of the herd for branding. Interposing its body between the cow and the herd, the cutting horse deftly separated one cow after another with little guidance from the rider. Quarter horses were specifically bred and trained as sprinters, able to cover a quarter of

The Palouse in Washington State is the home of both the Nez Perce and the Appaloosa horse, which the Nez Perce successfully developed and bred. *Bradley J. Birzer*

a mile in great speed. Cowboys used these animals to ride down runaway steers and rope them. A draft animal, such as a Percheron, could weigh as much as 1,500 pounds and had great value for farm work or pulling heavy wagons (as with the famous Clydesdales in the Budweiser Beer ads). Well into the 1920s horses pulled heavy farm machinery, such as harvesters, on the Great Plains, with teams of 6 to 36 drawing plows, disks, and a variety of other implements.

Raising horses was cheap on the range—perhaps as little as five dollars a day, until the U.S. government started to impose range fees and until *barbed wire [IV]* began to seal off the open lands. Introduction of motorized tractors and gasoline-powered cars steadily reduced the need for draft animals, while military tactics even before the Civil War had started to diminish the utility of cavalry. By the 1930s motorized tanks, trucks, and armored cars had replaced most of the cavalry units in the U.S. Army.

Although the numbers of horses declined—about 45,000 wild horses are estimated to exist in the United States today—horse breeding remains a popular activity on western ranches. Specific breeds, such as the Appaloosa (a gray and black-spotted horse), the Palomino (a golden horse with a shaggy blond mane), the Arabian (white or black desert animals), and the Morgan show horse all remain favorites at horse shows. And despite the urbanization of America, frontier rodeos—often performed in modern domed football stadiums—are as popular as ever.

Hudson's Bay Company

In the tradition of earlier "joint-stock companies," which featured multiple stockholders as owners, the "Governor and Company of Adventurers of England into Hudson's Bay" was chartered in May 1670. Joint-stock companies included the Virginia Company (1606) and the Massachusetts Bay Company (1629). In addition to having multiple owners, whose return was based on the number of shares of stock each held, joint-stock companies had limited liability (meaning that stockholders' liability extended only to their direct investment in the company in the form of their stock) and unlimited life (meaning that the company did not cease to exist when a president or stockholder died).

England had chartered the Virginia Company, the Plymouth Company (1620), and the Massachusetts Bay Company for the express purpose of establishing trading settlements in the New World. Each of these companies had a monopoly on trade within their chartered lands. As part of the geopolitical struggle with other European powers, England sought to counter Spanish and French moves in North America. Specifically, the Hudson's Bay Company arose out of reports from Sieur de Groseilliers and his brother-in-law, Pierre-Esprit *Radisson,* a pair of French fur trappers in Canada, that the area called New Wales (or Hudson's Bay) was a more strategic area for the fur trade than even the St. Lawrence region, which had been dominated by the French since the 1620s. An expedition aboard the *Nonsuch* (1668–1669) confirmed the assessments of the trappers, leading the Crown to support formation of the company in conjunction with King Charles II's cousin, Prince Rupert (who had backed the expedition), Groseilliers, and Radisson. A governor (Prince Rupert) and committee of seven directed the New World operations of the company that claimed 1.4 million square miles under its charter.

From 1670 to 1713 Hudson's Bay Company competed with French interests in the region, until the Treaty of Utrecht transferred legal claim to the entire area to England. Brief internal struggles occurred, as in 1682, when Radisson suddenly shifted allegiance to France and controlled the company for two years before switching back to the English. After 1713 the company expanded its operations into western Canada and the Rocky Mountains. In 1784 a new competitor, the North West Company organized in Montreal, provided stiff competition to the Hudson's Bay Company but was finally coerced into merging with Hudson's Bay Company in 1821. Meanwhile, American traders had started to encroach on company lands after 1818, protected by the Anglo-American Convention of that year, which established a 10-year joint occupation of Oregon.

For the next 50 years, Hudson's Bay Company had a constant challenge from the Americans all along the Canadian border to Oregon. Although John Jacob *Astor [III]*, with his ***American Fur Company [III]***, had established a presence at Vancouver, the Hudson's Bay Company gained control of most of the trading grounds by the late 1830s. The British wanted to use the company for settlement, but the Crown paid little attention to the actual needs of farmers and settlers. A general store was established at Winnipeg, known as Fort Garry, which served as a source of some territorial activity. Only in the 1840s did the British government react to the steady expansion of Americans into Hudson's Bay lands in Oregon, especially under the new administration of James K. Polk, which claimed all land in the Oregon country up to the 54 degree 40 minute line. American expansionists thus raised the cry, "Fifty-four forty or fight." The British minister to the United States, Richard Packenham, working with U.S. Secretary of State James Buchanan, hammered out an agreement establishing the Oregon line at the existing 49th parallel.

With the Americans effectively out of the way in Canada, the Company only had to concern itself with profits and administration, but the fur trade declined and American railroad terminals, such as St. Paul, started to siphon off some of the business. In 1863 the governor and directors of the Hudson's Bay Company resigned and the company was sold to the International Financial Society, which tried again to unload the assets. Finally, the British government purchased the territories from the company, allowing the Company to continue trading on the lands. Gradually the firm relocated its administrative offices to Winnipeg and began shifting its business operations from furs into retailing. By 1980 the company was running Canada's largest chain of department stores.

Iroquois

In the 17th and 18th centuries the Iroquois were one of the most powerful native societies in North America. Made up of the five powerful tribes—Mohawk, Oneida, Onondaga, Cayuga, and Seneca—the Iroquois Confederacy is the longest-lived political institution in the New World. Some scholars argue that it helped inspire Benjamin Franklin's understanding of an American confederacy. The Iroquois Confederacy's origins remain a matter of myth and legend, but the confederacy existed long before the arrival of Europeans. Estimates range from 1142 to 1525. "We, the five Iroquois nations, compose but one cabin; we maintain but one fire; and we have, from time immemorial, dwelt under one roof," an Iroquois stated in 1654.

Prior to the establishment of the confederacy, the five tribes brutally warred with one another. According to an Iroquois legend, a distraught Onondaga chief, *Hiawatha [II],* encountered a mysterious Huron, known as the Peacemaker. He convinced Hiawatha that peace and unity served society better than war and strife. He gave to Hiawatha the laws, known as the "Great Laws of Peace," necessary for peace and unity to work.

Once unified, the Iroquois (a French misinterpretation and mispronunciation of an Algonquian word for them) called themselves the Hodenosaunee, meaning "People of the Longhouse." It was in the longhouses that the Iroquois lived, held religious liturgies, and discussed political and cultural policies. European visitors and witnesses frequently expressed amazement at the longhouses, likening them and the surrounding village structures to European castles.

In addition, with unification, the Iroquois could focus on expansion, and they expanded quickly. Armed first with Dutch and later with English weaponry, the Iroquois expanded rapidly to the west, harassing the native peoples of the western Great Lakes and dominating the fur trade. Indeed, the Iroquois and their enemies, the French-backed Hurons, initiated nearly a century of warfare. Known as the *Mourning/Beaver Wars*, the conflicts of the 17th century were intensely bloody. They ended with the Grand Settlement of 1701.

Throughout the 18th century, the Iroquois continued to play an important role in the imperial and, after the establishment of the United States, national rivalries for the eastern half of North America, especially under the leadership of Mohawk Joseph *Brant [II]*. In 1722 the Tuscaroras joined

IN THEIR OWN

Iroquois Attack on the Miamis, Early 1680s

The Jesuit priest Jean Lamberville witnessed this Iroquois attack on the Miami Indians in the early 1680s.

Six hundred men, women, and children near Virginia, surrendered voluntarily, for fear that they might be compelled to do so by force. They [the Iroquois] Bring prisoners from all parts and thereby increase their numbers. They are beginning to attack some of our allies called the Oumiamis [Miamis], a nation of the bay des Puants; and They have already burned 6 or 7 of these, Without counting those whom they have massacred. The killing of one of their people, They say, through treachery, by an Oumiamis, will cause their ruin. Three of that tribe were Brought here some Days ago,

whom it was Impossible to save from the fury of the drunkards. No one would Undertake to Bring them to the chapel before they were burned, through fear of being beaten by the drunkards. They were treated with great cruelty, even those who had not been drinking. I tried to save them from the hands of those rioters but in vain; for, as soon as I proposed it, I was told not to say another word about it, and that as the anger of the drunkards was so great I would do well to withdraw. Hardly could they be prevented from tearing the prisoners into pieces on their arrival, and only The prospect of the greater torture that was being prepared for them induced the Iroquois to restrain their fury. . . . Three Days afterward, they brought a captive woman who had been taken with the others. She endured the same tortures; she received the same grace of baptism in the chapel, whither she was led by two warriors and by an old man of note. These are all people whose good services, as well as those of my Interpreter, We must acknowledge.

—SOURCE: S. J. JEAN DE LAMBERVILLE, *TRAVELS AND EXPLORATIONS OF THE JESUIT MISSIONNARIES IN NEW FRANCE, 1610–1791, VOL. 62* (CLEVELAND: BURROWS BROTHERS, 1900), 71–79.

the Iroquois, becoming the sixth nation. The Iroquois remain a viable political and cultural entity at the beginning of the 21st century.

Kennewick Man

In the summer of 1996 a 9,300-year-old skeleton was uncovered on the
Columbia River in Kennewick, Washington. Researchers speculate that he
is either of Ainu or Caucasian ancestry. Unfortunately for scholars, a local
Indian tribe, the Umatillas, confiscated the Kennewick man under the 1990
Native American Graves Protection and Repatriation Act. Since then, various
groups have vied for control over the skeleton in court. Regardless, the possibility of a pre-Columbian Ainu or Caucasian presence in the American
Northwest has reopened fundamental questions regarding Native American origins and the date of their migration(s) to North and South America.

King Philip's War

In June 1675 settlers from a coalition of New England colonies (Massachusetts, Plymouth, Connecticut, and New Haven) responded to attacks
by the Wampanoag Indians under Metacomet, known to the whites as "King
Philip." The war represented a continuation of white-Indian conflict that
had stalled into an uneasy truce after the Pequot War of 1636, but was not
the regionwide uprising of all the tribes feared by the English. Instead,
Metacomet had enlisted the help of the Narragansett, the Nipmuck, and
Pocomtuck, but found many other tribes, including the Mohican, Pequot,
Nauset, Massachusett, and others allied against him with the English. This
epitomized the North American Indians' central difficulty in resisting whites,
in that they frequently saw other Indians as the greater threat.

In the war, English settlers got a taste of the backwoods warfare that
they would have to adopt to drive out the French and, later, the troops of
the British Crown itself. Dozens of small, isolated engagements were fought
over remote farms and in deadly ambushes. Often, only the support of the
friendly Indian tribes kept the colonists from being overwhelmed. But
against the Narragansett in 1675–1676, the coalition of white colonists
attacked in the dead of winter, while the Indians were pinned down in
their camps. After that campaign, the Connecticut troops, relying heavily

on the Mohicans, gradually cleared the hostile Indians out. Plymouth co-lonial Captain Benjamin Church then led a force against Metacomet and the Wampanoag, culminating in a victory in 1676 for the colonists and Metacomet's death. Surviving Indians relocated in the west, where they encountered the Mohawks, then settled in the Hudson River Valley. Many remained in New England on reservations.

Both white and Indian casualties, as a proportion of the total popula-tion, were high. The experience gained by the settlers began to convince them that they had to adapt traditional European military methods to the woods and hills of North America.

kiva

A kiva is a sacred building used by numerous southwestern tribes as early as the ancient *Anasazi* up through the modern-day *Pueblos*. It is the spiri-tual center for many New Mexican Pueblo communities. The kiva is a cov-ered dugout in which male participants smoked much and communed with nature as well as with the spiritual world. Through its design—half in the ground and half above ground—the building serves as a gateway between this world and the spiritual world. It also represents the place from which the Pueblos emerged from the earth. Pueblo Indians consider the design to be preordained by spiritual beings. One enters a modern kiva via a ladder through the roof. An altar stands in the middle of the kiva, adorned by fetishes, detailed statues of spirit beings. Early Franciscan *missionaries* condemned the kivas as pagan and possibly satanic, demand-ing that the Indians practice their newfound Christianity in officially sanc-tioned churches and around blessed altars. Despite the warnings and an-ger of the priests, many of the kivas survived, and the 1930s witnessed a huge revival of the use of the kivas among Pueblos. Pueblo rules today forbid non-Pueblos from entering or looking into the kivas. Zunis and Hopis, from whom we derive the word "kiva," also use them as spiritual centers.

Las Casas, Bartolomé de (1474–1566)

Bartolomé de Las Casas, born to wealth in Seville, Spain, in 1474, had a uni-versity education and traveled to the New World in 1502. He arrived in His-paniola to run a plantation and mining operation using Indian slave labor.

After taking the vows of a priest, he served as the chaplain for the Nárvaez expedition through Cuba. He witnessed the capture of a chief leading the resistance to the Spanish, and the Spanish governor's decree that the chief be burned alive. Between 1510 and 1514, he focused on improving the conditions of Indians—especially the elimination of slavery—and resisted the *encomienda* system. This system involved tributory labor where the inhabitants of conquered lands were obliged to render personal, feudal-type service to the landowner. Returning to Spain in 1516, he found an ally in Cardinal Francisco Jimenéz de Cisneros, who named Las Casas "Protector of the Indies." When he sailed for the New World again, arriving at Santo Domingo, he created what he hoped was a model community for Indians. That effort, which lasted from 1520 to 1521, failed due to an already ongoing war between the Spanish and Indians. Depressed, Las Casas retreated to a monastery, where he joined the Dominican order. He then set out for Mexico, then Peru, where he had obtained a royal decree from Charles V called the "New Laws" in 1542, which arranged to end the *encomienda* system. He worked in Guatemala for a brief time.

Las Casas's support for the abolition of slavery among the Indians at first did not extend to Africans, who were imported to South America, but he quickly reconsidered and observed that blacks should be subject to the same laws as Indians. Subsequent administrators modified the "New Laws" so as to nullify them, but Las Casas continued to toil on behalf of the Indians as Bishop of Chiapas from 1544 to 1547. He was now an old man and in constant danger, and he decided to return to Spain that year. He continued to be an advocate for the Indians through his influential writings, especially the *Historia de las Indias* (1875–1876). In these, Las Casas developed what historians later termed the "Black Legend" of Spanish rule, relating a repressive, hard, and destructive reign in the Spanish New World. This sparked a reaction by the court to sponsor writers to produce a counterpart called the "White Legend," which stated that Spanish rule was benign and beneficial to the Indians. Las Casas provided useful anthropological and sociological studies of the lands he observed, which remain valuable to the present.

The Marquette and Jolliet Expedition

French Jesuit Jacques Marquette (June 1, 1637–May 18, 1675) and Louis Jolliet (ca. September 1645–ca. May 1700) led an important expedition down the *Mississippi River* in 1673. The two hoped to find a passage to the Pacific Ocean.

Leaving *Michilimackinac [II]* on May 17, 1673, the two men and five companions traveled across Lake Michigan. With the aid of two Miami guides, the seven traveled across the Fox-Wisconsin portage and down the Wisconsin River to reach the Mississippi. Reaching the great river on May 17, they traveled down it to the confluence of the Mississippi and Arkansas rivers. Along the way, they found the *Missouri River*, recognizing it as a potential route to the Pacific if the Mississippi would not work. There, Quapaw Indians informed them they were getting close to the Gulf of Mexico. Fearing the Spanish who were settling and exploring the gulf, Marquette and Joliet turned back on July 17, 1673. Upon arriving at the

IN THEIR OWN Words

Father Marquette's Journal

Between 1673 and 1675, Father Jacques Marquette founded a mission among the Illinois Indians near Chicago. Despite severe hardships and declining health, he continued to minister to the Indians until he died in 1675. His unfinished journal was addressed to the Superior of Missions, and in this passage he related his encounter with Maskouten Indians.

[November 23] After embarking at noon, we experienced some difficulty in reaching a river. Then the cold began, and more than a foot of snow covered the ground; it has remained ever since. We were delayed for three days, during which Pierre killed a deer, three bustards, and three turkeys. . . . The others proceeded to the prairies. A savage discovered some cabins, and came to get us. . . . two hunters also came to see me. They were Maskoutens, to the number of eight or nine cabins, who had separated from the others to obtain subsistence. With fatigues almost impossible to Frenchmen, they travel throughout the winter over very bad roads, the land abounding in streams, small lakes, and swamps. Their cabins are wretched; and they eat, or starve, according to the places where they happen to be. . . .

[December 15] [The Chachagwessiou and Illinois Indians] left us, to go and join their people and to give them the goods that they had brought, in order to obtain their robes. In this they act like traders, and give hardly any more than the French. . . . Being thus rid of them, we said the mass of the Conception. After the 14th, my disease turned into a bloody flux.

—SOURCE: "THE JOURNAL OF FR. JACQUES MARQUETTE," REPRODUCED IN LOUISE PHELPS KELLOGG, *EARLY NARRATIVES OF THE NORTHWEST, 1634–1699* (NEW YORK: CHARLES SCRIBNER'S SONS, 1917), 262–266.

Illinois River, the two explorers decided to chance it. The river took them back to Lake Michigan, via the Chicago portage.

The two explorers failed in their mission to discover a water route to the Pacific, but they did encounter and befriend several Indian tribes—the Mascouten, the *Miami [II]*, the Illinois, and possibly the *Shawnee [II]*. Most of the Indians encountered seemed downtrodden because of the *Mourning Wars* with the *Iroquois*. The French explorers discovered the incredible fertility of the Illinois country, leading to an eventual permanent French presence at the Indian village Kaskaskias. The Marquette and Jolliet expedition paved the way for future French exploration of the region. *La Salle [II]* followed their course down the Mississippi River in 1682, reaching the Gulf of Mexico in April.

Finally, the expedition opened the country to Jesuit missionary expansion. The Jesuits opened a mission at Kaskaskias almost as soon as Marquette and Jolliet returned, and Marquette returned to the Illinois Indians in the autumn of 1674.

mestizos and mulattos

As Europeans intermarried and/or had sexual relationships with Indians and African slaves, the races mixed, producing people who did not entirely belong to the clearly defined European class divisions that were imposed on the New World. Colonists, *españoles* in New Spain, who were white, came up with new terms to describe the descendants of interracial relationships. Those of European and African descent were called *mulattos*, those of European and North American Indian descent, *coyotes*, and those of European and Mexican Indian descent, *mestizos*. Another term, less frequently seen, was *zambos*, referring to those of African and Indian descent, and even more infrequent were the terms *pardos* or *color quebrados* to describe mixtures of all three ethnic groups. Spanish governors and early settlers intended that rigid class distinctions be enforced, based on these designations, which proved impossible. Mulattos regularly passed for white European, not only in New Spain, but all through the English colonies, and few could really tell if a person was a "coyote" or a "mestizo."

Nevertheless, *within* the racial subgroups, extreme prejudice occurred. By the late 1800s in New Orleans, for example, social clubs for blacks had a "paper bag" test, where a person's skin color had to be lighter than a paper bag to gain admittance; and mestizos generally looked down upon those of pure Indian blood, even as Europeans discriminated against them. It is estimated that intermarriage took over in New Spain quite quickly; the majority of those who trekked from Sonora to San Francisco in 1774 under Juan Bautista de Anza were mestizos and mulattos, while the wave of settlers to the San Jose/San Francisco region in the late 1700s counted only one-third pure *españoles*. Ultimately, the assumptions were reversed, in that land ownership implied pure blood, thereby making any *don* an *español*. Such facility with the truth promoted economic opportunity for those of mixed races and, over time, began to weaken the distinctions themselves.

missionaries (Franciscans and Jesuits)

Spanish, French, and English settlers in the New World arrived with God, glory, and gold on their minds, and not necessarily in that order. Preaching the Gospel was accepted as a principal purpose for exploration and conquest. Priests from the Roman Catholic Church accompanied Spanish explorers, tending to the spiritual life of soldiers, helping to pacify and control conquered territory.

Two religious orders within the Catholic Church composed the "shock troops" of missionary work: the Franciscans and the Jesuits. Franciscans, members of an order founded in the 13th century by St. Francis of Assisi, took vows of poverty, chastity, and communal living. Only the first order within the Franciscans, the friars—known by their brown robes tied with a single rope—reached the New World in numbers. They worked well among poor Indians because they had already adapted to having no possessions. Jesuits descended from an order founded by St. Ignatius of Loyola in 1540, which included priests ("fathers"), brothers, and scholastics. Over time, Jesuits became renowned for their rigorous study of scriptures and their intellectualism. Distinctively dressed in their black robes—leading the Indians to call all missionaries "Black Robes"—Jesuits often had a much more comfortable lifestyle than their Franciscan counterparts.

Jesuits came with the French, converting the Hurons, Algonquians, and *Iroquois* in the Great Lakes region. Missionaries possessed funds to purchase tools, seed, clothing, blankets, and other goods for the Indians, and the economic relationships proved helpful in securing conversions. However, once the Indians were baptized, missionaries expected them to remain on the mission grounds, and if they left, soldiers forced their return. Missions thus became a combination of political, religious, economic, and social life change for the Indians.

As missionaries traveled from tribe to tribe, however, they extended European influence and often served as peacemakers between Indians and whites. Father Jacques *Marquette* penetrated the Mississippi River valley, and other Jesuits (perhaps no more than about 50 prior to the American Revolution) converted thousands of Indians, including some 20,000 Ottawa Indians by 1763. A decade later, when the American colonies declared independence from England, missionaries had sufficient influence to convince many tribes to support the Americans. Even though France was evicted from Canada by 1763, the impact of the Black Robes was such that they could travel through lands no other whites (save a few trappers) could without fear of harm from the local tribes.

Franciscans arrived in present-day Santa Fe with Juan de *Oñate* in 1598, where within a few years dozens of friars converted—or, at least, baptized—thousands of Indians. Many have challenged the validity of these conversions as truly Christian. The Pueblo Indians, for example, adapted parts of Catholicism that were convenient but never abandoned pagan practices, despite occasional harsh penalties, such as flogging, meted out by the Franciscans. To the Indians, any medicine man demanded respect, and if friars could speak to the spirit world for the natives, it certainly could only help the crops and harvests. Further north, in Canada, Jesuit missionaries accompanying the French made inroads among some tribes, particularly the Hurons. Jesuits suffered torture and death at the hands of the first Indian contacts, but through their suffering they eventually commanded the respect of Indian chiefs and white lay leaders. At least 80 missionaries were executed by Indians prior to the American Revolution, including possibly the first, Juan de Padilla, in Kansas in 1540.

In both the cases of the Jesuits and Franciscans, Indians found the missionaries' efforts at conversion an aggravation, but the missionaries' moral authority and physical presence constituted a source of protection from white abuses. Besides taking the Gospel to the lost, the missionaries had a secondary purpose of seeing that local Spanish colonists did not abuse the natives. The force of scripture and, if necessary, excommunication usually proved sufficient to restrain oppressive colonial landowners.

The Spanish mission system, based on Jesuit models in South America, created a series of *reducciones* (communities), each consisting of several thousand Indians and a few missionaries. The town featured a market, plaza, and mission, plus outlying agricultural areas. Missionaries taught Indians agricultural techniques, music, and, of course, religion, facilitating the incorporation of the Indians into a docile workforce under the Spanish *encomienda,* or "trust," system.

By 1630 Franciscans had established 50 missions in New Mexico, changing Indian lifestyle to conform to that of Europeans. But in the 1680 Pueblo Revolt, led by *Popé*, Indians launched a coordinated assault on the Spanish, killing 400 residents, including 21 of the 33 missionaries in the region. The church and military regained control, and by 1776 Franciscans had authority over 18,000 Indians in 20 missions. Some individuals had extraordinary records of proselytizing. Jesuit Eusebio Francisco *Kino [II]*, who erected more than 20 missions, such as San Xavier del Bac in Tucson,

IN THEIR OWN Words

Kaskaskia and Peoria Indians Attempt to Counter the Influence of a Jesuit Missionary

Thou wouldst attach thyself to the Black Gown, and he has . . . thee, We do not thus despise thee; We have Pity on thee, and thou shalt have a share in our feasts. Let the Kaskaskia Pray to God if they wish and let them obey him who has instructed them. Are we Kaskaskia? And why shouldst thou obey him, thou who art a [Peoria]? Since he has vexed thee, thou must declare publicly that thou abandonest Prayer; that it is worthless." "I shall hold a feast," said the [Peoria] chief, "and I shall invite all the old men and all the chiefs of bands; thou also wilt be invited. After speaking of our medicines and of what our grandfathers and ancestors have taught us, has this man who has come from afar better medicines than we have, to make us adopt his customs? His Fables are good only in his own country; we have ours, which do not make us die as his do."

—SOURCE: *JESUIT RELATIONS AND ALLIED DOCUMENTS*, VOL. 64, 171–173.

covered 20,000 miles, drawing accurate maps of the Spanish holdings. Despite such heroic efforts, the missionary movement began to falter. In 1767 the Spanish government's suppression of the Jesuits as a political threat impeded the missionary influence by all religious orders, while political turmoil in the Spanish empire and the Mexican independence movement in 1821 retarded missionary activity.

IN THEIR OWN

First Person Narrative, Peter John de Smet, *Western Missions and Missionaries*

Rev. Peter John de Smet, a Jesuit Priest (January 30, 1801–May 23, 1873), was ordained in 1827 and began his mission work at Council Bluffs, Iowa, with the Potawatomi. From there he traveled to Flathead Indian land in Montana, to southern Oregon, and through the Dakotas. De Smet returned to St. Louis in 1846. He made another trip west in 1851, with his letters and recollections from these journeys comprising *Western Missions and Missionaries*, first published in 1859. In this passage de Smet described a ceremony with the remnants of the Delaware tribe, which had been moved west of the Mississippi.

After the banquet a fire is kindled in the centre of the lodge. Twelve stones, each one weighing three pounds, are placed before the fire and heated to redness. The victim, which is a white dog, is presented to the jugglers by the great chief, accompanied by all his grave counsellors. The sacrificant, or master of ceremonies, attaches the animal to the medicine-post, consecrated to this use, and painted red. After making his supplications to Waka-Tanka, he immolates the victim with a single blow, tears out his heart, and divides it into three equal parts. At the instant they draw from the fire the twelve red-hot stones and arrange them in there heaps, on each of which the sacrificant places a piece of the heart enveloped in the leaves of the kinekinie, or sumac [shrubs].

While these pieces are consuming, the jugglers raise with one hand their idols, and holding in the other a gourd filled with little stones, they beat the measure, dance, and thus surround the smoking sacrifice. At the same time they implore the Waka-Tanka to grant them a liberal share of blessings. After the heart and the leaves are entirely consumed, the ashes are collected in a beautiful doeskin, ornamented with beads and embroidered with porcupine, and presented to the sacrificant.

—SOURCE: PIERRE-JEAN DE SMET, *WESTERN MISSIONS AND MISSIONARIES: A SERIES OF LETTERS* (1859; REPRINT, SHANNON, IRELAND: IRISH UNIVERSITY PRESS, 1972), 228.

A new wave of Franciscans stepped in to revive the movement, led by Father Junípero Serra, who accompanied the Gálvez expedition to California in 1769. Serra was known for his self-flagellation, pounding his chest with stones, and burning himself with candles as penance. But he was also a tireless evangelist and mission builder who erected 21 missions along a road called El Camino Real (the "Royal Highway") running from San Diego to Sonoma. Missions were soon joined by *presidios*, or military forts, which further fused religious and political interests in the region. While some missionaries, such as Kino, championed the Indians' cause, others in the new California system viewed them as a source of imperial labor. Many missionaries never forgot that they were agents of the king. Indians attached to the missions died at a faster rate than those outside of it—largely due to their exposure to European diseases, but also partly due to the harsh treatment imposed on them by their missionary fathers. Protests over cruel treatment of the Indians added to the "Black Legend," introduced years earlier by Bartolemé de *Las Casas*.

After Independence, missionary activity continued under a new wave of priests, including the Dominican order. A St. Louis diocese created in the 1820s supervised new missions to the Indians of the Great Plains, sending Father Pierre Jean De Smet to the Sioux in the 1830s. De Smet emerged as the most trusted and respected of the priests, traveling among a hundred tribes and publishing in numerous languages. He evangelized among the Cheyenne, *Sioux [IV]*, *Crow [III]*, *Blackfoot [III]*, Bannoc, Mandan and many others. Nevertheless, De Smet's achievements tended to unravel once he left.

While Franciscans and Jesuits maintain a presence in the West to the present day, they made significant contributions to the early conquest and settlement of Mexico and Canada. Sometimes they conquered, sometimes they coopted, and occasionally they protected the Indians, but they always played a pivotal role in the spiritual and economic development of the frontier.

Mississippi River

The lifeline of trade for the early West, the Mississippi River runs 2,350 miles from Lake Itasca, Minnesota, to the Gulf of Mexico. Known as the "Father of Waters" and the "Mighty Mississip," the river is joined by a number of other rivers and tributaries, including the Minnesota River, the St. Croix, the Rock River, the Illinois River, the *Missouri River*, the Ohio River, and others. After being joined with the waters of the Ohio and the Missouri Rivers, the Mississippi expands to more than a mile across.

Several states have fixed their borders by the Mississippi, including Minnesota, Wisconsin, Illinois, Iowa, Missouri, Kentucky, Tennessee, Arkansas, Louisiana, and Mississippi. Early explorers included Jacques Marquette and Louis Jolliet, (see *Marquette and Jolliet Expediton*) and *La Salle [II]*, who explored the major part of the Mississippi River valley. The French established trading posts such as St. Louis, before ceding control of the Louisiana territory to Spain in 1762; it briefly returned to France before the *Louisiana Purchase [II]* of 1803. As trade increased along the river, it became the source of literature and song, most notably the stories of Mark *Twain [III]* (Samuel Clemens).

After 1873 a series of jetties were constructed allowing ships to reach harbors during periods of low flow; then after 1927 a program was established to control floods from the Mississippi. Debates erupted between those who saw nature as an element to control and manage and the pristine conservationist groups (such as the Sierra Club) who favor returning the Mississippi River (and other rivers) to their natural conditions. Either way, the Mississippi has long been viewed as the "gateway to the West" in America, as symbolized by the St. Louis arch.

Missouri River

Extending 2,464 miles from Three Forks, Montana, where it is formed by the Gallatin, Madison, and Jefferson Rivers, the Missouri River flows to the *Mississippi River* across the Great Plains, passing through Montana, the Dakotas, and parts of Nebraska, Kansas, and Iowa through a drainage basin of nearly 530,000 square miles. Modern cities of Sioux City, Iowa, Omaha, Nebraska, and Kansas City, Missouri, touch the Missouri, and its tributaries, such as the North and South Platte, extend to such cities as Greeley and Denver, Colorado, and Casper, Wyoming.

The Missouri, or "muddy waters," was first observed by Europeans when Father Jacques Marquette and Louis Jolliet explored the Mississippi and found Indians known as the Missouris ("the people of the big canoes") where the Missouri joined the Mississippi (see *Marquette and Jolliet*

Expedition). Later, Etienne Veniard de Bourgmont followed the river to the mouth of the Platte River, constructing Fort Orleans in 1723 at the junction of the Grand River.

Picking up melting snow from the Rocky Mountains, the Missouri actually has less flow than other major rivers because its course runs through so much arid land. Known as the "Big Muddy" because of its high sediment content deriving from the Missouri Basin's sparse fauna, the Missouri nevertheless constituted a major thoroughfare for trappers and traders. Indians and French *voyageurs* used the Missouri for years before the ***Lewis and Clark Expedition [III]*** of 1803 followed it to the Pacific Coast. The steamer *Independence* sailed up the river in 1819, and by the early 1820s, steamboats regularly transited the Missouri, but the river never developed as a central route to the West because travelers found it easier to take the overland route along the Republican River to the South Pass in Wyoming, or later, to take the transcontinental railroad. Still, several towns developed as a result of trade coming from the Missouri, including Atchison, Kansas, and St. Joseph, Missouri. In 1944 the U.S. Army Corps of Engineers started a reclamation project to build dams and reservoirs for flood control and irrigation on the Missouri; then 20 years later, the corps deepened the channel from Sioux City, Iowa, to St. Louis, keeping the river open much of the year.

Monument Valley

A scenic region of nearly 2,000 square miles in northeastern Arizona and southeastern Utah, Monument Valley is part of the Colorado Plateau. Its

A famous backdrop for numerous John Ford movies, Monument Valley, Arizona, is also frequently featured in automobile commercials. *Bradley J. Birzer*

tall, red sandstone buttes, mesas, and arches rise up to 1,000 feet from the plain. It is part of the Navajo Indian Reservation, and Navajos have occupied the region since the mid-1800s. The valley has been the location for numerous western movies, and its picturesque rock formations characterize the ruggedness of the American West.

Mourning/Beaver Wars, 1608–1701

A strategic decision on the part of Samuel *Champlain* in 1608 touched off nearly a century of warfare between the central Algonquian Indians and the *Iroquois*. Champlain decided to prove French loyalty to their new allies, the Hurons, by sending some musketeers on a war party with them. As the Hurons confronted a surprised Mohawk war party, the French musketeers opened fire, killing far more than was normal in a Indian skirmish. In response, the Iroquois, fueled by Dutch weapons and a desire to expand their control of the fur trade west, pushed the Hurons and central Algonquians west for nearly three-quarters of a century.

The war, from the Iroquois point of view, was about more than beaver. It was also about mourning, a process in which the Iroquois replaced dead members of their confederacy by capturing alien Indians and adopting them. This, of course, led to a vicious cycle in which the Iroquois warred to adopt, but lost many in the warring process and therefore had to war more to adopt more.

The Iroquois made great advances against the Indians of the western Great Lakes, wedging them between themselves and the Great Plains, in an area called the *Pays d'en Haut* (modern Illinois and Wisconsin). The war could be intensely brutal at times. In the 1650s, for example, a Seneca war party captured a number of Miami babies. On their way back to upstate New York, the Senecas cannibalized one Miami baby per night, leaving its head on a stick the following morning to taunt the pursuing Miami warriors.

In 1687 a French-Algonquian alliance launched a major counter-offensive against the Iroquois, striking them hard at present-day Kalamazoo, Michigan. After continuing success against the Iroquois in the 1690s, both sides ended the war in 1701 with the Grand Settlement. Though still aggressive, the Iroquois rarely expanded militarily west of New York after 1701.

Navajo

Closely related to the Apache (with whom they were probably one people in the distant past), the Navajos entered what is now the American Southwest in the 1300s. They most likely migrated from the north (probably from somewhere in Canada). They may have been one of the nomadic peoples that destroyed the high civilization of the *Anasazi* centered around *Chaco Canyon*. Anthropologist Edward Spicer notes that for all the environmental disadvantages of the Southwest, it has always served as a nexus and a palimpsest, in which cultures and peoples have participated in the "cycles of conquest." The Navajo are one of many such peoples.

The Navajo have resided in the Four Corners region of the Southwest since roughly 1600. They refer to themselves as the Diné, which simply means "the people" or "the people who cultivate the fields." They call their land Dinétah, or "land of the people who cultivate the fields." As with all native North Americans, the Navajos center their institutions around kinship, with the extended family living in what they call a hogan, a building housing the extended family. The kinship system is matrilineal, as the husbands join the family of the wife after marriage. Politically, the kinship system and hogan kept the Navajo decentralized. Unity simply meant a number of hogans, or extended families, temporarily acting in concert.

The Navajo in the last 400 years have sustained their economy through shepherding and farming, and they especially impressed the Spanish with their farming abilities in the desert. Sometime in the 17th century, the Navajos adapted Spanish-originated horses to their culture.

Prior to the 20th century, the Navajos rarely lived at peace with the neighbors. Their enemies (and sometimes their allies) have included the Pueblos, the Utes, the Hopis, the Spanish, the Mexicans, and the Americans. The Navajos first met the Spanish in 1598, but the Franciscan *missionaries* never successfully converted them. Instead, the Navajos and the Spanish warred and enslaved one another incessantly. San Antonio and Zacatecas served as the major Spanish trading depots for the Navajos. With the success of the Pueblo Revolt of 1680 (see *Popé*), many of the Pueblos sought refuge with the Navajos, thus transferring Spanish culture, language, and technology to their new protectors.

Though the Mexican government simply exacerbated the mutual animosity the Spanish and the Navajos had felt for one another, the United States fared better. Under Lieutenant Colonel Alexander Doniphan, the

United States signed its first peace treaty with the southwestern tribe in 1846, the first year of the Mexican War. America needed this powerful tribe either to remain neutral or come in on its side. Tensions developed after the *Mexican War [III]* as the Navajos failed to understand that the New Mexicans were now American citizens rather than Mexican citizens. They still seemed to be the enemy.

With the outbreak of the American *Civil War [IV]*, *Kit Carson [III]* forcibly removed the Navajos to the Apache Reservation. Carson employed total war against them, destroying their crops and their homes, forcing them to surrender. Not until January 1864 did the Navajos surrender. Carson then forced them to march to the reservation at *Bosque Redondo [IV]*. The Navajos bitterly remember this as the "*Navajo Long Walk*" *[IV]*. Their four years at Bosque Redondo were disasters on an unparalleled scale, as the Americans attempted to remake the Navajos in their own image.

With the obvious failure of the reservation experiment, the United States gave the tribe its traditional homelands back, though with reduced acreage. By 1880 the Navajos were again fairly autonomous and economically successful. During *World War II [V]*, despite their resentment against the collectivist New Deal, the Navajos served proudly and indispensably as Code Talkers. More than 420 Navajos served in this unique function. The Japanese never broke the code. Today more than a quarter of a million Indians make up the Navajo nation, and its reservation is the largest in the United States, with more than 25,000 square miles of land.

New France Exploration, 1524–1763

New France, as the French presence in North America was known, existed from roughly 1608, the establishment of Quebec, to its official demise in 1763 with the treaty ending the Great War for Empire. In reality, though, exploration and preparation for New France began as early as 1524 with Giovanni de Verrazano's explorations. New France's remnants and cultural influence lasted well into the 19th century, and some remains may be found in the present, especially in former French cities such as New Orleans and St. Louis in the United States. The strongest presence and remnant of New France, of course, resides in Canada with the strong French culture, language, Roman Catholicism, and nationalism of the Province of Quebec.

Francis *Parkman [III]*, the 19th-century Boston Brahmin historian, shaped and adulterated Americans' vision of New France. His seminal several-volume history of the French in North America presents a heavily skewed morality play. Parkman's distorted version presented the French as socially regressive, morally backward, miscegenationist Roman Catholics, seeking to spread the worst of the Middle Ages into North America. Their brave and stalwart counterpart, the English, were socially progressive, morally upstanding, Protestant, and, therefore, highly enlightened. They were attempting to carry North America into a progressive future. The Indians, in Parkman's view, served as mere pawns of the "wrong side." They'd chosen Christianity, but it was a paganized, barbaric Christianity according to Parkman.

In reality no such conspiracy existed. The French were rarely organized enough to present such a papist plot for domination in the New World. Instead, rather haphazardly, they explored, traded, and married their way into North American Indian society. New France was widespread, as the French explorers, priests, and fur trappers followed the lakes and rivers, using them as highways. At its height, New France controlled the St. Lawrence, Mississippi, and Missouri river valleys, and the land and lakes surrounding the tributaries of each of the three major rivers.

In the early 16th century two explorers, Giovanni de Verrazano and Jacques *Cartier*, paved the way for French claims to North America. Verrazano's good relations with the Indians began a French tradition that, with some important exceptions, lasted well into the 19th century. Cartier also established good relations with the Indians he met and made the significant discovery that the native peoples often preferred trade to warfare. Cartier attempted to colonize New France in 1541, but his efforts failed.

Because of the Reformation Wars and internal struggles between the Catholics and Huguenots, the French ignored North America for 70 years. Following the paths taken by de Verrazano and Cartier, Samuel de *Champlain* officially established New France and Quebec, its capital, in 1608. To his amazement, disease brought by the two explorers more than three generations earlier had wiped out many of the tribes they had encountered. In 1609 Champlain created a significant alliance when he aided the Hurons in an assault on the Mohawks, members of the powerful

Iroquois Confederacy. Champlain's actions, though strengthening French control of the region, led to almost a century of warfare, known as the *Mourning/Beaver Wars*, between the Iroquois and various central Algonquian tribes.

With Quebec as an established and defensible base, French exploration expanded. The most important in terms of physical and mental prowess of the French explorers were the Roman Catholic Jesuit *missionaries*. Their records, the *Jesuit Relations and Allied Documents,* remain the best historical and ethno-historical documents of native cultures from the 17th and 18th centuries. The first priest to explore and missionize in New France was Father Gabriel Sagard, a non-Jesuit. He lived with the Hurons for two years in the 1620s and said of them: "these would be families among whom God would take pleasure to dwell."

In 1625 the first stalwart Jesuits arrived. At first the Indians rejected the "Black Robes." The Jesuits encountered five problems in their missionary efforts. First, the Indians considered them demons, especially as they were celibate. With the martyrdom of the first Jesuits, though, the native people began to respect the members of the order, seeing them as possessing unusual stoic power and self-discipline, traits admired by all native societies.

Second, the Iroquois targeted Jesuit missions among the Algonquian missions, as the Jesuits taught the Christianized Indians nonviolent resistence. The missions were also relatively wealthy as well as being stationary. Third, disease killed the Indians as well. This especially frustrated the Jesuits, as the members of the order failed to understand why God would take souls prior to their salvation. Fourth, the Jesuits had to compete with the typically immoral French fur traders who saw the Christianizing of the Indians as a hindrance to potential profits and their exploitation of native labor. Finally, the sheer mental and physical prowess of the Jesuits probably led to many Indians converting to Christianity for reasons other than theology. Instead, they were simply attracted to the power of the Jesuits, thus leading to a fusion of Catholic and pagan beliefs.

French exploration continued well until the 1740s. In 1673 Jesuit Father Jacques Marquette and Louis Jolliet traveled the Mississippi River past present-day Cape Girardeau, but they did not reach the Gulf of Mexico. Ren *La Salle [II]* first discovered the Gulf in April 1682. In the 1710s and 1720s Etienne Veniard de *Bourgmont [II]* explored the Missouri River. Sieur de La Verendrye and his son explored the northern Great Plains in the 1730s and early 1740s, and the *Mallet [II]* brothers explored the central Great Plains, 1739–1740, discovering a route to Santa Fe.

With the official demise of New France militarily in 1761 and diplomatically in 1763, official French exploration of North America ended as well. French exploration initiative remained, however, and some of the best British and American fur trappers and explorers were French Creoles, left behind when their government departed in 1763.

New Netherlands

The Netherlands was one of the four most important European imperial powers seeking control over North America in the 17th century. Unlike its rivals—England, Spain, and France—the Dutch worked to establish a mercantile empire, hoping for control over the fur trade as opposed to land acquisition. They took their rivalry with the other three major powers seriously, especially given their recent separation through rebellion from the Spanish Hapsburgs.

The Dutch West Indies Company controlled the settlement of the New Netherlands, further indicating the importance of profit for the Dutch. The North American Dutch embraced commerce and Calvinism at virtually all levels of their society, leading to somewhat close ties with England.

In 1609 the Dutch West Indies Company hired an English explorer, Henry Hudson, to explore northern North America and find the fabled Great Northwest Passage to Asia. Though Hudson failed, he laid considerable claim to the Hudson River region, where he spent much of his time. He made it as far north as present-day Albany. During a second expedition, Hudson's crew mutinied, stranding their former captain in a lifeboat. He was never found.

In 1624 the Dutch West Indies Company settled 30 families in Albany and in 1626 sent colonists to New Amsterdam (modern New York City). Rarely, however, did the Dutch attempt to intermarry with or convert the Indians. Much of New Netherlands society revolved around the *handeltijd*, or business season, from the first of May to the first of November. In comparison with European rivals, the Dutch were quite liberal. Women, for example, while not as numerous as men, worked as merchants and in the fur trade. Jews, too, were allowed to trade and encouraged to settle.

Despite their liberality on issues of sex and religion, the Dutch could be brutal when it came to Indians and the fur trade. Dutch arming of the *Iroquois* Confederacy led to the nearly century-long *Mourning/Beaver Wars* in which the Iroquois ruthlessly expanded westward in search of new areas rich in fur.

In 1664 English troops seized New Amsterdam, the capital, and re-named it New York. As an imperial power, the New Netherlands only lasted from roughly 1614 to 1664, but it had long-ranging consequences. First, the Iroquois maintained their imperialistic expansion, having been first prompted by the Dutch, until 1701, when they finally signed the Grand Settlement. Second, a number of Dutch families, the Rensselaers and Roosevelts, to name just a few, remain significant culturally, economically, and politically to this day.

Oñate, Juan de (ca. 1550–1626)

A devout Roman Catholic and imperialist, Oñate was born into a promi-nent Spanish Creole family in New Spain in the early 1550s. After roughly 60 years of Spanish neglect of the region north of the *Rio Grande*, Oñate led a colonizing expedition to what is today New Mexico in 1598. He did so as a private citizen, but under license from the Spanish Crown. He took with him nearly 500 persons, including 130 soldiers and their families and 10 Roman Catholic priests. Upon reaching what is today El Paso, Oñate gave an impassioned speech, likening his expedition to the divine impera-tive given in the Book of Genesis: to have dominion over the earth, to name the unnamed flora and fauna, and to multiply. He and his men also performed a conversion play for the Indians. As Oñate's party moved north, they repeated the plays in each Pueblo village. Much to the surprise of Oñate and his priests, many of the Indians accepted baptism. The Span-iards, of course, saw this as providence. While some of the baptisms may have been legitimate, others were simply to avoid the punishment *Coronado* had dealt them nearly three generations earlier.

Geopolitics also played a role in Oñate's efforts. With Sir Francis *Drake* expanding his privateering efforts along the Atlantic coast, the Spanish Crown desired to further its control of the New World. Spain hoped Oñate would set up a permanent presence in the heart of North America, as well as open up a port on the Pacific Ocean. Such a goal demonstrates how little the Spanish understood North American geography. Other Spanish goals included the creation of mining and ranching enterprises.

Oñate and his men established their headquarters at the confluence of the Rio Grande and Chama River, renaming the already existing Tewa Pueblo, San Juan. Oñate moved the headquarters twice, once to San Gabriel, and finally, in 1608, to Santa Fe.

Oñate met resistence from his men, many of whom mutinied only months after arriving in New Mexico, and from the *Ácoma* Pueblos, who resented Spanish acquisition of their food stores during the first harsh winter. Oñate's men quickly subdued the Ácoma uprising. It proved to be the first of several such native revolts.

From his base in central New Mexico, Oñate launched several expeditions. He searched for Cibola's gold and silver deposits and mines as well as for a Pacific port. He failed to find either. With Oñate's failure to find

IN THEIR OWN Words

Don Juan de Oñate's Letter from New Mexico [1599]

Don Juan de Oñate, in a March 1599 letter to the Viceroy, the Count of Monterey, gave a report of his expedition to New Mexico. He continued to pass along rumors of incredible wealth in the region and requested further support, aid, and protection for settling and pacifying the region.

There is another nation, that of the Cocoyes [i.e., Pecos Indians], an innumerable people with huts and agriculture. Of this nation and of the large settlements at the source of the Rio del Norte and of those to the northwest and west and towards the South Sea, I have numberless reports, and pearls of remarkable size from said sea, and assurance that there is an infinite number of them on the coast of this country. And as to the east, a person in my camp, an Indian who speaks Spanish and is one of those who came with Humana, has been in the pueblo of the said herdsmen. It is nine continuous leagues in length and two in width, with streets and houses consisting of huts. It is situated in the midst of the multitude of buffalo, which are so numerous that my sargento mayor, who hunted them and brought back their hides, meat, tallow, and suet, asserts that in one herd alone he saw more than there are of our cattle in the combined three ranches of Rodrigo del Rio, Salvago, and Jerónimo López, which are famed in those regions.

—Source: Herbert Eugene Bolton, *Spanish Exploration in the Southwest, 1542–1706*
(New York: Charles Scribner's Sons, 1916), 212–221.

anything of significance on his expeditions and the continued revolts of the Pueblos, the Crown removed him from office and disgraced his name in 1614. It took a number of years for Oñate to regain favor with the Crown, and the Spanish court eventually named him "chief mining inspector" of Spain. In 1626 while inspecting a mine shaft, Oñate died.

Pays d'en Haut/Middle Ground

Early *missionaries* to North America, such as the Jesuits, saw the Central Algonquians as the perfect proto-Christians. Comparing the militantly expansionist *Iroquois* of the 17th century to the persecuting Romans of the first and second centuries, the "Black Robes" found inspiration and hope that the Indians, who were not as aggressive as "those who have Empires and Republics, Princes and Kings," would convert to Christianity. The Central Algonquians, living in relative squalor and in fear of the aggressive Iroquois, seemed culturally ready to accept Christianity, and according to the missionaries, they loved prayer, charity, and suffering.

The priests proved correct in their assessment, though it is doubtful that the Central Algonquians loved suffering. They did, however, endure it, as they had no choice. The Iroquois' aggressive campaigns of the *Mourning/Beaver Wars* had indeed forced the once powerful Central Algonquian Illinois-Miami confederacy to move west during the middle and late 17th centuries. Iroquois expansion wreaked sheer havoc upon the Central Algonquians, who were caught between their Dutch-inspired eastern aggressors and the Siouan tribes in the northern Great Plains. Unfortunately for the Central Algonquians, the Ohio Valley and western Great Lakes, with its numerous rivers that served well as trade highways, also provided enemies easy access into the area, a geographic vulnerability that the Iroquois naturally took advantage of.

In their cramped area centered around the western Great Lakes, the Central Algonquians readily mixed with one another, trading goods, cultural norms, and genetic traits. Out of sheer necessity, they did indeed practice the virtues of charity, primarily through reciprocal gift exchanges and mutual aid. Their unity provided an effective barrier against further Iroquois penetration. The Indian tribes intermixing in the Pays d'en Haut (modern Wisconson and Illinois) included the *Miami [II]*, the *Potawatomi [II]*, the Illinois, the Hurons, the *Fox*, the Ottawas, the Ojibwas, and the

Winnebagos, to name a few. Unfortunately, the sharing also included mortal European-originated diseases that spread quickly through the dense refugee population. The Iroquois essentially pushed the Algonquians into a deadly region in which smallpox and measles exacted a greater toll than the Iroquois.

With the immense cultural and genetic intermixing, as well as the massive population decline, the Central Algonquians, never highly centralized politically, decentralized even more. Their system of government, if one can label it as such, revolved around the village. Kinship, religion, and loyalty tied members of the tribe together. No centralized state unified them; instead, "wise" leaders led villages.

It was in the shattered world of the mid-17th century, with population dramatically falling and cultural mixing, that the Central Algonquian Indians first met the French. The French provided several things that proved to be godsends for the troubled Indians. The French offered new weapons, new tools, and new clothing.

By the 1680s, after only two decades of trade, the Miamis and the French were major trading partners. Indeed, the Miamis were providing more fur than the European market could bear.

Trade did provide new goods and new markets, and the French ably served as negotiators and mediators for the mixed and declining peoples under siege by the Iroquois. The French used their literacy to coordinate the various Central Algonquians through trade and warfare, resulting, by the end of the first several decades of "friendship," in the expulsion of the powerful Iroquois from the western Great Lakes area. "Onontio," the Indian name for the French king, became a powerful ally and friend. The Grand Settlement of 1701 effectively ended Iroquois power and the Mourning/Beaver Wars in the Ohio Valley, thus ending the significance of the Pays d'en Haut.

Popé (d. 1688)

Little is known regarding the Pueblo nativist leader and medicine man Popé. In 1675 the Spanish whipped him publically (one of the worst punishments a Pueblo male could receive), accusing him of sorcery. They may have also imprisoned him after he attempted to unite the Apache with the Pueblos. In the next five years, Popé organized an uprising of the Pueblos against the Spanish. He led a successful revolt secretly from a *kiva* in Taos on August 10, 1680. After driving away the Spanish, though, Popé established a brutal dictatorship over the Pueblos. In one Pueblo village after another, Popé ordered the destruction of all Catholic churches and relics, the death of any Spanish religious, and the forced "unconversion"or "unbaptism"of all Christians. His bitterness and tyrannical rule became too much for the Pueblos. They did not want to trade one form of control for another, and in events that remain clouded in mystery, the Pueblos forced Popé to step down. He most likely died in 1688, though some sources claim his death date in 1692. The Spanish did not fully regain control of the Pueblos until 1696. After the brutality of Popé's revolt, though, the Spanish governed with a lighter hand.

Pueblo Bonito

One of the greatest architectural achievements of northern American Indians, Pueblo Bonito ("pretty village") was built by the *Anasazi* Indians in *Chaco Canyon*, New Mexico. Construction began around A.D. 700, with more intense construction occurring between A.D. 900 and 1100. The site consisted of several sophisticated dwellings containing two- and three-story buildings, plus ceremonial structures known as *kivas*, and had a population of up to 1,200 people. A drought in the region around 1150 depopulated the area, which was rediscovered by American soldiers in 1849. In 1920 the National Geographic Society began a restoration of the site.

Radisson, Pierre-Esprit (d. 1710)

Radisson was the quintessential explorer. He loved being outside of European civilization and craved power. "We were Caesars," he wrote, about his experiences in the wilds of North America, "being nobody to contradict us." After bypassing traditional French-allied Indian businessmen and trading directly with the interior tribes, Radisson returned to France loaded with pelts. The French government, however, punished him for avoiding their Indian allies and confiscated his goods. Radisson then offered his services to the English, creating the *Hudson's Bay Company*, which greatly bolstered the English presence in the New World.

repartimiento

In the New World, the Spanish developed system of labor organization called *repartimiento*, under which Indians were required to contribute 45 days a year in labor in return for protection and Christianization. It was part of the broader *encomienda* policies of the Spanish empire in New Spain.

Rio Grande

Flowing some 1,800 miles from the Colorado Rockies at Stony Pass to the Gulf of Mexico at Brownsville, Texas, the "Great River" constitutes part of the modern boundary line between Mexico and the United States. The Rio Grande, the fifth longest river in North America with a drainage area of 172,000 square miles, crosses New Mexico, angles southeast at *El Paso*, heads north until it joins with the Pecos River above Del Rio, Texas, then continues through Laredo to the Gulf.

Early Spanish explorer Álvar Núñez *Cabeza de Vaca* encountered the Rio Grande during his travels as an Indian captive. Later, in 1598, Juan de *Oñate* gave the waterway its name. By 1600 Spanish settlers had moved into the midsection of the Rio Grande valleys. In 1806 Lieutenant Zebulon *Pike [III]* led a party of Americans into the region, camping on the banks of the Rio Grande in the San Luis Valley, and his reports brought more Americans seeking trade with the Spanish. After Mexican independence in 1821, regular lines of commerce between the United States and Mexico opened along the Santa Fe-Chihuahua Trail. Access to the northern Mexican territories via Missouri proved less daunting than carrying goods from coastal cities. As a result, *Santa Fe* became a leading commercial center.

Disputes over the southern boundary of Texas contributed to the *Mexican War [III]*, with the United States claiming the Rio Grande as the border, while Mexico insisted that the more northern boundary of the Nueces River was correct. The American victory in the war settled the issue, but legends of bandits escaping across the Rio Grande to the relative safety provided by the vast expanses of the Mexican deserts are a staple of western lore. More recently, in the 20th century, the river has been viewed as the symbolic line of defense against illegal immigrants, who, due to their willingness to swim across to the United States, were derogatorily referred to as "wetbacks." Although the Rio Grande's flow is considered barely able to meet the demands placed on it, it nevertheless floods routinely, and in 1915 the Elephant Butte Reservoir at Truth or Consequences, New Mexico, was constructed to reduce the likelihood of flooding.

San Gabriel

New Mexico's first capital and first European settlement, San Gabriel was founded in 1598 along the west bank of the *Rio Grande,* above the Chama River. Prior to their establishment of San Gabriel, New Mexico colonizer Don Juan de *Oñate* and his colonists had resided at San Juan Pueblo, where the Indians amiably shared their food and homes. Soon after the move to San Gabriel, Oñate set out in search of potential mines. When he returned in 1601 after a five-month absence, he found the settlement all but deserted. In 1610 Oñate's replacement, Don Pedro de Peralta, removed the San Gabriel settlement to a site further from Pueblo settlements and renamed it *Santa Fe.*

Santa Fe

The capital of the state of New Mexico, Santa Fe, founded in 1610, has been a seat of power in the Southwest for almost 400 years. Don Pedro de Peralta, at the order of the viceroy of Mexico City, established Santa Fe, or "Holy Faith." It is located on the Santa Fe River at the base of the Sangre de Cristo Mountains. Early Spanish settlers laid out a city plan around a governor's palace, using Indian slave labor to construct the buildings. A wall was later erected for defense of the tiny settlement, which in the mid-1600s numbered under 300. Supply trains brought food, staples, weapons, and news from home every three years.

In 1680 the Pueblo Uprising (see *Popé*) reached Santa Fe, placing the town under siege. The population retreated to the palace, holding off the Indian attackers until Governor Antonio de Otermín led an escape on August 21. Twelve years later General Diego de *Vargas* headed an army from *El Paso* that defeated the Indians. The population again rose in the

1700s, attracting several landowners as well as the soldiers and royal officials administering the territory. Intermarried Indians and detribalized natives, known as *genízaros*, constituted a significant part of the population, which numbered in the thousands by the early 1800s.

American explorers, led by Zebulon *Pike [III]*, reached Santa Fe in 1807, and after Mexico won independence from Spain in 1821, the Santa Fe Trail from Missouri was opened to regular trade between the two countries. During the *Mexican War [III]*, Brigadier General Stephen Watts *Kearny [III]* led an American expedition into New Mexico. Finding the local administrators had abandoned the defense of Santa Fe, Kearny established an American military government there and constructed Fort Marcy. Once Kearny moved on, however, locals staged a rebellion, killing Governor Charles Bent. The Mexican Cession turned New Mexico territory over to the United States and a formal government was organized in 1850. During the Civil War, the Confederates briefly held Santa Fe under General H. H. Sibley until Union volunteers from Colorado ejected them.

Following the extension of telegraph and rail lines to Santa Fe in the mid- to late-1800s, New Mexico Territory started to become more integrated into the United States culturally and politically. The Santa Fe Ring, a group of political operatives in the 1870s, dominated territorial politics with the selection of judges, sheriffs, the control of territorial legislature and of the Maxwell Land Grant Company. After 1912 when New Mexico was admitted into the Union as a state, the Santa Fe Ring lost most of its influence.

Modern Santa Fe became known first as a refuge for those suffering from tuberculosis, then later as an artist colony. Although Albuquerque surpassed Santa Fe as the commercial center of New Mexico, the capital city remains a cultural and intellectual haven.

smallpox

A viral disease spread by direct contact, smallpox was fatal and had no known cure in the 1600s and 1700s. The virus incubated for a few weeks; then the infected person developed high fevers, muscle aches, pains, and then broke out in a rash of blisters. When Europeans first came to America, smallpox wiped out most of the settlers in some colonies and decimated Indian tribes. The impact of European diseases such as smallpox on native American depopulation remains in dispute among scholars.

St. Augustine

The oldest city in the United States, St. Augustine, Florida, was settled by Spanish in 1565. Ponce de Léon, in April 1512, had claimed the land for Spain, but established no permanent settlement. Other explorers, including Nárvaez in 1526 and *de Soto* in 1539, crossed the territory, and the French built Fort Caroline near the St. John's River. Admiral Pedro Menendez de Aviles destroyed the French colony and founded St. Augustine, named after the fifth-century Catholic saint. The region remained in Spanish custody until the Adams-Onis Treaty of 1819 except for a 20-year period. Over the years, military expeditions ravaged the town, including Sir Francis *Drake*, and the Union Army held it during the Civil War.

Straits of Anian

The Straits of Anian was a mythical passage between Hudson's Bay and the Pacific Ocean. During the 18th century, explorers searched in vain for it. After lengthy discussions with the Ojibwa Indians in 1716, explorer James Knight convinced himself of the single river leading from the bay to the ocean. He mounted an expedition in 1719 to explore the Straits of Anian, but severe winter weather in northern Canada destroyed his ships and crew.

Treaty of Tordesillas

Following *Columbus*'s return from the New World, Spanish exploration had caught up to that of Portugal. Spain appealed to Pope Alexander VI for an edict giving lands discovered by Columbus to Spain. In 1494 the Pope set a line at 100 leagues west of the the Cape Verde Islands, and ruling that beyond the line, Spain was entitled to lands not claimed by a Christian monarch as of December 1492. This infringed on Portugal's South American territories. Subsequent negotiations produced the Treaty of Tordesillas in 1494, which moved the line to 370 leagues west of the Cape Verde Islands, giving Portugal the lands that remained east of the line.

Tucson

Founded as the presidio of San Agustín del Tucson on the banks of the
Santa Cruz River in December 1775, the town took its name from a nearby
Papago village. Although Apaches attacked the town regularly, settlers
moved in, protected by the presidio. After the Gadsden Purchase of 1853
added the town and its surrounding region to Arizona, commerce and
settlement accelerated. During the Civil War, Confederate troops occupied the city, after which Tucson briefly became the territorial capital. The
arrival of the *Southern Pacific Railroad [IV]* added to the population. In
1891 the legislature established the University of Arizona there, and defense industries located in Tucson over the years. Several high-tech firms
moved to Tucson in the 1950s, and by the mid-20th century, the city was
the second largest in Arizona.

Vargas, Diego de (1643–1704)

A middling member of the Spanish gentry, Vargas was appointed governor of the exiled colony of New Mexico in 1690. His mission was to recon-
quer and recolonize New Mexico. He arrived in 1691 in *El Paso*, home of
the New Mexicans since the successful Pueblo Revolt of 1680. Less than a
year later he launched an expedition into the heart of New Mexico. To his
surprise, he and his Pueblo Indian allies encountered little resistance and
gained the allegiance of 23 Pueblo communities. With victory seemingly
at hand, Vargas set out to recolonize New Mexico. He returned in 1693
with 800 soldiers, colonists, and allied Pueblo Indians, only to find resistance rather than allegiance. The Pueblos had no qualms about Vargas's
diplomatic overtures when his visit was temporary; when he returned to
settle the region permanently, the Pueblos quickly changed their stance. In
light of the Tewa and Tano refusal to relinquish *Santa Fe*, Vargas successfully attacked the city.

The Spanish victory provided Vargas with a stronghold from which
he conducted a difficult military campaign against the Pueblos throughout 1694. The Pueblos answered his campaign with another revolt in 1696,
killing 5 Franciscan priests, and 21 other Spaniards and burning churches
and convents. Determined to subdue the Pueblos, Vargas launched a war
of attrition that lasted six months, targeting food supplies as well as rebel-

lious natives. By the war's end, all but the three western pueblos (*Ácoma*, Zuni, and *Hopi*) were subdued. Ácoma and Zuni soon followed suit, but Hopi remained independent for another century. The resumption of trade in European goods beckoned the rest of the Pueblos, and they fell in line. Some communities split into pro-Spanish and anti-Spanish factions, with defiant individuals fleeing to a less fettered existence among the Apache or the *Navajo*.

To guard against future rebellions, Vargas established a presidio at Santa Fe in 1693 and founded a civilian town at Santa Cruz de la Cañada in 1695. In the early years of the 18th century, Vargas turned his attention toward marauding Apaches. In the midst of a 1704 campaign against Apache raiders, the governor contracted dysentery from a soldier. He died in Bernalillo after dictating a will and specifying the details for an elaborate funeral.

Vizcáino, Sebastián (ca. 1550–1628)

Sebastián Vizcáino, born in approximately 1550 to Antonio Vizcáino in Corcho, Spain, joined the Portuguese army while a teenager. In 1585 he sailed to Mexico but quickly saw the profits available in trade. In the late 1580s he made a voyage to Manila to investigate the markets in the Far East. After being captured by British pirates, Vizcáino lost much of his fortune before starting a company for the purpose of exploring California.

Vizcáino sent out one expedition under Perez del Castillo, which floundered badly; then in 1596 Vizcáino himself left Acapulco with 230 men, which accomplished little; he undertook yet another expedition in 1602. That voyage explored the coastline of lower California, staying in San Diego before going further north to Monterey Bay. In 1603 two of his ships (the third returned to Acapulco with the sick and infirm) reached Cape Mendocino. Vizcáino saw the advantages of having a port at Monterey and sailed to Spain where the Council of the Indies gave him a royal decree that placed him in charge of the port of Monterey. When the plan was disapproved by the new viceroy in Mexico, Vizcáino was given command of an expedition to discover the "Rica de Oro" islands thought to exist near Japan. Leaving for the Asian coast in 1611, the expedition returned in 1614 empty-handed. The following year, Vizcáino enlisted in a force to fight the Dutch, then disappeared.

Yaquis

The Yaquis are an Indian tribe claiming land that is now in northern Sonora and southern Arizona. They speak a Uto-Aztecan language. In 1529 explorer Nuño de Guzmán, a Spaniard, was the first European to make contact with them. Fathers Perez de Rivas and Tomás Basilio first missionized the Yaquis in 1619. With the Mexicans persecuting the Yaquis, most members of the tribe fled to the United States in 1884. In 1978 the federal government finally recognized them as an official tribe.

PART II

From LaSalle's Expeditions to the Louisiana Purchase (1682–1803)

As the era of exploration and colonization gave way to settlement and development, the frontiers gradually receded and the colonizing powers increasingly found themselves in conflict on their borders. French fur trading posts, Spanish missions and forts, and English trading settlements soon mixed Europeans of various nationalities with a diverse range of Native Americans and African Americans, both slave and free. Already, however, a key dynamic in the British system of landholding had taken root and shaped the British American colonies in such a way that they would technically surpass other cultures, European or Indian.

Land abundance in North America, especially to a culture that cherished individual—as opposed to collective—property rights, generated a "feedback loop." Available land meant labor scarcity, because workers could leave at any time to start a farm. Labor scarcity led to high wages, which in turn required businesses to constantly search for more improved machinery instead of additional labor. (Labor scarcity had also produced the failed attempts by the Spanish to enslave the Indians; the barely successful system of indentured servitude in the British colonies; and the more successful introduction of African slaves into the New World.) By substituting machinery for labor when possible British entrepreneurs stayed on the cutting edge of technical change, and thus consistently outpaced the French and the Spanish. This was not readily apparent in the 1700s but was abundantly clear by 1810, when English and American adoption of steam power far surpassed that of Spain. Even before that, by the early 1700s, the more capitalist and less mercantile England and Holland had leapfrogged Spain in musket and, especially, cannon technology.

Individual property rights led to inevitable conflict with the Indians, even with those Native American tribes who valued private property rights. But the inevitability of such clashes was not so apparent prior to the French and Indian War, when control of most of North America was still in dispute. Early hostilities in North America erupted over surveying parties and encroachments into French territory, on the one hand, and French fort building in the Ohio Valley on the other. Virginia Governor Robert Dinwiddie dispatched Major George Washington in 1753 to warn the French to stop their expansion into an area claimed by both England and France. When the French refused, Washington returned to Virginia, reorganized, and led two companies of volunteers to evict the French, and at Fort Necessity, he essentially started the Seven Years War in North America. However, the struggle between France and England had been building worldwide, involving geopolitical and religious elements that transcended North American issues. After seven years' worth of bloody fighting—and some horrendous defeats for the British—England nevertheless emerged victorious when Quebec fell, leaving Britain in control of Canada.

During the war, the Ottawa, under Pontiac, had aided the French and helped defeat General Edward Braddock. After the British gained control, they naturally stood to lose from their alliance with the French, and following a disastrous policy by British administrator Lord Jeffrey Amherst, Pontiac led a rebellion that besieged Forts Detroit and Pitt in 1763. British reinforcements finally forced the tribes to seek peace. But even the allies of the British, the Iroquois, who had fought the French in hopes of forcing France from Canada, learned that the removal of France did not work to the Indians' benefit. With their victory in 1763 also came seeds of their defeat: the British fur trade moved down the St. Lawrence, benefiting the more western tribes. The end of Iroquois dominance came with the American Revolution, when the Iroquois again sided with England.

English success in the Seven Years War also produced unhappiness with the Crown among the American colonists. Anxious to move across the Appalachians and trade or settle, English colonists moved westward, encroaching on Indian lands. Confronting a possible frontier uprising by the tribes, the British government issued the Proclamation Line of 1763, prohibiting new land purchases from the Indians west of the line and requiring English traders to obtain permits to conduct business there. In two ways, the Proclamation Line outraged American colonists. First, although it did not do so, the proclamation appeared to prohibit new settlement—which, after all, was one of the motivations for English men and women to come to America. Second, the presumption of a monopoly power for the established traders threatened competition from a rising group of entrepreneurs, who saw the Proclamation as an abridgment of the "rights of Englishmen."

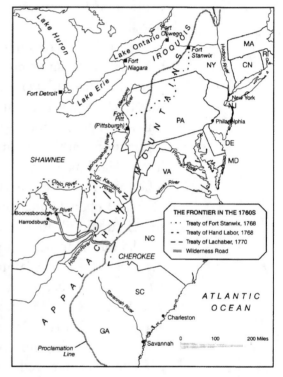

The frontier in the 1760s. *Ron Acklin, University of Dayton Print and Design*

The French and Indian War produced other pressures on the relationship between England and the colonies in North America, specifically the financial demands of defending the frontier. A series of taxes designed to pay for frontier defense only provoked outrage from the Americans that escalated into the events of Lexington and Concord and the Declaration of Independence. George Washington, the commander of the Continental Army, dispatched diplomats to arrange the neutrality of most of the Indian tribes, thus relieving the pressures on the frontier. With the Treaty of Paris in 1783, the balance of power in North America now involved five major players: England in Canada, France in Louisiana, Spain in Mexico and the Southwest and Florida, the Indian lands, and the United States of America.

Already though, colonists from the young United States, led by trailblazers such as Daniel Boone, moved into frontier areas of the Northwest Territory and Kentucky. The author of the Declaration and the leading voice of the Revolution, Thomas Jefferson, immediately saw the dangers and the promise of settlement in the new lands. An agrarian—though not, as commonly thought, a thinker focused on small-farm self-sufficiency—Jefferson did not want the new territories to turn on the mother country the way that the colonies had been alienated from England. He saw an opportunity to create a land system in which colonists became citizens, and in which new lands transformed themselves into equal states. Working through the Articles of Confederation Congress, Jefferson authored the Land Ordinance of 1785 and the Northwest Ordinance of 1787; these became the fundamental "law of the land" when it came to the territories. Jefferson proposed a system of survey and land sales in an orderly manner that provided for effective defense by only opening up new lands for sale after existing surveyed lands had been sold. More importantly, the second ordinance allowed for between three and five potential states out of the Old Northwest and set up a system in which settlers could apply for territory status, then, when the population rose, for statehood.

French exploration of the Louisiana region had continued, establishing important trading posts across the midwest. But France was preoccupied after 1789 with her own revolution and could devote few resources to the New World. When Napoleon Bonaparte acquired the Louisiana Territory from Spain in 1800—which had acquired it from France in 1762—he soon found that the demands of his ongoing war in Europe and the rebellion in Haiti made Louisiana too costly to defend. Meanwhile, President Jefferson had grown concerned about the right of deposit in New Orleans. He sent Robert Livingston to acquire the port for $10 million and was surprised and pleased when Livingston returned with an agreement to purchase all of Louisiana for $15 million. The Louisiana Purchase doubled the area of the United States, and although it only added a population of 10,000, the acquisition paved the way for the subsequent states of Arkansas, Missouri, Iowa, Minnesota, the Dakotas, Nebraska, Kansas, Oklahoma, and parts of Colorado, Wyoming, and Montana, as well as, of course, Louisiana. Jefferson then immediately ordered Meriwether Lewis and William Clark to head an expedition to explore and map the newly acquired land. Taken together, the Northwest Ordinance and the Louisiana Purchase marked the transition from a colonial land policy under England to a policy of national expansion as a new nation.

CHRONOLOGY   From LaSalle's Expeditions to the Louisiana Purchase

1682	*Pennsylvania settled*
1682	*LaSalle's expedition down the Mississippi*
1648–1711	*Father Francisco Kino's journeys through New Mexico*
1667	*LaSalle's expeditions to the Mississippi*
1696	*Board of Trade and Plantations formed*
1763	*Proclamation Line of 1763 established*
1763–1764	*Pontiac's Rebellion*
1768	*Treaty of Fort Stanwix*
1774	*Lord Dunmore's War*
1785	*Land Ordinance passed by Congress*
1786	*Treaty of Fort Finney*
1787	*United States Constitution drafted*
1787	*Northwest Ordinance adopted by Congress, debated, ratified*
1790–1795	*Miami-Federalist War*
1794	*Battle of Fallen Timbers*
1795	*Treaty of Greenville*
1803	*Louisiana Purchase*
1803	*Treaty of Vincennes*

Baranov, Aleksander (1747–1819)

As first governor of Russian America, Baranov, an autodidact and full of wanderlust, helped establish Russia's significant foothold in western North America at the beginning of the 19th century. A strong manager, Baranov ran an effective fur trading business in Alaska, bringing Orthodox missionaries to the natives, and often finding himself embroiled in conflict with the native Tlingits. He died in the Indian Ocean in 1819.

Beaubien, Charles ("Black Snake") (late 1700s)

A prominent trader, second husband of the Miami chieftess *Taucumwah*, and British Indian Agent to the *Miami* since 1777, Beaubien held considerable sway among the Miami and *Shawnee*. Americans in the Old Northwest despised Beaubien, rightfully seeing him as the instigator of innumerable war parties against them between 1777 and 1790. A traveler in 1777 described Beaubien as "zealous in appearance for the service of the King." British officers credited him with the capture of Daniel *Boone* in 1778. In 1779 Lieutenant Governor Henry Hamilton, captured by George Rogers *Clark*, blamed Beaubien for betraying him, though no formal charges were ever pressed against Beaubien. The French freebooter August *de la Balme* led an expedition against him in 1780, destroying his warehouse in Kekionga. De la Balme had correctly noted that Beaubien's warehouse had supplied the war parties hitting Americans along the Ohio and in the Illinois country. Miamis Little Turtle and *Pacanne* successfully defended Beaubien, who disappeared from the records after 1783.

Bering, Vitus (1681–1741)

In 1728 Vitus Bering, a Dane exploring for the Russians, was the first European to sail through the Bering Straits, between Alaska and Siberia, and to discover Alaska and the Aleutian Islands. In 1741 Bering led a second expedition to Alaska. Losing control of his crew as they became ridden with scurvy and neared mutiny, Bering wrecked his ship on an island off of Kamchatka, where he died. His journeys laid the path for Russian claims in North America.

Blue Jacket (1750–1810)

Blue Jacket was a heavy drinking *Shawnee* war chief and second in command of the military effort of the *Miami* Confederacy from 1790 to summer 1794 during the *Miami-Federalist War*. In August 1784 Blue Jacket's superior, Miami war chief Little Turtle, resigned in fear that "Mad" Anthony Wayne would defeat them solidly. Blue Jacket took command and rashly led his forces to defeat at the Battle of Fallen Timbers in 1794. Blue Jacket firmly believed in protecting the territorial sovereignty of the Old Northwest Indians. Though he recognized the American victory at the 1795 *Treaty of Greenville*, Blue Jacket continued to desire a pan-Indian Confederacy under British protection. He even advised *Tecumseh [III]* and the Shawnee Prophet in their nativist efforts.

Boone, Daniel (November 2, 1734–September 26, 1820)

One of the most famous frontiersmen in American history, Daniel Boone opened Kentucky to settlement and won fame as a backwoods master. Born in Berks County, Pennsylvania, to Squire Boone, a blacksmith and weaver, and Sarah Morgan, Daniel learned to hunt, trap, and even read and write. Much of his early life was spent moving from one location to another, and at age 15, his family arrived in the Yadkin Valley of North Carolina. By age 19 he had become an excellent marksman, pathfinder, and scout. In 1756 Boone married Rebecca Ryan and started a family. At about that time he joined a military expedition in the *French and Indian War*, where he met future partner John Finley, who told Boone about the western lands of Kentucky.

He had made several hunting forays to other parts of the frontier, including one to the St. Johns River in Florida and a hunt to the eastern part of Kentucky in 1767. Along with Finley and four other men, Boone crossed the Cumberland Gap to set up camp at Station Camp creek in June 1769. Boone left his companions and explored alone for almost two years, going as far west as the modern site of Louisville. He encountered Indians—not always friendly—then linked up with his brother, Squire, for a return to North Carolina in 1771. Two years later, he led a party, including his family, to start a settlement, but the group was attacked by

Cherokee [III] Indians at the Cumberland Gap, where his son was killed. After building a cabin at Harrodsburg, the Boone Party turned back.

Boone was in Kentucky the following year, though, as a messenger to a surveying party authorized by colonial governor Lord Dunmore. In March 1775 Colonel Richard Henderson of the Transylvania Company (who hoped to make Kentucky a state) hired Boone and 28 others to blaze a path through the Cumberland Gap, which became known as the "Wilderness Road." The group succeeded despite repeated Indian attacks, and at the Kentucky River, he constructed Fort Boonesboro, effectively opening Kentucky to settlement.

Boone continued to battle on the frontier between 1775 and 1778, at one point getting captured by the *Shawnee* at the Licking River. After overhearing the chief and a British officer discussing plans to raid Boonesboro, he escaped, warned the town, and helped in its defense. The defense of Boonesboro enhanced Boone's legend in the West, although he was eventually court-martialed because of his capture. At the same time, he lost his holdings in Kentucky due to an improper registry—a point that later generated great public sympathy for him.

Boone surveyed parts of the Ohio River region. In 1798 he left Kentucky for West Virginia. After just more than a year, he moved again, this time with his family to Missouri, where he remained a trapper and woodsman until his death in 1820, at the age of 85. Boone's wife had accompanied him into Kentucky, apparently as one of the first white women in the territory not brought in as a captive of the Indians.

Boone's legend spread among contemporaries—Lord Byron's "Don Juan" contained seven lines related to him, and he was the inspiration for Natty Bumppo, the James Fennimore *Cooper [III]* character. But it also continued through the ages. In 1964 the "Daniel Boone" television series premiered, featuring Fess *Parker [V]* (who had already become famous playing Davey *Crockett [III]* in the Walt Disney television programs) as Boone. The show ran for six years, reinvigorating Parker's career and the Boone myth.

Bourgmont, Etienne Veniard de (ca. 1680–1730)

The military historian of New France, W. J. Eccles, labels Veniard one of "the most colorful and intrepid of all French explorers of the Southwest." In 1695, most likely for harming the prominent family name, his parents exiled Veniard to French North America. By 1700 Veniard had joined the military as a cadet in the Troupes Frances de la Marine and was promoted to ensign in 1706. That year saw the young Veniard put in charge of one of the most important French forts, Fort Detroit. While there, Veniard sided with certain French-allied Indians, the *Miamis,* over other French-allied Indians, the Ottawas, ordering the killing of a number of the latter. During his tenure at Fort Detroit, Veniard ran afoul of his commanding officer, La Mothe Cadillac, and he deserted the French military. From 1706 to 1712 Veniard lived with a variety of different Indian tribes, evading French soldiers.

Citing the experience gleaned from six years of "wilderness living," Veniard met with French bureaucrats in Mobile, Alabama, and took up the task of exploration and diplomacy with the Indians along the *Missouri River [I]* and into the Great Plains. Bourgmont commanded two important expeditions. The first was in 1714 and lasted until 1718. During those four years, Bourgmont mapped the Missouri to South Dakota and opened strong trading and diplomatic relations with a number of Indian tribes. Veniard had to proceed cautiously, though, as many of the tribes feared the French attempts to negotiate with their economic rivals. The Pawnees, for example, refused to allow Veniard to travel through their country en route to the Comanches.

Rejoining the French military, Veniard was promoted to captain in 1718. Four years later, Veniard established a fort on the Missouri River. The French demanded three things of Veniard: (1) treat with the Comanches; (2) open trade ventures with the Spanish; and (3) find a passage to the Pacific Ocean. After two years at the fort, located in east-central Missouri, Veniard departed for Comanche country, traveling as far west as the Great Bend of the Arkansas River in what is today Kansas. Friendly Comanches and innumerable buffalo greeted Veniard's party. The Comanches promised open trade through their country as well 2,000 warriors, should the French ever need them. Though he had met two of the three objectives of his 1722–1724 mission, the treaty with the Comanches would ultimately fail for lack of French traffic across the plains. Veniard returned to New Orleans and made his way back to France. After marrying a well-to-do woman, he retired.

Braddock, Edward (1695–July 13, 1755)

Known for "Braddock's Road," a passage cut from Will's Creek near Cumberland to modern day Somerfield, Pennsylvania, General Edward

Braddock, the son of a general, arrived in Virginia in 1755 to lead British forces in North America against the French. George Washington, a lieutenant colonel, was under his command. Braddock mounted a campaign against Fort Duquesne (Pittsburgh) through the Allegheny Mountains. Roughly eight miles from Duquesne, the forward column was ambushed and destroyed. Braddock was wounded and died not long after.

Brant, Joseph (ca. 1742–November 24, 1807)

One of the most significant figures in late colonial and revolutionary history, Joseph Brant, whose Mohawk name was Thayendanega ("He who places together two bets"), received his English name from his stepfather, his mother's second husband. In addition, Brant was also connected by marriage of his sister to Sir William Johnson, a prominent British officer stationed in North America during the *French and Indian War*. During his teens, Brant served in a number of battles with Johnson. The connection with Johnson allowed Brant to study at Eleazer Wheelock's school in Connecticut (now Dartmouth College). In the 1760s Brant joined the Anglican Church and started a family. In the mid-1770s Brant visited Britain, met King George III, and, upon his return, led four of the six *Iroquois [I]* nations against the American patriot movement. Operating from Forts Oswego and Niagara, Brant and his Tory allies continually harassed the New York frontier. For his efforts, the British promoted Brant to the rank of captain. With the British loss in the rebellion, Brant and his allies sought sanctuary in Canada. During his last years, Brant promoted a pan-Indian alliance against the American Republic.

Carver, Jonathan (1710–1780)

Carver was born in Massachusetts and raised by an uncle in Connecticut. He served during the *French and Indian War* and was wounded while defending Fort William Henry in 1757. Unemployed after the war, Carver learned the basics of cartography and surveying.

With the British takeover of the Northwest, the English wanted to explore the western Great Lakes as well as find the Northwest Passage. A 1744 British law offered a reward (equivalent to $20,000) to the first person to find it. One who desperately wanted to do so was the officer in charge of Fort *Michilimackinac*, Robert Rogers, who also hoped to open new fur trading routes in old French territory and compete with the Spanish.

In 1766 he persuaded Carver to take a group of Indians and traders west of Michilimackinac. Carver followed the route originally taken by the *Marquette and Jolliet Expedition [I]* and ended up on the upper *Mississippi River [I]*, at the site of present-day Minneapolis. He traveled another 200 miles and wintered with the Dakotas, who told him of the Cheyenne and Mandans to the west. The following spring, Carver returned east, arriving at Fort Michilimackinac by August 1767, having traversed more than 1,000 miles, the longest exploration between 1763 and 1775.

Much to his dismay, he found that Rogers had gotten into trouble with British authorities, and Carver was never paid. He left for England in the late 1760s to become an author, writing an account of his travels and a text on Indian cultures. Others accused him of lying and plagiarizing, and he died in extreme poverty.

Charbonneau, Touissant (ca. 1760–ca. 1840)

On November 4, 1804, the *Lewis and Clark Expedition [III]* hired Toussaint Charbonneau as an interpreter and guide for their famed journey. More important to the Corps, however, was one of Charbonneau's wives, *Sacagawea [III]* ("Bird Woman"), a *Shoshone [III]* Indian who proved invaluable to the expedition as a guide and translator. The other men of the Corps regarded Charbonneau as a bore and a bully, though he proved useful as an interpreter.

Chouteau, Auguste (September 7, 1749–February 24, 1829)

At the age of 14, the French Creole Chouteau cofounded St. Louis with his stepfather. Both would remain leading citizens of that city for the remainder of their lives. With the death of his stepfather in 1778, Chouteau inherited the family fur trapping business. He turned it into a mercantile empire. Chouteau built an imposing castle-style manorial mansion in St. Louis, and the Osage Indians, with whom he had a monopoly on the fur trade, delivered their furs to him on his manorial lands several times a year.

Unwittingly, Chouteau aided the Burr Conspiracy in 1805 by joining forces with Burr's collaborator, General James Wilkinson, to explore Kansas and Oklahoma and pave the way for the Zebulon *Pike [III]* Expedition the following year. In 1816 Spanish soldiers arrested Chouteau's 25-man fur trapping party northeast of Taos, New Mexico. The governor at *Santa Fe [I]* regarded all Americans as spies and refused to acknowledge the *Louisiana Purchase*. The Spaniards requisitioned Chouteau's furs (worth more than $30,000), abused the men for more than 48 hours, sentenced the party to 48 days in a Santa Fe prison, and returned them across the plains with neither food nor arms. After the harrowing experience, Chouteau retired, spending the remainder of his life as the leading citizen of St. Louis.

Clark, George Rogers (November 19, 1752– February 13, 1818)

Born in Charlottesville, Virginia, George Rogers Clark grew up on a farm where he learned surveying techniques. From 1772 to 1774 he surveyed and explored lands along the Ohio and Kentucky rivers. He participated in *Lord Dunmore's War* against the Indians in 1774 and subsequently was the surveyor for the Ohio Company.

Clark joined others in advocating some degree of autonomy for Kentucky, which resulted in Virginia agreeing to provide lead and powder for the defense of forts. In 1776 the American Revolution provided an opportunity for the British and their Indian allies to overwhelm the frontier posts. After dispatching spies to learn the enemy's intent, Clark received permission to organize a foray against the British and Indian forces. He received a commission as a major, leading some 350 men to an outpost at modern-day Louisville, Kentucky, from which he took half his men in a strike against British-held Fort Massac on the Tennessee River. Following a victory there, his force took Kaskaskia on July 4, 1778, and eventually captured Fort Sackville (Vincennes) before British counteroffensives pushed him out. His units thereafter struggled to resist both the British and the Spanish at various forts. His efforts helped secure the Northwest for the United States at the end of the Revolution in the Treaty of Paris.

Clark served as an Indian commissioner, where he encountered Continental Army General James Wilkinson's schemes to establish an alliance with Spain from 1787 to1790. Wilkinson sought, successfully at times, to block Clark's career, and his military appointments placed him in a position to interfere with Clark's arrangements with the Indians. Although Clark engaged in milling and other economic pursuits, he remained committed to improving the region of Kentucky, which occasionally led him into agreements with the Spanish and French that were easily interpreted as disloyalty to the United States. He held a generalship in the French army, for example, that he refused to yield.

Clark's younger brother, William, accompanied Meriwether Lewis in the *Lewis and Clark Expedition [III]*. George Rogers Clark lived his final decade in ill health, partially paralyzed and having lost his right leg to amputation. Clark died in Louisville in February 1818.

Cresap, Michael (June 29, 1742–October 18, 1775)

Born in Old Town, Maryland, Michael Cresap had a mercantile business that failed, requiring him to find other work. He started a land improvement company, taking a party westward in 1774, traveling through modern Wheeling, West Virginia. During his land-clearing activities in April 1774, a number of small battles occurred between Indians and whites in what were the first battles of *Lord Dunmore's War*. Thinking himself surrounded, Cresap led a group of men to attack *Shawnee* warriors that later were mistaken for chief Tah-gah-jute (James Logan). Cresap is thus mistakenly blamed for starting Lord Dunmore's War. After the hostilities ended, Cresap again attempted to develop land, but when the Revolutionary War broke out he raised a regiment, at which time he died on the march to Boston in 1775.

de la Balme, August (d. 1780)

Little is known of August de la Balme prior to his arrival in America except that he had been a French officer and a self-proclaimed cavalry expert. In October 1776 he applied to the Continental Congress for a commission and, having significant ties to Benjamin Franklin, received the rank of lieutenant colonel and "Inspector General of the Cavalry" in the summer of 1777. By October 1777, however, de la Balme resigned, giving no reasons. By 1778 de la Balme regretted his resignation and applied again for a commission, which the Continental Congress refused. Traveling to the Illinois Country, he formed his own army of roughly 60 Creoles. They planned to attack Charles *Beaubien* at Kekionga, then attack Detroit, hoping the Creoles there would rise up against the British. In November 1780 his small expedition was ably defeated by the *Miami* Indians Little Turtle and *Pacanne*, and de la Balme was killed.

de Linctot, Daniel-Maurice Godefroy (1739–1783)

Born to a leading French noble and merchant family, Linctot carried considerable weight with the Americans and the Creoles in the western Great Lakes region between 1763 and 1775. As a successful fur trader, he operated mostly out of the Illinois country, especially Prairie du Chien and Cahokia.

During the years prior to the American Revolution, Linctot rejected British claims to the *Mississippi [I]* and *Wabash* regions. He traversed the Great Lakes region with 30 Indian allies, causing considerable mischief against the English.

Fluent in several Native American languages, Linctot acted the part of the courier of the French king, or "Onontio" as the Indians called him. He continued the tradition of the French "middle ground," distributing gifts to the Indians, even to the point of giving away his clothes to ensure their loyalty to France. August *de la Balme* said Linctot was a Frenchman worthy of the "greatest praise," an example of what French-Indian relations should be.

Like his Gallic comrade, Linctot's motives remain unclear. Though he held a commission from the Virginia government, Linctot often attempted to turn the Indians to the favor of the French rather than the Americans, causing the commandant of Detroit, A. S. de Peyster, to refer to Linctot as "that little babbling Frenchman . . . who poisons your ears." Despite de la Balme's praise of Linctot, his French companion failed to support him during de la Balme's failed attempt to take Kekionga and Detroit.

French and Indian War (Seven Years War)

The French and Indian War, also known as the Seven Years War, was fought in North America from 1756 to 1763, although it was more accurately a continuation of the French-English struggle that had intermittently gone on since 1689. At least four wars were involved in this larger conflict: King William's War (1689–1697), ending with the Treaty of Ryswick (1697), Queen Anne's War (1702–1713), ending with the Treaty of Utrecht (1713), King George's War (1744–1748), ending with the Treaty of Aix-la-Chappelle (1748), and the Seven Years War.

King William's war ended in a stalemate, while Queen Anne's War gave England Newfoundland, Nova Scotia, and French lands surrounding Hudson's Bay. King George's War resulted in no territory changing hands. As English settlers moved into the Ohio Valley, they encroached on French claims there, although the French were primarily traders, not farmers. Thus, English movement into the region tended to be more permanent, though resisted periodically by the powerful Iroquois Confederacy. France, however, could see that in a short time the English would intrude on their fur trade. In 1753 the French established a series of forts along the Allegheny River in Pennsylvania on land also claimed by the British. At one point, English pioneers had just completed a fort on the Allegheny and Monongahela Rivers only to be greeted by the arrival of French troops, who drove them out and erected a larger fort, Fort Duquesne (later, Pittsburgh).

Both the English and the French could calculate the high economic stakes if the other occupied the region. For France, the lucrative fur trade would be diminished and possibly threatened still further by English expansion further northwest. English colonists, equating liberty with land ownership, saw the French closing of the frontier as a direct assault on the growth of their colonies. Unaware that the French had driven off the English settlers and constructed Fort Dusquesne (which the English called "Ward's fort"), Governor Dinwiddie of Virginia dispatched young Colonel George Washington to reacquire the area. Washington, learning that the French were entrenched in Fort Dusquesne, planned to establish a base below the fort and wait for an opportunity to storm it. When his soldiers encountered a party of French, the brief battle officially set off the French and Indian War. Some 900 French advanced on Washington to exact revenge, whereupon Washington constructed a stockade called

Fort Necessity. Following a brief siege, Washington signed a surrender document on July 4, 1754. In the surrender document, he admitted (in French, which he could barely read) that he had executed all his French prisoners.

Armies from both nations arrived in North America, although before long the British fleet cut off the flow of reinforcements from France. English troops arriving under General Edward *Braddock* marched to take Fort Dusquesne. Marching through the forests in line formation with their red coats, Braddock's men were sitting ducks for the guerilla attacks of the Indians, supported by some French regulars. Washington had warned against Braddock's plan, and only through his efforts was the column saved. French troops counterattacked from Canada under the Marquis de Montcalm, threatening New York and forcing the British to extract supplies and men from the colonists. British Prime Minister William Pitt reversed course in 1758 and soon had the support of the Americans. Generals James Wolfe and Jeffrey Amherst, leading a large British army, supported by a fleet, attacked the French fortified city of Louisbourg, which protected the St. Lawrence River. The *Iroquois [I]*, perceiving that the tide had turned, convinced their allies to cease attacks on English frontier settlements.

While one British army marched toward Niagara, sealing the French off from the interior, Amherst took Fort Ticonderoga near Lake Champlain, New York. General Wolfe continued the advance on Quebec. Scaling the cliffs below Quebec, Wolfe's troops laid siege to the city, where Montcalm waited with the French army. Convinced British reinforcements were on the way, on September 13 Montcalm decided to leave the protection of the city walls and fight an open field battle on the Plains of Abraham, where the British prevailed. Both Montcalm and Wolfe were killed in the combat, which opened not only Quebec but Montreal and the rest of Canada to British influence.

The Treaty of Paris (1763), which concluded the war, gave Britain almost all of Canada. Spain, as a new ally of France, ceded Florida to Great Britain. Although the British gained vast new territory from France, including India, the war exacted a terrible cost on the economy of both France and England, who emerged from it with burdensome debts. Depredations by the French and Indians on the frontier led to a constant stream of calls from the colonists for protection by British regulars. Britain sought to impose new taxes to pay these for the troops and the war debt, in the process not only changing colonial trade policy but uniting the American colonies against England. The war also opened new land past the Appalachians to settlers, which forced England to issue the *Proclamation Line of 1763* to stem the flood of settlers.

fur trapping/fur trade

As early as 1534, members of the Jacques *Cartier [I]* Expedition encountered Indians in Chaleur Bay, New Brunswick, who offered them furs to barter, constituting the first recorded account of fur trading in North America. The Indians soon developed a practice of trading furs with Europeans, with the exchange being profitable for both. Seventy years later, Henry IV sent an expedition to America to acquire beaver hides, and before long, beaver furs and pelts were in demand throughout Europe for hats and coats. In most cases, the process was the same: Indians did the trapping, bringing the furs to European outposts to trade for iron utensils and textiles, and, at times, liquor and guns.

Most of the trade emerged along the St. Lawrence River, expanding to the interior with the explorations of Samuel de *Champlain [I]* and others. Although Indian tribes competed ferociously for the fur areas, Indian-white relations thrived at the posts, generating commercial and even military alliances between the Europeans and the favored Indians. The French traded extensively with the Hurons. That proved problematic in the 1640s, when the Hurons' enemy, the *Iroquois* Confederation, crushed them, disrupting all their trade area and posing a threat to New France. Forced to extend their trading areas further into Canada, toward the Great Lakes, and down the Mississippi, following the explorations of Louis Jolliet, Father Jacques Marquette, and Sieur de *La Salle*, the French initiated alliances with the Ottawa, *Miami*, and Illinois Indians. Montreal emerged as the primary trading city, with substantial numbers of Indians settling near the town, but the French also sent their own traders into the interior (called *coureurs de bois*) and in time they established more far-flung posts. Virtually the entire system was linked by rivers or the Great Lakes, with common birchbark canoes used to carry the furs to the posts and the goods back to the villages. Lake Superior featured a ring of posts that extended French influence further into North America. Indeed, by the late 1600s, the fur trade was losing money, yet France subsidized it for strategic purposes (to blunt British and Spanish expansion) and to secure Indian allies.

The Treaty of Utrecht (1713) turned the Hudson's Bay region over to England, which brought the British *Hudson's Bay Company [I]* into direct competition with French traders. Hudson's Bay Company had developed when Pierre-Esprit *Radisson [I]* and Medart Chouart, Sieur de Groseilliers, had discovered a faster way of delivering furs from the interior. The route they mapped from the Minnesota region, through Hudson's Bay, was much faster than the river passages through the Great Lakes. They presented the concept to French officials, who expressed little interest. Then they discussed the plan with English investors, who funded a return visit aboard the *Nonsuch* in 1668. When they returned laden with furs, the investors chartered the Hudson's Bay Company in 1670. That not only cut off the French but instituted a new business strategy of hiring independent traders such as Peter Pond to encroach in French territories, establishing a major post on Lake Superior called Grand Portage. Eventually, as the French constructed forts on Lake Erie to block further British expansion, conflict ensued, boiling over into the *French and Indian War* (1756–1763).

As a result of the war, England acquired Canada and the Canadian fur trade. The monopoly did not last long, however. Soon the new United States had its own traders of seal and otter furs in the Pacific Northwest, and as the country acquired the *Louisiana Purchase* territory, America also took over the important St. Louis fur center that the French had successfully developed. When the *Lewis and Clark Expedition* returned to St. Louis in 1806, their information spread rapidly, especially to Manuel Lisa, a local entrepreneur, who organized the Missouri Fur Company (1809). Lisa's operations were interrupted by the *War of 1812 [III]*, as were the early trade missions of John Jacob *Astor [III]* in the Northwest. Astor had created the Pacific Fur Company in 1810 to organize a trading operation from the *Missouri River [I]*, through the Pacific Northwest, into Russia and China. In 1811 Astor's employees completed Astoria on the mouth of the Columbia River, but shortly thereafter his partners sold the company to the North West Company in 1813. Astor had more success with his *American Fur Company [III]* and its operations on the Great Plains and in the Rockies, which used contracted river traders called *engages*. Astor's network ended the U.S. government's "factory system," in which government agents at posts, or "factories," exchanged goods for furs. That system failed due to several regulations and restrictions imposed by the government on the agents.

Astor and the St. Louis interests were often at odds, and sensing that the fur trade's days were numbered, he removed himself in the 1830s. Lisa had died in 1820, leaving the western fur trade mostly in the hands of the Hudson's Bay Company until the appearance of several new companies run by Americans such as William H. *Ashley [III]* that focused on the Rocky Mountain region. After a disaster in 1823 in which one of his trading parties was ambushed by Arikaras, Ashley developed the "Rocky Mountain trapping system." Instead of relying on Indian traders, Ashley used a mixture of Anglo trappers who worked for a salary or self-employed trappers who sold pelts and bought supplies from Ashley's firm at rendezvous points. His supply caravans would head west to Wyoming, Idaho, and Utah to the rendezvous with the trappers. Ashley sold his interests to William Sublette, Jedediah *Smith [III]*, and others in 1826.

Smith epitomized the "mountain man," a breed of trader/trappers who gained fame in this brief era. Sublette and Smith were convinced that silk would soon replace furs for clothing and hats. Therefore, they only ran the business for four years before selling it to Thomas Fitzpatrick, Jim *Bridger [III]*, and the Rocky Mountain Fur Company. That same year, the American Fur Company entered the Rocky Mountain trade, setting off a fur war on the frontier. Astor's company won, acquiring the Rocky Mountain Fur Company in 1834, marking one of the last times Astor was personally involved in the fur trade. By then, the price of beaver furs had started a steady fall, and while the trade continued to some degree—especially under the Hudson's Bay Company—it declined in influence in the West. For a brief time, interest in bison hides, then racoon skins, soared, but the prime legacy of the American fur trade was that it accelerated the expansion of Europeans westward, introducing them to Indians in an arena of business enterprise, providing one of the few areas in which whites and Indians operated on an equal footing. Moreover, by exposing Indians to early capitalism, it slowly encouraged them to move into a market economy, modifying their culture in some ways and flatly destroying it in others. The fur trade also created the legends of the "mountain man," and helped chart the vast interior of North America, first for the French, then the English, and finally, for the Americans.

Handsome Lake (ca. 1735–1815)

Brother of the great Seneca war leader Cornplanter, Handsome Lake spent much of his life prior to 1799 as an invalid and alcoholic. In the summer of 1799, Handsome Lake fell into a coma. When he awoke, he claimed three messengers from the Creator had visited him. The original three and several subsequent messengers, including one with the Christian stigmata, revealed a new religion to Handsome Lake. Known as the *Gaiwiio*, the new morality combined Christian—especially Quaker and Roman Catholic teachings—with traditional Iroquois norms. It argued that the *Iroquois [I]* must abstain from alcohol and vanities, use witchcraft only for healing, cherish marriage, family life, and children, embrace agriculture, live in peace with the United States, and confess sins. Handsome Lake further predicted the collapse of the world. Of the many nativist revivals in the late 18th and early 19th centuries (see, for example, *Neolin* and *Tenskwatawa [III]*), Handsome Lake's was relatively peaceful. Many Iroquois still follow Handsome Lake's teachings, regarding him as a true prophet.

headright

Within a few years of arriving on North American shores, English colonists found that they faced a constant labor shortage. To attract settlers, most charter companies offered land in the form of "headright," which granted acreage to any man who came to America. Headright included as much as 50 acres per "head," up to four, so a commoner in England who could save enough for transportation, or work as an indentured servant, could acquire up to 200 acres of land—far more than he could ever have dreamed of owning in England.

Hennepin, Louis (May 12, 1626–ca.1701)

Along with Henry de *Tonti*, the Belgian-born Hennepin served as a reliable and intelligent right-hand man and chaplain for *La Salle*. Filled with gross exaggerations, Hennepin's travelogue of the 1678–1682 Mississippi River explorations was the first to describe the region and served as an inspiration for many European explorers when it was initially published in French in 1683 and in English in 1697. Hennepin most likely remained in Europe until his death around 1701 in, many believe, a Roman monastery.

Hiawatha (ca. 1500s)

Hiawatha was an Onondaga Indian chief who, the Iroquois believe, founded the *Iroquois [I]* Confederacy. After losing three of his daughters in wars with a neighboring tribe, Hiawatha wanted revenge but, instead decided that blood for blood was not necessarily the best solution. While wandering in the woods and thinking, he came across Deganawidah (Peacemaker), who taught him mercy as well as the Great Laws of Peace. Recording their deeds and words on wampum, the two traveled throughout the surrounding villages, attempting to persuade the Indians to adopt these laws and concepts. Five groups did: the Onondagas, Oneidas, Cayugas, Senecas, and Mohawks.

Huronia

Located in what is presently southern Ontario, Huronia was the name given to the land of the Hurons. The French formed an alliance with the Hurons, creating a number of trading posts and missions in their land. Mortal enemies of the Hurons since 1608, the *Iroquois* began a concerted attack on Huronia beginning in 1648. Only a year later, the Hurons, believing they were defeated, burned their villages and abandoned them to the Iroquois.

Kenton, Simon (1755–1836)

Perhaps the quintessential stereotype of the Indian fighter of the Old Northwest, Simon Kenton killed numerous Indians (mostly *Shawnees*) during his life. Settling in Kentucky after a near fatal brawl over a lover in Virginia, Kenton became a scout and ally of Daniel *Boone*. He fought the Shawnees before, during, and after the Revolutionary War. In 1777 he saved Boone's life. He also served as a scout for George Rogers *Clark* during the American Revolution. With the end of the Revolutionary War, Kenton founded a small Kentucky settlement where the Limestone Creek flows into the Ohio River. Formerly Limestone, it is now known as Mayville. Between 1782 and 1795 the raids between Kentuckians and the Old Northwest Indians were relentless. Kenton's brutal attacks on the Shawnees in

1786—in what was the prelude to the brutal *Miami-Federalist Wars*—were made on men offering no resistance. Between 1793 and 1794, Kenton served with "Mad" Anthony Wayne and fought at the Battle of Fallen Timbers. Kenton returned home after the war to find that a Kentucky Court of Appeals had ruled in 1794 that he illegally possessed his lands in Kentucky. Broke, he ended up in debtor's prison and afterward remained dependent upon his children. He died near Zaneville, Ohio, in 1836.

Kentucky long rifle

The Kentucky long rifle originated in Pennsylvania but was used primarily by pioneers moving into the Ohio Valley and Kentucky. One of the earliest produced on American soil is dated to 1728. While the musket—which did not have rifled barrels—remained the standard weapon for armies due to their less expensive production and the dominance of the bayonet in combat, frontiersmen, who needed to hunt wild game at great distances, demanded greater accuracy.

The rifle consisted of a wooden maple or walnut stock supporting a metal barrel. Powder would be poured in a measured amount into the end of the barrel, often by a "powder horn," then a lead ball dropped in. This ball was "wrapped" with a cloth or cotton patch, which the shooter could lay on the end of the barrel while fitting the ball in. Thus, the patch kept the ball in place, and was pressed snug against the powder by a ramrod, which hung in a hook under the rifle. A tooth-and-gear device attached to the trigger worked a hammer, which struck a piece of flint inserted near the priming pan, generating a spark. The pan was primed with powder, and the spark set off the pan powder, generating a flash (from which we get the modern phrase "flash in the pan") and igniting the powder in the chamber ejecting the ball at high speeds. The patch would fly out as well. The "Pennsylvania" or "Kentucky" long rifle—a .40, .50, or .60 caliber weapon—was accurate up to 300 yards.

Kino, Father Eusebio Francisco (1644–1711)

Father Eusebio Francisco Kino, born in Italy, joined the Jesuit Order of the Catholic Church in 1665, studying mathematics, astronomy, and cartography in Genoa. In 1669 he gained full admission to the Jesuits, and in 1678 he left on a missionary journey to the New World, arriving in New Mexico in 1681. He spent two years studying the San Pedro and Santa Cruz Rivers, as well as Southwestern geography, making maps and exploring the region. Appointed to the expedition of Admiral Isidro de Atondo y Antillón to Baja California, Kino continued his scientific studies, demonstrating that California was not an island.

Kino journeyed constantly, on foot and on horse, covering thousands of miles and exploring the Gila River and the lands between it and the Colorado River, which he followed to the Gulf of Mexico. He set up a headquarters in Sonora, but seldom stayed there, establishing 24 missions, including San Xavier del Bac in 1700 near Tucson, Arizona. When not traveling, Kino was making newer and more accurate maps, engaging in cattle ranching, and encouraging Spanish colonization of Arizona, California, and northern Mexico. Father Kino remained active until his death in 1711 at the mission village of Santa Magdalena, which he founded, having earned the reputation as the "Apostle of Arizona."

La Salle, René-Robert Cavelier de
(November 21, 1643–March 19, 1687)

Born to a prosperous family, René La Salle flirted with becoming a Jesuit missionary and actually took vows. He left the order in 1667 and sailed for New France where his missionary brother worked. There, he joined an expedition heading out for the western Great Lakes, then abruptly disappeared for four years, leading to claims that he found the Ohio and *Mississippi Rivers [I]*. La Salle, however, never personally made such claims. He returned to Montreal in 1673, where the governor, Louis de Baude de Frontenac, employed him as an emissary to the Iroquois. He also engaged in fur trading on Lake Ontario.

In 1677–1678 La Salle returned to France, where he received authority to build forts at Niagara and a commission to explore the western territory. A year later, La Salle sailed to the Illinois River, where he built Fort Crevecoeur. When he left Crevecoeur to return to Fort Frontenac, Indians attacked the former installation and the defenders deserted it. La Salle planned another expedition down the Mississippi River that left in 1682. The party included 50 French and Indians who reached the Gulf of Mexico that April. La Salle established a French claim to the area, encountering several Indian tribes along the way before returning to *Michilimackinac*. He then returned to France in 1683 to gain support to establish forts in the region.

Given a command the following year to establish a settlement on the Gulf, La Salle was granted authority over the entire region from Illinois to Mexico. La Salle headed an expedition of more than 100 soldiers, workers, and missionaries, sailing through Santo Domingo to Matagorda Bay in Texas in 1685. La Salle's force built a settlement there while the explorer set out to find the Mississippi from the west. But the party came under repeated Indian attacks and lost its last ship. Low on supplies and mired in east Texas, members of the expedition killed La Salle. Meanwhile the settlers left on the coast were attacked and killed, except for several children adopted by the Indians.

Long Portage/Kekionga

The Long Portage, an eight-mile strip of land known to the *Miami* Indians as the "Golden Gate," is one of the three major portages leading from the western Great Lakes into the interior of the Old Northwest. The other two are the St. Joseph's at present-day Niles, Michigan, and the Grand Portage at present-day Grand Portage, Wisconsin. The Long Portage is the most efficient of the three portages, as one coming from the east does not have to sail around the Michigan Peninsula, which can be deadly over half of the year and is very well protected by Mackinac Island.

Located at present-day Fort Wayne, Indiana, the Long Portage connected the Wabash and Maumee rivers; hence, the Great Lakes and the Ohio River; and, therefore, the St. Lawrence and the Mississippi rivers. It was the best way—militarily and economically—into the Old Northwest and the interior of North America. Prior to the development of the railroad, land travel was extremely expensive. Rivers and waterways, instead, served as the highways of America.

History bears out the fundamental importance of the Long Portage's economic and strategic value. Old Northwest Indian tradition states, and French records verify, that the Miami Indians had at various points in their history controlled the three major portages. They understood the significance of the portages and used them for economic and military gains long before the Europeans arrived. The Long Portage at Kekionga, though, served as the most important of the three. Whichever Miami family controlled the Long Portage became the most prominent within the tribe. With the conclusion of the *Mourning Wars [I]*, the Miamis quickly returned from Wisconsin and Illinois to the Long Portage and created a multitribal village, Kekionga, overlooking and protecting the portage's northeastern end. From there, the Miamis set themselves as economic lords over the area and successfully plugged themselves back into the international fur trade.

By the late 1700s the famous Miami family of *Pacanne* and *Taucumwah* had full control of the Long Portage. After the *French and Indian War*, the British sent emissary Thomas Morris to take over Fort Miami. There from 1764 to 1774 tensions developed between the Miamis and the French traders still residing at Kekionga. Traders, led by Alexis *Maisonville* and Joseph Richerville, formed an organized protection scheme to take over the portage. Pacanne and the Miamis resisted by taking their case to a British court in Detroit that ruled in the favor of the Indians.

During the American Revolution, the Long Portage became a focal point for both the British and the Patriots. Henry Hamilton, British commander at Detroit, fortified it, thereby bringing Pacanne and the Miamis fully into the British effort against George Rogers *Clark* and the Americans. Despite his desire to do so, Clark never attacked the portage directly. Instead, an obscure French officer, August *de la Balme*, did in 1780. Leading a small army of Creoles, de la Balme successfully sacked a deserted Kekionga, only to be surprised and overwhelmed by a Miami counterattack led by Little Turtle and *Pacanne*.

Fueled by British agent Alexander *McKee*, the Miamis and *Shawnees* used Kekionga as a staging ground for attacks into Ohio and Kentucky in the 1780s and 1790s. In 1784 George Washington stated that one of the first military objectives of America should be Kekionga, which he believed to be the strategic key to the Old Northwest. The Articles of Confederation did not provide for a strong enough army to take Kekionga, but the 1787 Constitution did. Beginning in 1790 the Washington administration declared war against the Miami Confederacy. The four years of the *Miami-Federalist War* were brutal, but "Mad" Anthony Wayne finally broke the Miami Confederacy in August 1794. One of the major points of the peace, as ratified in the 1795 *Treaty of Greenville*, was the American military use, free of charge, of the Long Portage and the creation of an American fort to overlook it. The Miamis agreed, and the United States built Fort Wayne at the head of the Maumee River.

Miami Chief Jean Baptiste *Richardville [III]* inherited the Long Portage from his uncle and mother, becoming a millionaire by 1816. During the 1830s, under pressure from the state of Indiana and the federal government, Richardville and the Miamis sold significant portions of the portage to create the Wabash-Erie Canal.

Lord Dunmore's War

As white settlers and traders began pushing into the Indian lands of Kentucky and southern Ohio, despite prohibitions by the *Treaty of Fort Stanwix* (1768) and other treaties, the *Cherokee [III]* and *Shawnee*, both of whom hunted in those lands, resisted. By 1772 game was being depleted by hunters, and land speculators started to establish claims in the region. Settlers even began attacking tribes of Shawnee without provocation. In 1773, however, two boys were murdered in a display of Indian dissatisfaction with the encroachments.

Lord Dunmore (John Murray), the colonial governor of Virginia, laid claim to the western part of Pennsylvania and Kentucky in 1774, authorizing British subjects to defend themselves against the Indians. When the Shawnee sent a negotiating party to Pittsburgh, Dunmore held them as prisoners for more than three months. Finally, they were released, only to be attacked by colonial troops on their return. The Shawnee responded by killing 13 whites at Baker's Cabin on Yellow Creek, which in turn prompted whites under Daniel Greathouse to attack the peaceful Mingo tribe of Chief John Logan. Lord Dunmore's War had begun.

Dunmore dispatched Daniel *Boone* to locate surveying parties still in the region, and he also sent James Robertson and others to ensure the neutrality of other tribes, such as the Cherokee, *Iroquois [I]*, and Delaware. Then Dunmore personally led a column from Pittsburgh into Shawnee territory, while another militia force under Colonel Andrew Lewis moved up the Kanawa River. Lewis's command was engaged at Point Pleasant on October 10, 1774, while Dunmore moved on the Shawnee town of Chillicothe. Caught between two armies, the Indians agreed to the Treaty of Camp Charlotte, whereby the Shawnee gave up Kentucky, opening up the Ohio Valley to settlement, and perpetuating Indian hostility.

Louisiana Purchase

Upon hearing that Spain had transferred the region east of the *Mississippi River [I]* to France, President Thomas *Jefferson [III]* instructed Robert Livingston of New York to negotiate the purchase of the port of New Orleans as well as the land in Florida west of the Perdido River, all for under $10 million. Livingston, joined by James Monroe of Virginia, found a much different situation when they arrived in France—one alive with opportunities.

The Louisiana region had been explored by Hernando *de Soto [I]* in 1541, and by French explorer, Sieur de *La Salle* in 1682. La Salle traveled to the mouth of the Mississippi and claimed it for the king of France, Louis XIV, whereupon the region was called "Louisiana." But the area was in constant danger from English settlers from the Ohio River valley to the east. The population of the Anglo-Americans, in particular, had swollen in the decade prior to 1800, putting pressure on the administrator of Louisiana to ensure a robust (and costly) border defense. During the *French and Indian War*, rather than lose the territory to the British, France had ceded it to Spain. Pinckney's Treaty (1795) temporarily eased any tensions between the new United States and Spain by guaranteeing American rights of transit down the Mississippi and the right of deposit at New Orleans.

The new leader of France, Napoleon Bonaparte, soon brought Louisiana back under French control through two separate treaties, San Ildefonso (1800) and Godoy-Lucian Bonaparte (1801). It was news of the second treaty, which reached Jefferson in 1802, that provoked the mission of Livingston and Monroe to France. Meanwhile, Napoleon had experienced important military setbacks that made his ability to secure and supply the New World territories all the more difficult. The French navy had suffered a tremendous loss to the British at the Battle of the Nile (1798), and Napoleon had to maintain a constant naval presence in the Mediterranean and North Atlantic to counter the Royal Navy. Worse, a slave rebellion in France's Carribean territory of Haiti, which French troops had been unable to contain, convinced Napoleon that he had neither the troops nor the ships to spare for North America. Consequently, when Livingston and later Monroe arrived, Napoleon's negotiators, Foreign Minister Talleyrand and Finance Minister Barbe-Marbois, surprised them by offering all of the Louisiana region. Despite lacking authority to offer more than $9 million, Livingston and Monroe agreed on a payment of $11.25 million, and the United States also agreed to assume some $3.75 million in claims of American citizens against France. Exactly what the United States had purchased was not clear, and Talleyrand cautiously avoided fixing any boundaries, dismissing the negotiators by saying, "You have made a noble bargain for yourselves, and I suppose you will make the most of it." But even without clear boundaries, the Louisiana Purchase ran along the modern-day western border of Louisiana, just south of the modern Texas northern state line, crossed the Pecos River to reach the Rio Grande in the West, then ran northward, splitting Colorado almost in half. From there, the border angled across Wyoming to the northern line of Idaho, crossing the far western side of Montana, and even included some of Canada. Along the east, the territory stayed adjacent to the Mississippi River until it reached

IN THEIR OWN *Words*

Description of French Living in Spanish Louisiana, 1796

In 1826 Victor Collot published his observations of travels in North America, presenting the following disparaging portrait of the French in Louisiana when he passed through there in 1796.

These people [those living in the surviving French settlements under U.S. and Spanish control in North America] are, for the most part, traffickers, adventurers, hunters, rowers, and warriors; ignorant, superstitious, and obstinate; accustomed to fatigue and privations, and stopped by no sense of danger in the undertakings they form, and which they usually accomplish.

In domestic life, their characters and dispositions are similar to those of the Indians with whom they live; indolent, careless, and addicted to drunkenness, they cultivate little or no ground, speak a French jargon, and have forgotten the division of time and months. If they are asked at what time such an event took place, they answer, 'in the time of the great waters, of the strawberries, of the maize, of potatoes;' if they are advised to change any practice which is evidently wrong, or if observations are made to them respecting the amelioration of agriculture, or the augmentation of any branch of commerce, the only answer they give is this: 'It is the custom; our fathers did so: I have done well; my children will do the same.' They love France, and speak of their country with pride.

—Source: Victor Collot, *A Journey in North America*, vol. 1 (1826; reprint, Firenze: O. Lange, 1924), 232.

Minnesota, whereupon it crossed North Dakota. In all, the Purchase doubled the size of the United States, adding 828,000 square miles that eventually included the states of Iowa, Missouri, Arkansas, Louisiana, Oklahoma, Kansas, Nebraska, North and South Dakota, as well as parts of Texas, Minnesota, Montana, Colorado, and Wyoming. Even before striking the deal, Jefferson had requested funding for an expedition to survey the region all the way to the Pacific, and from 1804 to 1806, the *Lewis and Clark Expedition [III]* explored America's new acquisition. The "empire of liberty," as Jefferson called it, reflected a changing American attitude toward the continent and expansionism and set the stage for the "manifest destiny" of the 1840s.

Although some dispute remained over the assimilation of the territory, in 1828 the United States Supreme Court in *American Insurance Co. v. Canter* upheld the notion that the United States had the authority to govern the new territory as derived from its power to acquire it. Already, however, in 1812, Louisiana became the first new state admitted from the Louisiana Purchase.

MacKenzie, Alexander (ca. 1763–1820)

Alexander MacKenzie, a Scot who emigrated to Canada in 1779, joined a fur trading subsidiary of the North West Company as a partner. In 1788 he established a fur trading fort, Fort Chipewyan, on Lake Athabasca. Deciding to probe deeper into the interior, MacKenzie first explored the region north of Fort Chipewyan, following what is now known as the MacKenzie river, and moving into the Arctic regions. His joint British-Chipewyan Indian Expedition reached Whale Island in the Arctic Ocean on July 12, 1789. In 1793 MacKenzie led the first transcontinental expedition to the Pacific, following the Peace River into the Rocky Mountains and portaging to the ocean. His company reached the coast at what is today Vancouver on July 21, 1793. The following day, he carved on a rock: "Alex MacKenzie from Canada by land 22d July 1793." His journey predated the more famous *Lewis and Clark* Expedition by 12 years.

His travel account, *Voyages from Montreal* (1801), provided an argument for a transcontinental empire for the British. "By opening this intercourse between the Atlantic and Pacific Oceans, and forming regular establishments through the interior, and at both extremes, as well as along the coasts and islands, the entire command of the *fur* trade of North American might be obtained." Many scholars have argued that this one sentence, more than anything else, prompted Thomas *Jefferson [III]* to send out Lewis and Clark and their Corps of Discovery in 1804. His book became the standard source on western geography for more than a generation of Americans and Canadians, though it contained many mistaken assumptions. The British Crown knighted him in 1802 for his successes.

Maisonville, Alexis and Francis (late 1700s)

The Maisonville brothers were prominent French Creoles in the western Great Lakes in the second half of the 18th century. Fur traders and Indian agents, the Maisonvilles abused the power the British crown had given them in the 1760s and 1770s by attempting to take over the *Miami* Indian *Long Portage* at Kekionga in 1774. A British court forced them to step down. They continued to remain loyal to the British and both aided Henry Hamilton in his takeover of Post Vincennes in 1778. Francis committed suicide after George Rogers *Clark*'s men captured and scalped him.

Mallet, Pierre and Paul (ca. early 1700s)

French explorers Pierre and Paul Mallet left French posts in Illinois in 1739 to cross the prairie into Spanish New Mexico, roughly along the route of what was to become the *Santa Fe Trail [III]*. When they arrived in Santa Fe, the Spanish grew concerned that the French had designs on the region, but the two nations were not at war, and thus the Mallets were permitted to conduct their explorations. In 1740 the brothers returned to New Orleans, bringing to French authorities there the news of potential trade with the Spanish. Their visit sparked a trickle of Frenchmen into the New Mexico region until 1762, at which time Spain gained control of western Louisiana.

McKee, Alexander (ca.1735–January 10, 1799)

Introduced into the British Indian Department by his father, Thomas, Alexander McKee worked with Indian agent George Croghan to negotiate for the British government with many western Great Lakes tribes. He also played a role as mediator among Indian tribes. His arrangements cemented British Indian policy in the Northwest until the *War of 1812 [III]*. Often working as a trapper/trader, McKee profited from his royal contacts. He strongly opposed U.S. influence in the region—a position that ultimately ended in failure.

Miami

A central Algonquian, eastern-woodlands people, the Miami Indians met their first Europeans, the French, in the mid-17th century. In 1654 a part of the Miami tribe, residing far to the west of their traditional area of residence (pushed there by the Iroquois), encountered two traders, Pierre-Esprit *Radisson [I]* and Jean Baptiste Des Groseilliers, a famous early French Trader. Father Gabriel Dreuillettes, a member of the intrepid Society of Jesus (Jesuits), claimed that the village the traders encountered numbered an unbelievable "twenty-four thousand souls."

As the French found out immediately upon contact, the Miamis had an affinity for trade, both with other Indians and with the various European factions. They also realized that portages, in a time of significant river transportation, provided a solid economic income and a basis for material wealth. In other words, controlling a portage meant controlling wealth. Since Europeans first came into contact with the Miamis, the tribe at various times controlled the three major portages between the Mississippi and St. Lawrence River systems located at or near present-day Fort Wayne, Indiana; South Bend, Indiana; and Portage, Wisconsin.

What we now call the Miamis were really six separate groups around 1700. These groups included Atchatachakangouen (the Miami proper), Kilatika, the Mengakonkia, Pepikokia, Piankashaw, and Wea. Only the first three of these groups remain today. Scholars have not successfully determined what became of the remaining groups, but the Piankashaw and Wea remained independent, with the latter probably absorbing the Pepikokia during the 1740s.

In the decades following 1740, numerous French men intermarried with Miami women, precipitating even closer ties between the two peoples. Miami women, of course, served as the primary conduits between French and Miami culture, creating the Metis who would serve as effective traders and middlemen between the two cultures. With the French as allies, the Miamis slowly began to retake their traditional homelands along the Wabash in what is today northern Indiana. The Miamis exhibited great loyalty toward the French not only for unifying the Algonquians, allowing them to repel the Iroquois during the *Mourning/Beaver Wars [I]*, but also for providing new goods and markets for their services.

Despite the overt display of loyalty on the part of the Miamis, the French failed to trust their Indian allies completely. They rightly worried that the English, their most prominent and effective rivals for imperial control of North America, might make diplomatic and trade inroads into the traditional homelands of the Miamis, the Maumee and Ohio valleys. As early as 1700 English traders penetrated the area, seeking allies and new trading partners. To prevent an English alliance with the Miami, the French attempted to regulate, or at the least, encourage, where the Miamis would resettle after the Iroquois wars. For example, in 1682 the French built Fort St. Louis in Illinois, servicing the Miamis, Illinois, and Shawnees. By 1695, though, many of the Miamis had moved back to the Wabash region, and by the early 1710s the Miamis dominated their former homeland once again.

The French, unable to control the Miami migrations, placed forts among the Miamis in their traditional homelands. By 1720, despite the French forts on the upper Wabash, some groups of Miamis had already allied themselves with English traders. Though the French and Miamis shared years of loyalty and alliance, the English traders offered something the French failed to: free trade and lower prices. Never escaping the mercantilist mentality, the French attempted to regulate virtually all aspects of their own trade, including prices, the location of trade, and the quality of trade goods. This drove prices up and gave the less-regulated English an advantage.

Much to the chagrin of the French, by the 1740s the Miamis held divided loyalties. For a variety of reasons, including overly cumbersome regulations and the power of the British navy in the Atlantic, French prices rose by 150 percent in the early 1740s. The division of the Miamis between the French and English came to a head in 1747 with a Miami attack on Fort Miamis, the establishment of a British trading post in Ohio, and the rise of a pro-English Piankashaw chief, *Old Briton*. Though the French won militarily and Old Briton lost his life (eaten by French-allied Indians), the contest between the two European powers in the region remained a constant until the end of the French and Indian War. English traders, such as George Croghan and Christopher Gist, continued to make inroads into Miami trade networks throughout the 1750s and 1760s.

With the end of French Imperial power in the region in 1761, the British slowly and haltingly replaced their defeated rivals as the "Great Father" to the various Indian tribes in the Maumee and Wabash river valleys, including the Miamis. During the 1770s and 1780s the British formed very strong ties with the Miamis. With Kentuckians constantly harassing the Indians in northern Indiana, the Miamis viewed the British as natural allies. When the British failed to support the Miami Confederacy during the *Miami-Federalist War* in 1794, the Miamis, under the direction of Jean Baptiste *Richardville [III]* and Little Turtle, slowly turned their allegiance to the Americans. During the *War of 1812 [III]*, however, the Miamis returned their allegiance to the British.

After the war the Americans attempted to extract as much land from the Miamis as possible. Between 1818 and 1838 the United States and the Miamis signed a number of treaties through which the Miamis gave up unneeded land for exorbitant prices, annuities, and secure property rights for remaining land. Alcoholism and dependency upon government annuities ripped apart the tribe during the same decades. The death rate continued virtually unabated. In 1840 there were roughly 700 Miamis. Five years later, there were only 650. Only 1843 witnessed more live births than deaths.

In 1840 Richardville reluctantly signed a removal treaty. In 1846 nearly two-thirds of the tribe removed to Kansas. A year later nearly half of those returned to privately owned Miami lands in Indiana. As of 2002 there are three major Miami centers: Fort Wayne, Indiana; Peru, Indiana; and Miami, Oklahoma.

Miami-Federalist War, 1790–1795

Despite its desire to control the violence and the opposition of the *Miami Indians* in the Old Northwest, the American Army, weak under the Articles of Confederation, simply could not subdue the Indians of the northern Wabash in the 1780s. Warfare between the tribes of the upper Wabash and the Kentuckians became ingrained and all-pervasive between 1780 and 1790.

The United States attempted to treat with the Miamis in 1785, and they tried again in 1787, 1789, and finally, in the spring of 1790. In each case, however, the Miamis rebuffed them, adhering firmly to their Confederacy and to their alliance with the British.

The new federal government, ratified in 1787, instilled a sense of power and enthusiasm into the frontier army. Both sides had much both to lose and gain by fighting an all-out war. For the Miami Confederacy, victory meant the possibility of maintaining traditional homelands against the American demographic onslaught. It might mean an independent Indian nation, separating the United States from Canada, or it might mean the United States guarding the Ohio River, preventing settlers from creating homes north of the Ohio in the Miami and Shawnee homelands.

The British, wishing for a buffer state between Canada and the United States, encouraged and supplied the Indians as much as possible through the summer of 1794. "The defence of one's country, has been from the most early ages," a British officer told Blue Jacket, war chief of the Shawnees, "considered as Honorable, manly and praise-worthy." While the British may have truly believed in the Indian cause, they also knew that the Miamis represented a significant part of British wealth in North America. The *Long Portage* was the key, militarily and economically, to the Old Northwest.

For the United States, under the new Constitution, the war with the Miami confederacy was a test of courage, national strength, and vigor. Victory would mean declaring national sovereignty and hegemony over disputed frontiers and borders and protecting the United States integrity from British and Spanish intrigues.

Of the campaigns against the Miamis, the Harmar (1790) and St. Clair (1791) failed miserably from poor planning on the American part and brilliant planning by the Miamis. During the St. Clair campaign alone, which included nearly two-thirds of the United States Army, the Miami Confederacy killed more than 600 Americans and wounded nearly another 300. The United States suffered a serious loss with Harmar's defeat as well.

The Miami Confederacy, even with the brilliance of their leader, Little Turtle, and the backing of the British, met its match in "Mad" Anthony Wayne. General Wayne, a former Revolutionary War officer, attempted to treat with the Indians for peace several times between 1792 and 1794. Still exhilarated by their victories against Harmar and St. Clair, the Indians wanted to challenge Wayne as well, even going so far as to murder several of the peace emissaries.

In August 1794 just days before Wayne's invasion, Little Turtle, fearing that Wayne could not be beaten, resigned his role as head war chief of the Confederacy encouraging the Miami Confederacy to support a negotiated peace. Wayne, he feared, was "a chief who never sleeps." Other Indians mocked the Miami war chief for his views, appointing *Blue Jacket* to lead them.

Wayne openly proclaimed that his invasion throughout the region would be on August 17. While he started his march that day, he stopped his troops 10 miles from Fort Miami (near present-day Toledo, Ohio), where his force camped for 3 days. This delay had a purpose. Wayne knew the Indians fasted before battle, and he wanted to attack them just as they were feeling the overwhelming desire to eat. On the third day, August 20, 1794, the Indians began to return to the British garrison in search of food. As they did, Wayne attacked, achieving a swift victory at a dense patch of trees, Fallen Timbers, on the Maumee river.

The Indians, losing the battle, attempted to enter the British fort, but their English allies refused them. This action on the part of the British, more than any other single event of the Battle of Fallen Timbers, signaled the end of the war. The war concluded officially with the signing of the 1795 *Treaty of Greenville*.

The Indian defeat weakened Britain's grip on the Old Northwest and hastened Jay's Treaty, effectively opening the region for settlement by Americans.

Michilimackinac

Michilimackinac originally referred to the region around the Straits of Mackinac located between what are now the lower and upper peninsulas of Michigan. Until the 20th century, Michilimackinac encompassed what are now Mackinac Island, St. Ignace on upper peninsula, and the northernmost point of the lower peninsula. After the 19th century, the usage of the term "Michilimackinac" has been limited to the smallish Mackinac Island (nine miles in circumference).

Controlling the passage from Lake Huron to Lake Michigan, Michilimackinac has long been recognized for its strategic and economic importance. Various Indian groups have used it for centuries. When the French explored the region in the 17th century, they discovered numerous refugee Indians hiding from the deadly assaults of the *Iroquois [I]*. By the 1680s the French were using it as a base of operations. They built a semi-permanent fort there in 1715 but surrendered it to the English in 1763. During that same year Indians allied with *Pontiac* briefly took over the fort. In 1781 the British built another fort there, handing it over to the Americans in 1795. The Americans used it from 1796 to 1894, losing it to the British during the duration of the *War of 1812 [III]*. By 1830 nearly 1,200 traders and merchants, many of them Metis, lived there. Today, it is a state park.

moccasins

When the European settlers encountered Indians, they noticed that a common footwear among them—different from the hard shoes and leather boots worn by the colonists—was a soft shoe made of deerskin or moose skin called a moccasin. Irish and other medieval Europeans had worn similar soft shoes, usually laced high above the ankle or up the calf, but Indian footwear fit like a slipper, tied (if at all) only across the top of the foot. Moccasins were a natural clothing style taken from a hunting culture, and whites (especially trappers) soon adopted the footwear, often adding a fur lining and extending the shoe up the leg for colder weather.

Neolin (mid-1700s)

Little is known regarding the Delaware Neolin, and most historians associate him closely with his better-known disciple, Pontiac. Neolin inspired Pontiac through his creation of a nativist movement, an attempt to return to Indian religious and cultural fundamentals. Two things remain true for all Indian nativist movements: (1) they occur when a culture is in extreme distress, on the verge of collapse; and (2) they are always a synthesis of the old Indian religion and Christianity. The Delawares, a resilient people, who were forced to move from present-day Delaware to Pennsylvania and then into the western Great Lakes region, were ripe for such a movement. As a young man, Neolin claimed to have a vision in which a messenger from

God led him through heaven and hell. If the Indians refused to reject white ways, he said, they would go to hell. If they clung to their native ways, they would spend eternity in paradise. Neolin also attacked the practice of polygamy. Finally, he said that if his followers were faithful, the following seven years (1760–1767) would see the end of the British. When *Pontiac's Rebellion* failed in 1763–1764, Neolin's following collapsed. *Tenskwatawa's [III]* movement between 1805 and 1815 followed Neolin's as the next nativist movement.

Northwest Ordinance

Upon gaining independence from England, the original 13 colonies realized that they had territory that would soon become populated and that would, if not properly administered, attain a "colonial" status itself. Thomas *Jefferson [III]* especially wanted to ensure that no "American colonies" developed and that land—which he viewed as the possession of the people as individuals, rather than the state as a representative of the people—should be transferred into the hands of people as rapidly as possible. This required the government to establish policies for surveying and then disposing of the land.

In 1784 Jefferson drafted a land ordinance (Northwest Ordinance) to create out of the land within U.S. boundaries, but not already within the borders of an existing state, a number of territories that could eventually organize into states. Under his plan, the inhabitants would remain in a territorial status until the population reached a sufficient number to organize a state constitutional convention. At the time, however, the areas were so unsettled as to render the ordinance meaningless. Moreover, it could not take effect until the states had all ceded their western lands to Congress, which some delayed doing until as late as 1789. Meanwhile, in 1785 Jefferson drafted another land ordinance (Land Ordinance of 1785) that provided for a process of surveying the land, establishing a system of sections (one square mile) and townships (36 sections). Thirty-one of the surveyed sections would be put up for public sale, with the government retaining four for general purposes (armories or future sales) and one for a public school.

Jefferson's genius in this ordinance lay in the fact that while it provided Congress with steady revenues, it also consistently took resources out of the hands of government and put them in the hands of citizens. Thus, the government gained financial power, but only at the expense of political power.

When the region of the Old Northwest, especially Detroit, Vincennes, and other areas north of the Ohio River, started to develop, Congress responded by establishing a committee headed by James Monroe to determine a means of provisional government. On May 10, 1786, Monroe's committee drafted an ordinance to extend congressional control over the area until the old 1784 law could take effect.

On July 13, 1787, Monroe's much-revised bill amended the Northwest Ordinance of 1784. Entitled "Ordinance for the government of the territory of the United States North west of the river Ohio," the law was reenacted by the new United States Congress in August 1789. Although the "northwest territory" would originally be one district headed by a governor (appointed by the president), the significant portions of the law involved the process by which the residents became citizens of the new United States of America. First, a general assembly was to be elected that shaped the duties of the various appointed officials, although the governor retained a veto power over the assembly. Second, a territorial judicial

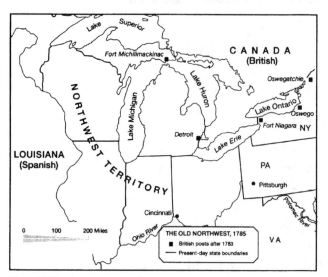

The old Northwest. *Ron Acklin, University of Dayton Print and Design*

system was established by the president's appointment of three judges to enforce the civil and criminal laws. After a census showed the territory had 5,000 free adult males, an election would establish a lower house of the general assembly, with one representative for every 500 voters up to 25 total representatives. A voter had to own 50 acres of land and be a resident of the territory, while a representative had to own 200 acres and be a resident. The upper house, known as a "legislative council," had 5 members who were territorial residents and who each had 500 acres of land. The general assembly could pass any laws not in opposition to U.S. federal law, and the governor retained a veto. Together, the upper and lower houses meeting in joint session could elect a nonvoting delegate to the U.S. Congress.

In the second section, the Northwest Ordinance declared a compact between the "original states" and the people in the new territory, granting religious freedom, trial by jury, civil rights, and other freedoms protected

IN THEIR OWN

Words

Moses Austin's Criticism of Government Neglect of Illinois Country, 1790s

Moses Austin, famous for responding to the Spanish plea for settlement in Texas, here criticizes U.S. policy toward the Illinois Country. Inhabited by French Creoles, Spanish officials, Indians, and Metis, Austin fears that the only U.S. presence in the region has been a poor one, pushing the inhabitants away from the United States and to the Spanish, thus creating instability on the frontier.

*I*t is not easy to account why this country has been Neglected by the Government of the United States, and when its considered that Its not onely [sic] a Frontier as to the Indians, but also as to Spain who are takeing Every step to make there Country Formidable incase of an attack, It is not unreasonable to suppose that the Executive of the united states, have not a Just Idia of the Importance of the Missisipe Country, or the Trade they are Daily looseing, and which will soon be so fix.d on the Spanish Shore as to be harde to with Draw. Some of the Standing Laws of Congress as they respect the Illinois Country are distressing and unjust in there Operation. the Law which make the Property of all the People forfeted to the United States who have left the Government of said States and do Not return with in five Years, is Cruel and severely unjust. It ought to be remember·d that in 1778 General Clark took the Illinois and left a Small Garrison at Kaskaskia onely, who instead of protecting the People Pillage.d them at Will and when that Garrison was with Drawn which i Beleave was in the Year 82 the whole settlement was unprotected and Notwithstanding Garrisons have been Established from Georgia North for the protection of much smaller settlements, Yet the Illinois have not recev.d the least assistance from Government from the Time of Clark untill the present Moment, Which Oblig.d many families to take Shelter under the Spanish Government, and because they did Not return and stand the scalping Knife they are loos thier property, for its to be Know[n] that all the Towns on the Missisipe have been at the mercy of the Indians untill the Treaty made by General. Wayn. that Government Should take away the property of a people they could not or would not Protect is something new more Especially a Government like Ours.

—SOURCE: "A MEMORANDUM OF M. AUSTINS' JOURNEY FROM THE LEAD MINES IN THE COUNTRY OF WYTHE IN THE STATE OF VIRGINIA TO THE LEAD MINES IN THE PROVINCE OF LOUISIANA WEST OF THE MISSISSIPPI, 1796–1797," *AMERICAN HISTORICAL REVIEW* 5 (APRIL 1900), 537.

by the U.S. Constitution. Slavery was prohibited—a move that Jefferson and others thought might set a precedent for the permanent elimination of slavery in the United States, and certainly in the territories. No one could anticipate that the *Louisiana Purchase* would occur, creating potential new slave territories. When the population reached 60,000 people, the territory could apply for admission as a state by holding a constitutional convention and submitting a constitution to the U.S. Congress. However, the Northwest Ordinance specifically stated that no fewer than three states be created and no more than five; this prevented one exceptionally large, populous state (such as modern-day California) from dominating either elections or the legislature and prevented the region from having an inordinate number of representatives in the House. Although the conditions limiting the numbers of states permitted in a new territory was eventually abandoned—with Alaska being both the largest state in the Union and the least populated—this framework worked well to maintain states as relatively coequal units. Only Texas (later admitted after status as an independent Republic) in size and New York, California, and Texas in numbers of representatives have challenged the intention of the framers in any way, and even then, population shifts in New York and Florida have proven that a population advantage is fleeting.

In 1788 the first provisional officials were appointed, with Governor Arthur *St. Clair* named as territorial governor, commencing management of the region from Marietta, Ohio, in October. St. Clair found that he not only had to carry out his stipulated duties but also handle local relations with the Indians. Within 10 years, Indiana Territory was established from the Northwest territory, including all the area outside of Ohio, and in 1803, Ohio became the first of the Northwest Ordinance territories to join the Union as a state. A succession of other states entered the Union through the same process, validating Jefferson and Monroe's vision of a growing Union rather than a colonial empire. The relatively smooth transition from territories to states confirmed the Founders' notions of turning subjects into citizens and of dispersing land to individuals.

Old Briton (d. 1752)

Also known as La Demoiselle and Memeskia, Old Briton, a Piankashaw chief, opposed the French fur and political monopoly in the western Great

Lakes. In 1747 he helped lead a multitribal uprising against the French, successfully attacking Fort Miami at *Long Portage/Kekionga*. Two years later, Old Briton built a trading post with British-Pennsylvania traders at Pickawillany, Ohio. Charles Langlade, a Metis, attacked Old Briton in June 1752 with nearly 240 Ottawa and Ojibwa warriors. Capturing Old Briton, the enemy warriors boiled and ate him.

Pacanne (ca. 1746–1815)

Pacanne ("the nut"), also known as Andre Roi, was born sometime in the mid-1740s to a prominent *Miami* Metis family. As was typical for many of the tribes along the Wabash River, his father was a French fur trader and his mother a Miami chieftess. Much of the family's wealth and prominence derived from their ownership of the *Long Portage* between the Maumee and Wabash rivers.

Pacanne gained considerable fame among the Miamis as well as among the British in 1764. The British government had sent an emissary, Thomas Morris, to inform the Indians of the western Great Lakes region and Illinois country that the area was now under British control. Only shortly after the failure of *Pontiac's Rebellion*, the Indians did not receive Morris kindly. Just as two Miamis were about to commence torturing Morris, young Pacanne jumped forward, cut Morris loose, and rushed him to a waiting canoe. There, his sister, *Taucumwah*, nursed Morris and sent him on his way to safety. Morris guaranteed Pacanne's fame in Britain by publishing the incident in his famous memoirs.

By the 1770s, as leader of Long Portage/Kekionga (present-day Fort Wayne, Indiana), Pacanne was the most prominent village chief among the Miamis. A rival trade faction, led by Alexis *Maisonville*, vied for control over the Long Portage in 1774, but Pacanne defended his claims to it in a British court in Detroit and won in September 1774.

Paying back with his support to the British for their aid in the Long Portage struggle, Pacanne offered his services to Henry Hamilton, the "hair buyer," in his attacks on Fort Vincennes in the fall of 1778. Throughout the American Revolution, Pacanne loyally fought with the British, attempting to stop the Patriots and their Indian allies in diplomacy and in battle.

When the British ignored the Indians in the Peace of Paris of 1783, however, a bitter Pacanne joined up with the Americans, moving his family to an area just north of the Franco-American village of Vincennes. He renounced Alexander *McKee*, the British Indian agent to Kekionga, as a cowardly instigator of violence. He left his young nephew, Jean Baptiste *Richardville [III]*, in charge of Kekionga. Pacanne worked as a scout for the American Army in Vincennes but was unable to thwart the murders of members of his family by American settlers who refused to distinguish one Indian from another.

In 1790 Pacanne moved his family to Spanish Missouri but moved back to Kekionga after the Miamis signed the *Treaty of Greenville*. Over the next 17 years, Pacanne and his family lived in relative peace in Kekionga, controlling the Long Portage and working as fur trappers. Pacanne's most significant challenges came from Little Turtle, the famed war chief, now falsely playing the part of a village chief, and from the Shawnee Prophet and his brother, *Tecumseh [III]*. Pacanne signed the infamous 1809 Treaty of Fort Wayne that ceded significant amounts of land in Indiana, which the Shawnee brothers deemed illegal. A year later, Pacanne claimed he had signed the document at the point of a gun.

When hostilities broke out in the summer and fall of 1812 in the Great Lakes, Pacanne attempted to remain neutral. Not trusting him, however, William Henry Harrison ordered his villages destroyed. Pacanne spent the winter of 1812 and 1813 in Detroit and formed an official Miami-British alliance. When that alliance collapsed at the Battle of the Thames, Pacanne signed the second *Treaty of Greenville* in 1814, declaring peace with the Americans. Pacanne, however, made one further attempt to form an alliance with the British, spending the fall and winter of 1814 and 1815 in northern Michigan under British protection. When the war came to an official close with the Treaty of Ghent, Pacanne moved back to the Wabash River and created a village in the "traditional" mode. He died in late 1815.

Pontiac's Rebellion

The Ottawa chief Pontiac, displeased by sudden changes in British Indian policies following the surrender of Detroit in 1760, led a series of strikes against British outposts beginning in May 1763. The conflict began when the British captured Detroit in November 1760. Indian tribes, including the Ottawa, had sided with the French, with whom they had close trading ties. When Indian leaders issued demands to the new English administrators for lower prices on traded goods and for ammunition, the British refused.

The British administrator, Lord Jeffrey Amherst, and his military commander, Colonel Henry Bouquet, despised natives and even plotted to give the Indians blankets riddled with smallpox. Amherst cut back expenditures for the Indian department and ceased offering gifts to chiefs to ensure their pacifism. This produced a meeting at Detroit in 1762, wherein the Indians discussed the likelihood of war. A Delaware prophet influenced their deliberations with talk of a new era for the western tribes, and Pontiac, the chief of three Ottawa tribes near Detroit, masterminded a

series of attacks on British outposts, including an unsuccessful surprise attack on Detroit itself. Pontiac had convinced the British to allow 300 Ottawa into Fort Detroit to hold a dance in May 1763, but the commander, Major Henry Gladwyn, had the garrison alert and cautious. On May 9 Pontiac abandoned stealth for a frontal assault, which was also defeated, and the Indians settled into a siege. By that time, Pontiac commanded 1,000 men, including representatives of the Potawatomi, Ojibwa, and Huron.

When news of the Detroit siege spread, other tribes, including the Shawnee and Delaware, attacked other British forts. Between May and July, Fort Sandusky, Fort St. Joseph, and several other outposts west of Niagara were captured or destroyed. Reinforcements sent by Amherst reached Detroit toward the end of July, allowing Major Gladwin to break out of the siege and fight a pitched battle at Bloody Ridge, where his forces were defeated. Again he had to withdraw to the fort, and the Indians again laid siege. The British fared better with the relief of

Ottawa chief Pontiac led a rebellion against British administrators in 1763 when they refused to improve the terms of trade with the Indians. He is pictured here debating with a British major. *Library of Congress*

Fort Pitt under Colonel Bouquet at the battle of Bushy Run. Indian tactics, however, were not suited to long sieges, and in November Pontiac, seeing many other tribes already signing peace agreements, lifted the siege of Detroit. By 1764 many of the tribes arrived at Fort Niagara for a peace conference.

British forces had continued to smash any tribes not participating in the Niagara talks. Colonel John Bradstreet took an expedition through the

Ohio Valley and destroyed any village that resisted. Pontiac, hoping to re-organize for a later campaign, finally agreed to a treaty with Sir William Johnson at Oswego on July 24, 1766. After promising loyalty to England, Pontiac ended his rebellion permanently. At least one version of his death suggests Pontiac was killed by a Kaskaskia Indian in 1769.

Potawatomi

The Potawatomis, a central Algonquian people, are generally associated with lands in the western Great Lakes, especially lower Michigan, northern Indiana and Illinois, and Wisconsin. Throughout the intense imperial rivalry of 17th and 18th centuries, the Potawatomis almost always sided with the French. From their initial contacts, the French intermarried, traded with, and missionized the Potawatomis. When the official alliance with the French government ended with the French defeat during the *French and Indian War*, the Potawatomis divided in their attitudes toward Europeans and Americans. A significant number of Potawatomis desired to maintain their political independence and cultural traditions, while others attempted to acculturate to an Anglo-agrarian lifestyle. After the *War of 1812 [III]*, many Potawatomis acquiesced to selling large portions of their lands to the U. S. government and, after the mid-1820s, to removing to a reservation in Kansas. Some Potawatomis, however, remained in Michigan and northeastern Wisconsin.

Proclamation Line of 1763

As settlers and traders flooded across the Appalachian Mountains in the mid-1700s, both treaties with the Indians and the monopolies of the British trading companies in the region were threatened. In 1763 the British Parliament issued a proclamation organizing the government of the provinces of Quebec, East Florida, and West Florida and reestablishing the charter powers of the trading companies west of the Appalachians. Colonists who had fought in the *French and Indian War* for promises of land in this area opposed this new law, and traders, lured to America by the prospect of trade, were outraged by these limitations.

Following *Pontiac's Rebellion,* during which virtually every British outpost on the frontier came under assault, the British government sought to end tensions by restricting white settlements on Indian land and to encourage British subjects to move instead to Quebec or the Floridas. But as the individuals running the Board of Trade changed, the policies were repealed then reinstated, until few knew what the official policy was. Since the entire issue of land restrictions struck at the very incentives offered to many to come to America, the Proclamation Line proved a badly flawed policy, either for maintaining solid Indian relations or for governing the colonies.

Provincias Internas

Part of the Bourbon Reforms, the Provincias Internas, or Interior Provinces, were created by the Spanish crown on the recommendation of visiting general José de Gálvez in 1776. The commandant general of the Interior Provinces oversaw the northern New Spain provinces of Texas, New Mexico, Alta California, Baja California, Nueva Vizcaya (the northern Mexican states of Chihuahua and Durango), Nuevo Leon (a state in northern Mexico), Sonora y Sinaloa, (now two states of the same names along Mexico's northwestern coast), and the colony of Nuevo Santander (now the Mexican state of Tamaulipas). Head of an independent military government, the commandant general of the Interior Provinces reported directly to the crown rather than to the viceroy. The commandant general's duties centered on increasing Spain's military presence to guard against foreign incursions and fostering peaceful relationships with borderlands Indian tribes. The latter goal was accomplished through a policy of "peace by purchase," that is, ensuring peace through supplying trade goods to Indians. As for the goal of a more visible military presence, the threat of foreign incursion failed to materialize during the heyday of the Provincias Internas.

Roman Catholic Missions

The Roman Catholic Church, seeking to convert American Indians to Christianity, dispatched priests on the earliest voyages to North America funded by European dioceses. Priests came from the ranks of the secular church order, or from any of the special missionary orders (Jesuits, Franciscans, Capuchins, and Marianists) that were formed. Known as "black robes" (a term that originally only applied to Jesuits, but eventually to all Catholic priests), missionaries accompanied French and Spanish expeditions from Mexico to Canada to evangelize the Indians. National governments saw an opportunity to use the church as a means to control rebellious natives and to ensure a docile labor force. Of course, priests were also expected to attend to the spiritual needs of the European conquerors.

IN THEIR OWN

A Quaker's Visit to Pennsylvania Indians

John Woolman, a Quaker from Mount Holly, New Jersey, traveled through the colonies to report to the Society of Friends, which had sent him on a visit to Pennsylvania. Although he does not identify the tribe, the Indians he encountered were from Wyoming, Pennsylvania in the Lehigh Valley.

*I*n conversation with [an Indian trader from the tribe] I perceived that many white people do often sell rum to the Indians, which I believe is a great evil. In the first place, they being thereby deprived of the use of reason, and, their spirits violently agitated, quarrels often arise which end in mischief, and the bitterness and resentments occasioned hereby are

frequently of long continuance. Again, there skins and furs, gotten through much fatigue and hard travels in hunting, with which they intended to buy clothing, when they begin to be intoxicated they often sell at a low rate for more rum; and afterwards when they suffer for want of the necessaries of life are angry with those who for the sale of gain, took advantage of their weakness. Their chiefs have often complained of this in their treaties with the English. . . .

I was renewedly confirmed in a belief that if all our inhabitants lived according to pure wisdom, labouring to promote universal love and righteousness, and ceased from every inordinate desire after wealth and from all customs which are tinctured with luxury, the way would be easy for our inhabitants, though much more numerous than at present, to live comfortable on honest employments, without having that temptation they are often under of being drawn into schemes to make settlements on lands which have not been honestly purchased of the Indians, or of applying to that wicked practice of selling rum to them.

—SOURCE: RICHARD N. CURRENT, JOHN A. GARRATY, AND JULIUS WEINBERG, *WORDS THAT MADE AMERICAN HISTORY: COLONIAL TIMES TO THE 1870S*, 3D EDITION (BOSTON: LITTLE, BROWN AND COMPANY, 1972), 35–38.

Missionaries led a life of sacrifice, traveling by foot or horseback to remote tribes. Many were killed or tortured by the Indians they sought to convert. Over time, their heroism impressed the Native Americans, occasionally bringing entire tribes to Christianity at one time. The Huron and Algonquian confederations and the Iroquois were converted after the steady effort of a few hundred Jesuits. Some of the missionaries were explorers in their own right, such as Jesuit Father Jacques *Marquette [I]*. When France lost its territory in the New World after the *French and Indian War*, the influence of the Catholic Church over many of the tribes diminished. Before then, the influence of the Church had been extensive, with more than 2 million baptized by the Jesuits alone in North and South America, and some 900,000 Indians still under the pastoral care of Jesuits or Franciscans by 1750.

The Catholic Church sought to bring Indians not only into the worship but also into the church structure, appointing Indians as a majority of American bishops by 1800. As the Spanish explorers fanned out through Mexico and the Southwest, still more came into the church. Dozens of missions dotted New Mexico, Arizona, Texas, and the northern Mexican landscape, many of them planted by Father Eusebio Francisco *Kino*—the "apostle of Arizona." Likewise, Father Junipero Serra founded a number of missions in California. Often the buildings became not only religious meeting places, but also the central location for the region's economy, often serving as the center of trade, farming, and business.

After the United States gained independence, the Indian tribes of the far West placed a steady demand on the Vatican to provide priests. One of the more successful, Father Pierre Jean DeSmet, became a virtual diplomat due to his ability to communicate with different Plains tribes. He lived, at one time or another, among 100 different tribes and won their trust. The work done by DeSmet and other missionaries paid off. A census estimate in 1873 put about 40 percent of the nation's 278,000 Indians as Catholics.

San Antonio

San Antonio de Béxar, founded by Martin de Alarcón on April 25, 1718, on the banks of the San Antonio river, became a major way station between northern Mexico and the capital of the province in Robeline, Louisiana. It immediately became a presidio, becoming the capital after 1773.

In addition, Father Antonio de San Buenaventura de Olivares established San Antonio de Valero, which soon became known by the name associated with the church building, "the Alamo."

San Antonio achieved fame in 1835–1836 during the *Texas Revolution [III]*. Texan troops captured the Mexican forces there in December 1835 and defended the Alamo against Antonio López de *Santa Anna [III]*, the new Mexican president, who had moved north to put down the rebellion. The Alamo fell on March 6, 1836, but after Texan independence, San Antonio revived and remained the largest city in Texas for several years.

After the United States annexed Texas, San Antonio became a major military training center, especially for the U.S. Army Air Force. It also attracted manufacturing, ranching, banking, and even breweries. In the mid-1960s, the city began a major renovation, including expansion of Riverwalk, a popular shopping area running adjacent to waterways, and HemisFair Park.

Sequoyah (ca. 1766–1843)

Sequoyah was a *Cherokee [III]* chief who, in the early 1800s invented a syllabary—a writing system with 85 symbols—for the Cherokee language. Sequoyah and his daughter taught many of their kinsmen the syllabary after 1822. Numerous Cherokees quickly realized the advantage of a written language, and the syllabary was used to translate part of the Bible and to print a Cherokee-nation newspaper, the *Cherokee Phoenix*. With the forced removal of the Cherokees during the Jackson administration, Sequoyah worked to unify the divided tribe (some supported removal, others did not), though with little success. Lost in a cave in 1843, Sequoyah was never seen again.

A Cherokee chief during the eviction of the Cherokee from their lands in the Jackson administration, Sequoya developed an alphabet, a written language, and a newspaper for the Cherokee. *Library of Congress*

Shawnee

The bulk of the Shawnees traditionally resided throughout the Ohio River Valley in what are now Indiana, Ohio, and Pennsylvania, with hunting grounds in Kentucky. Scattered bands, though, could be found in many parts of the American East prior to the American Revolution. They are a Central Algonquian people, and their name is Algonquian for "southerner." The five most important bands were the rivalrous Chalahgawtha and Thawegila, each known for its leadership skills, the Kispokothas, the warriors; the Maykujays, the healers and priests; and the Piqua, the warrior-priests. Frequently, the Shawnees split into two factions, the Chalahgawthas leading one faction, the Thawegila the other.

The Shawnees often remained aloof from European alliances, fighting the British in the *French and Indian War* and *Pontiac's Rebellion*, and the Virginians in *Lord Dunmore's War* in 1774. The Shawnees warred against the Americans during the Revolutionary War, the *Miami-Federalist War*, and the *War of 1812 [III]*. Between the latter two, a significant prophet, *Tenskwatawa [III]*, led a nativist, pan-Indian movement against American settlements in the western Great Lakes. William Henry *Harrison [III]* defeated Tenskwatawa's following at the *Battle of Tippecanoe [III]* in November 1811. During the War of 1812 Tenskwatawa's brother *Tecumseh [III]* attempted to recreate the alliance and fight with the British against the Americans. When the British reneged on their alliance with the Indians, and with Tecumseh's

---

IN THEIR OWN Words

The Shawnees Capture Daniel Boone

Daniel Boone, the preeminent backwoodsman, was captured by the Shawnees in April 1778, as recorded in this letter from Henry Hamilton to Guy Carleton.

April the 5th. Mr. Charles Baubin [Beaubien]. . . with a young man named Lorimier engaged four score Shawanese [Shawnees]. . . to go toward the fort on Kentuck River, east of the Ohio into which it discharges directly opposite the Great Mineamis or Rocky River. The fort is about 30 miles from the mouth. The number of men in it about 80. Here they had the good fortune to make prisoners Captain Daniel Boone, with 26 of his men, whom they brought off with their arms without killing or losing a man.

—SOURCE: HENRY HAMILTON, DETROIT, TO GUY CARLETON, 25 APRIL 1778, *FRONTIER DEFENSE ON THE UPPER OHIO, 1777–1778*, REUBEN GOLD THWAITES AND LOUISE PHELPS KELLOGG, EDS. (MADISON: WISCONSIN HISTORICAL SOCIETY, 1912), 283.

---

death in 1813 at the Battle of the Thames, any hope for Indian independence or autonomy in the Old Northwest vanished.

In 1826 the Shawnees migrated to Kansas. Their reservation was west of the Missouri-Kansas line and south of the Kansas River. Isaac McCoy, a Baptist missionary, ministered to them from the Shawnee Mission in what is now Kansas City, Kansas. Roughly 6,000 Shawnees now live in Oklahoma.

Sieur d'Iberville (ca. 1660–1706)

A Captain of the Quebec militia and an interpreter, Sieur Pierre d'Iberville was one of the early explorers of New France who sailed from France in 1698 to Pensacola, then in 1699 to the mouth of the Mississippi River. He then proceeded 200 miles upstream past the site of modern-day Baton Rouge, Louisiana. On his return, d'Iberville crossed Lake Ponchartrain into Bay St. Louis, confirming the routes of La Salle, and built a base at modern-day Biloxi, Mississippi.

South Pass

Located in southwest Wyoming near the Wind River Range, South Pass is a broad valley that was used by fur trappers as well as westering pioneers to cross the rather formidable Rocky Mountains. Whites, returning from Astoria in the Pacific Northwest in 1812, first located this 250-mile-wide extension of the Great Plains into the Rocky Mountain West. Jedediah *Smith [III]* rediscovered it in the 1820s, after discussing possible trans-mountain routes with the *Crow [III]* Indians. It also served as the site of the railroad tracks of the *Union Pacific Railroad [IV]*.

St. Clair, Arthur (March 23, 1736–August 31, 1818)

Known for commanding an expedition that suffered the greatest single loss by the U.S. Army to Indian forces (near Fort Wayne, Indiana), Arthur St. Clair was born in Thurso, Scotland, on March 23, 1736. He joined the

British Army, becoming an ensign in Lord Jeffery Amherst's expedition against the French in 1758. During the *French and Indian War*, St. Clair fought at Quebec and Louisbourg, before resigning in 1762 to farm his large estate in the Ligonier valley of Pennsylvania. His land acquisitions continued until he owned nearly 15,000 acres, and with his wealth and position came several local appointments.

When the American Revolution broke out, St. Clair joined the Continental Army and was later promoted by General of the Army George Washington to major general. Assigned to Fort Ticonderoga in June 1777 with 2,200 men to defend the fort, St. Clair faced a better equipped army under General John "Gentleman Johnny" Burgoyne, whose men commanded the heights around the fort. St. Clair, convinced his troops would all die if they remained, evacuated the fort in July 1777.

In November 1785 St. Clair was elected to the Continental Congress. A year later, he was elected president of the Congress, which also named him governor of the Northwest Territory in 1787. He traveled to Marietta, Ohio, where he officially named the town of Cincinnati.

Part of St. Clair's duties involved dealing with the Indians, and while he negotiated several treaties, such as the Treaty of Fort Harmar (1789), he could not keep the peace. One army was defeated that year, then, in 1791, President Washington and Congress ordered a second expedition against the natives. St. Clair led 3,000 men to engage the Northwestern Indian Confederation (including *Shawnee*, *Iroquois [I]*, Delaware, Ottawa, *Miami*, and *Potawatomi* Indians). His undisciplined recruits randomly raided Indian villages, further uniting the tribes. St. Clair's force encamped near the Ohio-Indiana border, when, during the night, the Indians under Miami chief Michikinikwa (Little Turtle) staged a surprise attack, dealing a humiliating defeat to the expedition. It was a staggering defeat for the regular army, and the worst at the hands of Indians until the *Battle of the Little Bighorn [IV]*. Although St. Clair requested exoneration and was cleared by (indeed, commended by) a court of inquiry and remained governor of the territory, the disaster ended his political ambitions.

On August 20, 1794, General "Mad" Anthony Wayne led a third, smaller but better trained army against the Confederacy, defeating the Indians at the Battle of Fallen Timbers. St. Clair, meanwhile, continued as governor, opposing Ohio statehood, until President Thomas *Jefferson [III]* removed him in 1802.

St. Denis, Louis Juchereau de (September 17, 1676–June 11, 1744)

St. Denis opposed Spanish-French rivalry in North America, believing the two countries had more in common and would benefit from strong trading relations and a common Roman Catholic mission front to the Indians. When Spanish priest Francisco Hidalgo opened a dialogue on the issue of joint French-Spanish missions to the Texas Indians in 1713, the French Canadian government sent St. Denis. Guided by two French children of the failed *La Salle* expedition who had been raised by Indians, he made his first exploration into Spanish territory in 1713 and 1714. But upon arriving at the northern Spanish frontier town of San Juan Bautista (currently Piedras Negras, Mexico) in the summer of 1714, St. Denis found only anxiety at his arrival. Spanish authorities removed him to Mexico City and interrogated him. The charismatic St. Denis charmed his way into Spanish society, even falling in love with a local Spaniard of a prominent family, Doña Emanuela, and becoming a Spanish citizen. In turn, the Spanish asked him to lead a mission back to east Texas to create a chain of forts to protect them from further French intrusions. St. Denis agreed and married Doña Emanuela.

Secretly, though, St. Denis had been sending information to the French government in North America. His information allowed the French to maintain a significant presence in Louisiana, despite Spanish build-up in the same region. When St. Denis violated Spanish law by moving French trade goods through Texas in 1717, the Spaniards arrested him as a French citizen illegally in Spanish territory. He spent more than a year in a jail in Mexico City. He broke out in late 1718, found his wife, and escaped to French Louisiana.

After his escape, St. Denis remained a significant player in French-Spanish rivalry. In 1719 he helped lead the attack against Spain's base in Pensacola. In 1721 he took charge of the French fort at Natchitoches, which he had established in 1714. St. Denis and Doña lived a happy and prosperous life in French Louisiana. They hoped to resettle in New Spain in 1744, but St. Denis died shortly after the decision to move.

Tabeau, Pierre-Antoine (dates unknown)

Born to a third-generation French fur trapping family, Tabeau traveled with the French expedition of Regis Loisel from 1803 to 1805. Exploring the Upper Missouri at the same time as the more famous American expedition of *Lewis and Clark*, Tabeau produced a fine journal of his exploits and encounters with the northern Plains Indians. Ethnohistorians regard his account of the Arikaras as especially important, ranking its worth even higher than the Lewis and Clark journals. His understanding of Indian intertribal politics is notably perceptive, and his view of Indian religious rituals and "magic" amusingly skeptical. After the expedition, Tabeau earned a formal education at Laval University, leaving his papers to a nephew, a parish priest.

Taucumwah (ca. mid–1700s)

Taucumwah, also known as Maria Louisa Roi, was born sometime in the 1740s to a prominent *Miami* Metis family. She was the sister of the famed civil chief, *Pacanne*, and the mother of Jean Baptiste *Richardville [III]*, also a famed civil chief. Her family rightfully controlled the *Long Portage* and served as chiefs over the main Miami village, Kekionga.

In the 1760s Taucumwah married a French nobleman and fur trapper, Joseph Richerville. Together they had four children, all baptized in the Roman Catholic faith. Her marriage was volatile and it came to a head in 1774, when Joseph began to beat Taucumwah severely, often threatening her with death. Taucumwah left Joseph and sought physical protection from her brother, Pacanne, and her new companion, Charles *Beaubien*. Involved in their separation was Richerville's attempt to take over the Long Portage.

In September 1774 a British court heard both sides regarding the divorce and the Long Portage. The British officer affirmed rightful ownership of the Long Portage to the Miamis, rather than the French. He also awarded Taucumwah a divorce, granting her custody of her property, preventing Joseph Richerville from obtaining any of it.

Taucumwah wielded considerable influence within her family and the Miamis. As a sister and mother, she most likely helped her brother and son attain their offices of chief. She also spoke frequently in tribal council meetings as a chieftess.

She was most likely rather wealthy for her day. Not only did August *de la Balme* raid her warehouse in 1780, but she owned part of the Long Portage, and records from 1790 indicate that she owned several fur trading posts along the Wabash River. Indeed, she spent her winters with the men, hunting. She disappears from the historical record after 1790.

Tonti, Henry de (ca.1650–ca.1704)

Tonti, an Italian by birth, is best known for being Ferdinand *La Salle*'s lieutenant and right-hand man. Between 1678 and 1682 La Salle and Tonti explored the Great Lakes and the *Mississippi River [I]*. They reached the Gulf of Mexico on April 9, 1682. In 1686 Tonti led an expedition to find the murdered La Salle, and three years later, he launched his last expedition, making his way up the Red River, only to be stopped by enemy Spaniards as well as mutinous soldiers. Tonti died of natural causes in 1704.

Treaty of Fort Finney, 1786

Fort Finney (1786–1793), near the site of present-day Louisville, Kentucky, at the mouth of the Great Miami River, served as the site of a short-lived truce between the *Miami* Confederacy and the United States. With the number of raids by both Americans and Indians increasing, George Rogers *Clark* and Richard Butler treated with the Miamis and *Shawnees* in January and February 1786, asking the Indians to end their raiding or to face real war against the United States. They also demanded that the Shawnees give up their claims to Ohio, threatening the lives of Shawnee women and children if the Indians failed to comply. Only a few intimidated Indian chiefs signed. Most Miamis and Shawnees believed the American attitude offensive. In addition, with the Articles of Confederation governing the United States, Clark and Butler's threats were hollow. The treaty only furthered the violence between the various factions and Indian and American raids continued, exploding into the *Miami-Federalist War*, 1790–1795.

Treaty of Fort Stanwix (First and Second Treaties)

In 1768 the British government negotiated a series of treaties with the Indian tribes on the then-western frontier, including the Creeks in the south and, with the Treaty of Fort Stanwix (November 5, 1768), the Iroquois in the north. This treaty, secured by Sir William Johnson, the head of Indian Affairs of New York, secured land for British settlers along a line running from Fort Stanwix (near Rome, New York) to the Unadilla River, then to the Delaware River, through Oswego, New York, then to Williamsport, Pennsylvania, then westward to the mouth of the Tennessee River. In addition, the "Walpole Group," headed by Samuel Wharton, Thomas Walpole, and George Grenville, obtained a grant of 20 million acres for the proprietary colony of Vandalia.

Following disputes between North Carolina, the independent state of Franklin (parts of modern-day Tennessee and Virginia), and the Indians, a second Treaty of Fort Stanwix was concluded on October 22, 1784, with the Six Nations of the Iroquois. Under the second treaty the Indians ceded to the United States all lands west of the Niagara River, although Ohio tribes rejected the treaty.

Treaty of Greenville

After the Battle of Fallen Timbers in modern-day Indiana, in August 1795, *Miami* chiefs Little Turtle and *Richardville [III]* signed the Treaty of Greenville with the United States, recognizing American political sovereignty over the land in the Northwest. General "Mad" Anthony Wayne negotiated the treaty, ensuring that if the United States owned land at both ends of the portage, it would be guaranteed free passage by land or water across Miami territory. Wayne also built a large fort that bore his name at the confluence of the St. Mary's and St. Joseph's Rivers to display American power, not only to the Indians but to the British, who still sought to maintain a presence in the region.

Treaty of Vincennes

On June 7, 1803, in the Treaty of Vincennes, the nine Indian tribes of the Old Northwest gave the United States title to disputed lands along the Wabash River. This treaty continued a process begun after the Battle of Fallen Timbers (1794) with the *Treaty of Greenville* (1795) that pushed the *Shawnee* and other tribes out of the Ohio Valley region. Indian leaders, such as *Tecumseh [III]*, later claimed that this, and the subsequent Treaty of Fort Wayne, defrauded them of their land.

Truteau, Jean Baptiste (ca.1750–1800)

In 1793 Truteau, a French Creole schoolmaster, led eight men up the *Missouri River [I]* under the auspices of the "Company of Explorers of the Upper Missouri," a Spanish-chartered company. Truteau's goal was to reach the Mandan Villages and open trade with them. To do so, he often traveled at night, so as to avoid being seen by other Plains tribes. The Teton *Sioux [IV]*, to no one's surprise, discovered the party and prevented Truteau and his expedition from reaching the Mandans. The Sioux feared the loss of their monopoly in the region. In 1795 Truteau attempted again to reach the Mandans but failed. His journal regarding the Teton Sioux remains one of the best extant ethnographies of the Lakota.

Vial, Pedro (?–1814)

Little is known of the early life of Pedro Vial (also known as Pierre Vial). Born in Lyons, France, he traveled to the American Southwest where he engaged in trade with the Indians until the Spanish government empowered him to explore a trail route from *San Antonio* to *Santa Fe [I]*.

Embarking in 1786, he and Cristóbal de Los Santos traveled up the Red River, arriving in Santa Fe in 1787. Vial apparently had extraordinary relations with the Indians, opening trails throughout the West and Southeast.

Villasur Expedition

In 1720 the Spanish government in Mexico dispatched a force of 40 soldiers and 70 Indian allies under Don Pedro de Villasur to exert pressure on the Pawnee Indians in Texas to cease trading with the French in Louisiana. Instead, the Pawnee attacked Villasur's force, killing the commander and most of the men before stragglers escaped to New Mexico. As a result, the Pawnee remained wedded to French trade and in 1750 declared a formal alliance with the French. When the Frence left Louisiana in 1763, the Pawnees came under attacks from *Sioux* and *Osage [III]*, which led to their withdrawal from the region and their migration to the Red River area, where they eventually merged with the Wichita Indians.

Wabash River

The Wabash River flows from Fort Wayne, in northeastern Indiana, in a southwesterly direction to the Ohio River. It runs for roughly 475 miles. The earliest recorded French documents reveal that the Wabash has always been a major highway for trade, especially as it connects, via the *Long Portage*, the Maumee River and Great Lakes to the Ohio and, ultimately, to the *Mississippi River [I]*. Prior to the 1830s, it served as a home to a large number of *Miamis*, *Shawnees*, Delawares, Piankishaws, and Weas. It became a part of the Wabash-Erie Canal in the 1830s.

IN THEIR OWN Words

Wabash River and Long Portage

In 1778 Thomas Hutchins published his observations of the Wabash River and Long Portage, made as part of a journey through Maryland, North Carolina, Pennsylvania, and Virginia.

The Wabash is a beautiful River, with high and upright banks, less subject to overflow, than any other River (the Ohio excepted) in this part of America. It discharges itself into the Ohio, one thousand and twenty two miles below Fort Pitt, in latitude 37° 41' at its mouth, it is 270 yards wide; Is navigable to Ouiatanon [Lafayette, Indiana] (412 miles) in the Spring, Summer, and Autumn, with Battoes or Barges, drawing about three feet water. From thence, on account of a rocky bottom, and shoal water, large canoes are chiefly employed, except when the River is swelled with Rains, at which time, it may be ascended with boats, such as I have just described, (197 miles further) to the Miami carrying place, which is nine miles from the Miami village [Kekionga]. . . . The land on this River is remarkably fertile, and several parts of it are natural meadows, of great extent, covered with fine long grass. The timber is large, and high, and in such variety, that almost all the different kinds growing upon the Ohio and its branches (but with a greater proportion of black and white mulberry-trees) may be found here.

—Source: Thomas Hutchins, *A Topographical Description of Virginia, Pennsylvania, Maryland, and North Carolina* (1778; reprint, Cleveland: Burrows Brothers, 1904), 98–99.

PART III

From Lewis and Clark to the Pony Express (1803–1861)

The acquisition of the Louisiana Territory by Thomas Jefferson and the subsequent exploration by the expeditions of Lewis and Clark and, in 1806, of Zebulon Pike, left the young republic with a vast new frontier and plenty of potential enemies on its borders. In addition to the numerous Indian tribes in the Old Northwest—most notably the Shawnee and the Miami—now the Americans had to deal with the French, Spanish, British, and Russians. At one time or another, all four of those European nations were at war with each other on the Continent, threatening to draw the United States into the conflict. Jefferson, seeking neutrality, carefully navigated a policy of nonintervention. British offenses at sea, including impressment of American sailors, made his task even more difficult, but he intended to follow the advice of George Washington, who had warned against foreign entanglements in his farewell address. Still, the wealth and openness of the West offered no end to scheming and adventuring, as seen in the Burr Conspiracy and the activities of John Wilkinson. The government not only sought to maintain peace when possible with the Indians, but to ensure that rogue elements did not spark a border war with Spain or France, a Jeffersonian policy continued by his successor, James Madison.

Ultimately, the new American government was concerned about British incursions in the Old Northwest and feared that the Indians would ally with England. As American settlers moved into the Wabash Valley, a dispute arose over which chiefs had authority to negotiate the Treaty of Fort Wayne, resulting in resistance from Shawnee chief Tecumseh and his brother, Tenskwatawa. William Henry Harrison, the territorial governor of Indiana, led a campaign to crush the Indian power of the Old Northwest, ending Tecumseh's power at the Battle of Tippecanoe. Already Indian and British power on the frontier had led to a new group of politicians, known as the War Hawks, to campaign for a war with England and an invasion of Canada. Several westerners were prominent among the War Hawks, including Henry Clay and Richard M. Johnson of Kentucky. Swept into power—Clay was elected Speaker of the House—the War Hawks succeeded in getting their declaration of war.

In the ensuing War of 1812 the West became a central battleground as Americans fought the British and their Indian allies around several key forts, especially Fort Detroit and Fort Dearborn. After early disasters William Henry Harrison regained the offensive in the Great Lakes region, while battles raged in New York and along the East Coast. Meanwhile, Andrew Jackson led a force south from Tennessee to deal with the Creek Indians, crushing them at the Battle of Horseshoe Bend. When a British armada showed up off New Orleans, Jackson led his troops there to defeat the redcoats at the Battle of New Orleans in January 1815, after negotiators from the United States and England had already concluded the Treaty of Ghent ending the war. Although the Americans failed in the invasion of Canada, the war had long-reaching effects in that it smashed Indian power in the Northwest.

In short order Ohio, Illinois, Indiana, Wisconsin, and Michigan, as well as Tennessee, Alabama, and Mississippi were added to the Union. Areas formerly uninhabited by whites now teemed with farms and factories, lumber mills and railroads, flatboats and fur posts. Already John Jacob Astor, after a failed attempt at establishing a colony at Astoria, Oregon, rebounded to build his American Fur Company into a thriving company that competed with both the British Hudson Bay Company and the government-owned and -operated fur trade. He out-dueled both of them, forcing the government to abolish government posts in 1821. When the fur trade trailed off, Astor turned to real estate in New York City.

Astor and other entrepreneurs increasingly depended on the river system, especially the Mississippi River, which became the focus of most shipping trade. Merchants could ship downstream to New Orleans, then across the Gulf of Mexico and up the Atlantic cheaper than they could carry goods overland. St. Louis, which had already served as the hub of trade for the French and Spanish, now assumed a central position in the fur trade enterprise of the West. Mountain Men such as Jim Bridger, William Sublette, and William H. Ashley, who fanned out across the Rockies and along the Missouri River, returned annually with their wares. These trappers developed the famous "rendezvous" system that replaced traditional trapping arrangements. Instead of leading large parties from St. Louis and other departure points, which gave Indians an easier target, the rendezvous system involved smaller groups traveling and trapping on their own, then meeting at an agreed point to return.

The introduction of steam power made the Mississippi and other rivers profitable to use for upstream as well as downstream trade, and soon steamships dominated traffic. Overland rates fell with the introduction of the railroads, which started to expand westward as part of the cattle trade. Extending the railroads soon brought calls to relocate the Indians yet further west. Already, land had been taken from the Cherokee and several tribes forced to move to Oklahoma on the "Trail of Tears." Despite the resistance of a few white reformers, the government pushed the Indians out to allow in more farmers.

Other groups, most notably the churches, followed a different strategy of "civilizing" and converting the Indians. Among the first dedicated efforts in that regard was that of the Methodists in Oregon, where the Oregon Trail brought steady streams of missionaries and settlers to the Willamette Valley. Early missionaries Elijah White and Jason Lee intended to Christianize the Indians as well as settle the land but found strong resistance among the Flatheads and other northwest tribes. Before long, Lee and White gave up, but other settlers followed, then headed south to Sacramento and San Francisco. Later Mormons (Church of the Latter Day Saints) under Joseph Smith and then Brigham Young settled in Salt Lake City, Utah, where they established a formidable settlement and prosperous church. Unlike the Methodists and Catholics, the Mormons engaged in minimal evangelization of Native Americans, which produced peaceful relations with the Utes and other Utah tribes. However, the Mormons also practiced polygamy, which created constant tensions with the federal government and delayed Utah statehood.

Farther south, the Texas region of Mexico had been the location of numerous adventurers who proclaimed independent states and republics.

In 1820 American Moses Austin proposed a plan of colonization of Texas that would encourage settlers from the United States. After his death, his son Stephen went to Mexico City shortly after the Mexican Revolution gained independence from Spain and helped draft the new nation's constitution. The government approved the colonization plan, and 25,000 people came to Texas within a few years. They remained substantially Americans in their customs and language, which concerned the Mexican government. In 1835 General Antonio López de Santa Anna overthrew the government and proclaimed the constitution null and void, an action that led to calls of rebellion from the Texans. Santa Anna moved to crush the rebellion and the Texans, smashing Texan forces at Goliad and the Alamo. But the Alamo's defenders bought time for Texan General Sam Houston, who rallied his army to stage a shocking defeat of Santa Anna's forces at San Jacinto in 1836. Texas declared itself a republic and elected Houston as the president.

For the next eight years, American relations with Texas were cordial, yet cautious. Few Americans wanted a war with Mexico, and many did not want new slave territories added to the Union. Nevertheless, sentiment grew to annex Texas, and on December 29, 1845, President James K. Polk annexed Texas and made it a state. Border disputes soon led to the Mexican War in 1846. Americans moved into Mexico, defeating the Mexican forces. With the Treaty of Guadalupe Hidalgo in 1848, Mexico ceded California, Arizona, New Mexico, and parts of Utah and Colorado to the United States. Those areas were quickly organized as territories, and California became a state in 1850. The discovery of gold at Sutter's Mill had already brought thousands of "forty-niners" to the region and made it all the more difficult for Mexico to control. After statehood, California quickly became an important part of the U.S. economy, if for no other reason than the steady stream of gold supplied to the U.S. Treasury.

California's admission to the Union had required a major sectional compromise as it extended above the Missouri Compromise line of 36° 30'—the imaginary line above which no slavery was allowed. Far from settling the slavery issue, the Missouri Compromise had only ensured that the nation would postpone dealing with the inflammatory issue. It guaranteed a titanic struggle over every new potential state, and in 1854 it gave rise to a purely sectional party, the Republican Party. The Republicans were relentless in their call to end slavery in the western territories. Southerners saw this as a direct assault on slavery in the South, which, to an extent, it was. Wherever slavery was declared an evil, it threatened slavery every-where. In the wake of the Dred Scott case in 1857, where the Supreme Court ruled that only a state had authority to prohibit slavery, both proslave and antislave forces raced to pack new territories with their own voters who could shape the new state's constitution. In Kansas, this produced violence touted in the Northern papers as "Bleeding Kansas" and involved radicals such as John Brown. Each side had its own capital, its own constitution, and its own groups of spokesmen in Congress. It was clear by 1860 that slavery was the central issue before the nation and that its future was being played out in the western territories.

CHRONOLOGY · From Lewis and Clark to the Pony Express

1804	*Lewis and Clark Expedition begins*
1806	*Zebulon Pike's Expedition*
1811	*Battle of Tippecanoe*
1812	*War of 1812 begins*
1815	*Treaty of Ghent ends War of 1812; Battle of New Orleans*
1816	*James Monroe elected President*
1818	*Andrew Jackson seizes Florida from Spain and Seminoles*
1819	*Adams-Onis Treaty*
1819–1822	*Missouri Compromises*
1823	*American Fur Company establishes Fort Union on Missouri River*
1828	*Andrew Jackson elected president*
1832	*Worster v. Georgia; Black Hawk War*
1836	*Texas Independence*
1837	*Panic of 1837*
1838	*"Trail of Tears"*
1840	*William Henry Harrison elected president*
1844	*James K. Polk pledges to annex both Texas and Oregon Territory*
1845	*Texas annexation*
1846–1847	*Mexican War*
1848	*Treaty of Guadalupe Hidalgo ends Mexican War; Annexation of Oregon Territory and Southwest (California, New Mexico, Nevada, and Utah); Zachary Taylor elected president*
1849	*Gold discovered at Sutter's Mill in California*
1850	*Compromise of 1850 admits California as a state in the Union*
1853	*Gadsden Purchase*
1854	*Kansas-Nebraska Act; "Bleeding Kansas"*
1857	*Dred Scott decision; Panic of 1857; Mountain Meadows Massacre*
1860	*Abraham Lincoln elected president*
1861	*Civil War begins*

American Fur Company

Founded by John Jacob *Astor* in 1808, the American Fur Company quickly became America's premier commercial fur trading operation. Astor had depended on Canadian and British sources prior to establishing the company, which had trade routes as far away as China. To provide for the China trade, he founded the Pacific Fur Company in 1810. Furs could be moved overland to the Pacific Coast, then shipped to the Orient more effectively and cheaper than the British could move their furs through Montreal or Hudson's Bay. Astor's parties reached the Columbia River, where they established Astoria in March 1811. But as the *War of 1812* swirled, some of Astor's partners sold Astoria to the British North West Company, causing Astor to fold the Pacific Fur Company.

Even with the tensions generated by the war, Astor and the Canadian North West Company reached an agreement on trade east of the Rockies in Canada and the Great Lakes in 1811 wherein Astor invested in the South West Company as well as continuing his American Fur Company's operations. He was able to take over the South West Company in 1817, establishing a key outpost at *Michilimaciknac [II]*, which soon dominated all fur trade in the region. In doing so, though, Astor virtually killed the U.S. government's "factory" program, whereby Congress had hoped to create posts called "factories" that would trade goods—but not liquor—to the Indians for furs. After 1818, when Congress ended the factory system under pressure from Astor, the American Fur Company, with its powerful new Western Department, expanded its trade operations to the Missouri River.

There, competition from Bernard Pratte and Company proved superior to Astor's Western Department, so he promptly bought out Pratte, renaming his company the Western Department and giving it control of the Missouri River trade. Building a new post called Fort McKenzie at the Marias River, the American Fur Company or its operatives had virtually all the trade east of the Rocky Mountains, which the Rocky Mountain Fur Company and the Sublette brothers still controlled. By 1834, though, Astor sensed that the fur trade had already reached its full business potential, and he sold his interests to Pratte and others. While the American Fur Company continued its operations, the fur trade dwindled, and in 1864 it came to an end when the company sold its assets to the Northwest Fur Company.

Arikaras

The Arikaras, also often referred to as the "Ree" in historical documents but calling themselves the Sahnish, spoke a form of Caddoan. Between the 17th and 19th centuries they lived along the *Missouri River [I]* in what are now the Dakotas, divided into 12 political bands. Long before *horses [I]* arrived and remade the cultures of the Great Plains Indians, the Arikaras were sedentary and practiced a complex form of agriculture along the river banks. Their traditional religion was tied to their horticultural practices, and village politics reflected their perceived order of the universe.

European exploration and trade fundamentally disrupted Arikara life. European-derived diseases flourished in the fixed villages, and the horse gave immense power to their enemies, especially the Lakotas, (i.e., *Sioux [IV]*) who reduced the Arikaras to a form of tributary serfdom. At the beginning of the 19th century, Frenchman Pierre *Tableau [II]* noted that disease and serfdom had reduced 18 Arikara villages to 3. By the 1830s fewer than 1,000 Arikaras made up the tribe.

In 1934 the remaining Arikaras joined with the Hidatsa and Mandan, forming the Three Affiliated Tribes. Today, many Arikaras still live on the Fort Berthold reservation in North Dakota.

Ashley, William H. (1778–March 26, 1838)

Famed for developing the "brigade-rendezvous system" for fur trading operations, William H. Ashley was born in Virginia, then moved to Missouri around 1803. After a brief period of soldering and politics, he plunged into fur trading. Ashley's first advertisements for traders brought the likes of Jedediah *Smith* and river boatman Mike Fink. His first expedition established a trading post (Fort Henry, later Fort Union) on the Yellowstone. The following year, however, the *Arikara* Indians ambushed his expedition.

Consequently, Ashley abandoned the notion of operating out of a fixed post and instead conceived of having the trappers meet at a preestablished rendezvous point. In 1824 he sent two parties to the Rockies from Fort Kiowa overland. This revolutionized the fur trade by moving the trappers from boats to horses. Indians found it harder to intercept the parties, and the mobility permitted greater range.

Ashley sold out his interests to William Sublette and Smith and moved to St. Louis, where he engaged in banking and mercantile business related to trapping. In subsequent years, Ashley again became involved in politics, eventually winning a Congressional seat.

Astor, John Jacob (July 17, 1763–March 29, 1848)

Considered one of the richest men in the early United States, a leading businessman and financier, John Jacob Astor established an American presence in the fur trade. Born in July 1763 in Germany, Astor was trained as a butcher. He left for London in 1779, where he and his brother made musical instruments, then sailed for America in 1783 with a few flutes. On his voyage, he engaged in extended discussions with officers of the Hudson's Bay Company, from whom he absorbed the essentials of the fur trade in North America. For a brief time after he arrived in New York, he worked as a fur peddler but also sold musical instruments to make ends meet. He expanded his peddling and mercantile business, then entered the fur trade directly, exchanging goods with trappers and traders before eventually employing trappers directly.

As early as 1800, Astor was considered one of the wealthiest men in America. He then opened trade with China, sending furs in exchange for silk, tea, and porcelain. He netted as much as $50,000 for a single voyage of one of his two ships. Buoyed by profits from the China markets and by the 1794 Jay Treaty, which resulted in the British abandoning western forts, Astor engaged in a direct competition with the powerful Mackinac Company, a Canadian fur trading enterprise. To facilitate this trade, he used his political connections to persuade the New York legislature to incorporate the American Fur Company in 1808 with an eye toward purchasing furs from the Pacific Northwest and selling them in China. This was followed by the incorporation of the Pacific Fur Company in 1810. Even then he envisioned these as only the first steps in a worldwide operation that would link the China trade through his Pacific northwest posts. Eventually, he planned to establish a string of posts along the Columbia River to the Missouri and, ultimately, St. Louis and hoped to ship furs and goods through the Great Lakes to New York. He dispatched a land party under Williams Price Hunt over the Lewis and Clark route and a ship, the *Tonquin*, to the mouth of the Columbia to construct a trading post, Astoria.

Astor's grand scheme ran into difficulties when the *Tonquin*, which arrived first, was boarded by Indians and destroyed under mysterious circumstances. The *Tonquin*'s captain, Jonathan Thorn, had apparently invited Indians aboard the ship after angering them on previous occasions. Ultimately, Astor's inability to reinforce or resupply Astoria—due in part to the declaration of war with England in 1812—led to pressure from his Canadian partners to sell the post to the British for $58,000. Despite these significant losses, Astor had managed to invest large sums in Manhattan real estate.

A political entrepreneur when necessary, Astor successfully lobbied Congress to pass an act that prohibited anyone except U.S. citizens from engaging in the fur trade on American soil. He also convinced Congress to end the system of government trading posts in favor of private posts, which of course, he dominated at the time. Throughout, Astor engaged in managerial innovation in his trading networks, dividing the territory into three separate business districts, each directed by an autonomous manager. His posts were sophisticated, well-stocked, and employed local traders or Indians. Critics, however, charged that Astor abused these agents, or *engages*, with low pay, while the managers skimmed the profits. It is true that Astor carefully tracked every penny in his operations, as seen in his detailed account ledgers. While he once fought against sales of liquor to Indians, by 1832 he supported sales of liquor as a trade item in his posts.

When John Jacob Astor died on March 29, 1848, he left a legacy as a visionary but stingy businessman. Few praised him in published postmortems, and his legacies to various institutions seemed exceptionally small for a man of such wealth. Overlooked, however, were the jobs he created, the expansion of American economic power into the West, and the managerial innovations over which he presided.

Austin, Moses (October 4, 1761–June 10, 1821)

Born in Durham, Connecticut, Moses Austin started his business career in a mercantile goods business in Middletown, before moving to Pennsylvania with his brother. The *War of 1812* interrupted his operations, after which Moses joined a group of entrepreneurs to form the Bank of St. Louis, which failed in 1819. He then planned to create a colony in Texas, traveling to San Antonio in 1820 to obtain permission from the Spanish government to obtain a land grant. In March 1821 he received 200,000 acres that would be sufficient to settle 300 families. Austin's health failed, though, and it was left to his son, Stephen, to oversee the establishment of the colony in Texas. Although he did not share his father's enthusiasm for the region, Stephen Austin carried out his father's wishes and is known as the Father of Texas. Moses Austin died on June 10, 1821.

Austin, Stephen Fuller (November 3, 1793– December 27, 1836)

The son of *Moses Austin*, Stephen Fuller Austin was born in Virginia but moved to his father's lead-mining town of Potosi, Missouri, in 1798. He obtained a university education and returned to Missouri to work in his father's businesses. Serving in the Missouri Territorial legislature from 1814 to 1820, Austin held a number of short-lived positions, including director of the failed Bank of St. Louis, lawyer, and writer for the *Louisiana Advertiser.*

When Moses Austin went to San Antonio to obtain a grant for colonizing the area of Texas, Stephen had little interest. But after his father's death in 1821, having promised to continue his father's dream of colonization, Stephen Austin completed the grant negotiations with Spanish authorities. However, the Mexican government established after independence did not recognize the grant, forcing Austin in December 1821 to go to the Brazos River where the colony was located, then on to Mexico City to cement the deal. In his capacity of *empresario*, that is, a landowner, Austin supported himself with a stipend of land, plus additional land for every family settled there. Naturally, he continued to press for more grants and to relocate more families. But Austin was not solely interested in his own gain, envisioning a growing industrial economy for the region that would bring prosperity to all. He used his authority to establish a militia to deal with Indians, to set up courts, and to develop trade.

Austin argued for conciliation with the Mexican government, realizing that most of the settlers were American Anglos, and many of them were slaveholders. In that respect, Austin sidestepped the issue of slavery by accepting the settler's disingenuous definition of the slaves as indentured servants. In 1830 the Mexican government grew sufficiently concerned about slavery to prohibit any further importation of such indentured servants or slaves. Three years later, the San Felipe Convention prepared a plan for a state of Texas. Austin took the colonists' demands to Mexico City to meet with the new President, Antonio López de *Santa Anna*, but the proposal did not receive a warm welcome. On his way home, Austin was arrested by Mexican authorities for inciting a revolution based on an earlier inflammatory letter he wrote. He was imprisoned or held under house arrest in Mexico City for more than a year.

During his absence more settlers who had never heard of Austin flooded into Texas. He reluctantly gave up his dream of a state within Mexico and joined the independence movement, but his late arrival made it seem that he was less committed than some of the other "Texican" rebels. Once the war started, though, Austin headed the forces at San Antonio, then was appointed as one of three commissioners to the United States in November 1835. Again, he was absent at a critical time when Sam *Houston* came to the forefront of the revolution, and he was defeated in a bid for the Texas presidency in 1836. Austin remains the Father of Texas, and despite later charges of profiteering, he never achieved great financial wealth from his efforts on behalf of Texas.

Battle of San Jacinto, 1836

Following the devastating loss of the Alamo (March 6, 1836) and the massacre of Colonel James Fanin's troops at Goliad, General Sam *Houston*, the commander of the Texan army and former governor of and congressman from Tennessee, began a strategic retreat to buy time for his poorly trained army. His Mexican adversary, General Antonio López de *Santa Anna*, while victorious, had lost at least 600 men of his force, estimated to be between 4,000 and 5,000 men. Houston, on the other hand, had perhaps 1,000 recruits, but many of them were unreliable and desertion was a common occurrence.

As Houston retreated eastward, toward the Brazos River, Santa Anna grew complacent, convinced he had already beaten the bulk of the Texan forces. Splitting his forces, Santa Anna led about 1,000 men after Houston, crossing the Brazos River on April 15 but failing to catch up to Houston. After receiving two cannons from the citizens of Cincinnati, Houston continued an eastward move toward Louisiana, experiencing near mutiny from his ill-trained troops, who nevertheless wanted to fight. But on April 17, well aware of the Mexican positions, Houston turned toward the San Jacinto River. Abandoning nearly one-fourth of his force that was too sick or fatigued to continue, Houston led the remaining 783 troops to the edge of the Mexican positions.

An artillery duel erupted on April 20, and the two sides prepared for a full battle. But while Houston allowed his men to eat and sleep, Santa Anna required his troops to build defenses all night. General Martin Perfecto de Cos arrived with an additional 500 Mexican troops, and it appeared that the Texans, outnumbered now nearly two to one, would have to attack entrenched positions. Houston also ordered Vince's Bridge burned, meaning neither side could escape or get reinforcements. Waiting until midafternoon—*siesta* time for the exhausted Mexican troops—Houston's men launched an assault screaming "Remember the Alamo!" and "Remember Goliad!" Small ridges had screened the advance of the troops until they were almost on top of the Mexican positions, and they smashed through with remarkable ease, crushing Santa Anna's army in less than 20 minutes. Santa Anna himself, although trying to flee in disguise, was captured, along with 730 of his troops. More than 600 Mexican soldiers died, compared to Texan losses of 2 killed and several wounded, 6 of whom died. Santa Anna, fearing he would be executed, signed a document withdrawing all Mexican troops south of the **Rio Grande [I]**. The Alamo had been avenged, and Texas remained an independent republic until it joined the United States in 1845.

Battle of Tippecanoe

The *Shawnee [II]* chief *Tecumseh*, who had formed a powerful confederation of tribes across Indiana and Illinois, and Indiana Territorial Governor William Henry *Harrison* viewed each other suspiciously. Although Tecumseh remained peaceful, Harrison saw the large confederation as a threat. When Tecumseh traveled south, leaving his brother, *Tenskwatawa*, known as "the Prophet," in charge, Harrison saw an opportunity to lure the Indians into a war without their best leader on the field.

Forming an expedition with more than a thousand troops, Harrison marched to the main village of Tecumseh. On November 7, 1811, the Indians, convinced the soldiers would attack, struck first and nearly overran

Harrison's camp above the Tippecanoe River. Nevertheless, the soldiers drove the Indians off and the Battle of Tippecanoe touched off a general war on the frontier. Tecumseh allied with the British in the *War of 1812*, and fell at the Battle of the Thames in October 1813.

Becknell, William (1790–1865)

William Becknell, known as the "father of the Santa Fe Trade," was the first American to profit from the commercial highway. As he and his fellow teamsters were crossing Raton Pass in New Mexico in 1821, they discovered that the Mexicans had successfully revolted against Spanish rule. Shaking off the shackles of Spanish mercantilism, Mexico briefly became a free-trade nation, and Becknell and his men made a huge profit before heading back to Missouri. He opened up other trade routes as well and later moved to Texas and fought there for its independence.

Beckwourth, Jim (1798–1866)

Beckwourth, the handsome son of an enslaved black woman and a white Virginian father, was one of the most prominent and interesting characters of the American West. Being of mixed race never limited him, and he moved frequently between various Indian, white, black, and Hispanic societies. He had four wives during his lifetime: two were American Indian, one was Hispanic, and one was black. He was highly regarded in all he did, whether it was trapping, managing businesses, or scouting for the army. The famous fur trapper, William *Ashley*, greatly admired him and said: "That Beckwourth is surely one of the most singular men I ever met."

Though he participated in the *Sand Creek Massacre [IV]*, he found the actions of *Chivington [IV]* and his men revolting and testified against them. In 1856 Beckwourth published his memoirs, a fascinating account of the West that is probably half truth and half fiction. In it, for example, he claimed to be the chief of the Crow Indians, though most likely he was merely an influential leader. In 1866 Beckwourth died while hunting with the Crows. Many suspect they poisoned him, believing him responsible for bringing *smallpox [I]* to them in 1837.

Benton, Thomas Hart (March 14, 1782– April 10, 1858)

An early advocate for the West, Thomas Hart Benton was born in North Carolina, the oldest of eight children. Expelled from the University of North Carolina for attempting to duel, Benton moved with his family to Tennessee, where he was admitted to the bar in 1806. In 1809 he won a state senate seat.

Benton had a notorious temper, landing him in a brawl with Andrew *Jackson* and his accomplices in Nashville; Benton shot Jackson, and Jackson's friends stabbed Benton. After that, Jackson blocked Benton's political career in Tennessee, forcing him to move to Missouri. There Benton edited the *Missouri Enquirer* and engaged in further dueling, eventually killing Charles Lucas, the U.S. district attorney. In 1820 Benton was elected to the U.S. Senate, where he served 30 consecutive years. He had already sponsored a "squatter's rights" bill in the Tennessee state senate. Throughout his life, Benton supported open land policies in the West, and he provided the model for the *Homestead Act [IV]* of 1862. His "Graduation Act" called for a steady decrease in the prices of western land until they reached 25 cents per acre. (This finally passed in 1854.) His views of St. Louis as the "gateway to the West" reflected his emphasis on opening the frontier, and as an editor, he argued his positions forcefully.

Despite his earlier battles with Jackson, Benton reconciled with "Old Hickory" and supported President Jackson's "Bank War." He was identified with a specie standard, earning him the nickname, "Old Bullion" Benton. He also sought to expunge the censure of Jackson from the senate journal.

As slavery came to dominate the national debate, Benton, a slaveowner, opposed the annexation of Texas, as it meant the expansion of slavery and posed the threat of civil war. This led Benton to split with the Democratic Party. As an advocate of the Union, Benton lost support of the slaveholders from Missouri and therefore lost his seat in 1850. He opposed Henry *Clay*'s Compromise of 1850, but in 1852, Benton won election to the U.S. House of Representatives. Although he had been an advocate of western development, he opposed subsidies to western railroads, and denounced the *Kansas-Nebraska Act*. After defeat in 1854, Benton began his *Thirty Years' View*, a memoir of his public life. When John C. *Fremont*, his son-in-law, ran as the first Republican candidate for president, Benton supported his opponent, James Buchanan. He also wrote a book challenging the decision in the *Dred Scott decision*. Thomas Hart Benton died in April 1858.

Black Hawk (1767–October 3, 1838)

Born near the Rock River in Illinois, Sauk warrior Black Hawk fought other Indian tribes as a young man but despised Americans and fought with *Tecumseh* in the *War of 1812*. A treaty signed with the Fox and Sauk Indians in 1804 had produced confusion and distrust in that the Indian delegates thought they had signed a cease-fire, while the white attendees thought the Indians had agreed to cede territory. When whites started to purchase the land in the 1820s, the Sauk and Fox opposed them. Although Black Hawk viewed the settlers as stealing Indian lands, he temporarily agreed to hold his warriors in Iowa in return for government supplies of corn.

By that time, although not formally a chief, Black Hawk wielded the authority of one, and he had the support of White Cloud, known as the "Winnebago Prophet," who nevertheless filled him with unrealistic expectations. Convinced the British and other Indians would support him, Black Hawk moved back across the Mississippi in 1832 with the intention of reclaiming the Sauk land. United States regulars soon moved to intercept him, leading Black Hawk to send diplomats under a white flag. One of the diplomats was killed by trigger-happy volunteers, and Black Hawk responded by ambushing the troops. But soon reinforcements arrived and Black Hawk, outnumbered, moved his villagers back across the Mississippi to Wisconsin. Troops pursued him, and again he sought to parlay, and again was fired upon, at which point most of the Sauk warriors were killed. Black Hawk was captured, taken on a tour of eastern cities, then returned to Iowa.

Black Hawk War

In 1832 the Sauk and Mesquakie (Fox) Indians under the leadership of *Black Hawk* formed an alliance to resist the intrusion of whites onto their lands in northwestern Illinois and southwestern Wisconsin. The cause of the conflict was the treaty of 1804, under which the government claimed the Indians ceded control of these territories and which the Indians maintained guaranteed them further use of the lands. When settlers moved into Black Hawk's home village, the Indians planned an attack, but the arrival of troops and a gunboat forced Black Hawk to retreat across the Mississippi. From April to August 1832, Black Hawk fought regulars and militia under General Henry Atkinson, until Black Hawk's forces were nearly wiped out by both Atkinson's men and the Sioux, who entered the war to destroy their Indian enemies.

The Sauk and Fox gave the United States a strip of land along the Mississippi in return for the government's payment of $40,000 of Indian debt and an annual sum paid to the tribes of $20,000. In addition, the government agreed to maintain the Indians' guns and to provide salt and tobacco. Some 70 settlers and between 400 and 500 Indians were killed in the conflict.

Blackfoot

Little known to Europeans and Americans before the 19th century, several bands—the Blood, Piegan, and Blackfeet proper—made up the fierce Blackfoot tribe. During the first seven decades of the 19th century, the tribe resided along the upper *Missouri River [I]* in what is now Montana and in the Saskatchewan River valley in Canada, dominating the two regions. Their first contact with whites was in 1806, when they encountered the *Lewis and Clark Expedition*. It had gone poorly. An American killed a Piegan, and the Blackfeet hunted down any white who entered their territory throughout much of the 19th century. There were only a few exceptions, the most prominent being Father Peter John de Smet, whom the tribe welcomed openly in the mid-1840s. By the late 1870s most Blackfeet had settled in Canada, leaving only a remnant near Glacier National Park. As of 2001 there were roughly 38,000 Blackfeet residing in the United States.

Boonesborough

The site of an Indian settlement for roughly 2,000 years, Boonesborough sat in a well-protected and easily defended area with plentiful supplies of salt. Situated on the Wilderness Road, northwest of the Cumberland Gap, Boonesborough was originally to serve as the capital of the never-realized colony of Transylvania (in present-day Kentucky).

The Transylvania Company wanted Boonesborough, founded by Daniel *Boone [II]*, to be a large palisaded village, but the settlers were too land hungry to remain confined in a fort, and they quickly spread out, staking land claims. In 1877 the Virginia House of Burgesses annexed the Transylvania Company's holdings, only two years after the founding of Boonesborough.

Border Ruffians/"pukes"

With the passage of the 1854 *Kansas-Nebraska Act*, the issue of slavery was determined by *"popular sovereignty,"* or the "will of the people" within a state. A group of Missourians, most of them drunk (hence the moniker "pukes") and heavily armed flooded into Kansas in 1855 to vote to make Kansas a slave state. While Kansas eventually came into the Union as a free state, the Border Ruffians prevented that from happening for over five years. Many other Missourians, under the umbrella of the Society of Missourians for Mutual Protection, settled legitimately in the towns of Leavenworth, Atchison, and Lecompton, and voted in vain for the extension of slavery.

Bowie knife

Named after Alamo hero "Jim" Bowie, this famous knife was actually designed by Jim's brother, Rezin P. Bowie, at Avoyelles, Louisiana. In 1827 Jim Bowie fought in a brawl in which several men were killed and Bowie wounded, and shortly thereafter Rezin invented the weapon. It featured a 9- to 15-inch curved blade, sharpened on one side and narrowing to a second tip that was sharpened on both sides. The walnut or bone handle, protected by a brass hand guard, made it an excellent close-combat knife. Useful for slashing and stabbing, especially in close quarters, the Bowie knife was not a practical hunting knife. In a duel in Alexandria, Louisiana, in 1827, Bowie disemboweled a man with one of his knives.

branding

Identifying cattle, horses, and other livestock on an open range was a problem easily solved by branding. This process involved roping an animal, laying it down and tying its feet together, then applying a red-hot iron to the hide. Branding irons were made of 36 to 48 inches of one-half-inch wrought iron—a long tube, usually with a curved or hooked handle (known as "free-handing" irons), with a unique symbol hammered out of the iron on the application end. The "stamp" or brand that went on the hide had to be clearly identifiable and difficult to alter. For example, a "∧" could easily be counterfeited as an "A" with a minor modification to the brand, and in such a way cattle with the first brand could be stolen through a quick rebranding. Consequently, ironsmiths came up with decidedly unalterable brands in the shape of a hat, a wine glass, scissors, a "Y" with a line through it (called a "Y cross" or "bar Y"), or a key. The brands took the name of a ranch—or vice versa—with ranches being known as the "bar Y ranch" or the "J A" ranch.

Branding was a necessity on the frontier for any rancher seeking to keep his cattle clearly identified as his property. A number of branding irons are displayed here. *Library of Congress*

On the trail, cowboys occasionally improvised by using an iron "cinch ring," which was an iron ring that was heated up, then applied by sticking two pieces of wood through it. Another easy-to-apply brand was a "running iron," which had a small 90° curve at the end, which, when skillfully used, could be artistically turned into almost any design. Both of these methods brought suspicion from established ranchers, and anyone carrying a "running iron" was likely to be considered a rustler.

Bridger, James ("Jim") (1804–1881)

The epitome of the "mountain man," James ("Jim") Bridger was born in Richmond, Virginia, in 1804 and moved to St. Louis at an early age. There he met William H. *Ashley*, who organized fur and pelt expeditions into the Rockies. Bridger made his first trapping journey in 1822 and thereafter made several trips to the mountains, crossing into the Great Salt Lake region in 1824 or 1825, becoming the first white man to reach what he thought was the Pacific Ocean. Bridger worked under several famous trappers, including Jedediah *Smith* and William Sublette. In 1830 he became an employee, then a partner in the Rocky Mountain Fur Company, during which time he was wounded by an Indian arrow that stayed in his back for three years until it could be removed.

As the fur trapping business began to decline, Bridger in 1843 joined with Louis Vasquez to build Fort Bridger on the Green River, providing an important trading post for travelers to Oregon. Ten years later, he sold his shares to the Mormons (see *Latter-day Saints*) and again became a guide for western expeditions. In 1850 as a guide for Captain Howard Stansbury, who searched for a route through the Wasatch and Rocky Mountains, he found what came to be called Bridger's Pass and Cheyenne Pass. Later, he acted as a guide for the U.S. Army on several occasions, including scouting for Colonel Albert Sidney Johnston's army during the Mormon War of 1857–1858. He assisted in the surveying of the *Union Pacific Railroad [IV]* for Grenville M. Dodge, led the Powder River Indian Expedition (1865–1866), and measured and recorded data on the *Bozeman Trail [IV]*.

A true western pioneer, Bridger married three different Indian women from different tribes, all of whom died before Bridger. He sent all of his six children to missionary schools or convents for a formal education, bought property in Westport, Missouri, near his old partner, Louis Vasquez, and finally retired there in 1866. When Bridger died 15 years later, he had become larger than life. Historian Bernard de Voto called Bridger an "atlas" of the West for his geographic knowledge, while writer E. Z. Judson's "Ned *Buntline [IV]*" novels romanticized his exploits.

Bureau of Indian Affairs (BIA)

The United States since its inception sought to deal with the various Indian tribes through official departments beginning in 1775 with three departments of Indian affairs (northern, central, and southern). Those departments negotiated treaties and sought tribal neutrality in the American Revolution. After Independence, the government of the United States established a superintendent of Indian trade, whose chief job was to oversee the operation of the factory trading system owned by the government. The first superintendent, Thomas L. *McKenney* held that position from

1816 to 1822, until competition by John Jacob *Astor* drove the government posts out of business.

When Congress eliminated the federal trading post system, in an effort to further centralize dealings with the Indians, the Bureau of Indian Affairs was created within the War Department on March 11, 1824. Again, McKenney was named to head the office, which handled appropriations for annuities, expenses related to the tribes; administered funds targeted for "civilizing" Indians; and had authority to adjudicate claims between Indian tribes. He also served as the Indians' liason to the War Department. Despite its official name, most people did not refer to this office as the Bureau of Indian Affairs, but as the "Indian Office." McKenney also found that while the Bureau's workload had increased, its authority and funding had not. In 1831 he proposed an Office of Indian Affairs, which would be headed by a General Superintendent of Indian Affairs, but Congress did not pass the bill he drafted.

Even before McKenney's proposal, Congress had appointed a separate Commissioner of Indian Affairs to serve within the War Department to assume many of the duties previously burdening the BIA. In 1849 the Bureau (also called "Office") of Indian Affairs was transferred to the newly created Interior Department.

With the removal of tribes to reservations under the Interior Department, the government became responsible for feeding the starving Indians. Distributing food, blankets, implements, and other supplies became a major cause for contention. Many agents were notoriously corrupt; the system was rife with political infighting, and few genuinely cared about their wards, the Indians, who now depended on them to survive. Matters grew so bad that in 1867, Congress appointed a Peace Commission to examine BIA policies. Although some of the worst abuses continued, the BIA improved in some areas. Following the Pendleton Act (1887), the impact of political patronage on agents was reduced. The BIA began to operate schools, handle supplies better, oversee land allotments, and in general take over all tribal government functions.

After 1938, when the government's Meriam Report was issued, more reforms were enacted by Congress in the Indian Reorganization Act. This sought to improve local economies, return power to the tribal governments, and place under the authority of the federal government the oversight of forestry, land acquisition and management, and agriculture on reservations.

The BIA was still often called the Office of Indian Affairs or the Indian Office, even in official correspondence, as late as 1947. By the 1960s responsibility for educating Indian children on reservations was transferred to the Department of Health, Education and Welfare (now Health and Human Services). Tribal demands for more autonomy in the 1970s led to the Indian Self-Determination Act, which restored some control over reservation policies to the tribes, marking a reversal of more than a century and a half of paternalism and, in many cases, outright oppression. The new emphasis changed the BIA from a management to an advisory role, seeking to encourage the tribes to manage their own lands and affairs, assist them with public resources, and to liberate them from economic dictates of the federal government. As part of the new policy, Indians were given preference when it came to hiring for positions in the BIA, and by 2002, more than 95 percent of the BIA's 12,000 employees are Indians.

Like all Indian-white relations, the history of the BIA has contained episodes of decency and honor, while at other times it was characterized by abuse and oppression. Completely forgetting past sins will never be entirely possible, nor can the ultimate role of the federal government as sovereign of the tribes be ignored, but the modern BIA continues to be an agency that is viewed positively at times and with ambivalence at others.

Butterfield Overland Mail

Founded by John Butterfield in 1857, the Overland Mail company was a stagecoach mail service that lasted until 1869. Butterfield drove stagecoaches as a boy and acquired controlling interests in many mail and stage lines over his career. In 1849 he organized the Butterfield and Wasson Express company, merging it with Wells and Company, and Livingston, Fargo and Company to create the American Express Company. (Wells and Fargo split with Butterfield over differences involving western routes, founding *Wells Fargo & Company [IV]* in 1852.)

The Overland Mail provided a daily mail service in the west, but Butterfield also envisioned a faster operation in which lone riders carrying only letters would carry mail nonstop, and in 1860 he created the *Pony Express*. Although the Overland Mail had a huge subsidy from the federal government, it still lost money, and the Pony Express concept did not excite the company's directors, causing Butterfield to be removed as president. In a giant consolidation of the major stagecoach operations, in 1866 Wells Fargo united the Overland Mail's routes with its own lines under the name Wells Fargo & Company, which provided mail service by stagecoach until the *Union Pacific [IV]* and Central Pacific Railroads were joined in 1869.

California Gold Rush

In January 1848 near Sacramento, California, John *Sutter* discovered gold along the American River near his mill, triggering the largest gold stampede in American history. California had been a quiet section of Mexico until the *Mexican War*, at which time numerous Americans entered the region and reported favorably on the fertile valleys and rich farmlands. But these small migrations paled beside the "hysteria," and the "flood proportions" of people flocking to the Sacramento area in the wake of Sutter's discovery. San Francisco, as the port of entry, boomed as did the gold fields all the way up the American Fork to the Sierra Nevada range. Gold seekers came from as far away as Great Britain, Europe, and even China.

The gold came out in phenomenal amounts. Thomas Berry estimated that gold exports from California from 1848 to 1860 reached $650 million at a price of $16 per ounce. In a single year, California gold production exceeded $35 million. Miners found gold nuggets on the ground, specks in the river that could be extracted with sluices (troughs with filters, known as "*placer mining*") or, further down, in solid rock ("hard rock mining"). Estimates suggest that California's population rose from 14,000 before the discovery of gold to 250,000 by 1852. By 1856 San Francisco alone had a population of more than 50,000. Daily income could reach between $16 and $20. Offsetting the tremendous incomes, prices in California reflected the difficulty of obtaining scarce goods: a single barrel of flour went for $45 and a shovel for $10.

Prospectors staked out a claim at a claim office. Courts and law enforcement officers were usually aggressive in supporting these claims, but in instances where they were not, mining camps quickly developed systems of vigilante justice. Indeed, the California mining camps in many cases created the camp culture that permeated other, subsequent rushes. It was in no miner's interest to allow anyone else's claims to be "jumped," in the parlance of the day. Once the prospectors had extracted the gold dust, they had to take it to an assay office to be weighed, at which point they were given a receipt for their gold or gold dust. Over time, the gold exchange offices began to discount against these receipts, creating an early form of checks or debit accounts.

The assay offices evolved into gold exchange businesses that provided the basis for modern banking activities. Gold was difficult to transport and expensive to secure, especially in wagons or coaches heading overland across Utah to the east, or down the coast through Panama for eastern seaboard ports. Consequently, when possible, merchants sought "exchange drafts," which were reliable paper substitutes for a specified quantity of gold that would easily be accepted at par in eastern cities. To obtain a draft, a miner or merchant only had to pay a small fee. Gold could be purchased at $16 per ounce in California and resold for $18 an ounce in the East.

California's brief but furious gold rush became a legendary part of the West, but the institutions it established—claims and mining laws and practices, banking establishments, and advances in mining technology—shaped the West long after the gold rush was over.

Placer gold was relatively easy for an untrained prospector to obtain using an inexpensive sluice and elbow grease. Using a pick and shovel, the prospector simply churned up the earth, then used the pan to filter out everything that did not glitter. These pans were soon replaced by rocking cradles that washed the material out faster. But eventually the placer gold grew scarce, and more sophisticated equipment was required to extract the gold from the hard rock that encased it. This mining only became popular and profitable in California after 1850, by which time the gold rush itself was technically over.

Carson, Christopher Houston ("Kit")
(December 24, 1809–May 23, 1868)

One of the best-known scouts and guides of the Old West, Christopher Houston ("Kit") Carson was born in Kentucky on December 24, 1809, but moved with his family to Missouri. His father died when he was nine years old, and the family apprenticed Kit to a saddlemaker. Carson disliked the boredom of leather work and ran away, joining a wagon train. By the time he got to New Mexico, Carson had become an experienced teamster, and then in 1829 he joined a fur trapping expedition to the Rockies. Unlike his associates, Jim *Bridger* and Tom Fitzpatrick, Carson never learned to run a fur business, but he distinguished himself as a scout and guide.

He also gained a reputation as an Indian fighter even though he married an Arapaho woman and then, when she died, a Cheyenne woman, living in Taos, New Mexico.

In 1842 John C. *Fremont* hired Carson to guide his expedition into Wyoming, then a year later, to California. After an incident in California where, acting on Fremont's orders, Carson shot three noncombatants, he was dispatched to Washington with official correspondence, only to be intercepted by General Stephen Watts *Kearney* and required to scout for the army through the Southwest. After several years, Carson returned to New Mexico to farm, then in 1853 was named Indian agent for the Ute, Apache, and Pueblo Indians.

When the Civil War came, Carson was made a colonel commanding the New Mexico volunteers and fought Confederates and Indians for the next three years, his career culminating with the Battle of Adobe Walls. There, he held off thousands of Kiowas, Comanches, and Apaches and withdrew with only a few losses. This and other actions brought Carson a promotion to Brigadier General. He resigned from the army in 1867 and died the following year.

Catlin, George (July 26, 1796–December 23, 1872)

After studying and practicing law briefly, Catlin decided on a career in painting portraits and Indians. Using government connections, he traveled to the American West numerous times in the 1830s, visiting several different Indian tribes and recording their culture on canvas as well as in books. His most famous ethnographic study was the *Letters and Notes on the Manners, Customs, and Condition of the North American Indians* (1841), a work heavily influenced by the Leatherstocking novels of James Fenimore *Cooper*.

Cherokee Indians

An Iroquoian people, the Cherokees migrated south from their original homeland around the Great Lakes sometime prior to Columbus's expeditions to the Americas. Many scholars believe that the Cherokees are the descendants of one of the upper-class castes of the Moundbuilders. Certainly, the respect shown them by other tribes—friend or foe—has helped convince many academics of this argument. At their height, the Cherokee Indians had a population of over 20,000 persons living in nearly 200 villages and controlled an immense amount of land in what is to-day the American South. The Cherokees, however, entered into nearly 40

IN THEIR OWN *Words*

Andrew Jackson on the Cherokee Removal

On December 7, 1835, President Andrew Jackson addressed the removal of the southern Indians, including the Cherokee, to Indian Territory. His comments reveal that whites continued to blame Indians for the inability of Americans to keep treaties and offer an unrealistic assessment of the prospects for the Indians in the new Territory.

The plan of removing the aboriginal people who yet remain within the settled portions of the United States to the country west of the Mississippi River approaches its consummation. It was adopted on the most mature consideration of the condition of this race, and ought to be persisted in till the object is accomplished, and prosecuted with as much vigor as a just regard to their circumstances will permit, and as fast as their consent can be obtained. All preceding experiments for the improvement of the Indians have failed. It seems now to be an established fact that they can not live in contact with a civilized community and prosper. . . .

To these districts [in new Indian Territory, i.e., Oklahoma] the Indians are removed at the expense of the United States, and with certain supplies of clothing, arms, ammunition, and other indispensable articles; they are also furnished gratuitously with provisions for the period of a year after their arrival at their new homes. In that time, from the nature of the country and of the products raised by them, they can subsist themselves by agricultural labor, if they choose to resort to that mode of life; if they do not they are upon the skirts of the great prairies, where countless herds of buffalo roam, and a short time suffices to adapt their own habits to the changes which a change of the animals destined for their food may require. . . .

No political communities can be formed in that extensive region [Indian Territory], except those which are established by the Indians themselves or by the United States for them and with their concurrence.

—SOURCE: HENRY STEELE COMMAGER, ED., *DOCUMENTS OF AMERICAN HISTORY, VOL. I: TO 1898*, 7TH ED. (NEW YORK: APPLETON-CENTURY-CROFTS, 1934), 259–261.

land sales with the English and the Americans, drastically reducing their holdings.

By the 1820s the Cherokees had adopted many of the republican and cultural features of United States. They had a written language, a constitution, a newspaper, and an advanced economy based on cotton production and slave labor. According to the norms of the time, Americans should have regarded them as the ideal Indians. Gold discoveries on Cherokee lands in the early 1830s, however, prompted many southerners to demand their removal. President Andrew *Jackson* complied, and with the 1835 Treaty of New Echota, a small group of Cherokees ceded all their traditional lands. General Winfield Scott and 7,000 troops forcibly removed any recalcitrant Cherokees to Oklahoma Territory in what has become known as the *Trail of Tears*. Removed in the winter of 1838 and 1839, nearly one out of every three Cherokees died en route to Indian Territory. Problems within the tribe continued as numerous assassinations and murders took place shortly after arrival in the new homeland, payback against those who had signed the 1835 treaty.

Despite the numerous obstacles and disadvantages, the Cherokees recreated a thriving economy and culture in the new territory under the U.S. policy of salutary neglect. By the beginning of the Civil War, the Cherokees had once again become a wealthy and cultured people. The Civil War, though, ruined their stability. Identifying culturally with the South, many Cherokees fought for the Confederacy. As punishment, the United States greatly reduced Cherokee land holdings and promises of political autonomy after the war.

Today, the Cherokees have a growing population due to lax requirements of blood quantum for tribal membership.

Cherokee Nation v. State of Georgia/ Worcester v. State of Georgia

Two cases brought before the United States Supreme Court in the 1830s questioned the jurisdiction of individual states over the Indian tribes, specifically what "nation" status meant in the context of federal dealings with the Indians. The first case, *Cherokee Nation v. State of Georgia* (1831), sought an injunction to block the state of Georgia's laws against the Cherokees. This case stemmed from a series of Georgia laws enacted in the late 1820s to confiscate Cherokee lands in the wake of revelations that gold existed on Indian property. Represented by William Wirt of Baltimore (in both cases), the Cherokee argued that Georgia had no jurisdiction over a foreign nation (i.e., the Cherokees), based on the existence of formal treaties between the Cherokees and the U.S. government.

The United States Supreme Court, led by Chief Justice John Marshall, ruled that the Indians were not a "foreign nation" in a technical sense because they resided inside the territory of the United States, and thus they could not sue. Nevertheless, the argument appeared rather specific to the nature of Wirt's brief, and the Court implied that it was sympathetic to future appeals. Thus, a year later, Wirt and the Cherokee brought another case before the court, *Worster v. the State of Georgia*. Samuel Worcester arrived in 1825 in Cherokee lands as a missionary, quickly establishing a mission there. Under the 1828 Georgia laws, though—the same laws designed to evict the Cherokee—no white man could reside in Cherokee territory without a license from the state. This time, Wirt argued that the state of Geogia sought to infringe a federal treaty between the Cherokee and the U. S. government. The Court agreed with this approach, agreeing that the laws of the United States treated Indians as "nations" (though carefully avoiding the term "foreign," which had undercut the earlier case). Chief Justice Marshall ruled that the laws of Georgia had no effect on the Cherokee nation, calling the 1828 acts "repugnant to the Constitution." Georgia refused to abide by the Court's decision, and President Andrew Jackson, siding with the state, reputedly said, "Chief Justice Marshall has made his decision. Now let him enforce it." Within a few years, the Cherokee were forced to evacuate their lands through a new, largely fraudulent treaty, along the *Trail of Tears*.

Clay, Henry (April 12, 1777–June 29, 1852)

A spokesman for western interests in the early national period, Henry Clay was born in Hanover, Virginia, remaining there when his family moved to Kentucky at age 15. Clay studied law, winning admission to the Richmond bar in 1797, at which time he left for Lexington. He developed a reputation for fiery speeches on behalf of the Jeffersonian Republican party, winning election to the Kentucky legislature in 1803. Clay was the defense counsel for Aaron Burr, who faced a grand jury investigation over his role in establishing an independent republic in the Southwest. Burr was acquitted, and shortly thereafter, Clay was appointed to fill an unexpired term for a U.S. Senate seat. When that term ended, Clay returned to the Kentucky legislature before receiving another appointment to an expired term in the Senate.

Clay established his mark on Washington as Speaker of the U. S. House of Representatives, where he led a group of disgruntled legislators who were outraged at British depredations against American ships at sea. These War Hawks, as they were known, rallied behind Clay to encourage President James Madison to enter the *War of 1812*. Clay later was a member of the U.S. Peace Commission that ended the war, gaining a British concession to abandon the rights to navigate the *Mississippi River [I]*. Yet it was Andrew *Jackson*, the hero of New Orleans, who emerged from the war as the next Washington "star." Clay, back in the House, started to forge a body of legislation referred to as the "American System," which included a national bank (such as the Bank of the United States), internal improvements for transportation, and protective tariffs for infant industries. Working alongside John C. Calhoun of South Carolina and Daniel Webster of Massachusetts, he envisioned federal expenditures for each region that would unite the sections in spite of slavery. In particular, Clay called for construction of roads and the clearing of waterways at federal expense.

In 1820 the admission of Missouri and Maine threatened to throw the nation into a civil war over slavery. Clay crafted the *Missouri Compromise*, a series of bills that admitted Missouri as a slave state and drew an imaginary line across the continent, above which would be free soil. His reputation as the "Great Pacificator" or "Great Compromiser" emboldened him to seek the presidency in 1824, but no candidate had a clear majority in the electoral votes. Clay threw his support to John Quincy Adams and was named secretary of state. Clay ran unsuccessfully against Jackson in 1832, largely on the issue of the Bank of the United States.

When the "Tariff of Abominations" was passed in 1828, Clay produced another compromise that averted conflict. In 1840 his presidential aspirations were again frustrated by retired General William Henry *Harrison*. He made yet another run at the presidency in 1844, but his failure to advocate the annexation of Texas cost him the election to James K. Polk of Tennessee. After the *Mexican War* brought California and other western territories into the Union—and again put the slavery issue at the forefront—Clay crafted the Compromise of 1850, with considerable help from Senator Stephen A. *Douglas* of Illinois. Having failed to gain the presidency, and in the long run to prevent a civil war, Clay died in Washington in 1852.

Colt handguns

Whether it was the Colt . 44 "Walker," the "Peacemaker," or the famous Colt . 45 "six-shooter," hand-held firearms known as "revolvers," developed by Samuel Colt, were a key element of the frontier West. Samuel Colt (1814–1862) had worked on the Eli Whitney musket. According to the Colt legend, while on a trip to China, Colt noticed the paddle wheels on his steamship and conceived the "revolver"—a gun in which a cylinder containing balls (later cartridges) was rotated with each shot, allowing for multiple shots before reloading. Colt patented his idea in 1836, but few orders came in, resulting in the gunmaker having to travel the country demonstrating laughing gas at carnivals. Finally, Colt obtained money to open a pistol factory, but by 1842 it closed in deep debt.

After a brief fling experimenting with aquatic explosives, Colt found a rising demand from the *Texas Rangers*, who had purchased some of his revolvers, for new supplies of his handguns. The publicity associated with the Rangers' orders led him to produce a six-shot .44 caliber weapon with a rifled barrel called the "Walker," named for Samuel Walker, the Texas Ranger who helped publicize the gun. When war broke out with Mexico in 1846, the U.S. government ordered 1,000 of the pistols, and in a single decade (1850–1860) Colt sold nearly 280,000 revolvers to civilians, mostly to those headed West.

Colter, John (1775–1813)

Colter is often regarded as the greatest of the original American mountain men, setting the example for the great generation of mountain men from the *Lewis and Clark Expedition* through the decline of the fur trade in the 1830s. Born in Virginia, Colter served as a vital member of the 1804–1806 Lewis and Clark Expedition. When the expedition ended, Colter worked for Spanish fur trader Manuel Lisa, attempting to making alliances with various Indian tribes during the winter of 1807–1808. During his 500-plus miles of travels that winter, Colter became the first white man to discover what is now *Yellowstone National Park [IV]*. Many refused to believe his tales of boiling springs and other natural wonders, earning Yellowstone the moniker "Colter's Hell."

Colter had two near-fatal encounters with the *Blackfeet* Indians. In the first encounter, Blackfeet discovered Colter and a friend, John Potts, trapping near the Forks of the *Missouri River [I]*. The Indians killed and tore apart Potts. Forcing Colter to strip, they made sport of him and chased him through the Montana snow and ice. Promising he would never return to the wilderness if God saved him, Colter survived a 200-mile journey back to the nearest trading post. Ignoring his promise to God, Colter returned to the Three Rivers area in April 1810, when a group of Blackfeet Indians again attacked and killed his companions. Making the same promise to God, Colter successfully escaped. He moved to Missouri, married, had children, and started a farm next to Daniel *Boone's [II]*. Colter died in 1813 of jaundice.

Comstock Lode

A rich silver vein running from Nevada to Colorado, the Comstock Lode was discovered in 1859, producing a new silver rush to the region. It was named after Henry Comstock, a sheepherder who owned rights to the land but sold it and died poor. The Comstock vein was discovered after the earlier gold rush in California had tapered off, draining many prospectors to the east from Sacramento and San Francisco. Estimates suggest as many as 100,000 miners came to the Nevada mountains, many of them exploring well beyond the Comstock, bringing permanent settlements to the territory.

Conestoga wagon

The famous long wagons that pioneers used to transport their possessions to the West were named after the Conestoga River valley in Lancaster County, Pennsylvania. They originated in the 1700s and were based on Dutch designs. Fur traders used them to carry their pelts from the valley to Philadelphia; later, in the *French and Indian War [II]*, the British army used the wagons to haul war supplies.

After the Ohio Valley opened to settlement in the 1760s, Conestoga wagons provided a common form of family transportation. A 12-foot-long wagon bed was 42 inches deep, curved downward slightly in the middle, with 8 to 16 large hoops of bent wood arching over the top of the bed, over which then was stretched canvas. Additional features included a feed trough at the back, so that some animals could eat as they walked behind; hooks, upon which to hang axes or shovels; and distinctive paint or color. Nevertheless, the wagons were intended primarily for freight transportation, lacking springs or interior seats to make riding easier on travelers. Instead, except for the driver ("teamster"), the settlers themselves often walked alongside, usually to the left of the lead oxen or mule.

The most popular vehicle for crossing the plains, the "prairie schooner," or Conestoga wagon, was based on a Dutch design and was 12 feet long and with a bed 42 inches deep. Pulled by oxen or horses, the wagon could carry all the necessities to start a new life in the West and, if the situation demanded it, could provide protection against Indian attacks. *From the collections of Carillon Historical Park*

Conestoga wagons, also known as "prairie schooners" or "covered wagons," rode on large hardwood axles reinforced by iron that attached to two sets of wooden wheels. Typically, the front set of wheels was smaller in diameter than the rear, to facilitate turning. A hand-operated brake could be engaged that pressed blocks of wood against all four wheels to stop the vehicle. Each wagon was capable of hauling up to 3,000 pounds, yet was light enough to be pulled by a standard yoke of four oxen, although when oxen were in short supply settlers used mules or horses. A wagon, without the oxen, sold for about $1,500, representing a sizeable investment for a family embarking on a new life. Still, the wagons could be sold once they reached their destination, and meantime, on the trail they provided good shelter against the elements and protection against the Indians. During raids, settlers quickly drove their wagons into a large circle, assembling a makeshift fort that attacking riders found difficult to penetrate. Few wagon trains were attacked after the large trains headed out from Missouri in the 1840s. Guides and wagon masters hesitated to send out any expedition that didn't contain a minimum number of wagons—usually 50, but as many as 120—meaning that the train contained at least 200 settlers, plus guides and teamsters, and as many as 500 to 600 people. Without question, the "prairie schooner" made settling the American West less burdensome than other alternatives.

IN THEIR OWN Words

Account of a Wagon Train Attack on the Plains (First Person Narrative)

Mary Perry Frost, on a trip to California in the summer of 1854, encountered Indians who attacked her wagon train. Several women kept diaries of their 1854 journeys. Frost's account differs from those of Nancy Hunt and Roxana Cheney—earlier that year—where the Indians were peaceable.

We had traveled perhaps an hour . . . Then Indians . . . came up squarely in front of our train and stopped the teams, but appeared friendly, shaking hands and asking for whiskey; upon being told that we had none they began to talk of trading with the men, and while my father was talking of trading a pistol for a pony, they opened fire on us, shooting my father, my uncle and my father's teamster . . . .

Thinking they wanted our horses, they were turned loose and the Indians departed after catching them all. Of those shot, my uncle was killed outright, my father's teamster was shot through the abdomen and lived until the following morning and my father was shot through the lungs and lived until the evening of the fourth day. . . . [He] was buried on the morning [of the fifth day]. The Indians also killed all the men in the forward party, leaving a boy of fourteen with an arrow in his chest . . . we stopped long enough to dig trenches and rude graves for the burial . . . The women and children [in the forward party] presented a sickening spectacle, having been burned by the savages.

—SOURCE: LILLIAN SCHLISSEL, *WOMEN'S DIARIES OF THE WESTWARD JOURNEY* (NEW YORK: SCHOCKEN BOOKS, 1982), 122–123.

Cooper, James Fenimore (September 15, 1789– September 14, 1851)

One of the first characteristically American writers, James Fenimore Cooper was born in Burlington, New Jersey. When Cooper was one, his family moved to Cooperstown, New York, which was founded by his father, William. The family had acquired large tracts of land—40,000 acres—near Otsego Lake. As a young boy, Cooper attended various schools, and even spent two years at Yale before being dismissed for misconduct.

From Yale, Cooper decided on a career in the Navy, sailing to London on a merchant vessel, the *Stirling*, then receiving his commission in 1808, at which time he served on the *Vesuvius* at Oswego, New York. After the death of his father in 1809, Cooper inherited all of his father's estate and a large sum of money. He left the Navy, married, and settled down in Westchester County in 1817. By then, he had depleted his inheritance and had to earn money through writing. His first book, *Precaution* (1820) gained the attention of reviewers in New York and brought him some income as a reviewer for a literary paper there. In December 1821 his story of the American Revolution, called *The Spy*, was successful, and he followed it with two other novels in a short time, *Tales for Fifteen* and *The Pioneers* (both 1823). He had since moved to New York City and become a mainstay in literary circles, where he produced one of his masterpieces, *The Last of the Mohicans* (1826) with its memorable character, Leatherstocking. In a series of three novels, he traced Leatherstocking from the **French and Indian War [II]** to his death in 1805. Cooper presented a sympathetic view of Native Americans that was not always warmly received by his countrymen.

From 1826 to 1833, Cooper and his family toured Europe, but he continued to write, turning out *The Red Rover* (1827). The Europeans knew Cooper's work well and feted him frequently. Caught up in the French revolution of 1830, he wrote on behalf of republican principles. But while in Paris, he produced three novels based on European themes, one of which, *The Bravo*, was attacked in American newspapers for its arguments that a democracy often concealed control by moneyed elites. When Cooper returned, he found anything but "moneyed elites" in the White House, and his attack on American foibles in *A Letter to His Countrymen* (1834) and his subsequent *History of the Navy of the United States of America* (1839) both earned him sharp criticism.

In 1841 Cooper wrote the second of his truly great works, *The Deerslayer*, and while his frontier works suffered from numerous inaccuracies—Cooper himself only went as far west as Detroit and mostly remained in New York—he captured the epic saga of adventure in the person of Natty Bumppo (Leatherstocking). Likely based on a real person, such as Daniel *Boone [II]*, Bumppo is a "mountain man" who understands both white and Indian ways and who can effectively argue the merits of either society. Using an elderly Bumppo, Cooper was able to comment on American society, not just its frontier.

James Fenimore Cooper continued to write numerous novels, maritime adventures, travel guides, editorials, and even a murder mystery. He was the quintessential professional writer, as opposed to a specifically western writer, but his commentaries on the early American frontier remain classics. Cooper died in Cooperstown on September 14, 1851.

The Creek ("Red Stick") War

Following the rebellion of *Tecumseh* in 1809–1811, Creek leaders were inspired to start their own uprising, called the Creek War of 1813–1814. Two factions had emerged within Creek leadership: the "White Sticks," who favored peace, and the "Red Sticks," who wanted war with whites. A full-blooded Creek, Big Warrior, led the White Sticks, while two mixed-bloods, Peter McQueen and William Weatherford, led the Red Sticks.

The war began when a Creek warrior band killed settlers along the Ohio River. White Stick leaders arrested and executed the head of the war party for the attack, but other Red Sticks soon acquired guns from the Spanish and in July 1813 attacked a party of settlers on Burnt Corn Creek. A month later, Weatherford (known as "Red Eagle") led 1,000 Creeks against Fort Mims, where the settlement fell and the Red Sticks massacred 400 settlers, then went on to attack White Stick camps.

An expedition under General Andrew *Jackson*, including a Tennessee sharpshooter named Davy *Crockett*, trapped the Red Sticks at the battle of Tallasahatchee in November 1813. The war ended in March 1814 when Jackson's troops defeated the Red Sticks at Horseshoe Bend. In the subsequent Treaty of Horseshoe Bend, the Creeks lost 23 million acres of land from both the loyal White Sticks and the warlike Red Sticks. The war contributed to the image of "Old Hickory" Andrew Jackson and remained alive in the memories of the Indians who were removed to the west.

Crockett, David ("Davy") (August 17, 1786–March 6, 1836)

Immortalized in folklore, literature, and Walt Disney's television series (in which he was played by Fess *Parker [V]*), David ("Davy") Crockett had a wide variety of experiences in his life: farming, fighting, serving as both judge and legislator, and creating his own persona even while still alive. Born in Greene County, Tennessee, on August 17, 1786, Crockett and his family moved to Franklin County, Tennessee. At about that time, Crockett joined the militia forces fighting under Andrew *Jackson* in the *Creek War*. After the war, Crockett was a justice of the peace, a militia colonel, and a state legislator until 1821, when he won election to the U.S. House of Representatives. There he clashed with Jackson over the Indian removal bill. He lost his seat in 1831 but regained it two years later.

Crockett was the subject of several national profiles that made him a legend even before the Alamo. His greatest fame, though, came from his role in the defense of that mission in February–March 1836, where, along with Colonel William *Travis* and Jim Bowie, he died when the Alamo fell to General *Santa Anna*.

A larger-than-life figure who took every opportunity to add to his reputation, Davy Crockett was a U.S. Congressman, a notoriously effective hunter, and an Indian fighter. *Library of Congress*

Crows

Known for their distinctive Mohawk-style hair, the Crows (also known as the Absaroke) controlled significant parts of Montana and Wyoming in the 18th and 19th centuries. Related to the sedentary Hidatsa, the Crows have two major divisions: the Mountain Crows and the River Crows. They most likely separated from the Hidatsa in the 15th century. Unlike their Hidatsa relatives, the Crows fully adopted the nomadic mounted horse and buffalo culture of the Great Plains, warring frequently with the *Blackfeet* and Lakota (see *Sioux [IV]*). Typically, though not always, the Crows allied themselves with the United States Army, serving as warriors and scouts. Most notably, they aided the Americans in the 1876 campaign against the Oglala and Hunkpapa Lakotas. Roman Catholic and Protestant missionaries visited the Crows in the late 1880s. As of 2001, many of the Crows live on a reservation in southeastern Montana, near Hardin, in their traditional homelands.

Donner Party

In 1846 a group of 89 settlers headed to California from Illinois under the leadership of two Illinois brothers, Jacob and George Donner. They followed a route outlined by Lansford W. Hastings and left the California Trail at Fort Bridger. When the Donner party left the trail at Fort Bridger in August 1846, they found that Hastings had already departed with another group and had left word that he would mark a trail for them. The Donner Expedition followed the trail to Weber Canyon, where Hastings had left another note for them, this time instructing them to wait for him to return and show them an easier trail. After more than a week, a messenger was dispatched to locate Hastings, and when the messenger returned, he had yet more instructions from the guide to follow another trail. They finally arrived at the Great Salt Lake valley after almost three weeks, with each delay pushing them closer to winter.

The party reached the base of the Sierra Nevada, sending riders ahead to California to return with supplies. When the riders returned on October 19 with mules and two Indian guides, the party started over the mountains. Camping at a high point in the mountains, the members of the party were confident they would soon be in California. However, an early winter storm set in, trapping the Donner party in the snowy mountains near present-day Truckee, Nevada. By December it was clear that the group would only survive with outside help. The party dispatched 15 of the strongest, including the 2 Indian guides, to reach California. This group, called the "Forlorn Hope," was struck by another violent storm, leaving two dead. Survivors sliced flesh from the bodies and ate it before moving on. Two more died, and when the two Indians refused to eat human flesh, they too were killed and eaten. On January 10, 1847, the seven survivors reached an Indian village, and by February rescue parties reached the main body, who, like "Forlorn Hope," had engaged in cannibalism. Only 45 of the Donner party survived.

Douglas, Stephen Arnold (April 23, 1813– June 3, 1861)

Called "the judge," Stephen Arnold Douglas was known for his debates with Abraham Lincoln and for his interest in opening the Nebraska Territory for settlement by whites. Born on April 23, 1813, in Brandon, Vermont, Douglas undertook the study of law at a young age, then moved to Cleveland, Ohio, in 1833. After nearly dying of typhoid fever, he pushed on to Illinois, where he became a schoolteacher. He opened a law office at the age of 21. Douglas was a lawyer, but at heart he was a politician, and he soon entered a series of politically appointed positions that gave him entry into the Democratic Party. A key influence in the establishment of a state nominating convention, Douglas served in a number of positions, including a judgeship, while he ran for office. After losing a House race in 1837, Douglas was elected in 1843.

In Congress Douglas led the fight for Oregon at 54°40' latitude and supported James K. Polk's war with Mexico in 1846. That year, the legislature of Illinois elected him to a vacant U.S. Senate seat at a time when the northern antislavery groups were gaining momentum. Douglas realized that Southerners, who exerted great power in the Democratic Party, would countenance no interference with slavery. In 1848 his new wife inherited more than 100 slaves from her father's estate, which tarnished his image in northern parts of Illinois. He continued, however, to emerge as a leader in the Democratic Party, especially after his efforts to extend railroads to the West. As chairman of the committee on territories, he received the bill to promote a Pacific railway across the Indian land in Nebraska Territory. In 1854 his committee reported out a bill that has come to be known as the *Kansas-Nebraska Act*, essentially destroying the compromise about slavery reached in the *Missouri Compromise* of 1820. The bill called for the creation of two new territories, Kansas and Nebraska, with the issue of slavery to be determined by the people of that territory. This position came to be called "*popular sovereignty*" and was forevermore associated with Douglas.

The issue involved the Constitution: can the people arbitrarily vote to do away with Constitutional rights, either for or against slavery? Although not a toady to the Southern states, Douglas seemed to be in their thrall with this bill. Over the next two years, bloodshed occurred in Kansas, which produced two legislatures and two constitutions—one free, one slave, both claiming popular sovereignty. For Douglas, who had his eye on the presidency, the concept started to become an albatross. He nevertheless privately withdrew his name from consideration for the presidency in 1856, bowing to James Buchanan of Pennsylvania rather than split the party. As events unfolded nationally, though, Douglas's popular sovereignty was in trouble in western territories.

In 1858 Douglas's opponent for the Illinois senate seat, Abraham Lincoln, came from a new party, the Republican Party, which had as its clearly stated purpose opposition to slavery in the territories. Lincoln, working at a disadvantage to the better-known Douglas, harassed Douglas into accepting a series of debates on the issue of slavery, which gave the Republican a statewide audience that he had lacked. Douglas had boxed himself in by accepting the *Dred Scott decision* by the U.S. Supreme Court (1857), which said that Congress did not have the power under the Constitution to prohibit slavery in the territories. Yet he also embraced popular sovereignty, which said that the people had the final say in matters of law. How, Lincoln asked, could the people prohibit slavery when the Dred Scott decision said they couldn't? Douglas's response, known as the Freeport Doctrine, was that the people could evade or skirt the law by electing officials who would not enforce it. The Freeport Doctrine sent chills up the spines of Southerners, who envisioned public officials refusing to arrest runaway slaves or enforce slave property laws. Douglas won the Senate seat, but his response cost him the general election in 1860, when the Southern delegates walked out of the convention.

At the onset of the Civil War, Stephen Douglas remained a patriot, pleading for the maintenance of the Union, then calling for volunteers to put down the rebellion. In his final days, he sent Lincoln a letter pledging to support him, and he spoke twice a day throughout Illinois, rousing crowds to rally around the Union cause. He last instructions to his sons were to obey the laws and support the Constitution.

Dred Scott decision

One of the most tumultuous Supreme Court decisions in history, the Dred Scott case helped push the nation toward Civil War and, arguably, instigated the *Panic of 1857*, having a decisive impact on westward expansion. Dred Scott was a slave and servant of an army surgeon, Dr. John Emerson, who took Scott from St. Louis, Missouri, to various posts, including Fort Armstrong, in Rock Island, Illinois, and Fort Snelling in Wisconsin Territory. Both of these posts were under federal authority; the first was in a free state, with slavery forbidden in Illinois by the Ordinance of 1787 (also called the *Northwest Ordinance [II]*); and the latter in a free territory by virtue of the *Missouri Compromise*, wherein slavery was prohibited above the 36°30' latitude line. From 1834 to 1838 Scott remained on free soil.

After Emerson died in 1843, Scott sued for his freedom in 1846 in Missouri, maintaining that his residence in a free state and a free territory made him de facto free. A lower court supported Scott's claim, but in 1852 the Missouri State Supreme Court overturned the lower court ruling and reversed its own previous position, which had stated that a slave became free in such circumstances. The case then went to the U.S. Supreme Court, under Chief Justice Roger B. Taney of Maryland, under the title *Dred Scott v. Sandford* (19 Howard 393). "Sandford" referred to John F. *Sanford* of New York, whose name was misspelled in the case.

The Supreme Court looked at three primary issues: (1) whether Scott had the right to sue as a citizen of the state of Missouri; (2) whether his temporary residence on free soil, either as a free state, free territory, or army installation, made him free; and (3) whether the Missouri Compromise was constitutionally valid, given its prohibition of slavery in Wisconsin Territory. Eight of the justices wrote a separate opinion, and one concurred with Taney. A majority of seven justices agreed that Scott (and all slaves) could not sue because he was not a citizen of Missouri. Taney wrongly claimed that citizenship only could occur through birth or through naturalization and that no state had ever conferred citizenship on blacks— a statement clearly contrary to practices of several northern states. He further held that Scott claimed freedom under Missouri laws, his place of residence, so the laws of the state of Missouri took precedence over those of subsequent states he lived in.

The most controversial part of the decision involved the question of the territories. Taney maintained that the Missouri Compromise was unconstitutional because it deprived citizens of their property (slaves), thus violating the "due process" clause of the Fifth Amendment, although he did not explicitly cite that amendment. This meant that Congress did not have the right to regulate slavery in the territories, overthrowing not only the Missouri Compromise but every "great compromise" since. Two dissenters, John McLean and Benjamin R. Curtis, stated that free blacks were citizens and that Congress had the authority to regulate slavery.

Since 1850 Congress had been operating on the principle of settling the territories according to "*popular sovereignty*," wherein the residents of the territory would determine whether they wanted slavery or not. But Taney closed off that option as well: if Congress couldn't regulate slavery, certainly the people of a territory could not, either. In essence, the Court had ruled that no law could keep slavery out of a region except for the state legislature, after the territory had become a state. Antislave forces realized this would be too late—that proslavery immigrants would fill up a state's voting totals until the state constitution was drafted, then leave after slavery was in place.

The decision had a significant effect on western railroads. Almost as soon as word of the decision got out, people realized that "Bleeding Kansas" would continue to be a battleground and, more important, that none of the territories that were considered "free" could in fact remain that way. Shock waves spread through all railroads running east and west (though almost none on the north-south axis), and their bonds tumbled. As railroad bonds collapsed, so did banks that were heavily invested in those railroads. At the very least, the Dred Scott decision made the Panic of 1857 deeper, and probably started it. The ruling also placed Democratic defenders of popular sovereignty (such as Stephen A. *Douglas*) in a difficult position, caught between the Court and their constituents.

Emerson, Ralph Waldo (May 25, 1803–April 22, 1882)

Born in Concord, Massachusetts, on May 25, 1803, Ralph Waldo Emerson emerged as the foremost poet of early America, capturing the vitality of the nation and its westward pull in an essay called "The Young American." In an address to Harvard in 1837 called "The American Scholar," Emerson outlined a vision of a national culture. His view of the frontier and the West was that the abundance of land best symbolized American liberty, calling land "the appointed remedy for whatever is false and fantastic in our culture." Any tilling of land "generates the feeling of patriotism." A powerful eastern intellectual voice, Emerson, as head of the group of philosophers called the Transcendentalists, saw the United States as possessing a unique character derived from working with the land and with nature.

Fort Dearborn Massacre

During the *War of 1812*, following the surrender of Mackinac, American forces under Captain Nathan Held at Fort Dearborn were ordered to evacuate the fort. On August 15, 1812, Held and Captain William Wells, who had delivered the orders, left the protection of the walls despite warnings by friendly Indians that the Pottawattomie were ready to attack. The party was only a few miles from the compound when 500 warriors attacked and killed half the forces and took the rest prisoner.

Forty-Niners

In the wake of the discovery of gold by John *Sutter* near Sacramento in January 1848, thousands of people anxious to cash in and get rich quickly streamed overland or arrived by boat in California. Known as "Forty-Niners" (because most of them arrived in 1849), these miners produced the largest gold rush in American history.

California had an estimated population of 14,000 before 1848 but by 1852 had nearly 250,000, most of them drawn to the states by gold. So-called *placer gold* could literally be picked up, easily panned using water, while subsequent gold-seekers had to mine for gold and silver ore.

"Free Soil, Free Labor, Free Men"

By the 1840s the issue of slavery in the western territories dominated political discussions. Frustration with the Whig Party's half-hearted opposition to slavery led a number of Democrats and Whigs to form new parties, including the Free-Soil Party, which held its convention in Buffalo in August 1848.

The party nominated New Yorker Martin Van Buren as president, pledged a national platform of freedom, supported the Wilmot Priviso's prohibition of slavery in the Mexican cession territories, and embraced the *Homestead Act [IV]*.

"Free Soil, Free Speech, Free Labor, and Free Men" was the party's slogan, referring to the exclusion of slavery from the western territories. Whig nominee Zachary Taylor was elected president of the United States, and the "Free Soilers" began to dissipate after that, quietly melding into the Republican Party.

Fremont, Jessie Ann Benton (May 31, 1824–December 27, 1902)

Jessie Ann Benton, the daughter of Missouri Senator Thomas Hart Benton, was born in Virginia and divided her childhood between Washington and St. Louis, much of the time tutored at home. Her education provided her with a sense of Washington politics and an appreciation for the role of the West in the nation's development.

On October 19, 1841, she married John C. *Fremont*, a soldier who had learned topography in the U.S. Army's Corps of Engineers. She took over writing most of Fremont's memos, reports, and letters (to which she occasionally signed his name), and completed his memoirs in 1887. She came to defend most of his controversial decisions, remaining strongly loyal to him, a loyalty that cost her friendships and which involved her in Washington intrigue to obtain various positions for him. In 1844 to 1845 she wrote the report of Fremont's second western expedition. She published her first book, *The Story of the Guard*, about Fremont's bodyguard, in 1863, followed by a recounting of her trip to San Francisco in 1849 called *A Year of American Travel*.

After her husband retired from the army in disgust over a court-martial resulting from a clash with Brigadier General Stephen Watts *Kearny*, Fremont became the U.S. senator from California. That returned Jessie to Washington society, where she continued to support her husband's career. After a period of European travel, the Fremonts lost much of their fortune, causing Jessie to begin writing articles for the *New York Ledger* at $100 each. These articles were collected in several other books, such as *Souvenirs of My Time* (1887) and *Far West Sketches* (1890). After John Fremont died in 1890, Jessie relied on her writing fees and her widow's pension, living in Los Angeles until her death in 1902.

Fremont, John Charles (January 21, 1813–July 13, 1890)

Known as "The Pathfinder," John Charles Fremont was born on January 21, 1813, in Savannah, Georgia, to a French émigré, Jean Fremon, and Anne Beverley Whiting Pryor. The family moved to Charleston after Jean's death in 1818. After working in a law office, Fremont attended Charleston College without graduating from 1829 to 1831. Through the efforts of South Carolina politician Joel Poinsett, Fremont received a position on the USS *Natchez* in 1833, then again, through Poinsett's intervention, got a job on the survey team for the Charleston, Louisville and Cincinnati Railroad in the Tennessee mountains and into Georgia. These surveys prepared Fremont for his explorations, which he undertook in 1838 along with Joseph N. Nicollet, a French scientist, who was assigned by then Secretary of War Poinsett to explore the Upper Mississippi River, exploring as far as Minnesota. That year Fremont received a commission as a lieutenant in the U.S. Army's Corps of Topographical Engineers. In 1841 Fremont married Jessie Benton *Fremont*, the daughter of Senator Thomas Hart *Benton*, which only advanced "The Pathfinder's" career.

In 1842 Nicollet, too ill to travel, yielded his survey expedition to Fremont, who headed a party (with the famous Kit *Carson* as the guide) that mapped the *Oregon Trail* through the South Pass and beyond. In 1843 to 1844 Fremont explored the Great Basin from the Rockies to the Sierras. On that expedition Fremont reached the Pacific Coast. He was likely one of the first to term the region the "Great Basin" and, with the help of his wife, drew a detailed map that provided a detailed report to Congress that enhanced his reputation.

Known as "The Pathfinder," John C. Fremont surveyed large parts of the West, mapped the Oregon Trail, and participated in the "Bear Flag Revolt" in California during the Mexican War. In 1856 he was the first candidate for president on the newly formed Republican Party ticket. *Library of Congress*

Fremont's orders for the third exploration limited him to the Rocky Mountains, but James K. Polk assumed office and, given the state of affairs with Mexico, funded "The Pathfinder" to continue to the Monterey area, which Fremont's party reached in February 1846. Naturally, the Mexican authorities were suspicious of 60 armed Americans entering their territory and instructed Fremont to leave. Upon his withdrawal, Fremont was met by Archibald Gillespie, Polk's agent, who bore further instructions that took him into the Sacramento Valley. There he participated in the "Bear Flag Revolt," but he admitted lacking any support of the U.S. government.

When the Mexican War erupted, however, Fremont placed his men (known as the "California battalion") under the authority of Commodore Robert F. Stockton of the U.S. Navy, which had taken the California ports.

But Fremont battled his own superiors, including General Stephen Watts *Kearney*, who disputed Stockton's supremacy of command in the region. This produced a court-martial, resulting in Fremont's conviction and dismissal from the army. Nevertheless, the court recommended leniency, based on Fremont's service, and Polk reinstated him. Fremont resigned, but Polk again tapped him to head a western expedition, which he accepted. Start-

IN THEIR OWN Words

Report of Commodore Robert Stockton in California

In 1848 Commodore Robert Stockton, upon his return from California, filed the following report on the activities of the Americans there. Included in his discussion was a review of the episode in which Captain John C. **Fremont** was charged with violating the orders of General Stephen Watts **Kearny**. Stockton describes here the process of organizing Fremont's volunteers into the "California battalion" and its subsequent successful advance toward San Pedro, just north of Los Angeles.

Captain Fremont and Lieutenant Gillespie, of the marine corps, had already raised a body of 160 volunteers, prepared to act according to circumstances. I informed those gentlemen that if they, together with the men whom they had raised, would volunteer to serve under my command . . . that I would form them into a battalion, appointing the former major and the latter captain. These arrangements were all completed . . . . It was thus that the battalion of California volunteers was organized, which subsequently, under its gallant officers, took so patriotic and efficient a part in the military operations in that territory. . . .

Leaving . . . Monterey, for its protection, I sailed . . . for San Pedro. This town is situated about 28 miles from Ciudad de Los Angeles, in the vicinity of which the enemy was stated to be. On the way to San Pedro, we landed at Santa Barbara, of which we took possession . . . [W]e commenced our march towards the camp of the enemy [and] in the course of the afternoon . . . information reached us that the enemy's force, instead of awaiting our approach, had dispersed; that they had buried their guns, and that the governor and general had retreated, as was supposed, to Sonora. We continued our march toward Ciudad de los Angeles, and . . . having been joined by Major Fremont with about 120 volunteers, under his command, we marched into the city, which we quietly occupied.

—SOURCE: JOHN BIGELOW, *MEMOIR OF THE LIFE AND PUBLIC SERVICES OF JOHN CHARLES FREMONT* (NEW YORK: DERBY & JACKSON, 1856), 166–168.

ing in October 1848, this exploration proved a disaster. Fremont lost 10 men in the snow.

Reaching California, Fremont invested in gold mines and engaged in politics, winning election as the first senator from the state in 1850, but in a short-term circumstance; he had to run again in 1851 when he was defeated by proslave forces. Two years later he was on the trail again with his fifth expedition, searching for a railroad route through the Rocky Mountains. Again, he almost led his party into a snowbound disaster before it encountered a small Utah village.

In 1856, backed by powerful politicians and editors, Fremont was nominated as the first presidential candidate of the newly formed Republican Party. He opposed the extension of slavery into the territories and, while losing the popular vote, nearly won enough northern states to win the election with a slogan of "Free Soil, Free Men, Fremont."

Fremont spent the next four years attempting to address his problematic western mines. He was named a major general in the Union Army, commanding the Department of the West when the *Civil War [IV]* broke out. He immediately was embroiled in a controversy for emancipating slaves in Missouri, a state that President Abraham Lincoln desperately needed to keep in the Union. Fremont's subordinates also were corrupt, a problem Fremont failed to check. He won several early engagements with the Confederates, but Lincoln relieved him for his slave policy and placed him in a command in Virginia. There he was tactically outclassed by Confederate General Thomas "Stonewall" Jackson. After another transfer, he resigned, and from that point he remained a political liability for Lincoln.

After the war, Fremont served as territorial governor of Arizona, attempted some railroad promotions, published his *Memoirs* in 1887, and received a large pension, but nevertheless he never achieved financial prosperity. John C. Fremont died in New York City on July 13, 1890.

Goliad Massacre

When Texans declared independence from Mexico in 1836, General Jose Urrea, with 1,000 men, traveled up the coast into Texas. General James W. Fannin headed the resistance from Goliad.

Fannin, who had only about 350 men, retreated to the town of Victoria. As the Texans moved through the open prairie, Urrea's forces attacked. On

March 20, 1836, the Texans surrendered to Urrea, expecting to be paroled, then return home. General Antonio López de *Santa Anna*, however, had ordered that all rebels were to be executed, and on March 27, Urrea shot the prisoners. A handful escaped to spread the word of the "Goliad Massacre." When news reached Texas General Sam *Houston*'s men, along with the earlier news of the Alamo, which fell on March 6 with the entire complement of defenders killed, the phrases "Remember Goliad" and "Remember the Alamo" galvanized the Texans as they won the *Battle of San Jacinto* (April 21, 1836).

Gregg, Josiah (July 19, 1806–February 25, 1850)

Born in Overton County, Tennessee, Josiah Gregg spent his youth in Illinois and Missouri. A sickly youth, he moved in 1831 to Santa Fe for health reasons. When he recovered, he became a trader, whose trading activities took him into Mexico several times. During his travels, he took notes on western trade, geography, and animals, publishing his manuscript, *Commerce of the Prairies,* in 1844. The book went through several editions, including foreign language editions.

In 1846 he joined the U.S. Army, although the exact nature of his appointment is unclear. During the Mexican War, he traveled with the army in Mexico, New Mexico, and California, where in 1849 he crossed the Coast Range to the Pacific Ocean, in the process suffering from hunger and exposure so severe that he died.

Harrison, William Henry (February 9, 1773–April 4, 1841)

Having the unremarkable distinction of holding the presidency of the United States for the shortest time, William Henry Harrison was born in Virginia on February 9, 1773. He attended school in Virginia, briefly practiced medicine, and then joined the U.S. Army, where he was assigned to the Northwest Territory. In 1792 he was commissioned a lieutenant, then in 1797 promoted to captain. Later that year, however, he resigned and applied for the position of secretary of the territory, which he received. At the same time, the territory voted him its delegate to Congress. He received an appointment as governor of Indiana Territory in 1800, serving for 12 years. Both as secretary and governor, Harrison was active in shaping land law in the territories and helped separate Indiana and Ohio, working to organize the Ohio capital at Chillicothe.

As governor, Harrison negotiated several treaties with the Indians obtaining large blocks of land. But disputes arose over these treaties, with Indians later claiming they did not realize they had signed over territorial rights. Indian complaints ballooned into full-scale hostilities with the appearance of the Shawnee leader *Tecumseh*, who surprised Harrison's forces on November 7, 1811, at the *Battle of Tippecanoe*. Nevertheless, the Indians retreated in a close battle.

When the *War of 1812* broke out, Harrison was promoted to general and commanded the march on Detroit. He finally managed a decisive victory over the British and Indians at the Battle of Thames in 1813, where Tecumseh was killed. By then he had a reputation as a great military leader who had enthusiastic backing in the West but who faced stiff opposition in Washington.

Harrison assumed a number of elected positions in Ohio as a congressman, then a U.S. senator, where he supported "internal improvements" (especially canals) and slavery in the territories. The latter position cost him his senate seat and then, in 1822, he lost a congressional race. Despite his personal losses, Harrison worked for the campaign of his ally Henry *Clay* in 1824, prior to being chosen again by the Ohio legislature as the U.S. senator. From 1828 to 1829 he served as the ambassador to Colombia until he was recalled by the new president Andrew *Jackson*.

It may have seemed that Harrison's options were closed. He had been removed from almost every appointed or elected position available, yet he still had a strong national presence and, as a Whig, offered the only hope of unseating the Jacksonian Democrats in the White House. In a trial run in 1836, he did well in the North. Then, in 1840, the Whigs nominated Harrison to oppose the incumbent Martin Van Buren. Perceiving that politics had changed to emphasize "mass marketing," Harrison ran one of the first truly modern campaigns on the slogan "Tippecanoe and Tyler, Too." When lambasted by the Democrats as lazy (retiring to his log cabin with his hard cider), Harrison's managers turned this into an advantage with the phrase "Log Cabin and Hard Cider." Harrison won overwhelmingly. Then, contracting pneumonia after giving an extended inaugural speech in the rain, "Old Tippecanoe" died only six weeks after assuming the presidency.

Houston, Sam (March 2, 1793–July 26, 1863)

Born on March 2, 1793, in Virginia, Sam Houston moved with his mother to Tennessee at age 14, where he worked as a store clerk. Houston spent much of his time with nearby *Cherokee* Indians, who named him "the Raven." After three years, Houston left the Cherokees and joined the U.S. Army to fight in 1813 against the Creek Indians at the Battle of Horseshoe Bend (1814), where Houston was wounded. Promoted to lieutenant, Houston became involved in a disagreement with the War Department over the Cherokees and resigned in late 1817. He then went into law, opening a law office and winning an election as a district attorney.

In 1823 Houston was elected to the U.S. House of Representatives from Tennessee, then won the governorship of that state in 1827. But in a conflict with a powerful family, he resigned and moved to Arkansas to live with the Cherokee. He drank heavily, earning the Indian nickname, "Big Drunk."

Houston left for Texas in 1832, supposedly for Indian-related matters, but doubtless for opportunities in land speculation. Representing the Comanche Indians to the Texas convention discussing separation with Mexico, Houston moved to Nacogdoches and was elected to the statehood convention, where he supported statehood for Texas. When General Antonio López de *Santa Anna* assumed power in Mexico City in 1835, Texans called for a new meeting of representatives called the "Consultation." Houston represented his district. The meeting established a provisional government in Texas and named Houston commander-in-chief of the military forces that the colonists thought would be required to repel Santa Anna. He criticized the early plans for attacking Mexican forces on the Rio Grande and therefore requested a temporary relief from January to March 1836.

After the Texas declaration of independence on March 2, Houston was reappointed commander-in-chief and, with his forces east of the Alamo, knew of that little fort's plight but could do little. He led his forces on a steady withdrawal in the face of Santa Anna's superior numbers, drawing the enemy ever deeper into Texas while his own forces grew and trained. When the Mexican general divided his forces to capture the Texas government in April, Houston met him at the *Battle of San Jacinto*. Despite knowing the Texas army was in the vicinity, Santa Anna's troops were caught as if off guard, and the Texans utterly defeated the Mexicans under the cry "Remember the Alamo." Houston suffered an ankle wound in the battle.

Returning from medical care in New Orleans, Houston was elected president of the new republic in September 1836. He hoped that the United States would annex Texas, but the best he could achieve was diplomatic relations with the United States. In 1839, ineligible for reelection, Houston was elected to the Texas legislature and, a year later, was married to Margaret Lea, who brought him to religion and settled him into family life. During the years he was out of the presidency, Houston criticized the administration of Mirabeau B. Lamar, and he rode that criticism to win the election in 1841. This time, he succeeded at getting the United States to propose a bill to annex Texas in 1844, but the bill did not win Senate approval. When annexation did pass, Houston was elected a U.S. senator for a short term, then was reelected for a full term in 1847.

Noted for his Unionist views, Houston increasingly became unpopular in parts of Texas, expressing the desire that slavery might die out on its own. By the mid-1850s his pro-Union positions were a liability, and after he voted against the *Kansas-Nebraska Act*, the legislature denounced him and indicated he would not be reelected, so he ran for governor in 1857. There he suffered the only defeat of his political career, but in a rematch, in 1859, he won. Although he remained strongly pro-Union, he bowed to the will of the people when the state voted to secede, but he refused to support the Confederacy and was removed in March 1861. Sam Houston died on July 26, 1863, always a Texan first.

Indian Removal Act of 1830

Anxious to acquire *Cherokee* lands in Georgia, in 1830 the U.S. Congress required the removal of Indian tribes west of the *Mississippi River [I]* to a territory established in June 1834 in Arkansas. This act defied treaties negotiated with the Cherokee beginning in 1791, under which the tribe was allowed to remain on its lands in Georgia. Whites constantly violated these treaties, both on Cherokee and Creek lands, while the states of Alabama and Mississippi violated treaties with the Choctaw and Chicasaw tribes. In 1828 the state of Georgia declared the laws of the Cherokee Nation null and void after June 1, 1830, opening the door for removal. A year later gold was discovered on Indian lands. At this time the Cherokee sued on the grounds that it was a "foreign nation" with a treaty with the United States government.

This case reached the U.S. Supreme Court, which, while sympathetic to the Indians' position, nevertheless ruled in 1831 (*Cherokee Nation v. State of Georgia*) that the tribes were not "foreign" nations as they resided within U.S. territorial boundaries. Nevertheless, the Court made clear that it would entertain other arguments.

When Georgia passed an 1830 law requiring whites to obtain a license from the governor and to take an oath of allegiance to Georgia before they could reside on Indian lands, the Indians had a chance to advance their case again. Two New England missionaries, Samuel A. Worcester and Elizur Butler, openly violated the law as a test and were convicted and sentenced to four years in prison. The case reached the U.S. Supreme Court in March, 1832, whereupon the court, under Chief Justice John Marshall (*Worcester v. Georgia*) stated that Indian nations were indeed distinct entities capable of making treaties that the state of Georgia and the United States were bound to honor. The state of Georgia simply refused to comply with Marshall's ruling, and President Andrew *Jackson* refused to enforce the law, saying "John Marshall has made his decision, now let him enforce it."

The federal government now threw its entire weight behind the removal, eliminating Indian land titles and forcing the Creek, Choctaw, and Chicasaw into new treaties that removed them from the Old Southwest. In 1835 the Cherokee, likewise, were forced out and relocated to the new Indian Territory in Oklahoma, with the government assuming the costs. Nevertheless, the relocation was difficult, with Cherokee especially lacking proper transportation, shelter, or clothing, and has become known as the *Trail of Tears*.

Jackson, Andrew (March 15, 1767–June 8, 1845)

A flamboyant symbol of the young West, Andrew Jackson was born to meager means in South Carolina. As a youth he fought in the Revolutionary War, during which he was captured by the British. When he refused to shine an officer's boots, he was slashed with a sword, and the incident left him with a deep hatred for the British his entire life. After the war he studied law in North Carolina and practiced somewhat unsuccessfully for a brief time before moving to the new territory of Tennessee. There he participated in the state's constitutional convention, then parlayed his minimal understanding of the law and his personal magnetism into a seat as the congressman to the United States House of Representatives. In the House, he sided with the Jeffersonians and, following the expulsion of speaker William Blount from the Senate (after Blount's attempt to wrest Florida from Spain), was named Blount's successor.

Jackson had difficulty with his financial dealings, eventually coming to distrust and despise banks. His Hermitage plantation struggled, and in his private life, his marriage to Rachel Robards—who at the time, technically, remained legally married to Lewis Robards as their divorce had not yet been finalized—produced a constant stream of allegations, defenses by Jackson, and even duels. He killed Charles Dickinson of Nashville in a duel in 1806, was wounded in a scuffle resulting from another duel, and attempted to fight still many others. The struggle with Jesse and Thomas Hart *Benton* left him with a serious wound and put him in constant suffering.

Jackson's election to judge of the Tennessee Supreme Court in 1798, makes it ironic that he would later challenge the authority of the U.S. Supreme Court. Law, however, was not his forte: fighting was. During the *War of 1812*, Jackson was given a commission as a major general, but he disobeyed orders and returned his troops to Natchez, where they were discharged. In 1814 he led an expedition against the Creek Indians at Horseshoe Bend that annihilated the Indians. Jackson then pursued the fleeing natives to the Gulf of Mexico. With the council at Fort Jackson in August, 1814, he extinguished Indian power in Alabama.

Since Jackson was already in the area, he was the natural choice to defend New Orleans against a British invasion force in January 1815. The British troops were routed, creating the myth of "Old Hickory" or the "Old Hero" as a romantic figure in the public eye. Later ordered to patrol southern Georgia, Jackson invaded Florida in the Seminole War. There he captured some chiefs but also took prisoner two Englishmen, whom Jackson hanged as spies. Nevertheless, after the Adams-Onis Treaty (1819) Jackson became the territorial governor of Florida.

He allowed his name to be put in nomination for 1824 by Martin Van Buren, but John Quincy Adams and Henry *Clay* pooled their votes (in

Following a successful career fighting Indians in Florida and Alabama, then a successful defense of New Orleans against the British in 1812, Andrew Jackson represented the first politician of the post-Appalachian West to become President of the United States. *Library of Congress*

what some termed the "corrupt bargain") to elect Adams president and have Clay named secretary of state. Outraged, Jackson and his party organizers developed a new political party entirely around "Old Hickory," called the Democratic Party. Based on patronage and the "spoils system," it represented the first truly modern political party. With this structure behind him, Jackson succeeded in winning the presidency in 1828.

His administration featured several critical points in which western interests were involved. Jackson vetoed the bill to spend federal money on the Maysville Road and opposed the recharter of the Bank of the United States. In keeping with the "small-government" practices of Jefferson, Jackson saw federal spending for a local or state road as excessive and viewed the Bank of the United States as a "monster" that sought to oppress the "common man." Perhaps more significant for the West was his policy toward the Indians. Under the Indian Removal Act of 1830, he implemented the forced removal of the Indians in the South to Oklahoma in 1832, and when the Supreme Court, in *Worcester v. Georgia* (1832) ruled in favor of the Cherokees, Jackson ignored the decision and allowed Georgia to remove the Indians anyway.

While in many ways the first truly western president, Jackson often took positions contrary to the best interests of his section—which Henry Clay of Kentucky took great pains to point out. Nevertheless, Jackson remained popular and powerful until the end of his second term in 1836, when he retired.

Jayhawkers

The name given to the anti-slavery, "free soil" forces prior to and during the Civil War, the term "Jayhawker" was associated with Charles R. Jennison, a New Yorker who came to Kansas in the territorial period and who led a group of guerilla fighters in 1861 into western Missouri. They struck both Harrisonville, Missouri, and Independence, Missouri, so brutally that even Union troops in the area were apprized of their activities. Later, taking the more respectable name of the Seventh Kansas Regiment, the unit deposed Jennison as commander and was redeployed to Mississippi. Jennison and his henchmen reappeared as a group called the "Red Legs," for the red stripe down their pants. The reputation of the Seventh Kansas, not Jennison's bandits, dominated after the war, and virtually all Kansans went by the nickname "Jayhawkers." The University of Kansas adopted the Jayhawk as the official nickname of its athletic teams.

Jefferson, Thomas (April 13, 1743–July 4, 1826)

The author of the Declaration of Independence had a remarkable career, much of it tied to the opening of the early West. Thomas Jefferson was born in Shadwell, Virginia, on April 13, 1743, to Peter Jefferson, a farmer in the Shenandoah Valley. Jefferson's early life on a large farm/estate influenced his thought, while the wealth generated by the estate allowed him to attend William and Mary, exposing him to classical political thinkers, literature, mathematics, and science. Life in the country deeply affected Jefferson, who came to view cities as cesspools. Instead, the ideal life was that of an agrarian philosopher—not a "subsistence farmer"—who had enough land to permit him to engage in a variety of pursuits, including politics, art, literature, and music. Jefferson himself was an avid reader, played the violin, drafted blueprints to his own magnificent house, Monticello, and of course penned some of the most influential political documents in history.

Although Jefferson studied law and was admitted to the bar in 1767, he spent as much time managing his estate as he did practicing law. Sent to the House of Burgesses in 1769, Jefferson emphasized property law, helping to end "primogeniture" (wherein the eldest son inherited all the land) and "entail" (wherein all land was handed down to a stipulated descendant), thereby hoping to discourage English-style large manorial estates in America. In a letter to James Madison published after Jefferson's death, he had stated that the "earth belongs in usufruct [trust] to the living." He in essence proposed a universal entail, stripping away claims of past generations, and went so far as to argue that all debts ought to expire at the end of 19 years.

Jefferson helped convince Virginia to hand over its lands west of the Appalachians to the Confederation and in 1784 proposed an ordinance creating the Northwest Territory, in which several states would emerge as fully functioning parts of the Union. Laying out a system of surveying and dividing land in a grid around sections and townships, Jefferson developed a plan for systematic and organized settlement. This became the basis for much of the territorial expansion thereafter, providing a way in which a region, after it reached a prerequisite number of people, became a territory, then a state. The *Northwest Ordinance [II]*, which superseded it, was nevertheless based on Jefferson's principles of democratic representation in the new territories. It established no more than five and no fewer than three new states to be formed out of the old Northwest.

When he became president in 1801, Jefferson fought to open up lands in the West by reducing the acreage minimum that had to be purchased, lowering the amount from 320 acres to 160. The price was reduced to $1.25 per acre in 1820.

In 1801 Napoleon secured a transfer of Louisiana back to France, which profoundly disturbed Jefferson. Less than a year later, Spanish officials in New Orleans interfered with American shipments out of that city, making any potential French takeover of New Orleans all the more trouble-

IN THEIR OWN Words

Thomas Jefferson on the Importance of New Orleans

Writing to Robert R. Livingston, the American Minister to France on April 18, 1802, President Thomas Jefferson reiterated America's concerns over the French acquiring control of New Orleans and urged Livingston to conclude negotiations to purchase the city.

The cession of Louisiana and the Floridas by Spain to France, works most sorely on the United States. . . . It completely reverses all the political relations of the United States, and will form a new epoch in our political course. . . . It is New Orleans, through which the produce of three-eights of our territory must pass to market, and from its fertility it will ere long yield more than half of our whole produce, and contain more than half our inhabitants. France, placing herself in that door, assumes to us the attitude of defiance.

I have no doubt you have urged these considerations, on every proper occasion, with the government where you are. They are such as must have effect . . . Every eye in the United States is now fixed on the affairs of Louisiana. Perhaps nothing since the revolutionary war, has produced more easy sensations through the body of the nation. Notwithstanding temporary bickering that has taken place with France, she has still a strong hold on the affections of our citizens generally. I have thought it not amiss, by way of supplement to the letters of the Secretary of State, to write you this private one, to impress you with the importance we affix to the transaction . . . .

—Source: Henry Steele Commager, ed., *Documents of American History, vol. 1: to 1898,* 7th ed. (New York: Appleton-Century-Crofts, 1934), 189–190.

some. Jefferson instructed his minister in Paris, Robert R. Livingston, to procure either some land on the lower Mississippi for a port or to secure the right of deposit at New Orleans, no matter who owned the city. Six months later, in January 1803, Jefferson named James Monroe as the minister plenipotentiary to France with instructions to purchase New Orleans and West Florida for up to $10 million. Other developments in the Western Hemisphere convinced Napoleon he could not support any empire there, and he offered all of Louisiana for $15 million. This meant that Jefferson had doubled the area of the United States, acquiring 828,000 square miles of western land.

Jefferson anticipated that Americans would settle this land slowly, in an organized fashion based on the principles of the Northwest Ordinance, expanding the agrarian frontier. To determine exactly what the United States had purchased, Jefferson sent William Clark and Meriwether Lewis from St. Louis to explore the *Missouri River [I]* and its tributaries westward. The president was fascinated by the notion of a "northwest passage" but also had genuine scientific and technological interests in the region. The *Lewis and Clark Expedition* returned, having crossed some 7,000 miles over the Continental Divide, up the Columbia River, then to the Pacific Ocean. Jefferson also sent Zebulon *Pike* on an expedition up the Mississippi, where he followed the Arkansas river to the Rocky Mountains.

When it came to the Indians on the western lands, Jefferson supported the campaigns against the tribes in Indiana under "Mad" Anthony Wayne. As president he urged the Indians to turn to agriculture. He thought that intermarriage could occur between Indians and whites, even as he disparaged the practice of intermarriage between blacks and whites.

Associated with an "Empire of Liberty" that would be grounded in citizen-farmers, Jefferson resisted large-scale efforts to improve roads, canals, or harbors at government expense. His secretary of the treasury, Albert Gallatin, proposed a giant government-funded canal system which received no political support. In foreign affairs Jefferson resisted any expansion of the army or navy, constructing a fleet of some 200 coastal gunboats that were utterly destroyed in the *War of 1812* while the 6 large frigates constructed under the Federalist presidents, John Adams and George Washington, acquitted themselves well in combat.

Toward the end of his life, the *Missouri Compromise* threatened to revive the clash over slavery—Jefferson called it the "death knell of the Union"—and it was the expansion of slavery into the western territories that ultimately brought about the rise of the Republican Party, which was associated with manufacturing and industrial interests. His views on small and limited government remain popular in the West, even to the present, but his ideal of an agrarian republic had largely vanished by 1900.

Kansas-Nebraska Act

In January 1854 Senator Stephen *Douglas* proposed a bill to form two new states out of Indian lands west of Missouri. Organizing these two new territories, Kansas and Nebraska, would facilitate construction of a transcontinental railroad. Instead, the Kansas-Nebraska Act set off a firestorm that contributed to the coming of the Civil War.

Territorial organization had been governed by the *Missouri Compromise*, which prohibited slavery above the 36°30' line. With little land above the line, the Compromise virtually guaranteed the exclusion of slavery from the territories. During the *Mexican War*, new concerns arose over the disposition of newly acquired territories, many below the Compromise line. The Wilmot Proviso, which failed to pass, had attempted to prohibit slavery in the Mexican Cession territories and necessitated the Compromise of 1850. By that time Douglas contended that the Missouri Compromise was null and void, superseded by the concept of "*popular sovereignty*," in which the residents of a territory would decide the status of slavery there.

Both pro- and antislave groups organized immigration into Kansas to tilt the vote in their favor. Proslave forces from Missouri, then Alabama and Georgia poured in, while the New England Emigrant Aid Society supported

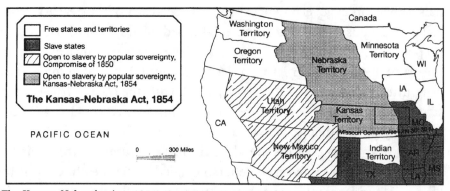

The Kansas-Nebraska Act, 1854. *Ron Acklin, University of Dayton Print and Design*

Free-Soil settlers to move to Kansas. Slave forces set up a territorial government at Lecompton, while free-soilers established a rival capital at Topeka. Violence between the two groups inevitably occurred. Proslave forces spread intimidation in Lawrence, then, in May 1856 John Brown and a group of antislave men murdered five southerners in the *Pottawatomie Massacre*. Northern newspapers referred to "Bleeding Kansas" or "Bloody Kansas," although overall there was little fighting, and even fewer slaves.

President James Buchanan, a Pennsylvania Democrat who hardly wanted to be responsible for starting a civil war, stood behind efforts to bribe the Kansans into accepting the Lecompton constitution. Shortly thereafter, Republican Abraham Lincoln gave his "House Divided" speech, predicting the divisions in Kansas would only foreshadow a more serious conflict in the entire nation over slavery.

By that time, Stephen Douglas, who had intended that popular sovereignty determine the status of slavery, sided with the Republicans against the bill. The Senate did pass it, but the House, with the aid of anti-Lecompton forces, required a new vote on the whole Lecompton constitution. The vote failed in August 1858, although slavery remained legal in Kansas because of the *Dred Scott decision*.

Kearny, Stephen Watts (August 30, 1794– October 31, 1848)

A career soldier, Stephen Watts Kearny was born on August 30, 1794, in Newark, New Jersey, and went to public schools, then Columbia College, before entering the army during the *War of 1812*.

Kearny continued to move up the army career ladder, commanding a dragoon regiment that constructed Fort Des Moines. He published a textbook on mounted operations in 1837 and led several expeditions in the trans-Mississippi region before tensions with Mexico led the army to place him in command of the Army of the West in 1846 as a brigadier general. That summer he set out from Fort Leavenworth, Kansas for Santa Fe, arriving in August with his force of 1,600 men. Capturing the city without resistance, Kearny administered the territory as military governor for just over a month. In September he set out for California with a fraction of his force, sending two-thirds of his men back to Santa Fe upon hearing that California already had been conquered. In fact, Mexican resistance in the region remained stiff, as Kearny found out at San Pasqual, where he attacked a larger Mexican force with near-disastrous results. Only a relief expedition from Commodore Robert Field Stockton rescued his expedition, at which time he regrouped and marched to San Diego. Stockton and Kearny captured San Diego, moving north to Los Angeles, where the California forces surrendered in January 1847—not to Kearny or Stockton but to a separate force commanded by Lt. Colonel John Charles *Fremont*. A struggle over command of the government ensued between Kearny, whom Stockton had named military commander, and Fremont, whom he had named civil commander. In March 1847 Kearny formed his own civil government, yet Fremont refused to obey his orders. Three months later, when Kearny marched back east, Fremont accompanied his senior officer, and upon arriving at Fort Leavenworth, Fremont was arrested and escorted to Washington, charged with insubordination. Found guilty, Fremont resigned from the army.

Kearny returned to action; then, while civil governor of Mexico City, he contracted a severe disease. He was promoted to major general shortly before he died in October 1848.

Larkin, Thomas Oliver (September 16, 1802– October 27, 1858)

Born in Charlestown, Massachusetts, Thomas Larkin traveled in search of wealth. He moved to the Carolinas where he operated a general store in Wilmington, then in 1827 investing in a sawmill. The mill ultimately failed and Larkin had to return home to Massachusetts in defeat in 1831. At that time, he accompanied his half-brother John B. R. Cooper to California, arriving in 1832. On the journey, he met his future wife, Rachel Holmes, with whom he had an illicit affair on board the ship. They married in 1833.

Using part of Rachel's inheritance, Larkin constructed a successful double-geared flour mill in California, later adding a general store and engaging in trade with Mexico. Larkin managed to speculate in land as well, becoming an all-around prosperous merchant. As a California merchant with commercial ties to Mexico, Larkin interacted with the financial elite in the region and thereby became a store of useful information for the United States government, which recruited him as the consul to Mexico in 1844. In that capacity, Larkin promoted American business interests, helped U.S. citizens who ran afoul of Mexican authorities, and unofficially supplied the government with important information about California. He consistently overestimated Britain's interest in the region, but by 1845 he had the additional charge of working as a "confidential agent" to help pry California from Mexico. President James K. Polk gave Larkin specific orders to prevent the transfer of California to Britain or France.

Whether Larkin would have been successful in persuading the Californians to secede from Mexico remains an open question, but the turmoil caused by John C. *Fremont* and the Bear Flag Rebellion made it a moot point. The *Mexican War* delivered California to the United States, and Larkin served as a member of the state constitutional convention in 1849. From 1847 to 1849 he served in various positions with the U.S. Navy, in which he performed routine record keeping and procurement functions.

After the Mexican War, Larkin returned to business enterprises, where he speculated in ranches, town lots, and other real estate, acquiring great wealth. In 1850 along with his family, Thomas Larkin moved to the east, before coming back once again to San Francisco in 1851. Larkin died in California on October 27, 1858.

Latter-day Saints, Church of Jesus Christ of ("LDS" or "Mormons")

A truly American-originated church, the Church of Jesus Christ of Latter-day Saints (known as the "Mormons") was first organized in 1830 in Fayette, New York, through the leadership of a young man named Joseph Smith (1805–1844). It grew to international proportions and, in 2002, remains one of the fastest-growing churches in the United States.

Born in Sharon, Vermont, to a relatively poor family of farmers, Joseph Smith grew up at Palmyra, New York, in part of the "burned over district," an area "scorched" by evangelists of the Gospel. Although his parents were Christians, they did not attend churches regularly, but the training in some of the scriptures sank through to Joseph, Jr., who prayed regularly at age 14 for enlightenment. In 1820 Smith claimed to have had a visitation from both God and Jesus Christ, when he was admonished not to join an existing church (an event called the "First Vision" by Mormons).

Smith's crucial vision came in 1823, when the angel Moroni informed him that a historical record of the spiritual life of the Americas was written on gold plates and buried near Smith's house. Although the angel showed Smith those plates, he was forbidden to remove them four times—once each year when he visited the location on the same day. At each visit he received instruction and revelation, until, in 1827, the angel instructed him to take the plates home. Smith proceeded over a two-year period to "read" and interpret the plates using two "lenses" ("seer stones," Urim and Thummim) given him by Moroni, dictating the translation to an associate, Oliver Cowdery, a schoolteacher. Cowdery and several other witnesses at various times claimed to have seen the plates, though none except Smith were allowed to translate them through the lenses. In 1830 Smith published the transcriptions as the *Book of Mormon*, named (according to Smith) after a fourth century prophet. Almost immediately, Smith organized a church called the Church of Christ, but over time becoming known as the Church of Jesus Christ of Latter-day Saints (LDS), or simply "Mormons."

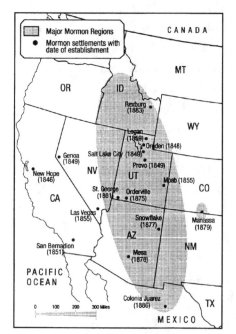

Major Mormon regions in the West. *Ron Acklin, University of Dayton Print and Design*

The *Book of Mormon* purported to describe the history of the ancient Americas, based on a group that migrated from the Middle East in 600 B.C. These people received prophecies of the coming of the Messiah to the New World, and the *Book of Mormon* presented a history of a titanic struggle between Indian tribes ("Lamanites" and the "Nephites") in North and Central America. Smith and his close cadre of followers and immediate family led the new church based on the teachings contained in the *Book of Mormon* and, over time, an equally important book, *Doctrine and Covenants* (1835), containing the writings, visions, and prophecies of Joseph Smith. (It was this book and not the *Book of Mormon* that contained Smith's institutionalization of polygamy.)

Smith prophesied that he was to move the church to a "New Jerusalem," where all converts would gather in a society called Zion to prepare for the Second Coming of Christ. Smith knew that Zion lay in the West, but the church needed to relocate before the actual location of Zion was revealed. Locals in New York had grown uncomfortable with the church's doctrines, so in 1830 Smith moved the congregation to Kirtland, Ohio, where the church was affiliated with a bank that Smith founded—and that collapsed in the *Panic of 1837*. The locals blamed Smith and the church for the bank's failure and the region's economic problems, which forced another move, to Independence, Missouri, where the rapidly growing membership had already established a foothold. From 1833 to 1838 Smith and the authorities of Jackson County clashed over the presence of the large number of Mormons there, but finally the Missouri government gave them an area in north central Missouri organized as Caldwell County.

No sooner had the Mormons arrived in large numbers than locals began to see them as a threat. Mormons, with their majorities, could dominate elections, and as Whigs, proslave elements feared the Mormons would consistently vote against their interests. Following the arrest of Smith and others in October 1838, Smith moved the church yet again, to Nauvoo, Illinois. There he introduced polygamy and presided over a town that was essentially Mormon-only. Nauvoo's size, and potential voting power, posed a threat to the existing political parties in Illinois, and the threat only grew as Mormon missionaries brought in more converts every day. When Smith announced he was running for the presidency of the United States in 1844, many saw their worst fears realized, with a huge Mormon "voting bloc" of about 25,000 capable of dominating Illinois elections. The few dissenters and non-Mormons in Nauvoo resisted, publishing a paper, the *Nauvoo Expositor*, to expose Smith and Mormonism. Smith, as mayor, closed the paper. Charged with inciting a riot, Smith and his brother Hyrum were held for trial at the county seat of Carthage, where a mob broke into the jail and shot the two men.

Smith left behind a gigantic family, having been "legitimately" married to Emma Hale (who bore eight children) and secretly married to more than 45 other women. Upon his death, the leadership of the church fell to Brigham *Young*, and many of Smith's family agreed.

Young had taken over many of the leadership functions when Smith was in jail or under legal attack. Although he oversaw the completion of the Mormon temple at Nauvoo, Young realized that the Mormons had to relocate. In 1846 Young led the Mormons on the great trek over the Mormon Trail to "Winter Quarters" at Omaha, Nebraska, then, the following year, to the Salt Lake Valley, where he allegedly said, "This is the place." The Mormons immediately cleared land and built the foundations of Salt Lake City. They also began work on a new temple.

Aside from the Indians, the Mormons were the most populous group in Utah (perhaps 6,000 in 1849). Despite Utah's status as a United States territory, Young essentially ran the colony as a theocracy, making civil positions and church service inseparable. For a decade, the federal government ignored or worked with the Mormons, seeking their help when necessary. In 1852, however, 1 of the 12 "apostles" appointed by Joseph Smith, Orson Pratt, made an official church announcement sanctioning polygamy. Federal officials grew wary, and the Mormons were again under attack in various public forums. President James Buchanan removed Young as Territorial Governor and, on the basis of reports of federal officials in Utah, became convinced that the Mormons planned a rebellion. He ordered federal troops into the territory,

IN THEIR OWN

Exposé of Joseph Smith, Founder of Mormonism, 1844

Most non-Mormons in the 1830s and 1840s considered Joseph Smith a charlatan, a dealer in the occult. His murder, though, in 1844, elevated him to the status of martyr for his followers. Typical of the time, George Davis's account considers Smith no more than a savvy con man, attacking life, liberty, and property on American soil.

The founders of the Mormon faith, consisting of Joe Smith, his father and brothers, admitted on all hands to be of all absurdities the most absurd, were originally citizens of the State of New York, and there first commenced imposing their delusions, and practicing their impositions upon the credulous and unsuspecting. While in that State they did not acquire much strength in numbers, or notoriety as a sect. From thence they removed to Kirkland, in the State of Ohio, commenced building up their Zion, and finding more favor among the masses in the West than they had done in New York, their leader and the chief of imposters, JOE SMITH THE PROPHET, acquired a fame for either evil or good, which extended throughout all portions of the Union. Of their conduct while in the State of Ohio, and the causes which immediately led to their again removing and seeking another place of resort, it is no part of my design to speak. It is sufficient for me to state, that public opinion rendered it absolutely necessary for "Joe" to remove.

About this time, the Prophet as he asserted, was favored with a revelation from the Almighty, in which the western part of the State of Missouri was designated as the promised land for the chosen people of God, upon which Zion was to

which fed Mormon paranoia that the forces intended to annihilate them.

Meanwhile, a wagon train of non-Mormons was attacked in August 1857 by Indians at Mountain Meadows, Utah. The settlers drove the Indians off, but the Indians met with Mormon officials and threatened war with them if the Mormons did not aid them in destroying the "gentiles." Some Mormon leaders—though not Young, who ordered that the emigrants be left alone—feared that federal troops would attack them at any moment. They concluded they could not fight a "two-front war" against both the Indians and U.S. Cavalry. Thus, the Mormons sent Indian agent John D. Lee and some prominent leaders with a militia group to "escort" the wagon train to safety. The Mormons set a trap, killing the able-bodied

be built, and they to await the second advent. Selecting a location upon unentered lands in one of the most fertile and desirable portions of that State, there JOE SMITH and his deluded followers took up their abode, and a second time commenced erecting their Zion. Here they increased for a season with almost unexampled rapidity, and as their strength increased, the designs of their Prophet became more and more apparent. Emboldened by success, depredations were committed by them, through the injunctions of their Prophet, upon the liberty, the property, and the lives of many of the citizens of Missouri. There, as the sequel will disclose, is the case in our own state—they were so fortified as to be beyond the reach of the law. And the only alternative on the part of the citizens was submission or extermination. The history of the country shows that the latter alternative was resorted to, and that under the authority of then Governor of Missouri, the Mormons were compelled to flee that State and seek a refuge in some other land. All the circumstances surrounding the expulsion of the Mormons from Missouri, and the reasons offered in justification of their course, has by the Legislature of that State, been long since spread before the public in the shape of a report, its repetition here would consequently be alike uninteresting and superfluous. It may not, however, be improper to mention that the PROPHET was subsequently indicted in that State for the crimes of theft, arson, murder and treason. And that although requisition upon requisition was made by the Executive of Missouri upon the Executive of Illinois for the delivery of JOE SMITH for trial, by the aid of his political as well as monied influence, he was always successful in escaping, and evading the ends of justice.

—SOURCE: GEO. T. M. DAVIS, AN AUTHENTIC ACCOUNT OF THE MASSACRE OF JOSEPH SMITH, THE MORMON PROPHET, AND HYRUM SMITH, HIS BROTHER, TOGETHER WITH A BRIEF HISTORY OF THE RISE AND PROGRESS OF MORMONISM (ST. LOUIS: CHAMBERS AND KNAPP, 1844).

men while the Indians raced in to exterminate the women and children. The Mountain Meadows Massacre of 120 innocents was a horrid stain on Mormon history, but Young made it worse, learning the truth but hiding it from federal authorities. Eventually, after much stonewalling by Young, the federal government tried and convicted Lee, but none of the other ringleaders or Young, for obstruction of justice.

As for the U.S. troops and the "Utah War," it failed to materialize. Young ordered the evacuation of Salt Lake City and a scorched earth policy to greet the advancing forces, but at the same time he explored negotiations with federal authorities. In 1858 an agreement was reached, and federal forces soon left the territory. Nor did Uncle Sam press the case against polygamy, which was outlawed by the Morrill Act of 1862. Still, plenty of grounds for conflict existed between the Mormons and the federal government.

During the Civil War, President Abraham Lincoln, needing to focus military energies elsewhere, told Brigham Young he would "plow around him" and not interfere with Mormon activities there. But after the war, in the 1870s, a new offensive was launched on the practice of polygamy with an 1879 Supreme Court decision that upheld the constitutionality of the antipolygamy law. Congress expelled George Cannon, a Mormon polygamist in 1882, and the federal government began to increase the number of arrests of polygamists under the 1882 Edmunds Law. The conflict reached a crisis with the Edmunds-Tucker Act in 1887, which disincorporated the LDS church, threatening to seize all LDS church property. LDS leader John Taylor offered a compromise to Congress by making polygamy a misdemeanor in exchange for statehood for Utah. Taylor's death, and the ascension of Wilford Woodruff, did not change the Mormon-federal relations. Quite the contrary, U.S. officials began to refuse naturalization for LDS immigrants on the grounds of their belief in polygamy. There was even a movement to disenfranchise all Mormon voters.

In 1890 Woodruff announced he had had a revelation, and he delivered an edict to all church members, urging them to comply with the laws against polygamy. Tensions eased and Utah was admitted to the Union in 1896.

In the 20th century the Mormon church grew rapidly and expanded. Once polygamy was brushed aside by all but a few holdouts in remote parts of the West (most of whom are known to church authorities, but tolerated), the Mormons developed an image as family-conscious, wholesome, and patriotic. The church's famous Mormon Tabernacle Choir began weekly broadcasts on national radio in 1929, and Brigham Young University gained a reputation as a legitimate place of higher education. Important Mormons, such as Marriner S. *Eccles [V]* and George Romney, held high political positions, while entertainers such as Donny and Marie *Osmond* gained national television audiences.

By mid-century, though, in the wake of the Civil Rights movement, new criticisms arose about the LDS practice of denying the status of the priesthood to African Americans. In June 1978 Church President Spencer Kimball announced that he had a revelation that the priesthood was to be made available to all worthy male members without regard to color or race. The church's position on African Americans has been ironic considering that the Mormons have been one of the leading churches in evangelizing Hawaii and the South Seas, particularly American Samoa. Nevertheless, as of 2002, the perception remains that the LDS is predominantly a "white church."

A second LDS church exists, called the Latter-day Saints, Reorganized. This church came from a succession crisis following Joseph Smith's death, which created "congregational" churches that did not join Young and the other Mormons in Utah. Primarily, these Mormons followed James Strang, one of Smith's close advisers who claimed a special appointment by Smith. Nevertheless, contention set in until 1852, when leaders of several congregations simultaneously had revelations saying that no one other than a Smith son should lead the church. In 1853 at Zarahemla, Wisconsin, the

The Mormon Tabernacle in Salt Lake City, Utah. *Bradley J. Birzer*

LDS Church, Reorganized, was established, but when no descendent of Smith stepped forward to assume leadership, it fell to Jason Briggs of the Wisconsin congregations. Eventually, however, Joseph Smith III announced that he would lead the church, which, unlike the Utah Mormons, rejected polygamy. A number of other differences with the Utah Mormons arose, though. In 1974 the president of the LDS Church in Utah and the Reorganized Mormons exchanged historical documents, leading to a warming of relations between the two churches.

The Reorganized Church continued to liberalize, ordaining women in 1985. Based in Independence, Missouri, the RLDS also avoided the secret and mysterious temple ceremonies of the Utah Mormons. In 1993 the RLDS consecrated its temple in Independence.

Lee, Jason (June 28, 1803–March 12, 1845)

Jason Lee was born in Stanstead, Quebec (later Vermont). At age 23 Lee experienced his call to Christ and began religious training in the Methodist Church. In 1833 the Methodist Episcopal Church ordained him and assigned him to go on a mission to the Flathead Indians. En route he decided instead to go to the Willamette Valley in Oregon, becoming the first missionary to bring Christianity to the Chinook Indians. A dedicated evangelist, Lee spread the faith throughout the region. In 1837 the church sent Elijah White to Oregon, allowing Lee to travel to Washington for fundraising. When he returned to Oregon he encountered little success converting the Indians and soon concentrated more on improving their material well being. In the process Lee played a key role in obtaining Oregon territorial status. The deemphasis of evangelization and immersion in territorial politics led to Lee's removal in 1843. Although the church exonerated him, he never regained his Oregon position.

Lewis and Clark Expedition

After American independence, Thomas *Jefferson* had been pondering an exploration of the western territories, particularly up the *Missouri River [I]*. Always concerned with the advance of science, Jefferson also well knew the tales of the "Northwest Passage"—the water route across North

America—and wanted to know if there was any merit to that concept. In 1803 Jefferson asked Congress for $2,500 to send an expedition to explore the Missouri River to its source in the Rocky Mountains, then on to the Pacific Ocean. He pointed to the value of the fur trade in that region and the necessity for scientific information, but at the time, the United States did not own the land. Louisiana was the property of France, having recently been ceded back by Spain. The area of the Pacific Northwest was claimed by several powers, including Russia, England, Spain, and the United States. By April the government completed the *Louisiana Purchase [II]* for $15 million, thus legitimating the expedition as a survey of American land.

Jefferson selected Captain Meriwether Lewis of the U.S. Army, and Lewis requested that his friend, William Clark, who had resigned his commission in 1796, be recalled to active duty as an officer. Clark, commissioned a lieutenant, was nevertheless viewed as Lewis's equal. On July 5, 1803, the expedition headed west, taking the Ohio River to Louisville, then ascending the *Mississippi River [I]* to a location opposite the Missouri River called Camp Wood. After several months of preparation, intelligence gathering, and training, Lewis and Clark set out with 27 soldiers, an interpreter, Clark's black slave, York, and a handful of other men who were slated to return with the records of the first season's work. Called the "Corps of Discovery," the expedition departed on May 14, 1804, moving up the Missouri in a keelboat and a pair of canoes. After four months, the party reached North Dakota at the mouth of the Knife River, where the troops erected Fort Mandan and sat out the winter.

Lewis and Clark treated times such as those, when they were not on the march, as opportunities to gather intelligence from Indians and to work on their scientific observations and maps. The party again set out in April 1805, having gained Toussaint Charbonneau, an interpreter, and his Indian wife, *Sacagawea* (or "Sacajawea"). By August they could no longer navigate the Missouri, at which point they began to climb the Rocky Mountains. Sacagawea, a *Shoshone*, provided assistance in obtaining horses, facilitating their crossing of the Continental Divide. They moved along the Salmon River, then into Montana near modern-day Missoula, crossing the Bitterroot Mountain Range over the Lolo Trail. At that point, they again took to their canoes and sailed down the Clearwater, Snake, and Columbia Rivers, reaching the Pacific on November 18, 1805. Erecting Fort Clatsop, the party again gathered supplies and worked on maps.

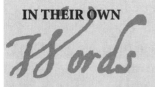
Lewis and Clark's Journals

In August 1805 Meriwether Lewis and William Clark's party crossed the Great Divide. They met Shoshone Indians, who invited Lewis and Clark into a lodge for a meal. Lewis then inquired of the chief named Cameahwait for details of the geography of the country.

This he undertook very cheerfully, by delienating [sic] the rivers on the ground. but I soon found that this information fell far short of my expectation or wishes. He drew the river on which we now are [i.e., Lemhi] to which he placed two branches just above us, which he shewed me from the openings of the mountains were in view; he next made it discharge itself into a large river which flowed from the S.W. about ten miles below us, then continued this joint stream in the same direction of this valley . . . he placed a number of heaps of sand on each side which he informed me represented the vast mountains of rock eternally covered with snow through which the river passed. . . . the chief further informed me that the had understood from the persed nosed [i.e., Nez Perce] Indians who inhabit this river below the rocky mountains that it ran a great way toward the seting [sic] sun and finally lost itself in a great lake of water which was illy tasted, and where the white men lived. . . .

I thanked him for his information and gave him a knife with which he appeared to be much gratifyed [sic] from this narative [sic] I was convinced that the streams of which he had spoken as runing [sic] through the plains and that on which his relations lived were southern branches of the Columbia, heading with the rivers Apostles and Collorado [sic], and that the rout he had pointed out was to the Vermillion Sea or the gulph [sic] of California. . . . [I then asked] if he could inform me of any except that of the barren plain which he said joined the mountain on that side and through which it was impossible for us to pass at this season. . . . I now asked Cameahwait by what rout the Pierced nosed indians, who he informed me had inhabited this river below the moutains [sic], came over to the Missouri; this he informed me was to the north, but added that the road was a very bad one . . . however knowing that Indians had passed, and di [sic] pass, at this [sic] season on that side of this river . . . my route was instantly settled in my own mind. . . . I feld [sic] perfectly satisfyed [sic] that if the Indians could pass these mountains with their women and Children, that we cold [sic] also pass them . . . .

—Source: Reuben Gold Thwaites, ed., *Original Journals of the Lewis and Clark Expedition, 1804–1806* (New York: Antiquarian Press, 1959), 2:380–382.

In March 1806 Lewis and Clark headed for home, along the same route they had covered. But after reaching Lolo Creek, the party split, with Lewis taking nine men to explore northern Montana, while Clark went into the Yellowstone River area, where eventually Lewis caught up with him. There, they convinced a local chief to accompany the party back to Washington. On September 23, 1806, Lewis and Clark reached St. Louis, surprising many who had concluded they were dead. Having covered more than 8,000 miles and mapping much of the Great Plains area—with the extraordinary loss of only one soldier—Lewis and Clark had effectively opened the West for America.

Mangas Coloradas (1795–1863)

Mangas Coloradas was an Indian born in New Mexico who engaged in raids against Mexican settlers from New Mexico to the Sierra Madre Mountains in the 1840s. When Americans entered the region in 1846 under General Stephen Watts *Kearny*, Mangas Coloradas sought an alliance. After a respite of several years, he resumed raiding in New Mexico in the 1850s.

When the *Civil War [IV]* took troops from Arizona in 1861, *Cochise [IV]*, Mangas Coloradas, and others accelerated their attacks on whites. Forces under Captain Thomas Roberts routed the natives and wounded Mangas Coloradas. In 1863 troopers captured Mangas Coloradas and held him at Fort McLane, New Mexico, where he died, reportedly trying to escape. However, according to one account, he was murdered in the process of being tortured.

Manifest Destiny

A term used to describe the attitudes of Americans in the 1830s and 1840s, the expression "Manifest Destiny" has been attributed to John L. O'Sullivan in the July 1845 issue of the *Democratic Review,* who said that the United States should annex Texas to fulfill "our manifest destiny to overspread the continent. . . . " Others, though, as early as Benjamin Franklin, expressed such opinions in a variety of contexts. This ill-defined concept included notions that the United States should rule the entire continent, including Canada and Mexico, that God or Providence had determined in advance that this would be the case, and that it was America's mission to spread its democracy and prosperity to the Western Hemisphere.

Manifest Destiny undergirded the Oregon boundary fight ("54°40' or fight") and, of course, Texas. President James K. Polk accepted the principles of Manifest Destiny when he engaged in a war with Mexico, as did President William McKinley in the Spanish-American War. Yet other than the presumption that democracy, association with the United States, and free markets would generally benefit anyone whose territory was taken through Manifest Destiny expansions, there were few unifying details common to the territorial acquisitions of the 1800s. For example, Cuba, taken in the Spanish-American War, was handed its independence quickly due to concerns over a large influx of Hispanic immigrants. There is some evidence that the United States never attempted to incorporate Mexico, even as U.S. troops guarded the "Halls of Montezuma," for similar reasons.

Nor are there clear economic principles involved in Manifest Destiny. In some cases expansion brought in new markets, but in others, it brought in low-paid labor. The acquisition of Hawaii was clearly influenced by the sea power concepts of Alfred Thayer Mahan who maintained that the United States needed coaling stations for continued growth and prosperity.

In the 19th century it is clear that the Oregon boundary, the acquisition of Texas, Florida, California and the Mexican Cession territories, Hawaii, Cuba, Alaska, and the Philippines all fell under the rubric of Manifest Destiny. When it came to international affairs, Manifest Destiny was applied by the Monroe Doctrine, which, if it did not flatly advocate American expansion, at least prohibited powerful competitors from entering the hemisphere. The Spanish-American War was the last invocation of Manifest Destiny. Running an empire was harder than some had thought, and Americans were not comfortable with groups coming into full citizenship outside the territorial system established in the 1780s. World War I dealt a death blow to the concept with Woodrow Wilson's internationalist League of Nations.

Resistance to concepts of Manifest Destiny came from a wide array of groups. Anti-war pacifists, such as Ralph Waldo *Emerson* and Henry David Thoreau, questioned America's involvement in the *Mexican War*. Nativists, concerned about the influx of Hispanics, blacks, and Asians, opposed American participation in the Spanish-American War and the subsequent Filipino insurrections. Union leaders, such as Samuel Gompers, feared that new territories opened the door for cheap labor that would compete with whites. Cynical editorialists asserted that the United States' actions made it no better than the Europeans.

Marcy, Randolph (April 9, 1812–November 22, 1887)

Born in Massachusetts, Marcy attended West Point. Following his graduation in 1832 (ranked 29th in his class), Marcy spent his life as a career officer. During his long career, Marcy led five significant expeditions into the West, the most famous being his 1852 trip along the Red River in the American Southwest. He mapped much of what is now southern Oklahoma and northern Texas and discovered several new species of mammals as well as enormous prairie-dog towns. Marcy participated in the *Mexican War*, the "Mormon War of 1857," and fought on the Union side during the American Civil War. His son-in-law was Major General George McClellan, and Marcy served as his chief of staff while McClellan was in charge of the Army of the Potomac. Marcy also wrote the famous 1859 guide to the Overland Trails, *The Prairie Traveler*. During the last decades of his life, Marcy wrote a semiregular column for *Harper's Weekly*, as well as publishing several accounts of his life and adventures in the West, including *Thirty Years of Army Life on the Border* (1866) and *Border Reminiscences* (1872). He retired in 1881 with the rank of brigadier general.

McKenney, Thomas Loraine (March 21, 1785–February 20, 1859)

Thomas McKenney conceived the U.S. government's "factory" system for fur trading with the Indians designed to turn Indians to the "white man's ways." Congress gave McKenney enormous sums to set up trading posts, but these posts failed to provide quality goods at reasonable prices and could not compete with the private fur business of John Jacob *Astor*. Named the superintendent of Indian trade in 1816, a frustrated McKenney continued to appeal to Congress for more money until the factory system was abolished in 1822. In 1824, in return for his support for the new Democratic Party, he was appointed head of the Office of Indian Affairs, until 1830, when President Andrew Jackson fired him. McKenney's efforts to turn Indians into farmers failed, and this failure was used to justify the

Cherokee Removal. He later wrote parts of the *History of the Indian Tribes of North America*.

Mexican War

Provoked by a boundary dispute over the newly annexed Republic of Texas, the Mexican War lasted from May 13, 1846 to February 2, 1848. Since the *Texas Revolution* Mexico had looked suspiciously at American intentions with regard to Mexico's former colony and had refused to recognize the *Rio Grande [I]* as the boundary between the two nations. President James K. Polk, who assumed the presidency in 1845, had already anticipated trouble and dispatched troops under General Zachary Taylor from Louisiana to the Nueces River, which Mexico claimed as its northernmost boundary. In March of that year the House and Senate adopted a joint resolution annexing Texas, but hoping to forestall trouble, the newly inaugurated Polk dispatched James Slidell to Mexico to offer $30 million for a recognition of the Rio Grande boundary and for the territories of New Mexico and California. Mexico had no intention of giving up such rich territory, and the mission failed.

Taylor then crossed into the disputed territory just north of the Rio Grande, where on April 25, 1846, Mexican General Mariano Arista's troops attacked U.S. soldiers. Many suspected Polk had provoked the attack, and among those who were skeptical of the location of the battle was Illinois Congressman Abraham Lincoln, who demanded in the "Spot Resolutions" to know the exact spot blood was shed. Congress, nevertheless, declared war, called for volunteers, and voted funds to invade Mexico. During the course of the war, some 90,000 troops were called up, and most of the famous names in the American Civil War experienced battlefield training in this conflict. Among those who saw action were Robert E. Lee, Ulysses S. Grant, Winfield Hancock, and Thomas "Stonewall" Jackson. Many Europeans predicted the war would be over quickly—with Mexican armies marching into Washington!

U.S. strategy involved a three-pronged assault: one force would head directly south through Monterrey for Mexico City; a second force would cut across the southwest to California; and a naval blockade would seal off the seaports and, if necessary, land troops on the coast. Taylor's men were already on the move, fighting Mexican forces at Palo Alto (May 8) and

Resaca de la Palma (May 9), both American victories. Early in the conflict, it became apparent that while Mexico enjoyed a manpower advantage, American artillery was superior. In September 1846 U.S. forces captured Monterrey, whereupon Taylor announced an armistice. Polk sharply rebuked him, but an attack by General Antonio López de *Santa Anna* (conqueror of the Alamo and the defeated general at the *Battle of San Jacinto*) made the truce moot.

Santa Anna's attack (February 23, 1847) with 15,000 men at the Battle of Buena Vista nearly proved successful, but Taylor, who had been in the rear inspecting defenses, arrived with fresh troops and more artillery to seal the victory. Ironically, Taylor, learning he was to be replaced immediately thereafter by General Winfield Scott, asked to be relieved. He had fought four battles against numerically superior troops, won them all, and controlled three Mexican states.

The second "prong," under Brigadier General Stephen Watts *Kearny*, left Kansas in June 1846 for New Mexico with more than 1,500 men. He found no opposition in *Santa Fe [I]* and, after establishing a government, instructed Colonel Alexander Doniphan to enter Chihuahua and Captain Philip Cooke to find a wagon path to California. Kearny headed for Los Angeles, where he and Commodore Robert Stockton, along with the "Bear Flag" contingent of John C. *Fremont*, captured Los Angeles on January 10, 1847, and effectively wrested California from Mexico. Meanwhile, Doniphan's troops headed south and captured El Paso, then Chihuahua City, and then moved on to the Gulf Coast. Cooke took another force and

In September 1847 American forces stormed "the Halls of Montezuma" to capture Chapultepec in Mexico City, essentially ending the Mexican War. *National Archives*

swung southwest through *Tucson [I]*, then crossed Arizona to link up with Kearny.

The final phase of the war ensued when Scott's 12,000-man invasion force arrived took Vera Cruz (March 27, 1847) as a staging ground to invade Mexico City. By that time Doniphan's army pressured the Mexicans from the north, and Scott's forces swung south of the city to surround Santa Anna, taking Contreras and Churubusco. As Taylor had, Scott then paused, sending another emissary to negotiate a peace. Nicholas Trist failed as Slidell before him had, and on September 14, 1847, at the Battle of

---

IN THEIR OWN *Words*

A Journal of Colonel Doniphan's Santa Fe Expedition

Private Jacob Robinson's journal of the 1846 expedition to Santa Fe under the command of Colonel Alexander Doniphan traced the command's departure from Fort Leavenworth to Santa Fe, then back to New Orleans. The year-long trip covered more than 1,000 miles and conquered Chihuahua and New Mexico. Here, Robinson describes the victorious entry into Santa Fe.

After a march of 35 miles, without grass for our horses, we at length came in sight of Santa Fe. The city at a little distance more resembles a parcel of brick yards than anything else; but in passing through we found it of considerable extent. The houses are all built of adobes. The city is full of corn and wheat fields; the corn is now fit to roast, and the wheat not quite ready to harvest. The people supply themselves with water from three beautiful streams that run through the town, having their sources in a lake to the north-west. With them they also irrigate their cornfields. We entered the city just as the sun was sinking behind the distant mountain; and as its last rays gilded the hill top, the flag of our country triumphantly waved over the battlements of the holy city; minute guns fired a national salute, and the long shout of the troops spoke the universal joy that was felt at the good fortune that has attended us.

—SOURCE: JACOB S. ROBINSON, *A JOURNAL OF THE SANTA FE EXPEDITION UNDER COLONEL DONIPHAN* (1848; REPRINT, NEW YORK: DA CAPO PRESS, 1972), 24–26.

Chapultepec, Scotts' forces captured Mexico City. The U.S. marines stood guard in the "halls of Montezuma."

Outside of Mexico City, at the town of Guadalupe Hidalgo, Trist and Mexican officials concluded an agreement, the *Treaty of Guadalupe Hidalgo*, on February 2, 1848, that ended the war. Mexico ceded the Southwest, including New Mexico, Arizona, Colorado, Wyoming, Nevada, California, and parts of Utah and Oregon to the United States. American forces, having lost 1,721 troops killed and many thousands more dead of disease, withdrew in July 1848. The war added a vast new territory to the United States, as well as new populations of Mexican Americans, and finalized the admission of Texas, with slavery, as a state in the Union. The status of slavery in these new territories, raised with the Wilmot Proviso, was not immediately settled, but festered until the Compromise of 1850 temporarily addressed it.

Missouri Compromise

In 1819 applications for statehood came before Congress from the territories of Missouri and Maine. At the time, there were 22 states in the Union—11 free and 11 slave. Until that time, political balance had been maintained by alternating admission of free and slave territories as states. Gradually, however, the larger population of the North led to a growing disparity in Congress against the South, even using the "three-fifths" rule, whereby three out of every five slaves would count toward representation in the U. S. House of Representatives. Since Missouri Territory was large, it opened the possibility of slavery throughout modern-day Iowa, Nebraska, Oklahoma, Kansas, Montana, and parts of the Dakotas. In short, it would certainly threaten to overwhelm the balance in the Senate and also, eventually, the House, in favor of the slave states.

A number of amendments were introduced to the application of Missouri for statehood prohibiting slavery in the new state, all of which were defeated. Finally, a compromise was reached with an amendment by Jesse B. Thomas of Illinois, in which both Missouri and Maine would be admitted, with no restriction on slavery in Missouri, but slavery prohibited north of the 36°30' line in all the remaining Louisiana Purchase territories. For territories below the line, however, the state legislatures could choose to have slavery or not.

Henry *Clay* had helped construct the compromise behind the scenes after Missouri submitted a state constitution with a clause excluding free blacks and mulattos from the state. Clay's "Second Missouri Compromise" bill required the state of Missouri to guarantee that the rights and privileges of American citizens would not be abridged; it was agreed to in March 1821. The final bill was thought to have provided a remedy for sectional strife, and Clay thought it would prevent an eventual war over slavery. Problems arose quickly, however. Southerners could count, and they realized that there was more territory above the line than below and that the option of choosing meant that even the territories below were not assured of admitting slavery if they became states. Many politicians, far from seeing a solution to the slavery issue, viewed the Missouri Compromise as a disaster. The aging Thomas Jefferson called it the "death knell of the Union," and said that news of the bill's passage awoke him like a "firebell in the night." Martin Van Buren and Georgian William Crawford immediately laid plans to overcome the sectional bias that they thought would inevitably result in a civil war. Their concept was to construct a new political party based on the "spoils system" and patronage, which would use jobs as a reward to enforce party discipline over the slavery issue. Specifically, Van Buren and Crawford wanted no congressional discussion of slavery, while procedurally they began to build a coalition between Northerners and Southerners through the new Democratic Party. Van Buren thought a war could be prevented if this national party could hold the presidency and

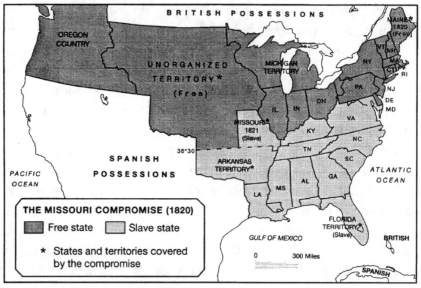

The Missouri Compromise. *Ron Acklin, University of Dayton Print and Design*

elect "Northern men of Southern principles" or westerners. This became the strategy for the newly formed "Jacksonian Democratic Party" (or merely "Jacksonians" or "Democrats") for the next 40 years.

International affairs soon superseded the Compromise. First, the annexation of Texas added a large slave-holding state to the Union. Then, the *Mexican War* added California, which lay both above and below the 36°30' line. This forced Clay to come up with yet another great compromise, the Compromise of 1850, which satisfied no one. Finally, the Nebraska Territory was organized by Senator Stephen A. *Douglas* of Illinois around an entirely different concept, "*popular sovereignty*," in which the people of a territory would decide whether or not to admit slavery. None of these half-measures worked, but in the meantime, Northern population increases and the growing dominance of the North in Congress, combined with the appearance of the antislave Republican Party, made it clear that sooner or later slavery would face national legislation. The final nail in the coffin of the Missouri Compromise was the *Dred Scott decision* of 1857, in which the United States Supreme Court declared the Compromise null and void, and asserted that Congress had no constitutional authority to act on slavery in the territories—only a state legislature could determine the status of slavery.

mountain men

A term given to the hunters and fur trappers who plied their trade in the western mountains during the period 1810 to 1850, mountain men lived for long periods in the territory in which they hunted and trapped. Dressed in their recognizable furs and skins, mountain men such as Jedediah *Smith*, William Sublette, and William *Ashley* were skilled managers as well as woodsmen. Sublette and Ashley built large trapping enterprises, but the image persists that these were illiterate hunters in fringe rather than early entrepreneurs.

mustangs

Wild horse herds covered North America for long periods, disappeared, then were reintroduced by *Columbus [I]* in 1493 and *Cortés [I]* in 1519.

Spanish colonists, settling in northern Mexico, used riders to tend large cattle herds that grazed freely on the plains. Domestication of *horses [I]* quickly spread through the Rockies, then into Montana, and as far north as the Great Lakes by 1730.

As both whites and Indians raised horse herds, unclaimed, released, or escaped animals soon bred and their numbers grew. Gradually, all wild horses were referred to as "mustangs," although this term technically meant only wild horses of Spanish blood. Both Indians and whites soon engaged in the mustang trade. In the 20th century, as public interest in the animals grew, herd numbers increased. Federal lands were set aside for mustangs, which, as of a 1982 estimate, totaled nearly 45,000 in the United States.

National Road

Interest in a "national road" dated to the 1740s, and reflected concern for military support of western areas and access to land. In 1802 Albert Gallatin developed a plan to fund a national road, and state enabling acts contained further financing provisions. In 1806 Thomas *Jefferson* officially established the national highway to run from Cumberland, Maryland, to the *Mississippi River [I]*. Construction started in 1811, reaching Wheeling, West Virginia, by 1818. The road consisted of layers of graded stone, a process called "madacamization." In the 1830s it terminated in Vandalia, Illinois, short of its destination due to lack of funds.

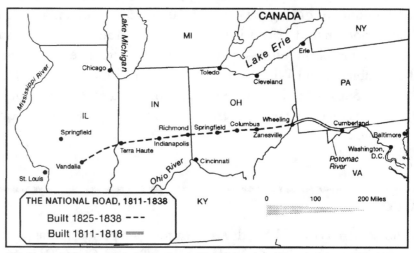

The National Road, 1811–1838. *Ron Acklin, University of Dayton Print and Design*

Oregon Trail

The longest-used of the western trails, the Oregon Trail covered about 2,000 miles from Independence, Missouri, to the mouth of the Willamette Valley near the mission established by Jason *Lee*. Explored by the Wilkes Expedition in 1841, then in 1843 by John C. *Fremont*, who provided an accurate map, the path started to be known as the Oregon Trail as early as the 1840s. The trail traveled westward along the Platte River, through the South Pass, then turned northwest to the Columbia River.

Over time, several forts had been established that provided resupply and resting stations along the way. Some 660 miles from their departure, parties reached Fort Laramie, then traveled along the North Platte to the Wyoming area to the gateway to Oregon, the South Pass. From there, parties would cross the Green River Valley to Fort Bridger, roughly 1,070 miles from their point of origin, before turning into Idaho and Fort Hall on the Snake River, then to Fort Boise. Crossing the Blue Mountains to the Columbia River, pioneers could follow that river to the mouth of the Willamette River. At that point they turned south into the Willamette Valley and their general destination.

One of the most important sites on the Oregon Trail, Independence Rock. Custom declared that all travelers on the trail must reach this rock by Independence Day, or they would fail to make it to Oregon before the first snowfall. *Bradley J. Birzer*

Many of the early immigrants across the Oregon Trail were Methodists under Jason Lee who sought to establish missions in the region. Elijah *White* guided one such group in 1842, then in 1843 led the "Great Migration" of nearly 1,000 settlers. Two years later another 3,000 arrived, followed by 4,000 to 5,000 in 1847. Several pioneers left well-known journals or records of their travels, including Narcissa Whitman of the *Whitman mission* and Francis *Parkman*.

Osage Indians

A Siouan-speaking people, the Osages originated in Virginia and migrated west. French explorers discovered them in Missouri in the 1670s. Throughout the colonial period of frontier history, the Osages served as important fur trappers, middlemen, and soldiers for various imperial rivalries—especially the French and Spanish. Though their culture resembled the culture of many eastern woodlands tribes, the Osage also adopted characteristics, especially the buffalo hunt, of the Great Plains tribes. In the American *Civil War [IV]* the Osages fought for the Union. After the war the United States removed the Osages to northeastern Oklahoma, where they soon discovered immense oil supplies. Today, there are roughly 5,000 Osages.

Major wagon trails in the West. *Ron Acklin, University of Dayton Print and Design*

Panic of 1837

In 1837 the United States experienced the worst panic in its brief history. Bankruptcies were numerous, hundreds of banks defaulted in paying gold or silver for paper money, and land values plummeted. Because of the difficult experience, many state legislatures passed laws banning banks altogether, or severely limiting their activities.

Many scholars long thought that the western lands played an important role in the Panic of 1837. In fact, like the previous panic (or depression) of 1819, money issues shaped the economic downturn that lasted from 1837 to 1842. For many years scholars saw the panic as developing out of the policies of President Andrew *Jackson*. In his "war" with the Bank of United States (BUS), Jackson withdrew the government's assets from the BUS in 1833. Without the BUS, private-owned, state-chartered commercial banks were free to issue notes without restraint, according to the theory, and the ensuing inflation was brought to a screeching halt by the Specie Circular, which decreed that all western land purchases had to be paid for with specie, which was gold or silver coin. The collapse of western land sales, along with the monetary disruptions made still worse because of the redistribution of the government surplus, was seen as causing the worst depression in 19th-century American history.

More recent scholarship has shown that Jackson's actions had little to do with the panic. When Mexican silver mines dried up in the late 1820s and early 1830s, less silver flowed into the United States. This had the effect of eroding trade between the United States and China, because Americans merchants used silver to purchase tea and porcelain from China. In the process, this forced the British to raise their interest rates due to the reduced China trade. Higher interest rates, not presidential policies, sent the economy into a tailspin. The panic had an added impact on the West in that several state legislatures prohibited banking altogether. As a result, many states did not again have banking services until years later.

Panic of 1857

In the fall of 1857 New York banks experienced sharp runs. Though the downturn is often viewed as tied to western grain production, which indeed played a part, more recent evidence has traced the initial collapse to uncertainty associated with the Supreme Court ruling in the *Dred Scott* case, which opened up western territories to slavery. Significantly, the panic started when the stocks of railroads running east and west began to slide, while those running north and south were not affected at all. Once the railroad bonds collapsed, eroding bank assets, the banks began to weaken.

Parker, Cynthia Ann (1827—ca. 1870)

Little is known about Cynthia Ann Parker, the mother of Comanche leader Quanah Parker, because her life was spent in captivity and because her story was used by both pro- and anti-Indian writers to stir support for their positions. She was born in Illinois in 1827, then moved with her family to east Texas in 1832. Four years later, Indians attacked Fort Parker, where she and her family lived, and killed Cynthia's father, Silas. They abducted all the children, including Cynthia. Over time, efforts to rescue Parker faded, and she adopted the Comanche culture as her own. One article stated that she had married a chief and that she rebuffed attempts to bring her back to "white" society.

In 1860 *Texas Rangers* attacked a Comanche village and recaptured Parker and her daughter, Topsannah, then sent her back to live with her white family, who proceeded to limit her contacts with the Comanches. It is even disputed when Cynthia Parker died, with the dates off as much as four or five years. Her son, Quanah Parker, became a Comanche leader and managed to attain a lasting peace between the Indians and the whites in Oklahoma and Texas.

Parkman, Francis (September 16, 1823– November 8, 1893)

Parkman was one of the most successful historians of the 19th century. He suffered from depression, poor physical health, and bad eyesight, but he toured the places he described in his books, whether down the St.

IN THEIR OWN Words

First Person Narrative: Francis Parkman, *The Oregon Trail*

In 1846 Francis Parkman, an inveterate explorer, traveled west to observe the Indians. He moved up the Oregon Trail, observing prairies and mountains, Indians and buffalo. It was his quest for buffalo that led him to write the following passage:

The buffalo now broke into several small bodies, scampering over the hills in different directions, and I lost sight of [my companion]; neither of us knew where the other had gone. . . . the fugitives, indeed, offered no very attractive spectacle, with their shaggy manes and the tattered remnants of their last winter's hair covering their backs in irregular shreds and patches, and flying off in the wind as they ran. At length I urged my horse behind a bull, and after trying in vain, by blows and spurring, to bring him alongside, I fired from this disadvantageous position. At the report Pontiac [Parkman's horse] swerved so much

Lawrence River, or traversing the Oregon Trail. Raised in a Boston Brahmin Unitarian household and educated at Harvard, Parkman was fascinated by Roman Catholicism. He found much to like in it, but he ultimately viewed it as a regressive force in western civilization. His famous seven-volume *France and England in North America* attempted to posit the forces of regression, the French Roman Catholics and their Indian pawns, against the forces of Enlightenment, the English Protestants. Parkman's works helped fundamentally shape America's view of itself as a progressive, enlightened force in the world. Parkman's most famous work as it pertained to the West was *The Oregon Trail* (1849), where he recounted his travels across the Great Plains in 1846. But it was only one of his many historical works on the West, including *The Jesuits in North America* (1867), *La Salle and the Discovery of the Great West* (1869), and *Half-Century of Conflict* (1892).

Pawnee Indians

Excellent farmers, the Pawnee Indians lived along the Republican and Platte rivers in what is now Nebraska during the first three-quarters of the 19th

that I was agin [sic] thrown a little behind the game. The bullet, entering too much in the rear, failed to disable the bull; for a buffalo requires to be shot at particular points, or he will certainly escape. . . .

But in the meantime my ride had been by no means a solitary one. The face of the country was dotted far and wide with countless hundreds of buffalo. They trooped along in files and columns, bulls, cows, and calves, on the green faces of the declivities in front. They scrambled away over the hills to the right and left; and far off, the pale blue swells in the extreme distance were dotted with innumerable specks. Sometimes I surprised shaggy old bulls grazing alone, or sleeping behind the ridges I ascended. They would leap up at my approach, stare stupidly at me through their tangled manes, and then gallop heavily away. . . . Again and again I looked toward the crowded hillsides, and was sure I saw horsemen; and riding near, with a mixture of hope and dread, for Indians were abroad, I found them transformed into a group of buffalo. There was nothing in human form amid all this vast congregation of brute forms.

—SOURCE: FRANCIS PARKMAN, *THE OREGON TRAIL: SKETCHES OF PRAIRIE AND ROCKY-MOUNTAIN LIFE* (1885; REPRINT, NEW YORK: MODERN LIBRARY, 1949), 71–74.

century. They grew 8 types of beans, 10 types of corn, and 7 types of squash. Like other Great Plains tribes, the Pawnees also hunted buffalo. The hunt was an important religious ceremony for the tribe, and it offered the hunt to Tirawa, a god who ordered all things. Pawnees carefully studied the stars, believing they offered a patterning of life and a guide to the natural seasons.

The imperialistic Lakotas (see *Sioux*) and disease offered the greatest threats to the Pawnees in the 19th century. Warfare between the Lakota and the Pawnees devastated the latter over 40 years. To make matters worse, a disease epidemic in 1839 killed nearly half of Pawnees. When the Lakota launched a major assault against them in 1873, the Pawnees requested protection from the United States and moved voluntarily to a reservation in the Indian Territory.

Generally, the United States and the Pawnees were allies, with the Pawnees often serving as scouts and warriors for the United States during the Indian Wars of the 19th century.

Pike, Zebulon Montgomery (January 5, 1779– April 27, 1813)

Born in Trenton, New Jersey, Zebulon Montgomery Pike was a career soldier, enlisting at age 15 and serving with General "Mad" Anthony Wayne. Commissioned a lieutenant in 1799, Pike was instructed by General James Wilkinson to explore the upper *Mississippi River [I]* from 1805 to 1806. Leaving from St. Louis, aboard a keelboat, Pike's party was to not only gather scientific data, but to search out Indian tribes that had not met with Wilkinson and encourage them to do so. After reaching Little Falls, Minnesota, and meeting with the *Sioux* at modern-day St. Paul-Minneapolis, he failed to locate the source of the Mississippi at Lake Itasca, which lay along a different branch of the river.

Commissioned a captain upon his return, Pike received new orders from Wilkinson to explore westward into Nebraska and Colorado along the Republican River. Again, the purposes of his mission were both diplomatic and scientific. The expedition explored the Arkansas River, eventually observing a tall peak that the men failed to scale, but which still bears the name Pike's Peak. His party then ventured toward the *Rio Grande [I]*, where it encountered Spanish troops who took him into custody.

The Spaniards brought Pike's party to *Santa Fe [I]*, New Mexico, then on to Chihuahua, before finally releasing him at Natchitoches, Louisiana, in June 1807. As a result of his travels, Pike published *An Account of Expeditions to the Sources of the Mississippi and through the Western Parts of Louisiana* in 1810. However, immediately upon his return, he was suspected of being an accomplice in the Burr conspiracy, which he was not.

In the *War of 1812*, by then a brigadier general, Pike died in the attempt to capture Toronto when a powder magazine exploded.

placer (gold) mining

An early form of gold mining dating from the late 1700s in the Appalachian region was placer mining. In its simplest form, placer mining involved panning. A prospector filled a two- to three-inch pan with earth from ground where he expected to find gold, then submerged the pan in water, shaking the contents through a sieve until all that remained were minerals. A visual inspection then confirmed the presence of any gold. A miner picked out and cleaned the gold, then took it to an exchange dealer for sale. Miners had to discern real gold from pyrite, or "fool's gold," which has a brassy yellow color, then ensure that they had mineral rights to it, defined by the General Mining Laws of 1872. At least one discovery of mineralization is required per claim, and since 1958, the U.S. government has accepted geological, geochemical, and geophysical surveys as evidence of such "reasonable prospect of success."

plow

Prior to the late 1700s, farmers used crude wooden plows which easily dulled and which broke the earth only with great effort. In 1797 Charles Newbold patented the first cast-iron plow, and in 1819 Jethro Wood patented an iron plow with interchangeable parts. These metal plows not only cut through ground better but could be resharpened and used again. Improved plows contributed to the rapid surges in agricultural productivity in the West throughout the 19th century.

Pony Express

Until the completion of the *telegraph [IV]* in 1861, communication between the last outposts of "civilization" in Missouri and on the West Coast was difficult. Mail was delivered by packet steamer, which involved shipping mail by a lengthy and tedious route from New York to Panama, across Panama by land, then on another vessel to San Francisco. Overland routes pitted the Central Overland California and Pike's Peak Express Company against the Overland Mail Company, both of which relied on stagecoaches to carry mail. This situation presented a classic opportunity for an entrepreneur to meet a critical need.

In January 1860 William Russell created the Pony Express to deliver mail more rapidly. This 1,966-mile mail route from St. Joseph, Missouri, to Sacramento, California used individual riders to carry light mail. It was based on tales of Mongol riders in China. The first rider, John Frye, left St. Joseph on April 3, 1860, while Billy Hamilton left from Sacramento. Riders were expected to make 100 miles before resting, changing horses every 10 to 15 miles. Changing horses occurred on the gallop at 1 of the 165 stations placed along the route, with horses making about 10 miles per hour. Special mailbags, called "mochilas," were developed to allow the riders to swing from one saddle to another in a fluid motion, transferring the mail without unbuckling the saddles. Riders often only carried a pistol for protection, seeking to further reduce weight on the horse. Indeed, weight restrictions were that riders not exceed 120 pounds, and with 25 pounds of supplies and 20 pounds of mail, the total weight allowed was 165 pounds.

Riders departed once a week until June 1860, when the departures increased to twice a week. The fastest delivery, of Lincoln's Inaugural Address, was in 7 days, 17 hours between the completed telegraph lines, but the average delivery took 10 days in summer or up to 16 days in winter. Robert "Pony Bob" Haslam covered the longest route, once riding 370 miles from Friday's Station to Smith Creek (both in Nevada) and back.

Russell drew his riders predominantly from the Mormon communities in Utah, due to their familiarity with the territory and their cordial relations with Ute, *Shoshone*, and Utah Indians. The company also preferred younger boys, who were lighter, and thus less burdensome on the horses. Some carried bugles to alert the station attendants that they were near, so that the fresh horse would be ready. The arrival at Sacramento of the first rider from St. Joseph in 1860 set off celebrations and parades. Many of the 183 men who rode for the Express became western legends, and, as pay rates in the 1800s went, the Pony Express riders were well compensated, receiving $100 per month.

Mail costs were $5 per ounce when the route started but had dropped to $1 per ounce when the Pony Express ended. Although it is difficult to verify, "official" Pony Express legend maintains that only one mail mochila was lost and only one rider killed in the brief history of the business.

When the telegraph was completed in October 1861, the Pony Express came to an end, its role eclipsed by superior technology. By that time, its riders had made 300 runs each way covering a total of 616,000 miles and carrying some 35,000 pieces of mail. Most of the riders, who were instantly unemployed by the telegraph, went on to more lucrative and successful professions. In its brief history the Pony Express left a giant-sized western legend.

"popular sovereignty"

As slavery threatened to disrupt the American political structure in the 1850s, politicians desperately looked for ways to defuse the issue. The *Mexican War* had reopened the slavery issue by adding new territories below the 36°30' invisible line drawn by the *Missouri Compromise*. In the Wilmot Proviso debates of 1846–1847, Lewis Cass used the term "popular sovereignty" to describe a process whereby the people of a territory, not Congress, could decide whether to permit or ban slavery. In the Compromise of 1850, drafted by Henry *Clay* and Stephen *Douglas*, new territories in Utah and New Mexico would be organized on the basis of popular sovereignty, with territorial legislatures given express permission to legislate on slavery.

Douglas proposed to organize the Nebraska Territory in 1854 (with what later became known as the *Kansas-Nebraska Act*). The act allowed slavery into an area previously prohibited by the Missouri Compromise. Douglas included a phrase that permitted states to enter the union "with or without slavery, as their constitution may prescribe at the time of admission." Douglas further argued that the Compromise of 1850 and the principle of popular sovereignty had superseded the old Missouri Compromise. Clearly, the side that gained control of the territorial legislatures would decide the slavery issue in new states, and in Kansas this led to the importation of virtual mercenaries for both the proslave and the abolitionist positions. Immigrants flocked in, with violence erupting and the region becoming known as "Bloody Kansas." Nevertheless, in 1856 the Democratic Party endorsed popular sovereignty again in its national platform. However, that same year the Republican Party appeared, having as its overriding principle the limitation of any further expansion of slavery into the territories, and in the *Dred Scott* case of 1857, the Supreme Court ruled that Congress could not prohibit slavery in a territory, and implied that a territorial legislature could not keep it out—only a state constitutional convention could do so. Douglas, running against Abraham Lincoln for the Illinois U.S. Senate seat the following year, came under sharp attack from his Northern constituents, who said that he endorsed the expansion of slavery into the territories. He developed a position, brought crisply into focus in the Lincoln-Douglas debates, called the "Freeport Doctrine," which held that the people of a territory could keep slavery out by electing officials who would not enforce slavery provisions. In essence, Douglas advocated keeping the law on the books but electing people who would not enforce it! Lincoln skillfully exploited the absurdity of this position, carving Douglas away from his Southern support. Southerners were dismayed at his instructions on how Northerners could evade the law. While Douglas won the 1858 Senate seat, it cost him the national election in 1860 by splitting the Democratic Party. By 1860 popular sovereignty was dead insofar as it related to slavery, doomed by Lincoln's moral arguments that slavery was either right or wrong, and if right, it should be a national policy, and if wrong, eliminated.

Pottawatomie Massacre

Led by John Brown (1800–1859), a group of local militia called the "Pottawatomie Rifles," responding to attacks by proslavery men on the night of May 24, 1856, murdered five proslavery men along the Pottawatomie Creek. Kansans and slaveholders everywhere were outraged at the Pottawatomie Massacre, seeing it as the beginning of a national war against slavery. That year, fighting between proslave and free-soil forces throughout Kansas led newspapers to refer to it as "Bloody Kansas." Brown left Kansas for New England, and staged a failed raid on the Harper's Ferry arsenal in 1859. Brown was tried for treason, found guilty, and hanged in December, but he was never charged with any crimes for his actions in the Pottawatomie Massacre.

preemption and squatter's rights

After 1820 Congress established a policy whereby almost all public lands put up for sale could be acquired for the small price of $1.25 per acre. But numerous settlers had already migrated onto public lands and improved them. These settlers wanted to live on the land and farm it for several years before having to pay for it. They also wanted a "preferential right" known as "preemption" that would allow them to purchase the land at $1.25 per acre without having the price raised by speculators. The southern colonies had all adopted "preemption," also called "squatter's rights," because the settler "squatted," or stayed, on the land prior to owning it, and as settlers moved westward, they wanted preemption laws to move westward as well.

Although Congress acted in a number of specific cases to grant preemption rights to settlers on public lands, westerners wanted a general law, and Congress responded in 1841 with a general preemption law that applied to all surveyed lands, expanding it further in 1850 to extend to all unsurveyed lands. Preemption and "squatter's rights," plus the taxation of property, made it difficult for large, landed estates to develop in America. Any owner who did not routinely visit every section of undeveloped land could anticipate that sooner or later squatters would appear. Meanwhile, the land was taxed, virtually forcing owners to develop the land or sell it.

Quaker missions

Members of the Society of Friends (Quakers) served as some of the most prolific of Christian missionaries to the American Indians. In the Colonial period, they proselytized only reluctantly. Their relations with the Indians, though, were exemplary, and Indians and non-Quakers alike viewed the Quakers as peace-loving and just. Viewpoints among the Quakers changed dramatically during the 18th century, fearing missionizing competition from the Catholics as well as abuse by whites in general. Reflecting this new attitude, Quakers were missionizing throughout the Pennsylvania and Ohio frontiers by the time of the American Revolution. In the early republic, Quakers missionized to the tribes of the Old Northwest, especially the Shawnees and Miamis. After the Civil War, the Grant administration recognized Quaker success in missions and appointed 18 as either a superintendent or an agent at various Indian posts in the American West. Though only a minority of superintendents or agents were Quaker, many referred to Grant's Indian policy as the "Quaker Policy." In the postbellum period, the Quakers proved especially important among the Kiowa and the Wichita. One of the most important post–Civil War Quakers was Albert Smiley, who organized the highly influential Lake Mohawk Conference of Friends of the Indian.

Unlike other prominent proselytizing Christian denominations—such as the Roman Catholics, Methodists, or Presbyterians—the Quakers believed that one must first teach the Native Americans the culture, agriculture, and industry of Western civilization. Once that was accomplished, Christianity would necessarily follow according to Quaker beliefs. The Quakers, therefore, often sent farmers and specialists to teach the Indians new farming techniques, rather than to preach the Gospel. Indeed, they believed preaching the Gospel counterproductive if the Indians had yet to be westernized. Such preaching before civilizing seemed only grandstanding to the Quakers. The real and patient work came with civilizing.

Richardville, Jean Baptiste (1760–1841)

Jean Baptiste Richardville was one of four children born into the volatile marriage of Miami [II] chieftess and Metis *Taucumwah [II]* (a.k.a. Maria Louisa) and French fur trader and nobleman Joseph Richerville. As his mother was a Metis, Richardville was most likely one-quarter Miami and three-quarters French. Legend has it that he was born under a famous apple tree, not indigenous to the area, on the Maumee River in *Long Portage/Kekionga[II]*. Richardville spent part of each year in Kekionga and along the Wabash learning the portage and fur trades, and he spent the remainder of the year with his father in Three Rivers, Canada, attending school. He was fluent in Miami, French, English, and Delaware.

Though Miami males inherited the office of chief from their maternal uncles, they still had to earn the title. As a young man, Richardville followed the example of his uncle *Pacanne [II]* and rescued a white man about to be tortured by his fellow Miamis. While the crowd was understandably upset that it could not witness a torture, it was equally impressed at the audacity of young Richardville and confirmed his office as chief.

In the 1780s Pacanne and his immediate family increasingly distanced themselves from the violence of the British, Miamis, and *Shawnees [II]* emanating from Kekionga. As he departed, he left his nephew Richardville in charge. In the winter of 1789 and 1790 Kekionga was rife with rumors as the U.S. Army prepared for the *Miami-Federalist War [II]* (1790–1795), and Little Turtle, the Miami war chief, consulted with Richardville frequently. Richardville refused to go on the warpath or the hunt that winter. Instead, he lived the life of a French gentleman. He and several other French traders spent the winter at leisure-time events—serenading women from canoes, playing cards, singing songs, dancing, and considerable drinking—usually enjoyed late into the long winter nights.

Most likely, Richardville did not participate as a warrior during the Miami-Federalist War. He was, however, the first chief of the Miami Confederacy to offer the olive branch in January 1795. He promised General Anthony Wayne unrestricted access to the highly lucrative Long Portage. Richardville even agreed to supply the U.S. Army, stationed at the newly created Fort Wayne, with goods.

During the relative peace between 1795 and 1811, Richardville continued to develop his skills and business as a fur trader and as the rightful owner of the Long Portage. Richardville was in a good position politically and economically. He was so successful at business that by 1816, when Indiana became a state, he was a millionaire.

Despite the increase in wealth, Richardville faced two serious problems prior to the *War of 1812*: Little Turtle and the Shawnee Brothers, *Tenskwatawa* (the "Prophet") and *Tecumseh*. The first, a great warrior, was merely a pretender. That is, Little Turtle obtained his position as chief by distributing government monies/annuities to the Miamis. According to tradition, only those deemed chiefs by the Miami at large could distribute such monies. The second problem was more serious. The Shawnee Brothers created a nativist movement, opposing all forms of assimilation. Not only did they oppose everything for which Richardville stood, their movement brought an angry U.S. Army into the region in November 1811 at the *Battle of Tippecanoe*.

Though successfully weathering both threats prior to the war, Richardville failed during the War of 1812. At the beginning of the conflict, although the Miamis declared themselves neutral, Richardville aided the Americans whenever possible. William Henry *Harrison*, though, saw Richardville's villages as a threat and ordered them destroyed in December 1812.

Furious, Richardville, Pacanne, and a majority of the Miamis fled to Detroit and joined the British side. Richardville earned the rank of captain in the Indian Service. When the British effort collapsed at the Battle of the Thames, all of the Miamis except Richardville surrendered to Harrison. In 1814 Richardville, Pacanne, and their families went to *Michilimackinac [II]* to live with the British but finally returned to Fort Wayne in the summer of 1815, realizing they were part of a lost cause.

From 1816 to 1841, Richardville served as the first of only two head chiefs of the Miamis in their history. He served the Miamis faithfully, repeatedly fighting off the United States' efforts to take Miami land. United States treaty agents feared to come up against the Miami chief, knowing the master diplomat would best them. Finally, in 1840 at the age of 80, Richardville sold the vast majority of Miami land to the United States and accepted removal for roughly two-thirds of his tribe to Kansas.

Ross, John (October 3, 1790–August 1, 1866)

Born to a Scottish father and Metis-Cherokee mother, Ross grew up in the Cherokee culture but was formally educated in Tennessee. His Cherokee name was Tsan usdi. Throughout his career, Ross attempted to use non-violent means to protect Cherokee lands from U.S. purchase and acquisition. The United States briefly imprisoned him for his opposition, but Ross eventually oversaw the forced removal of the *Trail of Tears*. He had hoped to attenuate its brutality on his people. Ross helped rewrite the Cherokee constitution for the new Cherokee lands in Indian Territory and continued to serve as head chief. During the Civil War, Ross opposed the Confederacy and secession, but he failed to keep his tribe unified and a significant number of Cherokees fought both for and against the Union.

Sacagawea (ca.1790–1812)

A *Shoshone* Indian and a captive of French-Canadian fur trader Toussaint *Charbonneau [II]*, Sacagawea joined the *Lewis and Clark* expedition in 1804 when Charbonneau was hired as an interpreter. She proved invaluable at interpreting the Snake Indian language but also facilitated peaceful exchanges with the Shoshone. Sacagawea also provided information about the geography of her native Montana. After the expedition returned east in 1805, Sacagawea's subsequent history is unclear. Some suggest she died in 1812, but one report placed her in Wyoming in 1884, making her 94 years old.

Salt Lake City, Utah

On July 23, 1847, a band of Mormon pioneers reached the Salt Lake Valley in Utah. Mormon leader Brigham *Young* and the main body of 147 pioneers arrived the following day. Soon they named the town Great Salt Lake City, after the salty inland lake that dominated the valley between the Wasatch and Oquirrh mountain ranges (the "great" was dropped in 1868). Fur trappers had known of the valley for decades; John C. *Fremont* explored there.

Under Young's direction, the Mormons farmed the surrounding land and built a model city, with streets 88 feet wide—wide enough to turn a *Conestoga wagon* around in. One city block was dedicated to the Mormon temple. As the seat of territorial, and later, state government and as the main home of the Church of Jesus Christ of *Latter-day Saints*, Salt Lake City has been the center of Utah's population and commerce and, more recently, a regional hub for Delta Airlines and a departure point for the state's *skiing [V]* industry.

Santa Anna, Antonio López de (1794–1876)

Born in Vera Cruz, Mexico, Antonio López de Santa Anna Perez de Labron grew up in a royalist household, joined the army, and battled revolutionaries in 1813. After 1821 he supported independence, and in 1823 he participated in a federalist overthrow of the government of Augustin de

Iturbide. Six years later, he led federalist forces to defeat a Spanish invasion at Tampico, then in 1833 was elected president by a popular majority.

More a military leader than a governor, Santa Anna struggled with a number of armed revolts in the north, particularly in Texas where a group of rebels resisted his rule from a small mission called the Alamo. Santa Anna led a large force north and crushed the Alamo defenders, also killing four hundred prisoners in the *Goliad Massacre.* The Texas revolutionaries under Sam *Houston* regrouped and defeated Santa Anna's forces at the *Battle of San Jacinto* in April 1835. Texas was given its independence.

After losing the presidency, Santa Anna returned to power in 1841, although a new revolution cast him out again in 1844, when he was exiled to Cuba. During the *Mexican War,* he returned yet again to battle the United States. When the Americans defeated the Mexican armies, Santa Anna went into exile again, only to be brought back still another time by the government in 1853, when he sold the Mesilla Valley to the United States in the Gadsden Purchase. Losing power for the last time in 1855, Santa Anna spent the next 19 years plotting to regain the reins of government, until he died in 1876.

Santa Fe Trail

Also known as the "Santa Fe and Chihuahua Trail" and the "Camino Real," the Santa Fe Trail was one of the most important routes of transit from Missouri to the Southwest in the early 1800s. The trail from Missouri, across the Cimarron Desert, through the Raton Pass to Santa Fe, New Mexico, was explored by William *Becknell*, a Missouri Indian trader, who had come with a company of Mexican soldiers to sell goods in Santa Fe in 1821–1822. This gained Becknell the sobriquet, "Father of the Santa Fe Trade," although Indians and other traders had used parts of this route for many years.

Trains of settlers traversing the 700 to 800 miles from Franklin or Independence, Missouri, consisted of dozens of *Conestoga wagons* (also called "prairie schooners") capable of covering 15 miles a day for a two- to three-month trip. At night, the wagons would circle to provide protection, and guards and scouts would take turns watching for attackers. A typical train might travel from Independence to points in Kansas, then across the Arkansas River to the Cimarron River. Eventually, the expedition would arrive at the Pecos River, then through the Glorieta Pass. Another approach ran westward to Bent's Fort in Colorado, then came southward through the Raton Pass. Each had its advantages. Josiah *Gregg*, in his 1844 book, *Commerce of the Prairies*, described a typical western wagon train. When the group finally arrived in Santa Fe, it was a public event marked by celebrations.

From Santa Fe, the trail moved south along Rio Grande to modern-day Albuquerque, then to Socorro, then, departing the river, crossed the "Deadman's March" (*Jornada del Muerto*) for some 90 miles. Rejoining the river and following it to *El Paso del Norte [I]*, the trail again crossed desert to Chihuahua, Zacatecas, then finally Mexico City, covering more than 1,600 miles.

The difficulty of the crossing due to parties of Indian raiders meant that large parties had to be mustered before beginning the journey. Typically, several hundred people up to 1,000 may have made a single trek from Santa Fe to Mexico City. Santa Fe's remote location also dictated high costs to travelers, requiring that virtually all manufactured items had to be imported across the difficult route. After Mexico gained its independence in 1821, more Americans began to appear along the trail. Military escorts began accompanying Americans in the late 1820s, by which time the government had already authorized and paid for surveys.

The key to the trail was commerce with Mexico. As early as 1824, nearly $200,000 a year in commerce moved up and down the trail, while a decade later, half of all the products brought in by the Americans continued on to Mexico. Along the way, they encountered Mexican tax collectors, known for their corruption. Some traders disliked the customs collectors so much that they off-loaded their goods onto mules and crossed eastern New Mexico on back trails. In addition to the national tax, local governors occasionally imposed their own, additional, duties. As tensions between the United States and Mexico increased, the Mexican government regulated trade even more strictly. Then, in 1846, General Stephen Watts *Kearny* took his expedition into the territory and captured Santa Fe, soon followed by the Army's Corps of Engineers, who built roads into the region. Regular stage routes crossed the trail by the 1850s, bringing the total value of trade to more than $5 million. Even that only accelerated after gold was discovered in California. In 1880 rail lines finally reached into the region, eliminating the need for overland trails.

Shoshone Indians

A Uto-Aztecan people, the Shoshones consist of two subgroups, the eastern Shoshones, traditionally residing in central Wyoming, and the northern Shoshones (including the Bannock and Lemhis) in central Idaho. Some 19th-century witnesses referred to them as the Snake Indians or Snakes. They are distantly connected to the Comanches, from whom they most likely obtained the horse in the early 18th century.

From their first meeting with the Americans of the *Lewis and Clark Expedition*, the Shoshones and the United States have typically enjoyed strong ties with one another. Lewis and Clark were especially fortunate to have a Shoshone woman, *Sacagawea*, as a guide and translator. Enemies of the more aggressive tribes of the Great Plains—such as the Lakota, *Blackfeet*, and Cheyennes—the Shoshones continued to ally with the United States, serving as scouts and warriors in several major engagements of the post–Civil War Indian Wars.

Shoshone relations with individual whites, however, often went awry. In 1812 the Shoshones wiped out a fur trading post in their territory. During white migrations to Oregon and California, Shoshones often raided wagon trains, causing further conflict. Shoshones especially attacked Mormon settlements in northern Utah and southern Idaho. In retaliation, California volunteer troops massacred 400 Shoshones, most of whom were women and children, in January 29, 1863, at the Bear River village of Chief

Crow's Heart Butte is an important geological and cultural feature of the Wind River Indian Reservation. Local legend claims that the Wind River Shoshone sacrificed a Crow at the top of the butte for insulting a white man. *Bradley J. Birzer*

Bear Hunter. The troops tortured many of the Shoshone survivors, and Mormon settlers in Cache Valley praised the soldiers as divinely inspired heroes.

Post–Civil War alliances with the United States, however, allowed both divisions of the Shoshones to gain reservations on their traditional homelands. Discoveries of gold, illegal white settlement, and various other factors, however, slowly whittled away both reservations for roughly 60 years after the formation of each.

Smith, Jedediah (1798–1831)

Born in Bainbridge, New York, in 1798, Jedediah Smith, an explorer, mountain man, trapper, scout, and guide, began his career as a teen clerk on a Lake Erie ship. In 1822 after traveling to St. Louis, Smith joined the expedition of fur trader William H. *Ashley* up the Missouri River. Smith proved capable enough that in 1823, Ashley appointed him to direct a second Missouri River expedition, which was attacked by *Arikara* Indians. He then led a third group from Fort Kiowa overland to the Dakota Black Hills, then to Wyoming. This time, friendly encounters with Indians brought them information of a pass through the Rockies called the South Pass (which originally had been discovered by the returning party from Astoria in 1812–1813, but the location of which had been lost). This route along the Platte and Sweetwater Rivers to the fur trapping areas in the Rockies was easier than going up the *Missouri River [I]* and provided a more direct route for wagon trains headed to Oregon or California.

While traveling in the Snake River region in 1824, he encountered an expedition of the Hudson's Bay Company, Ashley's main competition, and during the time he accompanied the group to the Flathead Post, he observed key details of the Canadian enterprise, which he later reported to Ashley. Smith's loyalty and skills made him so valuable that in 1825 Ashley offered him a partnership in the business. From that point on, Smith headed one of Ashley's field parties at all times. A year later, Smith and William L. Sublette bought out Ashley's interests, then undertook a massive expedition from Cache Lake southward to investigate new hunting grounds. He explored the Great Salt Lake, then the Colorado River and the Mojave Desert, arriving at San Gabriel, California. This marked the first American overland expedition through the Southwest. Smith headed northward through the San Juaquin Valley, then made a difficult crossing over the mountains along the American River to the Great Basin. The party reached the rendezvous point in July 1827, becoming the first whites to make the round-trip circuit across the Sierras and back across the Great Basin.

Smith, a deeply religious man, was no uncivilized bumpkin. He made careful records and wrote intelligently. He had his share of frontier experiences, including being mauled by a bear in the Black Hills and being 1 of only 3 survivors of an 18-man party attacked by Indians in July 1828. What remained of the 1828 expedition reached Fort Vancouver, then traveled through Hudson's Bay territory to reach the rendezvous point again. During a time when tensions over Oregon remained high between the British and the Americans, Smith's meticulous notes assisted U.S. diplomatic efforts to settle the border dispute. Smith attempted to retire after the 1830 expedition but scouted for a supply route through New Mexico, where, after riding ahead of his party, he was attacked by Indians and killed in 1831. Smith's contribution to western folklore, while great, paled compared to his trail-blazing and path-finding activities, which significantly enhanced western trade and settlement.

This is a reconstruction of the Spalding Mission to the Nez Perce Indians. *Bradley J. Birzer*

Spalding, Henry (1803–1874)

Mentally unbalanced, Spalding a Protestant missionary, found it very difficult to work with others. Despite that, he and his wife, strong-willed but an invalid, traveled to the Oregon Country in 1836 with the *Whitman mission*. To make matters worse, he had years earlier unsuccessfully courted Narcissa Whitman. Finding little success with the Indians of the Northwest, Spalding found scapegoats in the Catholics of the region, especially Father Peter Jean DeSmet. After the Cayuse massacre of the Whitmans in 1847, Spalding blamed the Jesuit missionary. Other Protestants, however, blamed Spalding for his own failures.

After the massacre, Spalding took up farming as well as anti-Catholic missionizing.

IN THEIR OWN

Character of Missionary Henry Spalding

When Cayuse Indians attacked and killed the Whitmans and 12 of their missionary companions in 1847, Henry Spalding, a fellow Presbyterian missionary, blamed the Roman Catholic missions in the Pacific Northwest. He claimed the Catholics had convinced the Cayuse to kill the Whitmans. The Roman Catholic Bishop of the Pacific Northwest, the Right Reverend J. B. A. Brouillet, responded with a book defending Roman Catholic missions as well as attacking the character of Henry Spalding. The following segment is one testimony against the character of Spalding, by John Baptist Gervais in 1848.

I spent last fall and last winter among the Nez Perces. I arrived there at the beginning of October. But I have known the Nez Perces for over twenty years, having been in the habit of trading and travelling with them almost every year; and it was at their request that I had gone to settle in their country. For many years I have heard the Nez Perces very often speaking badly of Mr. Spalding. It appeared to me that the greatest part of those Indians disliked and hated him. According to their reports, they were very often quarrelling with him; they complained that Mr. Spalding was too quick tempered. He fought with them twice, and tried to fire at them once. The Indians ill-treated and insulted him in a great many ways. They threw down his mill, pretending it was theirs.

Mr. Spalding told me himself last fall that for three of four years back he had ceased entirely to teach the Indians, because they refused to hear him.

> (Signed)
> John Baptist Gervais.
> St. Paul of Willament, Oct. 15, 1848.

—SOURCE: REV J.B.A. BROUILLET, *PROTESTANTISM IN OREGON* (NEW YORK: M.T. COZANS, 1853), 18.

Spencer Repeating Rifle

Christopher Spencer, a Boston firearms maker, conceived of a spring-loaded, lever-ejected repeating rifle that could use a rimfire cartridge. Spencer had built the weapons for cavalry beginning in 1863, using a concept similar to that of Sharp's rifle. During the war, the Spencer Repeating Rifle Company sold more than 100,000 weapons to the Union Army.

The Spencer Repeating Rifle provided the soldier with the ability to fire several shots from horseback without the multiple steps required by a musket. The Spencer carbine, in addition to having a rifled barrel, had a magazine in the butt that held seven .56 or .44 caliber rounds, with a new round inserted into the chamber with the ejection of the old through the lever action.

spurs

A critical and functional part of any cowboy's wardrobe, spurs were iron fittings worn over the boot heel, held in place by a leather strap, that featured a rolling star-shape extending off the heel. The cowboy used this to control the horse but not to break animals. Many cowboys rounded off the star points to do minimal damage to the horse. A spur looked like a rounded tuning fork or horseshoe, with the sides fitting around the heel of the boot, and the "handle" sticking backward toward the horse. A leather strap over the top of the foot and a small chain or leather strap right under the heel secured the spur to the boot. Spur designs sometimes became ornate, with intricate etchings on the side and different curvatures on the handles angling the spurs. Some cowboys kept their spurs on at all times, but others wore spurs only when actually riding.

stagecoaches

Evolving from European coaches, stagecoaches operated on a regular basis in America beginning in 1785. The Lewis Downing–established company, Abbott-Downing Company of Concord, New Hampshire, began making American coaches in 1826. A pivotal feature of the Abbott design was the placement of the center of gravity equidistant between the wheels by using a curved lower body in a half-oval shape. Likewise, the sides bulged out slightly for more interior space. Typical coaches had luggage racks on top of the coach, but often had seats on the roof facing forward and back. Naturally, such designs were only useful in areas where the roads were reasonably well maintained. The unloaded coach came in at about 2,500 pounds and cost just over $1,000, not including horses.

The Concord coaches were finely crafted and were artistic wonders. Most coaches were red, but the paint wore off quickly, especially in desert locations. Artists decorated the outside of the coaches with gold leaf scroll-work; then the coach was covered in a coat of wax.

Coaches were pulled by teams of four to six horses; teams of eight proved too difficult to control. Drivers used breast straps attached to the stage coach tongue and controlled the coach with traces, or reins, running through loops to the horses. This arrangement allowed the tongue to move one direction completely away from the coach itself, which proved effective when coaches hit potholes or rocks. Nevertheless, riding in a coach was not pleasant. The body rested on large steel springs, but the vehicles lacked shock absorbers. They were dusty, monotonous, and cramped, even under the best conditions.

When not subject to elements, coaches were particularly well suited to robberies. The *Butterfield Overland Mail* and *Wells Fargo & Company [IV]*, two of the most famous of the coach companies, constantly battled holdups. Most coaches traveled with a driver and an armed guard, especially when carrying cash. Even as coaches declined as a source of mail and passenger transportation, the coach companies diversified into wagons, ambulances, and specialty vehicles. Wells Fargo emphasized its banking functions. Abbot-Downing finally ceased production of coach-type vehicles in 1920.

steamboats

After Robert Fulton demonstrated his *Clermont*, the first steam-powered ship, in 1807 in New York, it was only a matter of time before steamboats would find their way into the nation's interior. In 1810 a side-wheeler, steam-powered vessel called the *New Orleans* set out from Pittsburgh for New Orleans, finally arriving in January 1812, after which it ran a regular route from that city to Natchez. Other vessels, including the *Enterprise* and the *Aetna*, followed. The central advantage of steam power was that it could sail upriver efficiently and at lower cost than other forms of shipping. This was demonstrated by the *Washington* in 1817, which sailed up the ***Mississippi River [I]*** with a full cargo, making Louisville after 25 days. Within a few years, more than 60 steamboats regularly plied their trade on the Mississippi, and by 1850, the number reached 750.

Some of the vessels were truly impressive and were designed for passengers as well as cargo. Passengers could travel in luxury or could choose the barest of necessities. Some steamboats were four-deckers with carpets, inlaid furniture, staterooms, with their own barbershops, nurseries, and orchestras. But at the other end of the scale, there were boats where passengers slept on open decks on bales of hay, drank the river water, ate what they could bring or catch. But it was cheap; the lowest fares were $1 per 500 miles! By midcentury the tonnage on the Mississippi and the Great Lakes exceeded all shipping from New York City by 200 percent, while western rivers alone carried more than 3 million people a year.

Steamboats reached their peak in the 1850s, having squeezed all the efficiency possible out of river travel, and they were soon displaced by railroads. Steam power not only opened the rivers but soon was applied to ocean-going vessels that could sail from the East Coast to Panama, transfer cargo and people overland, who then boarded a new vessel for San Francisco. This trade ensured the growth of California and the West Coast prior to the railroads, and a healthy competition with government-subsidized firms, led by Cornelius Vanderbilt, kept prices low.

Sutter, John Augustus (February 1803–June 18, 1880)

Known for discovering gold in California, John Sutter (originally Johann August Suter) was born in Baden, Germany, in 1803. He served in the Swiss army and came to the United States from Switzerland in 1834 to escape creditors. Sutter arrived in the Mexican province of California in July 1839, where he won the favor of Governor Juan Bautista Alvarado after presenting a grandiose plan for establishing a colony in the north.

"Sutter's Fort" was located near modern-day Sacramento. News of Sutter's discovery of gold on the American River on January 24, 1848, brought thousands of miners and treasure-seekers to Sutter's Fort. By then, Sutter had the worst of all worlds: lands that he could not protect from outsiders and no claim to the gold in the streams or hills. By 1852 the damage done to his crops left him bankrupt, and he never profited from the immense gold fields on his property.

Tecumseh (ca. 1768–October 5, 1813)

Tecumseh, the brother of *Tenskwatawa*, the "Prophet," was born approximately 1768, likely near Chillicothe, Ohio. His father, who was a Shawnee chief, died in the Battle of Point Pleasant (1774), and as Tecumseh matured he gained a reputation as a warrior and leader. He won the respect of whites for opposing the torture of prisoners and was known for the reliability of his word. Tecumseh and his brother were removed by whites to Greenville, Ohio, near Indiana, in the early 1800s, and the tribe settled on the Wabash River, sharing the region with the *Potawatomi [II]* and Kickapoo. The settlement they founded was called Tippecanoe or "Prophet's Town."

The Prophet wielded great influence among the Shawnee, but Tecumseh was the organizing force, arguing that the tribes should all work together to defeat— or at least resist— the whites. He claimed that no treaty with any tribe was valid unless all signed it. Working to form the tribes into a confederacy, Tecumseh came to the attention of the governor of Indiana Territory, William Henry *Harrison*, who recognized the threat posed by such a united Indian effort. In addition to working in concert, Tecumseh got the tribes to avoid alcohol and to farm effectively. He also endeavored to bring the British in on his side, although Britain, involved in wars with Napoleon, diplomatically refused. From 1803 to 1811, Tecumseh continued to appeal to the British for help against the Americans. As the United States was drawn into war with England, Tecumseh expected the British to finally support him.

After informing Harrison that he was displeased with the Treaty of Fort Wayne, wherein a few Indian chiefs again had spoken for all, Tecumseh announced that he was going to visit the southern tribes. He expected the

A powerful Shawnee chief who formed an Indian confederation in the early 1800s, Tecumseh was away when General William Henry Harrison lured the Indian warriors out into the open to defeat them at the Battle of Tippicanoe. *Library of Congress*

peaceful conditions that were in place to remain, but Harrison moved, reasoning that the Prophet, Tenskwatawa, would not be able to maintain control over the tribes in the face of a military invasion. At the *Battle of Tippecanoe*, a close struggle finally turned in Harrison's favor and the dream of a confederation collapsed. After the *War of 1812* broke out, Tecumseh and some of his braves joined the British army, whereupon he was given the rank of brigadier general. After the British, contrary to their promises, withdrew from Detroit, Tecumseh only fought reluctantly and died at the Battle of the Thames on October 5, 1813.

IN THEIR OWN *Words*

An Anonymous Participant's Account of Various Indian Tribes in the Battle of Tippecanoe, November 1811

With respect to the number of Indians that were engaged against us, I am possessed of no data by which I can form a correct statement. It must, however, have been considerable and perhaps not much inferior to our own: which deducting the dragoons, who were unable to do us much service, was very little above seven hundred, non-commissioned officers and privates, I am convinced there were at least six hundred. The Prophet had three weeks before 450 of his own proper followers. I am induced to believe that he was joined by a number of the lawless vagabonds who live on the Illinois river as large trails were seen coming from that direction. Indeed I shall not be surprised to find that some of those who professed the warmest friendship for us were arrayed against us – 'tis certain that one of this description came out from the town and spoke to me the night before the action. The potowatimie chief whom I mentioned to have been wounded and taken prisoner, in my letter of the 8ᵗʰ inst. I left on the battle ground, after having taken all the care of him in my power, I requested him to inform those of his own tribe who had joined the [unrecognizable word] and the Kickapoos & Winebagoes that if they would immediately abandon the Prophet and return to their own tribes, their past conduct would be forgiven and that we would treat them as we formerly had done. He assured me that he would do so, and that there was no doubt of their compliance. Indeed he said that he was certain they would put the Prophet to death.

—SOURCE: *WESTERN INTELLIGENCER* (WORTHINGTON OHIO), JANUARY 15, 1812.

Tenskwatawa (1775–1836)

Tenskwatawa was one of the most important religious leaders in American Indian history. Like *Handsome Lake [II]*, *Neolin [II]*, and Wovoka, he created and led a powerful pan-Indian nativist revival. Each of these prophets arose during times of intense cultural stress, and each promised that adhering to the "old ways" would bring favor from the Creator. Each movement, while claiming to be traditional, in fact synthesized various elements from Indian and white cultures.

Later known as the Shawnee Prophet, Tenskwatawa (the "Open Door") was originally called Lalawethika (the "Noise Maker," because he was loud and complained frequently). Few persons among the Shawnees liked him. He was unskilled and he found little favor with his family. With the exception of the 1794 Battle of Fallen Timbers, during the *Miami-Federalist War [II]*, he participated in few battles. When he did fight, his older brother *Tecumseh*, a great warrior, overshadowed him. He was so inept that he blinded one of his own eyes with an arrow from his own bow.

Lalawethika married when just a teenager. Unable to provide for his family through the hunt, he turned to alcohol. Between the 1795 *Treaty of Greenville [II]* and 1805, Lalawethika assumed an apprenticeship with the shaman, but as a medicine man he failed again.

In the spring of 1805 while in a drunken stupor, Lalawethika collapsed, and most of the Shawnees assumed he had died. Several hours later, he awoke, claiming that he had met the Creator. In a journey reminiscent of Dante's, Lalawethika had seen heaven and hell. Heaven, he said, was a paradise, a "rich fertile country, abounding in game, fish, pleasant hunting grounds and fine corn fields." In paradise, one could hunt or play games as he so wished. Hell, though, was a place of never-ending fire. The tortures found in hell were also similar to those described by Dante. Alcoholics drank molten lead, and other sinners had their arms or legs burned off.

Lalawethika also claimed that the Creator showed him the origin of white Americans. Unlike the Shawnees, the offspring of the Creator, Americans sprang from the Great Serpent of the Atlantic Ocean. Crawling onto the shores of North America, Americans first looked like a giant crab and settled in what is now Boston. Lalawethika exempted the British, French, and Spanish from this creation for they were also the offspring of the Great Spirit and, therefore, brothers of the Shawnees. He forbade contact with the Americans, however, as they were evil. Indians should never trade with Americans or have relationships of any kind with them. Because the Americans were evil, though, they had corrupted some Indians ("witches"), and those Indians must be removed.

The Creator also gave Lalawethika a set of rules to give to the Indians. First, they were to reject all American ways of living and return to their native ways. Second, they were to avoid alcohol and eat only native crops. He deemed all European-derived livestock unclean. Finally, they were to give up sexual promiscuity and polygamy. In reality, of course, the Shawnees could no longer remember a time that did not mix European and Indian ways; the multiple strands had become too intertwined. But they convinced themselves that what they were doing was purely native. If they followed these divine laws, Lalawethika announced, the dead would return to live among them, and the game would flourish in the forests.

After the vision, Lalawethika proclaimed himself Tenskwatawa (the Open Door), and others, stunned by his transformation, referred to him as the Shawnee Prophet. Not only did Tenskwatawa speak with authority, but he practiced what he preached. He began to treat his wife well, and he gave up alcohol. He further solidified his position by "predicting" an eclipse of the sun in the summer of 1806, information about which he had obtained from a chance encounter with some scientists.

Between 1805 and 1811 Tenskwatawa's following grew dramatically. At first Indians from all over the western Great Lakes gathered around Greenville, Ohio, but they soon had to move to Prophetstown (present-day Lafayette, Indiana) because of logistics. Using Prophetstown as a base, Tecumseh, Tenskwatawa's brother, continued to unite the various tribes of the Old Northwest.

Fearful of the Prophet's intentions, Indiana Territorial Governor William Henry *Harrison* attacked Prophetstown in November 1811. With Tecumseh in the South recruiting Indians for a new confederacy, the Prophet provided poor leadership against Harrison's army. This battle destroyed much of the Prophet's hold over the Indians, as they now saw him as a fraud for failing to protect them. Tecumseh, upon returning, assumed control of the alliance that he and his brother had created.

During the *War of 1812* Tenskwatawa fled to Canada and remained there until 1825 when the United States invited him back, if he would help remove his band to Kansas, which he did in the following year. In November 1836 he died near present-day Kansas City.

Texas Rangers

Loosely organized in 1826, then given more formal status during the *Texas Revolution* in 1835, the Texas Rangers were state law enforcement officers stationed on the Indian frontier, specifically charged with overseeing the area between the Brazos and Trinity Rivers. Members had to furnish all

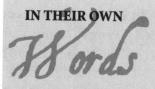

IN THEIR OWN Words

Memoirs of a Texas Ranger

James G. Gillett wrote his recollections of service in the Texas Rangers from 1875 to 1881. In this passage he relates the exploits of the Rangers in tracking the outlaw Sam Bass and his gang of train robbers. In 1877 Bass and five other men robbed a Union Pacific train at Big Springs, Nebraska, leading to a massive manhunt. News soon reached the Texas Rangers. Bass increasingly showed up in Texas, and when the Rangers learned of his whereabouts, 10 Rangers set out in pursuit.

We had ridden sixty-five miles that short summer night . . . We halted on the Gabriel [River] for a breakfast of bread, broiled bacon, and black coffee. . . . We did not halt again until we reached the vicinity of old Round Rock between one and two o'clock in the after-

noon of Friday, July nineteenth. . . . Bass, Barnes and Jackson rode into town, hitched their horses in an alley just back of the bank, passed that building, and made a mental note of its situation.

[When confronted by Deputy Sheriff Grimes] the robbers pulled their guns and killed Grimes as he backed out the door. He fell dead on the sidewalk. They then turned on [Deputy Sheriff Moore] and shot him through the lungs as he attempted to draw his weapon. At the crack of the first pistol [Ranger] Dick Ware, who was seated in a barber shop only a few steps away . . . rushed into the street and encountered the three bandits . . . Bass and his men fired on him at close range, one of their bullets striking a hitching post within six inches of his head . . . The bandits had now reached their horses, and realizing their situation was critical they fought with the energy of despair. . . . [Frank Jackson, one of the bandits] was holding Bass, pale and bleeding, in the saddle. . . . The battle was now over and the play spoiled by two over-zealous deputies bringin on a premature fight, after they had been warned to be careful. . . . From the moment he was shot until his death three days later Bass suffered untold agonies.

—SOURCE: JAMES G. GILLETT, *SIX YEARS WITH THE TEXAS RANGERS, 1875–1881,* ED., MILO M. QUAIFE (1925; REPRINT, NEW HAVEN: YALE UNIVERSITY PRESS, 1963), 123–127.

their own equipment and soon gained a reputation as excellent horsemen and ferocious fighters, defeating larger numbers of Indians on several occasions in 1840. This led to the subsequent phrase, "One riot, one Ranger." It was the Texas Rangers that provided the first orders for the famous Colt .45 handgun. After 1867 the Texas Rangers became a permanent state-funded organization with a Frontier Battalion (assigned to deal with Indians and frontier problems) and a Special Force that patrolled the Mexican border. The latter group arrested or killed numerous well-known outlaws, including Sam Bass and John Wesley *Hardin [IV]*. In 1935, after a series of reforms, they were merged with the Texas Highway Patrol. To this day, there is no official "Texas Ranger uniform," and as of 2000 there were 107 active Rangers in Texas.

Texas Revolution

In the early 19th century Anglos had been encouraged to emigrate to the northern part of Mexico, called Texas, in an effort by the newly independent country of Mexico to populate that region as a buffer against the Indians. In the process, the settlers had not only been given large tracts of land, but a relative degree of autonomy. In 1833 General Antonio López de *Santa Anna* gained control of the Mexican government, intending to crush any resistance to his programs in the northern province. Groups of rebellious Texans, calling for a return to the Constitution of 1824, had been growing in number and audacity. They had faced down customs collectors and their guards at Anahuac in a move not universally supported by other American Texans.

Stephen F. *Austin*, who had been under house arrest in Mexico City, returned to Texas following his release and endorsed calls for a convention to present grievances to Santa Anna. The government's forces were defeated at Gonzoles on October 2, 1835, and the next week Texans took control of the arsenal at Goliad. Texan rebels then took the town of *San Antonio [II]* and obtained the surrender of 800 Mexican troops, threatening the Mexican army's supply lines.

The Texans were not calling for independence but rather a return to the constitution of 1824. Forming a provisional government, Texas sent emissaries to the United States and began to build up military forces. But the forces in the field were divided and ill-organized. Sam *Houston*, appointed commander-in-chief of this "army," took a furlough while the bickering continued. Santa Anna, meanwhile, moved north with an army of over 8,000 men.

In February 1836 the lead elements of Santa Anna's army arrived at the Alamo and began shelling it. Several days later, the main body arrived and stormed the Alamo, killing all the defenders. Meanwhile, General Jose de Urrea captured James Fannin's 300 men at Goliad, where they were executed after surrendering. Word of both massacres soon reached the ears of Houston and his men, who nevertheless did not have enough troops to stand and fight. He therefore lured Santa Anna deeper into Texas, while building up his own forces. A new convention met on March 1, 1836, and declared independence, naming David

A symbol of courage, sacrifice, and resistance to oppression, the Alamo stood against General Santa Anna's army for nearly two weeks before being overwhelmed. Among its defenders were "Jim" Bowie, Davy Crockett, and William Barret Travis. *Daughters of the Republic of Texas Library at the Alamo 9784 (FR.44)*

Burnet to head the interim government and confirming Houston's position of commander in chief.

As Santa Anna advanced further into Texas, his supply lines grew more extended. Despite knowledge that the Texans were in the area, his troops were not on alert when Houston's army attacked, and in the *Battle of San Jacinto*, on the San Jacinto River (April 21, 1836), the Texans smashed Santa Anna's vanguard and captured the president, who complied with Houston's demands to order his remaining troops in Texas to withdraw. The Treaty of Velaco gave Texas its independence, while Santa Anna was released, although in the general's absence a coup had occurred in Mexico City. Texas, and its borders, remained a thorny issue for both Mexico and the United States until the end of the *Mexican War* in 1848.

Trail of Tears

A name given to the trek in 1838–1839 of the Cherokee Indians from their lands in Mississippi to Indian Territory in Oklahoma, the Trail of Tears is a classic example of mistreatment of Indian tribes by the federal government. In

1830 Congress passed the *Indian Removal Act* to force the "Five Civilized Tribes" (*Cherokees*, Chickasaws, Choctaws, Creeks, and Seminoles) off their lands between the original American colonies and the *Mississippi River [I]*. Over the next 20 years more than 100,000 Indians were moved west. The United States Supreme Court (*Worcester v. State of Georgia*) upheld the Cherokee's position, but President Andrew *Jackson* ignored the ruling. Working with a minority of Cherokees who thought it futile to fight the government, negotiators effected the Treaty of New Echota (Georgia) in 1835. None of the Cherokee chiefs were present, but under the terms of the treaty, the Cherokee exchanged their lands east of the Mississippi for $5 million and new homelands in Oklahoma (Indian Territory). In 1836 the Senate narrowly passed the treaty.

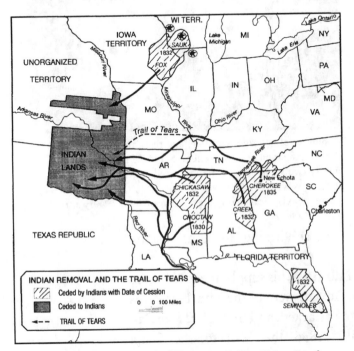

Indian removal and the Trail of Tears. *Ron Acklin, University of Dayton Print and Design*

Chief John *Ross*, among others, did not think the treaty was binding, and sought to discredit those Cherokee who had signed it. Troops moved in to round up the Cherokees into stockades in May 1838, and that summer, the Indians began the trek along the Trail of Tears where three to five Indians died each day. Although authorities thought much of the journey could be accomplished by boat, the river levels were too low. By March 1839 the last of the survivors, including Chief John Ross, who had been trapped icebound on the rivers, arrived in Oklahoma, and a few months later John Ross was elected chief of the reconstituted Cherokee Nation.

Travis, William Barret (August 9, 1809– March 6, 1836)

One of the heroes of the Alamo, William Barret Travis was born on August 9, 1809, at Red Banks Church, South Carolina. After several jobs and a brief marriage, Travis moved in 1831 to San Anahuac, Texas, where he opened a law practice, which failed. He ran afoul of Mexican officials, landing in jail for a month on one occasion. This primed him to agitate against the Mexican government, and he led a coup against the Anahuac officials in 1835. Travis joined the newly created Texas army, where he was appointed a lieutenant colonel, and led 30 men to Bexar, arriving on February 2, 1836.

IN THEIR OWN *Words*

To the People of Texas & all Americans in the World

After an army numbering about 4,000 Mexican soldiers under Mexican dictator and General Antonio López de Santa Anna began to surround the Alamo in late February 1836, the commander of the garrison, William Barret Travis, issued this desperate appeal for help from other Texans involved in the revolution. No aid came. On March 6, after the full complement of Santa Anna's army arrived, the Mexicans overwhelmed the defenders of the Alamo, killing all but a few women and children. Among the dead were Travis, Davy Crockett, and Jim Bowie. Travis's letter remains an example of loyalty to a cause—even in the face of sure death—and of heroism.

Commandancy of the Alamo
Bexar, Fby. 24th, 1836
To the People of Texas & all Americans in the world.
Fellow Citizens & Compatriots

I am besieged by a thousand or more of the Mexicans under Santa Anna. I have
sustained a continual bombardment & cannonade for 24 hours & have not lost a man. The enemy has demanded a surrender at discretion, otherwise the garrison are to be put to the sword if the fort is taken. I have answered the demand with a cannon shot, and our flag still waves proudly from the walls. I shall never surrender nor retreat.

Then, I call on you in the name of Liberty, of patriotism, & of everything dear to the American character, to come to our aid with all dispatch. The enemy is receiving reinforcements daily & will no doubt increase to three or four thousand in four or five days. If this call is neglected, I am determined to sustain myself as long as possible & die like a solder who never forgets what is due to his own honor & that of his country.

Victory or Death
William Barret Travis
Lt. Colonel Comdt.

—TRAVIS'S SPEECH CAN BE FOUND ON THE INTERNET AT www.lsjunction.com/docs/appeal.htm AND IS ON DISPLAY IN THE TEXAS STATE LIBRARY IN AUSTIN.

There he met "Jim" Bowie, who led a group of Texas volunteers. After attempting to exercise command over the volunteers, Travis developed a feud with Bowie. Nevertheless, with the imminent arrival of the Mexican army under General Antonio López de *Santa Anna*, Travis and Bowie agreed on a joint command.

Bexar was undefendable, and when Santa Anna's advance forces surprised the Texans, they withdrew to the Alamo mission. Bowie fell ill the next day, leaving total command in Travis's hands. He organized a well-conceived defense of the Alamo, despite overwhelming odds. According to a legend, Travis knew everyone inside the fort would not survive, and he used his sword to draw a line in the sand. All but 1 of the 190 defenders, including Bowie and Davy *Crockett*, stepped across the line to join him. On March 6 some 4,000 Mexican troops overwhelmed the tiny garrison, and Travis died of a gunshot wound only moments after the assault began. In death, however, Travis was victorious. The siege bought time for Sam *Houston*'s army and ensured victory by the Texans at the *Battle of San Jacinto* on April 21. In addition to delaying Santa Anna, the Alamo defenders had bled the Mexican army, weakening it, and had also provided the rallying cry—"Remember the Alamo" that went up from the Texans as they won independence at San Jacinto.

Treaty of Guadalupe Hidalgo, 1848

On February 2, 1848, the United States of America and Mexico signed the Treaty of Guadalupe Hidalgo, named after the villa in which it was signed. The agreement effectively ended the *Mexican War*, won by the Americans, and transferred 1.2 million square acres (including Texas, whose annexation had essentially started the war) to the United States. This increased U.S. territory by 66 percent, and with the exception of the Gadsden Purchase (1853) and the purchase of Alaska (1867), the treaty completed the map of the modern continental United States.

In 1845 the United States annexed the independent Republic of Texas, with a dispute arising over what constituted the southern boundary of Texas, the Nueces River (based on maps drawn by Stephen F. *Austin*) or the *Rio Grande [I]* (based on the *Louisiana Purchase [II]* maps). President James K. Polk dispatched troops under General Zachary Taylor to the north bank of the Rio Grande in 1846, at which point a skirmish ensued. On

May 13, 1846, Congress declared war, and over the next two years, U.S. forces under Taylor, General Winfield Scott, and General Stephen *Kearny* won several victories at Monterrey, Veracruz, and Puebla, and then captured Mexico City in August 1847. In the process Kearny's troops conducted an expedition through New Mexico, Chihuahua, and California.

Polk had sent an emissary, Nicholas Trist, to conclude a peace. Trist drafted the Treaty of Guadalupe Hidalgo, which was highly favorable to the United States. Under the treaty, the United States received New Mexico, California, and the establishment of the Texas boundary at the Rio Grande. The United States agreed to pay the government of Mexico $15 million and to assume all claims by U.S. citizens against the Mexican government—a provision that benefited Southern interests, which had lost slaves and territory to Mexico. Mexican nationals living inside the new U.S. borders were to be granted property protection and civil rights but were in no way guaranteed protection of language or culture, as some later argued. The Senate ratified the treaty in May 1848, at which time U.S. troops left Mexico City.

Twain, Mark (Samuel Langhorne Clemens) (November 30, 1835–April 21, 1910)

One of America's greatest fiction writers, Mark Twain was born Samuel Langhorne Clemens in Florida, Missouri, on November 30, 1835. After the family moved to Hannibal, Missouri, where Clemens encountered some of his early frontier experiences. His father died when Clemens was 12, and thereafter he quit school to work on a newspaper. Seeking work, he moved around the country, eventually sailing down the Mississippi on a steamboat, where he paid the pilot to train him in the art of maneuvering the large craft. When the Civil War shut down private steam-boating, Clemens headed for Nevada, where his brother was territorial secretary. Once he arrived in the rich Carson City area, he engaged in prospecting and mining, before taking a full-time job at a Virginia City newspaper.

By that time he was using the pen name Mark Twain, had developed his own publications, and had made numerous enemies with his acerbic writings. He was forced to go to San Francisco, where he worked as a reporter, before again returning to the goldfields. He wrote of his experiences in "Jim Smiley and His Jumping Frog," which impressed San Francisco editors enough that they funded a trip for him to Hawaii, from which he wrote a series of travel letters to the papers. When he returned, Twain gave lectures about his experiences and found he could made a good living for these public talks. His columns had reached newspapers in Chicago and New York, which began to carry his work as well. Using money from the father of a female acquaintance, Twain bought part of a Buffalo paper. Twain also got a contract for *Innocents Abroad* (1869), and then in 1872 he published *Roughing It.*

Twain continued to write and circulate in New England literary and intellectual circles. In 1876 he produced one of his greatest works, *The Adventures of Tom Sawyer*, followed 12 years later by *Adventures of Huckleberry Finn.* These stories returned Twain to his childhood setting in Missouri where Tom Sawyer, Huckleberry Finn, and Becky Thatcher encountered interesting people and dangerous situations, all with a feel of childhood whimsy. *Huckleberry Finn* was published by Twain's own firm, founded in 1885 as Charles L. Webster. His company also published the memoirs of Ulysses S. Grant. The latter work brought Twain substantial income, some of which he spent on improved typesetting machinery.

After 1891 Twain rarely lived in the United States, but when he did return, he was hailed as a conquering hero. Mark Twain died on April 21, 1910, easily the most famous writer in America. He had managed to capture in his writing not only the early trans-Mississippi west of Nevada, but the Wild West of the California mining camps.

Vanderbilt, Cornelius (May 27, 1794–January 2, 1877)

One of America's first great entrepreneurs, Cornelius Vanderbilt was born in New York on May 27, 1794, and at a young age was sailing for profit, making more than $1,000 during his first full year in business. During the *War of 1812*, Vanderbilt acquired a fleet of vessels, and then began to operate a steamship line between New York City and New Brunswick, New Jersey. The competition produced by his service under Thomas Gibbons produced the interstate commerce ruling by the United States Supreme Court, *Gibbons v. Ogden* (1824). Vanderbilt expanded his enterprise to dominate shipping throughout New York and the eastern seaboard, eventually turning his eye to California.

Vanderbilt's Pacific Ship Canal Company, running from New York to California via Nicaragua, slashed passenger prices in half. Government-subsidized competitors could not defeat Vanderbilt, and finally bought his business, but prices to California remained a fraction of what they had been before the "Commodore," died in 1877.

Walker, Joseph R. (December 13, 1798– November 13, 1872)

Joseph R. Walker was born on December 13, 1798, in Tennessee, and moved to Missouri at age 21, where he began to hunt and trap with parties of mountain men. After spending four years as a sheriff in Independence, Missouri, he assisted a fur trading operation in the Rocky Mountains under the command of Captain Benjamin Bonneville in 1832. With a party of about 40 men under his direction, Walker explored California, following a trail from the Great Salt Lake, then taking the Humboldt River to a point where he encountered and defeated a tribe of Digger Indians. Some think Walker's party was the first group of Americans to view the Yosemite Valley. After his return, Walker had opened a new trail to California that added to the knowledge of the terrain and the climate.

After this expedition, Walker engaged in trapping for the *American Fur Company* and served as a guide for John C. *Fremont* on his second and third expeditions to California. By the 1850s Walker was engaged in a number of business enterprises, including ranching in California. He never quit exploring and soon led a party to Arizona to search for gold, which he found near Prescott, Arizona. He was eagerly sought out to lead expeditions throughout the Southwest, including the campaigns against the Apache chief *Mangas Coloradas*. After prospecting in Arizona for several years, Walker returned to California in 1867, where he died five years later.

The War of 1812

Often called the "Second War of American Independence," the War of 1812 had its origins in the Franco-British conflict in Europe, which had divided Americans since the presidency of George Washington. Great Britain, taking advantage of her superiority at sea, had blockaded Napoleon's Europe, while France proclaimed an embargo of British ports. But the Royal Navy could make the blockade stick, while France could do little. Attempting to trade with both nations, the United States, first under Thomas *Jefferson*, then under James Madison, invoked "freedom of the seas." The British, however not only boarded U.S. merchantmen but took their crews and "impressed" them into service for the Royal Navy.

In 1811 a group of congressmen known as the "War Hawks," including a number of southerners and westerners, such as Langdon Cheves and John C. Calhoun of South Carolina, Felix Grundy of Tennessee, and Richard Johnson and Henry *Clay* of Kentucky, came into office demanding war with England. While the West was little affected by the trade policies, Indian uprisings on the frontier—which many thought were instigated by the British—motivated their desire for war. The uprising by *Tecumseh* and his brother, *Tenskwatawa* in 1811, and the resulting *Battle of Tippecanoe*, confirmed the fears of the westerners.

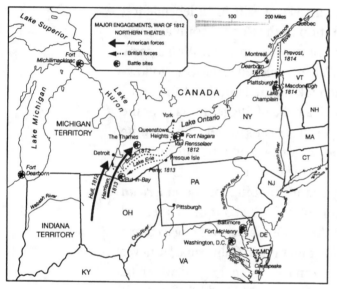

Major engagements in the War of 1812, Northern Theater. *Ron Acklin, University of Dayton Print and Design*

Congress declared war on June 18, 1812, although General William Hull had already taken command of the U.S. Army in Dayton, Ohio, before leading his forces toward Detroit. This marked a continuing effort by Americans to convince Canada, by reason or arms, to join the United States, and as before, the Canadians resisted. Hull's forays were deflected, and the British caused him to take refuge in Fort Detroit, whereupon Hull surrendered. Other western armies in Illinois and Michigan also dissipated. General Henry Dearborn's attempts to take Montreal likewise failed when his army nearly mutinied.

A second commander of the Northwest, William Henry *Harrison* (chosen by his men) led a campaign into the Detroit area in the fall of 1812. Attacking in the middle of winter, Harrison struck at Frenchtown in January 1813 and suffered a horrible defeat. Nothing could happen in the West until the United States gained control of the Great Lakes. After rebuilding the army during the summer of 1813, at which time he received a large body of Kentuckians, including Richard M. Johnson, Harrison got the break he needed when Commodore Oliver Hazard Perry defeated the British Great Lakes fleet at Put-In-Bay. Spreading sawdust on his decks to soak up the blood, Perry, seeing his own gunboat lose the use of all of its guns, sailed a nearby vessel and continued to lead the attack until the British surrendered. He marked the event with his famous line, "We have met the enemy and they are ours."

This opened the West for Harrison's advance into Canada. Johnson's cavalry scouted Detroit, then crossed into Canada in advance of Harrison's army. Fifteen miles away, British General Proctor, with 700 regulars and 1,200 Indians, continued to retreat up the Thames. Tecumseh had given Proctor an ultimatum to fight, or he would leave with the Indian forces, and on October 5, the British drew up to fight. Richard Johnson led a cavalry charge that disorganized the Indians—Tecumseh was killed early in the battle—and the British forces broke. While insignificant to the overall military results of the War, the Battle of the Thames smashed Indian power in the Northwest—the only long-term positive outcome in the war for the United States.

Other combat occurred in New York, where regular army ("Those are Regulars, by God!") forces fought British veterans to a draw. Andrew Jackson's Tennesseans, originally intended to reinforce General James Wilkinson at New Orleans, were dispatched to Alabama, where Creek warriors had massacred the defenders at Fort Mims. In March 1814, on the Tallapossa River, Jackson's troops defeated the Creek at the Battle of Horseshoe Bend. Jackson, promoted to major general, now moved to New Orleans, where he encountered a large force on January 8, 1815, under British General Edward Pakenham. The British were trapped in a funnel-shaped clearing and mounted an ambitious assault that was short-circuited by the sudden lifting of the fog that had concealed their movements. Pakenham was killed, the British force shattered, and the fighting over (the treaty having been signed in December 1814).

The negotiators had agreed to a *status quo antebellum*, with neither side gaining any significant territory or war aims. But for the West, the War of 1812 was significant: both in the Southwest and in the Southeast, Indian resistance had been crushed. And, despite the inability of American forces to win important open-field battles with the British, the war marked the second time that substantial numbers of British regular troops had themselves been unable to defeat either American militia or regulars on a consistent and decisive basis.

western art before the Civil War

Prior to the *Lewis and Clark* Expedition, there were few genuine western artists. Perhaps the first was Charles King Bird (1785–1862), who painted 150 portraits of Indians from west of the Mississippi commissioned by the Office of Indian Affairs. Later, a number of artists, including Titian Ramsay Peale (1799–1885), John Stanley (1814–1872), and Arthur Schott (1813–1875), illustrated the natural beauty of the West's sunsets, flora, fauna, mountains, and Indians. Some of these artists, especially George Catlin (1796–1872), who traveled up the Mississippi on a steamboat, painting *Blackfoot*, *Crow*, and Lakota Indians for his Catlin's Indian Gallery. This was one of the largest collections of art about the West to exist in the mid-1800s, and his work influenced Karl Bodmer (1809–1893) and Alfred Miller (1810–1874), who likewise painted Indians. All of these artists engaged in a romanticism about nature and Native Americans. This approach to art changed after the advent of photography, when Albert Bierstadt (1830–1902) began to copy the realism in photographic pictures into his paintings.

The emphasis prior to the Civil War remained landscapes and Indians. Seth Eastman (1808–1875), Charles Deas, and Paul Kane (1810–1871), all inspired by Catlin's gallery, determined to found their own Indian galleries, but only Stanley succeeded by opening a collection of 154 oils of Indians in 1850. These paintings went on display at the Smithsonian in 1865 and, along with several Charles Bird portraits, were destroyed in a fire.

Although the greatest decades for western art, with the works of giants such as Bierstadt, Charles Russell, and Frederick Remington, only appeared after the Civil War, the early painters had produced a solid foundation upon which the new generation could build.

western music before the Civil War

Music in the early West consisted of combinations of Irish and Scots-Irish jigs, African and African-derived melodies and rhythms, and Indian chants. The fiddle, brought from England and Ireland, provided a portable and popular instrument, which, combined with handclapping and foot stomping, was music enough for a reel or square dance. Other popular instruments were banjos and harmonicas, both of which were also portable.

As settlers crossed the trans-Appalachian West, the Irish influences in their music soon melded with the Spanish vaquero songs. Ballads tended to be songs imported from England, such as "Barbara Allen" and "Green Grow the Lilacs." By 1860, though, the cowboy West had started to develop its own musical styles and lyrics that dealt specifically with the trail or life in cow towns. "The Streets of Laredo," "The Cowboy's Lament," and "Chisholm Trail" were typical of this genre, which often adapted American western commentary to English tunes. Guitars, popular with the Spanish, also became common instruments on the trail, while in towns, every saloon had its piano. Settlements brought churches and religious songs, mostly English imports, and these melodies and African American spirituals also wove their way into the musical fabric.

The Whitman mission

The Whitmans were two of the most famous missionaries to venture into the antebellum American West. Marcus Whitman (1802–1847) was a physician from upstate New York. As a young man, Marcus decided to travel west and live as a missionary among northwestern Indians. In 1835 he toured the Pacific Northwest looking for mission sites. A year later, he married Narcissa Prentiss back in New York. That same year the American Board of Commissioners for Foreign Missions, the missionary branch of the Presbyterian church, sent the Whitmans to the Pacific Northwest. The Whitman party founded a mission at what is today Walla Walla.

Serious problems plagued the Presbyterian mission from the beginning. First, Whitman's missionary partner was Henry *Spalding*, who had once unsuccessfully courted Narcissa and remained a bitter person, losing more converts than he gained. Second, the Whitmans settled next to the hostile Cayuse Indians. When the *Oregon Trail* developed next to the mission, whites spread rapidly among the local Indian populations, who blamed the foreign invasion on the Christianity of the Whitmans. In 1847 angry Cayuse Indians slaughtered the Whitmans as well as 12 of their companions.

Young, Brigham (June 1, 1801–August 29, 1877)

The successor to Joseph Smith as the leader of the Church of Jesus Christ of *Latter-day Saints* ("Mormons"), Brigham Young was born in Whitingham, Vermont, to a large family, and grew up in New York, where he worked on the family farm doing a wide range of tasks. In 1815 he left home to become a carpenter, learning the trade well enough to establish a shop and mill in Mendon, New York. Young had read the *Book of Mormon*, becoming baptized as a Mormon in 1832 and meeting with Joseph Smith in Kirtland, Ohio, later that year. Young abandoned his carpentry profession to become a preacher and missionary. The church leaders named him an "Apostle" in 1835, and after following Smith to Missouri in 1838, Young was assigned the direction of the 12,000 Mormons to Illinois when the state of Missouri evicted them that year.

As senior Apostle, Young undertook a missionary trip to England in 1840, returning to Nauvoo, Illinois, in 1841, where he was named president of the Twelves Apostles. As Smith's special assistant, Young was in the East, raising funds for the temple to be constructed at Nauvoo, when Joseph Smith and his brother were killed in 1844. That elevated Young to the de facto leader of the church and required him to deal with the hostilities surrounding Smith's death. Nauvoo had become the largest city in Illinois and the Mormons had tremendous political influence, which marked them as a threat to the non-Mormon "gentile" citizens of the state. Then, 500 Mormon men and some 70 women volunteered for an expedition during the Mexican War. Payment for that service financed the Mormons' expedition into the Salt Lake Valley in 1847. There, on July 24, 1847, Young said "This is the place" and immediately set groups to farm, build housing, and clear land. He returned to Winter Quarters in December 1847, at which time he was ratified as church president. The second large migration of Mormons under Young's leadership arrived in Salt Lake in 1848. During the gold rush of 1849, Salt Lake City thrived as a major outpost along the trail to California. Virtually all of the Mormons from Illinois or along the Missouri River had migrated to Utah by 1852, growing and refining sugar, growing and ginning cotton, and establishing a network of businesses, from lumbering, to banking, to lead mining.

When Congress created Utah Territory in 1850, Young was appointed governor and superintendent of Indian Affairs, a position that fit him well in that he had made extensive overtures to the local Indians for amicable relations. But the unity of the Mormons, and their (to gentiles) odd religious beliefs, remained a potential threat. In 1857 President James Buchanan removed Young as governor and dispatched troops to the region to enforce his decision. Young organized a defense, sending the territorial militia to defend Utah against the federal incursion. Colonel Albert Sidney Johnston, at the head of the federal column, finally marched into Salt Lake City, only to find that Young and the Mormons had abandoned the city and withdrawn to southern Utah. In 1858 the "Utah War" was over, and four years later the army left Utah to fight Confederates.

During the Civil War, President Abraham Lincoln was unsure of the Mormons' loyalty but could only send a single regiment to Utah. Young, meanwhile, built telegraph lines, roadbeds, and bridges for the transcontinental railroad, and generally supported the mining economy of the hills. He continued to govern the Mormons as a "theocracy," even though countless federal judges and other territorial officials came and went. Brigham Young had a hand in virtually every major cultural or economic development in the region, from the Salt Lake Theater, to the University of Utah (then University of Deseret), Brigham Young University (then Brigham Young Academy), as well as a number of cooperative stores in almost every town. He dispatched missionaries to Arizona, Nevada, and Idaho, establishing large Mormon communities in those territories.

Along with his social, economic, political, and cultural activities, Young dominated church developments during this time. He had accepted the Smith doctrine of plural marriages and had at least 20 wives and 57 children and was once tried, but not convicted, of bigamy. Young died in Salt Lake City on August 29, 1877, having accomplished enough in a lifetime for 10 people.

PART IV

From the Civil War to the Closing of the Frontier (1861–1893)

In the popular imagination, the "West" is overwhelmingly associated with the events that occurred in the period from 1865 to 1890, that is, from the end of the Civil War to the Battle of Wounded Knee. It was in this period, for the most part, that the prominent images of cowboys and Indians, Wild West shows, cavalry charges, farming, buffalo, barbed wire, railroads, mining towns, gunfights, lawmen, and desperadoes all emerge.

America's Civil War had a great impact on the West, even though few actual battles took place on either the Great Plains or in the Far West. If the frontier did not run red with the blood of Yankee and Rebel dead, it nevertheless felt the effects of numerous Civil War policies enacted by the Union government. Wartime legislation gave land grants to transcontinental railroads, established a system of national banks, provided for cheap land sales through the Homestead Act, and set up a series of technical schools through the Morrill Act. The war stimulated a market for western wheat, corn, and livestock, brought to eastern markets by the steadily expanding network of railroads. Moreover, the war marked the triumph of "free soil, free labor, free men" as a working definition of America's attitudes toward expansion.

After the war, miners and cattlemen headed west, creating legendary towns in remote locations—Dodge City, Abilene, Reno, Sacramento, and

Tombstone. As the railroads followed, the market economy further integrated the West with the rest of the nation. For 30 years, and more in some locations, the frontier elements of the Wild West remained strong. Lawmen, such as "Bat" Masterson, Wyatt Earp, and Wild Bill Hickock, gained as much notoriety as the criminals they chased, including famous outlaws such as Billy the Kid, Calamity Jane, Butch Cassidy, and the Dalton Gang. Often the line between the two groups was blurred. But while gunfighters dominated some of the roughest towns, the overall level of violence and crime in the West stayed consistently low. Bank robberies were particularly rare, and as civilization and urban growth followed the frontier days, even the more rugged western towns became centers of economic and commercial growth. Technology steadily linked West to East: first, the Pony Express, then the telegraph, then finally the transcontinentals. Once communication and transportation over the Rockies became routine, a certain air of civility was inevitable.

Expansion in the postbellum period occurred at the expense of the Plains Indians, who found themselves consistently pushed further west and onto worse lands. Efforts to find a solution to the "Indian problem" swung between assimilation and annihilation, with religious reformers holding the former view and warriors such as General Phil Sheridan, General George Crook, and Lieutenant Colonel George Armstrong Custer holding the latter position. Ultimately, even the assimilationists realized that their goal of turning Indians into "white men in buckskins" was as deadly to Indian culture as military actions. As much as the greed of miners plunging into the Black Hills, the government's inconsistent Indian policies precipitated several disastrous military expeditions, including the Fetterman massacre, the Battle of Little Bighorn, and the army assault on Wounded Knee. Indian chiefs such as Geronimo, Red Cloud, Sitting Bull, and Crazy Horse were all well known to Americans living on the East Coast. Nevertheless, their resistance only delayed the inevitable white conquest of the West, and alternative outcomes to the reservation system are hard to conceive.

The stories of gold lying on California hills and silver buried just beneath the surface of Nevada mines produced a steady [II] influx of treasure hunters, then, right behind them, of merchants who could supply their needs. Land for cattle or for large-scale commercial agriculture beckoned, pulling thousands of farmers, ranchers, and laborers westward. These new migrations were interspersed with religious groups, such as the Latter-day Saints ("Mormons"), who moved en masse to Utah. Already, former frontier outposts such as St. Louis, Chicago, and Cincinnati had become commercial and cultural centers attempting to match eastern cities in refinement and opportunity. Now a host of new economic centers appeared—Denver, Laramie, Kansas City, El Paso, Albuquerque, Los Angeles, Portland—each demanding rail links to major markets. Yet even as the frontier faded, entrepreneurs such as Leland Stanford, David Moffat, and Frederick Weyerhauser built railroads, dug mines, cleared land for farms, and cut timber to bring the West into the mainstream of the American economy.

Cattle ranching gave life to the cities along the rail lines. Cattle were driven northward from huge ranches, such as the King Ranch in Texas, along famous cattle-drive trails, including the Goodnight-Loving Trail, to cattle towns. A culture associated with the cowboy arose that remains with us to the present. Cowboys bred their own special horses for cutting and running down cattle, honed their skills at roping and pulling down steers, and then marked the animals with a brand. All of the practices associated with the cattle drives found their way into competitive events in rodeos.

Politically, the West emphasized issues related to the land—property and water rights, conservation, irrigation—and to the capital needed to develop the land. It is not surprising that the silver and greenback issue generated more intensity among westerners than in any other region, and not just because silver was mined in the West. Rather, westerners sensed that the scarcity of money and credit demanded political responses, culminating in the Bland-Allison Act and the Sherman Silver Purchase Act. Railroads also became the focus of partisanship, and the land grants brought government investment in western railroads under scrutiny.

The West started to assume a mythical status in American culture, with legends of cowboys, lawmen, famous Indians, and outlaws reaching large numbers of the reading public through dime novels and in Wild West shows. History books, such as those written by Hubert How Bancroft, celebrated American expansion. The region took on its own distinct dress, through the pants produced by Levi Strauss, the garb of the cowboys (including chaps, hats, and spurs), and clothing items assimilated from the Indians. By 1890 the West had started to produce its own music, its own painting, its own cultural events unique to the cattle culture, and its own form of dress. Its entrepreneurs had opened the land for growth, while conservationists preserved parts of it for posterity. The Indians, having lost most of their lands, nevertheless survived and retained a form of autonomy. A true "western character" had started to emerge.

CHRONOLOGY — From the Civil War to the Closing of the Frontier

1861–1865	American Civil War
1862	Homestead Act; Land Grant College Act (Morrill Act); Battle of Glorieta Pass; Minnesota Sioux War
1863	Levi Strauss Company founded
1863–1864	National Bank and Currency Acts
1863–1868	Bozeman Trail opened
1864	Sand Creek Massacre
1865	Goodnight-Loving Trail blazed
1866	Fetterman Massacre
1867	Medicine Lodge Treaty
1868	Battle of Washita
1870s–1890s	Agrarian unrest, rise of the Farmer's Alliance, the Grange, and the Populist Party; Santa Fe Ring operates in New Mexico
1872–1917	"Buffalo Bill" Cody tours with his "Wild West Show"
1873	Modoc War; Panic of 1873; barbed wire invented
1874–1875	Red River War
1876	Little Bighorn; Hickok killed in Deadwood, South Dakota
1877	Dawes Act
1878	Meeker Massacre; Nez Perce War; Bland-Allison Act; James J. Hill founds the Great Northern Railroad
1879	Bureau of Ethnography founded
1881	Billy the Kid killed by Sheriff Pat Garrett; gunfight at the O.K. Corral, Tombstone
1882	Chinese Exclusion Act
1885	Rock Springs Massacre
1886	Geronimo surrenders to General Nelson Miles
1889	First Oklahoma Land Rush; Omnibus Bill passed
1890	Sherman Silver Purchase Act; Johnson County War begins; Dalton Gang robs banks in Kansas; Wounded Knee Massacre
1893	Panic of 1893; Frederick Jackson Turner presents his "Frontier Thesis" to historians

Bancroft, Hubert Howe (May 5, 1832–March 2, 1918)

Born in Granville, Ohio, on May 5, 1832, Hubert Howe Bancroft worked around books as a teenager and in 1852 transported a large shipment of books to California, where his father had moved in order to mine gold. Four years later, he opened a mercantile and bookshop business, which had success enough to allow Bancroft to engage his dream of developing an encyclopedia of the West. He relied on a staff of assistants, including his librarian, Henry L. Oak (1844–1905), to catalogue, index, and even write drafts of the topical volumes.

Bancroft personally wrote *The Native Races of the Pacific States of North America* (1875–1876), a 5-volume anthropological and historical study of native Americans, while relying on staff to help him produce *History of Central America*, 3 volumes (1882–1887); *History of Mexico*, 6 volumes (1883–1888); and 19 other topical volumes covering virtually all aspects of the West. In 1890 he published two volumes that dealt with the project and which were autobiographical, *Literary Industries* and *Works of Hubert Howe Bancroft, Essays and Miscellany*.

Bancroft hired a corps of salesmen to publicize the encyclopedia throughout the country, eventually producing gross sales of more than $1 million on some 6,000 sales of the 39-book set. But his writing associates were angered by his failure to cite their contributions, and Oak published his own book, *"Literary Industries" in a New Light* in 1893. Nevertheless, despite shortcomings of research and editing—often Bancroft did not examine archival materials, as in the case of Mexico—the volumes remain a classic work of American historical scholarship. Bancroft sold his library to the University of California at Berkeley for $250,000 in 1905 and continued writing until his death in 1918.

barbed wire

The Great Plains presented a difficult problem for farmers: how could they fence their land in a region that often was devoid of trees for wooden fences? New Englanders solved this on occasion with stone fences, but stones were as scarce as trees on the plains. As long as merely identifying boundaries remained the central problem, farmers could get along without fences. But when herds of cattle began overrunning farmlands, the issue of keeping animals out grew extreme, and at a cost of 60 to 300 percent more than fencing in other areas, plains farmers needed relief.

In response, Henry Rose apparently developed the first prototype barbed wire, which he displayed at a De Kalb, Illinois, fair in 1873, where some farmers, Farwell Glidden, Isaac Ellwood, and Jacob Haish, spotted the wire and began to improve upon it. Glidden's patent featured spur wires held in place by two other wires twisted around them, making it easy to mass produce. Ellwood soon joined Glidden in a partnership, and in 1878 hired a young salesman named John Warne Gates (later nicknamed "Bet-a-Million" Gates because of his outrageous wagers). Gates took the wire samples to Texas, where the wire sold itself, and Gates realized that the real money to be made was in manufacturing, not selling the wire. He established a plant in St. Louis to compete with the Glidden/Ellwood facility.

Glidden sold his interest to the Washburn and Moen Company of Massachusetts. By 1880 the company was churning out some 80 million pounds of barbed wire a year. Farmers saw clearly the value of the cheap, easily installed wire. This single invention instantly leveled the playing field of property rights between large cattle ranchers and small farmers. Gates, meanwhile, had persevered in his dream of consolidating all the wire companies, and in 1898 he formed American Steel & Wire Company, in New Jersey, which he sold four years later to U.S. Steel.

Battle of the Little Bighorn, 1876

The most famous battle of the Indian wars, the Battle of the Little Bighorn is also known as "Custer's Last Stand," where, on June 25, 1876, a large portion of Lieutenant Colonel George Armstrong *Custer*'s regiment of Seventh Cavalry soldiers was massacred by *Sioux* and *Cheyenne* warriors under Chiefs *Sitting Bull* and *Crazy Horse*. It marked the worst single defeat by the *United States Cavalry* on the Great Plains.

In the Second Treaty of Fort Laramie (1868), the Indians received exclusive possession of the Dakota territory west of the *Missouri River [I]*. Six years later, the discovery of gold in the sacred Black Hills generated a flood of white prospectors and provoked reprisals by Sioux. The U.S. government found it could not keep the prospectors out, nor could it persuade the Sioux to sell the territory. Consequently Indian agencies instructed the Indians that they all must return to designated reservations by January 31, 1876, or be viewed as "hostiles," subject to military action. Even had the Indians chosen to comply, hunting parties already out on the plains would not have received the instructions, ensuring a conflict of some type. When the Sioux and Cheyenne did not move, the government dispatched an army to round up the Indians in the Powder River area of Montana and remove them to the reservations.

Brigadier General Alfred Howe Terry commanded the operation, which left from Fort Abraham Lincoln with a large column of infantry, several Gatling guns, and the Seventh U.S. Cavalry under the command of Colonel Custer. Moving from the east, Terry's column was to meet a second force directed by General George *Crook*, coming up the Yellowstone River from the south. Terry's column was delayed, arriving at the Powder on June 7. Terry dispatched Major Marcus *Reno* and six companies to scout the Powder and Tongue Rivers, coming back down the Yellowstone. After locating indications of large villages, Reno reunited with Terry at the Yellowstone, where Terry and General John Gibbon planned to have yet another separate column under Gibbon move to the confluence of the Bighorn and Little Bighorn Rivers, where they expected the Indians to have camped. Custer was sent up the Rosebud and across the Little Bighorn River to crush the Indians between three armies, with Crook blocking any escape to the south. (Crook was defeated on June 17, but the news did not reach Custer's column.)

Custer, who had the only column comprised entirely of cavalry, had to slow down in order to coordinate his arrival with the other armies. The Seventh Cavalry, with more than 700 troops plus a pack train, departed from Terry's command on June 22. Contrary to orders, Custer made forced marches to the area, arriving on the morning of June 25. Custer had already received several reports from his white and Indian scouts that large Indian concentrations lay ahead—somewhere between 2,500 and 5,000 warriors. Told his own troops had been discovered, and concerned the Indians would escape, Custer planned a reckless and unorthodox attack on the villages.

Rather than wait for Terry, he determined to attack in the middle of the day and divided his regiment into three columns. Major Reno took three troops to Custer's left; Captain Frederick W. Benteen commanded three troops even further to the left, so as to prevent the Indians from escaping to the south. Custer took five troops in what he anticipated would be the main assault force, leaving one troop with the pack train. Every indicator suggests that well into the battle Custer still believed that his main difficulty lay in preventing the Indians from escaping, not in preserving his regiment.

Benteen disappeared from view in the sharp ravines and gullies, drifting back to Custer's left behind him and Reno. The pack train dropped even further behind. When the columns led by Custer and Reno reached a high spot overlooking modern-day Reno Creek, where they rode side-by-side for some distance, they observed a party of warriors riding away from them—a rear guard of a small lodge, it turned out. But it convinced Custer the village was in flight, despite repeated warnings from his scouts who told him that a huge village lay ahead.

Custer instructed Reno to attack, promising the entire Seventh would support him. Reno's command crossed the Little Bighorn (known to the Indians as "Greasy Grass"), riding toward the village when the soldiers discovered that the Indians were attacking, not retreating. Warriors poured out of the village, and Reno ordered his troops to dismount and form a skirmish line, but the Indians quickly flanked him, whereupon Reno ordered a retreat to the river. Indians now rode among the cavalry, generating confusion and terror. After reaching the river, Reno indecisively ordered his men to move to the bluffs across the river, then to dismount and form a skirmish line, then to mount up again. Finally, after the loss of nearly one-third of his command, Reno reached the bluffs overlooking the Little Bighorn.

At almost the same time, Benteen, having encountered no resistance on the left, rode to the sound of the guns to find himself under fire with Reno.

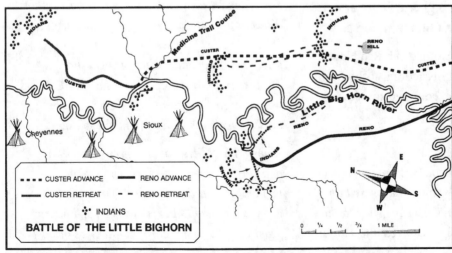

The Battle of the Little Bighorn. *Ron Acklin, University of Dayton Print and Design*

All of what remained of Reno's and Benteen's companies, or about 250 men, took up defensive positions on the bluffs. Reno refused to move, despite good evidence that a battle was going on downstream. Instead, he waited for the remainder of the pack train to arrive. In short, Reno with more men than Custer had failed to reinforce his superior officer.

Custer, meanwhile, had advanced north of the Little Bighorn along bluffs heading to the Medicine Tail Coulee. Hoping to take the Indian village in the rear, he rode into an ambush planned by Crazy Horse at the bottom of the coulee. Crazy Horse admonished his warriors with the call, "Today is a good day to die." Driven back by large numbers of Indians, Custer's troops dismounted, assumed a defensive position, and waited for assistance that he wrongly assumed was coming from Benteen. Nevertheless, Custer's request to McDougall with the baggage to "bring packs, p.s., bring packs" indicated he thought he would need plenty of ammunition for a longer battle.

Instead, overwhelmed and broken into several confused, panicked, and divided units, Custer's five troops dismounted and fought where they were as Indians came at them from every direction. The battle did not last long. Most

IN THEIR OWN Words

Battle of the Little Bighorn, First Person Narrative of Lakota Chief Red Horse

In 1881 the Lakota Sioux chief, Red Horse, gave this account of his actions at the Battle of the Little Bighorn, commemorated as "Custer's Last Stand."

Five springs ago I, with many Sioux Indians, took down and packed up our tipis and moved from Cheyenne river to the Rosebud river, where we camped a few days;

then took down and packed up our lodges and moved to the Little Bighorn [sic] river and pitched our lodges with the large camp of Sioux. . . . I was a Sioux chief in the council lodge. My lodge was pitched in the center of the camp. The day of the attack I and four women were a short distance from the camp digging wild turnips. Suddenly one of the women attracted my attention to a cloud of dust rising a short distance from the camp. I soon saw that soldiers were charging the camp. . . . The Sioux mount horses, take guns, and go fight the soldiers.

Among the soldiers was an officer who rode a horse with four white feet [evidently, Capt. French, Seventh U.S. Cavalry]. The Sioux have for a long time fought many brave men of different people, but the Sioux say this officer was the evidence suggests that Custer's command was wiped out in less than 45 minutes. Custer's men were courageous, according to the Indians, and the positions of the bodies indicated that to the last, Custer used the most sensible defensive tactics, organizing what was left of his troops into skirmish lines.

Benteen, Reno, and McDougall had reorganized and attempted an advance downstream toward the gunfire, not knowing that the battle by then was nearly over. The Indians, turning from Custer's position, drove the reinforcements back to Reno Hill, where the troopers held out through the night of June 26. Terry's column soon arrived, rescuing the survivors on Reno Hill. Subsequent investigations blamed Custer and/or Reno for poor military judgment. Although the Indians won a tremendous victory, as Sitting Bull warned, white men would soon overwhelm the Indians.

Battle of the Washita, 1868

The Battle of the Washita was one of many hostile acts resulting from the failed Medicine Lodge Treaty of 1867. Fearful that the United States meant

bravest man they had ever fought. I don't know whether this was Gen. [George Armstrong] Custer or not. Many of the Sioux men I hear talking tell me it was. . . . This officer saved the lives of many soldiers by turning his horse and covering the retreat. Sioux say this officer was the bravest man they ever fought. I saw two officers looking alike, both having long yellowish hair.

The soldiers charged the Sioux camp about noon. The soldiers were divided, one party charging right into the camp [Maj. Marcus Reno's command, no doubt]. After driving these soldiers across the river, the Sioux charged the different soldiers [i.e., Custer's troops] below, and drive them in confusion; these soldiers

became foolish, many throwing away their guns and raising their hands, saying, "Sioux, pity us; take us prisoners." The Sioux did not take a single soldier prisoner, but killed all of them; none were left alive for even a few minutes.

The Sioux took the guns and cartridges off the dead soldiers and went to the hill on which the soldiers were, surrounded and fought them with the guns and cartridges of the dead soldiers. Had the soldiers not divided I think they would have killed many Sioux. The different soldiers [again, Custer's troops] that the Sioux killed made five brave stands. Once the Sioux charged right in the midst of the different soldiers and scattered them all, fighting among the soldiers hand to hand.

—SOURCE: GARRICK MALLERY, "PICTURE WRITING OF THE AMERICAN INDIANS, 10TH ANNUAL REPORT OF THE BUREAU OF AMERICAN ETHNOLOGY, 1893," ON-LINE AT www.pbs/org/weta/thewest/wpages/wpgs660/bighorn.htm.

to overturn their traditional way of life, roughly 2,000 southern plains war-riors attacked farming settlements in western Kansas following the sign-ing of the treaty. Major General Phil *Sheridan*, in charge of western armies, ordered peaceful Indians to remain on the reservations so that the army could chase down the hostiles. Lieutenant Colonel George Armstrong *Custer* and his cavalry struck *Black Kettle*'s band of Northern *Cheyenne* in their winter villages along the Washita River near present-day Elk City, Oklahoma, in late November 1868. Though Black Kettle had desired and counseled peace, many of his young men wanted war and had been guilty of attacking the Kansas settlers. When Custer hit the village, he failed to distinguish guilt from innocence. After two hours of close combat, the United States claimed victory, having killed the Cheyenne chief and 102 warriors. Black Kettle's band had already suffered great losses at the *Sand Creek Massacre* exactly four years earlier. Custer ordered the total destruc-tion of the remains of the Cheyenne village.

Bean, Roy (1825–March 16, 1903)

A self-styled judge whose shingle over his saloon read "Law West of the Pecos," "Judge" Roy Bean was born in Kentucky, where he led a rough and tumble life. At age 22, he and his brother left for Mexico, then San Diego, then Los Angeles, in each case leaving just ahead of the law. Following the murder of his brother, Bean became a saloonkeeper. He fought with a Mexican officer, whom he killed, and a mob hanged him, at which point the rope stretched just enough that his girlfriend could free him. The incident prompted Bean to leave for New Mexico, where he joined up with Confederate troops for a brief time. For much of the Civil War, Bean was a blockade runner, operating out of San Antonio for many years.

In 1882 he moved west of the Pecos River, opening a tent saloon. Later, he established a more formal business at Dead Man's Canyon under the name "Jersey Lilly." He had gained an appointment as justice of the peace, despite lacking a law license, and the *Texas Rangers [III]* supported his decisions. At the Jersey Lilly, the law and liquor mixed freely. Bean handed down rulings that were often practical, but occasionally odd. He refused to find a man who murdered a Chinese guilty because there was no law against killing "a Chinaman," Bean said. His reputation grew, as did his self-spun stories that came from his court rulings. Roy Bean died in the town he founded in Texas on March 16, 1903.

Billy the Kid (Henry McCarty or William H. Bonney) (September 15, 1859–July 14, 1881)

A western legend, Billy the Kid was born in Brooklyn, New York, as Henry McCarty, and when his mother remarried, he briefly took his stepfather's name of Antrim, then settled on William H. Bonney. Most people just called him "the Kid."

In 1874, after his mother died, Bonney landed in jail for a minor incident, and after that decided on a life of crime. He engaged in horse rustling, killed at least one man by age 17, and gained a reputation as a member of the "regulators" in the Lincoln County War of 1878 in New Mexico. Allied with the forces of John Tunstall against Lawrence Murphy, Billy the Kid was in the party of vigilantes who captured two men accused of murdering Tunstall. While escorting them to jail, the men were shot, most likely by the Kid. Billy the Kid was also involved in an ambush of Sheriff William Brady in Lincoln. In July 1878 he participated in a shootout with a sheriff's posse reinforced by army troops.

Billy the Kid soon ended up with cattle rustlers near the Pecos River. He was captured by Sheriff Pat *Garrett* in December 1880 and tried for the murder of Sheriff Brady. Sentenced to hang, the Kid escaped in April 1881 and holed up in Fort Sumner until July 14, when Sheriff Garrett shot him. National publications such as the *Police Gazette* had already made him a legend, and Garrett contributed to the myth in his book, *Authentic Life of Billy the Kid*. The short life and significance of Billy the Kid is disproportionate to the legendary status his name still retains in the popular imagination.

Black Hills

The Black Hills of South Dakota, which contain ridges that are darkly colored, were home to numerous Indian tribes in the 1700s and 1800s. Because of the abundance of wildlife, many tribes hunted and settled in the region, including the *Sioux*, *Cheyenne*, *Kiowa*, and *Arikara [III]*, although the Sioux soon pushed the others out. White explorers came in the 1740s, then settlers followed after the Civil War, when the Treaty of 1868 set aside the Sioux Reservation for the Lakota Sioux. Gold was discovered there in 1874, and the rush started, with soldiers incapable of protecting the boundaries. After bloody warfare between whites and Indians, the Black Hills Act of 1877 ended Indian claims to the area.

Along with the natural beauty, which attracts visitors, and casinos in such refurbished "*ghost towns*" as Deadwood, tourists today are attracted to the Black Hills for the Mount Rushmore Memorial, a gigantic granite cliff sculpture of the faces of presidents George Washington, Thomas *Jefferson [III]*, Abraham Lincoln, and Theodore *Roosevelt [V]*. Carved out of the mountainside by sculptor Gutzon Borglum in the 1930s, the faces on the memorial stand 60 feet tall. The Sioux, meanwhile, have mounted numerous suits to reclaim the land of their ancestors.

Black Kettle (ca. 1803–November 27, 1868)

A pro-American Northern *Cheyenne* peace chief, Black Kettle spent the last decade of his life witnessing American atrocities committed against his people. In 1864 former Methodist preacher and hero of the *Civil War* Battle of Glorietta Pass, Colonel John M. *Chivington* led a group of Colorado volunteers against Black Kettle's village on the *Sand Creek* in eastern Colorado. Though the village was ostensibly under the protection of the *United States Cavalry* stationed at Fort Lyon, Chivington and his men massacred hundreds of women and children. Though Black Kettle survived the 1864 slaughter, George *Custer*'s troops killed him at the 1868 *Battle of the Washita River*.

Bland, Richard P. (August 19, 1835–June 15, 1899)

Richard P. "Silver Dick" Bland gained notoriety as the House leader of the "free silver" movement in the late 19th century, authoring the Bland-Allison Act of 1878. Born in Hartford, Kentucky, Bland moved to Nevada in the 1850s, working as a miner and prospector.

He also dabbled in politics and law. Elected to Congress from Missouri as a Democrat in 1872, Bland, as chairman of the Committee on

Mines and Mining, supported the remonetization of silver by requiring the government to coin and mint silver at "16:1," or 16 ounces of silver to 1 ounce of gold. That ratio, established in 1834, had contributed to the demonetization of silver by overvaluing gold for many years. After new silver discoveries in Nevada, combined with the adoption of the gold standard by several European countries, silver prices fell low enough to make coinage of silver by the U.S. government attractive again.

Populists, farmers, and miners wanted inflation to pay off debts in money that steadily lost value, while the "stability" factions—businesses and banks—wanted "sound money," which made the real cost of loans higher because the dollars would be worth more. To combat the deflation that swept through the United States after the Civil War, Bland crusaded for a bimetallic standard. In 1878 the "free silver" movement won its first victory with the Bland-Allison Act, which required the federal government to purchase between 2 and 4 million ounces of silver at market prices and to coin it. This only increased the money supply slightly. In 1890 the *Sherman Silver Purchase Act* required the government to purchase even more silver, at a fixed price above the market—above 16:1, which the silverites wanted, though not nearly in line with the 17:1 real price of silver. The mismatch in real costs of silver versus the requirements of the law created an opportunity for speculators, and gold flowed out of the country as silver poured in at artificially inflated prices. As the economy weakened, Congress repealed the Sherman Act. In the 1890s Bland resisted U.S. involvement in Cuba, and he died in 1899.

Bosque Redondo

After the devastating forced *Navajo Long Walk*, the Navajo spent the next four years (1864–1868) on the Bosque Redondo reservation in eastern New Mexico. The Bosque Redondo was the first attempt by the United States not just to contain an Indian peoples, but to "Americanize" them. Bosque Redondo was to be a testing ground for all future reservation policy. Its American leader, Brigadier General James H. Carleton, believed he could make the Navajos into Christian farmers in a matter of years. He also hoped the old would die quickly so that he could concentrate his efforts on the young Navajos. The former goal quickly eluded the frustrated Carleton, as the Navajos experienced numerous problems at the reservation: They were forced to live with their traditional enemies, the Mescalero Apaches; the soil in the region was worthless for farming; the water was alkaline and caused dysentery; the government failed to provide adequate rations, clothing, or shelter; and the *Kiowas* and *Comanches* frequently attacked them. Conditions proved so bad that by 1868, the Navajos simply refused to comply with the United States any longer. That same year William Tecumseh *Sherman* visited the reservation. Horrified by what he saw, Sherman used his influence in Washington to resettle the Navajos on their traditional lands and provide them with livestock.

Bozeman Trail

Running from Julesburg, Colorado, to Fort Laramie to the Powder River, then to the Yellowstone River into Virginia City and the goldfields in Montana, the Bozeman Trail was named for John M. Bozeman, who mapped the trail beginning in 1863. The trail ran through *Sioux* territory and the goldfields brought hundreds of miners who intruded on Sioux lands. Although the federal government had to establish Forts Reno and Kearny to protect the prospectors and keep them out of Indian lands, the presence of the army did little to correct the situation. *Red Cloud* launched an offensive against the miners that shut down the trail by 1868. After the Sioux Wars, however, the trail was reopened as a main cattle route to the north.

buffalo (bison)

Vast herds of large, thick-haired animals of the cow family, called buffalo, or bison, roamed the North American Plains long before Europeans arrived. Just how many buffalo were in North America remains a matter of sharp debate. Claims of Europeans that they saw "millions" of animals were doubtless in error by several orders of magnitude. *Lewis and Clark* observed a herd of 20,000 and led to errors or exaggerations of the total number of animals on the plains. Recent estimates, based on the "carrying capacity" of the grasslands, put the number of buffalo at about 27 million or fewer.

These animals were mobile, with the average animal standing 5 to 6 feet tall and weighing 2,000 pounds, making a buffalo the largest animal in the United States. A bison lived 20 to 30 years and had few natural predators. Wolves, wild dogs, and some wild cats could attack herds. Indians hunted buffalo far more ruthlessly than has been previously thought. Several new studies by historians and anthropologists confirm that Indians regularly engaged in burning prairies to kill herds, drove them off cliffs, and hunted them through a variety of clever methods. Of course, the lack of technology in the hands of Indians limited their overall detrimental effect on the herds, which were close to extermination after the arrival of European hunters on the plains. White hunters such as the famous William Frederick "Buffalo Bill" Cody killed the animals by the thousands to provide food for railroad workers. Using long-range, rapid-fire rifles, white hunters could kill in a few days herds that might take Indians weeks to eliminate. By 1900, according to some estimates, the North American buffalo herd numbered as few as 1,000.

A great mythology has grown up about the Indians' relationship with the buffalo. It was a religious symbol to many tribes, and Plains Indians used every part of the buffalo for something—dung for fire, bone for arrow tips and ornaments, hides for blankets, muscle for string, blood for paint, and so on. However, that does not mean that the Indians used all the buffalo they killed. Missionaries and scouts frequently came upon entire herds rotting in the sun. But if Indians used only a portion of the animals they killed, whites used even less: except for the meat and the hides, buffalo had little utility for the hunters. Hides sold for a few dollars, and one ton of bones went for $4 to $12. As more farmers moved to the Great

The modern buffalo is the descendent of Bison Antiqua. Unlike its forefathers, the modern buffalo lives according to a herd mentality. The herds are resilient, surviving with significant adaptive skills as well as with a short gestation period. *Bradley J. Birzer*

Plains, the buffalo became a nuisance. Fenced cattle lands cut off buffalo grazing grounds, further destroying the herds.

The most important aspect of the buffalo's near extinction was the rescue by both the government and the private sector. Buffalo were protected inside *Yellowstone National Park*, then inside other federal parks. Ironically, "Buffalo Bill *Cody*'s Wild West Show" exposed the plight of the buffalo to easterners, who rallied to rescue the animal. Small buffalo farms appeared; then in 1902 Theodore *Roosevelt [V]* established a game warden at Yellowstone specifically to restore the buffalo herds. The American Bison Society worked to publicize the problem and solicit support to restore the herds. By 1996 more than 200,000 bison existed in mostly private herds.

Buffalo Soldiers

The name "Buffalo Soldiers" was given by the Indians to African Americans in the U.S. Army on the frontier. Blacks had fought in American conflicts since the Revolution and served in Kansas Volunteer regiments during the Civil War. In 1866 there were four black regiments, two each of cavalry and infantry, stationed throughout the West, performing typical military duties but also used to control strikers and to chase outlaws.

Buntline, Ned (Edward Zane Carrol Judson) (March 20, 1823–July 16, 1886)

Known as the "king of the dime novels," Edward Zane Carrol Judson, who wrote under the pseudonym Ned Buntline, was born in Stamford, New York, on March 20, 1823. Conflicts with his father led him to join the Navy as a midshipman in 1838, and he served along the Florida coast and Cuba, before his attitude again got him in trouble with authority figures, at which time he resigned to take up writing. He had written numerous essays, and, having reconciled with his father, the two published *Ned Buntline's Magazine* in 1844. After his wife, who had lived apart from him for years, died in a Mexican poorhouse, Buntline moved to Boston, where he began to produce "dime novels," then to New York where he started a newspaper. After writing *The Mysteries and Miseries of New York* in 1848, he increasingly sought information on the city's seemier side. His actions as part of the Astor Place Riot landed him in prison. In the 1860s Buntline met William *Cody* (whom Buntline claimed to have provided the nickname "Buffalo Bill"), and he wrote a play with Cody as the lead, which was performed in Chicago. He married at least seven times (with some controversy over whether one marriage was legally ended), and he made and lost several fortunes from his prodigious writing. He died on July 16, 1886, in Stamford, New York.

Calamity Jane (Martha Cannary) (May 1, 1852–August 1, 1903)

Born Martha Cannary, "Calamity Jane" wandered the West with a transient lifestyle that involved menial jobs and possibly prostitution. Wherever she went, she encountered trouble with the law, usually for drunkenness. She married several times, although some were common-law marriages, and between 1880 and 1895 married a South Dakota teamster, who apparently dubbed her "Calamity Jane." Made famous in dime novels such as *Deadwood Dick* and others, toward the end of her life she cashed in on her image by performing in western shows. Calamity Jane died in 1903 and was buried next to "Wild Bill" *Hickok* in Deadwood.

One of the famous females in the West, Martha Cannary, known as "Calamity Jane," held her own with any man when it came to riding or shooting. *Library of Congress*

Cassidy, Butch (Robert LeRoy Parker) (April 13, 1866–?)

Born Robert LeRoy Parker, in Beaver, Utah, on April 13, 1866, Butch Cassidy was trained by cowboy Mike Cassidy and joined local gangs in the mid-1880s. He was a member of the "Wild Bunch," joining the *Johnson County War* in Wyoming. Arrested and jailed for theft, Cassidy returned to crime upon his release in 1896. His most famous heist was with Harry Longabaugh (the "Sundance Kid"), robbing a Winnemucca, Nevada, bank in 1890, after which he and four companions stood for a photo in Texas. He then sent a copy to the *Pinkerton* Agency, which hunted him. From here, Cassidy, the Kid, and Etta Place went to New York, then to South America, where they continued to rob banks. After that, Cassidy's life became a blur, with some accounts having him killed by Bolivian troops in 1908 and others having him living under an assumed name until the 1930s.

cattle drives

Cattle ranching and grazing had been a staple of the early American economy since the early 1800s. In the 1840s the famous speculator Daniel Drew already had perfected the technique of "watering stock" being

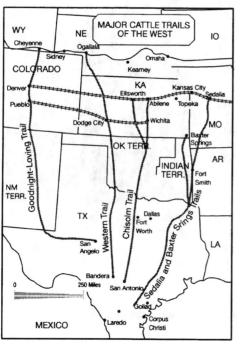

Major cattle trails of the West. *Ron Acklin, University of Dayton Print and Design*

shipped to New York by stopping his herds outside the city, feeding them salt, then letting them water so that they added weight at the time of delivery. By the *Mexican War [III]*, the open spaces and rich grasslands of Texas made it the perfect region to raise cattle, which were driven to New Orleans. Still, the mythic cattle drives of the West did not start until after the Civil War, when herds in Texas were driven to railheads in the *cattle towns* in Kansas.

The extension of the railroads provided a direct link to the stockyards of Chicago. Owners had to organize large drives from the Laredo, San Antonio, and Corpus Christi areas northward to the railheads across land in the public domain. There the herds roamed freely and grazing was open. The federal government certainly lacked the resources to police these regions, and the Indians had been systematically removed from them. And if a would-be cattle king did not have much stock of his own, wild cattle could be rounded up and made his by *branding [III]*. Any animal not bearing a brand became the property of the cowboy or ranch hand who found it.

Between 1866 and 1885 the golden era of cattle drives saw millions of head of cattle driven from Texas to Kansas. One of the first pioneers in the cattle drives was Charles Goodnight and his partner Oliver Loving, who in

1866 blazed the famous Goodnight-Loving Trail which ran some 700 miles from Fort Worth, Texas, to Fort Summer, New Mexico, to Colorado. A more direct route, the Chisholm Trail, following the map of Jesse Chisholm and running along a line from San Antonio, Texas, to Abilene, Kansas, was really the work of cattleman Joseph McCoy. It became the primary trail from Texas. Another major artery, the Eastern Trail, originated at the King Ranch in Texas and, like the Chisholm Trail, terminated in Abilene, while the Western Trail followed the Chisholm Trail before turning toward *Dodge City*. Dozens of trails soon crisscrossed the West, as well as the Northwest, where the *Oregon Trail [III]*, and the Northern Trail brought cattle to Montana, where livestock were more highly valued.

Drives were tedious, uncomfortable, and often dangerous, with cowboys spending days on end in the saddle, eating simple meals from the chuck wagons that accompanied the drive, and playing harmonicas, cards, or roping practice for entertainment. Cowboys had their own blankets, usually sleeping on the ground with their saddle as a pillow. It took only a couple of cowboys to watch the herds at night, and this shift was rotated. During the day, the herd kicked up clouds of choking dust under a sun that was usually blazing hot. On these drives, the cowboy's gear was not only important, but often meant the difference between life and death. Thick boots could protect against rattlesnake or other snakebites; *chaps* absorbed the razor-like thorns of the prairie bushes; and hats and bandanas offered some escape from the sun and dust. Boredom was the most common enemy, but occasionally lightning or fire could spook a herd, in which case the cowboys had to try to stay with the stampede as best they could and round up strays when it finally wound down. All cattle had to be branded, and any stray that came in would be roped and processed.

The great drives ended in the 1880s. By that time the further extension of railroads into Texas made them unnecessary.

cattle towns

Following the Civil War, cattle were raised on vast ranches in Texas, then herded to railroads for transportation to the stockyards and slaughterhouses of Chicago. Most of the "railheads"—the termini for the railroads—were in Kansas, where several boomtowns emerged as the focal point for the cattle business, saloons, gambling, and gunfights. The cattle towns that sprang up along the railroads found that the cattle drives were both a blessing and a curse. Local farmers, who had settled there first, struggled to keep the herds from destroying their crops, while city founders, who at one time were anxious to get the cattle trade, soon learned that it brought more than its share of criminals, prostitutes, and general "low-lifes."

The combination of alcohol, guns, and hordes of cowboys with time and money on their hands meant trouble, requiring most of the towns to hire the fastest gun, regardless of his ethical code or commitment to the law. Famous western names, such as Wyatt *Earp*, "Bat" *Masterson*, and "Wild Bill" *Hickok*, all donned badges and made reputations as lawmen, even though some, such as Earp, skirted or ignored the law when convenient. Subsequent studies on the violence in these cattle towns has shown that aside from the dynamics of the saloon, these towns were relatively normal in their levels of gunplay. When gunfights are accounted for, the streets of Wichita or *Dodge City*, Kansas, could be deadly places, but the street shootout between a sheriff and outlaws was more myth than reality. Neither Wyatt Earp nor Bat Masterson ever killed any cowboys during their time as lawmen in the cattle towns, while Hickok killed just five men in his law career in Abilene and Hays.

Abilene, Kansas, was probably the first of the cattle towns, following the 1867 arrival of the Kansas Pacific Railroad. Less than five years later, farmers and townspeople organized to stop the drives, which in turn moved southwest to Ellsworth. Wichita began to boom just as Abilene fizzled, following the withdrawal of the Wichita Indians in 1867. The first cattle arrived in Wichita in 1872. Again, through quarantine laws and other restrictions, farmers limited the trail areas for cattlemen to drive their herds. These restrictions discouraged cowboys, who again switched their business to Dodge City by 1876. A year later, the town was full of cattle and cowboys. Dodge City remained a viable railhead until the mid-1880s, when Caldwell started to siphon its business. By the end of the decade, though, virtually all of the cattle drives to Kansas had ended, and many of the once-thriving towns dried up or struggled to remain farm centers.

chaps

A central component of cowboy clothing, chaps developed from the riders' habits of throwing animal hides over their saddles while riding on the range. Eventually, the cowboys hung the hides on themselves, tying or lacing the supple leather onto their legs. Chaps were essentially leather pants with the seats cut out that protected the legs from thorns, stones, barbed-wire, and saddle sores. The word "chaps" comes from Spanish *chaparejos* ("leather breeches"). While few cowboys could ride without chaps, they were hot and cumbersome, especially over Levi *Strauss* blue jeans. Nevertheless, they became a staple of the distinctive cowboy look.

Cheyennes

The Cheyenne name derives from a Siouan word for "crazy talker." The Cheyennes call themselves, Tsistsistas, which can be translated as "The Called Out People."

A Central Algonquian people, the Cheyennes began a century-long migration from the western Great Lakes to the central Great Plains, beginning around 1680. By the 1770s the Cheyennes resided in earthen mound lodges on the *Missouri River [I]*. In 1780, the Cheyennes faced attacks by Ojibwas from the east, who destroyed a number of their villages. With these events, the Cheyennes decided to move onto the plains and adapt the buffalo and horse cultures. They would also serve as middlemen between the trade centers of the northern plains and the Southwest.

Their successful transition was astounding. By 1800 the average Cheyenne owned 10 horses, and by 1810, the Cheyennes proudly displayed their wealth to anyone crossing their path. Their language had 27 words for bison, each revealing a different aspect (size, sex, age, condition) of the animal.

Their territory became huge. Its boundaries were the Rockies, the Missouri River, the Arkansas River, and the Yellowstone. Like the Hebrews' escape from Egypt, or the Mormons' move westward in the 1840s, the Cheyenne trek to the plains became an essential part of their history, a reorientation of their entire way of life, culture, and economy. Hence, they called themselves Tsistsistas.

During their transition to the Great Plains, according to their own legends, they camped near Bear Butte in the Black Hills. It has subsequently become the holiest site in the Cheyenne world. Maheo, the All-Being, invited a Cheyenne prophet, Sweet Medicine, into his lodge, where he lived for four years. Maheo introduced Sweet Medicine to the lesser beings as well as to the laws of the universe.

Though trade created wealth for the Cheyennes, it also led to divisions. In the 1820s the tribes split into Northern and Southern divisions, based on loyalty to either Bent's Fort or Fort Laramie. When the Cheyennes first encountered whites, they viewed them as new trade partners, but that too had its downsides. Numerous whites brought their ravaging animals and diseases with them as they crossed from Westport, Missouri, to Utah, California, and Oregon in the 1840s. Disease was so bad in 1849, during the *California Gold Rush [III]*, that the Cheyennes named the year "When the Big Cramps Take Place." In 1864 a group of frustrated American officers and Colorado militia took their anger out on the Northern Cheyennes, in what became known as the *Sand Creek Massacre*. After several hearings regarding the massacre, the U.S. government decided the Northern and Southern Cheyennes would live best on protected reservations. The Cheyennes agreed, at least in theory, to forsake their nomadic way of life in exchange for an agrarian life, with the United States providing teachers, food, supplies, churches, and schools.

Not content with their new lifestyle, both divisions of Cheyennes rebelled, leading to hostilities between the United States and the Indians between 1868 and 1879. In 1868 George Armstrong *Custer* successfully attacked *Black Kettle*'s band of Northern Cheyenne on the Washita River (present-day Elk City, Oklahoma). Between 1874 and 1875 the United States and the Cheyennes again fought in what was called the Red River War. Between 1878 and 1879, Little Wolf and Dull Knife led 300 Cheyennes off their reservation in an attempt to make it to southeastern Montana. The United States forced them to a surrender at Fort Robinson, Nebraska, where they remained until 1883, when the federal government granted them a reservation in Montana.

Chief Joseph (ca. 1840–ca. 1904)

Born to a prominent *Nez Perce* family in the Wallowa Valley in roughly 1840, Joseph received a Christian education by missionaries in the 1840s and 1850s. It remains unknown if Joseph embraced Christianity, but like most of the Nez Perce, he had strong friendships with white settlers and the United States federal government. Joseph became the prominent peace chief of the Wallowa band of the Nez Perce upon the death of his father in 1871. Though he attempted to maintain strong ties to the U.S. government, a series of unfortunate events led to the *Nez Perce War* of 1877. Reluctantly, Joseph, along with several other Nez Perce chiefs, led his people on a 1,000-plus-mile trek, unsuccessfully trying to reach the safety and protection of the Canadian Mounted Police.

After the failure of the retreat, the U.S. Army sent Joseph and the remaining Nez Perce to a nine-year stint at Fort Leavenworth, Kansas. In 1885 the U.S. Army allowed them to return to Idaho. Joseph spent much of the last 20 years of his life defending Indian rights.

Chief Joseph epitomized everything "noble" about the American Indians to the 19th-century American mind. His image—developed near the end of the Indian wars—had a powerful effect on the sentimental Victorian culture of America's Gilded Age. Americans believed the Indian would soon be gone, his nobility with him. Joseph became their symbol; in his pictures and portraits of the time, he is always presented in classical (Greek or Roman) style. The November 17, 1877, issue of *Harper's Weekly* captured the noble image of Joseph very well. "Joseph has a gentle face, somewhat feminine in its beauty but intensely strong and full of character. A photograph could not do him justice. A bullet scratch left a slight scar on his forehead. In each shirt sleeve and in the body of the shirt are bullet holes, and there was also a bullet hole in one of his leggings, a bullet scratch on his wrist, and one across the small of his back." General Nelson *Miles* begged his shirt as a curiosity, so full was it of visible evidence that Joseph had been where "lead was flying." Today, the image and life of Chief Joseph remain powerful, especially to those Native Americans of the Pacific Northwest.

Chinese Exclusion Act

The extension of the mining frontier and the continued construction of the railroads in the West created demands for thousands of laborers. Chinese merchant-creditors on the West Coast had already determined that they would issue tickets to America in return for the labor of the immigrants until the debt was paid, creating a system of debt peonage. These merchants sold laborers to mining camps or other businesses that needed gang labor, in essence forming a type of "slave labor" in the West.

Two forces combined to end new immigration from China. First, the labor unions saw these Chinese debt-laborers as competition, driving down wages. Second, racist elements in America did not want any more Chinese coming into the country—about 105,000 already lived in the United States by 1880. The result was the Chinese Exclusion Act of 1882, which ended free immigration of Chinese laborers. Following the Geary Act of 1892, all Chinese workers in the United States could be deported if they did not have certificates of residence at the end of one year. In 1943 the wartime alliance of the United States and China forced Congress to repeal these acts.

Chivington, John M. (January 21, 1821– October 4, 1894)

Known for leading 1,000 Colorado Territorial volunteers against the peaceful *Cheyenne* village along Sand Creek, resulting in the *Sand Creek Massacre*, John M. Chivington was born in Ohio and was a minister in the Midwest prior to arriving in Denver, Colorado, in 1860. After gaining a commission during the Civil War, Chivington led a company at the Battle of Glorieta Pass (New Mexico). Chivington's November 1864 attack on the Cheyenne prompted an investigation and attempted court-martial. He resigned from the army in 1865, and battled the reputation he had gained from the massacre for the remainder of his life, which he spent as a farmer and an editor.

Civil War

Although the western territories, especially "Bloody Kansas," played a central role in the growing sectional schism that split the nation in 1861, the Civil War itself largely ignored the frontier West. The territories had seen the introduction of slaves into Kansas, New Mexico, and Utah, and pockets of Confederate support existed in California, as well as the actual western Confederate states of Texas and Arkansas and the border states of Missouri and Kentucky.

Abraham Lincoln's view that slavery had "natural limits" that would prohibit its expansion had been proven wrong, and indeed by 1860 the South politically, constitutionally, and morally had concluded that slavery had to expand into the territories if it were to survive. The prospect of an institution existing that had been deemed illegal and immoral by a majority of the states simply was untenable.

When the Southern states began to secede starting in December 1860 and continuing into 1861, the crisis soon erupted into war when South Carolina batteries opened fire on Fort Sumter on April 12, 1861. In June a convention at Wheeling, Virginia, sided with the Union government and formed a new state, West Virginia, which was admitted into the Union on June 20, 1863. Other states from the early West—Kentucky and Missouri—remained loyal to the Union. Two battles were fought in Missouri—at Wilson's Creek (August 1861) and Pea Ridge (1862)—that sealed Union control of that state. Traditional accounts of the Civil War in the West deal mainly with the territorial West, but at the time the "western theater" of operations consisted of Tennessee, Mississippi, and Louisiana.

By the end of April 1861 Union military strategists had developed a plan later known as the "Anaconda Plan" to divide the Confederacy into three sections: first, a move in the west down the Mississippi and north through New Orleans would sever Texas and Arkansas from the states east of the river; second, a slash southeast from Tennessee through Georgia to the coast; and third, a strangling naval blockade that would keep supplies from reaching the Confederacy from the sea. Of course, the Union intended a major thrust to come from the Washington area southward to the Confederate capital of Richmond as well. By May 1862 the Union navy had New Orleans and moved up to Baton Rouge by August. Although Vicksburg held out until July 1863, the trans-Mississippi south was effectively severed after the Yankees controlled most of the Mississippi River. Smuggling continued through the Texas coast, but by 1863 the Union Navy had shut down even that traffic.

Texas presented the most significant threat to the far western territories, with Colonel John Baylor's force moving from El Paso into the Mesilla area of New Mexico in July 1861. Briefly, a separatist movement appeared, which encompassed southern Arizona. This "new" Confederate territory even sent a delegate to the Confederate Congress. Soon, Texas sent another, larger force under General Henry Sibley up the Rio Grande valley toward Albuquerque with the intention of possibly invading Colorado and severing California. Union forces under Colonel E. R. Canby moved from Fort Craig to intercept the Confederates and were dealt a defeat at Valverde on February 16, 1862. However, after the Confederate forces pressed on, they met Colonel John Slough's forces at Glorieta Pass in New Mexico, on March 26 to 28. With regular troops reinforced by Colorado volunteers, the Union troops benefited by a flanking maneuver from Colorado Volunteer Colonel John M. *Chivington*, who rode to the Confederate supply train and destroyed its food and ammunition. Moreover, word that the "California Column" was on its way with still more reinforcements effectively ended the Confederate dream of capturing the Southwest. Glorieta Pass, known as the "Gettysburg of the West," marked the only true Civil War–style battle fought in the western territories.

The California volunteers, under General James H. Carleton, arrived in Arizona in the spring of 1862, fighting a small battle at Picacho Peak on April 15. This point, just northwest of Tucson, marked the Civil War's westernmost combat. It also brought the California Column into contact with hostile Apaches under *Cochise* in July, and Navajo in 1863–1864 throughout the New Mexico region. In response to the Navajo's uprising, the government temporarily evicted the tribe from its lands and moved them to the Pecos River—an exile which ended when the Navajo guaranteed no further actions against the government and were allowed to move back to the northern Arizona/northwestern New Mexico areas. Carleton assumed control of the New Mexico Territory, and after Arizona received territorial status, he insisted the capital be moved from *Tucson [I]*, a Confederate stronghold, to Prescott. California regiments also entered Utah to keep an eye on the *Latter-day Saints [III]* (Mormons), to construct Fort Douglas, and to ensure that the supply routes to the East remained open. But the forces there feuded incessantly with the Mormon leaders and battled most of the Indians in the area.

The war made it difficult to police ambitious white officials who saw an excuse to grab more Indian lands. Such was the case in Colorado in 1864, when Governor John Evans sought to acquire titles to Indian territory. After several skirmishes, Colorado volunteers under Colonel Chivington attacked a peaceful *Cheyenne* village at *Sand Creek* and massacred the inhabitants. The *Sioux* were not caught unawares as were the Cheyenne, and in the subsequent *Minnesota Sioux Uprising of 1862*, some 800 settlers were killed before militia units defeated the Indians and captured and hanged a number of the instigators. In Oklahoma territory Confederate representatives negotiated a series of treaties with Creek, Choctaw, Chickasaw, Seminole, and *Cherokee [III]* tribes. These Indians, many of whom owned slaves, provided a brigade of troops for the Confederate army in Arkansas.

Efforts to gain the allegiance of *Kiowa* and *Comanche* Indians in Texas proved less successful. Carleton dispatched Kit *Carson [III]* in November 1864 to end raids on the *Santa Fe Trail [III]*. Carson's forces encountered a large force of Indians at Adobe Walls, where his cannons destroyed the village. Outnumbered, Carson had to retreat, and the raids continued.

Although the Union controlled Missouri's government, large bands of pro-Confederate guerilla raiders raised havoc throughout the war. The worst of these, *Quantrill*'s Raiders, staged a full-fledged invasion of Lawrence, Kansas in August 1863, killing 150. Quantrill's men, and other Kansas *Jayhawkers [III]*, were little more than organized criminals who used the war as a facade to plunder helpless towns. The Union Army thus had to battle regular Confederates, guerilla raiders, and Indians.

Further to the north, Generals George H. Thomas and Ulysses S. Grant drove into Tennessee and, after securing Forts Henry and Donelson, drove the Confederates from Nashville by late February 1862. Thus, any support the Confederacy might have received in the form of food, horses, or men from much of the territorial West had effectively been cut off.

Meanwhile, Lincoln's appointees in the western territories proved loyal. He organized the western territories into political units, making Arizona and Montana territories during the war, and transferring dependable governors to such territories as Colorado (William Gilpin) and California (Stephen Field). Utah especially concerned Lincoln, as he did not know the intentions of Brigham *Young [III]*, the leader of the Mormons, who dominated the territory. Likewise, the Mormons were suspicious of federal attempts to rein in their practice of polygamy, something Lincoln had no inclination to do during the war. A series of meetings with Mormon officials resulted in Lincoln telling the representatives of the Latter-day Saints a parable about a large tree stump in one of the fields he plowed. It was too large to pull and too green to burn; so, he told the Mormons, he plowed around it, and that was what he intended to do with Utah: let it operate in relative peace if the Mormons would remain loyal and guard the communication lines to California.

Keeping routes to California and Colorado open during the war ensured a supply of gold, silver, and horses, all of which were vital to the war effort. In 1860 the *Pony Express [III]* had started to carry messages from St. Joseph, Missouri, to Sacramento, California, and employed Mormon riders for much of the route. It was made obsolete in October 1861 by *telegraph* lines that, in combination with the *Butterfield Overland Mail Company [III]*, provided mail, freight, and communication services that linked Missouri to the Far West. With Southern representatives gone, the

Union legislators in Congress in 1862 also passed a bill to construct the *transcontinental railroad*, and by the end of the war, construction had started on the Central Pacific Railroad.

Other Union legislation passed during the war was specifically aimed at ensuring a loyal, and Republican, West after the conflict. The *Homestead Act* (1862) provided land at low prices for settlers; the Morrill Act (1862) established land grant colleges to provide education in agriculture and engineering; and the *National Bank and Currency Acts* (1863–1864) opened new national banks in most major western cities. The Civil War helped ensure that the frontier West would be favorably disposed to the Republican Party for generations after the war ended in April 1865.

Cochise (1810–June 8, 1874)

Born in southeastern Arizona, Cochise, a Chiricahua Apache Indian, led raiding parties against the Mexicans in the 1830s and was part of a major Chiricahua setback in May 1832 when the Mexican army defeated three hundred Indians at the Gila River. A few years later, Cochise began organizing more raids, violating a treaty in the process. He married the daughter of the powerful Apache chief *Mangas Coloradas [III]*, adding to his prestige. Over the next decade, Cochise and the Mexicans engaged in a pattern of fighting, followed by an armistice, followed by new hostilities.

When Americans moved into the region, Cochise negotiated with them, and in 1858 agent Michael Steck and Cochise agreed to keep Indians and whites apart in return for regular delivery of rations by the government. This agreement ended in 1861, when a runaway white captive brought new army units under Lieutenant George Bascom to the area. Cochise, traveling under a flag of truce, was nevertheless taken prisoner along with some family members. Although he escaped and captured four Americans, the situation escalated until he tortured his prisoners to death and Bascom hanged several of Cochise's family. A nine-year war ensued, in which Mangas Coloradas joined Cochise in attacking white settlements. When the Civil War ended, and more troops arrived, Cochise retreated into guerrilla war on the Mexican-American border. General Oliver Otis *Howard* and Thomas Jeffords, made a peace treaty in 1872 with Cochise, giving the Chiricahua the ancestral lands they desired, where Cochise died in 1874.

Code of the West

The Code of the West was an informal way of western thinking regarding justice and violence that formed on the 18th- and 19th-century American frontiers. It derived originally from English common law and natural rights theories, especially those coming out of the English Republican/Whig traditions. Americans on the frontier, however, took the logic to its extremes. To back up their ideas, Americans took the Second Amendment to the Constitution seriously, the "right to bear arms" without limitations of ordnance, and they heavily armed themselves.

Historian and social theorist Richard Maxwell Brown has argued that there were four parts to the Code of the West. First, one had "no duty to retreat" from an attacker. According to English common law, a defender could not harm an attacker without first resorting to purely defensive tactics, such as running away, even if the attacker had invaded the defender's home. The defender, according to the English, could not use physical force to protect himself until chased to an unmovable barrier, such as a wall. But in the West, the "no duty to retreat" rule meant that not only did many men and women legitimately defend themselves, but also that the code could be used as an excuse for a minor barfight to degenerate into a gun battle or even a clan/family war.

A punishment box, typical at most western military forts for enforcing discipline. This one is at Fort Larned, Kansas. *Bradley J. Birzer*

Second, Americans on the frontier accepted "the imperative of personal self-redress." Not only did one have the right to defend one self from an attacker, but the defender had the duty to take out the attacker. Such an attack, however, did not have to constitute a violation of property—it could be merely an insult, a dig at someone's reputation. In the fluid 19th-century world of frontier life, reputation meant everything. One defended it at all costs. But it also involved protection of the family structure and marriages: one study found low levels of violence against women on the frontier, precisely because everyone (including a woman's relatives!) was armed and took reputation seriously.

Third, and closely related to "no duty to retreat," is the "homestead ethic." According to classical and English Republican theory, the best way of life was that of an independent or yeoman farmer. Not only was a farmer highly independent, but he also worked with nature, "mixing his labor with the soil," as John Locke put it. The Book of Genesis's divine imperative, to work the land and have dominion over the earth, lent powerful credence to this as well. A true man defended his homestead from all opponents, white or Indian.

The fourth and final element of the Code of the West was the "ethic of individual enterprise." An obvious one, this argued that one had the right to own property and to make a living, unburdened by physical insecurities or government regulations or taxation. This allowed one to develop his or her own gifts without hindrance.

Travelers to the American West, from eastern America or Europe, usually expressed a fascinated disgust at these four elements of the Code of the West. The West, though, was a social and political vacuum for whites, and the absence of government, according to their way of thinking, necessitated such an unwritten code. Indeed, for most western Americans, it proved essential as they recreated themselves socially and economically on the frontier. In the long term the Code of the West also informed the frontier rugged individualism of 20th-century conservatives such as Barry Goldwater [V].

Cody, William Frederick ("Buffalo Bill") (February 18, 1846–January 10, 1917)

William Frederick "Buffalo Bill" Cody, a name synonymous with "Wild West Shows," was born in Scott County, Iowa, on February 18, 1846. His father, Issac Cody, was a politician in the Kansas free-state legislature and had been stabbed in 1854 for his abolitionist leanings. After Issac's death in 1857, young Bill took on work as a rider for Russell, Majors, and Waddell dispatch service. In 1860 when this firm helped found the *Pony Express [III]*, Cody carried the mails, building a reputation as an accomplished horseman, a trusted scout, and a fearless Indian fighter.

Cody joined the Union Army in 1864 and was assigned to teamster duty in the Seventh Kansas Cavalry, after first serving with militia units that were as much renegade bands as they were soldiers. After the war, he worked under contract as a scout, messenger, and guide stationed at Fort Ellsworth, Kansas. As the *Union Pacific Railroad* extended westward, Cody shot buffalo for meat to feed the workers, killing more than 4,000 head of buffalo in just eight months to gain the sobriquet "Buffalo Bill."

From 1868 to 1872 Cody worked almost nonstop as a scout, often assigned to the Fifth U.S. Cavalry. That service put him in the middle of numerous Indian fights including the battle of Summit Springs against the *Cheyenne* in 1869. In 1876, following the *Battle of the Little Bighorn*, Cody fought with a group of Cheyenne, scalping the warrior "Yellow Hair" (also known as "Yellow Hand"), claiming it was in retaliation for the *Custer* massacre. His exploits won him a Medal of Honor in 1872. It was revoked in 1916 because Cody was a civilian scout, but the army reversed itself and restored the medal in 1989. Cody saw action in at least 16 engagements with the Indians, some of which were embellished for reports to the East or for the famous "*dime novels*," such as those written by Ned *Buntline*. He eventually was the subject or more than 1,700 dime novels produced by more than 20 western writers. His biography appeared in 1879, adding to his legendary status.

Two of the West's most famous personalities were captured in this rare photo staged as a promotion for Buffalo Bill Cody's "Wild West Show." Sitting Bull made one tour with the troupe and was enthusiastically greeted in both Europe and America, while Cody was already starting to feel the competition from other "Wild West Shows," such as those run by Gordon Lille, with whom he merged operations in 1903. *Buffalo Bill Museum and Grace, Lookout Mountain, Golden, Colorado*

The publicity Buntline and other novelists gave Cody encouraged him to consider dramatizing the West. His first experience came with an acting job in Buntline's *The Scouts of the Prairie* (1872), in which Cody began to hone his acting skills. For several seasons thereafter, Cody alternated acting in the winter with scouting or serving as a trail or hunting guide for wealthy Europeans, such as the Grand Duke of Russia, in warmer months.

In 1883 Cody formed the first of his Wild West Shows, under the name "Buffalo Bill's Wild West." These were outdoor exhibitions featuring riding, shooting, an attack on the Deadwood, South Dakota, stagecoach, a buffalo "hunt," Pony Express rides, and plenty of cowboys and Indians. He hired a star cowboy, Buck Taylor, female shooting phenomenon Annie *Oakley* (known as "Little Sure Shot"), and, in 1885, Chief *Sitting Bull* for one season. Cody employed many Indians when they could find little work off the reservation. His troupe played London in 1887 for Queen Victoria's Jubliee but had its greatest performances at the 1893 Chicago World's Columbian Exposition.

Cody's show started to lose money after his partner, Nate Salsbury, died in 1902, even though Cody temporarily merged his show with a competitor, "Pawnee Bill" (Gordon William *Lillie*). Nevertheless, Buffalo Bill's Wild West influenced western *rodeos* and exhibitions for decades, adding a touch of theater to the hard work of roping and riding.

Buffalo Bill, whose name had become equated with buffalo hunting, did much to preserve the species by keeping buffalo in his show. He exposed audiences to the huge animals, raised awareness, and maintained small herds. By romanticizing the Wild West, Cody kept it alive, even if he misrepresented reality from time to time. Cody died in Denver, Colorado, on January 10, 1917, having lost most of his fortune but performing right up to the end.

The Buffalo Bill Historical Center in Cody, Wyoming, was created in 1917 to celebrate western culture. Its galleries contain memorabilia related to Cody and the Wild West Shows, as well as the Whitney Gallery of Western Art, which contains the Frederic *Remington [V]* Studio Collection, and the Winchester Arms Collection, donated by the Winchester Arms Company, containing a variety of western firearms. Even in death, then, Buffalo Bill Cody continues to publicize and celebrate western lore.

Comanche Indians

Often regarded as the best horse warriors, the fiercest and cruelest of all American Indians, the Comanches were often referred to as the "Lords of the Southern Plains." Even the term *Comanche* is revealing. A Ute Indian word, it means "people who fight us incessantly." The Comanches speak a Shoshonean dialect and are regarded as Uto-Aztecan. The first evidence of the "proto-Comanche" peoples comes from the beginning of the 16th century. At that time, Comanche-like peoples hunted buffalo on foot in the Great Plains and returned to the Rocky Mountains for shelter after the hunt. With the Pueblo Revolt of 1680, the Comanches obtained *horses [I]* and became one of the first Indian tribes—if not the first— to use them effectively for the hunt and war, making the horse an integral part of their culture. Horses became the basis of all wealth, and Comanche society became one of the most decentralized and individualist of all American Indian tribes. All glory came from skill in the hunt and in war. Only appeals to history and tradition kept their social structure in check.

Between 1715 and 1786 the Comanche and the Spanish were in a constant state of war. In 1715 the Comanches attacked *San Antonio [II]*. The Spanish retaliated two years later by hitting Comanche villages in present-day Colorado. The warfare continued throughout the 18th century. In 1779 Spaniard Juan Bautista de Anza successfully subdued the Comanches, and obtained a relative peace from them in 1786.

The peace with the Spanish allowed the Comanches to solidify their control over northern Texas and New Mexico. By 1800 they began moving into the southern Great Plains and quickly established a Comanche hegemony over a territory ranging from the Rocky Mountains to the eastern edge of the Great Plains, from the Arkansas River to the hill country of central Texas. As with the Lakota expansion in the northern plains, the Comanches established a system of tributaries on the southern plains. Like medieval European lords, the Comanches demanded tribute—in the form of food and sometimes labor—from the more agriculturally oriented tribes in their domain. The Comanches treated their captives with little regard, either enslaving them, torturing them, or killing them.

The Comanches chose their allies and enemies wisely. While the Plains Apache became tributaries and vassals of the Comanches, the *Kiowas*, a recently arrived tribe from the northern plains, the *Cheyennes*, and the Arapahoes became their allies. In addition, they maintained friendly relations, typically, with Mexican and Anglo traders on the *Santa Fe Trail [III]*, which traversed much of their territory. Such relations gave the Comanche access to advanced weapons, and durable goods such as steel knives and pots. The Comanches hated Texans, though. They fiercely attacked a Texas trading party in 1837 after an outbreak of *smallpox [I]*, which the Comanches assumed the Texans had brought them. The Comanches also raided Texas and northern Mexico to steal horses and sell them at Bent's Fort in Colorado.

The Comanches signed two significant treaties with the United States. In 1853 they agreed to a permanent peace with the United States in exchange for $18,000 a year. At the 1867 Medicine Lodge Treaty in southern Kansas, the Comanches agreed to settle in western Oklahoma, maintaining hunting grounds on the northern Texas panhandle. When white hunters set up a trading post at the old post known simply as the "Adobe Walls" in the middle of Comanche hunting territory, 700 Comanche warriors attacked them in June 1874. Fortified, the 28 white hunters held them off and claimed victory. Comanches also participated in the Red River campaign of that same year against the Americans.

The 20th century witnessed the allotment of Comanche land to Comanche individuals. The Comanche reformed as an official tribe in 1963, and their current population is nearly 12,000.

cotton industry/cotton production

Cotton growing proved an essential part of expansion to the South and then later, the West. The early "cotton frontier" involved a southern and westward movement from the region of South Carolina through Georgia, then on through Alabama, Mississippi by the 1820s, Arkansas and Texas by the 1830s and 1840s, then (after jumping over the arid zones of New Mexico) the Salt River Valley in Arizona in the late 1800s, followed by the fertile valleys of California. Eventually, California emerged as the largest cotton-producing state in the nation.

Cotton grown in the antebellum South was shipped from New Orleans or Charleston to British textile plants. On the eve of the Civil War, American producers grew more than 4.5 million bales of cotton, accounting for 90 percent of the world's raw cotton market. As more western farmers began to grow cotton, the prices plunged further. Growers sought refuge in government through price supports. During the New Deal, the Agricultural Adjustment Administration began to provide subsidies to farmer who would take land out of cultivation, in theory reducing supply. In reality, farmers merely planted more on the land they *kept* in cultivation. Foreign competition, meanwhile, drove down U.S. production to 18 percent of the world total by 1983. The number of cotton farmers shrank accordingly.

Introduction of mechanical cotton pickers, though, had reduced the cost of picking cotton, as did the introduction of irrigation in the Southwest. By 1992 the United States produced 17.9 million bales of cotton, and in 1995 Congress ended the farm subsidies on cotton, reducing the number of farmers, but ensuring that those who remained were competitive enough to make a profit.

cowboy poetry

Seemingly endless days riding trail or the monotonous life on the ranch left plenty of room for introspection and reflection on nature, which cowboys expressed through poetry. Ranch life, campfires, wild animals, magnificent sunsets—all appeared in cowboy poetry, which usually told a story, recorded a significant event, or described the loneliness of the frontier, the warmth of the fire, or the pleasure of faithful friends. Some trace cowboy poetry to English, Celtic, and Gaelic roots. Whatever its background, by the 1880s it was a distinct literary form.

Predictably, the titles of some of the early poems speak to life on the trail: "The Peco Puncher," "The Stampede," "The Dying Cowboy." Major cowboy poets included Francis Henry "Frank" Maynard ("The Cowboy's Lament," "Bill Springer's Hand"), Lawrence "Larry" Chittenden ("Texas," "The Ranchman's Song"), and the author of perhaps the most famous frontier poem of all time, "Home on the Range," written by Brewster Higley.

Later, cowboys who could sing these poems, such as Gene *Autry [V]*, gained an even wider audience for the art. In the late 20th century cowboy poetry festivals had become common, and by the 1980s there were more than 150 festivals annually, while in 1988 the first annual National Cowboy Symposium in Lubbock, Texas, drew more than 25,000 visitors.

cowboys

Men on horseback herding animals were not unique to North America. Mexico had its *vaqueros* and *caballeros*, *gauchos* plied their trade on the Argentine pampas, and cowboys controlled cattle in Hawaii. Cowboys of the American West developed a folklore to go along with their work—a lonesome, violent, rugged individualist whose distinctive garb and difficult life created a unique world view. In fact, cowpunching was a business, and the successful cattlemen followed solid business practices. When the industry reached its golden era, from about 1870 to 1900, cowboys constituted a major part of the population in the West, and certainly left enough memories to write countless books and produce endless movies. Early cowboys worked in the southern United States, borrowing skills from the Mexican herders that they encountered in Spanish Texas. Although Irish cattle herders existed, most of the American tradition of cowboys descends from the Mexicans.

Typically, cowboys had three main tasks. First, they had to herd animals—usually cattle or horses—from one spot to another, for grazing, *branding [III]*, feeding, or selling. This process reached its peak in the famous cattle drives of the late 1800s along the trails that ended in railheads. When herding cattle or horses, cowboys themselves rode superior animals specially trained for cutting animals out of herds or for outrunning their targets. Cowboys held a "roundup," in which they would gather animals in the spring for herding to grazing lands, and, if necessary, branding. Branding was required to ensure ownership of animals, and it involved placing a heated piece of iron in a distinct shape onto the hide of cows and horses. Since branding could only occur one cow (or calf) at a time, the cowboy "cut" an animal from the herd by using his horse to separate the animal, roped it, then tied its legs together in a quick knot, long enough to permit the branding. At that point, the cowboy released the animal and moved on to another.

IN THEIR OWN *Words*

"The Cowboy's Lament": Cowboy Poetry and the "The Streets of Laredo"

"The Cowboy's Lament" (a poem by Francis Henry "Frank" Maynard that was the basis for the Marty Robbins song, "The Streets of Laredo").

As I walked out in the streets of Laredo, as I walked out in Laredo one day, I spied a poor cowboy wrapped up in white linen, Wrapped up in white linen as cold as the clay.

Oh, beat the drum slowly and play the fife lowly, Play the dead march as you carry me along; Take me to the green valley, there lay the sod o'er me, For I'm a young cowboy and I know I've done wrong.

"I see by your outfit that you are a cowboy"— These words he did say as I boldly stepped by. "Come sit down beside me and hear my sad story; I am shot in the breast and I know I must die.

"Let sixteen gamblers come handle my coffin. Let sixteen cowboys come sing me a song. Take me to the graveyard and lay the sod o'er me, For I'm a poor cowboy and I know I've done wrong.

"My friends and relations they live in the Nation, They know not where their boy has gone.

Cutting horses were exceptionally good at quickly segregating a cow. Still, the work was dangerous. A full-sized steer, which outweighed the rider and horse combined, could turn and gore the animal or cowboy. If the steer was a Texas Longhorn and did not come along somewhat willingly, the cowboy might have to "bulldog" the animal, wherein the rider leaped from a moving horse, grabbed the steer's horns while digging in his boot heels, and by twisting the steer's neck used leverage to take him to the ground.

Roping required extreme skill. Occasionally, to save time, cowboys would team rope, wherein one cowboy would take the "head" (really, the neck) of a cow and the other would take the heels. With the "head" rider holding the animal motionless, the "heel" man would flip the cow, apply a quick brand, and release the animal.

A second roundup occurred when it was time to drive the cattle to market. All strays were collected, then the herd moved along dusty trails to the railheads. These trail drives involved horrific dangers, including prairie storms, wild and poisonous animals, extreme temperatures, and,

He first came to Texas and hired to a ranchman, Oh, I'm a young cowboy and I know I've done wrong.

"It was once in the saddle I used to go dashing, It was once in the saddle I used to go gay; First to the dram-house and then to the card-house; Got shot in the breast and I am dying today.

"Get six jolly cowboys to carry my coffin; Get six pretty maidens to bear up my pall. Put bunches of roses all over my coffin, Put roses to deaden the sods as they fall.

"Then swing your rope slowly and rattle your spurs lowly, And give a wild whoop as you carry me along, And in the grave throw me and roll the sod o'er me, For I'm a young cowboy and I know I've done wrong.

"Oh, bury beside me my knife and six-shooter, My spurs on my heel, my rifle by my side, And over my coffin put a bottle of brandy, That the cowboys may drink as they carry me along.

"Go bring me a cup, a cup of cold water, To cool my parched lips," the cowboy then said; Before I returned his soul had departed, And gone to the round-up—the cowboy was dead.

We beat the drum slowly and played the fife lowly, And bitterly wept as we bore him along; For we all loved our comrade, so brave, young and handsome, We all loved our comrade although he'd done wrong.

—Source: Lyrics attributed to Francis Henry "Frank" Maynard; lyrics origianlly published in N. Howard "Jack" Thorp's songbook, *Songs of the Cowboy*, 1908.

something that many cowboys dreaded the most, stampedes. In addition, cowboys were expected to protect the herd from rustlers and Indian raiders.

At the end of a 14-hour day, cowboys would take turn watching the herd at night, while the rest curled up with their saddle for a pillow and a single rolled blanket or two for warmth. Cowboys obtained meals at the chuck wagon that accompanied every drive. The cook who drove the chuck wagon also served as a tailor, doctor, dentist, and leathersmith. Meals consisted of beans, potatoes, onions, coffee, bread and hardtack, and occasional game, although without preservatives it was difficult to keep meat on the trail.

A trail boss rode a the head of the drive, which could cover more than 1,000 miles and last for several months. The trail boss determined the schedule and route and managed the cowboys who rode at the flanks of the herd, and whenever a stray would wander off, the cowboy would use his lariat to lightly whip the animal back toward the herd. Except when spooked, herds tended to stay together. But fire, gunshots, sudden noises, or lightning could panic a herd and send it off at full gallop, at which time the cowboys struggled to get out of the way, keep up with the runaway cattle, and spot any that drifted too far from the main body to be rounded up later. A cowboy at the tail of the herd, in the "drag" position, kept a careful eye on stragglers and was accompanied by a "wrangler," who managed a small herd of fresh mounts for the cowboys. On the trail, cowboys wore out at least one horse a day, and sometimes more.

A second major task of cowboys was to care for the ranch and its facilities when not on the trail. Many cowboys, who were not on the full-time payroll but who were just hired for a drive, spent much of their winters on other ranches doing "grub-line riding." Ranch work and "grub-line riding" involved fence-mending, construction, painting, digging fenceposts and wells, and other assorted menial labor. Countless hours were spent riding isolated fence lines looking for breaks. The ranch house, which belonged to the owner, might provide entertainment on special occasions, such as dinners or a dance, but the cowboys lived in the bunkhouse, which was a small cabin with sparse creature comforts. Like the sodbuster dwellings, these bunkhouses were oppressively hot in the summer and freezing cold in winter and all year were infested by a number of bugs, lice, mice, and other critters that could make a cowboy's life miserable. An outhouse usually stood separate from the bunkhouse. Meals were taken in a cookhouse or mess hall, while a cowboy stashed his saddle and trail gear in barns and saddle houses. Entertainment consisted of gambling, drinking, shooting, roping competitions, and writing music or poetry. Given this absence of excitement on the ranches, it is understandable why cowboys saw range work, despite its loneliness, as more appealing.

The third set of tasks that some cowboys engaged in was breaking or "busting" horses. Since most cowboys fancied themselves excellent horsemen, it became a matter of pride to be able to tame a wild bronco. Typically, several cowboys, using lariats, would hold a wild stallion or mare steady while the daredevil cowboy climbed on the animal's back. Normally, cowboys saddled the horse first, but bareback bronco busting also was popular, wherein the cowboy held on only by the pressure of his legs and the grip of a single rope around the horse's muzzle. The ropes were released, and the horse immediately took off, leaping and kicking. If the cowboy held on long enough, the animal would get used to the feel of a rider and be broken. If the horse won, the rider was on the ground and another cowboy got the chance to break the horse. This found its way into the cowboy heritage in the *rodeos*. Rodeos were merely organized competitions that featured cowboys doing what they did on a daily basis, except for cash and honors.

A cowboy's clothing derived from his occupation. Virtually every part of a cowboy's garb was functional. The wide brimmed *Stetson hat* protected the cowboy's eyes from the sun and shielded his face, and cowboys could drink from their hats or provide water to a horse from it. Cowboys wore bandanas around their necks, again for protection from the sun, but also to pull over their mouth and nose during dust storms. If necessary, the bandana could serve as a tourniquet. Durable shirts, with long sleeves, and leather jackets protected the arms and torso from brambles; Levi blue jeans became popular as near-impenetrable pants (see *Strauss*); and many cowboys wore leather *chaps* over their jeans, adding still another layer of protection. The cowboy's boots were thick enough to protect the leg from a snakebite and, sometimes, shield the foot from a cow's misplaced hoof.

Most western saddles featured a high "horn," which allowed the cowboy to tie a rope around for the purposes of subduing an animal or pulling a stump. A saddle also had room for bags on each side to carry ammunition, food, or other supplies, and a spot on the rear for the cowboy's blanket. The single most important piece of a cowboy's gear, however, other than perhaps the lariat or rope, was his gun. All cowboys wore sidearms, such as the famous *Colt [III]* .45 or Colt .44 revolvers, and some carried more than one pistol. In addition, many cowboys had a sheath for a rifle, such as a *Winchester* or *Spencer repeating rifle [III]*. Besides coming in handy for fending off wolves, snakes, lizards, and other predators, cowboys often needed these firearms to defend themselves against rustlers or hostile Indians. In addition to these weapons, many cowboys carried a *Bowie knife [III]* for close combat or cutting rope or wood.

The cowboy life has achieved near mythical proportions in modern America, but in reality it was a hard, demanding job with occasional flashes

IN THEIR OWN *Words*

Granville Stuart's Life on the Range

In the 1880s Granville Stuart was engaged in cattle ranching in Montana. In this passage of his book *Forty Years on the Frontier*, he recounts the "laws" of the trail as they applied to cowboys.

A herd was perfectly safe in the hands of a "boss" and his outfit. Every man would sacrifice his life to protect the herd. If personal quarrels or disputes arose while on a roundup or on a drive, the settlement of the same was left until the roundup was over and the men released from duty, and then they settled their differences man to man and without interference from their comrades.

They often paid the penalty with their lives.

Cowpunchers were strictly honest as they reckoned honesty but they did not consider it stealing to take anything they could lay their hands on from the government or the Indians. There was always a bitter enmity between them and soldiers.

A shooting scrape that resulted in the death of one or both of the combatants was not considered a murder but an affair between themselves. If a sheriff from Texas or Arizona arrived on one of our northern ranges to arrest a man for murder, the other cowpunchers would invariable help him to make his escape. . . .

When on night herd it was necessary to sing to the cattle to keep them quiet. The sound of the boys' voices made the cattle know that their protectors were there guarding them and this gave them a sense of security. There were two songs that seemed to be favorites. . . . I know that their songs always made me drowsy and feel at peace with the world.

—SOURCE: GRANVILLE STUART, *FORTY YEARS ON THE FRONTIER*, PAUL C. PHILLIPS, ED., VOL. II
(CLEVELAND: ARTHUR H. CLARK COMPANY, 1925), 182–184.

of danger and frequent bouts of boredom. Modern cowboys may use pickup trucks and a wide variety of mechanized gear, but cowboy work still comes down to isolation, tedium, and a struggle of the individual against nature and animals.

Crazy Horse (ca. 1840–September 5, 1877)

Throughout Crazy Horse's life, he was intimately involved in the art and practice of warfare. Many considered him, in addition to being a great warrior, a mystic and recluse. Crazy Horse understood the profound implications of the American movement onto the Great Plains, and he understood his role in attempting to prevent his own Oglala *Sioux* culture from collapsing in the face of it.

Born in 1840 in what is today South Dakota, Crazy Horse was first known as Light Hair and later as Horse Stands in Sight. He eventually adopted his father's and grandfather's name, Crazy Horse, after performing bravely in the hunt and in battle. Crazy Horse first encountered whites in August 1854 at Fort Laramie. As an emigrating group of *Latter-day Saints [III]* (Mormons) passed by, one of their cows strayed from the wagon train. Several Sioux captured it. Furious, Lieutenant John Grattan and 31 men ordered the Sioux to surrender the thieves. Conquering Bear, a bewildered peace chief, attempted to negotiate with Grattan, but the Americans refused to listen and opened fire on Conquering Bear's village. Retaliating Sioux warriors quickly killed Grattan and his men.

After the incident, Crazy Horse experienced a vision that he would never be harmed in battle, but that his life would end when fellow Sioux betrayed him. This vision gave Crazy Horse the assurance of victory in battle, and he never suffered from a lack of bravery. Crazy Horse achieved fame and infamy in his successful 1866 ruse that resulted in the *Fetterman Massacre* during *Red Cloud's* War.

Despite success on the battlefield, not all went well for Crazy Horse. Two of his friends were killed; then an affair he was having with Black Buffalo Woman turned deadly. After he eloped with her, Black Buffalo Woman's husband, No Water, shot Crazy Horse through the head, the bullet barely missing vital parts of his brain. To make matters worse, while Crazy Horse was recovering from the gunshot, Black Buffalo Woman and

No Water reestablished their marriage. Because of the incident, the tribe stripped Crazy Horse of his formal office as war chief.

Crazy Horse led or participated in the major battles, including Rosebud and the *Battle of Little Bighorn*. In 1877 though, Crazy Horse decided that the Americans had too much might and determination, and he surrendered at Fort Robinson, Nebraska. On September 5, 1877, true to his vision, two Sioux guards trapped him in the guardhouse and bayoneted him. He died later that day.

"Crime of '73"

Following the Civil War, international economic forces drove price levels down. Farmers in the West, combined with "prosilver" forces (especially miners), sought to inflate the currency through a number of policies, including reissuing of the greenbacks (legal tender issued during the Civil War, convertible only into National Bank notes) and/or "free and unlimited coinage of silver at 16:1." Due to the shortage of money in the West, the deflation hit rural areas especially hard.

Critics argued that the deflation was a deliberate policy choice by the government, which sought to reduce the supply of greenbacks to the point that they could be brought into line with the gold reserve and thus redeemed in gold at a specified date. The government rejected calls for new issues of paper money, leading western farmers and "silverites," along with their allies in the cash-starved South, to press for monetization of silver. Monetization would require the government to purchase specified quantities of silver and mint it into dollars on a fixed exchange ratio with gold.

In practice, this had occurred for many years, but in 1873 Congress refused to remonetize silver at fixed exchange rates, leaving the United States on the mono-metallic gold standard. Critics labeled Congress's action the "Crime of '73" and renewed their efforts to expand the money supply through the "free and unlimited coinage of silver at 16:1." Had such a policy been adopted, it would have in fact overvalued silver, which was being mined at a ratio of about 17:1. Led by Missouri Congressman Richard P. "Silver Dick" *Bland* and Iowa Senator William Allison, Congress attempted to mollify the "silverite" forces, through passage of the Bland-Allison Act in 1878, then later, the *Sherman Silver Purchase Act*. While Bland-Allison had little impact on the economy, the Sherman Silver Purchase Act overvalued silver enough that speculators and foreign governments could exchange overvalued silver for overvalued gold, resulting in a massive gold outflow from the U.S. Treasury that was stemmed only by the repeal of the Sherman Silver Purchase Act and a financial bailout of the U.S. government by financier J. P. Morgan in 1893.

Crook, George (September 23, 1829–March 21, 1890)

Viewed by many as the greatest Indian fighter of all U.S. soldiers, George Crook was born in Ohio and attended West Point, where he graduated near the bottom of his class. He viewed his Indian opponent as a human who needed to be protected and dealt with honorably. Serving in the Pacific Northwest with the Fourth U.S. Infantry, Crook built forts before the *Civil War* and fought against the Paiutes after the Civil War.

Appointed a colonel in the Union Army, Crook fought in West Virginia, then at Second Bull Run, Antietam, and the Shenandoah campaign. He preferred frontier, guerilla-type operations to set-piece battles and was transferred back to the Pacific Northwest at war's end. Crook fought the Paiute in Idaho, then, in 1871, was assigned to pacify the Apache in Arizona. During this time, he learned to appreciate not only the weaknesses of volunteers and the lack of discipline in the army, but also the strengths of his enemy. Two years later he was promoted to brigadier general. The Apache war especially suited Crook's freewheeling skills as a commander, and by 1873 he had achieved some order in Arizona. Assigned to the Platte offensive to clear the Black Hills of miners encroaching on *Sioux* lands, Crook was part of a three-way pincer designed to trap the Sioux and *Cheyenne*. His forces were defeated at the Battle of the Rosebud on June 17, 1876, preventing him from rendezvousing with the cavalry units of George Armstrong *Custer*, whose command was massacred at the *Battle of the Little Bighorn*. But this was only a small blemish on Crook's otherwise bright career. His use of Indian scouts and his willingness to negotiate, rather than attack, enhanced his effectiveness.

In 1882 hostilities broke out in Arizona again, and Crook was reassigned to again fight the Apache. Eventually, he pursued the Chiricahua chief, *Geronimo*, into Mexico, where he forced the Apache to surrender, although Geronimo himself escaped. General Nelson A. *Miles* replaced Crook before he could recapture Geronimo. Crook was then assigned a second time to the Department of the Platte, then, in 1888 headed the Division of the Missouri, where he became a leading voice for Indian rights, especially for his scouts. General George Crook died on March 21, 1890, in Chicago, having worked to improve the conditions of the Indians he had fought to defeat on the battlefield.

Custer, George Armstrong (December 5, 1839– June 25, 1876)

A legend for his "Last Stand," George Armstrong Custer was a soldier all his life. Born in New Rumley, Ohio, he entered West Point in 1857, where he established a reputation as a poor student and graduated at the bottom

Pictured here with his brother Thomas Custer, who also died at the Battle of the Little Bighorn, George Armstrong Custer and his wife, Elizabeth Bacon Custer, were a powerful husband and wife team. After a brilliant career in the Civil War, Custer became a controversial figure in the Indian Wars, yet his wife carefully massaged his public image through her writings. Even after the Little Bighorn, where Custer and a large portion of his command were killed, Elizabeth glamorized and immortalized him in her 1885 book, *Boots and Saddles. Library of Congress*

of the class. In the *Civil War,* he led a Michigan cavalry troop, under General Phil Kearny. The youngest brigadier general in the army's history at age 23, Custer was fearless, if not reckless, defeating the heralded J. E. B. Stuart's Confederate cavalry at Gettysburg, perhaps sealing the Union victory there. Married to Elizabeth Bacon, who proved a capable publicist, Custer was assigned to the Seventh *United States Cavalry* on the Great Plains, where he was court-martialed in 1867 for abusing his troops. He was brought back for the *Battle of the Washita* River, then was transferred to Dakota Territory in 1873.

Known to the Indians as "Yellow Hair," Custer inspired both fear and hatred, although he also had impressed them with his courage. After exploring *Sioux* lands in the Black Hills, Custer triggered a gold rush with his comments about large quantities of gold in the area. When the army could not keep the settlers out, it undertook to remove the Indians. During the campaign under General Alfred Terry, Custer was sent with the Seventh U.S. Cavalry to scout the Indians' location and to prevent them from escaping. Instead, he chose to attack with a divided force against vastly superior odds, and, at the **Battle of the Little Bighorn**, his immediate command was wiped out by Sioux and Cheyenne under *Sitting Bull* and *Crazy Horse*. Custer achieved mythic status for his "Last Stand," which, although depicted in countless paintings and movies, likely never happened. Nevertheless, the massacre was almost entirely the result of Custer's recklessness and poor generalship in the face of vastly superior

IN THEIR OWN *Words*

Personal Narrative: Elizabeth Bacon Custer, *Boots and Saddles*

Taken from her 1885 tribute to her husband, called *Boots and Saddles, or, Life in Dakota with General Custer*, Elizabeth Bacon Custer recalled her last days with Custer:

O ur women's hearts fell when the fiat went forth that there was to be a summer campaign, with probably actual fighting with Indians. Sitting Bull refused to make a treaty with the government, and would not come in to live on a reservation. . . . The morning for the start came only too soon. My husband was to take Sister Margaret and me out for the first day's march, so I rode beside him out of camp. The column that followed seemed unending. . . .

When our band struck up "The Girl I Left Behind Me," the most dispairing hour seemed to have come. All the sad-faced wives of the officers who had forced themselves to their doors to try to wave a courageous farewell, and smile bravely to keep the ones they loved from knowing the anguish of their breaking hearts, gave up the struggle at the sound of the music. . . . From the hour of breaking camp, before the sun was up, a mist had enveloped everything. Soon the bright sun began to penetrate this veil and dispel the haze, and a scene of wonder and beauty appeared. The cavalry and infantry in the order named, the scouts, pack-mules, and artillery, and behind all the long line of white-covered wagons, made a column altogether some two miles in length. As the sun broke through the mist a mirage appeared, which took up about half of the line of cavalry, and thenceforth for a little distance it marched, equally plain to the sight on the earth and in the sky.

On the 5th of July—for it took that long for the news to come—the sun rose on a beautiful world, but with its earliest beams came the first knell of disaster. A steam came down the river bearing the wounded from the battle of the Little Big Horn, of Sunday, June 25th. This battle wrecked the lives of twenty-six women at Fort Lincoln, and orphaned children of officers and soldiers joined their cry to that of their bereaved mothers.

—SOURCE: ELIZABETH BACON CUSTER, *BOOTS AND SADDLES, OR, LIFE IN DAKOTA WITH GENERAL CUSTER* (1885; REPRINT, WILLIAMSTOWN, MA: CORNER HOUSE, 1969), 261–268.

odds. Custer's legend was enhanced by the flattering biography written by his wife, *Boots and Saddles, or, Life in Dakota with General Custer* (1885).

Dalton Gang

The Daltons were a large family—15 children, including 10 boys—born to Lewis and Adeline Dalton of Coffeyville, Kansas. The eldest brother Frank Dalton served as a deputy U.S. marshal out of Fort Smith, Arkansas, working for the "hanging judge" Isaac Parker, while some of the other children became farmers. Frank was killed in Indian Territory while serving a warrant on a horse thief, and this event not only shocked the family, but opened the door for revenge. Grattan Dalton (1861–1892) was invited to become the U.S. marshal for Indian Territory and named his brother Bob (1870–1892) as his deputy (and later, chief of the Indian Police for the Osage Nation). Whereas Frank had established a stellar reputation for upholding the law, Grattan and Bob complained that they were being swindled on fees that were owed them by the administration. Whether the brothers were fired or quit, it is clear that for some time as lawmen they were engaged in horse rustling operations, although it is also clear that they were blamed for crimes they could not possibly have committed.

Following his stint as U.S. marshal, Grattan went to California, where he was involved in an attempted train robbery. He escaped from jail in 1891 and returned to Kansas where he, Bob, Emmett, and other malcontents (including Bill Doolin) engaged in a number of train robberies. In October 1892 they planned a daring and overly ambitious raid against both banks in Coffeyville, Kansas. (Robbing any bank in the West was difficult—only a handful of successful robberies occurred during the entire frontier period—but hitting two was near impossible.) Almost as soon as they rode into town, the gang was recognized and armed citizens took up positions. The gang managed to get the cash out of First National Bank, but when the gang members came out of the Condon Bank, the townspeople opened fire. In the moving gun battle that followed, all the gang members but Emmett were killed. He was wounded, captured, sentenced to life in prison, and paroled after 14 years, whereupon he wrote his recollections. Four citizens died defending the town. Bill Dalton did not participate in the raid and even tried to "go straight" before joining Bill Doolin's gang but, in 1894, was killed by law officers.

Daly, Marcus (December 5, 1841–November 12, 1900)

The "Copper King," Marcus Daly emigrated from Ireland, moved west in 1856, and worked in Comstock Lode mines at a variety of jobs. In 1880 he acquired enough money to purchase the Anaconda silver mine in Butte, Montana, for $30,000. This mine also produced copper, and it proved so rich that Daly built a railroad to support it. By 1895 it was the world's largest copper producer. A one-time friend of William Clark, another mine owner, Daly soon fell out with his former partner and began a long personal and political struggle. Clark became a U.S. senator from Montana but was forced to resign due to a bribery investigation spurred by Daly.

Daly built the town of Anaconda, Montana, which he tried but failed to have declared the state capital. In his later years, he engaged in horse breeding but remained president of Anaconda Copper until he died on November 12, 1900.

Dart, Isom (Ned Huddleston) (1849–1900)

Born into slavery in Arkansas in 1849, Ned Huddleston began stealing horses in Mexico after emancipation and bringing them across the Rio Grande. He then moved to Colorado and began work as a cowboy and broncobuster. In 1875 he joined a band of rustlers. A rancher and his cowboys ambushed the gang, killing all but Huddleston.

Attempting to escape his past, Huddleston changed his name to Isom Dart and returned to broncobusting. Eventually, he purchased his own ranch, but while he was engaging in a lawful and productive life, Ned Huddleston's past caught up with Isom Dart in the form of a bounty hunter, Tom Horn, who killed Dart in 1900.

Daughters of the Republic of Texas

Founded in 1891 as the Daughters of the Lone Star Republic, by Betty Ballinger and Hally Bryan, this organization celebrated the 300 pioneer families of the Republic of Texas. Today it encourages historical research in the early periods of Texas, establishes historical markers, promotes historical celebrations, and operates and supervises several historical sites including the Alamo. Membership in the DRT is limited to female lineal descendants of anyone who performed services for the Republic of Texas from 1836 to 1846, who had a Texas land grant under the Republic, who was a soldier under the Republic, who was a resident of the Republic, or who is a descendent of one of "*Austin*'s *[III]* Three Hundred" colonists.

Deadwood Dick (Nat Love) (June 1854–1921)

Nat Love (often misidentified as "Nate" Love) was a slave born in Tennessee in 1854. After the Civil War, Love's family raised tobacco on a farm, where Love learned to ride and shoot. He moved to Kansas in 1869, joining a group of trail hands, including several other black cowboys, around *Dodge City*, where he was nicknamed "Red River Dick." He became so skilled at reading brands that he was the outfit's top brand reader, and his travels throughout the Southwest led him to learn to speak Spanish. A top roper and rider, Love won so many shooting and riding contests that he was renicknamed "Deadwood Dick." He got in more than one gunfight and battled Indians on the trail. Once, Love found himself along with other cowboys in a buffalo stampede, which resulted in the death of one of his friends. On another occasion, in Mexico, Love rode his horse into a saloon to order a beer. When the locals protested, Love shot his way out. He was driving his herd on the trail to Deadwood when news of the *Custer* massacre reached him: Love returned home via the Custer battlefield to see the location for himself.

During one outing, Love was separated from the other cowboys and attacked by Indians, who pinned him down until his ammunition gave out. Surrounded and captured, Love was taken to the Indian camp where, after several days in captivity, he was made a member of the tribe. He escaped, riding 100 miles bareback with the Indians in pursuit.

During his travels, Dick met many famous western personalities, including Buffalo Bill *Cody* and William Bonney (*Billy the Kid*). In 1890 he gave up the range for a job with the railroads working as a Pullman porter. He continued to display broad thinking, working to develop a fund for a retirement home and hospital for Pullman porters. In 1907 he wrote his autobiography, *The Life and Adventures of Nat Love*, and for a brief time thereafter worked with the General Securities Company in Los Angeles.

dime novels

An early form of fiction first written by Erastus Beadle in 1860, dime novels included more than 30 series of cheap, short, mass-market works of fiction. Beadle alone sold some 5 million copies of his books during the Civil War alone, while Edward Ellis's *Seth Jones* sold 60,000 copies in 1860. Beadle and his editor, Orville Victor, hired writers who would follow a formula, producing an entire novel in a few days. One writer, Prentiss Ingraham, who churned out 600 of these novels and other works, managed to write a 35,000-word story in 24 hours.

The dime novels usually involved a colorful hero or outlaw, such as *Deadwood Dick,* or could come from real life, as was the case when Edward Z. Judson (Ned *Buntline*) glamorized William "Buffalo Bill" *Cody.* In the 20th century successful western writers such as Zane *Grey [V]* and Louis *L'Amour [V]* may have surpassed the dime novelists in skill and sophistication, but the genre remained much the same: an exciting story, a despicable villain, and an inspiring, if flawed, hero or heroine.

Dodge City

One of the booming *cattle towns* of Kansas, Dodge City originated in 1872 as a saloon to nearby Fort Dodge on the *Santa Fe Trail [III].* Locals obtained land titles from the Osage Tribe, and traders began to ship buffalo hides east along the railroad. Cattle pens appeared in 1876, and a year later more than 22,000 head of cattle were shipped out of Dodge City. Resistance by farmers to the cattle trade resulted in the formation of the Western Kansas Cattle Grower's Association. By 1884 local farmers had fenced their land, moving the cattle trade further west. During its heyday, Dodge City had a reputation for wild cowboys and legendary lawmen, such as "Bat" *Masterson*, Wyatt *Earp*, and William "Bill" *Tilghman*.

A recreation of the false store fronts of the post–Civil War cattle town Dodge City. *Bradley J. Birzer*

Earp, Wyatt Berry Stapp (March 19, 1848– January 13, 1929)

Born in Illinois along with four brothers, James C. (1841–1926), Virgil W. (1843–1906), Morgan (1851–1882), and Warren B. (1855–1900), Wyatt Berry Stapp Earp moved to California in 1868, then back to Illinois. In 1870 the family moved to Lamar, Missouri, where Wyatt first entered law enforcement as a constable.

His wife's death led him to leave for Indian Territory, where he ran afoul of the law, then moved to Kansas to work in a variety of positions as a law officer, serving in Wichita (1875–1876) and, in one of his most famous stints, in *Dodge City* (1876–1877, 1878–1879). His second appointment as assistant marshal resulted in his reputation as a gunslinger and allowed him to make the acquaintance of other western legends, "Doc" *Holliday* and "Bat" *Masterson*. Earp then left Dodge City when the cattle trade began to dry up, moving to New Mexico, then eventually *Tombstone, Arizona,* where he joined Morgan and Virgil.

After a brief job with *Wells Fargo*, Earp held a job as deputy sheriff of Pima County, Arizona, although he continued to gamble and work in the Oriental Saloon. Although the Earps prospered in Tombstone, they made enemies as well as friends. Some of the problems stemmed from political affiliations. The Earps were Republicans when many in Arizona were still Democrats who harbored memories of the *Civil War*, including local rancher N. H. Clanton and his sons Ike, Phin, and Billy.

As the town had grown, the increasingly rowdy behavior of the Clantons and their friends, known as the "cowboys," gradually generated a resistance against them from Tombstone civic elements, including the Earps. Wyatt thought he had a solution to the conflict when a stage robbery gave Wyatt the opportunity to become sheriff if he could generate a splash by arresting the robbers. He met with Ike Clanton and worked out an agreement where Clanton would give him the information to capture the thieves in return for the reward money. The deal never materialized, and tensions rose, until, in October 1881, Wyatt, Morgan, Virgil, and "Doc" Holliday, after a series of heated exchanges with the Clantons, confronted Ike and Billy Clanton, Tom and Frank McLaury, and Billy Claiborne at the *O.K. Corral* in the most famous single gunfight in western lore. Billy Clanton and the McLaurys were killed, while Ike Clanton and Claiborne escaped. Although the local sheriff tried to arrest the Earps, Wyatt would not be taken, and a subsequent hearing absolved him of any guilt in the matter.

The gunfight at the O.K. Corral did not end the hostilities. Virgil was ambushed and partially paralyzed in 1881, and Morgan was assassinated in 1882. Wyatt, Doc Holliday, and others took revenge on the cowboys, hunting down many and allegedly killing one of the cowboys' fastest guns, Johnny *Ringo*, although many doubt this claim. Wyatt traveled to Colorado, California, and even Alaska, finally settling in Los Angeles, where he saw his wealth steadily erode. Although he consulted on many early western movies, he was paid little. In 1928 he met a journalist who produced a biography that exaggerated Wyatt's image as a heroic and pure lawman. The real Wyatt Earp, who had straddled both sides of the law and had indeed shown courage and skill, died in Los Angeles on January 13, 1929.

Exodusters

One of the greatest rights any person can hold is the "right to exit," that is, the right and ability to depart a bad situation in search of a better one. With the failure and end of post–Civil War Reconstruction in 1877, numerous ex-slaves voted with their feet, leaving the South for the American West. The 1870s and 1880s witnessed the beginning of the plains settlement boom, and blacks migrated in significant numbers to western Kansas, western Nebraska, and Oklahoma. Known as Exodusters, these blacks shook the dust of southern prejudice off their feet. The *Homestead Act of 1862*, one of the most liberal and republican of all American laws, did not discriminate on basis of race, and any black males or single black females were welcome to take up a government-provided homestead. Though records were poorly kept, almost 40,000 blacks migrated to the new communities. Like many of the original European-derived Great Plains communities, few of these black Gilded Age settlements remain at the beginning of the 21st century. The most prominent of those still extant is *Nicodemus* in Graham County, Kansas. It had been the earliest of the Exoduster communities, founded in 1877. By 1890 blacks owned roughly 20,000 acres in Kansas. Inspired by the philosophy of Booker T. Washington, another 50,000 blacks settled in Indian Territory in the 1890s.

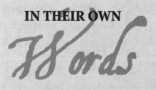

IN THEIR OWN

A Reporter Describes the Exodusters

When thousands of freed blacks moved to locations in Kansas after the Civil War, establishing such towns as Nicodemus, Kansas, they became known as Exodusters. A reporter for the *Atlantic Monthly* describes the "Negro Exodus" in 1879.

There is no doubt, however, that there is still a consuming desire among the negroes of the cotton districts in these two States to seek new homes, and there are the best reasons for believing that the exodus will take a new start next spring, after the gathering and conversion of the growing crop. Hundred of negroes who returned from the river-banks for lack of transportation, and thousands of others infected with the ruling discontent, are working harder in the fields this summer, and practicing more economy and self-denial than ever before, in order to have the means next winter and spring to pay their way to the "promised land."

"We've been working for fourteen long years," said an intelligent negro, in reply to a question as to the cause of the prevailing discontent, "and we ain't no better off than we was when we commenced." That is the negro version of the trouble, which is elaborated on occasion into the harrowing story of oppression and plunder.

"I tell you it's all owing to the radical politicians at [sic] the North," explained a representative of the type known as the Bourbons; "they've had their emissaries down here, and deluded the 'niggers' into a very fever of emigration, with the purpose of reducing our basis of representation in Congress and increasing that of the Northern States."

—SOURCE: JAMES B. RUNNION, "THE NEGRO EXODUS," *THE ATLANTIC MONTHLY*
(AUGUST 1879), 222–223.

Fetterman Massacre

Presaging the destruction of Colonel George Armstrong *Custer*'s troops less than a decade later, in December 1866, Lieutenant Colonel William J.

Fetterman's 80-man command was wiped out in an ambush by **Sioux,**
Cheyenne, and Arapaho warriors. Fetterman had been ordered by Colonel Henry Carrington to relieve a wood-gathering train outside Fort Phil
Kearny, Wyoming, which was under attack. Ironically, Fetterman had
boasted that he could "ride through the whole Sioux nation with eighty
men"—exactly the number under his command when it was destroyed.
Responsibility for the disaster, though, remains clouded, with historians
divided over whether Fetterman was obeying Carrington's orders.

Fletcher, Alice Cunningham (March 15, 1838– April 6, 1923)

Alice Cunningham Fletcher was born in Cuba to a New York City lawyer,
Thomas G. Fletcher, and Lucia Adeline Jenks. Her father had tuberculosis
and died less than two years after she was born. When her mother remarried, her stepfather's unwanted advances drove her from the house. Taken
in by her schoolmate's father, the wealthy merchant Claudius Conant,
Fletcher worked as a governess to the Conants, then was provided substantial means by the family. She became active in women's political organizations, organizing the Association for the Advancement of Women in
1873, then decided (partly because she had gone through her subsidies) to
find a career.

She met F. W. Putnam, who was one of the earliest practitioners of
anthropology in the United States, and soon studied informally herself.
When a group of Omaha Indians came to the Peabody Museum of Harvard,
where she worked, she accompanied them to Nebraska to study Indian
life. Arriving in 1881, Fletcher began a detailed examination of the *Sioux*
and Omaha Indians, publishing her notes as "Five Indian Ceremonies"
when she returned.

Her residence among the Indians led her to take up the cause of Native Americans in 1881, when she worked on behalf of the Omaha Indians
to allow them to retain their lands in Nebraska. After successfully appealing to Congress in person, Fletcher was named special agent for the *Bureau*
of Indian Affairs [III] to carry out the provisions of the act. While on the
reservation, she worked with the Omaha chief's son, Francis La Flesche. In
1885 she published *Indian Education and Civilization,* which criticized the
agency system. Fletcher supported the Dawes Act of 1887, which gave In-

dians their own land outside the tribal system, and which was viewed ulti-mately as a failure. After the Dawes Act failed to produce the results she had hoped, she left public service, taking a fellowship at the Peabody Museum, where she continued to write books and do research on Indian tribes. Fletcher died in Washington, D.C., on April 6, 1923.

Friends of the Indian

Reformers known as the "Friends of the Indian" ignited a reform move-ment in the 1800s following the Lake Mohonk Conference in 1883, at which time they formed the Indian Rights Association. These reformers held to the saying, "Kill the Indian and save the man." A number of Christian groups fought under this banner to educate Indian youth, especially at places such as the Carlisle Indian School. Among the noted participants at the Mohonk Conference were President Rutherford B. Hayes, General Oliver Otis *Howard*, and Helen Hunt *Jackson*, but virtually all of them were from the East, and only two had even seen an Indian.

Many of the Friends of the Indian hated westerners and saw sup-porting the Indians as a way to weaken the growing political power of the West. In the long run, the Friends of the Indian typified many (though not all) 19th century attempts at "reforming" Native Americans to resemble whites, yet without other equally important reforms in land rights and without large-scale social change that viewed Indians as fully capable citi-zens, the Friends of the Indians was doomed to fail. Some of their ideas were absorbed by other Christian groups, but in the short term, Indian policy actually went in the other direction—toward greater tribal autonomy. Ironically, by the late 20th century, the Choctaws, among others, found a practical mix of tribal government with free-market capitalism and mo-dernity to work well as they located business parks and traditional Euro-pean manufacturing on reservations.

Garrett, Pat (June 5, 1850–February 29, 1908)

Known for killing *Billy the Kid* (William H. Bonney), Pat Garrett was born in Alabama on June 5, 1850, and grew up in Louisiana, until he went to Texas at age 17 to become a cowboy. Later, he moved to New Mexico and became a deputy sheriff and then a sheriff involved in the pursuit of Billy the Kid over killings in the Lincoln County War. Garrett captured the Kid, but he escaped before the authorities could hang him. Chasing him down again in 1881, Garrett found the Kid at Pete Maxwell's ranch and waited for him in a darkened room, shooting him before the Kid could even see who had fired.

Garrett went into ranching, but in 1882, he became sheriff of Dona Ana County for 20 years. In 1906 he became a customs collector in El Paso, Texas, then resumed ranching in New Mexico, where he got into a dispute over the lease of a horse ranch. The owner of the ranch shot Garrett dead on an open road, but was not convicted of any crime.

Geronimo (June 1829–February 17, 1909)

Geronimo, or Goyathlay ("One Who Yawns"), was born in No-Doyohn Canyon, Mexico, in 1829 and grew up around the Gila River. In 1846 he was admitted to the warrior's council and began to raid Mexican towns in Sonora and Chihuahua. Mexican forces retaliated in a raid in 1858 that killed Geronimo's wife, mother, and children, branding him with hatred for the Mexicans. American troops, under Lieutenant Colonel (later General) George F. *Crook* subdued the Apache in Arizona, and in 1874 Geronimo accompanied the rest of the tribe to the San Carlos reservation (under Crook), where he emerged as their leader. Crook proved an effective soldier and administrator when it came to the Indians, but when he left to fight in the *Sioux* Wars, Geronimo and his warriors left the reservation and began raiding in southeastern Arizona and southwestern New Mexico. The Chiricahua would escape across the Mexican border if U.S. troops got too close, or vice versa if the Mexican units closed in.

The army recalled Crook to deal with Geronimo in 1882, whereupon he launched an effective campaign using Indian scouts to track down the Apache and force Geronimo's surrender in 1884. But a year later Geronimo escaped again, and again, Crook pursued him and convinced him to return to the reservation. Again, however, at the last minute, Geronimo and a handful of supporters escaped prior to the surrender, leading the army to replace Crook with General Nelson A. *Miles.* Using 500 Indian scouts, Miles forced Geronimo to surrender once and for all. Then 450 Apaches were shipped to Florida. Later, Geronimo was moved to Fort Sill, Oklahoma, where he farmed, joined a church, and earned a living by selling autographed photos. He was even on the army payroll as a scout and, prior to his death on February 17, 1909, dictated his life story to S. S. Barrett, *Geronimo: His Own Story*.

Ghost Dance

The Ghost Dance originated as a messianic, nativist, and millenialist liturgy—similar to the movements of the *Tenskwatawa [III]*, the Neosho, and *Handsome Lake [II]*—in the American Southwest. It quickly spread to the northern Great Plains, most strongly influencing the *Sioux*.

In 1870 a Paiute Indian in Masson Valley, Nevada, had a profound vision. The Indian, Tävibo, saw in his vision the earth swallowing all whites. Once the earth had consumed all whites, the Indian dead would create an earthly paradise. From this point forward, Tävibo claimed to communicate intimately with the dead. For his followers to do the same, they had to participate in a circle dance called the Ghost Dance. Though the movement spread from Nevada up along the West Coast to California and Oregon, Tävibo died the same year he had the revelations, and the movement seemingly died with him.

Two decades later, another Paiute known as Wovoka, or Jack Wilson, revived the Ghost Dance. Though Wovoka claimed to be the biological son of Tävibo, he was most likely merely a follower. When a solar eclipse occurred simultaneously with a fever, Wovoka claimed to have passed through a gate to heaven, led by God. There, he saw pure joy as all of the dead Indians were engaged in sports. God then handed to Wovoka four commandments: to love all beings; to live peaceably with whites; to work hard; and to perform the circle dance. The whites would disappear, but not through violence, after the Indians performed the circle dance a certain number of times. As with Tävibo, Wovoka claimed that the earth and heaven would become one. Finally, God imparted to Wovoka the gnostic rituals for controlling earth, fire, water, and wind.

To his disappointment, Wovoka recruited only a small number of followers in the areas where Tävibo had proselytized successfully. His religion spread, but in a violent form, among the Sioux in the northern Great Plains. Their traditional lifestyle only recently destroyed and their culture in near total collapse, the Sioux quickly adopted the Ghost Dance. To Wovoka's vision, the Sioux added the "Ghost Shirt." The Sioux believed it would protect them from bullets and other physical harm. Wovoka rejected the Ghost Shirt as a violent adulteration of his peaceful movement. It, however, had escaped his control. The Sioux en masse gave up work and regular daily life to dance the circle dance. They claimed to experience trances and visions of their dead relatives. The belief spread that whites would all disappear in the spring of 1891.

The Ghost Dance greatly alarmed American officials, and the ensuing struggle between the Sioux and the Americans over the new liturgy resulted in the 1890 *Wounded Knee Massacre*. With the bloody outcome, the Ghost Dance decreased in popularity, though it still remains in a watered down fashion in certain religious rituals among Indians.

ghost towns

The term "ghost towns" refers to any abandoned town or city, and in the West it has particular reference to those towns that once boomed with miners and prospectors, but that disappeared when the silver or gold dried up. In Arizona, *Tombstone*, though it remains a tourist location, was virtually a ghost town. Other such towns exist throughout the West: Bodie, Calico, and Yreka, in California, for example, or Goldfield, Nevada. Occasionally, however, the construction of a freeway can turn once-thriving communities into near–ghost

A well-preserved ghost town in Elkhorn, Montana, just south of Helena. *Bradley J. Birzer*

towns, as when Route 66 in Arizona was rendered obsolete by the interstate highway system. While mining usually caused the boom in "boom-towns," occasionally western towns saw their populations rise with *cattle drives* or the arrival of the railroad, only to disappear when the chief source of income left.

Great Northern Railroad

Founded in 1878 by Canadian James J. Hill, who purchased and combined the St. Paul and the Pacific Railroads, the Great Northern ran through Minnesota to Winnipeg, with a branch into Duluth and on to the Great Lakes. Hill built the railroad with private capital, in competition with the subsidized *Union Pacific* and Central Pacific transcontinental railways. Hill's railroad proved superior to any of the subsidized railroads and was the only transcontinental not to fail in the Panic of 1873. To encourage future business along the rail line, Hill gave land to farmers, brought in new breeds of cattle and strains of wheat, and sponsored farm improvement meetings. The Great Northern lacked the scenery of its competitors because it utilized only the lowest grades and easiest passages through the mountains.

Great Sioux War, 1876–1877

In a campaign most noted for the *Battle of the Little Bighorn* and the destruction of the Seventh *United States Cavalry* under George Armstrong *Custer*, the Great Sioux War originated with the government's decision to open the Black Hills of the Dakotas and the Wyoming and Montana regions to prospectors. That required clearing out the *Cheyenne* and Sioux tribes, and the government presented its demands in 1875, giving the Indians only a few months to comply. Chief *Sitting Bull* and *Crazy Horse* refused to move. The army organized a campaign against them, beginning with General George *Crook* who, in March 1876, attacked the Indians at the Powder River and won a victory. This was followed by a simultaneous advance from the south at Fort Fetterman (General Crook), and from the east at Fort Abraham Lincoln (General Alfred Terry), and Colonel John Gibbon coming from the northwest. Although Crook and Terry each had about 1,000 men, plus the Seventh Cavalry of just under 800 men under Custer, attached to Terry, the Indian strength was much greater than the army knew.

Crazy Horse struck Crook at the Battle of the Rosebud on June 17, 1876, and dealt him a severe enough blow that Crook withdrew to await reinforcements. Although Terry was unaware of Crook's halting,

Lieutenant Terry advanced, sending the Seventh Cavalry ahead to scout, but with orders to await the infantry support. Custer's ill-fated attack resulted in the destruction of one-third of the Seventh Cavalry. Terry and the remnants of the Seventh reunited to continue searching, while Crook marched to the Black Hills. Although Crook encountered some opposition at Slim Buttes, where he defeated American Horse, neither he nor Terry had fought the main body of Indians as hoped and had certainly failed to envelop them. During the winter, though, when the Indians were particularly vulnerable, the army continued its campaign. Colonel Nelson *Miles* chased Sitting Bull to Canada, while Crazy Horse finally surrendered at the Red Cloud agency in Nebraska in 1877. The Sioux would resist again, in 1890, with the resulting *Wounded Knee Massacre*, but for all intents and purposes the campaign of 1876–1877 ended the power of the northern plains tribes.

Greeley, Horace (February 3, 1811– November 29, 1872)

One of the most powerful newspaper editors in early America, Horace Greeley was known for his injunction "Go West, young man." Born in Amherst, New Hampshire, Greeley worked at printer's jobs until 1834, when he became the editor of a magazine called *The New Yorker* in New York City. There he became enmeshed in the political world of Thurlow Weed and published campaign materials—often little more than propaganda—for Weed and for New York Governor William H. Seward.

In 1841 Greeley founded the *New York Tribune*, an influential Whig paper which advanced the causes of the party but which also trumpeted temperance, antislavery, education for all, and the "free soil" movement. By the 1850s he was a Republican and his *Tribune* dedicated considerable print to the West, especially to the "free land" movement, in which Greeley wanted the government to give land to individuals (especially from the cities) as a means to reduce the size and congestion of cities and to equalize wealth. Greeley lost much of the good will he had built up, though, by opposing the renomination of Abraham Lincoln in 1864. He broke from the Republican Party in 1872 to run for president on the Liberal Republican Party but died shortly after the election.

Hardin, John Wesley (May 26, 1853– August 19, 1895)

At age 15, John Wesley Hardin killed his first man and continued a life of gambling, drinking, and gunfighting. Strongly pro-Confederate, Hardin excelled at killing blacks and Union troops during Reconstruction. Hardin was finally captured and tried for murder, receiving 25 years hard labor in 1877. Pardoned in 1894, Hardin settled down to a peaceful life in Texas for a brief time before returning to crime. In 1895 Hardin was shot in the

IN THEIR OWN *Words*

An excerpt from *The Life of John Wesley Hardin, as Written by Himself*

John Wesley Hardin, a notorious gunslinger, killed Charles Webb in 1874. He was captured in 1877 and served time in prison. Twenty years later, Hardin, writing his autobiography, justified his actions.

The simple fact is that Charles Webb had really come over from his own county that day to kill me, thinking I was drinking and at a disadvantage. He wanted to kill me to keep his name, and he made his break on me like an assassin would. He made his first shot at my vitals when I was uprepared, and who blames a man for shooting under such conditions? I was at a terrible disadvantage in my trial. I went before a court on a charge of murder without a witness. The cowardly mob had either killed them or run them out of the county. I went to trial in a town in which three years before my own brother and cousins had met an awful death at the hands of a mob. Who of my readers would like to be tried under these circum-stances? On that jury that tried me sat six men whom I knew to be directly implicated in my brother's death. No, my readers, I have served twenty-five years for the killing of Webb, but know ye that there is a God in high heaven who knows that I did not shoot Charles Webb through malice, nor through anger, nor for money, but to save my own life.

True, it is almost as bad to kill as to be killed. It drove my father to an early grave; it almost distracted my mother; it killed my brother Joe and my cousins Tom and William; it left my brother's widow with two helpless babes . . . I do say, however, that the man who does not exercise the first law of nature—that of self-preservation—is not worthy of living and breathing the breath of life.

—Source: *The Life of John Wesley Hardin, as Written by Himself* (Norman: University of Oklahoma Press, 1961), 124–125.

head by John Selman, Jr., a shady policeman from El Paso who had crossed Hardin previously. In 1896 Hardin's autobiography, *The Life of John Wesley Hardin, as Written by Himself*, was published posthumously.

Hickok, James Butler ("Wild Bill") (May 27, 1837–August 2, 1876)

Born in Illinois, James Butler Hickok moved to Kansas as a teenager and farmed, joined the militia, and worked briefly as a constable. He also scouted for the army, and drove *stagecoaches [III]* along the *Santa Fe Trail [III]*. His lifestyle inspired the name "Wild Bill": Hickok fought a bear with only a *Bowie knife [III]* and survived a shootout with a gang in Nebraska; during the Civil War, he was a scout and a spy for the Union forces; after the war, he continued to scout for the army, serving under Lieutenant Colonel George Armstrong *Custer*.

Hickok gained his reputation at Hays City (later, Hays), Kansas, and Abilene, Kansas, where he used his quick draw and steel courage to bring order to these *cattle towns*. For two years "Wild Bill" toured with "Buffalo Bill" in *Cody*'s "Wild West Show." In 1876 while playing poker in Deadwood, South Dakota, Hickok was shot by a drunk while holding two pair—aces and eights, which gamblers soon termed the "dead man's hand."

Holliday, John Henry ("Doc") (March 21, 1852–November 8, 1887)

A legendary figure known for his part in the gunfight at the *O.K. Corral* as an ally of Wyatt *Earp*, John Henry Holliday was born in Georgia, engaged in guerilla resistance against federal troops during the Civil War, then attended the Pennsylvania College of Dental Surgery, graduating in 1872. For a brief time he practiced in Atlanta, but he contracted tuberculosis and moved west for his health, settling in Dallas, Texas. There, he again worked as a dentist before finding himself immersed in gambling and saloon life.

By 1880 "Doc" Holliday, as he was known, had a reputation as a skilled gambler, especially at poker, a deadly shot, and a ladies' man. Although he traveled extensively—Pueblo and Denver, Colorado, Cheyenne, Wyoming, Deadwood, South Dakota—Holliday frequented *Dodge City*, where he met Earp and also encountered Mary Katherine Michael, known as Kate Elder. Some sources indicate the two were married, but like much of Holliday's life, truth is difficult to separate from fiction. Trouble followed Holliday, who eventually moved to *Tombstone*, where the Earp brothers had established themselves. In October 1880 Holliday's wild behavior resulted in his arrest at the hands of his friend, Wyatt Earp. With both his disease and his drinking growing worse, there were indications that Holliday robbed a stagecoach in 1881; charges were dropped because the primary witness was his wife. Despite the difficulties he caused the Earps, Holliday was immensely loyal, showing up at the O.K. Corral when the Earp brothers needed help against the "cowboys." Suspected of murdering a pair of cowboys who were thought by the Earps to have gunned down Morgan Earp, Holliday moved to Denver, where he was arrested and held for extradition to Tombstone. At that point, another of Earp's gunfighter/lawman friends, the legendary "Bat" *Masterson*, intervened to convince the Colorado governor to release Holliday. His tuberculosis bested him in November 1887 at Glenwood Springs, Colorado.

Homestead Act

As Americans moved westward, following the organizational plan established by Thomas *Jefferson [III]* in the Land Ordinance of 1785 (see *Northwest Ordinance [II]*), wherein land was subdivided into sections and townships, the U.S. government hoped for an orderly expansion. This expansion was in keeping with Jefferson's vision of a pastoral America with citizen-farmers. However, the government failed to survey land fast enough, and a vibrant market for land developed. After the *Louisiana Purchase [II]*, the distribution of land west of the Mississippi resulted in land speculation, a practice deplored by many politicians and the subject of many laws. But such speculation, in fact, was common among virtually all farmers, even dating to colonial times, when New England farmers would acquire more land than they needed for subsistence. Then, if crops failed, they could sell land rather than risk bankruptcy.

As westward movement continued, settlers began to complain about the price of $1.25 an acre charged by the government, arguing that the land had no value until they cleared it, fenced it, erected homes, and grew crops. They even reasoned that the government was forcing them into debt. In 1841 Senator Thomas Hart *Benton [III]* introduced the "Preemption Act." Preemption involved squatting, wherein a person could locate on someone else's land and, if not evicted in a period of seven years, could gain claim to a homestead.

Benton's bill legitimized squatting by allowing farmers to claim unsurveyed land and later purchase it from the government. Land policies quickly became enmeshed in the slavery issue. The South envisioned new free-soil states coming into the Union, bringing antislavery Senate and House votes with them.

Once the Southern states left the Union in 1861, following President Abraham Lincoln's election, Congress passed a homestead law in 1862, which allowed any citizen to claim government surveyed land of up to 160 acres, or one-quarter of a square mile of surveyed government land, for only a service and registration fee. After five years of uninterrupted residence on the land, the claimant owned the property.

Free land quickly lost its luster as settlers, who flocked by the thousands to the Midwest and West, found that railroads had often already received some of the choice ground. Many learned belatedly that farming was a tough business. Hot, dry summers alternated with freezing winters. Arid climates often made it impossible to obtain water, and hordes of insects, such as locusts, constantly threatened crops. Many farmers eventually unloaded their property to speculators, a testimony to the false prosperity promised through free land. Some estimates put the number of failed homesteaders at 50 percent by the 1890s. On the other hand, despite the high failure rate, the Homestead Act reaffirmed two key principles in the American political and economic system: property ownership and a bias toward wealth creation through property rights.

The act also succeeded in settling much of the prairie with farmers sympathetic to the Union, and it provided a growing breadbasket for the Union Army. Furthermore, as settlers formed population centers, a need arose for educational institutions.

Ultimately, more than 1.6 million homestead applications were filed, contributing to the settlement of the West and, indirectly, the collapse of slavery.

Howard, Oliver Otis (November 8, 1830–October 26, 1909)

Born in Maine on November 8, 1830, Oliver Otis ("O. O.") Howard gained fame as the "Christian General" during the Civil War. He advanced from the rank of colonel to major general, commanding troops at Sharpsburg, Gettysburg, and Chancellorsville, and lost his right arm to wounds at Fair Oaks. After the war, Howard was selected by Ulysses S. Grant to head the Freedmen's Bureau, where he campaigned tirelessly for black rights. In 1872 Grant selected Howard to parley with Chiricahua Apache chief *Cochise*, whereupon Howard traveled almost alone into Indian territory to secure a peace agreement. Howard's success in achieving peace with Cochise was not matched, five years later, in his dealings with the *Nez Perce* Indians under *Chief Joseph* in the Wallowa Valley of Oregon. There, the Indians, despite (in Howard's mind) having the law on their side, were forced to give up their valley. Chief Joseph refused, and Howard's troops chased down the Nez Perce until they surrendered. After that, Howard continued to serve in the army as superintendent of West Point, then as the commanding officer of the Department of the Platte until his retirement in 1894.

Huntington, Collis Potter (October 22, 1821–August 13, 1900)

One of the "Big Four" (with Leland *Stanford*, Charles Crocker, and Mark Hopkins), Collis Potter Huntington was born into a poor family in Connecticut and moved to New York at age 14, where he peddled watches and other items, making himself into a prosperous merchant in Oneonta, New York. In 1849 he moved to Sacramento, California, with the intention of opening a mercantile establishment, and there he met and became partners with Mark Hopkins. Along with Stanford, Crocker, and Hopkins, Huntington incorporated the Central Pacific Railroad in 1861, which sought to provide the western half of the transcontinental railroad. Construction began in 1863, at which time Huntington was the company lobbyist in the East. The "Big Four" constructed rail lines southward from San Francisco to Los Angeles, then westward to El Paso, forming the *Southern Pacific Railroad* (1865), of which Huntington eventually became president.

Indian Wars and reservation policy, 1864–1890

Numerous factors precipitated the Indian Wars of the post–Civil War period. Most of the factors, ironically, were well-intentioned. First, in reaction to the atrocities committed by Colonel John *Chivington* and the Colorado volunteers against *Black Kettle*'s village of Northern Cheyenne in the *Sand Creek Massacre* in 1864, the U.S. government decided that confining tribes to small reservations would allow for greater protection of native peoples from white violence. A committee comprised of three generals and four civilian commissioners recommended the small reservation policy as the greatest assurance of peace in the West, and the U.S. government decided to implement its recommendations. Second, with a top-heavy officer corps after the *Civil War* and little else to do, the military looked to Indians as their next responsibility. Tellingly, in 1867 and 1868 the government transferred the *Bureau of Indian Affairs [III]* to the War Department. Third, with the incorporation of the defeated Confederacy on the Yankee model, the U.S. government wanted to secure its holdings in the West. Other important factors such as gold discoveries, settlement of the Great Plains, and the destruction of the buffalo also played significant roles in the American adoption of the small reservation policy.

The idea of a "small reservation," however, was relatively new. Prior to the Civil War, the U.S. policy had promoted a "big reservation" policy, which had essentially defined the already preexisting and claimed territory of the various Indian tribes west of the 98th meridian. The 1851 Fort Laramie Treaty best exemplified this policy. U.S. commissioners asked Indian representatives of the numerous tribes to write or draw on a large map the extent of their territory. The *Sioux* claimed the most land, but few Indians dared challenge their claims, extravagant as they were.

The first attempt to implement the small reservation policy, the confinement of the Navajo at the *Bosque Redondo* in eastern New Mexico between 1864 and 1868, proved an unmitigated disaster. Not only did the Navajos reject forced Christianization and Americanization, but they suffered terribly from disease, malnutrition, and cultural and spiritual collapse. When General William T. *Sherman* witnessed the abuses at Bosque Redondo in 1868, he had the Navajos removed back to their native lands. Unfortunately, the American government failed to learn from the experience of Bosque Redondo and expended considerable effort to capture and contain nomadic Indian tribes. Wars broke out between most of the Great Plains tribes and the United States over the small reservation policy. Even tribes typically pro-American, such as the *Nez Perce*, were treated brutally, resulting in the *Nez Perce War* of 1877 and the longest military retreat of any peoples in world history. Small, decentralized tribes such as the Apache fought for their freedom throughout the early 1880s, finally surrendering to the Americans in 1886. Larger, more powerful tribes, such as the Sioux, fought in a variety of different ways. *Crazy Horse, Red Cloud* and the Oglala fought the United States directly, negotiating separate peaces with the federal government. *Sitting Bull* and the Hunkpapa fought from 1874 to 1877 and then retreated to sanctuary in Canada until 1881. The most significant event, in many ways, was the alliance between the Sioux and Cheyenne that led to the obliteration of George Armstrong *Custer*'s troops at the *Battle of the Little Bighorn* in 1876. Such alliances, however, proved the exception and not the rule.

Though all of the Indians who warred against the United States after the Civil War eventually agreed to remain on reservations, very few liked it, and Christianization and Americanization proceeded slowly and bitterly. Naturally conservative, Indians resented "progressives" telling them how to live, what to eat, and what to wear. The Sioux, for example, found on their many reservations in the Dakotas that they enjoyed ranching. Government policy, however, forbade Indians to ranch, for example, on the Pine Ridge Reservation. The Lakota were to become yeoman farmers, as ranching was too similar to the old way of life. Americans feared ranching would simply trap Indians in a primitive state. *Geronimo*'s multiple escapes to Mexico in the early 1880s and the *Wounded Knee Massacre* in 1890 best demonstrate the frustration the Indians experienced from the confining reservation policies.

Though large-scale violence between the native peoples and the Americans ended at Wounded Knee in 1890, the legacy of the reservation policy remains with us today. Many Indians on reservations still experience astronomically high rates of alcoholism, infant mortality, and unemployment. The heavy-handed socialism rampant in the Bureau of Indian Affairs today only serve to stymie real progress on the reservations.

irrigation

Water in the West was such a scarce commodity that Frank *Baum*'s [V] *The Wonderful Wizard of Oz* featured Dorothy killing the "wicked witch of the west" by pouring water on her. Most of the West had between 10 and 20 inches annual precipitation, making it necessary to store and transfer water from reservoirs or dams to the lower areas where it was needed for farming. Native Americans had applied irrigation to crops long before the Europeans arrived, putting some 250,000 acres under irrigation.

Early naturalists such as John Wesley Powell criticized the concept of irrigating the West, arguing that there wasn't enough water. But he did not foresee massive dams, such as *Hoover Dam [V]* and Grand Coulee Dam, or the Central Arizona Project, or other extensive water projects that could bring water to the parched deserts. Indeed, by 2000 the problems of releasing water regularly into Arizona's Salt River had become so troublesome that the state embarked on a project to keep water in the river at all times.

Generally, large canals bring water from dams in mountain areas to the lower elevations, with smaller tributary canals extending out to the farms like blood vessels. From there, farmers use any of several irrigation methods. For years, crops were planted in rows, then a standard suction-pipe which looked like an inverted "u" delivered the water over the side of the canal into the rows. It was started by the farmer closing off one end of the tube with his hand, pushing the pipe into the water to create a suction, then rapidly dropping the pipe into the row. Literally, the suction caused water to "run uphill," then down into the crops. Since the 1960s though, large sprinkler-type machines capable of dousing dozens of rows at a time could be seen in the fields. Some orchard crops employ "basin flooding," in which water is released to flood the entire orchard. Although periodic warnings about the falling water table appear, scientists continually find new sources of water, and the ultimate source—the oceans—is already in use in places such as the United Arab Emirates, where desalination plants have caused the desert to bloom.

Jackson, Helen Hunt (Helen Maria Fiske)
(October 15, 1830–August 12, 1885)

Best known for her nonfiction book on American Indians, *A Century of Dishonor* (1881), Helen Maria Fiske was born in Amherst, Massachusetts. Her first husband, an army engineer named Edward Hunt, died in an accident in 1863. Both their sons died by 1865. After moving to Newport, Rhode

Island, Jackson met writer Thomas Higginson, whose influence shaped her career in literature. She wrote novels and poems, including *Ramona* (1884), again about Indians. Helen Hunt met William Jackson in Colorado Springs and they married in 1875.

James, Jesse (September 5, 1837–April 3, 1882)

Born in Clay County, Missouri, on September 5, 1837, Jesse James became one of the most famous outlaws of the West. Robert James, Jesse's father, was a minister who later abandoned his calling and his family to search for gold in California. Jesse's mother, who remarried after Robert James left the family, owned several slaves and supported the Confederacy when the Civil War broke out. This put the family at risk to Union sympathizers, who harassed them and likely encouraged Jesse and his brother Frank to ride with various border raiders, such as the *Quantrill* gang, before starting their own outlaw gang.

By the early 1870s the James gang had met the Youngers (James, John, Robert, and Coleman) and began to specialize in train robberies. They attempted to cultivate a Robin Hood image, especially after a state fair robbery. But in 1876 the James/Younger gangs attempted to rob the Northfield, Minnesota, First National Bank, causing a gun battle with the staff and townspeople and failing to get any money. Several of the gang were captured, including Cole Younger (who later went on to try his hand at a "Wild West Show"). After another robbery, the Missouri governor placed a bounty on Jesse James's head, and on April 3, 1882, at St. Joseph, Missouri, one of his gang members, Robert Ford, shot Jesse James in the back. Frank James battled the courts and the law until 1915, when he died of natural causes.

Johnson County War

This Wyoming conflict erupted over cattle rustling by *cowboys* in the northern part of the state who had worked for the cattle barons near Cheyenne. The Wyoming Stock Growers' Association complained that the courts would not convict the rustlers, and after a failed attempt at using private detectives to ambush some of the cattle thieves, the Association mounted a full-scale invasion of the rustlers' territory in Johnson County, some 250 miles north of Cheyenne. Many of those who were hired by the Association had criminal backgrounds (as, it should be noted, did half the "lawmen" in the West!), and accompanying the 46 "regulators," as they were called, were an additional 20 hired hands, nearly as many Association members, and some reporters.

The invaders took a train to Casper, then rode by horse the remaining 100 miles to the Johnson County strongholds, hoping to surprise and ambush the rustlers in small groups. After killing two men on their "suspects" list, the vigilantes proceeded to a ranch south of Buffalo, Wyoming, where they found some 200 locals who had been alerted to their presence. Surrounded and outnumbered, the invaders were rescued by a cavalry troop dispatched by the governor in Cheyenne, and only two of the vigilantes were wounded in the "war." Both died of their wounds. In the legal process that followed, the Cheyenne and Buffalo forces battled over jurisdiction, with the Cheyenne group winning. Trial was to be held in 1893, but the leading witnesses against the vigilantes for their murder of the two men on the list suddenly disappeared, and the judge dismissed the case.

The Johnson County War had political overtones, allowing Democrats to temporarily gain ascendency in the state government, and it virtually bankrupted Johnson County. Guerilla warfare in the region continued between rustlers, cattlemen, and any invaders who remained, until the U.S. Army appeared in force to frighten off the remaining rustlers and restore order.

Kiowa Indians

According to Kiowa myth, Saynday, a trickster figure, allowed the Kiowas to escape from their underground world. They believed they appeared in the real world somewhere near *Yellowstone*. Anthropologically and linguistically, though, the Kiowa appear to be related to the Pueblos of Taos, New Mexico. As with all other North American tribes, kinship defined the social structure of the Kiowas. The Kiowa kinship system ignored the distinction between cousins and brothers and sisters. Instead, a Kiowa treated all cousins as brothers and sisters. The Kiowa structure extended further, as several kinship groups formed a "kindred." Kiowa religion centered around a single deity, the DWDW (pronounced "dwuh, dwuh") or "power," which manifested itself in a variety of ways. The concept of the DWDW and its various manifestations is quite similar to the Christian medieval notion of subsidiarity and the Blessed Trinity's "economy of grace." Not surprisingly, when the Kiowas first encountered Christian missionaries in 1887, they quickly embraced Christianity, as it seemed little different from their traditional theology.

Though the Kiowas despised Mexicans and Texans, sharing a long history of hostilities with each, they generally accepted Americans as allies. Kiowa Indians raided as deep into Mexico as Zacatecas. From their first encounter with Americans in the *Lewis and Clark Expedition [III]* at the Mandan villages through the Civil War, the Kiowas respected the power of the Americans. United States-Kiowa relations hit their high point, perhaps, when Nathan Boone returned a lost Kiowa girl to the tribe in the 1830s.

During the *Civil War* the Kiowas captured Texas cattle, selling them to the Union, and pushed the Texas frontier back to Austin. Impressed with their military prowess, Abraham Lincoln invited a delegation to Washington in 1863. Lincoln and the Kiowas negotiated a treaty offering the Indians $25,000 to protect commerce on the *Santa Fe Trail [III]*, even when the trade crossed northern Texas. The Senate, though, failed to ratify the treaty, greatly angering the Kiowas. When the Kiowas took up the warpath, Kit *Carson [III]* and a joint Indian-American force of over 400 warriors pursued them. The greatest battle occurred at the Adobe Walls in the Texas Panhandle in November 1864. The Kiowas fought long enough to allow their women and children to escape and to receive aid from allied *Comanches*. When the Kiowas and Comanches retreated, Carson's forces destroyed their winter supplies.

The United States and Kiowas remained belligerent until 1867, when they met at the treaty hearings at Medicine Lodge, Kansas. In addition, George Armstrong *Custer* had met with the leading war chief of the Kiowas, Satanta, in 1867 and was thoroughly impressed with his character. At Medicine Lodge, the Kiowas agreed to a reservation in southwestern Oklahoma and hunting grounds with the Comanche in the Texas Panhandle. Bored, Satanta and several Kiowa warriors renewed hostilities in 1871, striking Texans, whom they still considered separate from Americans. The final Kiowa hostilities occurred in the 1874–1875 *Red River War*, though Kiowas and Texans exchanged gunshots until 1879.

The Kiowas proudly fought in the major conflicts of the 20th century. One Kiowa, author N. Scott Momaday, has won the Pulitzer Prize in Literature.

Land Grant College Act of 1862 (Morrill Act)

In an effort to improve facilities to provide agricultural, mathematical, and technical education, in 1862 Congress pass the Land Grant Act,

---

IN THEIR OWN

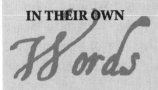 **Words**

Letter from the Carlisle School for Indians

In 1890 Paul Hayne, a Native American teenager attending Captain Richard Pratt's Carlisle School for Indians in Pennsylvania, related in a letter to a friend his education, particularly in the blacksmithing trade. The school's goal was to assimilate young natives by sending them to boarding schools where they learned trades in the "white" world.

Fort Peck Agency
Poplar Creek Mont
March 11, 1890

My Dear Friend
I got your letter and am glad to hear from you, and I am well.

please tell me how you are getting along up here, you ask me how, I like the Black Smith I like the other trades too, and I will tell you something I am going to go to Carlisle School that is in the Pennsylvania [sic]

40 childrens—15 girls + 25 boys = 40

Where is Mr Haskell now I never get letter from since I got letter from him last time I guess going stop Blacksmith we are all well down in Poplar Creek Mont don't write to me I might go to Carlisle School if I dont go. I will write to you and let you know What place I am going to. I must close my letter now. I hope this letter will find you in good Health.

From your friend
Paul H. Hayne
this is my own hand writing
I mean my name

—SOURCE: PAUL HAMILTON HAYNE PAPERS, 1815–1944, DUKE UNIVERSITY SPECIAL COLLECTIONS LIBRARY.

also known as the Morrill Act. Whereas previously most universities and colleges had been private institutions, the Morrill Act provided 30,000 acres for each senator and congressman. A state had to endow colleges specializing in the instruction of agricultural or mechanical arts. A second Morrill Act in 1890 made cash allotments available to the colleges. Among schools supported by the Morrill Act were Colorado State University, Iowa State University, Texas Agricultural and Mathematical (A&M), Utah State University, and many others.

After forming his own "Wild West Show" to compete with "Buffalo Bill Cody's Wild West Show" in 1881, "Pawnee Bill" merged his show with Cody's in 1903, bringing elephants and other wild animals in as attractions. The combined shows toured until 1913. *Buffalo Bill Museum and Grace, Lookout Mountain, Golden, Colorado*

Lillie, Gordon William ("Pawnee Bill") (ca. 1859–February 3, 1942)

Founder and operator of a "Wild West Show" that began in 1888, Gordon William ("Pawnee Bill") Lillie merged his operation with that of William Frederick "Buffalo Bill" *Cody* in 1903, under the title "Buffalo Bill's Wild West and Pawnee Bill's Far East," including elephants as part of the "east." The merged show had a life of several years, concluding around 1913—although Cody kept returning for "farewell appearances."

Loving, Oliver (1812–July 20, 1867)

Known for his section of the Goodnight-Loving Trail, Oliver Loving was born in Kentucky and moved to Texas in his thirties. He raised cattle in Lamar County, Texas, and shipped them to Shreveport. After moving his operations to Palo Pinto County, he started the first of his long cattle drives in 1858. After the Civil War, he met Charles Goodnight and the two drove a herd westward to New Mexico, then on to Denver. Loving also pioneered a trail from Texas to Chicago, and the Western Trail to Denver. In 1867 Loving died after suffering wounds from an Indian raid. His life became the basis for much of the novel *Lonesome Dove* by Larry *McMurtry[V]*.

Masterson, Bartholemew ("Bat") (later, William Barclay) (November 27, 1853–October 25, 1921)

Born in Henryville (East Quebec), Canada, as Bartholemew, Masterson changed his name to William Barclay Masterson, but went by "Bat." At age eighteen, Bat and his brother left home to become buffalo hunters, and in 1874, Masterson joined a hunting party that camped at Adobe Walls, Texas, where the expedition was attacked by 200 *Comanche* and *Kiowa* Indians. With 27 other men and 1 woman, the group poured accurate rifle fire at the attacking warriors until the chief, Quannah *Parker*, withdrew. The Adobe Walls fight quickly gained legendary status on the frontier.

Masterson then signed on as an army scout in Texas. At Sweetwater, he engaged in a gun fight over a girl, killing a U.S. soldier who drew on him. He was wounded in the hip, which forced him to carry a cane—later his trademark, along with his derby. He recuperated in *Dodge City*, where he was offered the job of assistant city marshal in 1876 by Wyatt Earp. His brothers served as marshal and deputy sheriff. When he was 22, his abilities with a gun led to his election as sheriff of Ford County in 1877. Dodge City lay within the county lines, requiring Sheriff Masterson to deal with drunken cowboys and violent vagabonds. His brothers served as town marshal and deputy sheriff, alongside assistant marshal Wyatt *Earp*. Within a couple of years, Masterson dealt with renegade Indians, such as Dull Knife, chased horse thieves, and kept Dodge City peaceful.

Turned out by the voters in 1879, Masterson moved to Denver, where he became an accomplished gambler. He then joined Wyatt Earp in *Tombstone, Arizona*, where the two operated the Oriental Saloon. Before long, he returned to Dodge City—and more gunfights—then various towns in Colorado, often serving as sheriff or marshal. As marshal of Trinidad, Colorado, Masterson helped prevent Doc *Holliday* from being extradited to Arizona for trial. He moved in and out of Dodge City, before returning to Denver, where he ran the Palace Theater and several saloons.

His gambling involved him in the new sport of boxing, and he attempted to establish a boxing organization in Colorado. When the rugged frontier became more civilized, even in places like Denver, Masterson no longer fit in. In 1902 the authorities of Denver instructed him to leave, whereupon he moved to New York City. There he entered yet another career, that of a journalist/writer, covering sporting events, hobnobbing with the elites, and serving as deputy U.S. marshal at the swearing in of President Theodore *Roosevelt [V]*. Masterson died at his newspaperman's desk on October 25, 1921.

Miles, Nelson Appleton (August 8, 1839– May 15, 1925)

Referred to as perhaps the most famous soldier in America, Lieutenant General Nelson Appleton Miles was born in Massachusetts, where, as a young man, he worked as a store clerk. When the Civil War broke out, Miles enlisted as a first lieutenant and advanced through the grades rapidly, achieving the rank of major general of volunteers by 1865. By that time, he had been wounded four times and had fought in every battle conducted by the army of the Potomac except Gettysburg. His courage at Chancellorsville gained him a Medal of Honor, awarded in 1892.

After the Civil War, Miles was placed in command of infantry during the *Red River War*, but his campaign against the *Sioux* in 1876–1877 gained him fame, and his role in forcing the *Nez Perce* to surrender in 1877 and in subduing the Bannocks the following year won him accolades. An ambitious man, Miles hoped for the presidency but found his path blocked. Instead, in 1886 he replaced General George *Crook* in the Arizona depart-ment and pursued the renegade Apache chief, *Geronimo*. Miles delegated the campaign to Captain Henry Lawton, who failed to track down the Apache, then sent Lieutenant Charles Gatewood, who arranged to bring Geronimo in. Transferred to the Military Division of the Missouri, Miles was in overall command when the Seventh *United States Cavalry* under Colonel James W. Forsythe massacred about 200 Sioux at *Wounded Knee* on December 29, 1890, despite having worked to secure a peaceful solution to the Sioux uprising.

Miles became commander in chief in 1895, and while he led troops in the Spanish-American War, he was assigned to the invasion of Puerto Rico, not Cuba. In 1903 Nelson Miles retired as a lieutenant general. Although he had an impressive record, Miles's disagreements with other famous soldiers, including George Crook and Oliver O. *Howard*, combined with his lack of political skills to tarnish his record.

Minnesota Sioux Uprising of 1862

In August 1862 the Santee Sioux led by Little Crow staged an uprising over white encroachments, on Indians' loss of lands, late government payments, and the corruption of agent Thomas Galbraith. When Galbraith withheld supplies from the Sioux, one of his colleagues, Andrew Myrick, told the hungry Indians they could eat grass. This comment started the uprising, whereupon outraged warriors murdered five white settlers. They then attacked the Lower Sioux Agency, killing 20 and capturing Myrick, whose mouth they stuffed with grass. A series of battles took place until finally the government troops defeated the Indians at the battle of Wood Lake on September 23. Some 400 to 800 settlers were killed in the conflict, and 38 Sioux were tried, convicted, and executed for rape and murder. Subsequently, the entire tribe was relocated to South Dakota.

Modoc War

The Modoc War had its origins in an 1864 treaty between the government and the Modoc Indians led by Keintpoos (called "Captain Jack" by whites), under which the Modocs were moved from the Lost Valley in southeastern Oregon onto lands once held by the Klamath Indians. Captain Jack led the Modocs in one exodus from the reservation in 1865, but he returned. Then, shortly thereafter, Captain Jack again took the Modocs back to Lost Valley, living near the California town of Yreka.

By that time, white settlers had staked claims and wanted to force the Indians to leave. After negotiations broke down, the Indian agent, T. B. Odeneal, along with 40 soldiers and acting without authority from the Department of War, marched into the Modoc camp on November 29, 1872, to disarm the Indians. Shooting broke out, and the Modocs escaped, taking up defensive positions in the Lava Beds near Tule Lake. Other Indians, hearing of the fight, soon joined Captain Jack, some of them bent on keeping him from any conciliation with the army. When new agents were brought in, including General Edward Canby, to negotiate a return to the reservations, Captain Jack was persuaded by the war faction to assassinate the general. After meeting under a white flag, Captain Jack killed Canby—the only general ever to die in the *Indian Wars*—ensuring a massive counteroffensive. At Dry Lake, the army won its first victory over the Modoc, whereupon deserters helped the soldiers find paths through the mountains and valleys to Captain Jack, who was captured on June 1, 1873. Jack and three other Indians were hanged for killing Canby, and the Modocs were moved to Oklahoma, although in 1909 they were allowed to return to the Klamath reservation.

Moffat, David Halliday, Jr. (July 22, 1839– March 18, 1911)

One of Colorado's leading bankers and businessmen, David Halliday Moffat, Jr., worked his way up the ranks in banking. Infected with the "gold fever" that swept the Midwest, Moffat left for Denver in 1860, where he formed a partnership with C. C. Woolworth to open a bank. He made the acquaintance of New Yorker Jerome B. Chaffee, miner Eban Smith, and territorial governor John Evans. Together, the men received a charter for the First National Bank of Denver, to which Moffat was appointed cashier in early 1867. At age 63 Moffat launched an ambitious project—the Denver, Northwestern & Pacific Railroad, which would become known as the "Moffat Road." The overextended nature of First National's investment in the road, combined with the Panic of 1907, essentially ended the project and bankrupted Moffat.

Moran, Thomas (January 12, 1837–August 25, 1926)

Thomas Moran was a prominent artist of the West, noted for his landscapes. He painted and studied in Europe, then settled in Philadelphia, where he furnished illustrations for *Scribner's*. When the magazine ran a series of articles on the Yellowstone area, Moran and the photographer William Henry Jackson produced a number of works of the expedition. Moran made contacts with railroad companies, which were eager to have him ride their rails and create illustrations for advertising and public relations. Moran made other trips—to Utah and Yosemite—painting memorable pieces such as *Mountain of the Holy Cross* and *The Grand Canyon of the Yellowstone*. Moran's illustrations prominently adorned the publications of the Denver and Rio Grande Railway. His career continued to develop, but he remained best known for his western work when he died in Santa Barbara in 1926.

Muir, John (April 21, 1838–December 24, 1914)

Born in Scotland, John Muir settled in Wisconsin in 1849. He worked in industrial jobs as a mechanic and in an accident lost his eyesight temporarily. After that incident, Muir toured America literally to see the sights. He kept a journal while exploring and encountered Ralph Waldo *Emerson [III]* in the Yosemite Valley in 1871, after which he took on the cause of conservation. Five years later, he lobbied the government for a federal forest conservation policy. In 1892 he founded the Sierra Club, an organization dedicated to conservation and environmental preservation. Muir and Gifford *Pinchot [V]*, Theodore *Roosevelt's [V]* secretary of the Interior, clashed over proper use and preservation of public lands. Although Roosevelt adopted many of Muir's positions, the government rejected his view that no national forests should be used for practical or utilitarian purposes.

National Bank and Currency Acts

The National Banking Act, passed as a wartime measure by Congress in February 1863, was intended primarily to create an institutional demand for government securities that would finance the war. Since the demise of the Second Bank of the United States, effectively killed by President Andrew *Jackson [III]* in 1833 when he withdrew all government deposits, the federal government had not issued charters to any banks. All charters— along with the authority to issue money (i.e., to print bank notes)—came from the states from 1833 until 1863. The National Banking Act established a new national banking system in which charters would come from the federal government, specifically the Treasury Department and the Office of the Comptroller of the Currency.

National banks had to hold appropriate government securities as collateral for all notes issued, as well as a fixed reserve of specie (gold and silver coin) established by the government. Banks were then free to print and circulate National Bank notes, which at the end of the war, would be redeemable in specie. Some other advantages accompanied having a federal charter: the bank could be named a depository bank for the Treasury's tax revenues, and the National Bank notes had a certain advertising value because each bank's name was on the notes it issued. Most important, to encourage state-chartered banks to join the system, Congress passed the Currency Act (an amendment of the National Bank Act) in 1865 placing a 10 percent tax on the issues of all non-national bank notes. That gave the national banks a monopoly on money issue, and ended "private" note issue.

The acts affected the West deeply, as obtaining a national bank charter required fairly high capital reserves. Many banks in small western towns could not afford such high capitalizations, and this in turn led to a disproportionate number of state banks in the West. That tended to restrict the issues of banknotes in the West, leading to complaints about money shortages—though not bank shortages. It was this concern that fueled the "free silver" movement and, later, the rise of the *Populist Party*.

Navajo Long Walk

After Kit *Carson*'s *[III]* successful 1863–1864 winter campaign against the *Navajo [I]*, the United States decided to move the surrendering Indians to Fort Sumner in the *Bosque Redondo* in western New Mexico. United States soldiers escorted the nearly 8,000 Navajos who made the infamous "long walk." The conditions proved horrific as the food and supplies were inadequate and the weather bitterly cold. Many Navajo starved during the forced trek, and the Navajo nation remembers the Long Walk in the same way that the *Cherokees [III]* remember the *Trail of Tears [III]*. It has become a mournful part of their history.

Nez Perce Indians

The Nez Perce are from the Shahaptian branch of the Penutian Indian language group. Some 13,000 years ago, the ancestors of the tribe migrated down the West Coast and up the Columbia River, settling in what is now northern Idaho, northeastern Oregon, and southeastern Washington. They lived according to a seasonal pattern, fishing whenever possible. Nearly 80 percent of their food came from the salmon runs of the Pacific Northwest rivers. Their other staple was camas flour, made from grinding the bulbs of the indigenous camas flowers.

In the early 1700s the Nez Perce obtained *horses [I]*, and their culture changed significantly. They were excellent horse breeders, having bred the Appaloosa, and they expanded their hunting and trading grounds onto the Great Plains of Montana. They pioneered and traveled the Lolo Trail (now U.S. Highway 12) between their homeland and the buffalo hunting grounds in Montana. Nez Perce aligned themselves with the Flatheads of Montana during their hunts and war parties. By 1800, just prior to their first contact with Americans, the Nez Perce population was roughly 7,000.

Though the Nez Perce forbade fur trapping on their lands—believing it immoral—they remained on very good terms with Americans after a good and friendly visit from the *Lewis and Clark Expedition [III]*. Good relations with the U.S. government continued until the 1860s. During the 1856 American expedition against the hostile Yakima Indians on the Pacific Coast, the Nez Perce supplied the U.S. Army with horses and scouts. In that same decade, the Nez Perce did what they could to protect Christian missionaries from attacks by unfriendly Indians.

Located in central Idaho, this is one of the most important Nez Perce holy sites. According to Nez Perce belief, this was their Creation Spot. Their theology has it that the mound is the leftover vomit of the Monster that created the Universe. *Bradley J. Birzer*

Relations soured in 1863 when the federal government purchased gold-rich areas from the Nez Perce. A significant minority of the tribe—mostly those who had remained unchristianized and were ranchers rather than farmers—opposed the sale because of the loss of good grazing land. Not until 1873, though, did the United States attempt to remove the Nez Perce ranchers from their land. Even then, President Grant protected the lands through an executive order. Justifying the support of the president, the Nez Perce aided the Americans against the hostile *Sioux* in 1874.

In 1877 the U.S. government ordered the Nez Perce off their traditional lands in what is now eastern Washington. Tensions increased to the breaking point when several Nez Perce warriors killed four whites in June. The misunderstanding resulted in the *Nez Perce War* of 1877. Between June and October 1877 the Nez Perce retreated from their traditional territory, across the Lolo Trail to Montana, south through *Yellowstone*, and then north to Canada. General Nelson A. *Miles* ended the Nez Perce retreat roughly 40 miles from the safety of the Canadian border.

The Nez Perce, thanks to the unrelenting efforts of *Chief Joseph*, won back some of their traditional lands in both Washington and Idaho. There are roughly 3,300 Nez Perce today, and the National Park Service has created a series of Nez Perce cultural, theological, and historic sites.

Fort Fizzle, Idaho, is a fort that failed. It was a post speedily built to observe the retreating Nez Perce tribe during the Nez Perce War of 1877. The military observers at Fort Fizzle were asleep as the entire tribe passed, unnoticed. *Bradley J. Birzer*

Nez Perce War

In 1877 new treaty demands on the Nez Perce Indians, who lived in the northeast section of Oregon, led to concerns the Indians would lose their hunting lands. After fruitless diplomacy, *Chief Joseph*, leading fewer than 150 braves and 500 noncombatants, fought U.S. Army units under General Oliver O. *Howard* across several states as the Indians tried to reach Canada. Colonel John Gibbon surprised the Indians at the Battle of Big Hole and pursued them eastward. Finally, 40 miles from the Canadian border, having covered 1,500 miles, the Nez Perce surrendered to Colonel Nelson A. *Miles*.

Nicodemus, Kansas

Nicodemus, Graham County, Kansas, founded in 1877, was the most famous of the Great Plains *exoduster [V]* communities of black immigrants. Though Nicodemus boasted a population of 700 persons by 1880, its earlier residents were far wealthier than the 1879 migration of poor black field hands. Tensions developed between the two groups, as the original residents feared that the newcomers would give them a bad name. In addition to internal strife the 1880s and 1890s witnessed severe droughts, natural disasters, and legislative discrimination that encouraged many blacks to leave the area by 1900.

Northern Pacific Railroad

Chartered in 1864, the Northern Pacific Railroad under the management of Jay Cooke, received a large land grant to run from Minnesota to the Pacific Ocean. The road collapsed in the Panic of 1873, and many of the lots were sold off to farmers in Minnesota and North Dakota. In 1883 Henry Villard merged the line with the Oregon Railway to form a genuine transcontinental railroad. Ultimately, in 1970, the line merged with the *Great Northern Railroad* founded by *James J. Hill*, the Spokane, Portland, and Seattle Railroad, and the Colorado and Southern Railroad as the Burlington Northern Railroad.

O.K. Corral

Easily the best-known single gunfight in western history, the gunfight at the O.K. Corral in *Tombstone, Arizona*, on October 26, 1881, pitted the Earps against the Clantons and the McLaurys. Most of the *Earp* brothers had worked in some form of law enforcement in various locations in the West. Wyatt worked with the Hays, Kansas, and *Dodge City* police, then was assistant marshal of Dodge. At the time of the shootout, the records differ as to whether he was already a deputy U.S. marshal, but he was a lawman for Pima County by 1880. His brother Morgan worked in Dodge City as well, then rode shotgun for *Wells Fargo* stages. Virgil was a U.S. deputy marshal when he arrived in Tombstone in 1879.

The Earps were involved in tracking down some stolen government mules that led to the McLaury ranch. Frank and Tom McLaury were sheep and cattle ranchers who had arrived in Arizona in 1877. Although the Earps could not prove the mules were on the McLaury ranch, local papers ran allegations that the McLaurys had stolen the animals, and the McLaurys blamed the Earps for encouraging the story. A third family, the Clantons (Newman and his sons Ike, Phin, and Billy), who also had a reputation as rustlers, were allies of the McLaurys. These groups generically were referred to as the "cowboys."

On the night of October 28, 1880, William "Curley Bill" Brocius, a Clanton gang member, shot the Tombstone marshal, Fred White, who had come to disarm Brocius. Apparently, the gun discharged in White's hand, but the Earps arrested Brocius and his friends. Brocius went free, later telling people he had indeed killed White, whose place as city marshal was temporarily filled by Virgil Earp. On another occasion, Wyatt, then a deputy marshal, broke up a lynch mob, further angering some of the locals, and yet at another time Wyatt's horse was stolen and was located in the possession of Billy Clanton. In March 1881 the stage to Benson was robbed and the driver murdered. A posse, including the Earps, Bat *Masterson* (visiting from Dodge), and Cochise County sheriff John Behan captured one of the perpetrators, who named members of the Clanton-run "cowboy" gang. Although the prisoner escaped—some think with Behan's help—he implicated John Henry "Doc" *Holliday* in the murder. (In later years, Holliday's girlfriend, Kate Elder [Mary Katherine Horony] said Wyatt Earp was also involved.)

The stage robbery soon caused problems in yet another way. Wyatt Earp cut a bargain with Ike Clanton, who promised to reveal the identities of the real robbers; Earp would get credit for capturing them, but Ike would get the reward money. Clanton backed out, and within a short time, another stage robbery led to the arrest of more cowboy gang members. Again, the Earps were blamed for the arrests, which led to a heated argument between Holliday and Ike Clanton on October 25. Although Virgil, then Wyatt, broke up the fight, Ike continued to wander the streets, making threats, at which time the Earps arrested him. After Ike left court, his friend Tom McLaury and Wyatt engaged in a heated exchange, until Wyatt pistol-whipped the cowboy. Other cowboy gang members soon arrived, including Frank McClaury, Billy Claiborne, and Billy Clanton. Virgil, hearing that a group of cowboys was threatening gunplay, left the saloon to disarm them.

On the way to meet the cowboys, Virgil was joined by Morgan and Wyatt, plus Doc Holliday, who was still looking for an opportunity to kill Ike Clanton. Both Morgan and Wyatt carried titles of "special officers," although Holliday had no legal authority whatsoever. At the O.K. Corral, near Fry's Photography Studio, the Earp party came face to face with Ike and Billy Clanton, Frank and Tom McLaury, and Billy Claiborne. Holliday had a shotgun, which he hid under his coat, but some historians suspect neither party wanted bloodshed. Whether the Clanton/McLaury gang put their hands up when ordered is in dispute, but within seconds, both Clantons and McLaurys were shot. All the Clanton/McLaury gang died immediately or soon thereafter, while Virgil was shot in the leg, Morgan in the back, and Holliday grazed on the hip. Wyatt was not shot, nor was Billy Claiborne, who ran before the shooting started. Sheriff John Behan, a known friend of the cowboys, attempted to disarm the Earps but backed down. In December a court ruled that the Earps had acted in a law enforcement capacity.

The cowboys sought revenge and subsequently ambushed Virgil in December 1881; he was wounded and left with a paralyzed arm, and Morgan, in 1882, was killed. After sending his wounded brother and female family members to California, Wyatt assembled a team and, under the authority of Virgil's U.S. deputy marshal's badge, hunted down several cowboys, including Frank Stilwell, Curly Bill Brocius, and, Wyatt later claimed, Johnny *Ringo*. A gunfight that was over in less than 30 seconds had compressed a lifetime of hatred and animosity among several pioneers of the Arizona frontier.

Oakley, Annie (Phoebe Ann Moses)
(August 13, 1860–November 3, 1926)

"Little Miss Sure Shot," or Annie Oakley, was born Phoebe Ann Moses on an Ohio farm. She learned to shoot before age 10, providing food for the family and even helping pay off the farm mortgage from her earnings as a sharpshooter. She defeated exhibition shooter Frank Butler in a match staged by one of Annie's sponsors in Cincinnati, after which the two courted, then married in 1882.

Butler trained Phoebe in horsemanship, handling dogs, and driving a stagecoach. At some point during this training she adopted the stage name Annie Oakley. Chief *Sitting Bull* saw her perform in St. Paul and adopted her, giving her the *Sioux* name Watanya Cicilia (Little Sure Shot). With Butler, Oakley joined Buffalo Bill *Cody*'s "Wild West Show" as one of its stars. Over the next 17 years, she continued with Cody's show, while Butler increasingly stepped into the background as her agent and manager as well as occasional stage hand. He held cigarettes in his mouth or coins in his hands for Oakley to shoot, all without incident. He billed her as the "peerless wing and rifle shot," and Oakley lived up to the billing. She could fire her rifle from a bicycle or standing on top of a galloping horse, or shoot a pistol aiming through a mirror over her shoulder. Her perfect placement of bullet holes in playing cards led to the term "an Annie Oakley" for a free pass marked with a punch in a ticket. Oakley's shooting skills were legendary: with a rifle she hit 943 out of 1,000 glass balls thrown in the air; with a shotgun she hit 4,772 out of 5,000 balls in nine hours.

Easily the greatest female shooter of all time, Annie Oakley (Pheobe Ann Moses) traveled with Wild Bill Cody's "Wild West Show," accomplishing feats of shooting virtually unmatched then, or since. *Library of Congress*

A small woman with piercing brown eyes, Oakley experienced two accidents later in her life that seriously impaired her health. The second accident forced her to wear a brace, although she continued to perform. After 1913 Oakley retired, having become an American legend. A 1950s television series—one of the few at the time starring a woman in an action role—fictionalized and glorified her career, and a Broadway musical by Irving Berlin, "Annie Get Your Gun," celebrated her life, which she captured in her autobiography, *The Story of My Life* (1926).

Opening of the Oklahoma Territory

The opening of the Oklahoma Territory, highlighted by the "land rush" of the 1890s, originated with the relocation of some 50 tribes on the lands once promised to the Five Civilized Tribes of the *Cherokee [III]*, Creek, Chicasaw, Choctaw, and Seminole Indians. During the *Civil War*, the Five Civilized Tribes had sided with the Confederacy, to the point of supplying troops to the Southern cause. As part of the punishment for their wartime activity, the tribes soon found that other Native Americans were admitted to their lands, including *Kiowa*, Arapaho, *Cheyenne*, Osage, and *Comanche*. More than 25 reservations were opened to accommodate these tribes, which were soon joined by Sauk, Fox, Seneca, and still others.

A section of the Territory was "unassigned," in which cattle grazed and which was crossed by railroads. As more whites saw the Indian lands, keeping ranchers and settlers out became increasingly difficult, despite the presence of many forts ringing the Territory. The Missouri, Kansas, and Texas Railroad soon stretched from Kansas, through Indian Territory, to Sherman, Texas. In 1887 the Atcheson, Topeka, and Santa Fe Railroad crossed the unassigned lands, bringing workers and support facilities. By the mid-1880s it became clear that the government could not keep settlers out. With the Dawes Act of 1887, the government provided for the purchase of Indian lands. Under the conditions of the Dawes Act, every Indian man, woman, and child was given 160 acres in exchange for extinguishing their titles to the lands, opening millions of acres for homesteads.

In 1889 President Benjamin Harrison authorized the opening of unoccupied lands and triggered the Oklahoma land rush in April, in which some 100,000 immigrants participated at the 226-mile Cherokee Outlet covering some 6 million acres of land. A bugle announced the start of the rush, whereupon thousands of men on horseback and families in wagons raced to unclaimed lands. One man fell immediately and was crushed; another was killed by a pistol shot fired by a rider to speed up his horse; and still many others were killed in confrontations over claims. Each person could receive up to 160 acres for a claim that was staked and held. Thus, the "boomers," as they were known, came both well-armed and unarmed; well-supplied and barely supplied. One wagon had a near-full house set on it. Others relied on speed, and others relied on their knowledge of the land. Before long, broken buggies, surreys, and wagons dotted the Oklahoma landscape. Railroads and for-hire, hastily organized wagon companies brought in still other settlers. At Arkansas City, Kansas, for example, some 10,000 people crammed into the station to catch one of the 15 Santa Fe trains collected to transport people to the available lands. Above 5 all, the land rush was a haven for bullies, who could threaten or cajole many off their territory.

Still others, who came late, sought to fake their way into ownership. These "sooners" did not begin at the starting line but hid or arrived early, trying to grab land claimed by others. Some lathered their horses so as to make them appear to have been ridden. When they could be caught, the sooners were driven off by marshals, but far too often they got away with their illegal activities. In one case, two riders arrived after a hard, unbroken ride, only to find the land they intended to occupy was already plowed. The riders found garden onions four inches tall on land that supposedly had not previously been inhabited. Immigrants gave birth to Norman, Oklahoma City, Edmund, and other Oklahoma towns and

IN THEIR OWN Words

Oklahoma Land Rush, from *Harper's*

When the Oklahoma Territory was opened to white settlement, Congress failed to provide for any form of civil government. The rules allowed the settlers to enter the territory on April 22, 1889, seek unclaimed land, and file a claim of ownership in accordance. Although federal marshals and others supervising the land rush supposedly were prohibited from owning lots, this restriction was violated regularly. William Willard Howard, writing in *Harper's Weekly* in 1889, recorded his observations of the "land rush."

In some respects the recent settlement of Oklahoma was the most remarkable thing of the present century. Unlike Rome, the city of Guthrie was built in a day. To be strictly accurate in the matter, it might be said that it was built in an afternoon. At twelve o'clock on Monday, April 22d, the resident population of Guthrie was nothing; before sundown it was at least ten thousand. In that time streets had been laid out, town lots staked off, and steps taken toward the formation of a municipal government. At twilight the camp-fires of ten thousand people gleamed on the grassy slopes of the Cimarron Valley, where, the night before, the coyote, the gray wolf, and the deer had roamed undisturbed. Never before in the history of the West has so large a number of people been concentrated in one place in so short a time. To the conservative Eastern man, who is wont to see cities grow by decades, the settlement of Guthrie was magical beyond belief; to the quick-acting resident of the West, it was merely a particularly lively town-site speculation.

The preparations for the settlement of Oklahoma had been complete, even to the slightest detail, for weeks before the opening day. The Santa Fe Railway, which runs through Oklahoma north and south, was prepared to take any number of people from its handsome station at Arkansas City, Kansas, and to deposit them in almost any part of Oklahoma as soon as the law allowed; thousands of covered wagons were gathered in camps on all sides of quickly found that the best lots were reserved for the marshals and other city officials who kept order. In Guthrie, Oklahoma, trains disgorged settlers who found that some 500 sooners already occupied the town. "Town companies," formed by criminal elements, also sought to acquire townships and sell off the lots later at inflated prices, and "confidence men" were in abundance. One detective counted 42 known thieves operating in Arkansas City.

the new Territory waiting for the embargo to be lifted. In its picturesque aspects the rush across the border at noon on the opening day must go down in history as one of the most noteworthy events of Western civilization. At the time fixed, thousands of hungry home-seekers, who had gathered from all parts of the country, and particularly from Kansas and Missouri, were arranged in line along the border, ready to lash their horses into furious speed in the race for fertile spots in the beautiful land before them.

As the expectant home-seekers waited with restless patience, the clear, sweet notes of a cavalry bugle rose and hung a moment upon the startled air. It was noon. The last barrier of savagery in the United States was broken down. Moved by the same impulse, each driver lashed his horses furiously; each rider dug his spurs into his willing steed, and each man on foot caught his breath hard and darted forward. A cloud of dust rose where the home-seekers had stood in line, and when it had drifted away before the gentle breeze, the horses and wagons and men were tearing across the open country like fiends. The horsemen had the best of it from the start. It was a fine race for a few minutes, but soon the riders began to spread out like a fan, and by the time they had reached the horizon they were scattered about as far as eye could see. Even the fleetest of the horsemen found upon reaching their chosen localities that men in wagons and men on foot were there before them. As it was clearly impossible for a man on foot to outrun a horseman, the inference is plain that Oklahoma had been entered hours before the appointed time.

Notwithstanding the assertions of the soldiers that every boomer had been driven out of Oklahoma, the fact remains that the woods along the streams within Oklahoma were literally full of people Sunday night. Nine-tenths of these people made settlement upon the land illegally. The other tenth would have done so had there been any desirable land left to settle upon. This action on the part of the first claim-holders will cause a great deal of land litigation in the future, as it is not to be expected that the man who ran his horse at its utmost speed for ten miles only to find a settler with an ox team in quiet possession of his chosen farm will tamely submit to this plain infringement of the law.

—SOURCE: WILLIAM WILLARD HOWARD, *HARPER'S WEEKLY* 33 (MAY 18, 1889): 391–394.

Over the next 12 years, a number of other runs followed, often regulated by on-the-spot law offices that registered titles. Equipment and supply stores did a "land rush" business at high prices, but merchants could get them with their monopoly status. Land office lines stretched on seemingly endlessly, and it often took days to register land. Other land titles were disposed of by lotteries, but one way or another, at the end of the rush period, virtually all of the Indian lands were distributed.

This resulted in two separate territories, Oklahoma Territory to the west, and Indian lands in the east. Still, there were only perhaps a million people in the two territories combined, and statehood for Oklahoma required the two sections, which did not wish to join, to form one entity, which became the State of Oklahoma in 1907.

O'Sullivan, Timothy H. (ca.1840–January 14, 1882)

A former apprentice in Matthew Brady's studio in New York, Timothy H. O'Sullivan photographed military sites and personnel during the Civil War, accompanying General William Tecumseh *Sherman*'s campaign in South Carolina. Working for Alexander Gardener's studio, he photographed soldiers and weapons at Gettysburg, Antietam, and Appomattox. After the war, he joined U.S. military survey teams in the West. He photographed natural wonders in Nevada, California, New Mexico, Colorado, and Utah. In 1873 he photographed Canyon de Chelly. Toward the end of his life, he worked for the U.S. Treasury Department, before dying of tuberculosis.

Parker, Ely S. (ca. 1828–August 30, 1895)

Ely S. Parker, a full-blooded Seneca Indian, was one of the most prominent Native Americans in the 19th century. On his mother's side, he was related to the great Indian Prophet, *Handsome Lake [II]*. Educated at a Baptist mission and at several private academies, Parker served the *Iroquois [I]* ably as both the chief of the Senecas and Grand Chief of the Iroquois Confederacy. During the *Civil War* Parker served as Grant's aide from Vicksburg in 1863 to Appomattox in 1865. When Robert E. Lee commended him on being the only "real American" in the courthouse at Appomattox during the grand surrender, Parker famously corrected him: "We are all Americans." After the war, Grant appointed Parker the commissioner of Indian affairs. Accused of corruption, Parker only served two years. After losing considerable investments in the economic downturn of the mid-1870s, Parker ended his career as an administrator for the New York City Police Department.

Parker, Quannah (ca.1852–February 23, 1911)

Parker, the famed son of an Indian chief and a captive white woman, was one of the most aggressive and warlike of the *Comanche* Indians. In 1874 Parker organized and led the joint Comanche, *Kiowa*, and *Cheyenne* forces against the buffalo hunters trapped in the Adobe Walls in the Texas Panhandle. Parker and his immediate followers were among the last to be captured by the U.S. military in 1875. Seeing the future clearly, Parker turned from warring to business, and became a successful businessman from the 1870s to his death in 1911. As leading chief of the Comanches, Parker's entrepreneurial adventures served as a powerful example to the other Comanche. Though a polygamist with five wives, Parker knew and associated with numerous political leaders, such as Teddy *Roosevelt [V]*, and political philosophers, such as the Englishman Lord Bryce. Indeed, he was a celebrity in and out of Comanche circles. In the 1890s Parker served as one of the creators of the *Native American Church [V]*, developing one of its two primary liturgies.

Pinkerton, Allan (1819–1884)

Born in Glasgow, Scotland in 1819, Allan Pinkerton arrived in the United States at age 23, settling in Kane County, Illinois. During brief employment as a cooper, he discovered a gang of counterfeiters and assisted the Chicago police with their capture. He then worked as a deputy sheriff of Kane County, then Cook County. In 1852 he started the Pinkerton Detective Agency with its famous logo, the "all-seeing eye."

Over the years Pinkerton's agency developed a reputation for using the most recent crime investigation techniques, such as conducting extensive compilations of the description of physical characteristics. The agency foiled a plot to kill Abraham Lincoln during his trip to Washington, D.C., after which, at Lincoln's request, Pinkerton organized the United States Secret Service under the control of the Treasury Department. Secret Service agents uncovered and foiled a Confederate plot for a prison break at Camp Douglas.

After the Civil War, the Pinkertons engaged in extensive industrial espionage against unions. They battled the Molly Maguires (a secret organization of Irish-American coal miners in Scranton, Pennsylvania) in 1874–1875, and, in 1892, supplied strikebreakers for the disastrous Homestead Strike. The Pinkertons' fate became intertwined with that of *Jesse James* and his gang and the Younger Brothers in the 1870s, when one Pinkerton detective was killed trying to infiltrate the gang. Pinkerton devoted increased resources to tracking the gang, and in 1875 Pinkerton agents found what they thought was the gang's hideout. Without confirming the identity of the occupants, the Pinkertons showered the cabin with gunfire, killing Jesse James's half brother and wounding his mother. Jesse James then embarked on a mission of killing Pinkerton, even traveling to Chicago once to assassinate the detective chief. The detectives crafted a reputation for finding criminals when others could not.

Pinkerton died of gangrene after biting his tongue in 1884, but his detective agency continued and became synonymous with "private eyes." The agency was successful in breaking up the Rube and Jim Burrows gang in 1888. Pinkerton agents also gained fame in their pursuit of the "Wild Bunch" and, subsequently, Butch *Cassidy* and the Sundance Kid.

polygamy

The practice of men having multiple wives was a practice condoned in the teachings of the Mormon Church of Jesus Christ of *Latter Day Saints [III]*. Technically, the Mormons approved of plural marriages for men only, as stemming from a revelation by the Church's prophet, Joseph Smith in 1843. (The date of the revelation apparently was two years earlier, but wasn't recorded until 1843, by which time Smith already had several wives.) Polygamy conflicted with American legal codes and also was resisted by some Mormons, who split off to form other Mormon churches, and some former members who wrote exposés. It was such an exposé that led to Smith's attack on the *Nauvoo Inquisitor*, which published some antipolygamy letters, and in turn led to Smith's murder while in jail in 1844. After moving to *Salt Lake City [III]*, the Mormon church hierarchy officially sanctioned polygamy as a church doctrine and as part of the process commanded by

God to establish a royal priesthood to provide bodies for spirits waiting to enter the earth. Mormon teaching also claimed that monogamy had led to immorality and promiscuity, which could be contained within church-sanctioned families.

The practice drew extreme criticism from traditional religions and from much of society. The Republican Party, in 1856, called for the end of the "twin relics of barbarism," slavery and polygamy. The existence of polygamy not only threatened to keep Utah from statehood but even led to government efforts to disincorporate the church. Church President Wilford Woodruff, in the Mormon Manifesto of 1890, instructed the church to cease further plural marriages, even though the religious sanction of polygamy did not change. Some isolated groups continued to practice polygamy under the auspices of Mormonism well into the 21st century.

Populist Party/Populism

The Populist Party was a third party that appeared in the 1890s that reflected agrarian discontent based on three main concerns: (1) railroad and grain elevator monopolies; (2) deflation and the unwillingness to monetize silver; and (3) improved position for laborers. The Populists emerged from the National Grange movement of the 1870s of the midwestern farm states, Iowa, Nebraska, and Kansas, but especially along the northern tier of Minnesota and the Dakotas. Ultimately, the Grange led to the formation of two main farm "alliances" called the National Farmer's Alliance (also called the Northern Alliance), and the National Farmer's Alliance and Industrial Union (known as the Southern Alliance). Despite several attempts to unite the two alliances, the efforts failed except for Kansas, North Dakota, and South Dakota. Attempts to unite the farmers soon took other directions.

In June 1890 the state People's party appeared in Kansas, and through the leadership of the Kansas delegation, a People's Party Convention occurred in Omaha to nominate a national presidential candidate in 1892. Ignatius Donnelly wrote the first platform, which called for government ownership of telegraph and railroad systems, and for a national currency that would provide a "safe, sound, and flexible" circulating medium. By that, Donnelly and the Populists meant bimetallism, or the purchase and coinage of silver at a ratio of 16:1 (silver ounces to gold). The Populists also endorsed an income tax to redistribute wealth. Although specific other retaliatory measures against corporations were not included, the Populists viewed them as oppressive and nondemocratic institutions.

The Populists nominated James B. Weaver (who had run for president on the 1880 Greenback-Labor party), and it managed to steal a handful of electoral votes from Democrat Grover Cleveland, the winner. Already the Congress had adopted measures that met the Populists' concerns: in 1890, the Sherman Antitrust Act prohibited combinations of

IN THEIR OWN *Words*

The Granger Resolutions

The farm movement known as the Granger movement, like that of the more radical Populist Party, was concerned with perceived unfair pricing and monopoly power of the western railroads. In some of the resolutions of the Farmers' Convention of 1873, the Grangers stated their objections:

1. Resolved, by the farmers of Illinois, in mass meeting assembled, that all chartered monopolies, not regulated and controlled by law, have proved detrimental to the public prosperity, corrupting in their management, and dangerous to republican institutions.

2. Resolved, that the railways of the world, except in those countries where they have been held under strict regulation and supervision of the government, have proved themselves arbitrary, extortionate, and as opposed to free institutions and free commerce . . .

3. Resolved, that we hold, declare, and resolve, that this despotism, which defies our laws, plunders our shippers, impoverishes our people, and corrupts our government, shall be subdued and made to subserve the public interest at whatever cost . . .

9. Resolved, that we urge the passage of a bill enforcing the principle that railroads are public highways, and requiring railroads to make connections with all roads whose tracks meet or cross their own . . .

12. Resolved, that we endorse most fully the action of those who tender legal rates of fare upon the railroads, and refuse to pay more; and that it is the duty of the legislature to provide by law for the defense of the State of Illinois of suits commenced . . . against individuals who have in good faith insisted, or hereafter may insist, upon the right to ride in railroads at legal rates.

—SOURCE: HENRY STEELE COMMAGER, ED., *DOCUMENTS OF AMERICAN HISTORY*
(NEW YORK: F. S. CROFTS & CO., 1934), 143–146.

business "in restraint of trade," and the *Sherman Silver Purchase Act* of the same year resulted in government purchases of silver at 16.5:1, close to what the Populists had demanded.

Those measures helped discredit the Populists in several ways. By overvaluing silver, the Silver Purchase Act helped ignite the Panic of 1893, and even though the act was repealed, it had already set in motion recessionary forces. The Sherman Antitrust Act effectively ended "trusts" (combinations in which subordinate businesses exchange 100 percent of their ownership shares for shares of the umbrella "trust" organization, thus ceding control to the trust), but it pushed American businesses into vertical combinations that made them more efficient, bigger, and more powerful than ever. In reality, that was beneficial for most Americans, and certainly for consumers, who saw steadily falling prices, but it did little to advance the Populists' goal of reining in corporations.

By 1896 the Populists had become entirely focused on two issues: railroad ownership and bimetallism. Then, thanks largely to the Party's candidate, *William Jennings Bryan [V]*, it became a single-issue silver party. Bryan, however, was also the Democratic Party's candidate, whose famous "cross of gold" speech to the Democratic Convention so inspired the Populists that they agreed to nominate him as the Populist Party candidate as well. The Republican candidate, William McKinley, ran on several issues, including a "full dinner pail," and stood behind the gold standard. He crushed Bryan in the election and Bryan's defeat completely deflated the Populist Party, which never recovered. However, in one of the most famous children's stories of all time, *The Wonderful Wizard of Oz* (1900), the Populist parable was immortalized with Dorothy (from Kansas), the Scarecrow (a symbolic farmer), the Tin Woodsman (Eastern labor), and the Cowardly Lion (Bryan). In the story the symbolism of Dorothy's silver shoes on the "yellow brick road" could not be missed. Meanwhile, the ideas of the Populists melded into either the Republican Progressive wing or the rising Socialist Party.

prostitution

Any location with large numbers of men and money is certain to encourage prostitution, and the West was no different. Cow towns, mining camps, and forts all provided the "demand-side" for prostitution in the West, where brothels often were contained within a saloon or "dance hall." The ages of prostitutes ranged from 11 to 30, although most were between 15 and 19. Estimates put the number of prostitutes on the frontier as high as 50,000. In St. Louis prostitution was regulated by requiring the prostitutes to be identified by a red light in the area and to have regular medical exams. Other districts were as well known, but less clearly marked, such as San Francisco's Barbary Coast.

Prostitutes' charges varied—some made $5 to $7 per "trick"—but often they had "overhead" in the form of payments or bribes to local police, the saloon or dance hall owner, cab or "hack" drivers, or madams. Some madams became wealthy (such as Madame Ah Toy in San Francisco), and women could work their way up to the status of madam and achieve a certain degree of financial success. Brothels established off-scene locations for sex, known as "cribs," which were both expensive and dangerous. Prostitutes also followed the army to remote locations, as they had in Roman times, and army prostitutes included many Indian women.

Quantrill, William Clarke (1837–June 6, 1865)

Notorious for the sacking of Lawrence, Kansas, during the Civil War, William Clarke Quantrill was born in Ohio. After teaching school for a time, he moved west in 1857 to Lawrence, Kansas. Despite coming from Ohio with a "free soil" view, he soon sided with the proslavery forces in "Bloody Kansas"and, when the Civil War broke out, organized a group of volunteers that usually numbered fewer than 30 but occasionally swelled to 300.

In August 1863 Quantrill's volunteer army entered Lawrence, burned most of the town, and killed most of the 150 defenders. Two months later, Quantrill's raiders captured a small party of federal noncombatants and massacred 17 of them near Baxter Springs, Kansas. He attracted such young fighters (and soon-to-be-outlaws) as Frank and Jesse *James*, and the Younger brothers. At first, Quantrill enjoyed the sympathy of many Kansas farmers, but over time, his excesses turned many against him. Many of his men left him, and the Confederate officers would not support him. On May 10, 1865, Union guerillas in Kentucky shot him, and he died on June 6.

Red Cloud (Makhpiya-Luta) (1822–1909)

An Oglala *Sioux* who developed a reputation as a fierce warrior and possibly a chief, although his rank remains in dispute, Red Cloud directed the *Fetterman Massacre* in December 1866. Red Cloud was born in Nebraska Territory, grew up an orphan, and joined war parties as a boy. He killed Bull Bear, an Oglala leader who was engaged in a rivalry with Red Cloud's uncle, Chief Smoke, a deed which created numerous friends and enemies. During the 1865–1866 conflicts with the U.S. Army over the *Bozeman Trail*, which ran through the Sioux hunting grounds, Red Cloud masterminded the Sioux offensive, so that it was named "Red Cloud's War." His ambush of Captain William J. Fetterman's expedition to relieve a wood-gathering party was a forerunner of the *Custer* massacre a decade later. Red Cloud's prominence in these actions confused whites, who assumed he was a chief and treated with him. In November 1868 Red Cloud agreed to the Treaty of Fort Laramie, in which he promised peace in return for a withdrawal of the army units in forts along the Powder River.

Red Cloud was rewarded with a trip to Washington in 1870, and two years later he brought the tribesmen he could persuade to join him at the Red Cloud (Indian) Agency. Although he only could account for some 20 percent of all the Sioux, over time more moved to the reservation. He never gained the leadership of the Sioux tribes because of his close relations with whites, and even his son refused to abide by his agreements. He resisted efforts to dilute Indian culture, however, making frequent appeals to Washington in person, and eventually he and his wife became Christians.

Red River War, 1874–1875

After the devastation of the 1864 *Sand Creek Massacre* and the 1868 *Battle of the Washita*, many *Cheyenne* Indians remained adamantly hostile to the United States. Other tribes, such as the *Kiowas* and the *Comanches*, joined in the hostilities, attacking trespassing buffalo hunters in June 1874 at the Adobe Walls, an area in northern Texas designated as Comanche hunting grounds by treaty. When the U.S. government gave permission to the military to strike Indian reservations, roughly 5,000 Cheyenne, Kiowa, and Comanche Indians headed for the Texas Panhandle on the staked plains, near Palo Duro Canyon. Though United States and Indian forces skirmished during 1874, most of the action between the warring parties was reduced to mere chasing and eluding. U.S. officials also destroyed Indian supplies and food whenever and wherever possible. The war tactics learned during the American Civil War proved effective. When war leaders headed back to the reservations for food and shelter during the winter of 1874 and 1875, U.S. officials imprisoned them. The U.S. chase and capture campaign of the so-called 1874–1875 Red River War proved highly effective. With only a few exceptions, U.S. actions prevented future hostilities from southern Great Plains tribes. Major General Phil *Sheridan* attempted a similar strategy against the Sioux and other northern tribes, only to experience dismal failure.

Reno, Marcus A. (November 15, 1834–March 30, 1889)

The highest-ranking officer to survive the *Battle of the Little Bighorn*, Marcus A. Reno was born in Illinois, went to West Point, and served in the Civil War. Assigned to the Seventh *United States Cavalry* under Lieutenant Colonel George Armstrong *Custer*, Reno had fought against the plains Indians in 1874 before the disastrous 1876 campaign. At Little Bighorn, Reno was ordered to attack the main village, and he led his men forward, only to be met with strong resistance. Custer, who had told Reno he would support him, had in fact moved far ahead and to the right, more than a mile away. As the *Sioux* and *Cheyenne* attacks grew stronger, Reno retreated to a stand of timber near the Little Bighorn River, and then, after still more Indians joined the onslaught, back across the river to bluffs, where his troops dug in. Meanwhile, a third column of some 150 men under Captain Frederick Benteen, who had been on Custer's right, heard the gunshots and arrived to reinforce Reno, finding themselves trapped. By that time, Custer's five troops were engaged and rapidly killed. Reno and Benteen made one foray to try to break through, but the Indians (who outnumbered Custer's entire command at least four-to-one) drove them back. Throughout the remainder of the day and night the troops held off further attacks until, on June 26, Colonel John Gibbon and General Alfred Terry arrived with reinforcements. Reno was hauled before a military board of inquiry in 1879, where he was cleared of charges of cowardice. A year later, however, he was court-martialed and discharged for dereliction of duty by an officer whose son had died at Little Bighorn. In 1967 a military board of review examining all the original documents and testimony, reversed the decision, changed Reno's discharge from general to "honorable," and ordered his remains interred along with those of the rest of Custer's command at the Little Bighorn battlefield.

Ringo, John Peters (May 3, 1850–July 14, 1882)

Born in Indiana, John Ringo moved with his family to Missouri, then on to California, eventually settling in San Jose near Coleman Younger. Ringo drank heavily, even as a young man, and left home at age 19 for Texas. There he became involved in a feud in Mason County, Texas, over the lynching of four cattle rustlers. Ringo became implicated in several murders but escaped from jail with the help of friends on at least two occasions. He was jailed but released yet another time before dropping out of sight. In 1879 he was seen in New Mexico and southern Arizona, where he, Curley Bill Brocius, the Clanton family, and the McLaury family were involved in cattle ranching and rustling. Always considered educated—some legends suggest he went to college, which is highly unlikely—Ringo was ill-tempered and quick to draw his weapon. He shot a man in Safford, Arizona, for refusing to drink with him; and another time, having lost a round of poker, he held up the players for $500.

Ringo's association with the Clantons and McLaurys put him in opposition to the powerful Earp family, especially Wyatt *Earp* and his friend "Doc" *Holliday*. Following the gunfight at the *O.K. Corral* in October 1881, Ringo and Holliday nearly had a shootout. Then, after the Earps left *Tombstone*, Ringo was found dead. Accounts of his death are confusing: some, including Wyatt Earp himself, claimed that Wyatt Earp shot Ringo in connection with the assassination of Morgan Earp in March 1882.

rodeos

Informal riding and roping contests were old traditions among *cowboys*, but the invention of the rodeo as an entertainment spectacle is attributed to Buffalo Bill *Cody*. When the legendary impressario staged horsemanship contests in his hometown of North Platte, Nebraska, during the 1882 Fourth of July celebrations, Cody realized that a traveling show exhibiting the aspects of the "Wild West" might provide exotic fun for the rest of the country. "Buffalo Bill's Wild West Show" became an international sensation, and well after a century the contests of strength and skill known as the rodeo remain. Indeed, the modern rodeo is big business.

Most modern rodeo competitors belong to the Professional Rodeo Cowboys Association (PRCA), based in Colorado Springs, Colorado. By maintaining rules, compiling scores, and presiding over championship ranking, the organization sanctions hundreds of otherwise unrelated rodeos across the United States and Canada. Regional championships are determined on 12 circuits across the nation, while full-time competitors may enter as many rodeos as they physically can.

Traditional rodeos include seven categories: calf roping, team roping, steer roping and wrestling, saddle bronco riding, bareback bronco riding, bull riding, and barrel racing. New events include "bullfighting," once reserved for rodeo clowns who protected downed riders from rampaging bulls. These unarmed contestants distract and manipulate bulls in the ring. Riding events are judged on the basis of how well a cowboy performs for a ride of eight seconds, and the rider receives no score if thrown prior to eight seconds. Roping events are evaluated solely on the basis of the time it takes a rider to rope and subdue a cow or steer.

In an etching from a "Wild West Show," both white hunters and Indians perform a "buffalo hunt" for an audience seated in the grandstands in the background. Note in the upper left "cowboys" are lassoing deer as part of the "hunt." *Buffalo Bill Museum and Grace, Lookout Mountain, Golden Colorado*

PRCA ranking is based on winnings revenue, with the top 15 earners in each event allowed to compete in the December National Finals at Las Vegas, Nevada. The title "all-around cowboy" goes to the contestant who has earned the most money that year in PRCA-sanctioned events. Many rodeos are televised, especially after the advent of ESPN, and such corporate sponsors as Chevrolet, Ford, and Levis boost the winnings. A purse that in 1959 totaled only $50,000, in 2000, exceeds $4 million.

Rodeo cowboys risk constant injury and live a life on the road. Many get only meager winnings after spending thousands in competition fees. Rodeo profits, though, have grown for the sponsors.

Wyoming's "Cheyenne Frontier Days," the world's largest outdoor rodeo and western celebration, began in 1897 as a local event to preserve regional traditions. In addition to its PRCA-sanctioned rodeo, the 10-day event is now held the last full week of July and celebrates the "Old West" with parades, country music concerts, dancing, food, art shows, and chuck-wagon racing. Sales for the rodeo and concert events at "Frontier Days" have hovered near 200,000 tickets per year, with the three free pancake breakfasts held during the event attracting 30,000 people.

Rodeos are no longer limited to seasonal or special events. The weekly Mesquite Rodeo near Dallas, for example, is televised by the National Network (TNN). Built in 1986, the Mesquite facility offers 5,000 seats, a banquet capacity of 2,000, and "Texas suites" similar to the "skyboxes" found in football stadiums such as the *Astrodome [V]*.

But as professional and glitzy as the rodeos have become, they essentially remain a contest between man and animal. Concerns for animals' health has led to the implementation of more than 60 regulations to govern treatment, care, and competition aspects of animal welfare. Human welfare is a concern, too, with Internet websites posting the lastest event information on broken limbs, concussions, or fatalities. Thus while a 1993–1994 survey of veterinarians showed that at 28 PRCA rodeos, there were 16 injuries among 33,991 participating animals (1 percent), the rate of human injuries and deaths remains higher.

Sand Creek Massacre, 1864

The Sand Creek Massacre, a blatant and unjustified attack on civilian targets, was the worst such incident conducted against American Indians during the 19th century. One of the heroes of the 1862 Civil War battle of Glorietta Pass, Colonel John M. *Chivington* considered himself maligned as the local Denver press labeled him "Bloodless Chivington," a reference to his inactivity since the famous New Mexican battle. Increasing tensions in Colorado, Indians had raided numerous settlements throughout the summer of 1864.

Humiliated by the press and angry at Indians at large, Chivington, a former Methodist minister, led a small but well-armed and determined force into eastern Colorado searching for Indian encampments. Even more significantly, an attack might further Chivington's political ambitions once Colorado became a state.

Chivington searched the Great Plains in vain for two months. In extreme eastern Colorado, along the Sand Creek, Chivington and his men ran across **Black Kettle**'s village of nearly 500 Northern **Cheyenne** Indians in late November 1864. Although Black Kettle's band had had conflicts with American settlers in the past, it was currently flying the American flag under the protection of Major Edward W. Wynkoop of Fort Lyon. That fort had also supplied the band with goods and provisions for the winter.

Though the village flew an American and a white surrender flag, Chivington and his forces struck at dawn on November 29, 1864. Within a few hours, the Colorado forces had killed and mutilated nearly 200 of the formerly 500-member tribe. Most of those killed and cut apart were women and children. Taking "scalps" from women (near the vagina) and children, Chivington and his men returned to Denver and proudly displayed their "trophies" to great applause of the Denver citizenry and the local press.

The massacre polarized the Indians on the Great Plains. It became apparent to them that they might become the next victims of unrestrained brutality. Their distrust of Americans increased significantly and they retaliated across the Plains. Most eastern Americans were horrified by the events in eastern Colorado, and Congress held several hearings investigating Chivington and the massacre. None found him guilty.

Sheridan, Philip Henry (March 6, 1831– August 5, 1888)

A superb cavalry commander during the Civil War, General Philip Sheridan presided over the Department of the Missouri during some of the most tumultuous times on the frontier. Sheridan was born in New York and worked a number of various jobs until he was given an appointment to West Point in 1848. He graduated well down in his class and was assigned to posts in the West. When the Civil War started, Sheridan was promoted to the rank of captain and was assigned to supply before being given command of the Second Michigan Cavalry, which was accompanied by a promotion to colonel.

After a brilliant deception at Booneville, Mississippi, he was promoted to brigadier general at the age of 31, then in 1863 was promoted to major general, fighting alongside Ulysses S. Grant and William T. *Sherman*. When Grant was appointed general in chief of the Union armies, he sent for Sheridan to head the cavalry of the army of the Potomac. Sheridan's destruction of the Shenandoah Valley proved crucial in ending the war.

In 1867 he was assigned to the Department of the Missouri, where he was to maintain control over the Indians. Grant promoted Sheridan to general of the army in 1869, where he directed the campaigns against the *Sioux* in 1876 and 1877. These campaigns successfully eliminated Sioux resistance and, as was Sheridan's intention, forced them onto reservations. Infamous for his alleged comment, "The only good Indian is a dead Indian," Sheridan was no different than most government officials who wanted to subdue the Indians, not destroy them.

Sherman Silver Purchase Act

In the political struggles over currency and the economy in the late 1890s, "free silver" became the antidote most looked to by westerners for relief from deflation. The *Bland*-Allison Act of 1878 had failed to sufficiently inflate the economy to raise prices, and the *Populist Party* had adopted the slogan "Free and Unlimited Coinage of Silver at 16:1" (meaning 16 ounces of silver to 1 ounce of gold) as its rallying cry. In 1890 Congress passed the Sherman Silver Purchase Act that required the U.S. Treasury to purchase 4.5 million ounces of silver each month at market prices for coinage into dollars. The amount was significant, but more important was the fact that the Treasury still could pay market prices, instead of the artificially inflated 16:1 that the Populists and silverites wanted. Nevertheless, by forcing the government to acquire silver, a small enough premium was placed on silver to encourage speculators to exchange silver for gold on a massive level, especially foreign speculators. The result was a massive run on gold at the U.S. Treasury, eventually triggering the Panic of 1893. Congress repealed the Sherman Act in a special session, and financier J. P. Morgan extended a gold loan to the U.S. government that warded off default, but the episode essentially ended the "bimetallism" debate. In 1896, running on a gold-only platform, William McKinley won the presidency, defeating William Jennings *Bryan [V]* of Nebraska.

Sherman, William Tecumseh (February 8, 1820–February 13, 1891)

Known for his statement "war is hell," William Tecumseh Sherman was born in Ohio on February 8, 1820, and attended West Point where he

achieved distinction before serving in the *Mexican War [III]*. After resigning from the army, he opened a bank in San Francisco in 1855. After that failed, he briefly practiced law and ran a military school. But soldiering was in his blood, and when the Civil War broke out, Sherman joined the Union Army.

At Shiloh, Sherman won a promotion to major general, then commanded troops under Ulysses Simpson Grant, whom he succeeded (March 1864) after the Battle of Chattanooga. Ordered to split the remaining Confederacy in half, Sherman marched to Atlanta, then on to the sea in a campaign that destroyed the South's ability to conduct the war.

After gaining fame in the Civil War, William Tecumseh Sherman headed the Division of the Missouri for the War Department, which clashed with the Interior Department over the direction of Indian policy on the Great Plains. *National Archives*

After the Civil War, Sherman remained in the army, commanding the Division of the Missouri with military authority over the Great Plains. He clashed with the *Bureau of Indian Affairs [III]*, arguing that the natives would have to be forced onto reservations and that the Department of War should handle all Indian policies. The best-known campaign reflecting Sherman's approach to pacifying the Indians was the *Red River War*. William Tecumseh Sherman retired in 1884 and died seven years later in New York.

Sioux Indians

The Sioux consisted of three separate branches: the Teton Sioux or Lakota proper; the Yankton Sioux or Nakota; and the Santee Sioux or Dakota. Within each branch, there are several tribes. Within the Teton Sioux are Sans Arc, Blackfoot, Brule, Miniconjou, Hunkpapa, Oglala, and Two Kettle; within the Yankton Sioux are Yankton and Yanktonai, and within the Santee Sioux are Mdwekanton, Sisseton, Wahpeton, and Wahpekute. Rarely did all Sioux work together, and rarely did they war against each other. The Teton

Sioux were the largest branch, maintaining a population in 19th century of roughly 25,000 persons.

All three branches originated in the western Great Lakes, living by the 17th century in what is today Minnesota. Though best known for being "lords of the northern Plains," the Sioux were primarily known as fur trappers in the 17th and 18th centuries, trading with the French, the English, and the Great Plains tribes. With the overhunting of the beaver by the late 18th century, the Sioux ventured onto the eastern Great Plains. The Oglala, a tribe within the Teton Sioux, had settled with the *Arikaras [III]* on the northern Missouri by the late 18th century but decided to more further into the plains to avoid European diseases spreading through the sedentary, agricultural villages.

From a historical and anthropological viewpoint, the conscious and relatively speedy decision by the Sioux to move onto the plains and adopt the mounted horse culture is nothing short of extraordinary. Within a generation, the Sioux changed almost every aspect of their culture and economy. As early as 1707, the Sioux had obtained Spanish *horses [I]*— most likely due to the Pueblo Revolt of 1680, a defining moment for all future western history. The Sioux launched their first raiding party in 1757 and 1758, but it failed, and the Sioux gave up adopting the horse culture for three more generations. Soon after adopting the horse culture in the last decade of the 18th century, the Sioux controlled most of the northern Great Plains. Imperialists without equal, they expanded not only territorially, but also economically, demanding tribute from the sedentary, agrarian tribes. *Lewis and Clark [III]* labeled them "the vilest miscreants of the savage race . . . the pirates of the Missouri" River. The Sioux expanded as rapidly as possible against the Arikara, the *Crow [III]*, and the *Pawnee [III]*.

From their first encounter with the Americans in the Lewis and Clark Expedition, the Sioux held tense relations with the United States. When the Arikara attacked an American fur trading party in 1823, the Sioux joined the retaliatory six infantry companies out of Fort Leavenworth. The Sioux wanted the United States to pursue a policy of genocide against the Arikaras. When the U.S. commander, Colonel Henry Leavenworth, dismissed the idea as horrific, the Sioux opinion of Americans decreased greatly. Americans, according to the Sioux, failed to even rate as "enemies." Instead, they considered Americans subhuman.

Unwittingly, the Americans proved a boon to Sioux expansion. In 1837 when one of the worst deadly disease epidemics swept the Great Plains

Indians, the Sioux used nearly all of the U.S.-provided inoculations and actually witnessed an increase in their population. In 1851 with the Treaty of Laramie, the United States ratified Sioux claims to most of the northern plains. The United States officers placed on the table a large map of the Great Plains and asked each tribe to identify as much of its land as possible. The republic hoped to prevent further Indian-versus-Indian wars by protecting the borders of each tribe, but the plan backfired miserably as the Sioux laid claim to far more than they controlled, even though they were at the height of their power. Either intimidated or cartographically ignorant—though most likely a combination of both—no other Indians

IN THEIR OWN Words

Sioux Abuse of the Crows, 1870s

During the 1870s the Crow Indians served as steadfast allies to the United States. Abused repeatedly by the imperialistic Sioux, the Crows turned to the United States for help and protection. This account, written by John F. Finerty, war correspondent for the *Chicago Times*, explores the specific abuses the Crows had suffered at the hands of their Great Plains rivals.

The Sioux had no legitimate claim to the Big Horn region. A part of it belonged originally to the Crows, whom the stronger tribe constantly persecuted, and who, by the treaty of '68, were placed at the mercy of their ruthless enemies. Other friendly tribes, such as the Snakes, or Shoshones, and the Bannocks, bordered on the ancient Crow territory, and were treated as foemen by the greedy Sioux and the haughty Cheyennes. The abolition of the three forts named fairly inflated the Sioux. The finest hunting grounds in the world had fallen into their possession, and the American Government, instead of standing by and strengthening the Crows, their ancient friends and allies, unwisely abandoned the very positions that would have held the more ferocious tribes in check. The Crows had a most unhappy time of it after the treaty was ratified. Their lands were constantly raided by the Sioux. Several desperate battles were fought, and, finally, the weaker tribe was compelled to seek safety beyond the Big Horn river.

Had the Sioux and Crows been left to settle the difficulty between themselves, few of the latter tribe would be left on the face of the earth today.

—SOURCE: JOHN F. FINERTY, *WAR-PATH AND BIVOUAC: OR THE CONQUEST OF THE SIOUX: A NARRATIVE OF STIRRING PERSONAL EXPERIENCES* (CHICAGO: DONOHUE BROTHERS, 1890), 39.

challenged the outrageous Sioux claims. Through the treaty of 1851, the United States committed itself to protecting Sioux land claims.

This failed to lessen tension between the Sioux and the United States. In 1862 the Dakota, under the leadership of Little Crow, an acculturated Christian Indian, killed over 400 whites on August 17 and 18, 1862. The United States, divided by the secession of the rebellious Southern states, was unable to squelch the *Minnesota Sioux Uprising* until October 1862. By then the Dakotas had murdered over 800 white settlers. Four years later, War Leader *Red Cloud* and the Oglalas attacked forts along the American *Bozeman Trail*, a highway the Indians considered illegal. The United States sued for peace in 1868, making Red Cloud the only American Indian leader to have won a war against America. Tensions erupted again between the Sioux and the Americans between 1874 and 1877, after the American Argonauts trespassed in the *Black Hills*, land the Sioux considered sacred. The most famous engagement of the two sides occurred at the *Battle of the Little Bighorn* in southeastern Montana and resulted in a completely one-sided victory for the Sioux under the leadership of *Crazy Horse* over Lieutenant Colonel George Armstrong *Custer*'s regiment of Seventh *United States Cavalry*. Crazy Horse surrendered in 1877, but *Sitting Bull* led a band of Hunkpapas into Canada under the protection of the Canadian Mounted Police. When Sitting Bull and his exiled followers returned to the United States in 1881, hostilities had ceased and the Sioux settled uncomfortably on a number reservations in the Dakotas. In December 1890, hostilities broke out again between the Sioux and the Americans over the U.S.-declared illegal ritual of the *Ghost Dance*. This tragic event resulted in the U.S. Cavalry killing nearly 200 Sioux and suffering 65 American casualties at *Wounded Knee* in 1890.

Today, most Americans regard the Sioux as the quintessential American Indian. Even eastern and southeastern tribes have adopted a number of Sioux rituals—especially in clothing and dance. Most of the Sioux reservations lie in the Dakotas. Well over 100,000 persons belong to the Sioux as of 2001.

Sitting Bull (ca.1832–December 15, 1890)

All of the mid– to late–19th-century Lakotas regarded Sitting Bull as the best of them. He embodied the ideals of Lakota manhood and especially the four virtues of manhood: bravery, fortitude, charity, and wisdom. In addition, from an early age, Sitting Bull seemed to have a strong connection with nature and especially with the animals. He claimed animal allies gave him insight into the future.

Generally, Sitting Bull held most whites in low regard. Aside from his good friend, Father Peter Jean DeSmet, whom Sitting Bull greatly respected, the Hunkpapa chief had contact only with white traders, whom he regarded as materialistic and boorish. Sitting Bull viewed the United States government as oppressive. He especially opposed the annuity programs. "See if I am poor, or my people either. The whites may get me at last, as you say, but I will have good times till then. You are fools to make yourselves slaves to a piece of fat bacon, some hard-tack, and a little sugar and coffee," he told a group of Assiniboines.

As whites continued to encroach on Lakota lands in the 1860s, several Lakotas took the unprecedented step of declaring Sitting Bull the chief of all Lakotas. A significant number of Lakotas, though, rejected Sitting Bull's leadership. During the Sioux War of 1874–1877, Sitting Bull resisted American claims to Sioux lands and helped protect Sioux villages during such important battles at the *Battle of the Little Bighorn*, where he directed the battle through his lieutenant, *Crazy Horse*. Fearing retaliation for George Armstrong *Custer*'s death at the hands of the Oglala Crazy Horse, Sitting Bull and his band fled to Canada, seeking protection from the Canadian Mounted Police. When the Canadian government refused to supply his people with food, Sitting Bull returned to the United States in 1881.

The four years during which Sitting Bull and his people had been gone were dramatic ones in the Dakotas. With the majority of Lakotas on reservations or hiding in Canada, significant numbers of whites settled in the former Sioux regions. Sitting Bull was stunned and fascinated by the white communities. Though he greatly missed his former pristine haunts, he very much enjoyed ice cream, manufactured boots, and the city fire department. Sitting Bull attempted to farm on the Standing Rock Reservation, but he clashed constantly with U.S. agency officials over policy. The U.S. agents regarded Sitting Bull as an enemy, intentionally leaving him out of decisions on the reservation. Sitting Bull especially wanted the Sioux to be able to ranch, as they had the necessary horsemanship skills and as well as land that lent itself to that livelihood. The agents rejected the idea as too primitive.

One highlight for Sitting Bull in the 1880s came from an invitation from Buffalo Bill *Cody* to travel with his "Wild West Show" in Europe. Cody treated Sitting Bull with dignity, and European audiences received the Lakota chief with great enthusiasm.

In 1890 Standing Rock officials feared that Sitting Bull was aligning himself with the Ghost Dancers among the Sioux. As a prominent medicine man, Sitting Bull was culturally obligated to investigate the Ghost Dance and take it seriously. No evidence exists, however, that Sitting Bull believed it to be true or advocated its adoption among the Sioux. At six A.M, December 15, 1890, Indian police arrested Sitting Bull, who was naked, and dragged him from his home into the freezing night. The arrest resulted in an unfortunate melee between Sitting Bull's supporters and the police. Sitting Bull was shot, and as he fell, the horse that Buffalo Bill had given him began to do its "Wild West Show" dance. Those around Sitting Bull assumed that his spirit had entered the horse and that he was telling them to continue fighting.

Southern Pacific Railroad

Fulfilling a dream long held by southerners to have a transcontinental route, the "Espee," as it is known, began when the "Big Four" (Collis P. Huntington, Leland *Stanford*, Mark Hopkins, and Charles Crocker) acquired the California Pacific Railroad in 1871 and started a route south through the San Joaquin Valley. By 1876 the road reached Los Angeles and the following year extended to Yuma, Arizona, where it encountered competition from the Texas and Pacific Railroad from El Paso. Eventually, Southern Pacific routes stretched all across California and into Portland, Oregon. In 1900 the *Union Pacific* under Edward H. Harriman acquired controlling interest in the Espee, only to see the U.S. Supreme Court rule in 1913 that the two roads had to be split. After years of prosperity, the road encountered financial trouble in the 1970s and merged with the Atchison, Topeka and Santa Fe Railroad in 1983 to form the Southern Pacific Corporation.

Stanford, Leland (March 9, 1824–June 21, 1893)

One of California's "Big Four" (with Mark Hopkins, Charles Crocker, and Collis P. Huntington), Leland Stanford joined his brothers in setting up a mercantile business in Sacramento, California. He, Hopkins, Crocker, and Huntington organized the Central Pacific Railroad to extend eastward and meet the *Union Pacific*, building westward. Stanford remained president of the Central Pacific until his death and in 1885 helped found the Southern Pacific Railroad. He was the U.S. senator from California from 1885 to 1893, and in 1885 Stanford endowed Stanford University in honor of his son, Leland, Jr.

Starr, Belle (Myra Belle Shirley) (February 5, 1848–February 3, 1889)

Born in Missouri as Myra Belle Shirley, Belle Starr fell in with guerrilla leader William C. *Quantrill*. In the early 1860s, she had encountered the *James* Gang and the Younger brothers and became involved with Cole Younger. Belle soon took up with another outlaw, Jim Reed, traveling with him to California, then returning to Texas. Only at that time did she change her name to Belle Starr. She referred to herself as the "bandit queen." She cut a striking figure in her velvet skirts and plumed hats. Arrested and tried before Judge Isaac C. ("Hanging Judge") Parker, who convicted Starr and Reed on charges of horse theft, Starr served time in federal prison. On her way to yet another trial for horse stealing with Judge Smith, Starr was shot in the back. There were several suspects in her shooting, but only Edgar Watson was arrested and later acquitted.

Stetson hats

Founded in 1865 by John B. Stetson in a rented room, the Stetson Hat Company began with capital of $10 worth of fur to become the "hat of the West." Trained by his father, a hatter, John Stetson produced a durable, quality product highlighted by its famous "*cowboy*" felt hat with the center crease. It was the trademark of the *Texas Rangers' [III]* clothing. The modern Stetson Hat factory in St. Joseph, Missouri, continues to produce the distinctively American western hat.

Strauss, Levi ("Loeb") (February 26, 1829– September 26, 1902)

Born in Bavaria in 1829 as Loeb Strauss, Levi moved to California in 1853, where he represented his family's dry goods firm under the name Levi Strauss. One of his most popular cloths was thick blue denim. Strauss's great break-through came in 1872, when he used metal rivets to secure pressure points, such as pocket corners. The following year, Strauss received a patent for "blue jeans," although they were called "waist overalls" at the time. Demand for the new product was so great that it required Strauss to set up several facilities in San Francisco. Eventually known solely by the name "Levis," blue jeans be-came a staple of western life, then later of all American informal wear.

Stuart, Granville (1834–1918)

A Montana pioneer who was born in West Virginia in 1834, Granville Stuart went to the California goldfields in 1852. After a brief, unsuc-cessful career in California, he headed back to the East in 1857 but moved into Montana. On May 2, 1858, he and his brother James dis-covered gold at Deer Lodge Valley Then the two moved around the region to different gold finds. Stuart opened a lumber business, a gen-eral store, and started a ranch, becoming a fixture in early Montana politics. He served on the territorial council, then in the territorial leg-islature. Like other cattlemen, he prospered in good times and went bankrupt in the severe winter of 1886–1887.

Swift, Gustavus (June 24, 1839–March 29, 1903)

Known for revolutionizing the slaughtering and packing of beef, Gustavus Swift was born in Sandwich, Massachusetts, and worked for his brother's butcher shop at an early age. At 16, he began purchasing and dressing ani-mals on his own in the Cape Cod area. By 1860 Swift had opened his own butcher shop in Eastham, Massachusetts. Other locations followed, such as Clinton and Freetown. His wagons made a regular route through Mas-sachusetts delivering fresh meat.

Through a partnership with James Hathaway of Boston, Swift began expanding westward, and in 1875 he arrived in Chicago. At the time, cows were loaded onto cattle cars and shipped east for final slaughter. Swift recognized the inefficiency and reasoned if he could keep the beef cold, he could slaughter the animals in Chicago and ship the more easily packed beef east. Employing a designer to develop a refrigerator car that used air passing over ice housed in parts of the car to keep the meat cold, Swift knew that the technological achievement was irrelevant if he could not convince eastern purchasers that his beef was fresh. Swift developed partnerships with local butchers, who acted as salesmen for his meats. He also secured a deal with the Grand Trunk Railway to transport the beef from Chicago.

Swift had stiff competition from Philip D. Armour and other meat packers in Chicago, but he focused relentlessly on eliminating waste and controlling his raw materials. This involved making sure that every part of the cow was used, leading him to constantly test water quality around his slaughterhouses for signs of fat in the water: if he detected fat, it meant there was waste. His hog production facilities had a slogan, "We use all of the pig but the grunt." Market pressures led Swift to insist on improving the environment. In 1885, when he capitalized Swift & Company, Swift was recognized as a leader in meat packing and business efficiency. Along with J. O. Armour and Edward Morris, Swift formed the National Packing Company, but the courts ruled it a monopoly and it disbanded in 1902. But Gustavus Swift had already changed America's grocery habits and had pushed the cattle frontier further west when he died on March 29, 1903.

Tabor, Elizabeth ("Baby Doe") (ca. 1855–March 7, 1935)

Considered one of the most scandalous and tragic "high-society" women in the Victorian West, Elizabeth McCourt Doe, a divorced woman, secretly married a divorced man, Colorado mining tycoon Senator Horace Austin Warner Tabor (1830–1899) in September 1882. Together they had two daughters. With a series of poor investments and the loss of government subsidies aiding the silver industry, Tabor lost his fortune in the 1890s and survived only by securing a minor political appointment. After his death in 1899, Baby Doe lived in extreme poverty in a shack in Leadville, Colorado, until her death in 1935.

telegraph

Invented by Samuel F. B. Morse, the design for the telegraph was finalized in 1837, five years after Charles Jackson demonstrated electromagnetism to Morse. Although Morse could not interest private business in his device, he received a $30,000 appropriation from the government to build a short telegraph line in 1843. Forging a partnership with Alfred Vail and Ezra Cornell, he connected Baltimore and Washington, D. C., in May 1844. Government support ended, but telegraph lines increased, from 40 miles in 1848 to 23,000 miles in 1852. A competitor, Hiram Sibley, acquired a similar patent to Morse's from Royal H. House, and in 1849, Sibley and partners organized a telegraphy company that merged with the Morse firms to form Western Union Telegraph Company.

The telegraph had a huge and immediate impact on the West. It instantly ended the *Pony Express [III]*, which shut down when the telegraph lines to California were connected in 1861. Over the long term, it linked the West with the rest of the nation and facilitated railroad scheduling, military efforts on the frontier, and the transmission of basic news and information.

Tilghman, William Matthew ("Bill"), Jr. (July 4, 1854–November 1, 1924)

A legendary lawman of the West, William ("Bill") Tilghman was born in Fort Dodge, Iowa, and steadily moved west, joining in buffalo hunting parties in the 1870s before falling in with various unsavory types. He engaged in horse stealing, part-time law enforcement, and buffalo hunting before moving to *Dodge City*, where he became a deputy sheriff, then a marshal. During that time, he built a reputation for fairness and honesty. In 1889 he moved to Oklahoma, where he again held a series of law enforcement marshal positions, capturing the outlaw Bill Doolin in 1896. Tilghman briefly was an Oklahoma state senator. When an old man, he unwisely became marshal in Cromwell, Oklahoma, and was killed by a man he was trying to arrest.

Tombstone, Arizona

A small mining town in southeast Arizona, Tombstone was founded in the 1870s. With the discovery of silver, the population grew in the 1880s, and it became the Cochise County seat. It also became a haven for famous gunfighters. Some of the great names of western lore walked the streets of Tombstone, including Wyatt *Earp*, "Texas" John Slaughter, Johnny *Ringo*, and "Doc" *Holliday*. In 1881 the famous Gunfight at the *O.K. Corral* occurred when the Clantons and the Earp families shot it out. When the silver dried up, the town did too, dropping to a population of barely over 1,000, but still remaining a popular "tourist trap" in recent decades with the reputation of the "town too tough to die."

transcontinental railroads

Largely financed through land-grant subsidies during the *Civil War*, the transcontinental railroads included the *Union Pacific Railroad*, which was built from Missouri westward, and the Central Pacific Railroad, which originated in Sacramento and ran eastward. In addition, there was the Northern Pacific, which was an extension of the Burlington and Quincy (1849) running from Chicago to Council Bluffs, Iowa, and also, in later years, to Minneapolis, Denver, Billings, Montana, and then on to the Pacific Northwest. In reality, the Northern Pacific was less a single line than a patchwork

Harper's Weekly of June 1869 offered an artist's rendering of the Union Pacific and Central Pacific Railroads and the driving of the famous "golden spike"—which was immediately removed, lest thieves steal it! *Library of Congress*

of merged companies that finally connected to Oregon. A fourth, largely unsubsidized line, James J. Hill's *Great Northern Railway*, left Minneapolis then ran to Winnipeg, Manitoba, before laying lines southward to Montana and the Pacific Coast, connecting in 1893.

Although great individual initiative was involved in all these roads—including the work of Collis P. Huntington, Charles Crocker, Leland *Stanford*, and Mark Hopkins with the Central Pacific—the nature of the government subsidies, which were allotted based on miles of track laid in competition with the Union Pacific, led to bizarre and perverse construction policies on the part of both railroads. The Central Pacific built over ice, up steep grades, and at times the two railroads built parallel to each other rather than connecting. In stark contrast, Hill's totally private operation selected only the lowest grades, built more slowly—but always brought "demand" with the railroad by giving land away to farmers—and avoided scenic, but costly, mountain routes. As a result, when the Panic of 1873 hit, the subsidized roads all were essentially bankrupt. Huntington labored to keep the Central Pacific from insolvency, and Congress investigated the railroad debacle, made worse by the 1873 Credit Mobilier scandal.

The Union Pacific and Central Pacific did link at Promontory Point, Utah, in May 1869, driving the famed "golden spike" into the track beds. Later, consolidations of other existing and new railroads added the Southern Pacific Railroad, which ran from Los Angeles through Texas to New Orleans.

Several myths persist about the transcontinentals. One, featured prominently in historian Stephen Ambrose's bestselling *Nothing Like It in the World*, is that only the government could have supported such a feat. Yet Hill's private railroad, while slower to connect Minneapolis to the Pacific Coast, accomplished the same objective without taxpayer money, and with a much more profitable and efficient railroad. Another myth is that the transcontinentals were built "ahead of demand." This is only true in terms of the government-sponsored roads; again, however, Hill's road was in full use, due to his insight that brought farmers (his customers) out with the railroad. But even at that, the "ahead-of-demand" story does not take into consideration that the subsidies were intended, in part, to extend lines westward during *war*, and that the railroads might have been a success even from the perspective of making available new crop lands, cattle and horse herds, and supplies of gold, to the extent that was accomplished in the three remaining years of conflict.

Ultimately, the greatest controversy over the transcontinentals involved the role of state and federal regulation. The fact that the railroads crossed state lines made them subject to interstate commerce provisions of the Constitution. Farm groups, especially the Grangers and the *Populists*, wanted the federal government to own and operate the railroads, claiming they had attained monopoly status. Recent studies, however, show that virtually all farm areas had competition in railroad rates, had access to more than one road, and had plenty of state laws controlling the lines. The federal government passed the Interstate Commerce Act in 1887 largely to deal with the railroads, then later (1914) used sections of the Clayton Act to further control railroad fee structures. Whether this regulation achieved its ends and benefited or harmed the farmers (and the railroads), remains a matter of hot scholarly debate.

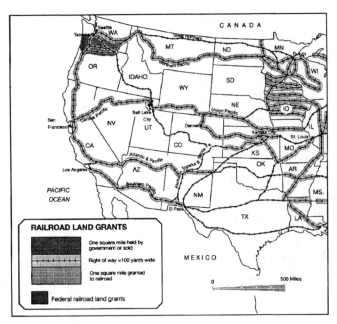

Railroad land grants. *Ron Acklin, University of Dayton Print and Design*

Union Pacific Railroad

The Union Pacific was the eastern part of the *transcontinental railroad* that reached Promontory Point in Utah on May 10, 1869. It originated with Asa Whitney as one of five routes to the Pacific authorized by Congress in 1853, and with the Pacific Railroad Act of 1862, the railroad received a large land grant and a subsidy of U.S. bonds worth $16,000 per mile of completed track. The government expected that the road would sell land for capital, building only on the narrow strip it needed. The railroad could sell the bonds immediately, then repay them over the 30-year life of the bond. But the nature of the subsidy—tied to miles of track built—led to circuitous routes and a tendency to ignore grades, which later would drive up costs. This contrasted sharply with James J. Hill's *Great Northern Railroad*, built entirely on private funds.

When the public expressed little interest in these bonds, Congress passed a second act that doubled the land grant and allowed the Union Pacific to issue its own bonds to raise still more capital. This proved difficult in the middle of the *Civil War*. One of the largest holdings of bonds was by Credit Mobilier company, a trust organized by Thomas C. Durant, which soon became embroiled in a massive scandal.

Laying the track was a dirty, dangerous, and slow business, with the work camps putting down approximately a mile of track per day. The competition with the Central Pacific Railroad, working its way east from California, occasionally got violent, with workers blowing up the competitor's tracks. General Grenville M. Dodge supervised the road until its meeting in Utah with the Central Pacific.

The combination of the Panic of 1873 and the Credit Mobilier scandal threatened to bankrupt the road, which was in part rescued by the Thurman Act of 1878, requiring the railroad's profits to go toward repaying the bonds. Jay Gould took over management of the road, attempting to form a pool that would keep prices up. Gould also acquired feeder lines, including the Missouri Pacific and the Wabash and the Kansas Pacific. But the railroad was tainted by the Credit Mobilier scandal and with its reputation dependent on government favors, the directors hired railroad critic Charles Francis Adams as president. Adams could not succeed where Gould and others had failed, and in 1893 the Union Pacific declared bankruptcy. It was a direct result of the road's subsidized origins and its failure to build using solid business practices.

The Union Pacific was reborn under Edward H. Harriman as part of a national network that included the *Southern Pacific*. Harriman ran afoul of the Sherman Anti-Trust Act, and in 1913 the Supreme Court required the Union Pacific and Southern Pacific to separate. Nevertheless, the Union Pacific regained its market share and by the 1980s again was acquiring railroads through mergers with the Western Pacific and the Missouri Pacific. Coming full circle, in 1996, the Union Pacific again acquired the Southern Pacific Rail Corporation to form the largest railroad in the United States.

United States Cavalry

Although all elements of the U.S. Army, including artillery, infantry, engineers, quartermaster corps, signal corps, and others, were involved in the frontier Indian wars, most of the burden fell on the mobile arm, the United States Cavalry. Cavalry units, at one time called "dragoons," existed since the Revolutionary War. In Europe they had lost much of their prestige as artillery and massed rifle fire made men on horseback highly vulnerable targets. But in the West, with its open spaces, fighting a foe who moved rapidly, the Cavalry had distinct advantages over other service arms.

Troopers typically carried a sidearm and a carbine as their standard weapons. The Sharps carbine, which used a metal cartridge, was a common weapon, although troops also used the *Winchester* repeating rifle, which proved exceptionally effective against Indians and the Henry.

The army had ceased using the saber, despite numerous popular paintings and movies to the contrary. Organization was based on the troop comprised of 50 men commanded by a lieutenant or captain, and a company of 100 men commanded by a captain or major. The regiment, which was considered more than sufficient to deal with any Indian opposition, was about seven companies, plus pack trains and quartermasters. (George Armstrong *Custer*'s command at the *Battle of the Little Bighorn* was just under 700 men total, but General Alfred Terry was en route to support him, and thus Custer did not need to take normal supply wagons). Cavalry units could also carry their own artillery, though few did. Companies generally used Indian scouts—four to eight to a regiment. In addition to white and Indian troops, there were two regiments of black *Buffalo Soldiers* in action on the frontier with the Ninth and Tenth Cavalry.

By the 1870s it was common for cavalry units to fight dismounted, in "skirmish lines" with a spacing of several feet between men. One man in four or five (depending on the desperation of the situation) would hold the horses for those deployed on the line. Since carbines lacked the range of longer-barreled rifles, the purpose of the skirmish line was to deliver fire for a brief time, then either attack or retreat. Commands to individual troop commanders were sent by messenger or, in battle, by bugle calls and movement of the guidons (battle flags).

Soldiers lived on $13 a month, were given their sidearms, clothes, carbine, mount, saddle, and supplies, and had to purchase any extras (some carried *Bowie knives [III]*, tomahawks, or upgraded weapons) on their own. Frontier life was extremely harsh and lonely, disease and drunkenness rampant, and discipline tough. Even so, to a distressed wagon train under attack, no greater sight could appear than a long blue column of U.S. Cavalry troopers.

Wells Fargo & Company

Wells Fargo & Company, a banking and express holding company, was founded in New York City on March 18, 1852, by Henry Wells and William G. Fargo. The firm competed with *Butterfield Overland Mail [III]* and other stage lines, eventually merging to form American Express. In 1852 Wells suggested American Express could extend its line to California, but when Butterfield and others resisted, Wells and Fargo organized Wells Fargo & Company. It had a thriving business, a network of 55 express offices and its own stagecoaches, and engaged in early banking activities, taking gold on deposit and issuing exchange drafts or extending credit. Wells Fargo ran stage routes through Texas as the Overland Mail and operated the famous *Pony Express [III]* service. In the 21st century Wells Fargo remains active in banking services, and was acquired by Norwest Bancor in 1998.

Winchester rifles

Winchester Repeating Arms, begun by Oliver Winchester as the New Haven Arms Company in 1857, specialized in either a .44 caliber (the famous 1873 weapon) or a .30 caliber rifle modeled on the *Spencer [III]* repeater, which held 12 rounds. With either weapon, each new round was pushed into firing position by the level action ejecting the spent round. Winchester's classic 1874 "Lever Action" was lightweight and accurate and, most important, its rapid-fire action made a Winchester-armed single cowboy or soldier the equal of many opponents using single-shot rifles. In 1866 a small group of troops and civilians held off a much larger Indian force under *Red Cloud* with such weapons until help arrived. The Winchester gained the reputation as the "gun that won the West."

Wounded Knee Massacre

During the summer of 1890 the Lakota adulterated the peaceful *Ghost Dance* into a philosophy justifying violent revolution against whites and especially white officials on the various Dakota reservations. During the autumn of 1890 the Ghost Dance religion spread through the *Sioux* reservations, and large numbers of Sioux simply left the official communities and any form of agricultural work and began to dance the Dance. President Benjamin Harrison moved federal troops onto the Rosebud and Pine Ridge reservations.

In December the Ghost Dancers, numbering roughly 600, assembled in the northwest corner of Pine Ridge Reservation. United States officials feared that two prominent Sioux, *Sitting Bull* and Big Foot, were instigating and precipitating the movement. Neither, however, had any real involvement in the Ghost Dance, a popular movement among average Sioux, which had taken on a life of its own. The U.S. attempt to arrest both Sitting Bull and Big Foot proved disastrous. Indian agents killed Sitting Bull during the arrest. Big Foot had fled, and President Harrison sent in the Seventh *United States Cavalry* to find him. This was the same regiment which, under the command of Lieutenant Colonel George Armstrong *Custer*, had been nearly destroyed by the Sioux at the *Battle of Little Bighorn* in 1876. It was a regiment out for revenge.

When the Seventh Cavalry arrived on December 28, 1890, it found roughly 300 ghost-dancing Sioux huddled together. Fearing a fight with the larger and

The Falls of the Yellowstone River in Yellowstone National Park, Wyoming, are one of the most famous spots of the park, visited annually by numerous travelers. *Bradley J. Birzer*

better armed force, the Sioux attempted to surrender. The Seventh Cavalry asked the Ghost Dancers to hand over their weapons on December 29, at which point the situation grew incredibly tense. A Ghost Dance medicine man began dancing, telling the Sioux that the sacred Ghost Shirts (an evolution on Wovoka's original teaching regarding the Ghost Dance) would protect them from bullets. When a U.S. soldier attempted to take a rifle from a deaf Indian, the Indian's rifle discharged, the dancing medicine man proclaimed an apocalypse, and for 30 minutes, close-range combat ensued between the Sioux and the Seventh Cavalry. The Sioux killed 25 U.S. soldiers and wounded another 40, but the army inflicted greater casualties, killing 150 Sioux outright. An additional 50 who were wounded froze to death.

Despite a few revenge-prompted skirmishes that occurred the following day, historians regard December 29, 1890, as the last day of frontier warfare between Americans and native peoples. Wounded Knee has great symbolism, not only as an end to the Indian military threat on the frontier, but also as a powerful loss to modern Native Americans. That symbolism was apparent in the *Second Wounded Knee [V]* and became one of the focal points of Dee Brown's pro-Indian book, *Bury My Heart at Wounded Knee* (1971).

Yellowstone National Park

Proclaimed a national park in 1872, Yellowstone National Park is located in northwestern Wyoming. It is known for "Old Faithful," a spectacular geyser, and for its all-around natural beauty. It was the nation's first national park. Indians lived in the region for years before John Colter, a member of the *Lewis and Clark Expedition [III],* crossed the area in 1807. After photographer William Henry Jackson and artist Thomas *Moran* visited the area, they played a role in publicizing its beauty to the American public. In 1872 President Ulysses S. Grant named the area a national park. It was administered by the army engineers until 1919, when the National Park Service took over. By the 20th century its 2.2 million acres had become a favorite tourist location. In 1988 fires ravaged the park, burning some 35 percent of it.

One of the West's most famous natural wonders is the "Old Faithful" geyser at Yellowstone National Park. *Library of Congress*

PART V

The Modern Era
(1893–The Present)

C hoosing a date for the "modern" era of the West is an exercise in futility. One can with some legitimacy point to the completion of the transcontinental railroad in 1869, or to the conclusion of the Indian wars in 1890, or to the statehood of Arizona in 1912—the last of the states attached to the other 47 states in the continental Union. Often, however, a convenient place to start the modern West is in 1893, with the publication of historian Frederick Jackson Turner's famous paper in which he argued that the frontier was closed. By that time (keeping in mind that statehood for Alaska was not yet on the horizon, nor had Hawaii, Puerto Rico, or the Virgin Islands been acquired by the United States), there was some rationale in Turner's claim that the frontier was closed. What Turner's message really meant was that no new territory would be annexed, and therefore all future debates about land allocation would take place within the constraints of economic scarcity.

In fact, people continued (and to this day, continue) to settle in the West. California remained a major point of relocation, mostly for mining, but increasingly in the 20th century, for the motion picture industry, farming, and then, after World War II, manufacturing. Colorado and Oregon also attracted miners, entrepreneurs, and farmers, and the Plains states, ranchers. Parts of the Southwest, however, which experienced harsh summers, saw any significant population growth substantially blunted. Aside from pockets in California and cities such as Denver, Portland, Seattle, Oklahoma City, Wichita, El Paso, Laramie, and Santa Fe, the West remained largely empty, populated mostly by dangerous predators and domesticated animals.

One of the first signs that the United States had become enormously wealthy, and that the West had become tremendously productive as a region, was the movement toward conservation of natural resources. It is something only a prosperous nation can consider, and yet by the early 1900s the United States, through the Department of the Interior, had already surveyed or organized most of the frontier land and established a National Park Service (1916) and the Reclamation Service (1902), both for supervision and conservation purposes. Construction of dams was undertaken not only with the needs of the farmers in mind, but with the health of the river systems.

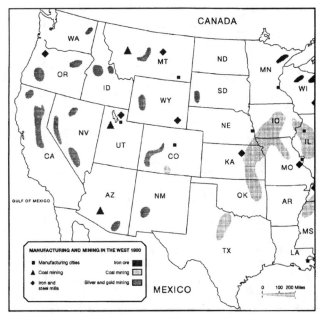

Manufacturing and mining in the West, 1900. *Ron Acklin, University of Dayton Print and Design*

America's first true "conservation president," Theodore Roosevelt, and naturalist John Muir, who organized the Sierra Club, led the effort to protect the wilderness.

Yet as the inevitable result of conflicting goals of "conservation" and "development" (which had a long history of support in American jurisprudence), it is not surprising that continual battles were waged by conservationists and entrepreneurs. In one of the first struggles between the two camps, Gifford Pinchot, the chief of the Forestry Division, took on Secretary of the Interior Richard Ballinger and was fired, becoming the first "martyr" to the cause of environmentalism. Increasingly though, the resources were not merely fought over by a few farmers and conservationists but by growing numbers of hotel owners and operators, miners, loggers, and urban planners.

This reflected the growing diversity of the West. Already, Bank of Italy (later Bank of America) under the brilliant A. P. Giannini, was on its way to its place as the largest bank in the country. The West's natural beauty and (in places) desirable climates attracted tourists and vacationers to a growing ski industry in Colorado and Utah, to natural wonders such as Yellowstone National Park, and to the coastal cities of California. World War I gave a small boost to the West, mainly in the form of increased demand for cotton and beef. But with the Great Depression a different kind of immigrant arrived in California, Arizona, and the Pacific Northwest—the "Okies," or immigrants escaping from the dust bowl of the Plains states, where farming had been badly damaged by droughts. The Far West offered new opportunities, away from the natural disasters of the Midwest, but also from the racial oppression in the South. After 1910 large numbers of African Americans streamed into California, where the black population already exceeded 20,000. New immigrants also came from across the Pacific, bringing more than 8,000 Japanese to California and the Pacific Coast. Mexican immigration into the United States, mostly for agricultural work, accelerated after the 1912 Mexican Revolution, whereupon San Antonio and other southwestern cities saw their Hispanic population grow. These new arrivals were not always welcomed: concerns over the numbers of foreign immigrants, especially Chinese and Mexicans, had led to a variety of national restrictions on immigration.

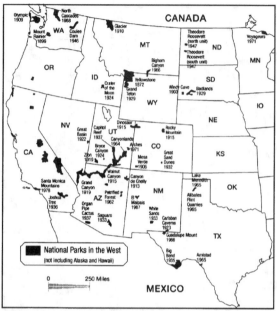

National parks in the West. *Ron Acklin, University of Dayton Print and Design*

The Great Depression did not spare the West. Entire banking systems were wiped out, including most of the banks in Wyoming and the total Wingfield chain in Nevada. Franklin Roosevelt's New Deal moved to bolster the nation's banks and attempted to address land erosion of the Great Plains states with the Civilian Conservation Corps. Federal dollars paid for construction of the Grand Coulee (later Hoover) and Bartlett Dams, and the West benefited substantially from New Deal spending on water projects.

Even during the Depression, while farming, ranching, and mining remained staples of western activity, new industries were slowly appearing. California's warm climate proved the perfect stimulus for the motion picture industry. Early filmmakers, such as Warner Brothers and Walt Disney, arrived in California to produce movies—one of the few sectors of the economy to grow during the 1930s. The industry evoked such romance and glamour that even an industrialist such as Howard Hughes felt he had to get involved. But the major surge in manufacturing did not occur until World War II. Ironically, the entrance of America into the war had come as a result of the attack on U.S. naval forces at Pearl Harbor, Hawaii—one of the newest western territories.

At that time, major aircraft manufacturers, such as Boeing, Lockheed, Convair, and Hughes, as well as the productive shipyards of Henry J. Kaiser, all moved west. The World War II constituted nothing less than the transformation of the American West, bringing in millions of families, thousands of new businesses, and billions of federal dollars. Shipbuilding dominated Oakland and Richmond, California, and the naval buildup boosted the economy of San Diego. Weapons production took place in virtually every part of the West: ammunition was made in Utah, bomb testing conducted in Arizona and New Mexico, and mining in the mountain states.

No single technology contributed to that shift more than Willis Carrier's air conditioner, which attracted people to live year-round in the extraordinarily hot climates of Arizona, south Texas, and central Califor-

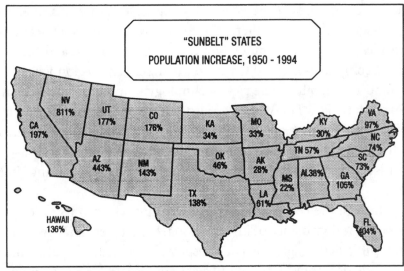

"Sunbelt" states population increase, 1950–1994. *Ron Acklin, University of Dayton Print and Design*

nia. Building on wartime exposure, booster groups mailed promotions and advertisements throughout the East with great success: Phoenix saw its population leap from 40,000 in the 1950s to more than 1 million by 1970, then double again in the next decade. Las Vegas, Nevada, home of the gambling industry, energized by the appearance of air conditioning, likewise saw its population soar. Similar rapid growth occurred in Denver, El Paso, Albuquerque, San Diego, Los Angeles, Portland, and other western cities.

This population shift produced an equally important political realignment, in which the West gained dramatically in congressional seats and electoral votes. By 2000, California and Texas, two "sun belt states," totaled more than 90 electoral votes between them. The tendency of inhabitants of the mountain and plains states to vote almost as a bloc allowed the western states, jointly, to do what many of them individually could not do. The election of Ronald Reagan in 1980, in which he swept virtually the entire West, illustrated the great electoral clout of the region. In fact the West had already produced three presidents since World War II: Kansan Dwight D. Eisenhower (R), Texan Lyndon Johnson (D), and Californian Richard Nixon (R). Excluding the caretaker president, Gerald Ford, since 1965 only two presidents—Jimmy Carter (D-GA) and Bill Clinton (D-AR), both Southerners—have broken the continued hold of the West on the presidency, which saw the ascension of George H. W. Bush (R-TX) in 1988 and his son, George W. Bush (R-TX) in 2000.

By the 1980s the West had largely become viewed as the home of "clean" industries and cutting-edge technologies. No clearer example existed than Silicon Valley in northern California, where the high-technology companies of Apple Computer, Sun Microsystems, Intel, and thousands of small, computer-oriented firms led the American economy in productivity and profitability. The new technology companies ushered in the "information age." The West was also home to Hollywood, which had emerged as the movie capital of the world, and the aerospace industry, which spanned the West from the Johnson Space Center in Houston to Edwards Air Force Base in California to the White Sands test range in New Mexico.

Although the computer industry went into a steep recession in the late 1990s, the dominance of information technologies is not going to disappear. Difficult immigration issues, especially involving illegal aliens from Mexico, still demand solutions, but even now, legal Mexican immigration continues to raise the populations of Texas, California, New Mexico, and

Colorado. Indeed, western cities not only keep growing, but by 2000 Las Vegas and Phoenix were among the top 10 fastest-growing cities in the United States. Thus, whether in technological change or in political power, the West remains a frontier that has never closed.

CHRONOLOGY	The Modern Era
1896	*Election of William McKinley and commitment to the gold standard ends "Populist" movement; William Jennings Bryan defeated; Klondike gold rush in Alaska*
1898	*Annexation of Hawaii*
1901	*McKinley assassinated; Theodore Roosevelt becomes president; oil discovered at Spindletop, Texas*
1902	*Newlands Reclamation Act*
1903	Lone Wolf v. Hitchcock *confirms congressional power over Indian tribes*
1904	*Theodore Roosevelt reelected*
1910	*Ballinger-Pinchot Controversy*
1905–1913	*Azusa Street Revival, Los Angeles*
1916	*President Woodrow Wilson orders General John Pershing to pursue the bandit Pancho Villa into Mexico*
1917	*U.S. declares war on Germany; Jeannette Pickering Rankin becomes first female member of the U.S. House of Representatives*
1918–1923	*Aimee Semple McPherson's evangelistic organization thrives in Los Angeles*
1921–1929	*"Roaring '20s"; Willis Carrier's air conditioners used on a wide scale*
1922	*Colorado River Compact signed; first "Rose Bowl" football game played*
1923	*Warner Brothers motion picture studios established*
1924	*Teapot Dome scandal; Immigration Restriction Act*
1928	*Herbert Hoover elected president; western films become popular*
1929	*Stock market crash*
1930–1941	*Great Depression*
1933	*Agricultural Adjustment Act; Indian Reorganization Act*
1934–1963	*Alcatraz operates as a federal prison*

The Modern Era (continued)

1935–1936	*"Dust Bowl" plagues American farms*
1936	*Hoover Dam completed*
1937	*Golden Gate Bridge completed*
1939	*Quintessential western film* Stagecoach *nominated for an Oscar*
1941	*U.S. declares war on Japan; Mt. Rushmore National Memorial completed*
1942	*Japanese Americans on the West Coast relocated to internment camps*
1943	*"Zoot Suit" riots*
1941–1945	*American defense industries move west; Los Angeles, San Diego, Phoenix, Albuquerque, El Paso, San Francisco, Seattle all witness strong growth; aircraft manufacturers Lockheed, Douglas, McDonnell, Boeing, and Consolidated Vultee relocate major operations in the West*
1945	*Atomic bomb detonated at Alamogordo, New Mexico*
1946	*Bureau of Land Management formed; RAND Corporation established*
1950s	*California surfing craze begins*
1951	*Texas Instruments founded*
1954	*U.S. Air Force Academy opens in Colorado Springs, Colorado*
1955	*Disneyland opens in Anaheim, California*
1960	*Dallas Cowboys given NFL Franchise; "Sagebrush Rebellion" begins in the West*
1961	*Seattle Space Needle completed*
1965	*Astrodome built in Houston, Texas; Watts riots*
1964	*Lyndon Johnson becomes first Texan elected to the U.S. presidency, defeating Arizonian Barry Goldwater; Berkeley "Free Speech" movement; Whiskey a Go Go opens in Los Angeles*
1966	*United Farm Workers founded by Cesar Chavez*
1967	*Monterey Pop Festival*
1968	*Richard Nixon becomes first Californian elected to the U.S. presidency; Intel Corporation founded*
1971	*"Silicon Valley" first used as a term to refer to the computer-rich area of the Santa Clara Valley, California*
1975	*Microsoft Corporation founded*
1976	*Apple Computer founded by Steve Jobs and Steve Wozniak*

The Modern Era (continued)

1978	*Proposition 13 cuts taxes in California*
1980	*Ronald Reagan of California elected president of the United States*
1981	*Women's Professional Rodeo Association*
1980s	*Branson, Missouri, becomes popular entertainment location; California fitness craze begins*
1981	*Sundance Institute for independent film founded by Robert Redford*
1988	*George H. W. Bush of Texas elected president of the United States*
1992	*Rodney King riots in Los Angeles*
1993	*Bureau of Alcohol, Tobacco and Firearms raids Branch Davidian compound in Waco, Texas*
1994	*O. J. Simpson trial*
1995	*Oklahoma City bombing*
2000	*George W. Bush of Texas elected president of the United States*

Adams, Ansel (February 20, 1902–April 22, 1984)

Considered one of the most prolific photographers of the American West, Ansel Adams was born on February 20, 1902, in San Francisco, where he grew up with a passion for piano. He was a talented composer who hoped to have a career in music, but at age 14 he went on a family vacation to Yosemite Park and took pictures with a Kodak "Brownie" camera. He was awed by the beauty of the park and began to visit Yosemite regularly, making photographic diaries of his ventures. From 1920 to 1924, he was the custodian of the Sierra Club headquarters there.

Nevertheless, he continued with his goal of becoming a concert pianist, and in 1925, purchased a luxurious concert grand piano. Two years later, though, he made the photograph that changed his life: "Monolith, the Face of the Half Dome" at Yosemite. To Adams, the photo did not just capture the mountain, but the dream of how it should appear. In 1928 he held his first solo exhibition and would later exhibit at the Smithsonian Institution in Washington, D.C., and at New York's Museum of Modern Art, supplementing his artistic side with commercial assignments. In 1967 Adams and other photographers and historians formed the Friends of Photography in Carmel, California, an international organization that promotes and encourages creative photography.

Adams's photos have a universal appeal and are often used as calendars or for art posters. Among his most famous are "Aspens, Northern New Mexico," "Moonrise, Hernandez, New Mexico, "Winter Sunrise, Sierra Nevada," "Frozen Lake and Cliffs," and "Clearing Winter Storm." Although he did not shoot scenes to promote environmental activism, he was active in the movement himself. Adams also published numerous books on photography. He died on April 22, 1984.

aerospace industry in the West

In the 1920s southern California's warm climate attracted many aircraft entrepreneurs to the state. The clear skies, open desert for safe testing, and the absence of unionized labor provided incentives to young firms to locate in California, as did the growing motion picture industry. Cecil B. DeMille experimented with aviation before becoming a director, and

Howard *Hughes* filmed the World War I movie *Hell's Angels* in California, purchasing RKO studios and establishing Hughes Aircraft.

Many aircraft entrepreneurs were from the Midwest: John Knudson Northrop came from Lincoln, Nebraska, and Glenn Martin moved from Liberal, Kansas. Others, such as Donald Douglas, came from the East. All of them founded companies in California that would grow into the core of the massive aerospace industry. In 1916 Allan and Malcolm Loughead set up a shop in Santa Barbara and hired John Northrup, and in 1923, Northrop left to work with Donald Douglas. The Lougheads changed the name of their firm to *Lockheed Aircraft* in 1926, building the "Vega," a successful aircraft actually designed by Northrop. By 1939 Lockheed was providing warplanes to England and showing a profit.

William Boeing, a Yale graduate, set up a plant in Seattle during World War I, selling aircraft to the Navy. In 1923, having produced pursuit planes for the navy, Boeing received a contract to make aircraft for airmail delivery. After Pearl Harbor, Boeing filled orders for the U.S. Army Air Corps, especially with its famous four-engined "Flying Fortress" B-17 bomber.

During World War II there was a tremendous boom in aircraft production. Southern California flourished with an influx of employees to turn out thousands of aircraft for the United States and the Allies. By 1941 Lockheed, in Burbank, had 50,000 employees and at its wartime peak in 1943 had 94,000 employees. *Douglas Aircraft* in Santa Monica built some 27,000 planes during the war; Hughes, in Culver City, Northrop in Hawthorne, and Convair in San Diego all contributed to the 301,000 planes turned out in the war.

As the military draft drew most able-bodied men into the armed forces, factory jobs, such as this tail assembly of a B-17F bomber at Long Beach were taken over by women. Even though Boeing built the B-17, this particular plant was a Douglas Aircraft facility. *National Archives*

After the war ended, though, the aircraft industry headed for a depression. Douglas Aircraft saw orders shrink to 127 in 1946, and all the manufacturers cut production dramatically. But the Korean War temporarily rescued the aviation industry. Douglas, Lockheed, Boeing, and Hughes all made aircraft, missiles, and high-tech weaponry.

In addition to the actual manufacturing of aircraft, the West became home to numerous large Air Force bases, including Edwards in California, Luke in Arizona, and Nellis in Nevada. White Sands, New Mexico, was a major test site, as was the Nevada Test Site north of Las Vegas. The close proximity to the vast Pacific Ocean, plus the open deserts, provided a margin of safety and secrecy for testing weapons. An educational/intellectual framework also developed at the large California universities, especially Berkeley, with its world-famous *Lawrence-Livermore Laboratory* and at the Jet Propulsion Laboratory at the California Institute of Technology. Mathematicians and operations specialists formed the *RAND Corporation* in Santa Monica to serve as a research and consulting group to the Defense Department. As missiles and rockets started to play more of a role, Hughes Aircraft and Hercules Corporation in Manga, Utah, as well as Lockheed's Sunnyvale, California, facility made weapons for the Cold War.

Threats from the Soviet Union reinvigorated the aviation/missile industry after the 1960s. In 1967 North American Aircraft merged with Rockwell, a Pittsburgh-based firm, and later produced the Space Shuttle and, still later, the B-1 Bomber. That same year, Douglas Aircraft sold out to McDonnell Aircraft in St. Louis, Missouri, to form McDonnell-Douglas. By the 1970s, more than 500,000 people worked in the aircraft industry in California, representing one-third of all manufacturing jobs in the state.

Such dependence on military purchases came at a price, and in the 1990s, when the United States began to scale back its military following the end of the Cold War, orders for aircraft and weapons declined precipitously, bringing a minor recession to California and affecting the entire West. More mergers followed, as the once-anticipated growth in space-related activities had not significantly offset aerospace job losses.

air conditioning

New Yorker Willis Carrier conceived of an atmospheric cooling system that removed humidity from the air in 1902. His first machine was installed that year in Sackett-Wilhelms Lithographing and Publishing Company of Brooklyn. In 1915 Carrier and other engineers founded the Carrier

Engineering Corporation, which had as its chief product the air conditioner. In the following decades, Carrier's air conditioner played a pivotal role in large-scale settlement of cities such as Phoenix, Arizona, and El Paso, Texas, and inland California regions. Populations in Las Vegas, Phoenix, and other cities began to grow dramatically. Combined with the new concept of indoor shopping "malls," which began to appear more frequently in the 1950s, air conditioners helped reshape every aspect of living and working in the West.

Alamogordo (Trinity Atomic Bomb Test)

On July 16, 1945, the world entered the atomic age when researchers and engineers set off the first atomic explosion at Alamogordo, New Mexico, culminating years of work and billions of dollars of investment in the "Manhattan Project." Alamogordo ("fat cottonwood tree" in Spanish) is located near White Sands, New Mexico, and was chosen for its remote isolation. After the bomb was constructed, it was placed on top of a giant tower, and at 5:30 A.M. the test went off as scheduled. The bomb lit up the southwestern sky for miles, and residents 100 miles away said that it was as if the sun rose twice. Enrico Fermi estimated the explosion at 13 kilotons, or 13,000 tons of TNT. The explosion gave off heat, light, x-rays, and other radiation, vaporizing the steel support tower and raising a vast cloud of dust.

Alcatraz

An island in San Francisco Bay, Alcatraz was first explored by Juan Manuel de Ayala in 1755. Alcatraz means "pelican," and the island was home to a large pelican population. From 1868 to 1933 it was home to a military prison, then from 1934 to 1963 it was a federal prison, from which it was considered impossible to escape. The prison (itself known as Alcatraz, and also called "the Rock") had 390 cells equipped with some of the most advanced escape-proof systems. Of the 36 attempted escapes, only 2 were successful. In 1969 a group of Native Americans occupied the island, claiming it as their own, before being forced off in 1971. The following year, Alcatraz was made a part of the Golden Gate National Recreation Area.

Amazon.com

One of the first "dot.com" giants, and a symbol of the "clean" economy of the New West, Amazon.com was founded by Princeton graduate Jeff Bezos in 1994 to sell books via the internet. Bezos did not particularly like books, but he loved computers and had searched for a product to sell over the World Wide Web. The physical company was based in Seattle, Washington, but its market was the world. Amazon's "virtual doors" flew open in July 1995. By the first quarter of 2000 Amazon had 20 million customer accounts, but for all its novelty and massive volume, the company still remained in the red. Amazon.com posted its first profit in the first quarter of 2002, and it projected profits for subsequent quarters as well.

Apple Computers

Founded by Steven Jobs and Stephen Wozniak in 1976, Apple Computer Company revolutionized the personal computer industry and epitomized the rise of "clean" industry in the New West. Located in the Santa Clara Valley, in California, the company's first product was the Apple I, a single-board computer with on-board read-only memory (ROM), which sold for about $650 without a monitor or keyboard. Orders instantly soared, and Jobs and Wozniak quickly brought out the Apple II, which included a keyboard, color monitor, and expansions for peripheral devices. In 1984, Apple introduced the Macintosh, which was aimed at the business and education markets, by which time the company had already not only changed American industry but had reshaped entire areas of the West around silicon.

In 1996, after a series of CEOs failed to keep Apple profitable, Steve Jobs returned under the rubric "interim CEO" and soon launched a new marketing and licensing relationship with Microsoft. In 2000 his direct sales concept, the "Apple Store," brought the company back to profitability.

Area 51/Groom Lake

In the early 1950s the federal government tested atomic weapons on land roughly 150 miles north-northwest of Las Vegas, Nevada, near the small town of Rachel. "Area 51" and the Groom Lake region, which encompasses some 38,000 acres, soon became home to testing top-secret weapons, including the F-117 "Stealth" fighter and B-2 bomber. To this day, the government refuses to admit that the facility exists, and it is patrolled by private guards. Mystery surrounding the base has generated numerous rumors associated with the *Roswell*, New Mexico, "UFO" crash in 1947, wherein pieces of a weather balloon were mistaken for wreckage of a crashed unidentified flying object. "UFO-ologists" have maintained that a government conspiracy exists to conceal the existence of the crash and that recovered "alien" bodies are stored at Area 51.

Ash, Mary Kay (May 19, 1918–November 23, 2001)

An example of a western entrepreneur in the burgeoning health and beauty industry, Mary Kay Ash developed her cosmetics company into a powerful presence in Dallas, Texas. Famous for the pink Cadillacs she presented for exceeding sales quotas, Ash began her career as a middle-aged divorcee with three children to raise. Born May 12, 1918, as Mary Kay Wagner in Hot Wells, Texas, she had an impoverished childhood. After graduating from high school, Mary Kay married a musician and local radio host. With three children, Mary Kay needed to supplement her husband's income with door-to-door sales of encyclopedias. She became very successful at this, exceeding in a day the monthly sales expectations for other representatives. Having mastered home sales, she joined Stanley Products after her husband returned from the service at the end of World War II and ran off with another woman.

Even as she outsold male coworkers in the company, she found that they were promoted instead of her. In 1952, out of frustration, she left Stanley for World Gift Company, where again, she achieved impressive sales. While at World Gift, she had met a woman who made skin care products, using a formula passed down to her by her father, who was a hide tanner. Mary Kay convinced the woman to make a new line of skin products for a new company she would start. In September 1963 Mary Kay Ash and her son Richard sank their life savings into Mary Kay Cosmetics of Dallas. By that time Mary Kay had also remarried, but just as she launched her new business, her second husband died of a heart attack. Supported by her children, Richard, Benjamin, and Marilyn, Mary Kay nevertheless forged ahead with her company, which reported $200,000 in sales in its first year.

Sales soared in part because Mary Kay—having experienced discrimination and lack of financial incentives for performance—insisted that her company emphasize self-worth, respect, and motivation. After rewarding top sales people with jewelry and vacations, she originated the practice of giving away a pink Cadillac as an incentive bonus. By the time Mary Kay Ash took the company public in 1968, she was a millionaire. She was the only woman featured in the *Forbes* "Greatest Business Success Stories of All Times."

Astrodome

Opened on April 12, 1965, the Astrodome in Houston, Texas—dubbed "the Eighth Wonder of the World"—was the first ball park to have a roof over the playing field. When first built, the Astrodome—which featured baseball and football games, as well as other attractions—had a Bermuda grass playing field, but it was discovered that the grass was too difficult to maintain. By 1966 the stadium utilized a new plastic grass carpet laid over a slab of cement, called "Astroturf." At its apex, the dome rises 208 feet high, with center field 400 feet away from home plate. Home to the Houston Astros of major league baseball until 1999, the Astrodome also hosted the Houston Oilers professional football team from 1965 to 1996.

Autry, (Orvon) Gene (September 29, 1907– October 2, 1998)

Known as the "singing cowboy," Gene Autry, like his contemporary Roy *Rogers*, pioneered the "horse opera"—a western that always contained a singing interlude. Born in Tioga, Texas, on September 29, 1907, Autry sang all his life but was working as a railroad telegrapher in Oklahoma when he met Will *Rogers*, who encouraged him to pursue a career in singing. In 1928 he appeared on Tulsa radio as a "yodeling cowboy" and had regular radio appearances on the "National Barn Dance" show. In 1935 he starred in his first movie, *Tumbling Tumbleweeds*. The following year, he was the top-ranked western star—a position he held until 1943.

Autry recorded more than 600 songs in his career. While many were related to the West (his signature song was "Back in the Saddle Again"), many were commercial hits in the general market, including "That Silver-Haired Daddy of Mine," and his three enduring Christmas hits, "Frosty the Snowman," "Rudolph the Red-Nosed Reindeer," and "Here Comes Santa Claus." He earned enough to branch into business interests such as cattle ranching, broadcasting, music publishing, and ownership of the California Angels baseball team. Gene Autry died on October 2, 1998, in Hollywood, California.

Azusa Street revival

In 1905 a movement within American Protestant churches, known as the "holiness" movement, reached Los Angeles. Elder William J. Seymour of the Holiness Mission on Santa Fe Street ignited the movement when he preached a doctrine that speaking in tongues, according to Acts 2, was the "only" evidence of being "filled with the Holy Spirit," which occurred at Pentecost. The people spoke with other tongues, known as "glossalalia." Consequently, those who spoke in tongues were known as "Pentecostals." Meetings ran 24 hours a day for days at a time at an abandoned church on Azusa Street where believers gathered. Azusa's believers came from all denominations: blacks, whites, and Hispanics worshiped together at a time when most churches remained ethnically segregated. Although the Azusa Street revival faded after 1913, the Pentecostal movement it originated continued to grow.

The Bakersfield Sound

Nashville's hegemony as country music's primary recording center was unchallenged until the early 1960s, when songwriters and musicians from rural California offered an alternative known as "the Bakersfield Sound." Located between the Mojave Desert and the San Joaquin Valley, Bakersfield was the western terminus for thousands of migrants searching for agricultural work during the Great Depression. By the late 1940s "Okies" and others who had fled westward had become a permanent part of the Bakersfield community. So were the musical tastes they brought along.

The postwar economic boom benefited the Bakersfield area. By the 1950s there were plenty of live musical venues, from dance halls to rougher honky-tonks. Country music was a staple of local radio, and Bakersfield was close enough to Las Vegas to tap into the talent there. Bakersfield's musicians had more of a rock 'n' roll influence than did the Nashville bands and featured electric guitars—especially the Fender Telecaster—and drum sets.

One of the most prominent Bakersfield musicians was Alvis Edgar "Buck" Owens, born in Sherman, Texas, in 1929. Owens grew up in dismal poverty, often lacking shoes. In 1951 he moved to Bakersfield and played honky tonks as a guitarist. In 1956 he received a contract with Capitol Records, and in 1963 Owens and his band, the Buckaroos, reached the top spot in the national country charts with "Love's Gonna Live Here," "Act Naturally," and "I've Got a Tiger by the Tail." Another prominent Bakersfield musician, Merle *Haggard*, also had a long string of successful hits, including his anthem for country singers, "Okie From Muskogee." A more recent country star adopting the Bakersfield Sound is Dwight Yoakam, who shared with Owens and Haggard a rougher counterpart to the slick Nashville songs.

Bank of America (BankAmerica)

Founded as the Bank of Italy in October 1904 by Amadeo Peter ("A. P.") *Giannini*, this San Francisco bank drew its customers from the North Beach Italian colony in that city. Giannini took advantage of branch banking laws in the California constitution that allowed a bank to open other offices under the original name and with all records, capital, and accounts subsumed under the original bank's name. This fostered tremendous stability and growth, for a bank could open a branch in an area long before it might have the resources to establish a free-standing "unit" bank. Beginning with the first Bank of Italy branch in San Jose in 1909, the Bank of Italy became a statewide presence by entering into Los Angeles (where it competed directly with another powerful California banker, Joseph Sartori). But Giannini had started with a solid foundation in San Francisco. After the earthquake and fire of 1906, the Bank of Italy resumed operations sooner than any other, attracting a wave of new customers.

In 1927 as part of an effort to increase the number of banks chartered by the federal government instead of the states—called "national" banks—

the McFadden Act permitted a bank to join the national system with all branches it previously held and, furthermore, allowed branching by national banks where state laws permitted it. The Bank of Italy agreed to recharter under national regulations, reorganizing itself as the Bank of America National Trust and Savings Association (eschewing the more traditional title of "National Bank"). Under Giannini's leadership, the bank continued to expand, growing to 538 branches in 317 California cities by 1954.

After Giannini's death in 1949, the Bank continued to be a powerful presence under his son, Mario Giannini, becoming the largest commercial bank in the world. After 1970 a combination of high inflation and poor foreign loans—especially to Mexico—ate away at the bank's profits and stability. In the early 1980s it wrote off billions of dollars in bad loans, while its deposit base dwindled. Just as several analysts had started to proclaim the death of "BofA," as they called it, the bank revived. By 1990 it was again profitable, with the highest profits of any American bank. Relaxed acquisition laws also allowed Bank of America to acquire banks in other states under the Bank of America name, although these were not pure branch banks.

Baum, L. Frank (May 15, 1856–May 6, 1919)

Best known for his 1900 book, *The Wonderful Wizard of Oz*, L. Frank Baum was born to Benjamin and Cynthia Stanton Baum on May 15, 1856. A sickly and shy child, Baum's first job was publishing a small newspaper called the *Rose Lawn Home Journal* for several years on a small printing press that his oilman father bought for him. In 1873 he started a second newspaper, called *The Empire*. He also became interested in the stage, writing original plays such as "The Maid of Arran," in which he was the leading man.

Baum married Maud Gage, whose mother was a nationally known feminist and whose father owned a dry-goods store. The Baums moved to Aberdeen, South Dakota, in the 1880s and opened "Baum's Bazaar," a general store. After the business nearly went bankrupt and eventually closed, Baum began selling advertising in local newspapers. His sales took him to Chicago, where he conceived of new marketing techniques using glass front windows, eventually publishing a leading trade magazine called *The Show Window*.

Meanwhile, Baum had begun to dabble in writing children's stories. His most influential and popular work was *The Wonderful Wizard of Oz* (1900), in which he told the story of Dorothy, a Kansas girl swept into a magical land called Oz. There are forces of evil, represented by the bad witches of the West and East, and forces of good, in the person of the witches of the North and South. The famous Wizard of Oz, who was ultimately only a little man with no real power, was all things to all people. Many modern scholars conclude that the Wizard of Oz was a parable on the *Populist [IV]* movement in the West.

Frank Baum died in May 1919. The *Wonderful Wizard of Oz* was extremely popular, and although Baum wrote 13 more "Oz" books, they never achieved the same connection with the audience that his first effort had.

The Beach Boys

The quintessential "*surf music*" band, comprised of brothers Brian, Carl, and Dennis Wilson, their cousin, Al Jardine, and friend, Mike Love, the Beach Boys captured the California surfing craze of the early 1960s and stood, at least for a while, as the American counterpart to the Beatles. Formed in 1961 in Hawthorne, California, the Beach Boys were the brainchild of Brian Wilson, who was the chief songwriter and inspirational talent. Wilson became obsessed with harmonic and melodic style of the Four Freshmen and the Hi-Lo's. The brothers' father, Murray Wilson, took over their career as a self-appointed manager and publicist and helped guide them temporarily to a series of hits. Brian's first major song, "Surfin', " reached Billboard's top 100 in 1962 when the band received a recording contract from Capitol Records.

At Capitol, the band took off, having 10 major hits and 4 albums within 2 years. Most of the songs were about girls, surfing, hot rods, and school, and the band appeared to be more innocent than some of the English invaders who competed for the radio market. One of the biggest of the Beach Boys' hits, "Surfin' USA," managed to break into the tough British market. But the Beach Boys were only just starting, releasing an astounding four more albums in 1964 alone, almost all of which were written and largely produced and arranged by Brian Wilson. Seeing his band as direct competitors to the Beatles, Wilson attained a measure of success when, in 1966, the Beach Boys were voted the number one band in Britain—ahead of the Beatles.

By that time, the Beach Boys had such classic hits as "I Get Around," "God Only Knows," "In My Room," "Wouldn't It Be Nice?" and the pop theme of the Golden State, "California Girls." Even then, the efforts artistically paled compared to the 1966 masterpiece, the album "Pet Sounds," or the exceptional single "Good Vibrations" released near the end of 1966. However, "Pet Sounds" was surpassed by the Beatles' "Sgt. Pepper's Lonely Hearts Club Band" the following year. After hearing it, Brian Wilson had a nervous breakdown. Soon thereafter, Wilson entered a spiral of self-destruction marked by stunning weight gains, psychological problems, and drugs. The band battled internally, especially Mike Love, who chafed at the "artsy" direction of Brian Wilson, and Dennis Wilson came within the psychotic orbit of Charles Manson. Struggles with Capitol Records, management, and one another intensified. By the mid-1970s, Brian Wilson was often incomprehensible, while Love and Jardine were rebellious; and the band often featured hired musicians who could not capture the sound of the brothers. In 1983 Dennis Wilson drowned, an event that temporarily brought the group back together for a tour.

Nevertheless, Brian Wilson bordered on insanity, and in 1990 the other Beach Boys took him to court to have him and his $80 million fortune declared a ward of the court. In 1998 Carl Wilson died of cancer, effectively ending any possibility of ever recreating the Beach Boys' harmony or energy. A 2001 televised "Tribute to Brian Wilson" featured the singer and dozens of artists, including his daughter Carnie Wilson (who had become a pop artist in her own right), playing and singing the songs that have, more than any other, come to characterize and describe California.

Beats

A counter-culture movement of poets, the San Francisco Beats later became known as the "Beatniks." Poets Lawrence Ferlinghetti and Allen Ginsburg and novelists William Burroughs and Jack Kerouac formed the nucleus of the group. Although they inhabited both New York and San Francisco, the presence of Ferlinghetti's bookstore and publishing house in San Francisco tended to identify the Beatniks with the West Coast. To be a "beat" meant to have an interest in jazz, a bohemian urban culture associated with New York's Greenwich Village before World War I, and to characterize oneself as "hip," "with it," and generally nonconformist in the tradition of 19th-century American transcendentalists, such as Emerson. The beats were displaced by the more radical "hippie" movement of the 1960s.

Berkeley "Free Speech" Movement

In 1964 students at the University of California at Berkeley, following a radical program laid out in the "Port Huron Statement" by the Students for a Democratic Society (SDS) led by Tom Hayden and Al Haber, produced a student strike over the closing of the Telegraph Avenue street corner traditionally used for political speeches. Before long, some 2,000 students joined the "sit in," and subsequently, led by Mario Savio, they formed the Free Speech Movement (FSM). Savio led student demonstrators to occupy administration offices, before police arrived to displace them. The tactics of the SDS and FSM soon spread from California to other American universities and set the tone for other student uprisings on American campuses for the rest of the 1960s.

Black Elk (1863–1950)

Black Elk, a *Sioux [IV]*, came to the attention of the American public when poet and novelist John G. Neihardt recorded and edited his autobiography, *Black Elk Speaks*, in 1932. Black Elk had witnessed both the *Battle of the Little Bighorn [IV]* in 1876 and the *Massacre at Wounded Knee [IV]* in 1890. After Wounded Knee, Black Elk slowly converted to Roman Catholicism, being baptized in December 1904. For the rest of his life, Black Elk served as a staunch Roman Catholic and catechist. Many scholars, however, doubt the legitimacy of a sincere conversion. Many assume that he merely acted as a devout Roman Catholic, using this as a smokescreen to continue traditional Sioux religious practices. Whether he did or not, Black Elk certainly helped revitalize religion and spirituality among the demoralized Sioux. He remains a symbol of Lakota spirituality to this day, and *Black Elk Speaks* has become since its publication.

Borah, William E. (June 29, 1865–January 19, 1940)

A noted opponent of America's entry into the League of Nations at the end of World War I, William Edgar Borah was born in Illinois. He was admitted to the bar in 1889 before moving to Idaho, which became his home. He practiced law in Boise, actively working in the state's Republican Party, where he was the Republican State Central Committee chairman in 1892. He parlayed that influence into a U.S. Senate seat in 1906, where he remained until 1940.

While in the Senate, Borah was known as an isolationist, opposing U.S. entry not only into the League, but also the World Court. He influenced the Washington Conference of 1920–1921, which resulted in the Naval Armament Limitation Treaty of 1922. But Borah did not oppose all foreign involvement, supporting the Kellogg-Briand Pact of 1928, which outlawed war.

Borah, despite coming from a western state, opposed the farm price bill known as McNary-Haugen, but he otherwise embraced the federal government's expanding role, sponsoring the establishment of the Department of Labor and the Children's Bureau. He also supported the income tax and firmly backed all of Franklin *Roosevelt*'s New Deal policies except FDR's overtures to send aid to England after Germany invaded Poland in 1939.

bracero program

Initiated in 1942 as a wartime measure to provide agricultural labor, the bracero program allowed for the importation of Mexican laborers into the United States. Mexico agreed to the program only reluctantly, after negotiating several safeguards to protect the employees, including having the employers guarantee a "living wage," transportation and shelter, and have contracts written in Spanish. The Farm Security Administration, under the Department of Agriculture, administered the program. Farmers distrusted the government and resisted the wage provisions, while laborers charged that farmers set the "prevailing wage" at the beginning of the growing season, when it was lower, thus discouraging American laborers from doing the jobs and opening the door for more braceros. The program expired in 1964.

Branson, Missouri

Located in southeastern Missouri in the Ozark Mountains, Branson has become a haven for country music. Several Nashville stars began building large music theaters in Branson in the 1980s, competing with the "Grand Ol' Opry" in Nashville. These music theaters provided greater artistic control, as the performers themselves owned the music halls. The town of Branson emphasized family entertainment and vacation features, and the popularity of these shows grew. Among the stars having their own permanent shows in Branson are Bobby Vinton, Mel Tillis, Glen Campbell, and Kenny Rogers.

Brown, Molly (July 1867–October 25, 1932)

A survivor of the *Titanic* sinking, where she commanded a lifeboat, Molly Tobin (also called "Maggie") was born in Hannibal, Missouri, and worked throughout much of her childhood and early youth. After moving to Leadville, Colorado, with her brother in 1884, she met and married a silver mine manager, James J. Brown, who hit a rich gold vein in 1894. Thereupon, the couple moved to Denver, where Molly entered the circles of "high society." Her husband left her but continued to send her money, and she visited New York, Newport, Rhode Island, and Europe, winning fame as a frequent party guest of the Astors, the Vanderbilts, and other wealthy families. The broadway musical, *The Unsinkable Molly Brown* (1960) was loosely based on her life.

Bryan, William Jennings (March 19, 1860– July 26, 1925)

Famous for his "Cross of Gold" speech to the Democratic Convention in 1896, then later, for his prosecution of Tennessee teacher John Scopes in the "Scopes Monkey Trial" in Dayton, Tennessee, in 1925, William Jennings Bryan epitomized the rising *Populist [IV]* sentiment in the West. Born in Illinois, Bryan was raised in a deeply religious family. He studied law and practiced in Illinois, then Nebraska, where he won a seat in the U.S. Congress. Known for his advocacy of "free silver," Bryan became a favorite of the rising Populist Party. Farm distress had led the Populists and "silverites" to favor "free and unlimited coinage of silver at 16:1"—in short, inflation of the currency.

Bryan also supported prohibition and the income tax during this time, but his efforts in repealing the *Sherman Silver Purchase Act [IV]* of 1890 identified him more with the "free silver" movement than any other issue. But after he failed in a bid to capture a Nebraska U.S. Senate seat, Bryan increasingly advocated "free silver" in his writings and speeches. Named a delegate to the 1896 Democratic Party platform committee, Bryan gave the a memorable speech to the convention known as the "Cross of Gold" speech: "You shall not press down upon the brow of labor this crown of thorns. You shall not crucify mankind upon a cross of gold." The speech was sufficient to give Bryan the Democratic nomination, after which the Populist Party also supported him.

Running against Republican William McKinley, Bryan made the gold standard the dominant issue in the campaign. Seeing himself vastly outfinanced by the traditional Republican elements (as compared to his "grassroots" effort), Bryan changed the nature of campaigning by traveling some 18,000 miles and giving speeches while McKinley remained at home and spoke from his front porch. Playing on class envy, Bryan mounted a strong challenge but fell short in the presidential election, which marked a realignment of the political parties and ensured Republican control of the presidency for an almost unbroken period until the Great Depression. (Woodrow Wilson, a Democrat elected in 1912, faced a badly divided GOP with two candidates, Theodore Roosevelt and William Howard Taft.)

Bryan briefly served in the military during the Spanish-American War and ran again in 1900 on the silver platform of the Democratic Party. But in that election, he lost the support of the Populists over his (as the Populists perceived it) lack of enthusiasm for opposing the Spanish American War. McKinley defeated Bryan by a wider margin in 1900, but Bryan remained popular among certain elements of the Democratic Party. He attempted a third run in 1908 and again was defeated. But in 1912, when Wilson won, the new president tapped Bryan as his secretary of state. Seeing himself as a peacemaker, Secretary Bryan set out to secure treaties among some 30 nations to reduce the risk of war.

These efforts unraveled in 1914 when European conflict broke out between the Central Powers and the Allies. Wilson proclaimed "strict neutrality," which to Bryan meant absolute noninvolvement. But Wilson soon found his administration siding in deed, if not word, with Britain and France. When a German U-boat sank the *Lusitania* in 1915, Wilson's strong protest note to Germany forced Bryan to resign rather than endorse the nation's direction.

IN THEIR OWN

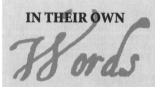

William Jennings Bryan's "Cross of Gold" Speech, July 8, 1896

William Jennings Bryan, a delegate from Nebraska to the Democratic National Convention in Chicago, addressed the explosive issue of the "gold standard" versus "free silver," a po-sition endorsed by the Populist Party. Bryan's memorable speech is considered one of the most influential in American history. It was laced with religious imagery.

*W*ith a zeal approaching the zeal which inspired the Crusaders who followed Peter the Hermit, our silver Democrats went forth from victory unto victory until they are now assembled, not to discuss, not to debate, but to enter up the judgment already rendered by the plain people of this country. . . . And now, my friends, let me come to the paramount issue. If they ask us why it is that we say more on the money question than we say on the tariff question, I reply that, if protection has slain its thousands, the gold standard has slain its tens of thousands. . . .

Three months ago when it was confidently asserted that those who believed in the gold standard would frame our platform and nominate our candidates, even the advocates of the gold standard did not think we could elect a President. And they had good reason for their doubt, because there is scarcely a State here today asking for the gold standard which is not in the absolute control of the Republican Party. But note the change. Mr. McKinley was nominated at St. Louis upon a platform which declared for the maintenance of the gold standard. . . .

If they dare to come out in the open field and defend the gold standard as a good thing, we will fight them to the uttermost. Having behind us the producing masses of this nation and the world, supported by the commercial interests and the toilers everywhere, we will answer their demand for a gold standard by saying to them; You shall not press down upon the brow of labor this crown of thorns, you shall not crucify mankind upon a cross of gold.

—SOURCE: HENRY STEELE COMMAGER, ED., *DOCUMENTS OF AMERICAN HISTORY, VOL. I: TO 1898*, 7TH EDITION (NEW YORK: F. S. CROFTS, 1934), 174–178.

Revisiting his early issue of prohibition, Bryan turned his oratorical skills toward enacting the 18th Amendment. His increasingly quirky positions, though, had become embarrassing to some mainstream Democrats, including his opposition to a proposal condemning the Ku Klux Klan at the Democratic Convention of 1924. Increasingly, political opponents pushed him to the margin, using his religious positions on evolution as a lever. The end, figuratively and literally, came for Bryan in 1925 when he assisted the prosecutor in Dayton, Tennessee, in a case against John Scopes, a high school teacher charged with violating the state's law prohibiting the instruction of evolution. Pitted against the famous barrister Clarence Darrow, Bryan has been portrayed as a bumpkin out of his league. Egged into taking the witness stand, Bryan reportedly folded against the superior Darrow. In fact, almost all local and regional news accounts described Bryan as winning the exchanges, and only a few Eastern journalists described Darrow as the victor. Bryan won the case—Scopes was found guilty—but the state supreme court later overturned the verdict, which was later romanticized (with a bumbling Bryan bested by the slick Darrow) in the play, and later movie, *Inherit the Wind*. Bryan died shortly after the trial, never getting out of Dayton, Tennessee.

Randolph Street, in Chicago, in 1903, reflected the hustle and bustle of a major metropolitan city at the turn of the century. It also reflected the steady expansion westward: Chicago once was one of the most far-western cities, but by the time of the photo was already considered "Midwest." *Library of Congress*

Bureau of Land Management

The Bureau of Land Management (BLM) originated with the *Northwest Ordinance [II]* and its requirements for a systematic survey of U.S. government lands. In 1812 Congress established the General Land Office (in the Treasury Department) to deal with government land, which remained in place until the government created the BLM in 1946 by merging the General Land Office with the Grazing Service. The BLM's mission is to "sustain the health, diversity and productivity of the public lands for the use and enjoyment of present and future generations."

Bush, George Herbert Walker (June 12, 1924–)

Born on June 12, 1924, into a wealthy political family, George Herbert Walker Bush attended private schools. In World War II he volunteered for service in the U.S. Navy, where he flew fighter planes in the Pacific, where he was shot down and earned medals for heroism. He attended Yale University upon his return, and graduated in 1948. Using his military pay, Bush moved to Texas to work in Dresser Industries, then in 1954, founded the Zapata Petroleum Corporation and Zapata Off-Shore Company.

Following in the footsteps of his father, who was a U.S. senator from 1952 to 1963, Bush ran for political office, losing the election to the Senate to Ralph Yarborough, although he ran ahead of the national ticket. In 1966 Bush won a seat in the U.S. House of Representatives from Houston, then in 1970, again ran for the Senate, only to be defeated by Lloyd Bentsen. Nevertheless, he gained valuable experience and earned a reputation as a "moderate." He mixed "eastern" and "western" influences, supporting liberal programs such as the Environmental Protection Agency and conservative legislation to oppose school busing. In 1976 President Gerald Ford named Bush director of the Central Intelligence Agency to replace the dismissed William Colby.

After an unsuccessful bid for the Republican nomination in 1980, where he lost to California Governor Ronald *Reagan*, Bush agreed to become Reagan's running mate on the national ticket. Following Reagan's win in the general election, Bush served as an effective and supportive vice president for eight years. In 1988 Bush ran as the GOP nominee on a platform of continuing the "Reagan Revolution" against liberal Democrat Michael Dukakis from Massachusetts. Bush won a landslide victory, which forced the Democratic Party to undergo a sharp internal redefinition of itself.

As president, Bush oversaw the final victory in the Cold War as the Berlin Wall was torn down in 1989 and the Soviet Union split into numerous independent republics and de-communized over the ensuing two years. He put together an improbable coalition when, in 1990, Iraq invaded neighboring Kuwait and threatened to invade Saudi Arabia. Forging an alliance among not only several Muslim states that routinely disliked one another, but also all of NATO, Bush rallied the United States to send more than 500,000 troops to the Middle Eastern deserts. His most significant achievements in this action remained hidden, though: Bush secured pledges from the Soviet Union/Russia—which itself was unraveling—not to intervene;

from Israel not to counterattack if struck; and from Japan to bankroll the entire operation. In Operation Desert Storm, a hundred-hour ground war resulted in an overwhelming victory for the allied forces. Bush allowed his military leaders to make the strategic and tactical decisions necessary for victory. When the brief war was over, Bush's approval ratings in the polls hovered above 85 percent.

But overriding Bush's foreign policy success, media attention and constant politicization of the deficits by the Democrats (who were now in the majority in both the House and the Senate) forced Bush, on the advice of Secretary of the Treasury Jim Baker, to agree to a tax increase. Breaking his "read my lips" pledge outraged and alienated large chunks of Bush's conservative base that had reluctantly supported him as Reagan's successor. It doomed him in the 1992 election, combined with a recession that arguably was *caused* by the tax increases. His inability to contain the Democrats' spending on social issues made him a target for disaffected conservatives. Bush's free-trade philosophy also led to a reaction by "Reagan Democrats," and those elements of the Reagan coalition abandoned Bush for third party candidate H. Ross *Perot*.

Perot's presence in the general election siphoned 17 percent away from the major parties and helped ensure the election of Democrat Bill Clinton, who received only 43 percent of the vote. Bush and his wife, Barbara, who remained a popular first lady, left Washington for retirement from government service, although Bush's sons, George W. *Bush* and Jeb Bush already had staked out successful political careers. When George W. Bush was elected president, it marked only the second time in American history that a father and son had both ascended to the highest office in the land.

Bush, George W. (July 6, 1946–)

The son of the 41st president of the United States, George Herbert Walker *Bush*, George W. Bush was born on July 6, 1946, and grew up in Midland, Texas. He attended Yale University and Harvard Business School, then served in the Air National Guard, where he flew F-104 aircraft during the Vietnam War years. After his guard service, Bush became involved in the oil business in Midland, working with various companies for more than a decade until he joined his father's campaign team in 1988. After his father was elected president, "W," as Bush was called, put together a group of partners to purchase the troubled Texas Rangers professional baseball team in Arlington, Texas. In 1989 he became the managing general partner and oversaw construction of the Rangers' new stadium in Arlington.

After six years at the head of the Texas Rangers, Bush ran for governor of Texas as a Republican and won a surprise victory in 1994 against incumbent Ann Richards. He quickly established himself as a coalition builder who worked with Democrats. Four years later, Bush became the first Texas governor to be elected to consecutive four-year terms, winning nearly 70 percent of the vote. Not long thereafter, he decided to run for the presidency, methodically building a huge "war chest" of funds and aligning all the 25 Republican governors behind him. In the 2000 general election, Bush won in the closest election in American history over the incumbent Democratic Vice President Al Gore, giving the GOP control of the House, Senate, and White House for the first time since Eisenhower. The result was not decided until, literally, the last votes in Florida were counted. Gore contested the election, demanding recounts, which had to be undertaken according to Florida law. As both sides fought in the courts over the legitimacy of the recounts, the Florida Supreme Court required a statewide recount just days before the national deadline for the voting in the Electoral College. The United States Supreme Court ruled that a partial recount would be illegal and a statewide recount would be impossible under the time constraints. This left standing the initial certification by Florida of Bush's victory with a state margin of 930 votes and a one-vote margin in the electoral college, making him the 43d president of the United States.

After getting his tax cuts through Congress, Bush settled in for a series of confrontations after a one-seat switch in the Senate gave that chamber back to the Democrats. But on September 11, 2001, when Islamic terrorists hijacked aircraft and flew them into the World Trade Center and the Pentagon, Bush saw his role change to that of a wartime leader. His September 20 speech to a joint session of Congress outlined the "Bush Doctrine" against terrorists and states that support terrorism, and several weeks later, the first military operations commenced against Afghanistan and its Taliban government. Bush attained the highest approval levels in presidential history, and for a longer sustained period than any other president. His approval numbers were well above 70 percent on most major polls by midsummer of 2002 as he continued to direct the "war on terror." He also proved the most prolific fundraiser in political history, raising $30 million in a few appearances for the GOP.

California fitness/aerobic craze

The fitness boom in America did not originate strictly in California, but certainly it took off in the West and achieved its highest form in California in the 1980s. Aerobic dance was introduced in 1969 by Jackie Sorenson in New Jersey, involving a continuous rhythmic movement to music intended to improve cardiovascular fitness. At about the same time, Dr. Kenneth H. Cooper, in Dallas, Texas, opened a medical clinic to study the relationship of exercise to health. His book *Aerobics* (1968) emphasized the use of oxygen through running, dancing, bike riding, or other activities.

By the mid-1970s various aerobic dance activities had begun, with strictly choreographed dances such as Jazzercize, introduced by Judy Sheppard Missett in California in 1977, gaining popularity. But the true aerobic fitness craze perhaps originated with the video produced by actress Jane Fonda in 1982, the "Jane Fonda Workout." Within months, gyms began to be flooded with requests for aerobic studios, and several pure dance studios converted to include aerobic classes. In 1984 LA Fitness opened its first club in West Covina, California, emphasizing aerobic classes as well as weight lifting. The Sports Connection gyms in California proved the hottest locations, with the 1985 movie *Perfect*, featuring Jamie Lee Curtis as a sexy aerobic instructor (filmed at the Sports Connection) adding to the craze. Up-tempo aerobic music, adapted from the top high-energy popular tunes of the day, became an industry unto itself, complete with its own competitions carried on ESPN. Professional associations, such as the Aerobics and Fitness Association of America (AFAA), founded in 1983, established standards for instruction and safety in aerobic workouts. While the fitness craze subsided in the 1990s, as Americans branched out into more varied forms of exercise, a variety of aerobic classes are still expected by anyone joining a health club.

Cash, Johnny (February 26, 1932–)

Born to a poor family in Kingsland, Arkansas, Johnny Cash served in the U.S. Army Air Corps, then briefly worked as an appliance salesman before signing with Sam Phillips's Sun Records in 1955, joining "the Million Dollar Quartet" of Carl Perkins, Jerry Lee Lewis, and Elvis Presley. In a short time, Cash was one of the top musical performers in the world, knocking out country and western hits such as "Folsom Prison Blues," "I Walk the Line," "Ring of Fire," and "A Boy Named Sue." After more than 40 songs on the top country charts along with bouts with drugs, alcohol, and jail, Cash restored his career, which he attributed to a born-again Christian experience in the late 1960s, and remains the legendary "Man in Black" for his audiences. Johnny Cash was the classic western singer, especially as he represented the new breed of "outlaws," which included Waylon Jennings and Merle *Haggard*. These new singers had often done time in jail and seemed to capture the rebelliousness of the West.

Cather, Willa (December 7, 1873–April 24, 1947)

Willa Cather was born in Virginia and moved with her family to Red Cloud, Nebraska, when Willa was nine. She was the oldest of seven children, and she was home-schooled by her parents and neighbors. Nebraska profoundly shaped her world view. Its religious and ethnic diversity especially astounded her. Germans, Poles, Bohemians, Moravians, Swedes, and Russians populated the region, and she absorbed as much of each culture as possible. In addition, the land and its profound if stark beauty fascinated her. As a child, Cather was overwhelmed and disgusted by the vastness of the Great Plains, but as an adult, she came to find the same land and its people beautiful.

Themes of ethnic diversity and contribution, the meaning of the land to an individual as well as to a community, and the role of the individual within the community permeate most of Cather's novels. The first of Cather's famous novels, *O Pioneers!*, reveals all of these themes.

Following her graduation in 1895, Cather worked as a journalist in Lincoln; Pittsburgh, Pennsylvania; and New York. In 1912 Cather decided to write fiction full time. Her works include: *April Twilights* (1903), *Alexander's Bridge* (1912), *O Pioneers!* (1913), *The Song of the Lark* (1915), *My Antonia* (1918), *Youth and the Bright Medusa* (1920), *One of Ours* (1922, for which she won the Pulitzer Prize), *A Lost Lady* (1923), *The Professor's House* (1925), *My Mortal Enemy* (1926), *Death Comes to the Archbishop* (1927), *Shadows on the Rock* (1931), *Obscure Destinies* (1932), and *Lucy Gayheart* (1935).

Words

O Pioneers!

Writer Willa Cather, who moved to Nebraska as a child, wrote *O Pioneers!* in 1913 when she was 40. It is the story of life on the Great Plains, reflecting the hopes and realities of life in the Midwest through the eyes of a Swedish girl in Nebraska named Alexandra Bergson. As Alexandra takes over the family farm, she takes on the characteristics of many of the immigrants in Cather's novels: nobility, tenacity, and love of the land, coupled with a concern that those who follow will not care for it as did the first generation. In these scenes dealing with Alexandra's dying father, Cather captures the difficult life on the prairie, as well as the dream of making the transition from farmers to landowners.

Of all the bewildering things about a new country, the absence of human landmarks is one of the most depressing and disheartening. The houses on the Divide were small and were usually tucked away in low places; you did not see them until you came directly upon them. Most of them were built of the sod itself, and were only the unescapable ground in another form. The roads were but faint tracks in the grass, and the fields were scarcely noticeable. The record of the plow was insignificant, like the feeble scratches on stone left by prehistoric races, so indeterminate that they may, after all, be only the markings of glaciers, and not a record of human strivings.

In eleven long years John Bergson had made but little impression upon the wild land he had come to tame. It was still a wild thing that had its ugly moods; and no one knew when they were likely to come, or why. . . .

Bergson went over in his mind the things that had held him back. One winter his cattle had perished in a blizzard. The next summer one of his plow horses broke its leg in a prairie-dog hole and had to be shot. Another summer he lost his hogs from cholera, and a valuable stallion died from a rattlesnake bite. Time and again his crops had failed. He had lost two children, boys, that came between Lou and Emil, and there had been the cost of sickness and death. Now, when he had at last struggled out of debt, he was going to die himself. He was only forty-six, and had, of course, counted upon more time.

Bergson had spent his first five years on the Divide getting into debt, and the last six getting out. He had paid off his mortgages and had ended pretty much where he began, with the land. He owned exactly six hundred and forty acres of what stretched outside his door . . .

John Bergson had the Old-World belief that land, in itself, is desirable. But this land was an

(Continued on page 398)

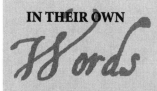

enigma. It was like a horse that no one knows how to break to harness, that runs wild and kicks things to pieces. He had an idea that no one understood how to farm it properly.

*****

Alexandra reached home in the afternoon. That evening she held a family council and told her brothers all that she had seen and heard.

"I want you boys to go down yourselves and look it over. Nothing will convince you like seeing with your own eyes. The river land was settled before this, and so they are a few years ahead of us, and have learned more about farming. The land sells for three times as much as this, but in five years we will double it. The rich men down there own all the best land, and they are buying all they can get. The thing to do is to sell our cattle and what little corn we have, and buy the Linstrum place. Then the next thing to do is take out two loans on our half-section and buy Peter Crow's place; raise every dollar we can, and buy every acre we can . . ."

Alexandra looked from one to the other and bit her lip. They had never seen her so nervous. "See here," she brought out at last. "We borrow the money for six years. Well, with the money we buy a half-section from Linstrum and a half from Crow, and a quarter from Struble, maybe. That will give us upwards of fourteen hundred acres, won't it? You won't have to pay off your mortgages for six years. By that time, any of this land will be worth thirty dollars an acre—it will be worth fifty, but we'll say thirty; then you can sell a garden patch anywhere, and pay off a debt of sixteen hundred dollars. . . . But as sure as we are sitting here to-night, we can sit down here ten years from now independent landowners, not struggling farmers any longer."

—FROM WILLA CATHER, *O PIONEERS!* (BOSTON: HOUGHTON-MIFFLIN, 1913), 12–13, 38–39.

Chavez, César Estrada (March 31, 1927– April 23, 1993)

Labor organizer César Estrada Chavez was born in Yuma, Arizona, to Mexican immigrants. His family lost its farm during the Great Depression and became migrant laborers. During World War II, Chavez served in the U.S. Navy.

Chavez spent his early career as his father had, as a migrant farm laborer, usually in strawberry fields. While in San Jose, California, in 1952,

Chavez came into contact with the Community Services Organization (CSO), an organizing group created and led by radical Saul Alinsky. During the next few years, Chavez was a paid staff member of CSO, traveling around California to learn union organizing techniques. He headed the CSO's voter registration drive and developed programs to help Mexican immigrants gain U.S. citizenship. It was also during this time that Chavez, who had little formal education and had not gone beyond seventh grade, learned to read and write. In 1958 Chavez was named general director of the national CSO but found the organization increasingly peppered with white middle-class professionals. He resigned in March 1962 when the CSO convention did not approve formation of a farmworkers' union.

Later that year, he formed the National Farm Workers' Association (NFWA) in Fresno and proceeded to enlist workers. He described the organization as a "union" for the first time in 1965, leading the NFWA on a strike against grape growers around Delano, California. The strike lasted five years, generating a boycott of grapes that gained liberal support. He not only faced struggles with the growers, but also with a rival union established by the Agricultural Workers Organizing Committee, prompting the two to merge in 1966 to form the United Farm Workers Organizing Committee (UFWOC) with the blessing of the national AFL-CIO.

Periodically, Chavez decried the militancy of some union members and fasted several times to show public penance for violence associated with some of the members. He received the support of U.S. Senator and presidential candidate Robert F. Kennedy, becoming a delegate to the Democratic convention for Kennedy. However, Chavez did not attend the convention after Kennedy was assassinated.

Meanwhile, the grape boycott continued to grow, to the point that by 1970 more than half of California grapes were being picked under UFWOC contract. When those contracts expired, however, the growers signed new contracts with another rival union, the Teamsters, which offered more favorable terms to the growers. Chavez's union membership peaked in 1972 with 72,000 members, then started a steady decline. He led a new round of strikes in the mid-1970s, drawing support from other national unions. The California state legislature enacted a collective bargaining agreement for farmworkers in 1975, in which the UFW, or *United Farm Workers*, as the union was now called, won nearly two-thirds of all certifying elections. But the UFW failed in its attempt to pass more wide ranging labor laws in 1976, and in 1977 the UFW and Teamsters reached an agreement that gave the UFW the sole right to organize farm workers.

Chavez tended to exercise dictatorial control over the UFW, driving off most of his loyal supporters, many of whom later claimed Chavez staffed the union with family members. He fasted regularly and subscribed to the nonviolent teachings of Gandhi and St. Paul. Over time, however, he also practiced holistic medicine, vegetarianism, and faith healing, often attempting to urge these concepts on union officials and members. This further alienated his supporters until unionized workers only accounted for about 10 percent of California's grape production. The UFW suffered another setback in 1987 when a superior court required it to pay $1.7 million to a lettuce grower stemming from union-sanctioned violence in a 1979 strike. Chavez's influence faded, although he still remained a liberal icon. Chavez died in Arizona in 1993, weakened by yet another fast.

Cheyenne Mountain (NORAD)

In 1956, concerned that the Soviet Union might launch a nuclear attack on American soil, possibly obliterating the military's command and control operations, General Earle Partridge, commander in chief of the Continental Air Defense Command, spearheaded a program to construct a massive underground operations center south of Colorado Springs that would be hardened to withstand nuclear blasts. The newly created NORAD (North American Aerospace Defense Command) was established in 1958 and was complete in 1964. NORAD has served as the early warning system for attacks on the U.S. mainland and has since become the home to the U.S. Space Command. Operations are conducted by 6 centers, which are manned 365 days a year, 24 hours a day.

Chicanos

Inspired by the radical elements of the black civil rights movement, politicized Mexican American university students took on the racial slur "Chicano" and redefined it as their name of choice. It connoted camaraderie and commonality of heritage and experience. Chicanos and Chicanas saw themselves as the descendants of Aztlán, the mythical homeland of the Aztecs, located in central-to-northern Mexico.

Political activism among Mexican Americans reached new heights after World War II, when veterans returned home expecting to be greeted with the first-class citizenship they had earned through their efforts in the war. Racial tensions had heightened during the war, especially in the Los Angeles area, with several incidents of violence between American servicemen and Mexican American youth. After the war, the heightened expectations of veterans were not met, leading them to form organizations

IN THEIR OWN *Words*

Life in the Barrio

Ernesto Galarza recalls his trip from Mexico and, in this section, his education in American public schools in post–World War II America. Attending Lincoln School in Tucson, Arizona, Galarza related the transition from being a Mexican to becoming an American.

At Lincoln, making us into Americans did not mean scrubbing away what made us originally foreign. The teachers called us as our parents did, or as close as they could pronounce our names in Spanish or Japanese. No one was ever scolded or punished for speaking in his native tongue on the playground. . . . I astounded the third grade with the story of my travels on a stagecoach, which nobody else in the class had seen except the museum at Sutter's Fort. After a visit to the Crocker Art Gallery and its collection of heroic paintings of the golden age of California, someone showed a silk scroll with a Chinese painting. . . .

The Americanization of Mexican me was no smoother matter. I had to fight one lout who made fun of my travels . . . [and my pronunciation of "diligence"]. He doubled up in laughter over the word until I straightened him out with a kick. . . .

I came back to the Lincoln School after every summer, moving up through the grades . . . [and] it was Miss Campbell who introduced me to the public library on Eye Street, where I became a regular customer. . . . We assembled to say good-bye to Miss Applegate, who was off to Alaska to be married. Now it was my turn to be excused from class to interpret for a parent enrolling a new student fresh from Mexico.

—SOURCE: ERNESTO GALARZA, *BARRIO BOY*
(NOTRE DAME, INDIANA: UNIVERSITY OF NOTRE DAME PRESS, 1971), 211–214.

such as the G.I. Forum, which worked to protect the rights of Mexican Americans as American citizens.

The political ferment of the 1960s encouraged agitation among Mexican Americans in labor, politics, land grant issues, and education. Farmworkers in California, led by César Chavez and Dolores Huerta, went on strike in the early 1960s, hoping to force growers to improve working conditions. In Tierra Amarilla, New Mexico, Reies Lópes Tijerina led a movement to regain possession of long-lost Spanish and Mexican land grants. Voters in the South Texas town of Crystal City elected a working-class Mexican American government in 1963. Crystal City native José Angel Gutiérrez returned home in 1969, establishing a third political party, La Raza Unida, which experienced some electoral victories, all in South Texas. This activism pushed Mexican American students to participate in a civil rights movement that became known as the Chicano Movement. Its most enduring legacies were the establishment of Chicano studies programs in universities across the nation and of a national student organization, the Movimiento Estudiantil Chicano de Aztlan (MEChA). The term *Chicano* encompassed their pride in their heritage, particularly their Mexican Indian roots, their youthful militancy, and their political and cultural agenda. The older generation of Mexican Americans, however, disliked the term *Chicano*, remembering its negative connotations, and did not appreciate the broad application of the moniker to cover all groups within the Spanish-speaking population.

chili cookoffs

Chili con carne is a stew of meat, *chili peppers [I]*, tomatoes, and spices. Debate over what constitutes "good chili" resembles theological argument over the acceptability of beans, onions, or the chili peppers. In 1947 the Chili Appreciation Society International was formed to trade recipes and held a cookoff on October 21, 1967. This may have involved a publicity stunt for humorist Frank X. Tolbert and his book, *A Bowl of Red*. H. Allen Smith, a New York self-proclaimed chili authority, was pitted against Texan journalist Wick Fowler in a cookoff at a remote ghost town, Terlingua. The two men battled to a tie, effectively killing the taste buds of a judge who held the deciding vote. Cookoffs have since occurred regularly in Texas, California, and currently, Reno, Nevada.

Chinatowns

In labor camps, port cities, and railroad towns throughout the West, Chinese immigrants established their own communities called "Chinatowns." The most famous were in San Francisco and Los Angeles, but other sizeable Chinese communities exist in Portland, Seattle, Denver, and Sacramento. The locus of traditional Chinese celebrations, Chinatowns tended to attract the most recent immigrants, while people

---

IN THEIR OWN Words

Leland Chin's Recollection of the 1906 San Francisco Earthquake

Leland Chin, a bank clerk and employee of the *Young China Daily*, whose father had come to America in 1877, recalls the April 1906 earthquake that struck San Francisco.

It was in April 1906. And it was around five o' clock in the morning. We were all in bed. In those days, we only had gas light, didn't have electricity in the house. But you could still have hot water, because people used to have a little hook . . . get a little wire, and get a pot, and let the jet, the flame of the gas light heat the water. So when you get up in the morning, there's the hot water. . . . So on the day of the earthquake . . . It happened they had the pot

there, and it struck out the gas light, and it sake [sic] and the water spilt. . . . And the water dripped on my head . . . . I wake up, and everything there is shaking. . . . I used to live on California Street, where the Dr. Sun Yat-sen statue is . . . and the first thing you know there's a big crack there. And the street had a big hole there. And then later on the sparks, the fire, the blaze began to start down around Montgomery Street, along the financial district. At that time only the Merchants' Exchange Building was there, that's about the highest building they have, and just about all . . . the whole building was enveloped in flame.

At six o-clock the flames began to spread. . . . My father had a shop down on Taylor street. And from there the whole family, and our employees and neighbors in the building, began to move . . . . Finally we got up to the park at Washington and Steiner and we rested. . . . In the morning the army came in and noticed a big group of Chinese all in the park there without any shelter or any food, so they got the army truck and took us to stay in the Presidio.

—SOURCE: VICTOR G. AND BRETT DE BARY NEE, *LONGTIME CALIFORN': A DOCUMENTARY STUDY OF AN AMERICAN CHINATOWN* (NEW YORK: PANTHEON, 1973), 76–77.

who have lived in the United States for a long time move to other diverse communities.

Church, Frank (July 24, 1924–April 7, 1984)

A senator from Idaho, Church is most famous for helping develop Lyndon B. *Johnson*'s environmentalist agenda. After gaining national prominence as the keynote speaker at the 1960 Democratic National Convention, Church became a leading advocate of environmental protection and oversaw the passage of the wide sweeping 1964 Wilderness Act. The Frank Church River of No Return Wilderness now bears his name. With close to 2.4 million acres, it is the second largest wilderness area in the United States (excluding those in Alaska). Church also helped shape and pass the various civil rights laws of Lyndon B. Johnson's so-called Great Society, but he vigorously opposed Johnson's escalation of the conflict in Vietnam.

During the 1970s he became most famous for his investigations into alleged Central Intelligence Agency abuse of power and for his sponsorship of legislation giving the Panama Canal to Panama. The 1980 *Reagan* revolution swept Democrat Church out of office.

Colorado River Community Compact

In 1922 representatives of seven western states signed an agreement that permitted them to share and manage the water in the Colorado River. The compact was undertaken, in part, to prevent the federal government from becoming involved. This became known as the "Law of the River," and was sparked by construction of Boulder (*Hoover*) *Dam*, which would give California more of a share of the Colorado River. A demarcation of "upper basin" states (Wyoming, Colorado, Utah, and New Mexico) and "lower basin" states (Arizona, California, and Nevada) allocated 7.5 million acre feet of water each per year, obviously with the "lower basin" states getting more. Arizona, as the geographic "owner" of much of the Colorado River, insisted on its share of the "basin," plus any tributaries flowing into it. Arizona finally approved the compact, but only after Carl *Hayden* and other Arizona politicians had secured federal funding for the Central Arizona Project canals to bring water from the river to urban areas.

commercial fishing in the West

Western commercial fishing, limited to California, Oregon, and Washington, accounts for about 10 percent of the 10 billion pounds of fish taken from the seas by the United States each year. In Washington the fishing industry has an annual return of more than $115 million, accounting for about 1 percent of the state's annual gross product. Of that amount, less than 1 percent comes from fresh water. Salmon accounts for about one-third of Washington's annual catch, followed by oysters, crab, shrimp, and other shellfish. Oregon, by comparison, has a return of about $80 million on Chinook and varieties of salmon, rockfish, and shrimp. Oregon's commercial fishing takes place on the continental shelf, although some occurs on the Columbia River. California has a fishing industry equal to that of Washington, both in dollar value and in percentage of state income. California's fishermen harvest crab, sole, rockfish, squid, and other fish.

As Americans have eaten more fish, the number of commercial fishing vessels in the United States has increased to peak at 130,000 in the mid-1980s, before tapering off in the 1990s. The increased demand for seafood has put pressure on marine fisheries, especially the Pacific salmon population, which is the cornerstone of the West's fishing industry. But salmon populations have declined in western states for reasons other than simply demand: logging, grazing, dams, and agriculture have taken some of the fishing habitats, and the government ownership of nearly half the land base in the Northwest means that private industry is often excluded from key fishing areas. Oregon and Washington have established agencies to provide hatcheries, restoration projects, and research to increase salmon populations.

"concealed carry" laws

Laws against carrying concealed weapons originated in states along the early western frontier, such as Arkansas, and often focused on knives—especially *Bowie knives [III]*—more than handguns. Eventually, laws prohibited carrying such weapons in certain places, such as legislative assemblies and churches.

In the 1990s several states adopted laws giving an individual a right to carry a concealed handgun. Florida, Indiana, Idaho, Texas, Utah, Washington, and Wyoming were just a few of the 22 states that had "concealed carry" laws on the books since 1986. In Texas—one of the most recent states to adopt a "concealed carry" law—the crime rate dropped 50 percent faster than in the nation as a whole. Opponents contend that such laws foster more gun fatalities and accidents.

credit cards

Both the major name brand revolving credit cards, VISA and Mastercard, originated or substantially evolved in the West. California's *Bank of America* introduced the BankAmericard in 1959, which was the nation's first true domestic credit card. The bank established a framework to administer card franchises, oversee collections, and deal with fraud. Several large California banks, in association with Phoenix and Seattle institutions, soon entered the market with another competitive card, called Master Charge. The two groups merged in 1967, and in 1979 the card's name was changed to "MasterCard." Two years earlier, the BankAmericard was renamed VISA to accommodate all those banks not affiliated with Bank of America.

Crystal Cathedral in Garden Grove, California, was completed in 1980 where it became the home of Rev. Robert Schuller's weekly "Hour of Power" broadcast. *Used by permission of Crystal Cathedral Ministries*

Crystal Cathedral

Home to famous "televangelist" preacher, the Reverend Robert Schuller, the Crystal Cathedral is located in Garden Grove, California, and was dedicated in September 1980. It is home for the international Crystal Cathedral Ministries, and to a local congregation of more than 10,000 members. The sanctuary seats 2,766 as well as another 1,000 singers and instrumentalists, while viewing is facilitated by a giant indoor television screen. Designed by American Institute of Architects gold medal winner Philip Johnson and his partner John Burgee, the building features more than 10,000 windows of reflective mirrored glass, giving it the effect of an all-crystal building. Two 90-foot-tall doors open electronically behind the pulpit to turn worship services into "open air" events. The Crystal Cathedral not only houses Reverend Schuller's local ministries, but is the originating point for the television ministry's weekly "Hour of Power" broadcast.

Curtis, Charles (January 25, 1860–February 8, 1936)

Charles Curtis was one-eighth Kaw-Kansa Indian mix. The Indian blood came from his mother's side; his father was an eccentric Civil War officer, a *Jayhawker [III]*, and an Indian (mostly *Cheyenne [IV]*) fighter. Americans considered Curtis a great success story, even comparing him to the characters of Horatio Alger novels. In his political speeches Curtis played up his "poor" frontier and Indian background. In reality he had inherited a significant amount of money and land from his Indian grandmother's government allotment. The same grandmother told the young Curtis to leave the reservation and "make something of himself." Curtis spent much of his childhood moving between the Kaw reservation near Council Grove and Topeka, between Catholicism and Methodism, and between Franco-Kansa culture and white American culture.

Curtis epitomized America's desire for "reformed" Indians; he made Americans feel comfortable with their policies toward the Indian. By all accounts, he was indeed a great success. As a young man in the early 1880s, he became a lawyer and a Republican. Curtis won his first House seat in 1892 and held that office until 1907, when the Kansas legislature elected him to the Senate. As a representative, Curtis was a straight-down-the-line Republican, never deviating toward progressivism. His colleagues joked that he believed the Holy Trinity to be "the Republican Party, the protective tariff, and the Grand Army of the Republic." Curtis hated any taint of progressivism and the "whims" of reform. Rather, he worked diligently for industry and war veterans. As a firm believer in individualism and private property, he also, importantly, sponsored the Curtis Act of 1898 which eventually dissolved Indian Territory, allowing it to become the state of Oklahoma in 1907. As a senator from 1907 to 1928, he was best known for "whispering," that is, making quiet political deals behind the scenes. In 1924 he became Senate majority leader; and in 1928, he attempted to secure the Republican nomination for president but instead became Hoover's vice-presidential running mate. As vice president (a job he disliked), he continued to support prohibition, high tariffs, isolationism, and the curtailment of the Federal Reserve system. He adamantly opposed Hoover's interventionist policies. In 1933, following Hoover's electoral defeat, he returned to law practice. He died three years later.

Dallas Cowboys

The Dallas Cowboys professional football team, given a franchise in 1960, has become one of the most consistent winning sports organizations and most valued franchises in history. Clint Murchison, Jr., the team's first owner, hired Tex Schramm as the general manager and Tom Landry as head coach. Although the Cowboys went 0-11-1 in the team's first season, in 1966 the Cowboys began an NFL record streak of 20 consecutive winning seasons, including 18 playoff appearances, 5 trips to the Super Bowl, and 2 Super Bowl trophies. During that time, the Cowboys were christened with the nickname "America's Team" for the team's popularity outside of Texas. After a dismal stretch in the 1980s, the new owner, Jerry Jones, and coach, Jimmy Johnson, returned the Cowboys to their glory, winning two consecutive Super Bowls. Johnson left, but Dallas kept winning, taking an unprecedented third Super Bowl trophy in four years in the 1990s, before falling back into the pack.

dam movement of the 20th century

While the federal government has involved itself in most aspects of frontier expansion since the *Lewis and Clark Expedition [III]* of 1804–1806, its involvement increased significantly in the 20th century. The Bureau of Reclamation and the Army Corps of Engineers dammed almost every major river in the West. In California alone, the United States government dammed every major river but one and created more than 1,251 reservoirs.

Led by the scretary of the interior, New Dealer Harold Ickes, projects increased at their greatest rate of the century during the Great Depression. Dam projects completed during the New Deal years were *Hoover Dam* (Nevada), Mansfield Dam (Texas), Big Thompson Project (Colorado), Conchas Dam and Tucumcari Project (New Mexico), Gila Project (Arizona), Provo River Project (Utah), Fort Peck Dam (Montana), Central Valley Project (California), and the Bonneville and Grand Coulee dams (Oregon and Washington). Typically, the New Dealers would contract the work of building the dams to large western corporations. After, the New Dealers regulated the prices and distributed the energy produced by the dams. Ironically, as Department of the Interior dams attempted to open up new lands to agricultural production, Henry Wallace's Department of Agriculture was attempting to limit production of crops and livestock (slaughtering millions of animals) to drive up prices for farmers.

With the precedent of the New Deal, politicians of the second half of the 20th century treated water projects as a source of government "pork." Throughout the Eisenhower years, dam development increased unabated, and bureaucrats would fly over western lands simply looking for any place that might be appropriate for a dam. Dam construction continued well into the 1960s. During that tumultuous decade, the rising environmentalist movement finally attenuated the growth of concrete poured in western arid areas.

As is typical for most bureaucratic involvement in the economy, every one dollar of government monies spent has yielded an economic return of only five cents. In addition, such monetary calculations fail to include the vast environmental destruction in the West caused by dams. Despite the massive construction and reworking of the western environment through American technology and public works projects, America has only created a Missouri-sized section of green through the political redistribution of water. In places such as western Kansas, reservoirs remain bone dry, as they have demanded too much of fragile ecostructures such as the Oglala aquifer. Historian Walter Prescott Webb once cautioned about American enthusiasm for remaking the environment: the desert holds "too dark a soul to be truly converted."

de Voto, Bernard (January 11, 1897– November 13, 1955)

The son of a Mormon mother and a Roman Catholic father, Bernard de Voto spent his relatively short life fighting what he perceived to be oppressive forces, especially religious intolerance and East Coast capitalism. As a western proponent of the New Deal, de Voto developed what he called the "plundered province" thesis. It stated that the American East had ravaged and exploited the West for its own purposes. The East had, in essence, colonized the West.

De Voto's numerous historical works include: *The Crooked Mile* (1924), *The Chariot of Fire* (1926), *The House of Sun-Goes-Down* (1928), *Mark Twain's America* (1932), (ed.) *Mark Twain in Eruption* (1940), *Mark Twain at Work* (1942), *Mountain Time* (1947), *Across the Wide Missouri* (1948), *The World of Fiction* (1950), *The Hour* (1951), *The Course of Empire* (1952), and he edited *The Journals of Lewis and Clark* (1953). During his lifetime, his writings earned him Pulitzer, Bancroft, and National Book awards. A national monument honors him at the Montana-Idaho border on U.S. Route 12.

Debo, Angie (January 30, 1890–February 21, 1988)

Born in Beattie, Kansas, and raised in Marshall, Oklahoma, Angie Debo observed life on Indian reservations firsthand. After writing a dissertation at the University of Oklahoma in 1933, *The Rise and Fall of the Choctaw Republic*, which won the John Dunning Prize, she became a freelance writer and historian, specializing in Indian topics. In all, Debo wrote nine books, coauthored another, and edited three more. She continued writing until her death at age 87 in 1988.

Denver, John (December 31, 1943–October 12, 1997)

Born John Henry Deutschendorf, in *Roswell*, New Mexico, John Denver took his stage name from the Colorado city in 1964. He performed with the Chad Mitchell Trio and wrote songs for Peter, Paul, and Mary, including "Leaving on a Jet Plane" (1969). Denver's first solo hit, "Take Me Home, Country Roads" (1971) exemplified his style of twangy country with messages about love, nature, and the West. Subsequent hits marked him as an optimist, and he had a brief movie career, appearing in "Oh God!" (1978). Denver spent time at his Aspen, Colorado, home and worked for charitable and environmental causes, becoming (in 1993) the first nonclassical artist to win the Albert Schweitzer Music Award. In 1997 Denver died when his experimental single-engine aircraft he was piloting crashed.

Disneyland

Conceived and funded by Walter Elias ("Walt") Disney (1901–1966) as a theme amusement park that would be clean, organized, and, most important, representative of traditional American values, Disneyland opened in 1955 in a former orange grove in Anaheim, California. Unlike Coney Island or other amusement parks, Disneyland was envisioned by Disney as grouping "attractions" (not rides) around themes, such as "Frontierland," "Adventureland," "Fantasyland," and "Tomorrowland." "Guests" (not customers) encountered employees who were "cast members" (not staff). While the number of attractions at first was limited, the public reaction was overwhelming. The Disney concept became so popular that the Disney corporation built larger parks in Orlando (just being completed at the time of Walt's death), Japan, and France, while expanding and refurbishing the original park. Among the innovations developed by Disney at his parks were circuitous routes for patrons waiting in line designed to keep large masses of people moving without clogging the thoroughfares.

Dobie, J. Frank (September 18, 1888–September 18, 1964)

Western storyteller, folklorist, historian, and author, J. Frank Dobie grew up on a ranch in Texas. As a young man he became interested in writing and poetry, and after spending time in the army in World War I, he returned to the University of Texas English department, where he worked with the Texas Folklore Society. Dobie became the society's editor in 1921, by which time he had started working on historical fiction books, including *A Vaquero of the Brush Country* (1929) and *Coronado's Children* (1930). He finished his career at the Huntington Library.

The Doors

The Doors were one of the premier psychedelic/progressive rock groups of the late 1960s/early 1970s. They remain one of the most influential rock bands of all time. Four young men made up the band: Jim Morrison (vocals), Ray Manzarek (organ and bass keyboards), Robbie Krieger (guitar), and John Densmore (drums and percussion). They recorded six albums, all with a relatively new record company, Elektra: *The Doors* (1967), *Strange Days* (1967), *Waiting for the Sun* (1968), *Soft Parade* (1969), *Morrison Hotel* (1970), and *L.A. Woman* (1971). In 1979 The Doors recorded music to some of Jim Morrison's poetry, entitled *An American Prayer*. The two founders, Manzarek and Morrison, met at the UCLA School of Film, and not surprisingly, their music was very cinematic and theatrical. It was at Maharishi Mahesh Yogi's Third Street Meditation center that Manzarek met the Mahesh's followers, Krieger and Densmore. Morrison named the band after Aldous Huxley's drug-inspired book *Doors of Perception*.

They were quintessentially western. Indeed, originating at Venice Beach, California, they revealed the sheer cultural power of the New West, and of California in particular. Their lyrics also dealt, frequently, with the West, and, while on drug trips, Jim Morrison often believed he had the soul of a deceased American Indian within him. They saw their concerts as mystical experiences, becoming one with the universe—"a public meeting called by us for a special dramatic discussion," Morrison explained.

Morrison, though, had a troubled career as lead singer. A purported alcoholic, drug abuser, and physically violent toward women, he was arrested several times. In 1967 police officers arrested him on stage as he was complaining about police brutality against him prior to the concert. In 1969 Miami police arrested him for public indecency. On July 3, 1971, Morrison was found dead from a drug overdose in a Paris hotel.

Douglas Aircraft Company

Founded by Donald W. Douglas, a pilot and civilian aeronautical engineer for the army's Aviation Section of the Signal Corps, Douglas Aircraft sprang from Douglas's engineering company in 1920 in Los Angeles. In 1928 the Douglas Company moved to Santa Monica, into an abandoned movie studio, where Douglas sold torpedo planes to the U.S. Navy. In 1933 Douglas rolled out the famous DC-1, the first of the famous "DC" series, which later included the DC-3 and DC-7. In 1967 Douglas Aircraft merged with McDonnell Company to form McDonnell Douglas Corporation, which became a giant defense contractor headquartered in St. Louis.

Dubois, Fred T. (May 29, 1851–February 14, 1930)

One of the most ambitious and prowestern senators of the Gilded Age and Progressive Eras, Dubois was born in Illinois to a devoutly Whiggish and Republican family. His grandfather, Touissant Dubois, had been an Indian fighter with William Henry *Harrison [III]* during the *War of 1812 [III]*, and his father, Jesse, had helped Abraham Lincoln secure the 1860 Republican nomination for president. After graduating from Yale in 1872, Fred Dubois moved to Fort Hall, Idaho, to live with his brother. In 1882 President Arthur appointed him a U.S. Marshal. Dubois used his four years in that office to prosecute Mormons vigorously.

In 1886 Dubois won the Idaho territorial delegate seat in the U.S. Senate. He spent his four years in that position learning as much as possible about the Senate as well as advocating high tariffs on Idaho raw materials and Idaho statehood. When elected Idaho senator after it gained official statehood in 1890, Dubois fought vehemently for Idaho's interests. Though only two years in the august body, the young Dubois led the fight against repeal of the *Sherman Silver Purchase Act [IV]* in 1893. President Grover Cleveland believed the act was the cause of the 1893 depression, and he demanded its repeal. Since much of the silver mined and subsidized by that act came from Idaho, Dubois wanted it protected. Creating a prosilver coalition between the West and the South, he led a filibuster. The fight over repeal became so nasty that many learned magazines predicted a new Civil War. By late October 1893 the Southern allies had fallen away, and the Senate passed the repeal.

In 1896 Fred T. Dubois and Henry Moore Teller led the prosilver forces in the Republican Party. When the party adopted a progold standard plank, Dubois and Teller initiated the walkout of the silver forces. They flirted with joining the *Populist Party [IV]* or the Democratic Party but instead created a third party, the Silver Republican Party. The new party ran candidates for several state and federal offices. The party lasted until 1901, when Dubois was elected to the Senate for a second term and joined the Democratic Party. During his second and last term as senator, Dubois supported progressive causes. After 1908, he held a variety of offices, but never again wielded the power he had in the Senate.

dude ranches

Western health and tourist resort hotels had operated since the late 1800s, and artists had flocked to Taos, New Mexico, after 1900. However, genuine dude ranches were, for the most part, a 20th century phenomenon. The object was usually to give tourists a taste of the frontier West. Typical dude ranches in Arizona, New Mexico, and Nevada provided horseback riding, camping, scenic hikes, and rudimentary training in roping or shooting. Later in the 20th century, tours offered customers the opportunity to participate in actual cattle drives, as was made popular in the 1989 film, *City Slickers*. As of 2001 so many dude ranches existed that they had their own organization and web sites.

Dust Bowl

During the 1920s farmers in the Midwest stripped land of natural grasses to plant wheat and other crops. Droughts and massive crop failures in the

As seen in this 1930s picture of a farmer's son in Cimarron County, Oklahoma, the Dust Bowl destroyed much of the agricultural base of the midwest. *Library of Congress*

early 1930s left nothing to hold the soil, as dust storms blew off millions of tons of topsoil. The most severe wind erosion occurred in 1935–1936, and the worst hit areas were Kansas, the panhandle of Oklahoma, and Texas. Thousands of families, labeled "Okies, whether they came from Oklahoma or not, left these parched farms for California. Conservation efforts and changing weather patterns eventually allowed the Dust Bowl to recover.

Eastwood, Clinton ("Clint") (May 31, 1930–)

Known for his classic line "Go ahead, make my day" and his steely, silent *cowboy [IV]* characters, Clinton "Clint" Eastwood, Jr., was born in San Francisco and grew up in California, yet he was never a cowboy. He took numerous bit parts in Hollywood before landing the second lead in the television series, *Rawhide* (1959–1966). Eastwood then starred in a series of Sergio Leone movies made in Italy (called "spaghetti westerns") known only as "the man with no name."

A quasi-Christ-like character, Eastwood arrived in western towns to mete out justice, then disappear, a theme revisited in some of his successful American westerns, such as *Pale Rider* (1985) and the Academy Award–winning *Unforgiven* (1992), which he directed. By the 1970s Eastwood had a new character for the new West, Inspector Harry Callahan of San Francisco, known as *Dirty Harry* (1971). His terse delivery of "A man's got to know his limitations" and "Do you feel lucky, punk?" are still often quoted by movie fans.

The cowboy characters played by Clint Eastwood differed significantly from previous on-screen portrayals of tough western men. Certainly they lacked the purity of a Gary Cooper in *High Noon* (1952), or the overall sense of justice in most John *Wayne* movies. After *Pale Rider*, Eastwood moved almost exclusively into broader roles, including comedy, drama, and traditional cop-type action movies. Eastwood became the last major star largely known for his western roles. Except for *Unforgiven*, modern western movies have been infrequent, though the genre has made something of a revival with *Tombstone* (1993), *Dances With Wolves* (1990), and the television movie miniseries *Lonesome Dove* (1989).

He also moved into the roles of director and producer. In 1986, after a zoning fight with officials of the city of Carmel, California, he entered politics and won the mayorship, serving a two-year term.

Eccles, Marriner Stoddard (September 9, 1890– December 18, 1977)

One of the three or four most influential bankers in the West, Marriner S. Eccles was born on September 9, 1890, to David and Ellen Stoddard Eccles. The oldest of nine children in a Mormon family, Eccles learned self-reliance and cooperation, responsibility, and enterprise. He worked in his father's businesses, including railroads, lumber mills, and banks. Marriner attended local elementary schools, then went to Brigham Young College in Logan, Utah.

Eccles managed some of his father's businesses after David died in 1912, including the Ogden First National Bank and the Ogden Savings Bank, which presented Eccles an opportunity to learn financial intricacies first hand. In 1925 he formed the Eccles-Browning Affiliated Banks with the Browning family from Ogden, and the company proceeded to acquire several banks. Three years later, the Brownings and Eccles, along with Marriner's brother, George, and E.G. Bennett of Idaho, formed the

First Security Corporation as a holding company for the 17 banks and a savings and loan company, considered one of the first multi-unit holding companies in the United States. Eccles was the president, putting him on a plane with other important western financiers, such as A. P. *Giannini* and Joseph Sartori of California and George Wingfield of Nevada.

As Utah sank with the rest of the nation into the Great Depression, Eccles fought to keep his businesses afloat but also worked on a personal level to understand the causes of the nation's economic distress. He was renowned for employing remarkable psychology to thwart a bank run during the banking crisis in 1931. Steeped in the communal doctrines of Mormonism, Eccles gradually adopted the "demand-side" positions of the Keynesians that called for more government relief and spending. After a speech to a businessman's luncheon attended by a Roosevelt administration official, Eccles came to the attention of the New Dealers in Washington.

He helped write the Emergency Banking Act of 1933; then in 1934 he was asked to serve as assistant secretary of the Treasury, where he helped draft the Federal Housing Act. Eccles's stock rose fast, and in November 1934 President Franklin Roosevelt nominated him as a governor in the Federal Reserve System. Eccles established himself as a counterbalance to Secretary of the Treasury Henry Morgenthau, Jr., who sought to rein in federal spending. In 1936 he became chairman of the Fed, during which time Eccles became a friend of virtually all taxes, supporting a tax increase in 1936 on undistributed profits, which contributed to the collapse of the economy in 1937 during the "Roosevelt Recession." At that point, he prevailed on the president to again increase public spending.

The Depression featured a distinctly western sideshow involving Eccles and A. P. Giannini, another Democrat banker. Both men had endorsed interstate branch banking, and Giannini supported the McFadden Act in 1927 on the assumption that it was the first step to national branch banking. Yet after Eccles gained a dominant place in the Treasury, he resisted efforts to liberalize branch banking, leaving Giannini feeling betrayed. When time came for Eccles to be reappointed in 1948, Giannini lobbied President Truman to remove Eccles. Truman did not reappoint Eccles as chairman, and while he remained on as vice chairman of the Board of Governors until 1951, his career in Washington wound down.

The Washington years also cost Eccles his marriage, which ended in divorce in 1950. After a failed Senate run, Eccles returned to the private sector, heading First Security Corporation as the chairman.

Eccles died in Salt Lake City at the age of 87, having made his mark as one of the most important American bankers of the 20th century.

Edwards Air Force Base

Edwards Air Force base was established as a major test facility for the Army Air Force in the 1930s as part of Muroc Air Force Base and as a gunnery range for the U.S. Army, which used the Rogers and Rosamond lake bed surfaces for live fire practice. In 1949 Muroc was renamed Edwards, in honor of Captain Glen Edwards, the copilot of the YB-49 flying wing that crashed in 1948. The base has become famous for many world-record feats, including Captain "Chuck" Yeager's X-1 flight that broke the sound barrier and the X-15 flights. In 1981 the space shuttle *Columbia* landed at Rogers Dry Lake following its orbital mission. The Air Force Flight Test Center, activated in 1951, makes the base a hub of aircraft and spacecraft testing.

El Teatro Campesino

Founded in the early 1960s as a street troupe of actors by Luis Valdez, El Teatro Campesino ("the Farmworkers Theater") evolved into a world-renowned performance company.

Valdez organized some of the striking workers to improvise comical skits and performed on the backs of flatbed trucks. The troupe also engaged in education and fundraising, but soon moved away from its farmworker origins to locate in San Juan Bautista. There, El Teatro Campesino developed a vaudevillian approach using Southwestern and Mexican humor. In 1987 the troupe's work was featured in a television adaptation of *Corridos*, and later, Valdez wrote *Zoot Suit*, then won widespread acclaim for writing and directing *La Bamba*, about Mexican American music star Ritchie Valens.

endangered species/"takings" clauses

Under the Endangered Species Act of 1973 the federal government gradually began to exert its authority to render private land unusable by claiming that the land was part of a habitat for an endangered species. Similar legislation allowed the U.S. Army Corps of Engineers and the Environmental Protection Agency to declare land "wetlands" even if it was dry 350 days a year. These and other environmental regulations were fought in courts by private individuals on the grounds that they represented unconstitutional "takings" of private property, arguing that if individuals were deprived of reasonable use of their property, the government had virtually "taken" it and should have to compensate owners.

Battles over wetlands, endangered species, and other use of "takings" flared in the West, where farmers and ranchers attempted to control predators (some of which were on the endangered species list), manage their farm lands, and build facilities or plant crops. One California farmer was assaulted by EPA agents in black jumpsuits and helicopters because he had plowed over the nest of a kangaroo rat. The courts, although usually siding with the federal government, have nevertheless enacted some restrictions on "takings," and no universally accepted legal guidelines have been settled on as of 2002.

The FaithDome

When the idea for the FaithDome was launched in the early 1980s, it was simply for a larger church for the Crenshaw Christian Center in Los Angeles. When it was completed, the FaithDome became the largest domed church sanctuary in the United States.

Frederick K. C. Price, the pastor of Crenshaw Christian Center, had sought land for a new church and finally discovered the 32-acre former site of Pepperdine University. Construction of the FaithDome began in January 1987 and was completed in 1989. The seating capacity is 10,146, contained inside a 320-foot-diameter, 75-foot-high structure. Built at a cost of $12 million, the ministry paid off the building in less than five years. It is the home to Dr. Price's "Ever Increasing Faith" weekly television series.

Fall, Albert B. (November 26, 1861–November 30, 1944)

The first American convicted of a felony while a member of a cabinet, Albert Bacon Fall was born in Frankfort, Kentucky, then moved to Texas and then New Mexico in the 1880s. He established a large ranch near Las Cruces, and participated in territorial politics, becoming a U.S. senator from New Mexico as a Republican in 1912.

In 1921 Fall was appointed secretary of the interior by Warren G. Harding. He approved the sale of public lands at Teapot Dome, Wyoming, and Elk Hills, California, to oil companies directed by Henry F. Sinclair and Edward L. Doheny. A Senate investigation found that Fall had accepted a $100,000 bribe to arrange the sale of the lands, for which he was convicted of bribery in 1929. Doheny was acquitted of offering the bribe Fall accepted. Fall's corruption was viewed as one of many in the Harding administration, while "Teapot Dome" became synonymous with government scandals.

"fern bars"

A California phenomena of the 1970s, "fern bars" were restaurants characterized by a light, breezy atmosphere and inevitably decorated with large numbers of potted plants, especially ferns. "Fern bars" specialized in "California food," such as tuna sandwiches and avocado, and helped pioneer the vegetarian and health fads, serving lentils, tofu, and soy dishes. These restaurants epitomized the California culture and its emphasis on the sexual revolution and its emphasis on the hip lifestyle, captured in Cyra McFadden's 1978 book, *The Serial.* "Fern bars" went out of vogue by the 1980s, replaced by "theme" restaurants such as the Hard Rock Cafe, with louder music and a stronger emphasis on being "hip."

Ford, John (February 1, 1894–August 31, 1973)

John Ford, arguably the greatest western-genre movie director, began his film career on movie sets doing odd jobs, stunt work, and appearing as an extra. His work in film editing allowed him to start directing short films by 1917, most of them westerns or cowboy movies, many starring Harry Carey. In 1917 he directed his first full-length film, *The Soul Herder;* over the next 18 years, his numerous films brought him into contact with Tom *Mix* and other stars of the silent era. In 1924 he made *The Iron Horse,* a true historical epic about the railroad. His career accelerated in 1935 when he directed *The Informer*, considered one of the great American films, and bringing Ford an Oscar for best director. Ford directed rising star John *Wayne* in the 1939 classic *Stagecoach* and teamed with another rising star, Henry Fonda, for several movies. During World War II, Ford filmed documentaries for the U.S. Navy, placing himself in harm's way with no protection other than a camera and winning Oscars for *The Battle of Midway* (1942) and *December 7th* (1943). After the war, Ford made his most critically acclaimed movies, again with John Wayne—the "Trilogy" of *Fort Apache* (1948), *She Wore a Yellow Ribbon* (1949), and *Rio Grande* (1950). Ford captured not only the beauty and scenery of the West but emphasized the individual's role in shaping early western society. Ford's cavalry outposts represented the advance of civilization into an untamed land, even while they brought some uncivil and even barbarous elements with them.

Giannini, Amadeo Peter ("A. P.") (May 6, 1870–June 3, 1949

Considered America's premier western banker—and arguably the most important western financial figure of the 20th century—Amadeo Peter Giannini parlayed a produce delivery business into a banking empire. After his death, the Bank of America (as it was called by then) struggled for decades to replace his vision and energy.

Amadeo Peter Giannini, usually referred to as "A. P.," was the son of Luigi and Virginia Giannini, a San Jose, California, hotel operator. After Luigi was killed in a dispute with a workman over a dollar, Virginia moved the family to a ranch outside the town. There she married a ranch produce delivery entrepreneur named Lorenzo Scatena. Giannini's stepfather taught him the wholesale produce business after the family moved again to North Beach, an Italian community in San Francisco. A. P. attended Washington Grammar School but soon worked full time in L. Scatena and Company, where by age 15 he conducted waterfront trading sessions, traveled all over the San Joaquin Valley to purchase produce, and then extended the company's area of operations to Santa Clara, the Napa Valley, and Sacramento.

When his wife's father, Joseph Cuneo, died in 1902, leaving a large estate, A. P. was appointed to manage the estate for a 25 percent share of any increase in capital value he effected. Two of the estate shares he administered, a North Beach savings bank and the Columbus Savings and

Loan Society, required his participation on a board of directors, wherein he gained valuable insight into the banking business.

While on the board of Columbus, Giannini formed a philosophy that characterized the Bank of Italy during its growth, namely to focus on new businesses that needed an initial capitalization. Although San Francisco was the money hub of the West, banks there had overlooked the small business market. When the other directors disagreed with Giannini's vision, he started his own bank.

Capitalized at $300,000, the Bank of Italy opened for business in October 1904, with Giannini as president. Emphasizing small loans, the institution grew rapidly, largely on the backs of the directors, who walked the North Beach area soliciting accounts on a personal basis. The bank also benefited greatly from a natural disaster, the devastating 1906 San Francisco earthquake and subsequent fire. Giannini's insight and opportunism enabled the bank to nearly double its assets, to $1.9 million, in 1906 alone.

The Bank of Italy always had a significant advantage over many competitors in Giannini's utilization of branch banking. Under many state laws (known as "unit banking laws"), the only way a bank could expand its operations was by creating a new bank, with a new charter. Branch banking laws allowed a bank to simply open new offices. Each new branch retained the original name and all resources, assets, and liabilities of branches and were considered inseparable from those

Along with Utah banker Marriner Eccles, Californian A. P. Giannini was one of the two most powerful western bankers in the United States in the 20th century, influencing branch banking policy and building the Bank of America into a world class financial powerhouse. *Bank of America Corporate Archives*

of the home office. This proved especially sound for larger states, such as California, where one region might experience an economic downturn while others remained prosperous.

Typically, Giannini established branches by purchasing existing troubled banks that nevertheless had large local customer bases. He took care to retain local employees and advisory boards. Although the first expansion phase of the bank occurred in the San Jose agricultural areas, offices soon appeared in San Francisco and other urban locations. Ultimately, Giannini had his eye on Los Angeles, intending to make the bank into a statewide presence. After Bank of Italy started to move into southern California, the new California superintendent of banking, Jonathan Dodge, grew concerned about the size of the operation and refused further branch permits.

In 1927 Giannini engaged in a massive consolidation effort resulting in the Bank of Italy Trust and Savings Association, which he converted to a national bank. He envisioned this as only the first step in a gigantic national interstate branch bank, which would have involved a restructuring of national banking laws. The McFadden Act, specifically passed to permit the extensive Bank of Italy system to come into the national banking network, liberalized many of the regulations governing national banks, and provided the incentive for Giannini to convert his state network of banks to national charters.

Anticipating interstate banking, Giannini purchased a controlling interest in the Bank of America in New York in 1928. The federal government grew concerned that Giannini's holding company, Bankitaly, would engage in trust activities through Bank of America. The Federal Reserve therefore required Giannini to sell the Bank of Italy to obtain the Bank of America. Giannini complied but immediately organized another new holding company, Transamerica Corporation, which then repurchased the Bank of Italy, now put under the name Bank of America.

Giannini met the Great Depression head-on, developing new leasing arrangements on California farm lands and keeping thousands of farmers in business during that difficult time. By 1936 Bank of America had regained its momentum and prestige, but the anticipated changes in interstate banking laws never came, leaving Giannini's dream unfulfilled. Giannini retired in 1936, succeeded by his son, Mario. He continued to serve as chairman but otherwise attempted to give his son a free hand in running the bank. In 1945 Bank of America became the world's largest commercial bank, providing a fitting time for A. P. Giannini to retire. In his last years, Giannini divided his time between travel and fighting federal government efforts to break up the Transamerica holding company. A. P. Giannini died on June 3, 1949, leaving a legacy as the premier western banker, who established a California financial institution on a par with any in the East.

Golden Gate Bridge

Designed by civil engineer Joseph Strauss, the Golden Gate Bridge resulted from acts passed in 1923 by the state of California to fund a bridge across the Golden Gate (the entrance to San Francisco Bay). Strauss completed the marvel in 1937. It opened on May 27, 1937, and was twice the length of any existing bridge. Strauss's design was a suspension bridge with a main span of 4,200 feet and suspending towers of 746 feet. Each main cable is more than a yard in diameter, while more than 80,000 miles of wrapped wire are used in the construction of the cables. Orange was chosen to accentuate the area's natural beauty.

The Golden Gate Bridge, completed in 1937, remains an engineering marvel of the West. *Bradley J. Birzer*

Goldwater, Barry Morris
(January 1, 1909–May 29, 1998)

Called "Mr. Conservative" by friends and foes alike, Barry M. Goldwater was a genuine Arizonian, born in Arizona Territory on January 1, 1909.He attended Staunton Military Academy in Virginia, where he graduated "outstanding cadet" in his class. As a young man, he worked in the family department store. Eight years later he was named president of the department store chain, where he remained until the outbreak of World War II.

In 1941 Goldwater enlisted in the Army Air Corps, where he became a group commander of the 90th Air Force Base Squadron, then chief of staff of the 4th Air Force. He flew the new P-47 "Mustang" fighters across the Atlantic and commanded air transport operations in the Azores, Casablanca, and India. When the war ended, Goldwater left active service as a lieutenant colonel, but he retired from the Air Force as a reserve major general in 1967.

In 1952 Goldwater defeated Arizona legend Ernest McFarland for the U.S. Senate seat, speaking aggressively against New Deal–style "big" government and in favor of states rights. That frequently put him in conflict with the civil rights movement in the 1950s and allowed critics to lump him in with extremists such as Democratic governor of Alabama George Wallace. A staunch anti-Communist, Goldwater supported U.S. policies of containment. In 1960 he outlined his views in his book, *The Conscience of a Conservative*.

As the Republican presidential candidate in 1964, Goldwater ran on a platform of ending Social Security, a hard line on communism, and rolling back the New Deal. His acceptance speech at the convention is best remembered for phrase, "Extremism in the defense of liberty is no vice. Moderation in the pursuit of justice is no virtue." His opponent, Lyndon *Johnson*, produced a television commercial implying that Goldwater was a

IN THEIR OWN

Words

Barry Goldwater's *The Conscience of a Conservative*

Whereas William Jennings Bryan's "Cross of Gold" speech reflected the western sentiments of the 1890s Populist movement in the Midwest, Barry Goldwater captured much of the 20th century West's individualism and hostility toward government. Other western presidents had come from large states such as Texas (Lyndon Johnson) or California (Richard Nixon), but Goldwater was the first western candidate of the 20th century to come from a smaller state. His book, *The Conscience of a Conservative* (1960), expressed his views of limiting the power of the federal government in favor of the states.

I caution against a defensive, or apologetic, appeal to the Constitution.

There is a reason for its reservation of States' Rights. Not only does it prevent the accumulation of power in a central government that is remote from the people and relatively im-mune from popular restraints; it also recognizes the principle that essentially local problems are best dealt with by the people most directly concerned. Who knows better than New Yorkers how much and what kind of publicly-financed slum clearance in New York City is needed . . . ? Who knows better than Nebraskans whether that State has an adequate nursing program? Who knows better than Arizonans the kind of school program that is needed to educate their children? The people of my own State—and I am confident that I speak for the majority of them—have long since seen through the spurious suggestion that federal aid comes "free." They know that the money comes out of their own pockets . . . .

Nothing could so far advance the cause of freedom as for state officials throughout the land to assert their rightful claims to lost state power; and for the federal government to withdraw promptly and totally from every jurisdiction which the Constitution reserved to the states.

—SOURCE: BARRY GOLDWATER, *THE CONSCIENCE OF A CONSERVATIVE* (SHEPHERDSVILLE, KY: VICTOR PUBLISHING COMPANY, 1960), 29–30.

warmonger who would involve the United States in a nuclear holocaust. The Arizonian was defeated in a landslide in 1964 but was reelected to the Senate in 1968, where he continued to press for improving the pay and effectiveness of the military. He and other top Republicans convinced President Richard Nixon to resign in 1974 during the Watergate crisis.

Even in defeat, Barry Goldwater emerged as the father of western conservatism and antifederalism. He paved the way for Ronald *Reagan*, who first gained the national political limelight when he gave the nominating speech for Goldwater in 1964. Long after he aligned himself with many liberal issues (such as prochoice) and made derogatory comments about Christian conservatives, Goldwater nevertheless remained the ideal of what a conservative politician "ought to be."

Arizona Senator Barry M. Goldwater gained a reputation as "Mr. Conservative" and sparked a reaction to New Deal liberalism with his ill-fated but influential presidential run against Lyndon Johnson in 1964. Among those who flocked to Goldwater's banner was Ronald Reagan, who would become governor of California and in 1980, president of the United States. *Library of Congress*

Grey, Zane (January 31, 1872–October 23, 1939)

Easily the most famous western storyteller in history, Zane Grey was born in Zanesville, Ohio on January 31, 1872. He produced well-known novels, biographies, and adventures of the American West. As a young man, Grey read the *dime novels [IV]*, played semiprofessional baseball, then practiced dentistry for a brief time before meeting Colonel C. J. Jones, who asked Grey to write a biography of him and took him west to gather research. There, Grey fell in love with the geography, the adventure, and the legends of the "wild West," and after publishing Jones's book as *The Last of the Plainsmen* (1908), Grey began a career in western writing.

His *Riders of the Purple Sage* (1912) remains a classic and has sold more than 1 million copies. He spent several months each year gathering experiences for the next novel, whether fishing or in the wilds of Colorado, leaving more than 60 western titles, 9 fishing books, and 3 family biographies, along with short story collections and juvenile fiction. Sometimes criticized as racist or simplistic, Zane Grey's adventures achieved beauty and spoke to a genuine American idealism. To those who loved a good, fast-paced story of the Old West, no one told it like Zane Grey. He died in October 1939.

Haggard, Merle (April 6, 1937–)

Born in Bakersfield, California, Merle Haggard turned a struggling and often depressing personal life into a musical career, ranking as one of the top country and western performers of the 20th century. For 15 years, Haggard ran afoul of the law, finally committing a burglary of a restaurant and landing in San Quentin prison. There, Haggard met author and death row inmate Caryl Chessman, who led him to turn his life around. After getting paroled, Haggard became a musician. Playing a number of local Bakersfield clubs when the popular Buck Owens's career was on the rise, Haggard had his first hit, "Sing a Sad Song." He developed a melancholy, sad, earthy vocal style that still retained the country music nasal twang, and in 1969 during the Vietnam War he penned a song called "Okie from Muskogee" that made him him a cult hero.

Harvey Girls

The name "Harvey Girls" was given to young women who came west in the 1880s to work for Fred Harvey in his chain of way stations known as "Harvey Houses" alongside the Santa Fe Railroad route from Kansas to California. The women, usually aged 18 to 30, were single and signed a one-year contract to work as waitresses 10 hours a day serving four-course meals. They lived at no charge above the restaurants in the Harvey Houses but were subject to strict rules and the supervision of a "house mother" who acted as a chaperone. In addition to the pay and free lodging, the Harvey Girls received free rail passes.

Hawaii

The youngest state in the Union, Hawaii, located almost 2,500 miles west of California, is the only state not connected to the North American mainland. It is the midway point between San Francisco and Japan. The Hawaiian islands consist of eight major islands—the largest being Hawaii, but the most populated being Oahu—and more than 100 smaller volcanic islands. Settled originally by Polynesians, the islands were discovered by British explorer James

Cook in 1778 when he named them the "Sandwich Islands." At the time, the population may have exceeded 300,000, but after European diseases ravaged the locals population numbers fell to below 60,000.

At the time Cook arrived, Hawaii was governed by leaders known as kahunas. The most important of these was Kamehameha I, who utilized English artillery to subdue opponents in the late 1700s. Western missionaries arrived in the 1800s, and their emphasis on Bible reading was associated with a public education system that made Hawaiians extremely literate. Continued contact with Europeans, including, by the 1850s, Americans, came from the whaling crews that made port calls in Hawaii. The islands proved excellent agricultural spots, producing bananas, sugar, coconuts, and other foods, which were eagerly sought during the Civil War. Indeed, as a result of the sugar business, King David Kalakaua became the first monarch to visit the United States when he arrived in 1874 to discuss trade treaties.

Upon his death, Kalakaua was succeeded by Queen Liliokalani. Local European settlers (*haoles,* pronounced "howlies") staged a rebellion against Queen Liliokalani's government with the support of the United States diplomats on the island. The Republic of Hawaii was established on July 4, 1894, but was not annexed immediately; rather, after William McKinley was elected, the Republic applied for, and was given, territorial status in 1898.

Hawaii's population always included a large number of Japanese, and an ongoing three-way struggle for power between Polynesians, European/Americans, and Japanese has ensued and continued to the present. The Japanese have emerged as the leading property owners in many of the cities, while American-born investors acquired many of the large fruit businesses, such as Dole Pineapple. Efforts to get Hawaiian sugar admitted into the United States duty-free led to a statehood movement in the 1930s, but Congress was concerned about the islands' large Japanese population.

The importance of Hawaii as a naval base was underscored on December 7, 1941, when Japanese planes from the Imperial Navy attacked Pearl Harbor and brought the United States into World War II. Subsequently, the large influx of mainland Americans anglicized the islands and later revived the statehood movement. On March 12, 1959, Hawaii became the 50th state. Substantially Democratic in its politics, the state is one of the best-known resort spots in the world and remains an important source of several key food items.

Hayden, Carl T. (October 2, 1877–January 25, 1972)

Except for Barry *Goldwater*, no public figure was more associated with Arizona's political history than Carl Hayden. By the time Arizona was granted statehood in 1912, Hayden already had experience lobbying for water rights in Washington. He was the first U.S. congressman elected from the new state in 1912, then ran for the U.S. Senate in 1926, where he remained until 1969. He focused on obtaining water rights for the young desert state. Hayden's father had started a ferry across the Salt River, and by the 1920s, a number of water projects were underway. Hayden worked to obtain Arizona's share of the Colorado River water—which was divided by Congress between California and Arizona in the 1920s—and won congressional approval for construction of Boulder (*Hoover*) *Dam*. In 1968 the climax of his career came with the approval of the Central Arizona Project to move Colorado River water to Phoenix and Tucson via canals and aqueducts.

Hayes, Ira (January 12, 1923–January 24, 1955)

Immortalized in the photograph by Joe Rosenthal raising the flag atop Mount Suribachi over Iwo Jima on February 23, 1945, Ira Hayes was born on the Pima Reservation at Sacaton, Arizona, on January 12, 1923. When the war broke out, he joined the U.S. Marines and went to parachutist school, earning the nickname "Chief Falling Cloud." The flag-raising changed Hayes's life. He was hustled back to the United States for a war bond drive. When the war ended, Hayes was unable to adjust to domestic life and was uncomfortable with what he saw as unwarranted adulation. He died at age 33 on January 24, 1955, when he fell into a ditch drunk and froze to death—a "hero to everyone but himself."

Haywood, William Dudley ("Big Bill") (February 4, 1869–May 18, 1928)

One of the leaders of the International Workers of the World ("Wobblies"), William "Big Bill" Haywood was born in *Salt Lake City [III]*, lost an eye at age nine, and worked as a miner from a young age. He was elected to the position of secretary-treasurer of the Western Federation of Miners, then became active in the Wobblies, chairing their convention in 1905. He was implicated in the murder of the former governor of Idaho, Frank Steunenberg, for which he was defended by Clarence Darrow and prosecuted by William *Borah*. Haywood was acquitted and the trial became a national sensation. A member of the fledgling socialist movement in America, Haywood soon became a featured speaker and organizer, while continuing to organize strikes for the Wobblies. His radical connections resulted in his expulsion from the Western Federation of Miners in 1907.

Haywood spent considerable time in jail or defending himself from various charges. In 1917 he was arrested and convicted on charges of sedition but was released on bail. While free, Haywood escaped to the Soviet Union, where he anticipated finding the ideal society. The Soviet government welcomed any capitalist defectors and promptly gave him a largely ceremonial administrative post. He had arrived in the Soviet Union ill and continued to grow sicker until he died there in 1928.

Hillerman, Tony (May 27, 1925–)

Born in Sacred Heart, Oklahoma, Hillerman attended a Catholic grade school and a public high school. During World War II he saw much combat and received several medals, including the Bronze Star with Oak Leaf Cluster, the Silver Star, and the Purple Heart. After recovering from his war injuries, Hillerman earned his bachelor's degree at the University of Oklahoma. From 1948 until 1962 he worked as a journalist in a number of western towns. Hillerman attended graduate school at the University of New Mexico and became a professor of journalism in 1966. He is most famous for his numerous mystery novels set on the *Navajo [I]* Reservation, including *The Blessing Way* (1970), *The Coyote Waits* (1990), and *Hunting Badger* (1999).

Hollywood

Though originally founded by Kansas prohibitionists in 1887, the city of Hollywood has come to represent all that is decadent in American society. Situated just northwest of Los Angeles, Hollywood became a filmmaker's mecca in the early 20th century. Men such as Cecil B. DeMille, Samuel Goldwyn, and D. W. Griffith were entrepreneurs who saw great opportunities in the profitability of motion pictures, assuming correctly that it represented the next great leap in entertainment. By the 1930s Hollywood had started to become associated with glamor (being dubbed "tinseltown") and the locals played to that image with galas, balls, and, of course, the motion picture awards (the "Oscars"), which debuted in 1929 at the Hollywood Roosevelt Hotel. In addition to the numerous motion picture studios, there are several landmarks located near Hollywood, such as Grau-man's Chinese Theater. Later, as the rock music industry became important, other Hollywood landmarks included the Capital Records Building and the Whiskey a Go Go.

Hoover Dam

Begun in 1931 as part of the Boulder Canyon project and completed in 1936, Hoover Dam contains the Colorado River, and its hydroelectric generators deliver 1.5 million kilowatts of power to Arizona, Nevada, and southern California. The dam, named for President Herbert Hoover, is 726 feet high and 1,244 feet long at its crest. Lake Mead, the artificially created reservoir behind the dam, covers some 233 square miles. After the Great Depression, with ill memories of President Hoover still lingering, the name of the dam was changed to Boulder Dam. But in 1947 the name reverted to Hoover Dam. At the time, it was considered one of the world's great engineering achievements, accomplished in part through the efforts of Henry J. *Kaiser*.

Completed in 1936, Hoover Dam on the Colorado River, built by westerner Henry J. Kaiser, was an example of the Bureau of Reclamation's efforts at irrigation in the West. *Bureau of Reclamation*

Hoover, Herbert Clark (August 10, 1874–October 20, 1964)

Known as the president with responsibility for the Great Depression, Herbert Hoover was born in West Branch, Iowa, graduated from Stanford University, and headed several mining operations in China, Africa, and South America in the years before World War I. During the war, Hoover directed the American Relief Committee in London, then headed the Commission of Relief in Belgium. Both of these activities brought him into close contact with agriculture in the United States. From 1921 to 1928, as the secretary of commerce under the Harding and Coolidge administrations, Hoover supported various farm relief programs. However, he brought an engineer's mentality to the problems of the economy.

After his election as president in 1928, Hoover presided over the worst economic downturn in American history. Although he had little control over the Federal Reserve's tight money policies, he signed the Smoot-Hawley Tariff that severely distorted American trade and enacted a variety of programs and taxes that presaged the New Deal of Franklin Roosevelt. His Reconstruction Finance Corporation, designed to aid struggling banks in the West and Midwest, had disastrously published the names of the loan recipients, triggering still more bank runs. His policies for farmers, however, proved a dismal failure for agriculture. Hoover was not the first true West Coast president in the sense Californian Richard Nixon was, but his impact on the West was important.

Hughes, Howard Robard (September 24, 1905–April 5, 1976)

Born in Houston, Texas, and inheritor of his father's company, Hughes Tool and Die Co., known for its famous "Hughes Drill Bit," Howard Hughes ran the family business for a while before moving to Los Angeles, where he simultaneously became obsessed with aircraft and women. He produced several films, including aviation movies in which he used most of his own personal aircraft collection for props. Among his most memorable films were *The Front Page* (1931), *Scarface* (1932), and *The Outlaw* (1942), which gave Jane Russell her break into movies. Gradually Hughes abandoned filmmaking for aircraft design, racing, and production.

Hughes's airplanes set several speed records, but his test aircraft crashed frequently, often with Hughes inside. After the FX-11 crashed in 1946, Hughes started to suffer from chronic physical disabilities. During World War II he produced small wooden scout airplanes and handled other contract work. Ultimately he teamed with shipbuilder Henry *Kaiser* to build the world's largest aircraft, an all-wooden seaplane ultimately known as *Spruce Goose*. Hughes came under scrutiny from the Congress for cost overruns and delays. To prove that *Spruce Goose* could indeed fly, in November 1947 he personally took the three-story, 320-foot-wingspan aircraft on its maiden—and only—flight.

After briefly owning TWA Airlines, in 1966 Hughes then turned his attention to *Las Vegas* casinos, purchasing several hotels in Nevada—the Frontier, the Sands, and the Desert Inn. Hughes resided on the top floor of the Desert Inn, became reclusive, and seldom spoke to many of his top lieutenants. Robert Maheu, who headed the Las Vegas casino operations, never saw Hughes in person. This eccentricity provided an abundant rumor mill in the tabloids, made all the more bizarre by Hughes's sudden departures from his Las Vegas hotel. Hughes's behavior grew increasingly bizarre: a virtual prisoner in his hotel room, Hughes' sole exercise for his 94-pound frame consisted of walking to the bathroom and back to his bed. His fingernails grew so long they curled over several times, and he refused to touch others physically. When he died in 1976, the public image of Howard Hughes was that of a bizarre billionaire rather than that of the younger daring and innovative pilot and aggressive businessman.

Howard Hughes, seen here in his director's chair, inherited his father's tool and die company, which he soon left to others to manage while he pursued filmmaking, then aircraft construction and racing. After several accidents, his physical and mental health deteriorated, but not before he had built an airline industry and a major electronics firm in the West. *Library of Congress*

illegal immigration

Illegal immigration refers to undocumented aliens, the vast majority of whom are from Mexico or South America, entering the United States and living as residents. What once was a troublesome but manageable problem, in the last few decades had reached near-crisis levels in the West. The 2000 census reported that based on the "head count" in the United States using birth, death, and other records, there should be 275 million U.S. residents. Instead, the surveys indicate that there are approximately 281 to 285 million. Both the Census Bureau and the Bureau of Immigration and Naturalization conclude that most of this discrepancy comes from illegal aliens. Texas, Arizona, New Mexico, and California have seen the burdens on their social systems grow as a result of the undocumented flood. One study found that California alone paid billions of dollars for the education of illegal alien children, and a study from Harvard's George Borjas found significant losses to U.S. workers from continued illegal immigration.

The United States Border Patrol, with its 7,000 immigration agents, is the agency mostly charged with stopping illegal immigration along the 3,200-kilometer border with Mexico. The number of agents has doubled since 1994, and the U.S. Border Patrol also uses radar and infrared cameras. But at least half the illegals are visa-"overstayers"—people who remain in the United States after their visas have expired. This became a particularly acute concern after September 11, 2001, when Arab terrorists destroyed the World Trade Center and subsequent searches for members of its terror network revealed thousands of Arabs linked to these networks, many of whom had entered the United States legally but remained after their visas expired.

Still, even in light of September 11, when most Americans think of "illegal immigration," they still picture Mexicans coming across the Rio Grande. Indeed, that remains the most popular point of entry for illegals, although thousands cross the Arizona and New Mexico deserts annually—often led by "coyotes," or guides, whom they pay to get them across the border and the desert beyond. In 1999, 356 illegals died attempting to cross the deserts.

Indian alcoholism

It is often argued that early contact between Europeans and Native Americans introduced Indians to alcohol, but it is now thought that alcohol was known to at least some Indian groups. When Europeans arrived and introduced new forms of alcohol, at first many tribes staunchly refused any association with liquor. Likewise some colonial governments sought to prohibit traders from giving alcohol to Indians.

By the 20th century, however, alcoholism was rampant on reservations, as was obesity. Scientific studies have shown that social factors, such as low self-esteem, explain the preponderance of both. Previously held views that Indians were genetically predisposed to alcoholism have been challenged by recent evidence that even within Indian groups, levels of alcoholism vary significantly.

Among North American Indians, the highest alcoholism rate occurs among the Inupiat of the region, but it appears to afflict Indians at a much higher rate across the board than other races. A national 1988 study showed that alcohol-related mortality rates were 5.4 times higher for Indians than for all other races. Another study in the 1990s found that for the age group 35 to 44, Indian alcoholism rates reached 50 per 100,000, and for the age group 65 to 74, the number reached 76 per 100,000. New research on the social context of drinking suggests that Indian environment and culture have contributed to the high levels of alcohol use compared to other groups. Combined with poverty and high unemployment, alcohol abuse on reservations remains at near-epidemic proportions.

Indian Reorganization Act

One of the most intrusive policies in federal government Indian relations, the Indian Reorganization Act was nothing less than an attempt to recommunalize American Indians in the vision of the director of the *Bureau of Indian Affairs [III]*, John Collier. Collier, a brilliant and idealistic reformer, had been heavily influenced by Friedrich Nietzsche, Lester Frank Ward, and various forms of socialist thought as a young man at Columbia University and in the European Cooperative movement. He attempted reforms in the American South, New York City, and California before working with Communist Mabel Dodge Luhan in Taos, New Mexico, in the 1920s. Living with the Pueblo Indians, Collier became the leading critic of the Bureau of Indian Affairs and especially of the allotment policies of the federal government. Such attempts to force privatization of the land, he believed, only led the Indians into destitution.

In 1933 Franklin D. Roosevelt appointed Collier as head of the Bureau of Indian Affairs. The New Deal secretary of the interior, Harold Ickes, had highly recommended him. In his first year Collier conducted an extensive study of living standards among the American Indians. His findings were shocking. First, almost half of all Indians owned no property. Second, the landless lived with relatives. Third, the government controlled almost every aspect of an Indian's life. Finally, the infant mortality rate among American Indians was double that of the white population.

To combat these problems, Collier developed the byzantine Indian Reorganization Act, known in Congress as the Wheeler-Howard Act. It had eight goals and became a central piece of the first New Deal. Its most significant aim was to redefine Indian nations not as dependent upon Congress but as "semi-sovereign" and autonomous internal nations. Specifically, it: (1) ended allotments; (2) allowed tribes to act as corporate entities; (3) helped tribes buy back land that had been bought by non-Indians; (4) allowed each tribe to write its own constitution; (5) offered $10 million of credit for tribal economic development; (6) offered livestock; (7) promoted native arts and religious beliefs; and (8) offered government monies for increased provision of education and medical care.

Despite the best of intentions, Collier and the IRA met considerable opposition. First, many of the American Indians, especially those who had become economically middle class or had converted to Christianity, viewed the new law as pure socialism. Second, those whites who had purchased land from Indians resented the implications that they might have illegally or immorally acquired it. In the end, though, 181 tribes adopted the IRA provisions and 77 rejected them. The greatest opposition came from the *Navajos [I]*, who resented the legislation (as well as the New Deal) as socialistic and were doing relatively well economically.

Even those who supported the provisions, though, soon discovered the flaws of the bill. First, Collier and the New Dealers, though often well intentioned, used their positions of power to manipulate tribal politics and tribal opinion. Second, the IRA tribes set up a series of liaisons between the tribe and the federal government. This often created tribal governments that were based on political influence rather than traditional norms. Third, and most important, despite promises of Indian autonomy, federal interference with Indian tribal autonomy increased dramatically, as federal monies and regulation soon affected numerous parts of tribal life.

Japanese internment in World War II

Following the attack on Pearl Harbor on December 7, 1941, and several other devastating U.S. losses to the Japanese in the following three months, Americans on the West Coast were terrified of a Japanese invasion. Concern about sabotage and a "fifth column" inside the Japanese American community led President Franklin D. Roosevelt to sign Executive Order 9066 on February 19, 1943, placing all persons of Japanese ancestry in California and other parts of the Far West under the authority of the War Relocation Authority, which was to remove all such persons from coastal areas to the interior western states. In the process of removing thousands of Japanese Americans—who left homes and businesses with no more luggage than they could carry—evacuees were removed from California to Arizona, Wyoming, Idaho, Utah, and even Arkansas, where they were housed in temporary facilities and guarded as prisoners. Some 120,000 were relocated, of whom 50,000 were not U.S. citizens, although most had lived in the United States for many years, denied citizenship by U.S. immigration laws.

George, Hisa, and Yasbei Hirano posed for this picture at the Colorado River Relocation Center in Poston, Arizona, after President Franklin Roosevelt ordered that all Japanese Americans on the West Coast be relocated to interior areas out of concern for a "fifth column" of saboteurs and spies during World War II. *National Archives*

In 1944 Fred Korematsu, a native of Oakland, who wished to remain with his fiancé when his family was transferred, was arrested. Aided by the American Civil Liberties Union and the Japanese American Citizens League, Korematsu appealed his conviction to the U.S. Supreme Court, which heard the case in 1944. The Supreme Court upheld the conviction on grounds of national security, upon which Korematsu was sent to a camp in Topaz, Utah. In 1981 still determined to prove he was wrongly arrested, Korematsu returned to the courts to charge that the government withheld evidence of the loyalty of Japanese Americans. A San Francisco federal judge overturned the Korematsu conviction and voided Executive Order 9066, also reversing the Hirabayashi case. The government passed the Civil Liberties Act in 1988, in which it apologized for the internment and paid reparations of $20,000 to each surviving detainee.

Johnson, Hiram (September 2, 1866–August 6, 1945)

Historians often regard Hiram Johnson as the leading western progressive of the early 20th century. He became famous in the 1900s for attacking the then dominant California political machine run by the *Southern Pacific Railroad [IV]*. In 1910 he successfully ran for the governor's office of California. His major proposal was to "kick the Southern Pacific out of politics," which became the mantra for his supporters. His first two years as governor saw a whirlwind of progressive-style reforms in the economy and education. His most important piece of legislation involved what was known as "cross-filing," which allowed an individual to run as a candidate for multiple political parties. Its stated purpose was to destroy the power of political parties. Its real purpose was to allow progressives to run on multiple tickets. Like many early 20th-century progressives, Johnson disliked non-Protestants and non-northwestern Europeans, and as governor he prevented Japanese from owning land through the 1913 sponsorship and eventual passage of the bigoted and nativist Alien Land Act.

He was so successful in getting his legislative agenda passed in California that Theodore *Roosevelt* remarked that the program was the "greatest advance ever made by a state for the benefit of its people." Johnson ran as Teddy Roosevelt's vice-presidential candidate for the Bull Moose Progressive Party in 1912. Dedicated and faithful to the progressive cause, Johnson campaigned vigorously, but Woodrow Wilson won the election.

As a U.S. senator, Johnson continued to advocate his progressive agenda. Most important, Johnson played a vital role in securing the controversial federal creation of Boulder (*Hoover*) *Dam* on the Colorado River. Johnson, an ardent isolationist, helped prevent America's entry into the League of Nations in 1920 and also Franklin Roosevelt's attempted war preparations prior to December 1941. Johnson served in the Senate until his death in 1945.

Johnson, Lyndon Baines (August 27, 1908– January 23, 1973)

Lyndon Baines Johnson was born in Johnson City, Texas, on August 27, 1908, and raised in poverty. After attending public schools, Johnson worked odd jobs before enrolling in Southwest Texas State Teachers College, where he temporarily dropped out due to lack of money. During that time he taught school at the southern Texas town of Cotulla, then returned to school to graduate. Like his father, he served in Congress, winning his first election in 1937, and when World War II broke out, Johnson served in the navy, where he earned a Silver Star.

The first of three U.S. presidents from the state of Texas since World War II (along with George H. W. Bush and George W. Bush), Lyndon Johnson used his ranch as a political prop. More at home in Washington, where as a senator he was one of the most effective legislators in history, Johnson never achieved acclaim as a president, although NASA's Johnson Space Center in Houston is named for him. *LBJ Library Photo by Frank Wolfe*

After six terms in Congress, Johnson won his first Senate seat in 1948, and just five years later he became the youngest minority leader in Senate history. When the Democrats won control of the Senate the next year, he became the majority leader. In the Senate Johnson gained a reputation as a masterful "log-roller," capable of getting legislation of either Democrats or Republicans passed. He hoped to become president in 1960 but was defeated for the Democratic Party nomination by John F. Kennedy. Although personally disliked by the Massachusetts senator, Johnson was tapped as the vice-presidential nominee for his sectional appeal and his ability to swing Texas to the northeastern presidential nominee.

After winning the election, Johnson was an active vice president, interested in civil rights issues, and a strong voice in the Kennedy inner circle. The assassination of John Kennedy in November 1963 elevated "LBJ" (as he was called) to the presidency. He was in Texas the day of the assassination and was sworn in on the airplane before it departed Dallas. Johnson inherited a rapidly deteriorating situation in Vietnam, which he hoped to keep, as he said, on the "back burner." Instead, Johnson hoped to advance his domestic agenda, which he termed the "Great Society." Renominated in 1964, Johnson ran against Arizona

Senator Barry *Goldwater*, whom he defeated in a landslide. Ironically, after warning in a national ad that Goldwater's election would lead to a nuclear war, Johnson found himself increasingly sucked into the undeclared war in Vietnam.

Benefitting from the Kennedy tax cut, which Johnson signed in February 1964, the economy under Johnson was thought strong enough to support both "guns and butter"—to fight the war in Vietnam and to pursue Johnson's "war on poverty." Johnson pursued his civil rights agenda with passage of the 1964 Civil Rights Act, which was opposed by southern Democrats in a record filibuster, marking his most important piece of domestic legislation. With a two-to-one margin of Democrats to Republicans in the Congress, Johnson encountered virtually no opposition to his Great Society programs.

The conflict in Vietnam had escalated steadily since the 1964 Gulf of Tonkin Resolution (approved 98-2 in the Senate), wherein Johnson had the full backing of Congress to send troops to Vietnam. American presence there rose from 16,000 in 1963 to more than 500,000 under Johnson. Yet even that number proved inadequate to address the Communist threat. By 1967 the Vietnam War dominated Johnson's attention. Along with his secretary of defense, Robert McNamara, Johnson took personal control of the war, to the point that he picked the bombing targets. Resistance to the war grew among the population in general, and opposition to Johnson appeared within the Democratic Party for the nomination in 1968. The economy had slowly deteriorated under the high costs of the war and the Great Society programs, and Johnson had responded by raising taxes, driving the economy down further. Bewildered by the vicious attacks on his policies and on him personally, Johnson, in a surprise announcement, declared that he would not run and, if elected, would not serve another term as president in 1968, paving the way for his vice president Hubert H. Humphrey from Minnesota. Humphrey, with the unpopular war dragging him down, lost to Californian Richard M. *Nixon*.

Lyndon Johnson and his wife, "Lady Bird" Johnson, retired to his ranch in Texas. Four years later, on January 22, 1973, he died from a heart attack. That year, the space center at Houston was named in his honor, as was the Lyndon Baines Johnson School of Public Affairs at the University of Texas in Austin.

Jordan, Barbara Charlene (February 21, 1936–January 17, 1996)

The first African American woman to enter the U.S. House of Representatives, Barbara Jordan worked as an administrative assistant to a judge in the Houston area before entering politics to run for a seat in the Texas House of Representatives. She lost that race, then another in 1964. In 1966 she ran for the state senate from the newly created 11th District in Houston, becoming the first black woman in that body since 1883. In 1972 Jordan ran for a U.S. House seat and became one of the first two African Americans in the Congress since Reconstruction. She served three terms, working for civil rights, minimum wage laws, and opposing the war in Vietnam.

Kaiser, Henry J. (May 9, 1882–August 24, 1967)

A man who lived almost four separate lives, Henry J. Kaiser was born in New York and opened a construction company as a young man. Kaiser's first industrial "life" involved the construction and fabrication of large public works. He developed a reputation as a master road builder and in 1931 headed the effort to build *Hoover Dam*. His companies also constructed Bonneville, Grand Coulee, Parker, and Shasta Dams, as well as the San Francisco–Oakland Bridge. During World War II he eclipsed even these feats in his second "life" as a shipbuilding marvel. Commissioned by President Franklin Roosevelt to build Liberty Ships, Kaiser opened several new shipyards in California, imported a huge new labor force to staff the yards, provided innovative prefabricated housing for some of his workers, and churned out ships at record levels.

Kaiser's shipbuilding feats almost defy imagination. His yards could construct a ship from scratch in 25 days after only a year into the war; and by 1944, Kaiser's yards set a world record by building the *Robert E. Peary* Liberty Ship in four and a half days. As much as any individual, Henry Kaiser helped win the war in the Atlantic against the German U-boats.

In his third "incarnation" Kaiser started an automobile company after the war. Although his company had rapidly rising sales every year and produced a reliable, sturdy car, even the wealthy Kaiser underestimated the capital demands of automaking, and his venture was unsuccessful. He then became interested in *Hawaii* and soon rebounded from his auto fiasco to develop real estate on the islands. Kaiser's reputation in other firms made him a natural public relations spokesman for Hawaii.

L'Amour, Louis (March 28, 1908–January 10, 1988)

Next to Zane *Grey*, Louis L'Amour may be the best known writer of western fiction. He lived a life of adventure, leaving school at age 15 to travel the world, and working a number of unrelated jobs, including a miner, elephant handler, and sailor. At one point, he also lived with Tibetan bandits and was stranded in the West Indies. During World War II he served as a tank commander in the U.S. Army, then after the war began to write western novels.

During his lifetime L'Amour produced more than 100 novels (some of which remain unpublished) that reached astonishing sales levels (230 million copies). He became not just one of the bestselling western writers of all time, but one of the bestselling overall authors ever. He published his first novel, *Hopalong Cassidy and the Riders of the High Rock* (1951) under the pen name of Tex Burns. With *Hondo* (1953), L'Amour reverted to his romantic name, and the book was made into a 1954 movie starring John *Wayne*. L'Amour dealt with the everyday life of *cowboys [IV]*, miners, Indians, cattlemen, explorers, and other western figures, all wrapped in furious action. L'Amour's women were tough, and despite their beauty, were able to stand up under the worst circumstances. People of all races and places in life could be presented by L'Amour in broad strokes that emphasized honor and nobility, or their opposite, criminal evil and immorality. His egalitarian approach to different groups meant that L'Amour did not offend even sensitive readers.

Critics ignored L'Amour until his following of avid readers was so large he could not be dismissed. Despite predictable plots and large chunks of western lore woven into the story, L'Amour's novels enthralled his audience. He knew the land and the history, and most of the time one could see L'Amour's own life-threatening experiences as the background for the action. Beginning in 1960 he introduced a recurring body of characters, the Sackett family, whose history was spread across 300 years and whose characters' stories intermingled with those of the Chantry and Talon families. Toward the end of his career, L'Amour began to write in other genres, and in 1989 published his autobiography, *The Education of a Wandering Man*.

Lange, Dorothea (May 25, 1895–October 11, 1965)

Dorthea Lange was born Dorothea Nutzhorn in Hoboken, New Jersey. Early in her life, she developed an empathy for the poor as she passed through the poorer sections of Hoboken on her way home from school. As a teen, she decided to become a photographer and studied as an apprentice in New York studios. At that time, she began to use her mother's maiden name, Lange, and embarked on a trip around the world, stopping in San Francisco. There she was robbed and stranded, putting her to work again in a photography studio.

Within a year, Lange had her own photo business and had met western artist Maynard Dixon. Photographing San Francisco's docks and low-rent districts, Lange published a classic Depression-era picture called *The White Angel Breadline* depicting a forlorn, grizzled man holding a cup. She received an offer to present a showing of her photography in 1934, attracting the attention of economist Paul Taylor, who championed the cause of the small farmer against "corporate agriculture." Lange provided the photographs for Taylor's studies, especially photos of immigrants, which received national attention. After Pearl Harbor she also photographed the Japanese American relocation to the internment camps. In addition to photographing much of the culture of San Francisco, Lange established the documentary photograph as a distinct art form.

Las Vegas

Although declared illegal in 1910, gambling in the state of Nevada was legalized in 1931 for the stated purpose of funding public schools. At the time, Nevada was the only state in the Union that permitted gambling. At first a handful of small casinos did a quiet business in the desert. Las Vegas was only slightly different from other towns with gambling venues. In 1941 the El Rancho Vegas Hotel-Casino was the first major casino on what would be called "the strip." Later, it was joined by the Last Frontier, the Thunderbird, and Club Bingo.

Five years later, a mobster named Benjamin "Bugsy" Siegel opened the Flamingo Hotel. While the other casinos all had a frontier theme, the Flamingo was a "carpet joint," as Siegel called it, emphasizing luxury over a western decor, and quickly several competitors opened with similar concepts: the Desert Inn, the Sahara, and the Sands. Each had a nightclub as well as a gambling area.

For the next 20 years Las Vegas and the state of Nevada waged a war to force the mob out of the casinos. Ultimately, however, the market overtook the mob. In 1967 eccentric millionaire Howard Hughes took up residence in the top floor of the Desert Inn. The attention he brought, plus an exposé by *Life* magazine, forced the mob to liquidate many of its holdings, and consistent pressure by the state gaming commission, along with competition from large, publicly funded corporations, finally pushed the mob out.

Steve Wynn, one of the new entrepreneurs responsible for the construction of the Mirage, exemplified the influence of Wall Street on the Vegas hotels. Downtown Vegas's "Glitter Gulch" was transformed into a landscaped, traffic-free Fremont Street Experience, complete with light shows. A number of new hotels were constructed as legalized gambling thrived, to the point that by the late 1990s, gaming revenues for Clark County (which includes Vegas and Laughlin) for the year 1997 exceeded $6 billion, or 87 percent of the state's total gaming revenues.

Seeking to expand beyond traditional gamblers, several hotels opened with a family theme, hoping to turn Vegas into the "*Disneyland* of the Desert." Virtual reality rides, several enclosed theme parks, and the world's highest roller coaster, as well as family-oriented theme hotels appealed to families looking for a vacation spot. But whether that strategy pays off remains uncertain. As of 1999 many of the hotels had quietly shifted back to luring traditional gamblers or couples without children. Shows no longer feature nudity as much as special effects, highlighted by the *Cirque du Soleil* circus troupe. Even the Hard Rock Cafe—the icon of the counterculture movement—had its own hotel and casino.

Lawrence Livermore National Laboratory

One of the world's best research laboratories, Lawrence Livermore National Laboratory was named for scientist Ernest O. Lawrence at Livermore, California. In 1952 Lawrence worked with Edward Teller to convince the

Atomic Energy Commission that a weapons development laboratory was needed to parallel the efforts of Los Alamos. Teller agreed to come to California if the lab focused on construction of the hydrogen bomb. Livermore Laboratory, as it was called, worked on innovative weapons technologies throughout the Cold War. By the 1980s the lab employed 8,000 scientists and other employees and had a budget of more than $1 billion. It became the leading lab for work on the Strategic Defense Initiative (SDI), which involves the use of X-rays from a nuclear laser that would destroy incoming missiles. The lab also emphasizes work in hydrogen fusion.

Lockheed Aircraft Company

A major western aircraft manufacturing firm, Lockheed Aircraft was synonymous with its highly innovative "skunk works" research facilities and its cutting edge high-speed aircraft, such as the SR-71 *Blackbird*. Formed in 1912 by two aircraft designers, Allen and Malcolm Loughead, as the Alco Hydro-Aeroplane Company, the firm flew a wooden seaplane over the San Francisco Bay in 1913. A few years later Allen Loughead formed a new company, Lockheed Aircraft in Hollywood, changing the name to be spelled like it sounded. Two years later a Lockheed *Vega*—a four-passenger monoplane—completed the first transcontinental flight. For a brief time, Lockheed came under the ownership of Detroit Aircraft, then was purchased back by private investors headed by Robert Gross.

By 1931 not only did Lockheed build revolutionary new fighter planes for the U.S. Army Air Force, but Lockheed aircraft were used by such notable pilots as Charles Lindbergh and Amelia Earhart to set records and chart new routes. Six years later, with Germany and Italy becoming more aggressive, Lockheed turned out its famous P-38 fighter. The company churned out fighter and transport planes during the war, then in 1947 produced the first American jet-powered experimental fighter.

During the Cold War Lockheed produced a variety of aircraft and weapons for military use, including the powerful C-130 *Hercules* transport, the secret U-2 spy plane, the navy's *Polaris* ballistic missile, and the F-104 *Starfighter*. In the 1960s and 1970s the company produced the *Trident* ballistic missile, the SR-71 *Blackbird*, and the F-16 *Fighting Falcon*. Many of these weapons came from the famous Skunk Works research facilities developed by Lockheed, which minimized "red tape" and rewarded team-work at unprecedented levels. In 1988 the Skunk Works turned out the famous F-117 *Stealth* fighter. The company also continued to build missiles, such as the army's *Pershing* missile, civilian-launch rockets, and conduct work on the space shuttle. In 1995 Lockheed merged with Georgia-based aeronautics company Martin-Marietta to form Lockheed-Martin.

London, Jack Griffith (January 12, 1876– November 22, 1916)

Author of the classic outdoor story, *The Call of the Wild* (1903), Jack London was born John Griffith Chaney in San Francisco and worked at a number of positions before going to Japan as a sailor. He had also become a militant socialist and joined a number of the protest marches on Washington, D.C., then headed for Alaska to participate in the capitalist enterprise of gold prospecting that he scorned. When he returned from Alaska, he began his writing career with short stories, published as *The Son of Wolf* in 1900. His masterpiece, *The Call of the Wild*, not only depicts life in the wilderness, but also man's interaction with animals and their natural—often vicious—struggles with each other. London battled alcoholism, which he wrote about in an autobiographical novel, *Martin Eden* (1909), and in *John Barleycorn* (1913). Alcoholism made his work erratic and uneven, and London's books were often cited by the Prohibition movement as examples of how alcohol could destroy lives. But they also depicted life in the wild, and often brutal, western frontiers.

Lone Wolf v. Hitchcock, 1903

A vital decision in the fight toward recognition of Indian persons as American citizens, the Supreme Court decision in *Lone Wolf v. Hitchcock* argued that Congress had complete control over Indian persons. In other words, Indian persons possessed no rights independent of what Congress bestowed upon them. The case originated with a controversy over an 1885 congressional law, the Major Crimes Act, which declared that Congress held all power over Indian tribal law. According to the ruling, Congress could "abrogate the provisions of an Indian treaty, though presumably such power will be exercised only when circumstances arise which will not only justify the government in disregarding the stipulations of the treaty, but may demand, in the interest of the country and the Indians themselves, that it should do so." Lone Wolf, a *Kiowa [IV]* Indian, had argued that the 1885 law as well as the various laws forcing allotment of communal land violated the letter and spirit of the 1867 Medicine Lodge Treaty. Some have called the Supreme Court ruling an Indian version of the 1857 *Dred Scott decision [III]*.

Los Alamos Nuclear Laboratory

In July 1943 the U.S. Army's Manhattan District in the Corps of Engineers, supervising the atomic bomb ("Manhattan") project, sought an isolated place in which to test the device. A bomb had become a possibility when Enrico Fermi demonstrated a nuclear reaction at the University of Chicago in 1942, and in September of that year, General Leslie Groves, who headed the Manhattan Project, acquired land near Los Alamos, New Mexico, to build the bomb. Robert J. Oppenheimer, a theoretical physicist, headed the team actually developing the bomb on site in New Mexico. The scientists were especially concerned with the detonation device known as the "lens," a device that used shaped conventional charges to implode subcritical plutonium into a subcritical ball of plutonium, instantly raising the plutonium to critical mass.

The test occurred at the "Trinity" test site 210 miles from Los Alamos on the Alamagordo test range on July 16, 1945. It was successful, meeting all expectations, and General Groves informed President Harry Truman that the bomb was ready. On August 6, 1945, the first of two atomic bombs was dropped on Japan, which had refused to surrender. Following the second atomic bombing—of Nagasaki on August 9—Japan surrendered.

Los Alamos continued to provide a home to the Los Alamos Nuclear Laboratory and was the subject of scandals involving national security in 1999. Several computer hard drives were discovered to be missing. The government charged a Los Alamos scientist, Wen Ho Lee, with leaking secret documents to the Communist Chinese. Eventually, however, the case eroded until Lee pleaded guilty to only one charge of mishandling classified information and was sentenced to time already served. Subsequent investigations did not determine who had stolen the materials either. If the investigations had identified culprits, no public announcement of any further progress in the case was made.

Los Angeles Dodgers/western sports expansion

One of the first professional sports franchises to move west was the Brooklyn Dodgers, who, in 1957, left New York for the West Coast. Despite winning several National League pennants and the World Series in 1955, the franchise played in a decrepit Ebbets Field. Owner Walter O'Malley urged the City of New York to provide a new stadium, but he also saw the potential offered by California, urging the New York Giants to move west as well. In the fall of 1957 the two teams announced they would move, giving the West its first major-league teams beyond St. Louis. Over the next few decades major league baseball added eight professional teams in the West, and other professional sports saw teams relocate west on a regular basis.

Lubbock and the sound of west Texas

As rock 'n' roll captured the American music scene in the 1950s, a southwestern outpost in the decade-long recording boom appeared in Clovis, New Mexico, near Lubbock, Texas. An independent producer named Norman Petty, using state-of-the-art recording equipment, offered an alternative studio for regional musicians who did not want to go to Memphis, New York, or Los Angeles. Roy Orbison, a teenager from Vernon, Texas, recorded his first hit in Petty's studio. Petty became well known for Buddy Knox and The Rhythm Orchids' song, "Party Doll," which he placed with a major label, even though the group never left Canyon, Texas.

Petty's greatest discovery was Charles Holly, a Lubbock singer who took the nickname "Buddy." After recording Holly's "That'll Be the Day" and placing it with Decca in 1957, Petty was part of an exceptional team that featured Buddy Holly and the Crickets. Together, they recorded "Peggy Sue," "Words of Love," "Oh Boy!" and other tunes. Holly died in a plane crash in

1959, and Petty went on to record a few other hits, including "Bottle of Wine" by Jimmy Gilmer in 1968. A distinctive sound had emerged from Lubbock and the Clovis, New Mexico, studio that continued well into the 1980s.

Lyndon B. Johnson Space Center

The Johnson Space Center in Houston has emerged as one of the most important installations of the National Aeronautics and Space Administration (NASA). Built in 1961, the Johnson Space Center's purpose is to direct the design and development of spacecraft and associated systems for human flight, selection and training of American astronauts, and planning and conducting the human flight missions. The center was famous for its "Mission Control," the brains of the NASA missions. Neil Armstrong sent his famous line "The Eagle has landed," to Mission Control in 1969, and since the 1970s, the center has been in charge of the space shuttle program.

MacDonald, Peter (December 16, 1925–)

Involved in the 1989 Window Rock riot, where two people died, Peter MacDonald was a *Navajo code talker* during World War II and became the leader of the Navajo Nation in 1974. A forceful proponent of Indian rights, MacDonald nevertheless became enmeshed in corruption and controversy and was sentenced to 14 years in prison in 1993 for the riot that ensued when he and his supporters tried to overthrow the tribal government that had replaced him. His sentence was commuted in the large number of "midnight commutations" by outgoing President Bill Clinton in 2001.

Mankiller, Wilma (November 18, 1945–)

Born in Tahlequah, Oklahoma, Wilma Mankiller is the first woman to serve as chief of the *Cherokee [III]* Nation. She is also the first woman chief of a large tribe. Trained in community service and planning as well as being a political activist in the 1960s and 1970s, Mankiller became vice chief in 1983. When the post of chief became vacant in 1985, she became chief according to the Cherokee constitution. The Cherokee people elected her chief in 1987, a post she kept until 1995, when she chose not to run again. She used her office to reclaim many Cherokee traditions through the Institute for Cherokee Literacy.

McMurtry, Larry (June 3, 1936–)

Born in Wichita Falls, Texas, Larry McMurtry wrote novels exploring the desolate past and often depressing present in the West. His first novel, *Horseman, Pass By,* was published in 1961, but his first renowned work, *The Last Picture Show* (1966), was made into a motion picture, as was *Terms of Endearment* (1975). His best known works, *Lonesome Dove* (1985), *Anything for Billy* (1988), and *Buffalo Girls* (1990), became a widely acclaimed television miniseries. *Texasville* (1987) was a sequel to *The Last Picture Show.* McMurtry's stories have a depressing tone, and in such works as *Lonesome Dove,* virtually every character ends the story worse than he or she started. Whether that is an accurate portrayal of the real West is left up to readers.

McPherson, Aimee Semple (October 9, 1890– September 27, 1944)

Born Aimee Elizabeth Kennedy in Ontario, Canada, on October 9, 1890, McPherson grew up around her mother's Salvation Army work. She began preaching as early as age 17, and the following year she married Pentecostal evangelist Robert J. Semple, whom she accompanied to China. Semple died two years later, and Aimee returned to the United States, where she married Harold McPherson. She entered full-time evangelism, emphasizing the Pentecostal doctrines of speaking in tongues and faith healing. By 1918 she had a large organization directed by her mother and headquartered in Los Angeles, where she built the Angelus Temple,

A modern-era Los Angeles–based evangelist—and one of the first nationally recognized female preachers—Aimee Semple McPherson held massive crusades in Los Angeles. McPherson founded a large Gospel church, but also staged her own mysterious "disappearance" in 1926. *Library of Congress*

which in 1923 was dedicated as the Church of the Foursquare Gospel. In 1921, she divorced Harold McPherson, but she kept her married name.

McPherson preached nightly in the temple to thousands of worshipers, her sermons broadcast by radio to millions of listeners. In 1926 McPherson disappeared for several weeks and claimed to have been kidnaped. The news media criticized McPherson harshly, investigating her finances, and her family filed numerous lawsuits against her. But her preaching continued unabated, and her Foursquare Gospel church grew to more than 400 branches with 22,000 members and is still in operation today.

Means, Russell (November 10, 1939–)

An Oglala and Yankton *Sioux [IV]*, Means was born in 1939 on the Pine Ridge Reservation in South Dakota. Means became the first national director of the activist American Indian Movement and in 1972 helped lead the violent takeover of the *Bureau of Indian Affairs [III]* in Washington, D.C. On February 27, 1973, he led the takeover of Wounded Knee, South Dakota, known as *Second Wounded Knee*. Federal marshals besieged the Indian protestors and exchanged gunfire until May 7, 1973. Means was arrested for his actions and spent more than a year in prison.

Continuing his pro-Indian activities Means founded the first all–American Indian radio station in 1980. On the world scene Means defended the Mosquito Indians of Nicaragua during the brutality and abuses of the communist Sandinista Regime in the 1980s. In 1987 and 1988 Means sought the nomination for the presidency on the United States Libertarian Party, but Congressman Ron Paul beat him for the third-party position. While not forsaking his activism, Means became a Hollywood actor in the 1990s, appearing in such movies as *The Last of the Mohicans* (1992) and *Natural Born Killers* (1994).

Microsoft

Along with fellow Harvard student Paul Allen, William H. (Bill) Gates founded Microsoft Corporation in 1975 to develop language and operator interface systems for computers. Gates (b. 1955) was born and raised in Seattle, the son of William Gates II, an attorney, and Mary Gates, a school teacher. At 13 Bill Gates was already programming computers and developing personal software. At Harvard he, Allen, and Microsoft president Steve Ballmer, all plunged into developing programming language called BASIC for the first personal computer, the MITS Altair.

Gates's break came when he dropped out of Harvard to establish Microsoft. He and Allen perceived that the personal computer would become a common device, found in every home and office. Allen flew to Albuquerque to demonstrate BASIC to the MITS Altair executives in 1975, then, in 1976, Microsoft developed its second language, FORTRAN. Shortly thereafter, Microsoft moved to Seattle, passing the $1 million in sales mark and creating a third language, COBOL. These remained complex, difficult-to-penetrate languages for a nonspecialist, and Gates increasingly realized that the key to personal computer usage lay in finding a language that any person could use with a minimum of training. To that end, in 1981, Microsoft unveiled MS-DOS, which became the first language truly accessible to an "average" professional.

A significant hurdle during this time was the diversity of computer systems. Microsoft had to develop a separate version of MS-DOS for each major computer manufacturer. In 1983 Gates's cofounder and partner, Paul Allen, resigned to pursue other interests. Even without Allen, though, the company marched toward introducing "user-friendly" operating systems, introducing MS Word, preparing a new graphical version of MS-DOS called "Windows," which debuted in 1985, offering a "point- and-click" operating system. All a user had to do was to move a "mouse" scrolling device to graphic images called "icons," and click on the image, which would initiate a computer function.

Microsoft's success triggered alarms in the U.S. Justice Department, which began investigating the company in 1990 for possible restraint of trade. Seven years later, the Justice Department filed a motion arguing that the company had linked sales of its Windows operating system to its Internet browser. A federal judge ruled that Microsoft was a monopoly and engaged in restraint of trade. Nevertheless, Microsoft remained, according to polls, one of the "most admired" companies in America.

military base closures in the West

No region of the country benefited economically from the Cold War more than the West. Dozens of military bases were created, others expanded in both personnel and operations, and Cold War–related industry boomed. But after 1988, when the Soviet Union's threat appeared to diminish, the federal government began closing military bases.

For years, legislators and researchers in think tanks had advocated streamlining the military base system, citing multiple (often redundant) bases in the same state. Several blue-ribbon panels had prepared "hit lists" in the 1980s for the purpose of getting local lawmakers off the hook. The base closure packages were presented en masse, so that legislators had to vote for it or against it, leaving them a way to explain to their constituencies that the base in their state was only one of many on the list. But clearly some states were hit harder than others. The Long Beach naval shipyard in California alone accounted for more than 4,000 armed forces jobs, plus thousands of civilian support positions.

To minimize the impact of the base closings on communities in the West, the Department of Defense Authorization Act of 1994, gave the secretary of defense the authority to transfer or lease military base land to state or private interests at favorable rates, or even free. Other federal acts established programs to help people forced out of their homes by base closures. In many cases, however, the expected economic decline did not occur. Of more immediate impact, in some cases, are the environmental hazards associated with abandoning military facilities that engaged in research or weapons testing. The Department of Defense allocated $25 billion to restore or clean up more than 10,000 sites closed across the nation.

Mix, Tom (January 6, 1880–October 12, 1940)

One of the most celebrated early cowboy actors, Thomas Hezikiah Mix was a star in the era of silent films. He represented one of several genuine cowboys who made a transition to playing cowboys on the screen. After working on ranches in Montana and chasing Pancho Villa with the American Army in Mexico, Mix started acting in 1910. Riding his horse "Tony," who also became famous, Mix made some 200 pictures, but he could not

The first cowboy film hero, Tom Mix paved the way for such superstars of the silver screen as John Wayne and Clint Eastwood. *Library of Congress*

make the transition to "talkies," and his popularity faded. His final years were spent directing a circus and Wild West show.

Monterey International Pop Festival

Conceived by Alan Pariser, the concert held on June 16, 17, and 18, 1967, at the Monterey County Fairgrounds in Monterey, California, took on legendary status. Among the most impressive acts, a young guitarist named Jimi Hendrix played with his teeth, set his guitar on fire, and otherwise astounded the audience with his virtuosity. The roster of performers was a "who's who" of the popular music world at the time, including Lou Rawls, the Mamas and the Papas, Big Brother and the Holding Company, the Byrds, the Who, Otis Redding, and the Grateful Dead.

Mount Rushmore

Located in the Black Hills of South Dakota, Mount Rushmore, as the official government web site states, "memorializes the birth, growth, preservation and development" of the United States. It was conceived by sculptor Gutzon

Borglum. A crew of 400 blasters and sculptors carved four 60-foot busts of American Presidents George Washington, Thomas Jefferson, Theodore Roosevelt, and Abraham Lincoln, chosen mainly to represent specific eras of growth as opposed to pure "greatness." Built between 1927 to 1941, the monument was dedicated in 1927 and placed under the National Park service in 1933. It remains an emotional and thrilling site.

National Aeronautics and Space Administration (NASA)

Formed in October 1958 out of the National Advisory Committee for Aeronautics (NACA), the National Aeronautics and Space Administration (NASA) had two major functions: conduct research in space launch, travel, and exploration and advance research in aeronautics. NASA has had an exceptional impact on the West in its short history. The *Lyndon Johnson Space Center*, which has served as "Mission Control" for the Apollo missions, has been the hub of much of NASA's launch activity, even though launches take place out of Florida.

National Cowboy Hall of Fame

The National Cowboy Hall of fame was founded in 1965 in Oklahoma City by Chester Reynolds, a Kansas City businessman, to commemorate the men and women who established western lore and legend. It features an American *Rodeo [IV]* Gallery, in which all of the inductees into the Rodeo Hall of Fame appear. There is also an art studio (Prix de West Award winners) that includes the works of Frederic *Remington* and Charles Russell, as well as sculptures by Albert Bierstadt. The American Cowboy Gallery celebrates real and film *cowboys [IV]*. In November 2000 the National Cowboy Hall of Fame changed its name to the National Cowboy and Western Heritage Museum.

National Rifle Association (NRA)

Founded in 1871 by Union Army veterans Colonel William C. Church and General George Wingate, who were dismayed at the poor marksmanship of their troops, the National Rifle Association (NRA) was formed to promote and encourage rifle shooting on a scientific basis. Former Union General Ambrose Burnside served as the organization's first president.

With support from the state of New York, the NRA developed a practice firing ground in 1872, commencing shooting matches soon thereafter. The organization soon moved to New Jersey. In 1903 the NRA began a program to establish rifle clubs at major colleges, universities, and military academies to encourage marksmanship among the nation's youth. By 2000 the NRA had more than 1 million youths enrolled in shooting events. Opposition to marksmanship training, however, intensified—indeed, it was that opposition that forced the NRA out of New York. In 1934 the NRA formed a "Legislative Affairs Division" to prepare and distribute facts related to firearms. The NRA also published *The American Rifleman* to keep members abreast of new firearms legislation.

When the nation needed firearms training on a large scale during World War II, however, it quickly turned to the NRA, which opened its ranges to the government. NRA members served as "home security" around domestic plants. In 1940 the NRA called on its members to help arm Great Britain, which resulted in more than 7,000 firearms sent to England for defense against a potential invasion by Germany.

After the war, the NRA emphasized hunting education and training, establishing hunter education courses in conjunction with the state fish and game departments across the nation. It also launched a second magazine for hunters, *The American Hunter*. Increasingly, despite its headquarters in New Jersey, the NRA became associated with the West and western interests, particularly hunting and self-defense.

Having addressed the education of hunters, the NRA turned to improving law enforcement training, becoming the only national trainer of law enforcement officers with a certification program in 1960, accounting in time for more than 10,000 NRA-certified police and security firearms instructors. The NRA also sponsored shooting matches for police, the National Police Shooting Championships, held in Jackson, Mississippi. By 2000 NRA instructors trained three-quarters of a million gun owners a year in handgun, shotgun, rifle, and muzzleloading firearms.

In the late 20th century guns (especially handguns and so-called "assault weapons") became the target of gun-control groups. Numerous gun-control laws, highlighted by the Brady Bill, imposed restrictions on gun owners (who called them severe impingements on the Second Amendment). Much of the debate involved the language of the Second Amendment, and whether the preamble referring to the necessity for a "well regulated militia" referred to state or individual gun ownership. The debate reached a critical juncture of sorts in 2002 with the *United States v. Emerson* decision in Texas, which ruled on local regulations prohibiting firearms. *Emerson* was important because it was the first case since the Great Depression, when the first true modern gun ordinances were enacted, to actually center on the "well regulated militia" phrase. In the ruling the United States Court of Appeals for the Fifth Circuit endorsed an "individual right" and not a "collective" right as claimed by gun control groups in their reading of the term "militia." The court did allow for "limited, narrowly tailored" regulations under "specific" cases that were not in violation of the general individual right to possess firearms. Although that final "regulation" phrase gave hope to gun control advocates, the NRA had won a substantial victory. Both sides promised to continue the battle over defining the Second Amendment, although following *Emerson*, in 2002, the NRA won a number of key liability suits in Chicago and Atlanta that had sought to implicate gun owners in metropolitan homicides.

Meanwhile, the NRA has grown to be a powerful lobbying group in Washington and has prominent political influence. The NRA's tenets are particularly appealing to westerners due to the frontier heritage of hunting, sport shooting, and self-defense. But the NRA has also made an important transformation from an enthusiasts' organization to a genuine political force.

Native American Church

Claiming to continue religious traditions more than 10,000 years old, the modern Native American Church began officially in Oklahoma in 1918. In 1944 it was reorganized as the Native American Church of the United States, and it adopted new amendments and practices in 1950 and 1955. The center of its worship is the sacramental act of ingesting some aspect of the *peyote* cactus. Within the "sacrament of peyotism," though, there are two liturgies, one following *Comanche [IV]* Chief Quanah *Parker [IV]*, the other following the Delaware/Caddo Indian Nishkuntu. Each developed separate practices at the end of the 19th century.

The purpose of the sacrament is to come into greater communion with God, learning some previously unrevealed truth. One local church states: "Where the Earth, the Sky, meet in Harmony, the physical and the Spiritual energy of each of us can enter into this area and find the Gifts of Being. The gifts vary from one to another. However, this variance is based on attunement to the Harmonic Convergence taking place. It is important that perceptual awareness be centered and open when you confront the apertures and emerse [sic] your 'self' at/in the Matrix. To receive the 'Gifts,' you have to personally participate with your energy into synergistic alignment."

Many of the local branches of the church practice a mixture of Christianity and native sacramentalism. During worship, singing, and prayer ceremonies, members often profess praise for Jesus Christ in a Charismatic style. But many native church branches prohibit Christian sentiment or practices, and Christian ministers are known as "road men."

The United States Congress recognized the native religion in 1978 with the passage of the Native American Religious Freedom Act. Nearly a quarter of a million persons representing 70 different Native American tribes belong to the Native American Church.

Navajo code talkers

During World War II, an engineer from Los Angeles, Philip Johnston, originated the idea of using native Indian speakers as code talkers. Navajo code talkers transmitted short messages over radios for marine units in the South Pacific using their language, which proved not only indecipherable to the Japanese, but also quick and efficient with an economy of words. As a boy, Johnston had lived at a mission for the *Navajos [I]*. Johnston and other linguists assigned Navajo words for modern military terms and weapons. Examples include "whale" for battleship, "chicken hawk" for a bomber, and "two stars" for a general. At the beginning of the experimental program, the marines limited the program to only 29 members. The marines also experimented with the speakers and the language modifications extensively before testing them in battle. The Navajos proved essential as forward observers in the United States strategy of island hopping in the Pacific Theater of the war. They served most famously at the bloody battle of Iwo Jima.

By the end of the war 420 Navajos had served. While other American Indian tribes participated as code talkers—including the Choctaws, Hopis, Ojibwas, Menominees, Creeks, and Comanches—the Navajos were the only tribe to maintain the integrity and security of their code during the war.

New Age movement in the West

The term "New Age" has become particularly associated with the modern West in part due to its popularity in California, but also because the openness of the West has provided several refuges for practitioners of cults. Idaho, New Mexico, Oregon, and other western states have seen the appearance of "New Age" centers and retreats.

The New Age nevertheless remains a nebulous term, loosely applied to many nontraditional religions, eastern philosophies, outright cults, and odd practices. Many date it from the late 1960s "Age of Aquarius" hippie movement, which was heavily linked to achieving a "higher consciousness" with the assistance of drugs. But many sought spiritual growth through meditation, Eastern religions, and even technology, including pyramids. While it is dangerous to generalize, one principle runs through most New Age thinking—that all world philosophies and religions are "alternate paths" to the goal of unification with a higher being and/or spiritual purpose. Most New Agers accept the Hindu concept of "reincarnation" (whereby a person's soul keeps returning for life on the earth in different physical forms, including animals), as well as in "karma," or the mystic sense of justice brought upon one's self.

Carlos Castaneda, an author of 10 New Age books, produced the "manifesto" of New Age works, *The Teaching of Don Juan* (1968), which traced the supernatural adventures of an Indian shaman with a boost from *peyote*. Many modern Indians have criticized the New Age's portrayal of all Indian practices as similar, or even of all Indians as shamans.

Other, more modern gurus have used the Internet as a recruitment tool and to facilitate the transmission of their message, including those involved in the multiple suicide pact by the "Heaven's Gate" cult, in which 38 men and women committed suicide over three successive days in March 1997. More broadly, many New Age groups tout the healing and regenerative power of pyramid shapes, some going so far as to sleep in pyramid-shaped structures.

Newlands Reclamation Act

The Newlands Reclamation Act, or simply the "Newlands Act" of June 17, 1902, set aside virtually the entire proceeds from the sales of public lands in 16 western states for the financing of irrigation projects. Named for Nevada congressman Francis Griffith Newlands, the Act empowered the Bureau of Reclamation to construct massive dams, such as *Hoover Dam* on the Colorado River and the Grand Coulee Dam on the Columbia River. Funds later went to develop the Central Arizona Project (thanks to extensive work by Arizona Senator Carl *Hayden*), which transferred water through 300 miles of canals from the Colorado River to the growing populations of Phoenix and Tucson.

Nixon, Richard Milhous, (January 9, 1913–April 22, 1994)

Easily one of the most controversial politicians in American history, Richard Milhous Nixon was born in Yorba Linda, California, on January 9, 1913, and raised by a Quaker family in Whittier, California. Nixon worked his way through Whittier College, then Duke Law School, graduating near the top of his class. When World War II broke out he briefly worked with the Office of Price Administration before joining the navy in 1942. He was a ground officer in the Pacific, attaining the rank of lieutenant commander.

Upon leaving the navy Nixon ran for a House seat against Jerry Voorhis. Nixon's claim that Voorhis was procommunist established his reputation as being tough on communism. Nixon served from January 1947 until 1951 in the House, where he achieved distinction with his investigation of Alger Hiss, who was convicted of perjury related to earlier espionage charges. In 1950 Nixon won a U.S. Senate seat against Helen Gehagan Douglas, wife of actor Melvyn Douglas. Gaining a reputation as a determined "Cold Warrior," Nixon was named by Dwight Eisenhower as his running mate in the presidential election. Accused by his opponents of having a "slush fund," Nixon responded with one of the early famous television speeches, the "Checkers Speech," in which he said the only gift he or his family had ever received was a cocker spaniel named Checkers.

A congressman from California, Richard Nixon was Dwight Eisenhower's vice president before losing a close race to John F. Kennedy for the presidency in 1960. Then, after losing the California governor's race, Nixon made a remarkable political resurrection to win the presidency in 1968. He was the first president of the United States from California. *Library of Congress*

As vice president, Nixon ran the government during several periods when President Eisenhower was ill, then ran for president himself in 1960 against Senator John F. Kennedy from Massachusetts. Kennedy won an excruciatingly close race—so close that Nixon was entitled to a recount but refused, saying he didn't want to damage the nation. Two years later he lost the California gubernatorial race to Pat Brown. Convinced the press had been hostile to him, Nixon angrily remarked to reporters, "You won't have Richard Nixon to kick around anymore." But with the unpopularity of the Democrats during the Vietnam War, Nixon again was on the public stage in 1968, when he won the presidency in a narrow contest against Vice President Hubert Humphrey.

Assuming the presidency at the peak of the Vietnam War, Nixon rapidly reduced U.S. commitments to Vietnam. When he took office, there were more than 550,000 U.S. service personnel in Vietnam, but by 1972 the number was around 50,000. Even so, civil protestors against the war tended to blame him for not withdrawing immediately.

In the 1972 presidential race Nixon easily won reelection over liberal Democrat George McGovern, but a group known as the "plumbers," formed to stop administration leaks, had been instructed by John Dean, Nixon's White House counsel, to break into the Watergate Building, where the Democratic National Committee Headquarters was located. Controversy remains about whether or not Nixon knew of this break-in, let alone ordered it. What is undeniable is that after the break-in, Nixon used his presidential powers to thwart the FBI's investigation, which constituted obstruction of justice. Under a congressional investigation, other improprieties and wrongdoing emerged, and articles of impeachment were drafted. Before Congress could vote on impeachment, leading Republicans estimated that Nixon would not survive an impeachment by the House or a vote in the Senate. A group of GOP leaders, including Barry *Goldwater* of Arizona, met with Nixon and convinced him to resign, which he did on August 9, 1974.

Following impeachment, although temporarily disgraced, Nixon gradually reclaimed a place in the public's esteem through his foreign policy accomplishments as president (opening Chinese American relations, improving relations with the U.S.S.R.) and through his authorship of several books on foreign policy. By 1986 even one of his most vociferous critics, *Newsweek* magazine, proclaimed him "rehabilitated." He was viewed as a senior statesman and adviser to presidents Carter, Reagan, and Bush. Richard Nixon died in San Clemente, California, on April 22, 1994.

Non-Partisan League

One of many agrarian revolts in the West between the Civil War and the Great Depression, the Non-Partisan League was the only truly—albeit temporarily—successful one in implementing a socialist program. It lasted in North Dakota from 1915 to 1922 and had lesser successes in neighboring states, and even very briefly at the national level.

Its founder and main organizer, Arthur C. Townley, originally of Minnesota, moved to the Golden Valley of North Dakota in 1907 and began farming. By 1912 he was nearly $80,000 in debt. Blaming his difficulties on "Eastern capitalists," Townley turned to the thriving Socialist Party. During the election year of 1912, the Socialist Party of North Dakota openly attacked the National Guard and supported the radically militant Wobblies. The party even denounced the Boy Scouts of America as the "hired Hessians of capitalism." When Socialist Party leader Eugene Debs visited the state in 1915, he happily noted that it was "red to the core" and had even taken over most of the platform and positions espoused by the Republican party.

In 1915 the state government failed to pass a constitutional amendment allowing a government-run and -owned grain elevator. When a group of angry farmers protested the state government's decision, a state congressman supposedly told them to "go home and slop the hogs," and Townley saw his Machiavellian moment. In February he met with prominent farmer and socialist Fred B. Wood, and they drew up a platform and a management plan for a new farmer's organization, the Non-Partisan League. The platform called for publicly owned flour mills, cold-storage units, packing houses, and grain elevators. It also proposed the creation of new agencies for safety and health inspections, as well as stringent regulations on banking laws. For its management program, the Non-Partisan League's ideals would be introduced to farmers on an individual basis in a missionizing style. A friend would introduce a spokesman for the league to another friend; the spokesman would take it from there.

The management tactic worked brilliantly, and the Non-Partisan League grew rapidly. By early 1916, only a year into its existence, the League claimed a membership of nearly 26,000. Its main newspaper, the *Fargo Nonpartisan Leader*, reached nearly 30,000. By the end of 1916, another 14,000 had joined the league. By 1918 the Socialist Party of North Dakota had disbanded, nearly all of its organizational staff and constituency having switched to the Non-Partisan League. To no one's surprise, the League dominated the 1916 elections. It won a majority of North Dakota house seats and all the state offices except one. The two sticking points were the governorship and the Senate, in which it only had one-third of the seats.

Under the direction of a nightly and semi-secretive caucus, to which the House members of the league pledged their complete allegiance, the Non-Partisan League introduced House Bill 44. This radical bill proposed the abolition of the North Dakota constitution. It was to be replaced by an adamantly socialist constitution. The Senate defeated it, thus thwarting many of the League's collectivist plans.

The very success of the Non-Partisan League ultimately undermined it. First, many of the members as well as opponents began to balk at the powerful nightly caucuses that controlled the members of the House. Second, many of the League-created state agencies failed due to mismanagement and corruption. Third, the movement fractured internally over the corruption and mismanagement. The split became so bad that sessions of Congress often ended in physical violence. Fourth, numerous North Dakotans filed lawsuits against the League, declaring many of its programs unconstitutional. Fifth, the Democrats and the Republicans joined together in 1920 to defeat the League at the polls. Finally, sixth, the federal government arrested Townley for attempting to prevent enlistments during World War I. His three-month imprisonment began at the end of 1921. When Townley stepped down as League president the following year, the organization fell apart.

O. J. Simpson trial

In 1994 when Nicole Brown Simpson and Ron Goldman were slashed to death in Brentwood, California, Nicole's former husband, Orenthal James ("O. J.") Simpson, the Hall of Fame former football player, emerged as the prime suspect. His criminal trial ran from September 26, 1994, to October 2, 1995, and was one of the most intensely covered events in history. Television was allowed gavel to gavel coverage of the trial, which ended in an acquittal on all counts. Nevertheless, the family of Ron Goldman sued Simpson for wrongful death damages in civil court, where a jury in 1997 unanimously found him guilty of all eight technical questions and ordered him to pay $8.5 million to the Goldman family.

O'Connor, Sandra Day (March 26, 1930–)

Sandra Day O'Connor was the first female justice appointed to the United States Supreme Court. When O'Connor graduated from law school, she could only find work with a private firm as a legal secretary. From 1965 to 1969 she was an assistant attorney general for the state of Arizona, and in 1974 she was elected a superior court judge of Maricopa County, Arizona. After her appointment to the Arizona Court of Appeals, President Ronald *Reagan* appointed O'Connor associate justice to the United States Supreme Court, where she developed a reputation as a centrist and "swing vote" on the Court. O'Conner opposes systematic affirmative action, supports *Roe v. Wade* on abortions, but leads the coalition to allow states to implement restrictions on abortions that don't constitute an "undue burden" on pregnant women.

O'Keeffe, Georgia (November 15, 1887–March 6, 1986)

Perhaps the most famous female western artist of the modern era, Georgia O'Keeffe was born in Wisconsin and studied art from an early age, culminating in her participation in the New York City Art Students League in 1907. After teaching in northern Texas for a while, painting the natural landscapes she saw in watercolors, O'Keeffe debuted her work in 1917 at the Alfred Stieglitz gallery, whereupon she and Stieglitz became lovers and eventually married. In 1929 O'Keeffe took a train trip to the Southwest, where she began her trademark work involving cow skulls and ram's heads, done in warm pastels and vibrant colors. Her western topics contrasted the death of the desert with the warm life of art.

Oklahoma City bombing

On April 19, 1995 a massive bomb exploded outside the Alfred P. Murrah Federal Building in downtown Oklahoma City, killing 169 and injuring many others. This marked the worst terrorist attack on U.S. soil, but it was conducted by Americans Timothy McVeigh and Terry Nichols. The conspirators claimed they acted out of outrage over the federal government's botched raid at *Waco*, Texas, on the Branch Davidians. Two days after the bombing, McVeigh, who had been arrested for driving without a license, was recognized as the bombing suspect and charged. His trial began in May 1997 and in June he was found guilty on all 11 counts of murder, conspiracy, and using a weapon of mass destruction. He was executed in June 2001.

Osage oil

The United States government resettled the Osage Indians, originally from Missouri, in Osage County in northeast Oklahoma in 1871. An area larger than Delaware, it is today widely known for its mineral abundance. Oil was first discovered there in 1897, and in the 1907 Indian allotment of tribal lands severally to individuals within the tribe, the Osage leaders/government wisely demanded the retaining of tribal property rights to the subsurface minerals. The wealth from the minerals found underground provided substantial material security for the Osages. That wealth peaked in the 1920s. By 1925, for example, each Osage earned $13,200 per year, roughly equivalent to $145,000 today, and by 1980, individual Osages were still receiving approximately $26,000 per year.

Oklahomans still laugh about the extravagant spending sprees of the Osage in the 1920s and 1930s—especially in the ownership of cars. While this naturally brought in unfathomable prosperity to the Osages, it also attracted the worst of humanity, a multitude of unscrupulous and conniving outsiders—various con men and whiskey traders—into the area. Consequently, the traditional Osage area became filled with lawlessness, corruption, and frequently violence. Bizarre murders involving love triangles, secret alliances, and deceit especially characterize the Osages in the 1920s. "Oil merely gave the Osages more money for white men to grab," Terry P. Wilson wrote. In terms of sheer numbers only a very few men actually defrauded the Osages. But white American culture at large viewed this exploitation as acceptable.

The Osmonds (Donny and Marie)

A true western musical family, the Osmonds of Utah featured several brothers who performed professionally and one who made music his career. In

1962 the Osmonds appeared on *The Andy Williams Show*, were signed to a five-year contract, and subsequently performed regularly in Las Vegas. During a 1973 performance at Caesar's Palace Donny and Marie Osmond sang together in a show for the first time. After cohosting the *Mike Douglas Show* in 1975 Donny and Marie were invited to start their own variety show, premiering in 1976 as *The Donny & Marie Show*. At this time Donny was 18 and Marie 16. They were the youngest hosts of a weekly prime-time television show in history. Coming from a Mormon family (see *Latter-day Saints [III]*), Donny and Marie presented a public face of Mormonism.

Owens Valley incident

On May 21, 1924, 40 outraged farmers in the California Owens Valley used dynamite to destroy a section of the Los Angeles aqueduct, which had diverted water from their farm lands for use in Los Angeles. Although the incident generated considerable sympathy for the farmers, as well as publicity, the resistance fell apart when Mark Watterson and Wilfred Watterson, who had led the resistance, were charged with various criminal counts relative to the Inyo County Bank they owned. By 1927 the state had closed their bank, although the Owens Valley Property Owners Protective Association won financial restitution for the farmers in the courts.

Parker, Fess (August 16, 1924–)

Few actors are indelibly identified with two separate characters—Sylvester Stallone as "Rocky" and as "Rambo" comes to mind—but Fess Parker, in the minds of many Americans, *is* both Davy *Crockett [III]* and Daniel *Boone [II]*. Parker began acting in 1951 and in 1954 got his big break when Walt Disney studios signed him to play Davy Crockett in a television series, which won him instant popularity. His coonskin cap was one of the best-selling clothing items of the 1950s, as was the song from the series, "The Ballad of Davy Crockett." After establishing the television persona of Davy Crockett, Parker played a second western legend, Daniel Boone, on a television series from 1964 to 1970. He later established a winery, and then a resort.

Perot, H. Ross (June 27, 1930–)

H. Ross Perot, born in Texarkana, Texas, in 1930, attended public schools and Texarkana Junior College. Early in life Perot worked odd jobs, including selling livestock, breaking horses, and marketing magazines and garden seeds. In 1949 he entered the U.S. Naval Academy, graduating in 1953, whereupon he went to sea as an officer on a destroyer and on an aircraft carrier. After his discharge from the navy, Perot and his wife, Margo Birmingham of Greensburg, Pennsylvania, settled in Dallas, Texas.

Perot worked for International Business Machines (IBM) as a salesman in the data processing division while Margot taught school. With a loan from his wife, Perot started Electronic Data Systems (EDS) in 1962. The company obtained numerous contracts from the state of Texas, then from automotive giant General Motors.

During the Vietnam War Perot's strong advocacy for rescuing U.S. prisoners of war (POWs) led the government to request that he intervene on behalf of the captives. He worked on the project for the next three years, receiving the Medal for Distinguished Public Service for his efforts. Several years later, when two EDS employees became hostages of the Iranian government, Perot masterminded a successful rescue mission led by Colonel Arthur "Bull" Simons, personally accompanying the party inside the Iranian prison to effect the rescue. This became the basis for the bestselling novel by Ken Follett, *On the Wings of Eagles*.

From 1979 to 1982 the Texas governor enlisted Perot's help in assessing better ways to eliminate the use of illegal drugs in the state and to address the deteriorating quality of public education in Texas. Exposure to these types of public issues gave Perot a wider experience than that of just a businessman, experience that he would tap into in 1992 and 1996 to run for president of the United States. Meanwhile, in 1984 he sold EDS to General Motors for $2.5 billion, which made Perot a member of the General Motors board and put him in conflict with GM chairman Roger Smith. In 1986 he resigned from the GM board, leaving EDS to the auto giant, and founded a new data company, Perot Systems.

His personal fortune and his dissatisfaction with the existing two political parties set the stage for Perot to run for president in 1992 as an independent with the new "Reform Party USA." Enlisting a former POW, retired Admiral James Stockdale, as his running mate, Perot failed to win a single electoral vote but did garner 17 percent of the popular vote—enough votes to shift the election from George Bush to Bill Clinton, who won with only 43 percent of the popular vote. Perot actively opposed Clinton's North American Free Trade Agreement (NAFTA), debating Vice President Al Gore on television, where most analysts agree he lost. Perot warned that the agreement would lead to the "pitter patter of little feet across the Rio Grande." Silent during the Clinton scandals of the 1990s, Perot resurfaced in 1996 to wrest the nomination of the Reform Party from former Colorado governor Richard Lamm, after pledging to support Lamm. In 1996 Perot received less than half the popular vote he won four years earlier, and by 2000, although he remained ostensibly in control of the Reform Party, he saw Patrick Buchanan win the nomination.

petroleum (oil) industry in the West

Since the 1860s petroleum extraction and crude oil production has occurred in California, but much of the rest of the West had little to do with the petroleum industry. However, after 1900 California's production, which had risen steadily, ranked fifth among all states, and discoveries of oil in Oklahoma, Louisiana, and Texas gradually increased the West's percentage of crude oil produced in the United States. The prevailing opinion that America's crude oil stocks would run out in the near future led the U.S. government to set up naval oil reserves at Elk Hills, California, and Teapot Dome, Wyoming, which became one of the scandals during the Harding administration under the supervision of interior secretary Albert B. *Fall.*

Yet not only did the oil industry stand on the threshhold of vast new discoveries in ground drilling, but in 1932 drilling for oil offshore started along the California coast, and five years later offshore drilling began in the Gulf of Mexico. Drillers steadily expanded the area within which they could operate, and in 1976 they passed the 1,000-foot marker in the Gulf of Mexico.

In 1901 oil was struck at Spindletop, Texas, leading to the formation of two major oil companies, Gulf Oil and Texaco. A third competitor, Sun Oil Company of Lima, Ohio, started to turn its attention to the Texas fields as well. Prairie Oil and Gas also had extensive leases in Kansas and Oklahoma. Soon, still other competitors joined these three, including Sinclair Oil, Phillips Petroleum, and Skelly. This domestic competition, along with foreign oil production, kept prices low and offset the powerful market position of Standard Oil.

The arrival of the automobile as a widely owned consumer item combined with the emergence of electrical power to redirect the petroleum industry toward oil as a fuel as opposed to a source of illumination. Refinable crude oil from Texas and California had a high gasoline content, with California's rich crude having high-octane hydrocarbons that gave it a high octane rating, making it more desirable for auto fuel.

Some regulation of the oil companies was exerted by state government corporation commissions, and, of course, oil was rationed during World Wars I and II. During the New Deal, the Roosevelt administration had sought to control drilling, limit production, and essentially fix prices. Many in the industry feared Roosevelt would in fact attempt to nationalize oil under the guise of "stabilizing prices."

Fortunately for consumers, discoveries of major oil reserves in the Middle East forced domestic producers to avoid monopolistic activities—and to continue exploration and drilling. In the mid-20th century, vast new fields were discovered in the Permian Basin of Texas, as well as in new locations in Oklahoma and California, plus New Mexico, Colorado, Montana, Wyoming, and other states. Offshore drilling continued as well, relying on gigantic offshore rigs to produce (by the 1990s) more than 20 percent of the total oil in the United States.

The petroleum industry proved vital to the economic growth of the West and the vitality of the United States. Oil production in Texas, Oklahoma, California, Colorado, and Alaska provided the lifeblood for the modern automobile age. *Library of Congress*

Environmentalists have opposed offshore drilling on two grounds. First, they argued that the rigs constituted an eyesore on some of the most beautiful beach areas in the world. The rigs in the Santa Barbara channel, for example, particularly offended them. Second, they expressed concern about accidental leaks or destruction of a rig during a storm. Here the record tends to support the oil companies, which can point to the nearly 4,000 oil and gas platforms in the Gulf of Mexico that have survived the worst hurricanes and storms on record and yet have lost fewer than 1,000 barrels spilled.

Environmentalists also fought, and lost, a battle over the Alaska Pipeline, a 787-mile pipeline constructed to take advantage of one of the largest discoveries of western oil at the North Slope of Alaska near Prudhoe Bay. Oil was first found there in 1968, and the ensuing "oil rush" resembled the Klondike Gold Rush of earlier days and brought windfall profits to the state of Alaska. An ice-free port of Valdez was available to get the oil out, but companies had to find a way to get the oil from the North Slope. Although environmentalists held up construction of the pipeline for several years, the 1973 energy crisis that hit the United States ended most of the opposition to the pipeline, which was completed in 1977. Ironically, one of the worst oil-related disasters involved neither offshore drilling nor the Alaska Pipeline but a ship disaster when the *Exxon Valdez* ran aground on March 24, 1989, spilling 232,000 barrels of crude oil into the bay. Cleanup cost Exxon Corporation $2 billion, plus another $1 billion in civil damages. As a result, the oil industry established the "Valdez Principles" in which it promised to recycle when possible, dispose of wastes promptly and efficiently, and minimize contributing to the "greenhouse effect."

The oil industry in the West suffered through an era of high regulation until the late 1970s, with President Ronald *Reagan*'s Economic Recovery Tax Act of 1981 again restoring production to high levels. Tax policies promoted a drilling boom, and in Oklahoma alone more than 100 deep wells were sunk in 1982. As new sources of oil appeared, prices fell, pushed downward by OPEC price cuts. This brought about a dramatic reduction in the number of domestic wells, and in 1993, domestic reserves hit a 15-year low, mainly related to regulatory costs associated with production. The Clinton administration also aided environmental groups in blocking further drilling. In late 2000 the dearth of domestic reserves and the cost of new environmental regulations had driven prices to a 10-year high, and California was affected by "rolling brownouts." Thus, the West's ability to supply Americans with a large part of their fuel needs was curtailed not by the inability of the land to provide resources, but by public policy.

peyote (mescaline)

A naturally occurring alkaloid from the flowering heads of the peyote cactus (*Lophophora williamsii*), mescaline produces hallucinations by affecting hormones produced by the adrenal glands. Indians in the Southwest and Mexico were known to use peyote in religious ceremonies, but peyote later became a favored drug of the "hippie" movement in the 1960s and early 1970s in the form of peyote "buttons." Author Carlos Castaneda wrote several books purportedly dealing with mystical powers endowed by mescaline, including *Teachings of Don Juan: A Yaqui Way of Knowledge* (1985). Although the drug is illegal, the *Native American Church* has been allowed to use it for ceremonial purposes.

Pinchot, Gifford (August 11, 1865–October 4, 1946)

The first national forestry "czar," Gifford Pinchot studied forestry at Yale and in Europe, then in 1892 returned to the United States to work on the estate of George W. Vanderbilt. Working on the National Forest Commission, he helped plan the use and preservation of American woodlands. He was appointed chief of the Division of Forestry in 1898; the name was later changed to the Bureau of Forestry, then to the Forestry Service. Although he held his position under Presidents McKinley, Roosevelt, and Taft, a dispute with Richard Ballinger, the secretary of the interior under Taft, led to Pinchot's dismissal in 1910.

He then worked with his former boss, Theodore *Roosevelt*, to found the Bull Moose Party in 1912 and taught at Yale. He was the state forester of Pennsylvania, then, from 1923 to 1927, and from 1931 to 1935, governor of Pennsylvania. In his term as governor, he managed to settle a coal strike in 1923. Considered an early voice in the conservation movement, Gifford Pinchot wrote several books on forestry and conservation before he died in New York on October 4, 1946.

Proposition 13

Started by California taxpayer advocate Howard Jarvis in the summer of 1978, Proposition 13 began the American "taxpayer revolt." California's high property taxes had threatened home ownership among the middle class in the state. Jarvis's initiative cut California's notoriously high property taxes one-third, then capped further increases. But with escalating home values, many California homeowners still found that they had to sell their houses in order to pay the taxes on their land. Unions, teachers' groups, lobbyists, and newspaper editors opposed the measure, but 60 percent of the California voters approved it. After Proposition 13 the state's economy grew at a rate 50 percent faster than the rest of the nation's, while the state budget grew more than 40 percent over the next 15 years. Based on Proposition 13, in 1981, the new president, Ronald *Reagan*, got Congress to approve a 25 percent across-the-board tax cut that spurred the largest economic boom since the "Roaring '20s."

RAND Corporation

The RAND Corporation, or Research and Development Corporation, emerged in 1946 from the U.S. Air Force's planning during the Cold War through the efforts of General "Hap" Arnold and aerospace scientist Theodore von Karman. For the first time in American military history, the nation had to plan for large-scale war in times of peace. This was especially important with the rise of nuclear weapons, which not only required production goals but required a new strategic war plan. Studies were needed to determine how foreign enemies, especially the Soviet Union, would respond to various limited conflicts if both sides possessed nuclear weapons. RAND was founded to provide the military with exactly those kinds of studies.

The air force provided up to one-third of RAND's original funding, but Arnold became concerned that RAND conclusions might be tainted by its association with the military. Consequently, RAND moved its facilities to *Douglas Aircraft* in 1948, then shortly thereafter, with a Ford grant, it left Douglas altogether for Santa Monica, California.

RAND's first study, *Preliminary Design of an Earth-Circling Spaceship* (1946), was followed by extensive research on nuclear war, especially "game theory," developed by 300-pound pool shark and *Sports Illustrated* writer, John Williams, and mathematician, John von Neumann. Applying a concept called "the prisoner's dilemma," which hypothesized that two guilty prisoners, kept in separate rooms, who were the only evidence against each other, had a dilemma: if either spoke, one would go to jail, but if neither spoke, both went free. Would one speak first? Von Neumann and Williams concluded that the best nuclear strategy would be one that would exact such a cost on an attacker that neither power would strike first. This concept, "MAD," for Mutual Assured Destruction, reflected the total absence of defense against nuclear weapons.

RAND would go on to generate other important studies under Bernard Brodie and tap the genius of Hungarian-born physicist and "father of the H-bomb," Edward Teller, on nuclear strategy. Eventually, RAND expanded its studies into space flight, antimissile defenses, trade policy, deficits, and other military and economic issues.

Rankin, Jeanette Pickering (June 11, 1880– May 18, 1983)

Born near Missoula, Montana, Jeannette Pickering Rankin became involved in the movement for women's suffrage. In 1911 she began lobbying the Montana state legislature to give women the vote, which became law in 1914. She ran as a Republican for Congress in 1916, becoming the first female representative on April 2, 1917. Rankin opposed the U.S. entry in World War I and was defeated in her bid for the Senate in 1918, but in 1940 she again ran for Congress and won.

Ray, Dixie Lee (September 3, 1914–January 3, 1994)

The first woman appointed to a full term on the U.S. Atomic Energy Commission and the second woman governor in the United States elected on her own, Dixie Lee Ray was a scientist who published several research papers on marine organisms. A consultant to the National Science Foundation, in 1963 she was appointed director of the Pacific Science Center in Seattle. In 1969 Ray served on President Nixon's task force on oceanography, and in 1972 the president named her to head the Atomic Energy Commission, the first woman to do so. In 1975 she became the second woman to win a governorship on her own when she was elected governor of Washington. Losing her bid for reelection in 1980, she then authored two books critical of the environmental movement that she had shaped: *Trashing the Planet* and *Environmental Overkill*.

Rayburn, Samuel ("Sam") Taliaferro (January 6, 1882–November 16, 1961)

"Sam" Rayburn was elected to the Texas legislature in 1906 and in 1911 was chosen as the Speaker of the Texas House. The following year, he was elected to the U.S. House of Representatives, beginning a remarkable career of 24 consecutive elections to that body from the Fourth District of Texas. During the Great Depression, he served on the Committee on Interstate and Foreign Commerce, during which time he coauthored the Rural Electrification Act. In 1937 he was elected Speaker of the House of Representatives.

Reagan, Ronald Wilson (February 6, 1911–)

Ronald Reagan, like Lyndon *Johnson* before him, westernized the White House. Unlike Richard *Nixon*, also a Californian, Reagan brought a truly western ideology to Washington, emphasizing low taxes, limited government, and a strong national defense. Called "the Great Communicator" for his ability to go over the media elites with his messages aimed directly at the American public, Reagan confounded his critics and implemented important national policies.

Born in Tampico, Illinois, in February 1911, Reagan attended Eureka College, then took a job as a sports announcer in Des Moines, Iowa. Politically, Reagan supported Franklin Roosevelt and was a registered Democrat. Roosevelt's compassion for the poor and helpless appealed to Reagan.

After moving to California in 1937, Regan embarked on an acting career, playing his most famous role as the Notre Dame coach George Gipp in *Knute Rockne, All American* (1940). He married actress Jane Wyman in 1940. From 1947 to 1952 Reagan was president of the Screen Actors' Guild, giving him experience in a union, but also drawing attention for his success in reducing the influence of the Communist Party in the guild. His attacks on some left-wing actors won Reagan praise from conservatives but became a point of contention with his wife, who divorced him in 1949.

It was through his work in the Screen Actors' Guild that Reagan met Nancy Davis, who had been falsely associated with Communist causes. Reagan had the guild look into her background and cleared her name. The two were married in 1952 and remained married thereafter.

Reagan's film career stagnated, but an appearance as an announcer in a series sponsored by General Electric led the company to hire him as a spokesman. This gave Reagan insight into the business side of the American economy, although he spent much time speaking to employees on shop floors at some 135 GE plants. He perfected his communications skills and built a substantial following. Increasingly, Reagan criticized the growing power of the federal government. By the late 1950s, as he would later say, he did not leave the Democratic Party—it left him. He supported the campaign of Arizonian Barry *Goldwater* for president and delivered a memorable speech on Goldwater's behalf to the Republican convention in 1964. Even in Goldwater's defeat, Reagan gained supporters, who urged him to run for governor of California.

The first western president who identified more with the West than Washington, Ronald Reagan was at home in a business suit, actor's makeup, or a cowboy hat. As the 40th president of the United States, Reagan played a critical role in winning the Cold War but also presided over a rapidly growing economy that especially benefited the western "Sun Belt" regions.
Courtesy Ronald Reagan Library

He won the governorship in 1966 on themes of opposition to big government, low taxes, and attacking welfare. But no one could accuse him of being a typical "country club Republican," and his message appealed to large numbers of people, enough to reelect him in 1970. At times Reagan's sharp wit and ability to get to a point were viewed by outsiders as ignorance: when faced with appeals for more money for university libraries to buy books, Reagan quipped, "Well, have they read the ones that they already have?" Yet comments such as these cut to the nub of the issues that most politicians preferred to "talk around," and they won Reagan immense respect from the public. He came across as honest, amiable, and possessing of common sense.

Taking his themes to the national stage, Reagan ran for the Republican nomination in 1976 in the wake of the Watergate scandal. More conservative than Nixon but more likeable than the incumbent president, Gerald Ford, Reagan nevertheless had not yet "paid his dues" nationally and could not oust Ford. A number of policy disasters by Carter opened the door for an effective challenge by the Californian. He ran again in 1980.

Reagan ran on three simple precepts: taxes were too high, government was too big, and the military was too weak. But he won largely on the basis of his ability to use Carter's own campaign words against the president, asking "Are you better off now than you were four years ago?" Shortly after he was elected president, bringing with him the first GOP Senate in a number of years, Reagan pushed through the first increment of a tax cut that began the longest period of economic expansion in history to that point. In March 1981 he survived an assassination attempt and in his Reaganesque way said of the doctors who operated on him, "I hope they're Republicans!" Faced with an air traffic controllers' strike, Reagan promptly fired the federal workers, sending a message that the union intimidation of the government would not be tolerated.

After a horrific terrorist bombing of U.S. peacekeeping troops in Lebanon, Reagan refrained from using American military forces except where the outcome was clear (Grenada) or where the threat demanded a response (Libya, 1986, after a terrorist bombing directed at U.S. troops that was linked to the Libyans). The exception remained the Soviet Union, where Reagan spared no expense to keep the pressure on the crumbling Communist state. He initiated the "Reagan Doctrine," which said that the United States would actively support populations under Communist rule who wanted to overthrow their dictatorial regimes, and he quietly sent antiaircraft missiles to freedom fighters in Afganistan. But his most effective efforts toward winning the Cold War came with his 1981–1982 military buildup, which funded new submarines, bombers, and missiles; in the 1983 "Star Wars" (Strategic Defense Initiative) program to defend against ballistic missiles; and in the 1986 deployment of intermediate-range nuclear missiles in Western Europe after a Soviet deployment of short-range missiles intended to shatter NATO. Taken together, these actions—continued by Reagan's Texan successor, George H. W. *Bush*, helped end the Cold War when the U.S.S.R. collapsed.

The nation's economy was able to subsidize these efforts because of Reagan's tax plans, which caused government revenues to grow by more than 50 percent in his eight years. Inflation fell at the hands of the Federal Reserve Chairman Paul Volcker, and at one point in the mid-1980s the United States had an inflation rate of zero, with unemployment rates of around 4 percent—a situation that confounded economists, who claimed it was impossible. Reagan instinctively understood that if people had more money, they

IN THEIR OWN
Words

Ronald Reagan's Radio Broadcast about Land Use

In 1974 California Governor Ronald Reagan—about to leave office—agreed to provide five-minute radio speeches, five days a week, to be syndicated nationally. From 1975 to 1979, Reagan, who was an aspiring presidential candidate, had a forum to express his views on a wide range of topics. In the 1990s researchers discovered boxes of handwritten drafts of these speeches, which put to rest the notion often touted by Reagan's opponents that he was intellectually shallow and merely read note cards. This February 27, 1975, speech dealt with western land use and planning.

The [crossed out] A majority of us are somewhere in an environmental middle between missionaries [crossed out] those who'd pave over everything in the name of progress and those who wouldn't let us build a house unless it looked like a bird nest.

People are ecology too and most of us are looking for answers that will preserve nature to the greatest extent possible consistent with the need to have places to [crossed out] where we can work & live.

The Fed. govt. pushes nationwide land planning which is the greatest threat in 200 yrs. To our traditional right to own property. Cong. debates a bill which if passed would destroy the right of counties & towns to have local zoning ordinances. And all of this is done in the name of environmentalism.

But what happens to freedom? What happens to your right to purchase or homestead a piece of land and make it bear fruit if an agency in Wash. can tell . . . YOU exactly what you [crossed out] YOU can or can't do with . . . YOUR land . . .

Is it oversimplification to suggest we don't need restrictive laws or govt. land planning but simply the law of supply & demand operating in the free mkt. [?] . . . . In some of our more scenic states the [crossed out] govt. ownership is as much as 90% of the total state. . . . If more is needed, we should do collectively exactly what we do individually—go buy it. What we must not do is give to ourselves collectively in the name of govt. rights we do not posess [sic] as individuals.

—Source: Kiron K. Skinner, Annelise Anderson, Martin Anderson, eds., *Reagan: In His Own Hand: The Writings of Ronald Reagan that Reveal His Revolutionary Vision for America* (New York: Free Press, 2001), 338–340.

would buy more, save more, and invest more. Criticized for running up high deficits, Reagan's policies in fact had deficits only slightly higher than those of John Kennedy and the debt levels of the United States as a share of GNP were lower than under Eisenhower, Truman, or, of course, Roosevelt.

Reagan was unsuccessful in two other priorities, limiting the number of abortions by curtailing *Roe v. Wade* and in reducing the size of the federal government. In large part this lack of success was due to the fact that despite holding the Senate from 1980 to 1986, the GOP never held the House in Reagan's eight years, then lost the Senate after Reagan's reelection. After endorsing George Bush as his successor, Reagan, urging the party to "win one for the Gipper," left the public stage in 1988. He made some speaking engagements in the next few years, but in 1994, in a public letter to the American people, he announced he had Alzheimer's disease, and his health continued to deteriorate. Nevertheless, more than Johnson, Nixon, or George H. W. Bush, Ronald Reagan was the quintessential western president of the 20th century.

Remington, Frederic, (October 4, 1861– December 26, 1909)

The premier western artist, sculptor, and illustrator, Frederic Sackrider Remington was born in Canton, New York. His father, Pierre, was a newspaper editor who provided young Frederic with enough money to attend Yale University, where he excelled in football. After Pierre's death, the inheritance allowed Remington to engage in some unprofitable ranching enterprises in Kansas. The ranch did not succeed, and when Remington sold it, he joined other partners in a saloon venture, where he was swindled out of most of his remaining money. Yet even at that time, he had already published his first sketch of a *cowboy [IV]* in *Harper's* magazine. After traveling throughout the Southwest in 1885–1886, Remington, having lost all his money but having a bulging portfolio of western drawings, decided on a career in art.

He moved to Brooklyn and his illustrations immediately became popular with eastern magazines. Seeking to improve and expand his talent, Remington enrolled in watercolor art courses at the Art Students League, immediately gaining such a grasp of the work that his illustrations were exhibited in 1887 at the National Academy of Design. These pieces drew the attention of Theodore *Roosevelt*, who requested the artist collaborate with him for an article on western life for *Century Magazine*. By that time, major magazines commissioned Remington to tour the West and produce illustrations regularly, many of which he used as the basis for future watercolors or other art. Close contact with the publishers also gave him entry into the world of book illustration, and he supplied art for Elizabeth Bacon Custer's *Tenting on the Plains* (1887) and Theodore Roosevelt's *Ranch Life and the Hunting Trail* (1888). To all this, he added an oil painting skill that made its debut in 1889 with *A Dash for Timber*.

His paintings now sold for up to $5,000 each, and his skill led the National Academy of Design to elect him as an associate member. Remington continued to scour the West, especially Indian lands, searching for new subjects, sketching the Blackfeet Indians and traveling to the Pine Ridge Agency to watch the **Ghost Dance [IV]** in 1891. He traveled to Russia and North Africa in 1892, expressing the energy and violence of North African Bedouin horsemen and Don Cossacks with the same broad heroic and inspiring strokes that characterized his cowboy, soldier, and Indian subjects in the American West.

Although he accompanied U.S. forces in the Spanish-American War and observed the charge of Roosevelt's Rough Riders up San Juan Hill, Remington spent much of the conflict aboard naval vessels, then returned to his studios. He had already begun working with bronze casting of horsemen. In 1895 his first sculpture, *The Bronco Buster*, proved he had mastered that skill as

The most famous western artist of all, Frederic Remington was one of many to depict the Indian wars. This painting, "The Last Stand," could be George Armstrong Custer's Seventh Cavalry at the Battle of the Little Bighorn or could be any other outnumbered unit, dismounted and fighting for their lives. *Library of Congress*

well, turning out 25 bronze sculptures in his life. Remington also engaged in writing a number of illustrated short stories—"Pony Tracks" (1895), "Crooked Trails" (1898), and "Men With the Bark On" (1900)—culminating in a western novel, *John Ermine of the Yellowstone* (1902), and even wrote a humorous novel about Indians, *The Way of the Indian* (1906).

But Frederic Remington remained best known for his art, whether paintings or sculpture. Unlike some other western painters, such as Albert Bierstadt or Thomas *Moran [IV]*, Remington always made people (mostly men) and animals the focus of his work. The West showed its rugged and violent character through the activities of its subjects, not through its majestic scenery. Like Charles *Russell*, he attended to every detail. Frederic Remington died on December 26, 1909, when complications set in after an appendectomy, having produced 2,700 paintings, of which more than 700 specifically dealt with men on horseback.

Roberts, Monty (May 14, 1935–)

One of the most acclaimed "broncobusters" or horse trainers in the West, Monty Roberts learned to ride well and early, becoming a child stunt rider and doubling for actors like Roddy McDowell in *My Friend Flicka* and even Elizabeth Taylor in *National Velvet*. By his teen years, Roberts toured the *rodeo [IV]* circuit, riding bulls and horses and earning a reputation as a first-rate equine handler. He had trapped *mustangs [III]* in the Nevada desert and rejected his father's more forceful "breaking" methods in favor of using a horse's own body language to train the animal. Roberts could tame a horse in minutes with a method called "join-up." His autobiography, *The Man Who Listens to Horses,* became a bestseller in the 1990s.

Rodney King and the Los Angeles riots of 1992

In March 1991 four white Los Angeles police officers chased a suspect fleeing at high speeds in a car, apprehending him. In the process of arresting the black driver, Rodney Glen King, the officers beat him repeatedly with nightsticks. The event was captured on videotape by a local resident and the tape given to a television station. Two weeks later, the officers were charged with felonious assault related to the beating and were tried in Simi

Valley, where the four were acquitted of most of the charges and a mistrial declared on one count of excessive force against one officer. Upon learning of the verdicts, the city of Los Angeles erupted in riots. By the time the rioting and looting were over, 42 people were dead and 700 buildings were destroyed by fire in the worst violence since the 1965 *Watts riots*.

The U.S. Justice Department filed civil rights charges against the officers, two of whom were convicted in April 1993. Both officers were sentenced to 30 months in prison and were released after serving 24 months. Rodney King filed a civil suit against the city of Los Angeles, winning $3.8 million in damages for medical costs, loss of work, and pain and suffering. Subsequently King was arrested again. The Los Angeles Police Department underwent a thorough internal study related to its use of force, alleged racism in the department, and corruption. Controversial chief Daryl Gates was replaced by Willie Williams, but the department continued to be steeped in racial controversy with the *O. J. Simpson trial* in 1996.

Rogers, Roy (November 5, 1911–July 6, 1998)

Born Leonard Frank Sly in Ohio, Roy Rogers started singing as a child. In California he began to sing country music in local clubs with a band called the Rocky Mountaineers. In 1934 he formed the Sons of the Pioneers, which was signed by Decca Records. When western star Gene *Autry* had a contract dispute with Republic Pictures, Rogers replaced him in a movie called *Under Western Stars*. By 1943 he became the top cowboy actor in the nation, starring in almost 50 western films with his horse Trigger. He married Dale Evans, his costar, in 1947, and the two had a successful television show from 1951 to 1957, building an empire of Roy Rogers comic books and merchandise. A dedicated Christian, Rogers toured with the Billy Graham crusades and appeared on behalf of Campus Crusade for Christ. He also loaned his name to the Willard Marriott Roy Rogers Roast Beef chain.

Rogers, William Penn Adair ("Will") (November 4, 1879–August 15, 1935)

Will Rogers was one of America's best-loved entertainers and perhaps the first truly western comedian. Born in Cherokee Territory, Oklahoma, William Penn Adair Rogers grew up on a ranch and became adept at rope tricks that earned him a spot in Wild West shows. While performing at Madison Square Garden, he came to the attention of media critics, and he sought employment in vaudeville, where he worked as a stand-up comic. Developing an arsenal of pithy one-liners ("I never met a man I didn't like," "Everyone is ignorant, only on different subjects," "Even if you're on the right track, you'll get run over if you just sit there"), Rogers was offered a part in a 1912 Broadway show, *The Wall Street Girl*. There he twirled his rope and spun homilies in the intermissions. Producer Flo Ziegfeld hired Rogers for the 1915 show, *Midnight Frolic*.

Rogers honed a clever, sarcastic humor about daily life, politicians, peoples' weaknesses (including his own), and Hollywood. Even while poking fun at Hollywood ("There is only one thing that can kill the movies, and that is education"), Rogers became a feature film star, acting in *Laughing Bill Hyde* (1918) and his first "talkie," *They Had to See Paris* (1929). He also made *Connecticut Yankee* (1931) and even produced some of his own silent movies. His most famous film was arguably *State Fair* (1933). Rogers regularly wrote newspaper columns, books, and articles and was a sought-after dinner speaker. Unlike many motion picture stars, he also had success on radio, capturing audiences with his western insights tempered by an obvious morality. "Rumor travels faster," he observed, "but it don't stay put as long as the truth," and "Everything is funny, as long as it is happening to someone else."

Although he remained generally nonpartisan he supported Franklin Roosevelt's New Deal in the Great Depression. Rogers died in a plane crash near Point Barrow, Alaska, in 1935, and later that year his last two films, *Steamboat 'Round the Bend* and *In Old Kentucky* were released.

Roosevelt, Theodore (October 27, 1858– January 6, 1919)

Although Theodore "Teddy" Roosevelt grew up in Oyster Bay, New York, and practiced politics in New York City or Washington, D.C., for much of his life, he nevertheless is viewed as a western president in many quarters. His conservation efforts, his first-hand experience at ranching, and his brief but successful leadership of the "Rough Riders" made this New Yorker seem perfectly at home on the range.

Roosevelt was born to a wealthy family, attended Harvard, then pursued a number of interests, including law, writing, and history. Between publishing his books *The Naval War of 1812* (1882) and *The Winning of the West* (1889–1896), Roosevelt went west in 1884 to start ranching. He even told his friends that he intended to stay there permanently. He made a name for himself in the Dakotas after standing up to a local bully in Mingusville (Roosevelt boxed for the Harvard boxing team) and taking part in an 1886 Montana hunting expedition.

Although an easterner by birth, Theodore Roosevelt identified with the rugged outdoors from his time in the Dakotas and his frequent hunting trips. After leading the Rough Riders in the Spanish-American War, Roosevelt became the first American president to actively address conservation issues. *Public Domain*

Despite his original declarations, within two years he was back in New York City, running for mayor. Even so, the West and its natural beauty impressed Roosevelt greatly. Over the next two decades he spent most of his working hours in big cities and in offices, but he never lost his enthusiasm for hunting, going so far as to publish a book on hunting in 1897. Roosevelt served as New York City police commissioner, and then as United States assistant secretary of the navy. While he was in that position, the Spanish-American War broke out, and Roosevelt resigned to form the Rough Riders, a volunteer cavalry regiment of men from western states and territories. The Rough Riders were involved in one of the more famous land actions of a substantially ocean-based war, the "Charge up San Juan Hill." This event, captured in paintings and myth, further enhanced Roosevelt's image as a no-nonsense, rugged hero, which he played upon to gain the governorship of New York.

In 1900 electors made Roosevelt the vice-presidential nominee on the ticket with President William McKinley, and when an assassin's bullet felled McKinley in 1901, Roosevelt stepped into the office. He facilitated the acquisition of a zone to build a canal across Panama and won the Nobel Peace Prize for his efforts in securing the Treaty of Portsmouth ending the Russo-Japanese War in 1905.

Although Roosevelt had a reputation as a "trust buster" who broke up many of the big conglomerates, his main influence on the West came in his ideas and policies related to conservation. Along with Gifford *Pinchot*, the head of the Forest Service, Roosevelt pushed an agenda of reclamation and preservation of natural resources. He supported the Newlands Reclamation Act of 1902 and established a Public Lands Commission in 1903 to examine the policies of selling public lands. Roosevelt sought to preserve the lands specifically for tourism and hunting. The conservation and land policies reflected the rugged individualism that Roosevelt himself possessed.

In 1908, after announcing he would not seek reelection, Roosevelt named William Howard Taft as his preferred successor. Taft won but then disappointed Roosevelt in a number of areas. By 1912 Roosevelt decided he needed to challenge Taft by creating a new, third party, the Progressive (or "Bull Moose") Party. Roosevelt indeed denied the presidency to Taft, but only by splitting the Republican vote and handing the election to Woodrow Wilson. Teddy Roosevelt died in New York in 1919.

The Rose Bowl

On January 1, 1890, the Valley Hunt Club of Pasadena, California, hosted the "Festival of the Flowers." Residents decorated buggies and, later, automobiles with flowers for a parade. In 1897 the Pasadena Tournament of Roses Association took over the festival, and five years later the University of Michigan and Stanford University capped the festivities with a football game held at Tournament Park. The Rose Bowl football stadium, completed in 1922, became the home for this annual game, which pitted the champion of the Pacific Coast Conference against any selected winning eastern team. In 1947 the Big Ten Football Conference agreed to match its champion against the Pacific Coast champion in a Rose Bowl game held on New Year's Day, which is always preceded by the Tournament of Roses Parade. This Pasadena parade featured 60 intricately and elaborately decorated floats—with only flowers allowed as the element of decoration, all representing a theme of the year—interspersed with marching bands, horses and riders, and other participants.

Roswell crash and UFOs

In June 1947 New Mexico rancher "Mac" Brazel discovered debris in one of his pastures. Brazel loaded the debris in his truck and took it to the sheriff in Roswell, New Mexico, who promptly called the U.S. Army Air Force base at Roswell. The Air Force had been testing high-altitude balloons, both for weather projections and in dropping human-looking dummies to test parachutes. Confusion arose when a public relations officer put out a press release in which he used the unfortunate term "flying disk." Indeed a part of the balloon apparatus contained a small, shiny disk. In conjunction with several unidentified flying objects sighted in Idaho earlier in June, the recovery of a "flying saucer," based on the earlier "disk" reference, led to a flurry of public interest. Although the Air Force put out clarifying remarks, the balloon project was classified, and the military could only release limited information.

By the 1980s the "UFO crash at Roswell" had attracted large numbers of UFO "researchers," convinced that the government not only was "covering up" the existence of UFOs but had actually recovered alien bodies from the crash that were secretly stored at either Area 51 in Nevada or "Hangar 18" at Wright Patterson Air Force Base in Dayton, Ohio. The citizens of Roswell, sensing an opportunity to gain from the hordes of visitors who trekked to their town annually, erected UFO "museums" and, in general, played to the pro-UFO crowds.

Russell, Charles Marion (March 19, 1864– October 24, 1926)

A contemporary of Frederic *Remington* and Albert Bierstadt, western painter Charles Russell was born in St. Louis, Missouri, and after an unfruitful stay at a military academy, went West to become a cowboy. Even while hunting, trapping, raising sheep, and punching cows, Russell sketched and painted the West. His first oil painting was shown in 1886; then his popularity increased with a lithograph called "The Cowboy Artist," a montage of several scenes from western life. Like Remington, he soon engaged in writing short stories and dabbled with clay modeling, often illustrating books for well-known authors. Like Remington, he also illustrated one of Theodore *Roosevelt*'s works.

Operating out of Great Falls, Montana, Russell eventually commanded top dollar for his paintings and statues, which included *Smoking Up* (1903). His work, somewhat like Remington's, focused on people rather than scenery—the cattle drive, the Indian camp, the hunting trip. By the end of his life, though, he was as well known for his books of prose, featuring home-spun narrators and laced with descriptions of range life, as he was for his fine art. These books captured in words what his oils captured on canvas, with great attention to detail and action.

Salamander Letter

With a clever forgery, Mark Hoffman, a collector of historical memorabilia disrupted life significantly for the Church of *Latter-day Saints (LDS)* in the 1980s. Hoffman claimed to have discovered a letter written by Martin Harris, one of the witnesses of the so-called Golden Tablets that made up the *Book of Mormon* as well as one of the earliest followers of LDS founder Joseph Smith. The forged letter, supposedly written in 1830, claimed that the golden tablets were protected by a "white salamander" that could transform itself into the figure of an angel and frequently attacked Joseph Smith as he translated the Tablets. The letter, if true, would have linked the founder of the LDS church to typical types of occultism found on the New York frontier. So complete was the forgery that even LDS President Gordon Hinckley feared it initially to be real. Hoffman is now serving time in the Utah State prison for murder.

Sandia

Sandia is the name for the main nuclear weapons complex located in the city of Albuquerque, New Mexico. Growing out of explosives work done there during World War II, the Sandia facilities were part of the Manhattan Project to build the atomic bomb. Other principal work was conducted at *Los Alamos* laboratories, some 50 miles away. Sandia, however, was first located at Kirtland Air Force Base as "Z Division" of the Los Alamos Labs, then later as Sandia Laboratory. The labs employed technicians, administrators, engineers, machinists, and experts in all kinds of explosives. After the war the government organized Sandia Laboratory separately from Los Alamos, and in 1949 Western Electric took over operation of the lab. Western Electric was replaced in 1993 by Martin-Marietta (now Lockheed-Martin.)

Located outside the Kirtland Air Force Base compound and next to Albuquerque International Airport, Sandia has seen its mission expanded and altered. The lab first focused on engineering the main parts of nuclear weapons, maintaining records and details of modifications to designs. In 1956 Sandia opened new facilities at Livermore, California, to support the hydrogen bomb work at *Lawrence Livermore* National Laboratory. Sandia also supplied parts and personnel to assist in the Nevada nuclear tests north of *Las Vegas* and on Pacific islands in the 1950s and 1960s.

Schroeder, Patricia Scott (July 30, 1940–)

As the most senior female member of the U.S. House of Representatives in the early 1990s, Patricia Scott Schroeder, a Colorado Democrat, wielded exceptional power, especially on the Armed Services Committee, where she repeatedly blocked procurement of new and more effective weapons. Born in Portland, Oregon, on July 30, 1940, Schroeder worked her way through the University of Minnesota and entered Harvard Law School, graduating in 1964. She took a job as a field attorney for the National Labor Relations Board, then entered a brief career in teaching. In 1972 Schroeder won election as a Democrat to the U.S. House of Representatives from Colorado's First District. She was a proponent of abortion rights and women's issues, and ran for president in 1988.

Seattle "grunge" sound

In the early 1990s a heavy, industrial rock sound emerged from a number of Seattle, Washington, bands such as Nirvana, Pearl Jam, Alice in Chains, and Soundgarden. The "Seattle sound" peaked, according to *Rolling Stone*, in 1989, when all of the major bands still were playing in Seattle. Some explained that the Seattle phenomenon—an outgrowth of punk music—thrived on Seattle's rainy environment, which bred isolation among the region's musicians. Described as "sloppy, smeary, staggering, drunken music" that reflected the noise of airplane construction and the musty feel of garages, the Seattle sound also sparked a new look in rock bands. Discarding the flashy sparkles, scarves, tight pants, and theatrics of the 1980s pop and heavy metal bands, the Seattle musicians wore denim, plaid workshirts, and Doc Martens shoes, had short hair, and kept an unkempt look that could best be described as "grungy."

By far, the most successful of the bands was Nirvana, fronted by singer Kurt Cobain, until his suicide in 1994.

The Seattle Space Needle

Conceived by Edward Carlson in 1959, the privately financed building was to be the centerpiece of the 1962 Seattle World's Fair. Completed in December 1961 at a cost of $4.5 million, it opened for visitors on the first day of the fair, April 21. The needle featured a rotating observation deck and restaurant sitting atop the 184-meter-high structure. Built to withstand wind velocities of 200 miles per hour, the Needle has nevertheless closed on occasion when gusts exceeded 70 miles per hour. In 1965 an earthquake of 6.5 magnitude on the Richter scale hit Seattle, but the radio broadcasts in the top of the Needle continued: the Connie Francis record that was being played never skipped a beat.

Second Wounded Knee

The armed occupation of Wounded Knee, South Dakota, was one of several spectacular protests led by the pan-Indian American Indian Movement (AIM) between 1969 and 1973. Other takeovers included the two-year occupation of Alcatraz, 1969–1971, the armed occupation of the *Bureau of Indian Affairs [III]* in Washington, D.C., in 1972, and the brief occupation of the Black Hills in 1981. George Mitchell, Dennis Banks, Eddie Benton-Banai, and Clyde Bellecourt founded the activist movement in 1968, hoping to increase public awareness of the plight of American Indians in the second half of the 20th century. Though not founders, Russell *Means* and Leonard Peltier also served as two of the most controversial and daring of the early leaders of AIM.

In January 1973 white law officials arrested several Lakota Indians on trumped-up charges, and they refused to hear the testimony of native witnesses. This tension, as well as tensions between various internal factions of *Sioux [IV]* (Lakota), led to an AIM commemoration and mourning of the tragic 1890 massacre at *Wounded Knee [IV]*. Nearly 200 Lakota Indians, under AIM's leadership, occupied Sacred Heart Catholic Church, a museum, and a trading post on February 27. They renamed the area as defined by the 1868 Fort Laramie treaty the "Oglala Sioux Nation," and they seceded from the United States. With only a few rifles and some homemade barricades and battlements, the AIM protestors held off the heavily-armed FBI, BIA police, and U.S. marshals for 71 days. Still, despite the military disadvantages, AIM used the time wisely, focusing the international media on the mistreatment of American Indians.

The Indians surrendered on May 8, 1973, after two of their side were killed and one of the other side seriously wounded. The two sides agreed to a "peace treaty," which traded a surrender for a presidential investigation into federal Indian policy. The AIM protestors also demanded internal reform of the Indian reservations, removing federally controlled and influenced tribal governments stemming from the supposed reforms of the New Deal under the *Indian Reorganization Act*.

Selena (Selena Quintanilla) (April 16, 1971–April 1, 1995)

Selena Quintanilla was born on April 16, 1971, in Freeport, Texas. After singing in the family band, Los Dinos, she emerged as the featured performer and in 1991 became the first female Tejano singer to earn a Gold Record. Two years later, she won a Grammy for Best Mexican American Album. As her fan base grew, she gained national, then international celebrity status, and became known only by her first name, Selena. In 1995 she recorded her first English-language album. Her father discovered financial irregularities in her business operations, run by Yolanda Saldivar, the head of the Selena Fan Club. When Selena confronted Saldivar over missing records Saldivar shot her. The news of the star's death shook Chicano communities in Texas, where candlelight vigils and wall murals celebrated her life and mourned her death.

Silicon Valley

This region, associated with "high tech" and computers, is a geographic area stretching from San Jose to Palo Alto, California, covering some 25 miles of the Santa Clara and San Jose Valleys. Major cities in the Valley include Sunnyvale, San Jose, Santa Clara, and Los Altos. The origins of the area date to the founding of Hewlett-Packard Company (1937) in Palo

Alto, and the expansion began during World War II when Hewlett-Packard, and other defense firms, interacting with Stanford University, attracted large numbers of people to the Valley.

When the microprocessor was developed in the late 1950s, making possible a smaller computer than the large units IBM was making, a number of researchers associated with Stanford, the University of California, Berkeley, and many private companies began to concentrate on developing computers. Both the Stanford Research Institute and Stanford Industrial Park accelerated the growth of "high-tech" activity in the Valley. The arrival of Fairchild Semiconductor in 1957 also enhanced the Valley's position as a center of computer-related activity, and the company spun off 10 other competitors within 8 years.

Journalist Don Hoefler coined the term "Silicon Valley" in a series of 1971 articles in *Electronic News*. Over time, the decentralized nature of Silicon Valley, combined with its emphasis on private firms (as opposed to government contracts or support) led to its triumph over all other high-tech regions in the country. The ease of job start-up, the rapid dissemination of information, and the concentration of high-tech personnel all contributed to make Silicon Valley one of the keys to development in the New West.

During the "dot.com" bust of 1999–2001 Silicon Valley faced its first major recession. In the first half of 2001, for example, Silicon Valley had more than 200,000 layoffs in the tech industry. Major producers such as Intel and Microsoft laid people off in significant numbers for the first time in their history. Nevertheless, despite claims of "dot.com speculation" as the cause of the downturn, some analysts have pointed to the decade-long deflationary policies of the Federal Reserve Board, which, they claim, have dried up venture capital. Others cited the delays in wiring the "last mile" of users with fiber optics, which has stalled in competing legislation before Congress. Finally, the September 11 terror attacks further weakened the economy and some overseas sales. But few observers expect these conditions to last, and the more optimistic observers have predicted another explosion once the "last mile" issues are solved and venture capital flows again.

skiing

Skiing as a recreation or hobby had begun in the East, but as early as the mid-1880s "Snowshoe" Thompson had introduced long, heavy skis in the

Sierras to deliver his hundred-pound mail load 90 miles away through the snow. In 1915 Seattle residents began having skiing races on Mt. Ranier, and by the 1920s, ski clubs had sprung up throughout the West. Even during the Great Depression, regular ski buses took skiers to Stevens Pass and to ski schools at Mt. Ranier, Mt. Baker, and Mt. Hood near Portland, as well as Yosemite, California. By the 1950s Snoqualmie Summit in Seattle, the region's most popular ski area, sold more than 12,000 lift tickets in a weekend, and some estimates put the number of skiers in the Seattle area at 100,000.

Anywhere in the West where large mountain ranges existed close to population centers, the ski industry had a natural market. Cities such as Portland, San Francisco, Los Angeles, Tucson, Denver, Salt Lake City, and Albuquerque all took advantage of nearby mountains to develop a thriving ski industry. Colorado's ski mecca in the Rockies featured many resorts, including Aspen, Breckenridge, Steamboat Springs, and others. The desirability of living in these "ski towns" pushed housing prices up so high that locals often could no longer afford to live there, making the once-isolated towns havens for the rich and famous.

Ski zones can be found in the Cascade Range, running through Washington and Oregon; the Sierra Nevadas, which run through California; the Rockies stretching from Northern Montana through Wyoming, Colorado, and into New Mexico; the Sawtooth range in Idaho; the Wasatch Mountains in Utah; and the White Mountains in Arizona. Weather systems that move from west to east dump damp snow from the ocean into the resort areas of Stevens Pass, Crystal Mountain, and Mount Bachelor in the Cascades, then on to Tahoe, Squaw Valley, Mammoth Mountain, and Heavenly in the Sierras. The deep, dense base of this snow fills in many irregularities on the mountain faces, and extends the ski season, in some cases, until the fourth of July.

Wasatch ski areas, including the resorts of Alta, Snowbird, Park City, Sundance, and Snowbasin, have drier snow for "deep powder" skiing, while the higher elevations of the Rockies at Jackson Hole, Wyoming, and Aspen, Vail, and Steamboat Springs, Colorado, also provide a fluffy dry powder. Further south, other Rocky Mountain resorts, such as Telluride and Purgatory, Colorado, and Taos and Santa Fe, New Mexico, often feature sunny days and few winter storms.

Downhill skiing techniques, as developed in the 1920s by the Arlberg ski school (headed by legendry Hannes Schneider of Austria), had begun to teach people to turn their weight from the uphill to the downhill ski in a "stem christie." This allowed many skiers on a hill without fear of running over each other. Since then, the search for more challenging ski experiences has led daredevils to jump from airplanes or helicopters to high, nearly inaccessible slopes, or to ski off sheer cliffs with a parachute.

Modern resorts, such as Sun Valley, Idaho, combine suitable terrain, accessibility to transportation, and entrepreneurial vision. In Sun Valley's case, Averill Harriman, whose family controlled the *Union Pacific Railroad [IV]*, identified a suitable location along the railroad's route. In 1936 he sent a friend who was very familiar with European ski resorts to determine the best spot to build a lodge. Harriman settled on a picturesque valley near Ketchum, Idaho, at the end of a spur line of the railroad. Skiing as a sport benefited from James Curran's invention in 1936 of the world's first chair lift on a cable conveyor system that the railroad had used to load bananas into boxcars.

During World War II resorts such as Sun Valley became training grounds for the U.S. Army's mountain divisions. The 10th Mountain Division trained at Camp Hale, Colorado, 160 miles from Aspen, but drew on experienced ski instructors from the resorts. Resorts also held ski competitions, such as the 1950 world championships held at Aspen. In 1960 Squaw Valley, California, hosted the Winter Olympic Games, attended by thousands of spectators and seen by millions on television. Other resorts, such as Vail, Colorado, emerged later but gained ground on the established lodges quickly. By 1996–1997 Colorado totaled 20 percent of all lift tickets sold in the United States. Meanwhile, Salt Lake City, overcoming charges of bribery and corruption, won the rights to hold the 2002 XIX Olympic Games, utilizing the Wasatch Mountains.

Spindletop

On January 10, 1901, the salt dome known as the "Big Hill" south of Beaumont, Texas, yielded its first gusher. This opened the Spindletop oil field that created the first oil "boom town" in Texas and made the state a leading producer of oil in the United States. Patillo Higgins (1862–1955), a Beaumont resident, was the first to find petroleum in the area, and Anthony Lucas, a geologist, along with James Guffey, or J. M. Guffey Petroleum, drilled the wells.

Stagecoach, the movie

The 1939 classic movie, directed by John *Ford*, *Stagecoach* is considered by most critics to be one of the finest western movies ever produced. It featured an all-star cast, including John *Wayne* in his quintessential role as the "Ringo Kid," John Carradine as "Mr. Hatfield," Claire Trevor as "Dallas," and Andy Devine as "Buck," the stagecoach driver. The plot involved a group of passengers on a stagecoach trip, which is interrupted by attacks by *Geronimo [IV]*. Nominated for a Best Picture Academy Award in 1939, the picture competed against some of the finest movies ever made, such as *The Wizard of Oz, Goodbye, Mr. Chips, Mr. Smith Goes to Washington*, and, of course, *Gone With the Wind*, which won the award.

Starbucks Coffee

Beginning as a small store in the Pike Place Market in Seattle in 1971 to provide coffee to existing restaurants, Starbucks emerged as a true "coffee bar" that grew by leaps and bounds in the 1990s. In 1987 the company officially became known as Starbucks Corporation. The first Starbucks stores outside of Seattle opened in Chicago and Vancouver, but in less than a decade, the Starbucks empire counted more than 1,000 locations across the United States and Canada, as well as in Japan and Singapore. By the end of the 1990s Starbucks' company name had become synonymous with "coffee" as much as Kleenex had become synonymous with "tissue." The company also epitomized the enterprises of the New West, based on retail, banking, sales, processed foods, aviation, and music.

Stegner, Wallace (February 18, 1909–April 13, 1993)

Born in Iowa in 1909, Wallace Stegner moved with his parents to the Canadian province of Saskatchewan to homestead in 1914; his family homesteaded for six years. In 1930 Stegner graduated with a B.A. from the University of Utah. He earned his Ph.D. in the University of Iowa Creative Writing Program in 1935. For the next 12 years, Stegner taught at a number of universities, finally settling at Palo Alto, California, in 1945 as the director of the creative writing program at Stanford University. He held the position until 1971, teaching such notable writers as Larry *McMurtry*, Edward Abbey, Wendell Berry, Tom Mcguane, and Ken Kesey.

During his adult career he produced a number of excellent works of fiction and history, including his Pulitzer Prize–winning *Angle of Repose* (1971). His other works include: *Remembering Laughter* (1937), *The Big Rock Candy Mountain* (1943), *Joe Hill* (1950), *Beyond the Hundredth Meridian* (1954), *A Shooting Star* (1961), *Wolf Willow* (1963), and *All the Little Live Things* (1967). During his career, he received several prominent awards, including the O. Henry Award, the National Book Award, the Robert Kirsche Award, a Guggenheim, and the National Medal of the Arts. Most of his works attacked the stereotypical notions of western individualism. They instead focused on community, family, and cooperative efforts to settle the West. He was also an ardent environmentalist, and in 1960, issued his famous "Wilderness Letters," which outlined his proposals for wilderness management and control.

Sundance Institute

Best known for its annual January film festival, the Sundance Institute was founded by actor Robert Redford in 1981 at Park City, Utah, to help artists pursue creative visions without industry demands. The institute offers year-round screenwriters labs, filmmakers labs, and a theater program. The Sundance Film Festival, founded three years earlier as the United States Film Festival (then based in Salt Lake City), included a national competition to highlight dramatic feature films made by independent film producers. The Institute joined with the University of California, Los Angeles' Film and Television Archive to establish the Sundance Collection at UCLA, an archive devoted to collecting and preserving independent films.

surf music

Pioneered by guitarist Dick Dale in the early 1960s, this beach music combined the manic intensity of jazz drummer Gene Krupa with a new guitar sound developed by amplifier manufacturer Leo Fender from Fullerton, California. Dale was a Bostonian, but his family had moved to California in 1954, and he had played in country bands when he was giving guitar lessons in Costa Mesa. A surfer, Dale wanted a new sound that would capture the roar of the ocean and the energy of surfing.

Fender had a new guitar, the Stratocaster, that featured a particularly twangy and edgy sound. Fender's amplifiers also had "reverb" or echo, an adjustable effect capable of creating the illusion of space. Dale had asked for an echo-type device to aid his thin singing voice, but he quickly saw the potential for channeling the guitar through reverb as well.

In a short time Dale was known as the "king of the surf guitar." With his group, the Deltones, he had a string of hits in the early 1960s, including "Let's go Trippin'," "Surf Beat," and "Misirlou." Although he dropped out of the music business for more than a decade, he returned in the 1980s to join popular Texas guitarist Stevie Ray Vaughn for the soundtrack to the film *Back to the Beach*.

The Ventures, from the state of Washington, followed the sound formula established by Dale, as did the Trashmen, who came from Minnesota. But despite the fact that many groups, and far more listeners, never actually surfed or were from California, the sound proved attractive across the United States—and not just with listeners, but also with film audiences. Hollywood cashed in with movies such as *Muscle Beach Party* and *Ride the Wild Surf*. But by far the most successful of all the surf music groups was the *Beach Boys*.

surfing

The sport of stand-up surfing came from Hawaii, where it was called "he 'e nalu" or "wave sliding." By the 1950s it had emerged as a popular sport all along the California beaches in addition to the Hawaiian islands. In 1953 Dale Velzy and Hap Jacobs started making balsa boards on Venice Beach, and soon Manhattan Beach and Sunset Beach became popular surfing spots as well. The sport involves the surfer paddling into the ocean on a 5'6" wooden board, waiting for a wave, then jumping upright on the board to "ride" the wave into the surf. While surfers traveled all over the world in search of the "perfect" wave, California developed a particularly vibrant surf culture with its own music by Dick Dale and the Deltones and the *Beach Boys*, its own clothing styles ("baggy" swimsuits), and its own transportation ("Woodies" or early sport utility vehicles capable of carrying the long boards).

Tan, Amy (February 19, 1952–)

Born in Oakland, California, Amy Tan began her career as a medical therapist in a center for the mentally retarded. She began writing emergency medical reports, then established her own business writing firm. After joining a writer's workshop, she had a short story published. Then, before she completed a volume of short stories, her mother, Daisy Chan, became ill. Fulfilling a commitment she made years earlier, Amy accompanied her mother to China to see daughters of a previous marriage that Amy's mother had left behind when she left China. This 1987 trip was the basis for her successful debut novel, *The Joy Luck Club* (1989). She followed with two other novels about Chinese American women and their mothers, *The Kitchen God's Wife* (1991) and *The Hundred Secret Senses* (1995).

Teapot Dome scandal

Secretary of the Interior Albert B. *Fall* transferred federal lands designated for oil reserves from the Navy Department to his own department in 1921–1922. Fall then awarded leases in Teapot Dome, Wyoming, and Elk Hills, California, to the Mammoth Oil Company. The United States Senate began hearings to investigate the sales, discovering that Fall had accepted $400,000 in loans from the executives of those companies. Fall, however, had already resigned before the hearings began. On December 18, 1924, President Calvin Coolidge created the Federal Oil Conservation Board to oversee the relationship between the federal government and petroleum companies. Although the scandal was a part of the presidential campaign of 1924, it was largely laid at the feet of Fall and President Warren G. Harding, who had died in 1923.

Texaco

After oil was discovered at *Spindletop*, Texas, Texaco was established in March 1901 as Texas Fuel Company by Joseph "Buckskin Joe" Cullinan and Arnold Schlaet, near Beaumont, Texas. A year later, the company started to use the term "Texaco" to describe the firm, which produced more than 300,000 barrels of oil in its first year. By 2001 Texaco was pumping more than 1 billion barrels of oil per day, and it remained one of the largest oil companies in the world.

Texas Instruments

Texas Instruments began as Geophysical Service Company, which used a new technique, reflection seismology, to find oil. By 1951 the company had been renamed Texas Instruments. In 1952 TI paid $25,000 to Western Electric for permission to make transistors out of germanium. In 1953 TI merged with Intercontinental Rubber Company and the capital from this move was used to fuel the rapid growth. With its $2 million investment in manufacturing, TI produced the first pocket transistor radio in 1954. This "transistor radio" became immensely popular, and transistors started to take the place of the old vacuum tubes that had powered radios, televisions, and electronic equipment.

One of the key breakthroughs in the "computer revolution" occurred in 1954 when TI made a transistor out of silicon, a material that could withstand far higher temperatures than germanium. Computer giant International Business Machines (IBM) saw the potential of the silicon transistor and in 1957 contracted with TI to become a major supplier of the transistors. The following year, Jack Kilby and Bob Noyce (later to found Intel) invented the integrated circuit. Before this invention, circuits for electronic equipment had to be soldered and wired together out of many different parts. But the integrated circuit was a single unit, and it made circuits much smaller, cramming together components onto a single semiconductor or "computer chip." This accelerated the revolution by driving down the sizes—and prices—of electronics. Seeing the capabilities of the transistors and integrated circuits, the government finally got on board, acquiring contracts from TI for the U.S. Air Force.

Within a few years, though, TI already had a hand-held calculator on the market, and sales soared from 3 million units in 1971 to 45 million in 1975. By that time IBM had started using integrated circuits in all of its computers, moving the technology into the civilian sector by lowering prices. But neither TI nor IBM recognized the consumer potential of a "personal computer," and both missed the "PC revolution" that was pioneered by *Apple Computers*. TI had stayed in the consumer electronics market and had a PC available in 1979. Its competitors, though, had already mastered the PC market, and by the mid-1980s, TI got out of consumer electronics and PC manufacturing to concentrate on chips.

Thorpe, James Francis ("Jim") (May 28, 1888–March 28, 1953)

Considered one of the greatest athletes of all time, James Francis ("Jim") Thorpe was of Sauk and Fox Indian descent. Born in Prague, Indian Territory (later Oklahoma), on May 28, 1888, Jim Thorpe attended Haskell Indian School in Lawrence, Kansas, and Carlisle Indian Industrial School in Pennsylvania. At Carlisle, Thorpe played football for Glenn Scobey "Pop" Warner, starring as a halfback on Warner's All-America teams in 1911–1912. He also competed in the international Olympics of 1912, winning the decathlon and pentathlon, only to have his medals taken from him when a 1913 Olympic investigation showed that he had played on semi-professional baseball teams in 1909 and 1910.

Thorpe then played professional baseball with several National League teams from 1913 to 1919, while at the same time becoming a "two-sport" star by signing with the Canton Bulldogs professional football team in 1915, becoming the first big-name athlete in the sport. In 1919 he made an astounding career move by switching from baseball to full-time professional football. Thorpe served as president of the American Professional Football Association (later the National Football League, or NFL) in 1920, winding up his football career with the Chicago Cardinals in 1928.

After a stint in Hollywood and an appearance in a few western movies, Thorpe engaged in a lecture tour, worked on Indian affairs, then, in World War II, joined the Merchant Marines, sailing on an ammunition ship. But once he could no longer play on a regular basis, he drifted into depression, bouts with alcohol, and poverty. Jim Thorpe, labeled the top American athlete of the first half of the 20th century over such notables as Babe Ruth and Jesse Owens, died in 1953. The following year the communities of Mauch Chunk and East Mauch Chunk, Pennsylvania, merged to form the borough of Jim Thorpe, Pennsylvania, and the next year a Jim Thorpe trophy was awarded to the Most Valuable Player in the NFL. In 1983 the International Olympic Committee reversed itself and declared Thorpe an amateur in 1912, restoring the Olympic gold medals to his family.

tourism development in the West

From the *skiing* industry to *surfing*, from the gaming tables of *Las Vegas* to the attractions of *Disneyland*, and from the beauty of Yosemite National Park to the splendor of the *Grand Canyon [I]*, the West offers tourists a wide range of experiences and pleasures. Although national parks such as Yosemite have long drawn tourists and people interested in the outdoors, after World War II the explosion of automobile sales made access to western sites easier. The Interstate Highway Act of 1956 provided freeways that further facilitated access to tourist sites.

World War II also left surplus army equipment, such as four-wheel-drive vehicles, rubber rafts for running rapids, knapsacks, winter and camping gear, which explorers and tourists swept up. As wealth increased after the war and Americans had more leisure time, they increasingly traveled. Camping became more popular; Kampgrounds of America (KOA), based in Billings, Montana, was the largest of the national commercial campground chains with 525 properties in the United States and Canada. Catering to the new camping mania, Detroit turned out large "recreational vehicles," which were essentially house trailers with an engine. People could travel in comfort in the facility that they would live in when they reached their destination.

Amusement parks also sprang up throughout America to attract tourists, none more important than *Disneyland* in Anaheim, California. Founded by Walter Elias "Walt" Disney in 1956, Disneyland was the first true "theme park" organizing attractions (not "rides") around specific themes. By the 1970s Disneyland's success had inspired many similar parks, including Magic Mountain in California, DisneyWorld and EPCOT Center in Florida, and the Six Flags parks around the country. Still later, Universal Studios in California and Florida, as well as the Sea World parks, vied for the tourist's dollar.

Perhaps no commercial location has had more success than the city of Las Vegas, which had long been a gambling haven. In the 1970s, however, Las Vegas began to emphasize its entertainment and shows as well as its roulette wheels and gaming tables. Then, in the 1980s, the city began to market to families by providing theme parks and attractions oriented toward children as well as adults.

Of course, it did not take a theme park or an exceptional natural wonder to bring tourists to the West. Towns such as Santa Fe, New Mexico,

Aspen, Colorado, and *Tombstone [IV]*, Arizona, still appealed to people for the beauty or history of their locations. The ocean also offered a desirable vacation option, with cruise lines sailing out of Los Angeles, San Diego, and San Francisco.

Turner, Frederick Jackson (November 14, 1861– March 14, 1932)

Considered one of the foremost American historians, Frederick Jackson Turner was born in Portage, Wisconsin, the son of a newspaper editor. After graduating from the University of Wisconsin in 1884, Turner himself briefly worked as a correspondent, then entered the Johns Hopkins University, where he studied under Herbert Baxter Adams. He focused on western and Indian history, completing a doctorate on the fur trade. Following his graduation, Turner was hired at the University of Wisconsin, where he taught until 1910, at which time he became the president of the American Historical Association. At that point, he moved to Harvard University, where he remained until his retirement in 1924, although he continued to research and write while a fellow at the Huntington Library in San Marino, California.

Turner is often described as the first truly original American historian for his so-called "frontier thesis," developed in his essay, "The Significance of the Frontier in American History" (1893). Although he would expound further upon this in two books, *The Frontier in American History* (1920) and *The Significance of Sections in American History* (1932), most students cite his essay, which he gave at the American Historical Association meeting in 1893 at the World's Columbian Exposition in Chicago.

According to the "frontier thesis," American democracy worked best on the frontier, where the harsh life and competitive circumstances pushed society forward. Much of the tension in society, he argued, was alleviated by the availability of land in the West. But, he argued, by 1893 the frontier was closed (he did not include Alaska as part of his frontier concept), and this had significant implications for American democracy. Turner's work was as important for its incorporation of the new "scientific history" of his mentor at Johns Hopkins as it was for his ideas on the West. Yet he rejected the notion that American civilization descended intact from European origins, arguing that the environment of the West had reshaped the American character. Individualism, nationalism, and the rugged frontier spirit were the result of this environmental pressure. Turner also argued that different sections of the country competed in a balance-of-power maneuvering to shape the political character of the country, although this concept was not so well received as his frontier thesis.

IN THEIR OWN Words

Frederick Jackson Turner's Frontier Thesis

In 1893 historian Frederick Jackson Turner presented a paper to the American Historical Association called "The Significance of the Frontier in American History." It represented the first truly distinctive historical theory to emerge from the United States, and it also proposed a novel analysis of American expansion in light of the availability of land.

The public domain has been a force of profound importance in the nationalization and development of the Government. The effects of the struggle of the landed and the landless States, and of the ordinance of 1787, need no discussion. Administratively the frontier called out some of the highest and most vitalizing activities of the General Government. The purchase of Louisiana was perhaps the constitutional turning point in the history of the Republic, inasmuch as it afforded both a new area for national legislation and the occasion of the downfall of the policy of strict construction. . . .

When we consider the public domain from the point of view of the sale and disposal of the public lands we are again brought face to face with the frontier. . . . It is safe to say that the legislation with regard to land, tariff, and internal improvements . . . was conditioned on frontier ideas and needs. But it was not merely in legislative action that the frontier worked against the sectionalism of the coast. The economic and social characteristics of the frontier worked against sectionalism. . . .

It was this nationalizing tendency of the West that transformed the democracy of Jefferson into the national republicanism of Monroe and the democracy of Andrew Jackson. . . . But the most important effect of the frontier has been in the promotion of democracy here and in Europe. . . . [T]he frontier is productive of individualism. Complex society is precipitated by the wilderness into a kind of primitive organization based on the family. The tendency is anti-social. It produces antipathy to control, and particularly to any direct control. The tax-gatherer is viewed as a representative of oppression.

—SOURCE: FREDERICK JACKSON TURNER, "THE SIGNIFICANCE OF THE FRONTIER IN AMERICAN HISTORY," *PROCEEDINGS OF THE NINTH ANNUAL MEETING OF THE AMERICAN HISTORICAL ASSOCIATION*, JULY 1893 (WASHINGTON: GOVERNMENT PRINTING OFFICE, 1893), 199–227.

Turner's last book, *The United States, 1830–1850*, was published after his death and won the Pulitzer Prize. His frontier thesis fell out of favor in the late 1930s but rebounded with the new social history of the 1960s.

United Farm Workers

Founded by César *Chavez* in 1966 out of a merger between the National Farm Workers Association and Filipino workers under the name United Farm Workers Organizing Committee, this union became the nation's most powerful farm union for a period during the 1960s and 1970s. Chavez had learned organizing techniques from Fred Ross of the Community Services Organization (CSO) in San Jose, California, and by 1959 Chavez was an executive director of the CSO. But when the CSO refused to fund a test program to organize farm workers, Chavez resigned and in Delano, California, began to organize farm workers in the San Joaquin Valley. In 1962 he established the National Farm Workers Association (NFWA), which sought to raise the minimum wage to $1.50 per hour, give farm workers unemployment insurance, and require growers to bargain collectively with farm workers.

After merging with the Filipino workers under the new name United Farm Workers Organizing Committee (UFWOC), the union began to picket and use nonviolent protest strategies to bring the growers to the negotiating tables. Some growers engaged in beating picketers, others fired participating UFWOC members, but Chavez used the incidents as opportunities to swing the public to his cause. Chavez called for a national boycott of grapes not carrying a union label, and eventually the growers in California gave in to the grape boycott and UFWOC pressure, signing contracts in 1970 with the union. In 1972 the union was certified as the United Farm Workers of America.

Meanwhile, lettuce growers agreed to let the International Brotherhood of Teamsters represent the workers, leading not only to violence between growers and workers, but also between the unions. Chavez tried another boycott, but this time the growers learned how to form their own public relations campaigns and to sue the unions for violence and property damage. Moreover, Chavez ignored the imperative to constantly organize the farms, focusing instead on the boycotts and losing many new potential members. When the balance of nonaffiliated workers to union members shifted, the growers renegotiated nonunion contracts. UFW membership plunged by two-thirds.

After César Chavez died in 1993, the UFW started to grow again under Arturo Rodriguez, Chavez's son-in-law and successor as president. Rodriguez again returned the UFW to its primary mission of organizing workers. But Rodriguez had to contend with the fact that the burgeoning economy that had originated in the 1980s had raised wages and improved working conditions on nonunion farms to the extent that nonunion farms were paying as much and providing as many benefits as unionized operations.

United States Air Force Academy

Chartered in 1954 and opened in 1959 at Colorado Springs, Colorado, the United States Air Force Academy is the only service academy located in the West. In its mission of developing air force officers, it provides a full college education in the arts and sciences as well as specific training in aeronautical arts and disciplines through a number of air training wings. The academy is easily recognized by its beautiful and prominent chapel and routinely educates about 4,000 cadets.

Villa, Pancho (June 5, 1878–June 20, 1923)

A soldier in the uprising against Porfirio Diaz in Mexico in 1909, Pancho Villa organized a large body of loyal revolutionary soldiers around him-

Following Pancho Villa's raid on Columbus, New Mexico, suspected Villistas were captured and executed by both American troops sent to the region and by Mexican Federales. *National Archives*

self. In 1912 General Victoriano Huerta, suspicious of Villa's role in a coup, placed a death mark on him, but Villa escaped to the United States and allied with Venustiano Carranza, who made him military governor of Chihuahua. Later, a split with Carranza made him an outlaw once again. Villa demonstrated his vicious side by killing Americans in Columbus, New Mexico, after he thought the United States turned against him. This prompted President Woodrow Wilson to dispatch General John Pershing with an expeditionary force into Mexico to catch him. Although Villa eluded Pershing, he was later assassinated on his ranch in 1923.

Waco and the Branch Davidians

On April 19, 1993, the FBI, the Bureau of Alcohol, Tobacco, and Firearms (BATF), *Texas Rangers [III]*, and national guard troops stormed the compound of a religious sect called the Branch Davidians at Waco, Texas, killing 82 men, women, and children. The Davidians were an offshoot of the Davidian Seventh Day Adventists, with this particular group under the leadership of David Koresh and established in Waco in 1935 by Victor Houteff. Under Koresh, Davidian behavior at the compound was bizarre, but whether it was illegal or not remains in doubt. Authorities had been called ostensibly due to reports of child abuse, yet subsequent trials did not confirm that charge. The Davidians certainly were armed and subscribed to a religious view that held that the "end times" were at hand. Thus, they saw acts of force against them as prophetic fulfillment.

BATF agents had watched the group for a year, suspecting it of dealing in illegal weapons. On February 28 the BATF moved in aggressively and recklessly, after Koresh had offered to negotiate. When agents arrived, a firefight ensued in which several agents and Davidians were killed, and Koresh wounded. A siege ensued, with the FBI placed in charge, but military forces were also brought in under circumstances that were questionable or possibly illegal. When the final assault was launched, C-4 gas was fired into the compound, and a massive fire broke out, killing most of those inside the compound, including Koresh. Subsequent hearings have been unable to prove whether military troops and helicopters firing into the compound started the fires or whether the Davidians, in a final burst of religious martyrdom, set the fires themselves. A 1997 film, and winner of the *Sundance Institute* award, *Waco: the Rules of Engagement*, unearthed new evidence, throwing both the government's explanations and the Congressional investigation into doubt.

Walton, Sam (March 29, 1918–April 5, 1992)

Born in rural Kingfisher, Oklahoma, on March 28, 1918, Samuel Moore Walton is best known for founding the largest retail chain in the United States, Wal-Mart stores. Walton, the son of Thomas and Nancy Walton, lived in Missouri for much of his early life, settling in Columbia. After attending the University of Missouri, Walton worked for J. C. Penney in Des Moines, Iowa, where he met James Cash Penney when he came to inspect the store. Drafted in 1942, Walton served in the Army Intelligence Corps.

In late 1945 Sam Walton purchased a Ben Franklin variety store in Newport, Arkansas. Five years later, the landlord refused to renew Walton's lease, whereupon Walton moved to Bentonville, Arkansas, again acquiring Ben Franklin stores. Walton researched his business, noting that other large chain stores, such as K-Mart, tended to build near large cities, ignoring smaller towns. Walton was convinced that small towns could support variety. In 1962 Walton opened Wal-Mart Discount City in Rogers, Arkansas, then a second store in Harrison, Arkansas. Within eight years he had 25 stores. Then the business took off. By 1972 Wal-Mart sales reached $125 million, and a decade later, the company had 642 stores in 19 states with sales of more than $4 billion.

Up until that time, most Wal-Marts were still being constructed in rural areas, but with the opening of stores in Little Rock, Arkansas, Kansas City, Missouri, and Dallas, Texas, Wal-Mart began to enter larger urban areas. The company branched into Sam's Wholesale Clubs, which were little more than giant warehouse outlets selling to bulk customers at less than 10 percent over cost.

Walton's personal wealth grew apace, exceeding $2 billion and landing him on the *Forbes* list of wealthy Americans. Yet he still donned his University of Arkansas "tractor" cap, refused to drive ostentatious cars, and until late in life, managed to visit every store on a continuous cycle. At each stop, he would lead the employees in a shout of "soooooooeeeeeeyyyyy Pig!"—the battle cry of the Arkansas Razorbacks. His stores hired elderly greeters, who had no other job but to say hello to every customer; he originated a finely honed distribution network; and at all times he strove to keep prices low. Sam Walton died in 1992, having revolutionized retailing and provided a new public image of the wealthy in America, showing that one of the richest men in the world was an "ordinary guy."

Warner Brothers

Founded by Jack Leonard Warner (1892–1978) and his brothers Samuel (1888–1927), Harry (1881–1958), and Albert (1884–1967) in 1923, Warner Brothers studios became one of the titans of *Hollywood.* The brothers were Canadian, changing their name from Eichelbaum in 1907 after settling in Ohio. Jack was an entertainer, while his brothers had a neighborhood film projection theater in the early 1900s in Pittsburgh. Incorporating themselves as Warner Brothers Pictures in 1923, the firm developed sound motion pictures that were the first to contain a fully synchronized musical score designed to complement the action. Warner Brothers made some of the most memorable movies or film scenes in history: *The Public Enemy* (1931), Errol Flynn's *Captain Blood* (1935), *Casablanca* (1942), *My Fair Lady* (1964), *Who's Afraid of Virginia Woolf?* (1966), *Bonnie and Clyde* (1967), and *Harry Potter* (2001). In addition to feature films Warner Brothers was responsible for the classic cartoon characters Bugs Bunny and Daffy Duck, which remain popular in the 21st century. In 1965 Seven Arts took over Warner Brothers, which continues to make popular and profitable big-screen films, and in 2001 Warner Brothers was acquired by AOL.

The Watts riots

On August 11, 1965, a white highway patrolman pulled over a driver in the predominantly black Watts area of Los Angeles, arresting him for drunk driving. The driver, Marquette Frye, along with his passenger and brother, Ronald Frye, were black. It was an extraordinarily hot evening, causing many of the local residents to be in the street. As more patrolmen and onlookers arrived, as well as Marquette and Ronald's mother, the situation turned ugly. The growing crowd was egged on by the Fryes, and rumors quickly spread. Within a few minutes, more than 1,000 people had gathered, and were becoming more hostile, and less than an hour after the car had been pulled over, the neighborhood erupted in a full-scale riot.

The following night, even larger crowds rioted, and it was a week before police and some 3,000 national guardsmen again declared the situation under control. Damage to buildings exceeded $40 million, 34 people had been killed, and more than 1,000 injured.

Although certainly not the first "race riot" in American history, Watts had important implications for race relations in the United States. It originated, and grew rapidly, out of perceived and real abuses by the Los Angeles Police Department, which was all-white, forcing several reviews and reforms of the department in subsequent years. Watts also was a harbinger of other race riots in the 1960s. Publicity of the event brought national public attention to the poor living conditions and seething resentment in the inner cities and raised national awareness to the perceived injustices of all-white police forces in largely black neighborhoods. Finally, Watts was a forerunner of the riots that erupted in the wake of the *Rodney King* verdict in 1992.

Wayne, John (May 26, 1907–June 11, 1979)

John Wayne was born Marion Michael Morrison on May 26, 1907, to Clyde Morrison and Margaret Brown, but known as "the Duke," John Wayne became a movie icon in America. Wayne lived in Palmdale, then Glendale, California, as a child and was a tall, rugged boy who played football on a scholarship at the University of Southern California. He worked part time at the Fox Film Studios as an extra and prop mover, where he met director John *Ford*, who set him up with his first film role in *The Big Trail* (1930). The movie was a flop, but it gave him his new screen name. Wayne then suffered through a long dry spell over the next nine years, working in a series of forgettable "B" movies for different studios. During this period, Wayne made nearly 70 films, some of which required less than a week to shoot.

Wayne got his next break, again, from John Ford, who cast him as the Ringo Kid in the classic *Stagecoach* (1939), which established Wayne's low-key western hero persona, replete with swagger and confidence. Still, he continued to make "B" movies, being paired with Marlene Dietrich in a series of pictures, before he was cast by Howard Hawks in *Red River* (1948). He followed that with the John Ford cavalry trilogy that emphasized tradition, American loyalty, and courage: *Fort Apache* (1948), *She Wore a Yellow Ribbon* (1949), and *Rio Grande* (1950). In 1949 he won his first Oscar nomination for *The Sands of Iwo Jima*.

During World War II, Wayne saw the movie industry becoming populated with Communists, and he helped found the Motion Picture Alliance for the Preservation of American Ideals in 1944. He helped compile the famous Hollywood blacklist and opposed Communism throughout his life. Many of his movies had clear references to the struggle he saw going on between America and its totalitarian enemies. His pet project, a titanic production called *The Alamo* (1960), featured Wayne as Davy *Crockett [III]*, leading a valiant resistance against the dictatorial General *Santa Anna [III]*. He not only starred in the film, but it was his first directorial effort, followed by *The Green Berets* (1968), a Vietnam movie he flatly stated was intended as a "prowar" feature. Although both movies were panned by critics, Wayne loved to point out that *The Green Berets* made money at the box office, and after his death, *The Alamo* became a movie classic. He won an Academy Award for best actor in 1969 for his role in *True Grit* as "Rooster" Cogburn, a one-eyed, often drunk bounty hunter, and quipped to the Academy that he would have worn an eyepatch 40 years earlier if he had thought that was all it took to win the Oscar. In his last movie, *The Shootist* (1976), he played an old gunfighter dying of cancer, which Wayne was also fighting at the time. He had boasted in 1964 that he "beat the big C," but in fact in 1979 it beat him.

John Wayne was the most famous "cowboy" actor of all time, and while no single character he played is immortalized, his overall image of a rugged western individualist was unmistakable. *Wisconsin Center for Film and Theater Research*

Wayne's personal life was a disaster, in part because of his commitment to his work. From 1933 to 1945, he was married to Josephine Saenz and the couple had four children. Then he married Esperanza Baur Diaz, from 1946 to 1953. His longest marriage, to Pilar Pallette Weldy, lasted from 1954 to 1973 and produced three children. Known for his professionalism and loyalty to friends, Wayne lacked any flexibility or versatility in his acting, but it hardly mattered. His on- and off-screen persona identified him with the rugged individualist and the American West. One of his best biographies captures this association perfectly in its simple title, *John Wayne: American*.

Webb, Walter Prescott (April 3, 1888–March 8, 1963)

Born in Texas, Walter Prescott Webb moved with his family throughout north-central Texas as his father drifted from job to job. Although Webb had early plans to become a writer, he took a number of teaching positions before finally enrolling in the University of Texas in 1909—a college career that took six years to complete due to financial pressures. Translating his interest in writing into a new passion for history, Webb began to interpret western development in terms of the environment and the land. This ran counter to the accepted historical theories of the day.

Offered a position at the University of Texas in 1918, Webb did not have a doctorate, and four years later he took a leave to enroll at the University of Chicago but failed his preliminary exams. Webb's failure led him to conclude that there was a prejudice in the history profession against scholars of the West. Even without a doctorate, Webb researched and wrote *The Great Plains: A Study in Institutions and Environment* (1931), wherein he developed a thesis, like Frederick Jackson *Turner*'s, that the West was a separate part of the country geographically, culturally, and institutionally. He claimed that the aridity of the West distinctly affected every area of activity, to the point that nature had created a new type of life past the 98th meridian.

When Turner died in 1932, Webb assumed his place as the leader of the new western studies field of historical writing. Throughout his career, as with his 1937 book, *Divided We Stand: The Crisis of a Frontierless Society* (1937), Webb argued that land-related policy factors, such as inexpensive or free land provided by the *Homestead Act [IV]*, laid the foundation of democracy. Yet although Webb continued to lecture and teach in a number of places, including Oxford, he did not write another major book until 1952 (*The Great Frontier*). In the meantime, he had battled the University of Texas administration and the Board of Regents over liberal ideology at the school. He increasingly grew cynical and pessimistic in his writing, with his predictions for the future West resembling the prognostications of economist John Kenneth Galbraith. However, for all his passion for the West, Webb rarely traveled there, never saw many of its natural wonders or spoke with people outside of Texas, and spent a great deal of time in New York—a place he had once disparaged as biased against western interests.

Webb directed the Texas State Historical Association for a number of years and was an important influence in the writing of western history. Yet he was often seriously wrong in his predictions—including his claims that the West's economy would never grow much—and his Turneresque view of western history already was under assault by a new generation of scholars by the time of his death in 1963.

"western" movies

If movies are quintessentially American, then the "western" film is the quintessential American movie. Although traditionally thought of as occurring in a "frontier" setting, increasingly the crossover of western stars, such as John *Wayne* and, later, Clint *Eastwood*, into police and crime dramas indicated that the western in fact extended beyond deserts and mountains and into 20th century urban landscapes. Even more recently—and somewhat tongue-in-cheek—the phenomenal popularity of martial arts movies has increasingly utilized Asian heroes and heroines in an essentially western setting. The ultimate example of this was the transformation of an "eastern" (Akira Kurosawa's 1954 film *The Seven Samarai*) into a western (John Sturges's film *The Magnificent Seven*), followed by a predictable transition to television in the form of the series *Kung Fu* and revived by Jackie Chan in *Shanghai Noon*.

Whether western film genre intends to depict reality in the West or substitute for that reality its own interpretation remains a matter of heated debate. Some of the earliest motion pictures by Thomas Edison (*Bucking Bronco*, 1894), used the West as its subject and proved more popular than European subjects that appeared on screens. Nickelodeons prominently featured western plots and settings in the early 1900s and even hired some of the Wild West Show stars to appear in them. One of the most influential of the early stars, G. M. "Bronco Billy" Anderson, acted in, wrote, and directed 375 westerns, before being eclipsed by a new western star, Tom *Mix*. Mix, another "Wild West Show" performer who made the transition to the silent screen, continued the tradition of an untarnished hero who battled evil on the frontier.

More than any other director, John *Ford* gave the western its modern form. In 1924 his film *The Iron Horse* celebrated the construction of a railroad. After the war, Ford and an actor named John *Wayne* rode an already strong consumer demand for westerns to team up for his epic western trilogy, *Fort Apache* (1948), *She Wore A Yellow Ribbon* (1949), and *Rio*

Grande (1950). Wayne, already critically acclaimed for his work in *Stagecoach* (1939) as the Ringo Kid, emerged as the biggest western star in history, working with director Howard Hawks to produce another trilogy, *Rio Bravo* (1959), *El Dorado* (1967), and *Rio Lobo* (1970).

Most of these films, including the classics *Shane* (1953), *High Noon* (1952), and *The Searchers* (1956), all emphasized the individual's struggle against injustice. Only a slight variation occurred with *The Magnificent Seven* (1960), where hard-bitten gunslingers, gold seekers, and glory hunters find redemption by defending a small Mexican town against a much larger force of *banditos*. Generally, regardless of plot twists, the hero (there were few female leads in westerns) overcomes great odds, personal demons, and often bad luck to establish justice with a gun. Nevertheless, the antiviolent messages were strung throughout. One of the "Magnificent Seven," Charles Bronson, tells Mexican children that their farmer-fathers are the real heroes for shouldering the daily burden of providing for a family. Gary Cooper's sheriff in *High Noon* finds that the otherwise decent citizens will not help him.

The motif of the virtuous hero began to fray during the Vietnam era, with Sam Peckinpah's *The Wild Bunch* (1969), one of the best of the new "antihero" movies, in which a group of aging adventurers insert themselves into an internal Mexican conflict, ending in a horrific, bloody gunfight. But *The Wild Bunch* was not the first to explore injustice on the frontier—that perhaps came from *The Ox-Bow Incident* (1943)—and certainly wasn't the last. Yet even as a number of preachy movies appeared, sometimes emphasizing real hardships of Indians or settlers and genuine inhumanity by the government (*Cheyenne Autumn*, 1964, for example), they were immediately eclipsed by "spaghetti westerns" made by Sergio Leone starring Clint Eastwood. A leading television actor in the United States, Eastwood filmed three of these westerns in Italy: *A Fistful of Dollars* (1964), *For A Few Dollars More* (1965), and *The Good, the Bad, and the Ugly* (1966). Despite being dubbed in English, these movies featured a silent "man with no name," who had no past as a criminal or lawman, and who arrived to dispense justice. Although Hollywood's inclination during this time was to blur the lines between the "good guys" and the "bad guys," films that succeeded still relied on a hero, and the American moviegoing public on the whole did not like to leave the theater depressed. Hollywood's inability to convert western heros into appealing villains failed most notoriously in *The Missouri Breaks* (1976), but the industry also failed to heed the lesson of *Heaven's Gate* (1980), which had a meandering plot, uninspired acting, and one of the most bloated budgets in film history.

More recent westerns, such as *Pale Rider* (1985, with Clint Eastwood), *Dances With Wolves* (1990, with Kevin Costner), and *Unforgiven* (1992, again, with Eastwood), won critical acclaim and two Best Picture awards by remaking their darker characters into heroes who nevertheless fight for justice.

Whatever its ability to move into other settings, the western film seemed to lack one characteristic—the ability to laugh at itself—until Mel Brooks produced *Blazing Saddles* (1973), followed by *The Villain* (1979), and *Silverado* (1985).

While it is unlikely that the moviegoing public will embrace westerns to the same degree it did in the 1940s and 1950s, the genre still remains viable for character studies, as seen in the immensely popular made-for-television miniseries, *Lonesome Dove* (1989). Modern audiences, however, seem to prefer faster plot lines than most westerns have provided.

the "western" on television

Almost from the beginning of television broadcasting, the "western" show was a staple of programming, beginning with *The Lone Ranger*, a long-running radio show that aired on television from 1949 to 1959. The program opened with the "William Tell Overture" and featured Clayton Moore as the Lone Ranger and Jay Silverheels as his "faithful companion," Tonto. This was followed by such shows as the *Life and Legend of Wyatt Earp [IV]* (1954), which opened with a barbershop-style quartet singing "Wyatt Earp, Wyatt Earp, brave, courageous and bold/Long live his fame, and long live his glory and long may his story be told." Television westerns (sometimes called "horse operas" as opposed to daytime dramas called "soap operas") glamorized the West and made mythic heroes of its characters, who fought injustice ("Hopalong Cassidy") and occasionally sang along the way (Roy *Rogers*). Walt Disney produced the highly popular *Davy Crockett [III]* series as part of his weekly television show.

By the late 1950s there were more than 40 different western-oriented series running on network television. Given the simple plots and the black-and-white nature of the characters, the shows used western weaponry as a "hook." Wyatt Earp carried a long-barreled pistol called a "Buntline Special" presented to him by Ned *Buntline [IV]*, a New York journalist. Steve McQueen's character on *Wanted: Dead or Alive* (1958–1961) packed a sawed-off shotgun.

Chuck Conner's pacifist farmer in *The Rifleman* (1958–1963) would not wear a pistol but wielded a Winchester repeater specially modified to fire like a semi-automatic. Bat *Masterson [IV]*, played by Gene Barry, had a gold-tipped cane that he employed as a sword and popped a deringer out of his belt-buckle when danger appeared. Chuck Conners, who returned for a show called *Branded*, portrayed a wrongly court-martialed cavalry officer who carried a broken sword honed into a minisaber.

No western was more popular than *Gunsmoke* (1955–1975). James Arness played Marshall Matt Dillon, a law-abiding, peaceful marshal required to employ his gun to maintain order. But the gunfight was always Dillon's last resort, and increasingly the shows began to resolve conflicts without guns. The nature of the half-hour or hour-long plots, however, meant that there could be little character development, although some shows began to emphasize the "loner" aspect of the West, notably Richard Boone's character "Paladin" in *Have Gun Will Travel* (1957–1963). And, as more women became viewers, emphasis on family shaped such shows as the popular *Bonanza* (1959–1973), where a widowed father and three grown sons ran a ranch. *The Virginian* (1962–1970), *The High Chaparral* (1967–1971), and *The Big Valley* (1965–1969) all reflected the family elements of running vast empires.

Complaints that these shows lacked "real people," even if true, ignored the basic fact that television was entertainment. Chinese in the West, black cowboys, the role of women, and more controversial religious movements such as Methodism and Mormonism were all either ignored or quietly blended into the main plots. But it is also a fact that "daily life" in the West was not a marketable commodity. *Little House on the Prairie*, a highly successful series from 1974 to 1982, based on the books of Laura Ingalls Wilder about her pioneer family, was an exception largely made possible by the highly popular character played by actor Michael Landon and the good supporting cast. The only women featured in early shows were Dale Evans, the costar of the *Roy Rogers Show*, and *Annie Oakley* (1954–1956), played by Gail Davis. But not until *Dr. Quinn, Medicine Woman*, (1993–1998) played by Jane Seymour, did a female star in a series in a role other than a gunfighter.

Likewise, the role of Indians was stereotypical in that Indians were almost always portrayed as either "hostiles" or "victims" that the white hero had to help. One exception was *Broken Arrow* (1956–1958) a touching series about the relationship between *Cochise [IV]* and Indian agent Tom Jeffords.

One attempt to break the mold was a television miniseries, *Centennial* (1978–1979), which had 25 episodes of the James Michener novel that chronicled the development of a Colorado city from the 1800s to the 1900s. In 1989 Larry *McMurtry*'s novel, *Lonesome Dove*, was a top-rated miniseries in which the characters played all-too-human roles. By the 1970s the traditional western had ceased to appeal to large audiences, although the most popular long-running nighttime drama in television history was *Dallas* (1978–1991), in which a wealthy Texas oil family battles outsiders and each other. Nevertheless, by the 1990s new, "softer" westerns had returned, including a television version of the *Magnificent Seven* film. The mythic West presented in the original westerns was often ridiculed, but the fact remains that television westerns spoke to classical American values of hard work, honesty, the rule of law, and resistance to oppression. The wonder is not that they lasted so long, but that they have disappeared at all.

western swing dancing

Emerging from the American jazz movement of the 1930s, a form of swing music called "western swing" coalesced in Texas and Oklahoma. Absorbing influences of the Irish jig and Scottish and English reels, the music also displayed hillbilly string band influences, as well as touches of Mexican folk music. Fiddling contests and dancing to string bands were common entertainments in the Southwest by the time that radio and record players introduced jazz to the region. Building on a strong 2/4 beat, known as a "two-step," the music had a strong dance appeal. Adding to the string sounds, swing bands added steel guitars, brass, mandolins, and later, electric guitars. Bob Wills, a Texas fiddler, performed daily on radio and became nationally known. Wills expanded the western swing sound by hiring many jazz musicians, forming a group called the Texas Playboys. By the 1990s country swing music had made a comeback with country line dancing, creating its own cowboy bar culture.

Wheeler, Burton Kendall (February 27, 1882– January 6, 1975)

Born in Hudson, Massachusetts, Burton Wheeler worked briefly as a stenographer before attending the University of Michigan, where he studied law and was admitted to the bar. He practiced law briefly in Butte, Montana, then in 1912 won a seat in the state legislature before being appointed as the U.S. district attorney for Montana. When that position ended, Wheeler returned to his law practice.

He was elected to the United States Senate in 1922 as a Democrat, then ran as Robert M. LaFollette's vice presidential candidate on the Progressive Party ticket, which was defeated in 1924. Wheeler then returned to the Democratic Party and his Senate seat, which he held until 1947, but he kept his reputation as the "fighting Progressive." Wheeler chaired the Indian Affairs Committee and the Interstate Commerce Committee and strongly supported Franklin Roosevelt's New Deal legislation. But as an isolationist, Wheeler broke with Roosevelt over policies that threatened to bring the United States into World War II. Defeated in 1946, Wheeler wrote an autobiography, *Yankee from the West* (1962). The University of Montana created the Burton K. Wheeler Center for the Exploration of Montana Issues in his honor.

Williams, Hank (September 17, 1923–January 1, 1953)

Singing on the streets in Montgomery, Alabama, from an early age, Hank Williams (born Hiram) played with his band, the Drifting Cowboys, developing the hillbilly sound associated with country and western music. After World War II, Williams had his first national hit, "Move It On Over." After moving to Shreveport, Louisiana, he emerged as a major star with "Lovesick Blues," which he followed up with "I'm So Lonesome I Could Cry." When he died in 1953, after a lifetime of alcoholism, he had changed the shape of country and western music and produced, with his wife Audrey Sheppard, a son, Hank Williams, Jr., who himself became a country star.

Wister, Owen (July 14, 1860–July 21, 1938)

After a normal, joyful childhood in Philadelphia and Germantown, Pennsylvania, Wister attended Harvard from 1878 to 1882, earning a degree in music with highest honors. He spent two years in Europe studying music, but he returned home in 1884 due to ill health. When his health failed to recover in

1885, Wister moved to Wyoming for a summer to live in the fresh, western air. His trip affected him deeply. "To ride twenty miles and see no chance of seeing human traces; to get up on a mountain and overlook any number of square miles," he wrote in 1885, "and never a column of smoke or a sound except the immediate grasshoppers—and then never to upstairs. You begin to wonder if there is such a place as Philadelphia anywhere."

From 1885 to 1888 Wister attended Harvard Law School. After graduation, he passed the Pennsylvania bar and opened a law firm in Philadelphia in 1889. But he hated his legal practice, and he longed for his life in the West. Indeed, he visited the region as often as possible. His good friend from his undergraduate days at Harvard, Theodore *Roosevelt*, convinced Wister to write about his summer convalescing in Wyoming as well as the experiences he had during other visits. Wister's first stories appeared in *Harper's* magazine in 1891. Thereafter came *Red Men and White* (1896), *Lin McLean* (1897), and *The Jimmyjohn Boss* (1900). In 1902, Wister published what many historians and literary scholars regard as the definitive western, *The Virginian*, a story about a school marm and a rough but virtuous cowboy who fall in love with one another. It was Wister's best and last novel. After the incredible success of *The Virginian*, Wister wrote only histories and biographies. He died in 1938 on Long Island.

Women's Professional Rodeo Association

Organized in Amarillo, Texas, in 1948 as the Girls Rodeo Association, the Women's Professional Rodeo Association provided a league for women who wanted to compete in *rodeo [IV]* events as a profession. Original membership consisted of 74 saddle bronc and trick riders, who competed in 60 contests for a total prize purse of $29,000. In 1981 the group officially changed its name to the Women's Professional Rodeo Association (WRPA), and by 1998 the organization had more than 2,000 women competing in 780 rodeos annually for nearly $3 million in prizes. The WPRA sanctions all-women rodeos, which have smaller prizes but include the same scope of competition as the male rodeos, sharing its rules with the Professional Rodeo Cowboys Association (PRCA), which sanctions its events as well.

World War II in the West

No single event spurred growth in the West more than World War II. In a few years, the western United States went from being a section of the country that seemed almost foreign to many easterners to one visited (voluntarily for work or involuntarily for military service) by millions of Americans. During the war some 10 million servicemen and women were stationed in the western United States. Many, if not most, liked what they saw, and a population boom ensued, with California's population rising by 1 million in a four-year span. The breakthrough technology of *air conditioning*, which became widely available, abetted the growth. However, population growth did not occur across the board in all western states: Montana, Nebraska, and the Dakotas lost population.

The war not only brought people westward but established several universities and cities as regional research and commercial hubs, bringing a vitality to the region that was often lacking east of the Mississippi. Population in the urban West rose rapidly, while farm states declined in population.

Technically, the war started in the West when the empire of Japan bombed Pearl Harbor in *Hawaii* on December 7, 1941. Initially, the government had grave concerns that Japan might attempt an invasion of the West Coast and prepared accordingly. After the immediate concern over an invasion lifted, the government set out to use the resources of the West and the proximity to the Pacific Ocean to full advantage. Los Angeles, San Francisco, and San Diego were transformed as thousands of people poured in, turning even smaller cities such as Richmond and Vallejo into metropolitan areas. A large percentage of the immigrants were minorities: the black population of California rose by 150,000, but Mexican American population also rose rapidly.

Japanese Americans were affected negatively by the war when President Franklin Roosevelt, in February 1942, ordered all Americans of Japanese descent living on the Pacific Coast to internment camps in Arizona, Colorado, Idaho, Utah, and Wyoming. In December 1944 the War Department allowed the detainees to go free, but only after they had lost jobs, homes, and reputations.

The Pacific Coast grew the most rapidly because of the opportunity for work that existed there. Huge shipyards and major aircraft manufacturing companies began to churn out the weapons of war. Boeing, *Douglas Aircraft*, *Lockheed*, Northrup, Hughes, North American, and Convair produced B-17s and B-24 bombers that by 1943 would raze the cities of Germany. Boeing alone employed 40,000 workers in Seattle and Renton, manufacturing 10,000 B-17 "Flying Fortress" bombers during the war. Between 1940 and 1945 employment in aircraft manufacturing in California alone rose from 1,000 to 300,000. California accounted for one-fifth of the more than 300,000 planes built during the war.

More impressive than the aircraft production figures was the work of steel magnate Henry J. *Kaiser*, who was charged by Roosevelt to construct "Liberty" ships as fast as possible. Kaiser recognized that before he built a single ship he needed a huge new workforce, which he enlisted by running ads in eastern cities. His engineers developed prefabricated housing that could support the new workforce and then constructed new shipyards in Richmond, Oakland, Vallejo, and San Pedro, California. The Bank of America generated $445 million in new housing loans during the war.

Kaiser's efficient yards built more than 800 ships per year, launching a vessel every 10 hours. Although his yards got Liberty Ship construction time to 25 days, Kaiser was not satisfied. By 1944 when his plants reached peak efficiency, the Kaiser shipyards produced the *Robert E. Peary* Liberty Ship in an astounding four and a half days from scratch. Oddly enough, hull sections for many ships of all sorts came from land-bound Denver, Colorado, which fabricated landing barges and other ship sections.

In addition to Kaiser's famous Fontana, California, integrated steel plant, new steel works were erected in Provo, Utah, while electronics and munitions work took place in Utah, Arizona, and New Mexico. Scientific research also relocated in the West at Cal Tech in Pasadena, the *Lawrence Livermore* Laboratory in Berkeley, and the *Los Alamos* government laboratories. While scientific groups working in these labs developed advanced torpedo tubes, worked on rocket motors and propellants, and laid the groundwork for jet engine research, some of the most important work involved the highly secret Manhattan Project, which yielded the atomic bomb. Under tremendously tight security, Los Alamos clustered some of the most brilliant scientific minds of the 20th century. Plutonium for the bomb was manufactured at the Hanford, Washington, facility. Ultimately, the result of their research and work, the atomic bomb, was tested in July 1945 at Los Alamos.

Beyond the sheer numbers in population shifts, the war brought fundamental changes to the West by introducing large numbers of "technocrats" to the major urban areas. These scientists, engineers, and managers brought more conservative attitudes to the West, marking a steady shift of the intermountain states to the Republican Party that has continued to the present. Temporarily, even California became more conservative due to the influx of the workers in the "clean" industries. Introduced to the scenic vistas and open lifestyle of the West, many wartime employees never left. Denver, Phoenix, El Paso, and Albuquerque benefited from these new residents to become "sunbelt" metropolises with new economic and political power.

Historians such as Gerald Nash argue that the rise of the New West depended heavily on federal spending for defense. It is certainly true that Uncle Sam sparked the relocation of millions, and provided funding for many western industries to take off during the war. But after the war, it was the residents, the entrepreneurs, and the "boosters" who solidified the gains temporarily provided by the federal government for the West.

Zoot suit riots

In 1943 groups of Mexican American youths adopted a status symbol of peg-bottomed trousers, wide-brimmed hats, and generally floppy suits reminiscent of the gangsters of the 1930s. They referred to these as "Zoot suits," and the Mexican Americans who wore them were derogatorily referred to as *pachucos*, implying that they were dangerous Mexicans. Servicemen stationed in Los Angeles resented the "Zoot-suiters" and violence soon broke out between the two groups, encompassing much of East Los Angeles.

Select Bibliography

Abbott, Carl. *Boosters and Businessmen: Popular Economic Thought and Urban Growth in the Antebellum Middle West.* Westport, CT: Greenwood Press, 1981.

Adelman, Jeremy, and Stephen Aron. "From Borderlands to Borders: Empires, Nation-States, and Peoples in between in North American History." *American Historical Review* 104 (June 1999): 814–841.

Allen, James B., and Glen M. Leonard. *The Story of the Latter-day Saints.* 2d ed. Salt Lake City: Deseret Books, 1992.

Allen, John Logan, ed. *A Continent Defined*, vol. 2, *North American Exploration.* Lincoln: University of Nebraska Press, 1997.

_____. *Western Rivermen, 1763–1861: Ohio and Mississippi Boatmen and the Myth of the Alligator Horse.* Baton Rouge: Louisiana State University Press, 1990.

Ambrose, Stephen E. *Undaunted Courage: Meriwether Lewis, Thomas Jefferson, and the Opening of the American West.* New York: Simon and Schuster, 1996.

Anderson, David. *William Jennings Bryan.* Boston: Twayne, 1981.

_____. *The New Urban America: Growth and Politics in Sunbelt Cities.* Chapel Hill: University of North Carolina Press, 1981.

Anderson, Terry, and P. J. Hill. "An American Experiment in Anarcho-Capitalism: The Not So Wild, Wild West." *Journal of Libertarian Studies* 3 (1979): 9–29.

_____, ed. *The Political Economy of the American West.* Lanham, MD: Rowman and Littlefield, 1994.

_____, ed. *Property Rights and Indian Economies.* Lanham, MD: Rowman and Littlefield, 1992.

Anonymous. *From Greene Ville to Fallen Timbers: A Journal of the Wayne Campaign, July 28–September 14, 1794*, ed. Dwight L. Smith. Indianapolis: Indiana Historical Society, 1794.

Anson, Bert. "The Early Years of Lathrop M. Taylor, the Fur Trader." *Indiana Magazine of History* 44 (December 1948): 367–383.

_____. *The Miami Indians.* Norman: University of Oklahoma Press, 1970.

_____. "Variations of the Indian Conflict: The Effects of the Emigrant Indian Removal Policy, 1830–1854." *Missouri Historical Review* 59 (October 1964): 64–89.

Aquila, Richard. *The Iroquois Restoration: Iroquois Diplomacy on the Colonial Frontier, 1701–1754.* Lincoln: University of Nebraska Press, 1997.

Argersinger, Peter H. *The Limits of Agrarian Radicalism: Western Populism and American Politics.* Lawrence: University Press of Kansas, 1995.

Arrington, Leonard J. *Great Basin Kingdom.* Cambridge: Harvard University Press, 1958.

_____. and Davis Bitton. *The Mormon Experience: A History of the Latter-day Saints.* 2d ed. Urbana: University of Illinois Press, 1992.

Aron, Stephen. *How the West Was Lost: The Transformation of Kentucky from Daniel Boone to Henry Clay.* Baltimore: Johns Hopkins, 1996.

Atherton, Lewis E. "The Santa Fe Trader as Mercantile Capitalist." *Missouri Historical Review* 77, (October 1962): 1–12.

_____. *The Cattle Kings.* Bloomington: Indiana University Press, 1961.

_____. *The Frontier Merchant in Mid-America.* Columbia: University of Missouri Press, 1971.

Bailyn, Bernard. *The Peopling of British North America: An Introduction.* New York: Alfred A. Knopf, 1986.

Ball, Larry D. *Desert Lawmen: The High Sheriffs of New Mexico and Arizona, 1846–1912.* Albuquerque: University of New Mexico Press, 1992.

Banning, Evelyn I. *Helen Hunt Jackson.* New York: Vanguard, 1973.

Barker, Eugene C. *The Life of Stephen F. Austin, Founder of Texas, 1793–1836.* New York: Da Capo, 1968.

Barnhart, John D., and Dorothy Riker. *Indiana to 1816: The Colonial Period.* Indianapolis: Indiana Historical Society, 1994.

Bartlett, Donald L., and James B. Steele. *Empire: The Life, Legend, and Madness of Howard Hughes.* New York: W. W. Norton, 1979.

Beckwith, Hiram W. "The Miamis." In *The Illinois and Indiana Indians,* 107–117. Chicago: Fergus Printing Co., 1884.

Benton, Elbert Jay. *The Wabash Trade Route in the Development of the Old Northwest.* Baltimore: Johns Hopkins Press, 1903.

Bernard, Richard M., and Bradley R. Rice, eds. *Sunbelt Cities: Politics and Growth Since World War II.* Austin: University of Texas Press, 1983.

Billington, Ray Allen. *The Far Western Frontier, 1830–1860.* New York: Harper and Row, 1956.

Billington, Ray Allen, and Martin Ridge. *Westward Expansion: A History of the American Frontier*. 5th ed. New York: Macmillan, 1982.

A Biographical History of Eminent and Self-Made Men of the State of Indiana. Vol. 2. Cincinnati, OH: Western Biographical Publishing Company, 1880.

Bird, Harrison. *War for the West, 1790–1813*. New York: Oxford University Press, 1971.

Birzer, Bradley J. "Silver, Discontent, and Conspiracy: The Ideology of the Western Republican Revolt of 1890–1901." *Pacific Historical Review* (May 1995): 243–265.

_____. "The Private West: Voluntary Associations in the American Wests." In *Frontiers of Western History: Origins, Evolution, and the Future of Western History*, eds. Michael Allen and Mary L. Hanneman. Carmel, IN: Simon and Schuster, 1999.

Bishop, Joan. "Vigorous Attempts to Prosecute: Pinkerton Men on Montana's Range, 1914." *Montana* 30 (1980): 2–15.

Bogue, Allan G. "The Iowa Claim Clubs: Symbol and Substance." *Mississippi Valley Historical Review* 45 (1958): 231–251.

Bolton, Herbert Eugene. *The Spanish Borderlands: A Chronicle of Old Florida and the Southwest.* Toronto: U.S. Publishers Association, 1921.

Bonadio, Felice. *A. P. Giannini, Banker of America*. Berkeley: University of California Press, 1994.

Boyle, Susan Calafate. *Los Capitalistas: Hispano Merchants and the Santa Fe Trade*. Albuquerque: University of New Mexico Press, 1997.

Brebner, John Bartlett. *Explorers of North America, 1492–1806*. New York: Macmillan, 1933.

Brice, Wallace A. *History of Fort Wayne from the Earliest Known Accounts of This Point, to the Present Period*. Fort Wayne, IN: D.W. Jones, 1868.

Brophy, William, and Sopie Aberle, eds. *The Indian: America's Unfinished Business*. Norman: University of Oklahoma Press, 1966.

Brown, Richard Maxwell. "Violence." In *The Oxford History of the American West*. Edited by Cleyde A Milner II, Carol A. O'Connor and Martha Sandweiss. New York: Oxford University Press, 1994

Bryant, Keith L., Jr. *History of the Atchison, Topeka and Santa Fe Railway*. Lincoln: University of Nebraska Press, 1982.

Burnet, Jacob. *Notes on the Early Settlement of the North-Western Territory*. New York: D. Appleton, 1847.

Bushnell, David L., Jr. "The Virginia Frontier in History—1778." *Virginia Magazine of History and Biography* 23 (October 1915).

Bushnell, David L., Jr., ed. "A Journey through the Indian Country Beyond the Ohio, 1785 [Journal of Samuel Montgomery]." *Mississippi Valley Historical Review* 2 (1915–1916): 261–273.

Butler, Anne M. *Daughters of Joy, Sisters of Misery: Prostitutes in the American West, 1865–90.* Urbana: University of Illinois Press, 1985.

Calloway, Colin G. *Crown and Calumet: British-Indian Relations, 1783–1815.* Norman: University of Oklahoma Press, 1987.

_____. *Our Hearts Fell to the Ground: Plains Indian Views of How the West was Lost.* Boston: Bedford, 1996.

_____. *First Peoples: A Documentary Survey of American Indian History.* Boston: Bedford: 1999.

_____. *The World Turned Upside Down: Indian Voices from Early America.* Boston: Bedford, 1994.

Calomiris, Charles, and Larry Schweikart. "The Panic of 1857: Causes, Transmission, and Containment." *Journal of Economic History* 51 (December 1990): 807–834.

Cambell, Randolph B. *Sam Houston and the American Southwest.* New York: HarperCollins, 1993.

Carely, Kenneth. *The Sioux Uprising of 1862.* 2d ed. St. Paul: Minnesota Historical Society, 1976.

Carpenter, John A. *Sword and Olive Branch: Oliver Otis Howard.* Pittsburgh: University of Pittsburgh Press, 1964.

Carriker, Robert C. *Father Peter John De Smet: Jesuit in the West.* Norman: University of Oklahoma Press, 1995.

Carstensen, Vernon, ed. *The Public Lands: Studies in the History of the Public Domain.* Madison: University of Wisconsin Press, 1968.

Carter, Clarence Edwin, ed. *The Territorial Papers of the United States.* Washington, DC: U.S. Government Printing Office, 1934.

_____. *The Life and Times of Little Turtle: First Sagamore of the Wabash.* Urbana: University of Illinois Press, 1987.

Cather, Willa. *O Pioneers.* Boston: Houghton Mifflin, 1913; 1988.

Caughey, John W. *Hubert Howe Bancroft, Historian of the West.* Berkeley: University of California Press, 1946.

Cayton, Andrew R. L. *The Frontier Republic: Ideology and Politics in the Ohio Country, 1780–1825.* Kent, OH: Kent State University, 1986.

_____. *Frontier Indiana A History of the Trans-Appalachian Frontier, eds.* Walter Nugent and Malcolm Rohrbough. Bloomington: Indiana University Press, 1996.

Chalfant, William Y. *Cheyennes and Horse Soldiers: The 1857 Expedition and the Battle of Solomon's Fork.* Norman: University of Oklahoma Press, 1989.

Chambers, William N. *Old Bullion Benton: Senator from the West.* Boston: Little Brown, 1956.

Chaput, Donald. "The Family of Drouet De Richerville: Merchants, Soldiers, and Chiefs of Indiana." *Indiana Magazine of History* 74 (June 1978): 103–116.

Childs, Marquis. *Mighty Mississippi: Biography of a River.* New Haven, CT: Ticknor and Fields, 1982.

Clarke, Dwight L. *Stephen Watts Kearny, Soldier of the West.* Norman: University of Oklahoma Press, 1961.

Cleaves, Freeman. *Old Tippecanoe; William Henry Harrison and His Time.* New York: Charles Scribner's Sons, 1939.

Coleman, Christopher B., ed. "Letters from Eighteenth Century Indiana Merchants." *Indiana Magazine of History* 5 (December 1909): 137–159.

Coletta, Paolo. *William Jennings Bryan.* Lincoln: University of Nebraska Press, 1964.

Coman, Katherine. "Government Factories: An Attempt to Control Competition in the Fur Trade." *Publications of the American Economic Association* 4 (April 1911): 368–388.

Conkling, Roscoe P., and Margaret B. Conkling. *The Butterfield Overland Mail,* 1857–1869. Glendale, CA: A. H. Clark, 1947.

Convey, Cyclone, trans. *Cabeza de Vaca's Adventures in the Unknown Interior of America.* Albuquerque: University of New Mexico Press, 1983.

Cooke, Sarah E., and Rachel B. Ramadhyani, eds. *Indians and a Changing Frontier: The Art of George Winter.* Indianapolis: Indiana Historical Society, 1993.

Coquillard, Mary Clarke. *Alexis Coquillard—His Time: A Story of the Founding of South Bend, Indiana.* South Bend: Northern Indiana Historical Society, 1931.

Cornelius, Wayne, Leo R. Chavez, and Jorge G. Castro, eds. *Mexican Immigrants and Southern California.* La Jolla: University of California, San Diego. 1982.

Cottman, George. "The Wabash and Its Valley: Part I—the Earlier History." *Indiana Magazine of History* 1 (1905): 59–67.

Cremony, John C. *Life Among the Apaches.* San Francisco: A. Roman, 1868.

Crockett, David. *Life and Adventures of Davy Crocket. An Autobiography.* New York: G. Munro, 1882.

Crockett, Norman L. *The Black Towns*. Lawrence: Regents Press of Kansas, 1979.

Croghan, George. "Journal of George Croghan, 1750–1765." In *Early Western Travels, 1748–1846*, ed. Reuben Gold Thwaites, 1, 47–173. Cleveland, OH: Arthur H. Clark, 1904.

Cronon, William. *Changes in the Land: Indians, Colonists, and the Ecology of New England*. New York: Hill and Wang, 1983.

Cronon, William, George Miles, and Jay Gitlin, eds. *Under an Open Sky: Rethinking America's Western Past*. New York: W. W. Norton, 1992.

Crosby, Alfred W. *Ecological Imperialism: The Biological Expansion of Europe, 900–1900*. Cambridge: Cambridge University Press, 1986.

Cruikshank, Ernest Alexander. "Robert Dickson, the Indian Trader." *Wisconsin Historical Collections* 12 (1892): 133–153.

Cusic, Don. *Cowboys and the Wild West: An A–Z Guide from the Chisholm Trail to the Silver Screen*. New York: Facts on File, 1994.

Cutter, Charles R. "The Administration of Law in Colonial New Mexico." *Journal of the Early Republic* 18 (Spring 1998): 99–114.

Dallek, Robert. *Lone Star Rising: Lyndon Johnson and His Times, 1908–1961*. New York: Oxford University Press, 1991.

Dary, David. *Entrepreneurs of the Old West*. Lincoln: University of Nebraska Press, 1986.

Davis, William C. *Three Roads to the Alamo: The Lives and Fortunes of David Crockett, James Bowie, and William Barret Travis*. New York: Harper Collins, 1998.

de Graaf, Lawrence B. "Race, Sex, and Region: Black Women in the American West, 1850–1920." *Pacific Historical Review* 49 (May 1980): 285–313.

de la Teja, Jesus Frank. "Discovering the Tejano Community in "Early" Texas." *Journal of the Early Republic* 18 (Spring 1998): 73–115.

DeArment, Robert K. *Bat Masterson, the Man and the Legend*. Norman: University of Oklahoma Press, 1979.

Descriptions of Nature, the Religious, Political, and Social Life Gathered from Letters by a Catholic Missionary–Augsburg 1845. Augsburg, Bavaria: D. Schmid Bookstore, 1845.

DeVoto, Bernard. *The Course of Empire*. Boston: Houghton Mifflin, 1952.

Dillon, John B. *The National Decline of the Miami Indians 1848*. Indianapolis: Bowen-Merrill Co., 1897.

Dippie, Brian W. *The Vanishing American*. Middletown, CT: Wesleyan University Press, 1982.

Dobie, J. Frank. *The Mustangs.* Austin: University of Texas Press, 1990.

Donnelly, Joseph P. *Jacques Marquette, S.J.* Chicago: Loyola, 1968.

Doti, Lynne Pierson, and Larry Schweikart. *Banking in the American West from the Gold Rush to Deregulation.* Norman: University of Oklahoma Press, 1991.

Dowd, Gregory Evans. *A Spirited Resistence: The North American Indian Struggle for Unity, 1745–1815.* Johns Hopkins University Studies in Historical and Political Science. Baltimore: Johns Hopkins University Press, 1992.

_____. *The Social Order of a Frontier Community: Jacksonville, Illinois, 1825–70.* Urbana: University of Illinois Press, 1978.

Drake, Samuel G. *Biography and History of the Indians of North America.* Boston: Benjamin B. Mussey, 1851.

Dubofsky, Melvyn. "The Origins of Western Working Class Radicalism, 1890–1905." *Labor History* 7 (Spring 1966): 131–154.

Dykstra, Robert P. *The Cattle Towns.* New York: Atheneum, 1970.

Edmunds, R. David. *The Potawatomis: Keepers of the Fire.* Norman: University of Oklahoma Press, 1978.

_____, ed. *American Indian Leaders: Studies in Diversity.* Lincoln: University of Nebraska Press, 1980.

_____. *The Shawnee Prophet.* Lincoln: University of Nebraska Press, 1983.

_____. *Tecumseh and the Quest for Indian Leadership.* Library of American Biography, ed. Oscar Handlin. New York: HarperCollins, 1984.

Edmunds, R. David, and Joseph L. Peyser. *The Fox Wars: The Mesquakie Challenge to New France.* Norman: University of Oklahoma Press, 1993.

Eid, Leroy V. "American Indian Military Leadership: St. Clair's 1791 Defeat." *Journal of Military History* 57 (January 1993): 71–88.

Eisenhower, John S. D. *So Far from God: The U.S. War with Mexico, 1846–1848.* New York: Random House, 1989.

Ekirch, Arthur A., Jr. *Man and Nature in America.* Lincoln: University of Nebraska Press, 1973.

Emmons, David M. *The Butte Irish: Class and Ethnicity in an American Mining Town, 1875–1925.* Urbana: University of Illinois Press, 1989.

Esarey, Logan, ed. *Messages and Letters of William Henry Harrison.* Vol. I: 1800–1811. Indianapolis: Indiana Historical Commission, 1922.

_____, ed. *Messages and Letters of William Henry Harrison [Concluded].* Vol. 2: 1812–1816. Bloomington: Indiana Historical Commission, 1922.

Etulain, Richard W., ed. *Writing Western History: Essays on Major Western Historians.* Albuquerque: University of New Mexico Press, 1991.

Faragher, John Mack. *Women and Men on the Overland Trail.* New Haven: Yale University Press, 1979.

_____. *Daniel Boone: The Life and Legend of an American Pioneer.* New York: Henry Holt, 1992.

Farnham. *Part I of Farnham's Travels in the Great Western Prairies, Etc., May 21–October 16, 1839.* Vol. 28 Early Western Travels, 1748–1846, ed. Reuben Gold Thwaites. Cleveland, OH: Arthur H. Clark, 1839.

Faux. *Part I of Faux's Memorable Days in America, 1819–1820.* Vol. 11 Early Western Travels, 1748–1846, ed. Reuben Gold Thwaites. Cleveland, OH: Arthur H. Clark, 1819.

Faye, Stanley. "Illinois Indians on the Lower Mississippi, 1771–1782." *Journal of the Illinois State Historical Society* 35 (March 1942): 57–72.

Fenin, George N., and William K. Everson. *The Western: From Silents to Cinerama.* New York: Bonanza Books, 1962.

Fitzgerald, Daniel. *Ghost Towns of Kansas: A Traveler's Guide.* Lawrence: University Press of Kansas, 1988.

Flores, Dan. "Bison Ecology and Bison Diplomacy: The Southern Plains from 1800–1850." *Journal of American History* 78 (September 1991): 465–485.

_____ ed. *Jefferson and Southwestern Exploration: The Freeman and Custis Accounts of the Red River Expedition of 1806.* Norman: University of Oklahoma Press, 1984.

Folsom, Burton W. *Empire Builders: How Michigan Entrepreneurs Helped Make America Great.* Traverse City, MI: Rhodes and Easton, 1998.

Font, Walter, ed. *A Garrison at Miami Town: Fort Wayne, October 1794–June 1795 [Lt. Massey's Orderly Book].* Fort Wayne: Fort Wayne-Allen County Historical Society, 1994.

Forbes, Jack D. "The Indian in the West: A Challenge for Historians." *Arizona and the West* 1 (Autumn 1958): 206–15.

_____. "Frontier in American History." *Journal of the West* 1 (July 1962): 63–73.

Foster, Mark S. *Henry J. Kaiser: Builder in the Modern American West.* Austin: University of Texas Press, 1989.

Fradkin, Phillip L. *A River No More: The Colorado River and the West.* Tucson: University of Arizona Press, 1984.

Frazer, Robert W. *Forts of the West: Military Forts and Presidios and Posts Commonly Called Forts West of the Mississippi to 1898.* Norman: University of Oklahoma Press, 1965.

Frederick, J. V. *Ben Holladay, the Stagecoach King.* Glendale, CA: Arthur H. Clark. 1940.

Frazier, Ian. *Great Plains.* New York: Farrar, Straus, and Giroux, 1989.

Garber, Paul N. *The Gadsden Treaty.* Philadelphia: University Press of Pennsylvania, 1923.

Gipson, Lawrence Henry. *The British Empire Before the American Revolution.* New York: Knopf, 1958.

_____. "The Fur Trade, the Long Portage and the Forks of the Wabash." In *The Forks of the Wabash: An Historical Survey*, eds. Dwight and Ann Ericsson, 7–26. Huntington, IN: Historic Forks of the Wabash, 1994.

Goetzmann, William H. "Exploration and Imperialism: 1805–45." In *Exploration and Empire: The Explorer and the Scientist in theWinning of the American West*, 1–198. New York: History Book Club, 1993.

Goetzmann, William, and Glyndwr Williams. *Atlas of North American Exploration: From the Norse Voyages to the Race to the PoleI.* New York: Prentice Hall, 1992.

Goldstein, Daniel. "Midwestern Naturalists: Academies of Science in the Mississippi Valley, 1850–1900." Dissertation, Yale University, 1989.

Gravlin, Steven C. "Josiah Harmar and the Army on the Northwest Frontier." *Valley Forge Journal* 5 (1990): 40–68.

Gregg, J. *Part II of Gregg's Commerce of the Prairies, 1831–1839*, vol. 20 *Early Western Travels*, ed. Reuben Gold Thwaites. Cleveland, OH: Arthur H. Clark, 1844.

Gressley, Gene M. *The American West: A Reorientation.* Laramie: University of Wyoming, 1966.

_____, ed. *Old West, New West.* Norman: University of Oklahoma Press, 1997.

_____. *The Turner Thesis: A Problem in Historiography.* Indianapolis: Bobbs-Merrill, 1949.

_____. *The Twentieth Century West: A Potpourri.* Columbia: University of Missouri Press, 1977.

Griffiths, David B. "Far Western Populism: The Case of Utah, 1893–1900." *Utah Historical Quarterly* 37 (Fall 1967): 397–407.

Griswold, Bert J. *The Pictorial History of Fort Wayne.* Chicago: Robert O. Law Company, 1917.

Grossman, James R., ed. *The Frontier in American Culture: Essays by Richard White and Patricia Nelson Limerick*. Berkeley: University of California Press, 1994.

Grubber, Frank. *Zane Grey: A Biography*. Roslyn, New York. Walter J. Black. 1969.

Haeger, John D. "Economic Development of the American West." In *American Frontier and Western Issues: A Historigraphical Review*, ed. Roger Nichols. New York: Greenwood Press, 1986.

Haines, Michael R., ed. *A Population History of North America*. New York: Cambridge University Press, 2000.

Haites, Erik F., James Jak, and Gary Walton. *Western River Transportation: The Era of Early Internal Improvement*. Baltimore: Johns Hopkins Press, 1975.

Hamilton, Holman. *Prologue to Conflict: The Crisis and Compromise of 1850*. Lexington: University of Kentucky Press, 1964.

Hardin, John Wesley. *The Life and Times of John Wesley Hardin as Written by Himself*. Norman: University of Oklahoma Press, 1961.

Harris, Marshall. *Origin of the Land Tenure System in the United States*. Ames: Iowa State University Press. 1953.

Harrison, William Henry. *A Discourse on the Aborigines of the Ohio Valley*. Chicago: Fergus Printing, 1883.

Helm, Thomas B., ed. *History of Allen County, Indiana, with Illustrations and Biographical Sketches of Some of Its Prominent Men and Pioneers*. Chicago: Kingman Brothers, 1880.

Heyman, Josiah McC. *Life and the Labor on the Border: Working People of Northeastern Sonora, Mexico, 1886–1986*. Tucson: University of Arizona Press, 1991.

Hicks, John D. *The Populist Revolt: A History of the Farmers' Alliance and the People's Party*. Lincoln: University of Nebraska Press, 1961.

Higgs, Robert. "Landless by Law: Japanese Immigrants in California Agriculture to 1941." *Journal of Economic History* 38 (March 1978).

_____. "The Wealth of Japanese Tenant Farmers in California, 1909." *Agricultural History* 53 (April 1979): 488–493.

Hill, Leonard U. *John Johnston and the Indians: In the Land of the Three Miamis*. Piqua, OH: 1957.

Hinckley, Ted C., ed. *Entrepreneurship in the West*. Manhattan, KS: Sunflower University Press, 1986.

Hine, Robert V. *Community on the Frontier: Separate but Not Alone*. Norman: University of Oklahoma Press, 1980.

Hodge, Frederick W., and Theodore H. Lewis, eds. *Spanish Explorers in the Southern United States*. New York: Barnes and Noble, 1959.

Hofsommer, Don L. *The Southern Pacific, 1901–1985*. College Station: Texas A&M University Press, 1986.

Hoig, Stan. *Tribal Wars of the Southern Plains*. Norman: University of Oklahoma Press, 1993.

Hollon, W. Eugene. *Frontier Violence: Another Look*. New York: Oxford University Press, 1974.

Horn, Miriam. "The Old West: The New View of Frontier Life." *U.S. News and World Report* (May 21, 1990): 56–65.

Horsman, Reginald. "Western War Aims, 1811–1812." *Indiana Magazine of History* 53 (March 1957): 1–18.

_____. "British Indian Policy in the Northwest, 1807–1812." *Mississippi Valley Historical Review* 45 (June 1958): 51–66.

_____. "American Indian Policy in the Old Northwest, 1783–1812." *William and Mary Quarterly* 18 (January 1961): 35–53.

Houck, Louis, ed. *The Spanish Regime in Missouri*. Chicago: R. R. Donnelley, 1909.

Houze, Herbert G. *Winchester Repeating Arms Company: Its History and Development from 1865 to 1981*. Iola, WI: Krause Publications, 1994.

Hoxie, Frederick E. *Parading through History: The Making of the Crow Nation in America, 1805–1935*. Cambridge: Cambridge University Press, 1995.

_____ ed. *Encyclopedia of North American Indians*. Boston: Houghton Mifflin, 1996.

Hoy, Jim, and Tom Isern. *Plains Folk: The Romance of the Landscape*. Norman: University of Oklahoma Press, 1990.

_____. "They Saw the Early Midwest: A Bibliography of Travel Narratives, 1727–1850." *Iowa Journal of History* 52 (1954): 223–234.

Hughes, John T. *Doniphan's Expedition*. Chicago: Rio Grande Press, 1962.

Hundley, Norris. *Water and the West: The Colorado River Compact and the Politics of Water in the American West*. Bloomington: Indiana University Press, 1984.

_____. *Dividing the Waters: A Century of Controversy Between the United States and Mexico*. Berkeley: University of California Press, 1966.

Hungerford, Edward. *Wells Fargo: Advancing the American Frontier*. New York: Random House, 1949.

Hurt, R. Douglas. *The Ohio Frontier: Crucible of the Old Northwest, 1720–1830* A History of the Trans-Appalachian Frontier, eds. Walter Nugent and Malcolm Rohrbough. Bloomington: Indiana University Press, 1996.

_____. *Nathan Boone and the American Frontier*. Columbia: University of Missouri Press, 1998.

Hutton, Paul Andrew. *Phil Sheridan and His Army*. Lincoln: University of Nebraska Press, 1985.

Ichihashi, Yamato. *Japanese in the United States*. New York: Arno, 1969.

Iverson, Peter. *Barry Goldwater, Native Arizonan*. Norman: University of Oklahoma Press, 1997.

Jacobs, Lewis. *The Rise of the American Film: A Critical History*. New York: Harcourt Brace, 1939.

Jacobs, Wilbur R. "The Indian and the Frontier in American History—a Need for Revision." *Western Historical Quarterly* 4 (January 1973): 43–56.

Jahns, Pat. *The Frontier World of Doc Holliday: Faro Dealer from Dallas to Deadwood*. New York: Hastings House, 1957.

James, Marquis, and Bessie R. James. *Biography of a Bank: The Story of Bank of America, N.T. & S.A.* New York: Harper, 1954.

Jameson, Elizabeth, and Susan Armitage, eds. *Writing the Range: Race, Class, and Culture in the Women's West*. Norman: University of Oklahoma, 1997.

Jefferson, Thomas. *The Writings of Thomas Jefferson*. Vol. 15, ed. Albert Ellery Bergh. Washington, DC: Thomas Jefferson Memorial Association, 1907.

Jennings, Francis. *The Ambiguous Iroquois Empire: The Covenant Chain Confederation of Indian Tribes with English Colonies from Its Beginnings to the Lancaster Treaty of 1744*. New York: W. W. Norton, 1984.

_____. *The Founders of America: From the Earliest Migrations to the Present*. New York: W. W. Norton, 1993.

Jensen, Joan M. *With These Hands: Working Women on the Land*. Old Westbury, NY: Feminist Press, 1981.

Johanssen, Robert W. *Stephen A. Douglas*. New York: Oxford, 1973.

_____. *To the Halls of the Montezumas: The Mexican War in American Imagination*. New York: Oxford, 1985.

Johnson, Dorothy M. *The Bloody Bozeman: The Perilous Trail to Montana's Gold*. Missoula, MT: Mountain Press, 1983.

Jordan, Terry G. *North American Cattle-Ranching Frontiers: Origins, Diffusion, and Differentiation.* Albuquerque: University of New Mexico Press, 1993.

Josephy, Alvin M., Jr. *The Civil War in the American West.* New York: Alfred A. Knopf, 1992.

Kappler, Charles J., ed. *Indian Treaties, 1778–1883.* New York: Interland Publishing.

Katz, William Loren. *The Black West,* 3d ed. Seattle, WA: Open Hand, 1987.

Keenan, Jerry. *Encyclopedia of American Indian Wars, 1492–1890.* New York: W. W. Norton, 1999.

Keleher, William A. *Violence in Lincoln County.* Albuquerque: University of New Mexico Press, 1957.

Kenny, Martin, ed. *Understanding Silicon Valley: The Anatomy of an Entrepreneurial Region.* Stanford, CA: Stanford University Press, 2000.

Kellar, Herbert Anthony, ed. *Solon Robinson, Pioneer and Agriculturalist: Selected Writings, 1825–1845.* Vol. 1. Indianapolis: Indiana Historical Bureau, 1936.

Klein, Maury. *Union Pacific: Birth of a Railroad, 1862–1893.* Garden City, NY: Doubleday, 1987.

Klingaman, David C., and Richard K. Vedder, eds. *Essays in Nineteenth Century Economic History.* Athens: Ohio University Press, 1975.

_____, eds. *Essays on the Economy of the Old Northwest.* Athens: Ohio University Press, 1987.

_____, ed *Anthony Wayne, a Name in Arms: Soldier, Diplomat, Defender of Expansion Westward of a Nation.* Pittsburgh: University of Pittsburgh Press, 1960.

Knopf, Richard C., ed. *Document Transcriptions of the War of 1812 in the Northwest.* Columbus: Ohio Historical Society, 1958.

Lamar, Howard Roberts. *The Far Southwest, 1846–1912: A Territorial History.* New Haven: Yale University Press, 1966.

_____ ed. *The New Encyclopedia of the American West.* New Haven, CT: Yale University Press, 1998.

_____. *The Trader on the American Frontier: Myth's Victim.* College Station: Texas A&M University Press, 1977.

Larson, Robert W. *Populism in the Mountain West.* Albuquerque: University of New Mexico Press, 1986.

_____. *Red Cloud: Warrior-Statesman of the Lakota Sioux.* Norman: University of Oklahoma Press, 1997.

Lea, Tom. *The King Ranch.* 2 vols. Kingsville, TX: King Ranch, 1957.

Leckie, Robert. *The Wars of America.* New York: Harper and Row, 1981.

_____. "Chief Jean Baptiste Richardville." In *The Forks of the Wabash: An Historical Survey,* ed. Dwight Ericcson and Ann Ericsson, 75–88. Huntington, IN: Historic Forks of the Wabash, 1994.

Leonard, Craig. *Historic Structure Report: The Indian House.* Huntington, IN: Historic Forks of the Wabash, n.d.

Leonard, Stephen J., and Thomas J. Noel. *Denver: Mining Camp to Metropolis.* Niwot: University Press of Colorado, 1990.

Light, Ivan, and Edna Bonacich. *Immigrant Entrepreneurs: Koreans in Los Angeles, 1965–1982.* Berkeley: University of California Press, 1988.

Limerick, Patricia Nelson. *The Legacy of Conquest: The Unbroken Past of the American West.* New York: W. W. Norton, 1987.

Limerick, Patricia Nelson, Clyde A. Milner, and Charles E. Rankin, eds. *Trails: Toward a New Western History.* Lawrence: University Press of Kansas, 1991.

Lindley, Harlow, ed. *Indiana as Seen by Early Travelers: A Collection of Reprints from Books of Travel, Letters and Diaries Prior to 1830.* Indianapolis: Indiana Historical Commission, 1916.

Loewenberg, Robert J. *Equality on the Oregon Frontier: Jason Lee and the Methodist Mission, 1834–43.* Seattle: University of Washington Press, 1976.

Logsdon, Guy, Mary Rogers, and William Jacobson. *Saddle Serenaders.* Layton, UT: Gibbs-Smith, 1994.

Lotchin, Roger. *Fortress California, 1910–1961: From Warfare to Welfare.* New York: Oxford University Press, 1992.

Lowett, Richard. *The New Deal and the West.* Bloomington: Indiana University Press, 1984.

Luebke, Frederick C. "Ethnic Group Settlement on the Great Plains." *Western Historical Quarterly* 8 (October 1977): 405–430.

_____, ed. *Ethnicity on the Great Plains.* Lincoln: University of Nebraska Press, 1980.

Malin, James. *History and Ecology: Studies in the Grassland,* ed. Robert Swierenga. Lincoln: University of Nebraska Press, 1984.

McCallum, Henry D., and Frances McCallum. *The Wire That Fenced the West.* Norman: University of Oklahoma Press, 1965.

Malin, James C. *Essays on Historiography*. Lawrence: privately published by author, 1946.

Malone, Dumas. *Jefferson and His Time*. 6 vols. Boston: Little Brown and Company, 1948–1981.

Malone, Michael P. *James J. Hill: Empire Builder of the Northwest*. Norman: University of Oklahoma Press, 1996.

Malone, Michael P., and Richard W. Etulain. *The American West: A Twentieth-Century History*. Lincoln: University of Nebraska Press, 1989.

Mangrum, R. Collin. *Zion in the Courts: A Legal History of the Church of Jesus Christ of Latter-Day Saints*. Urbana: University of Illinois Press, 1988.

Mansfield, Edward Deering. *Personal Memories, Social, Political and Literary, 1803–1843*. New York: Arno and the *New York Times*, 1970.

Marks, Paula Mitchell. *And Die in the West: The Story of the O.K. Corral Gunfight*. New York: Morrow, 1989.

Martin, Albro. *James J. Hill and the Opening of the Northwest*. St. Paul: Minnesota Historical Society Press, 1991.

_____. *Railroads Triumphant: The Growth, Rejection, and Rebirth of a Vital American Force*. New York: Oxford University Press, 1992.

McCoy, Isaac. *History of the Baptist Indian Missions*. New York: Johnson Reprint Corporation, 1970.

McCulloch, Hugh. *Men and Measures of Half a Century*. New York: Charles Scribner's Sons, 1888.

McMurtry, Larry. *Lonesome Dove*. New York: Pocket Books, 1985.

Meek, Basil, ed. "General Harmar's Expedition." *Ohio Archaeological and Historical Quarterly* 20 (1911): 74–108.

Merk, Frederick. *Manifest Destiny and Mission in American History: A Reinterpretation*. New York: Vintage Books, 1963.

Miller, Nyle H., and Joseph W. Snell. *Why the West Was Wild: A Contemporary Look at Some Highly Publicized Kansas Cowtown Personalities*. Topeka: Kansas State Historical Society, 1963.

Milner, Clyde A., II, ed. *A New Significance: Re-Envisioning the History of the American West*. New York: Oxford University Press, 1996.

Milner, Clyde A., II, Carol A. O'Connor, and Martha A. Sandweiss, eds. *The Oxford History of the American West*. New York: Oxford University Press, 1994.

Miner, H. Craig. *The Corporation and the Indian: Tribal Sovereignty and Industrial Civilization in Indian Territory, 1865–1907*. Norman: University of Oklahoma Press, 1976.

_____. *West of Wichita: Settling the High Plains of Kansas, 1865–1890.* Lawrence: University Press of Kansas, 1986.

Morgan, Dale L. *Jedediah Smith and the Opening of the West.* Indianapolis: Bobbs-Merrill, 1953.

Morn, Frank. *"The Eye That Never Sleeps": A History of the Pinkerton National Detective Agency.* Bloomington: Indiana University Press, 1982.

Morse, Jedediah. *A Report to the Secretary of War of the United States on Indian Affairs.* 1822; reprint, St. Claire Shores, MI: Scholarly Press, 1972.

Nasatir, Abraham P., ed. "Spanish Explorations of the Upper Missouri." *Mississippi Valley Historical Review* 14 (June 1927).

Nash, Gary B. *Red, White, and Black: The Peoples of Early America.* Englewood Cliffs, NJ: Prentice Hall, 1974.

Nash, Gerald D. *The American West in the Twentieth Century.* Albuquerque: University of New Mexico Press, 1973.

_____. *The American West Transformed: The Impact of the Second World War.* Bloomington: Indiana University Press, 1985.

_____. *World War II and the West: Reshaping the Economy.* Lincoln: University of Nebraska Press, 1990.

Nash, Gerald D., and Richard W. Etulain, eds. *The Twentieth-Century West: Historical Interpretations.* Albuquerque: University of New Mexico, 1989.

Nelson, Paul David. *Anthony Wayne: Soldier of the Early Republic.* Bloomington: Indiana University Press, 1985.

Nichols, David A. *Lincoln and the Indians: Civil War Policy and Politics.* Columbia: University of Missouri Press, 1978.

Nichols, Roger L. *Black Hawk and the Warrior's Path.* Arlington Heights: Harlan Davidson, 1992.

_____ ed. *The American Indian: Past and Present,* 5th edition. New York: McGraw Hill, 1999.

Nobles, Gregory H. *American Frontiers: Cultural Encounters and Continental Conquest.* New York: Hill and Wang, 1997.

Nugent, Walter. *Structures of American Social History.* Bloomington: Indiana University Press, 1981.

_____. "Frontiers and Empires in the Late Nineteenth Century." *Western Historical Quarterly* 20 (November 1989): 393–408.

Nuttall, Thomas. "Nuttall's Journal." *North American Review* 16 (1823): 59–76.

O'Donnell, J. H. "Alexander Mcgillivray: Training for Leadership, 1777–1783." *Georgia Historical Quarterly* 49 (1965): 172–186.

Overton, Richard C. *Burlington Route: A History of the Burlington Lines.* New York: Knopf, 1965.

Parker, Watson. *Gold in the Black Hills.* Norman: University of Oklahoma Press, 1966.

Parkman, Francis. *The Discovery of the Great West: La Salle,* 1879.

_____. *France and England in North America.* 2 vols. New York: Library of America, 1983.

Parman, Donald L. *Indians and the American West in the Twentieth Century.* Bloomington: Indiana University Press, 1994.

Parsons, Joseph A., Jr. "Civilizing the Indians of the Old Northwest, 1800–1810." *Indiana Magazine of History* 56 (September 1960): 195–216.

Pathways to the Old Northwest: An Observance of the Bicentennial of the Northwest Ordinance. Indianapolis: Indiana Historical Society, 1988.

Paul, Rodman W. *The Far West and Great Plains in Transition, 1859–1900.* Norman: University of Oklahoma Press, 1998.

_____. *Mining Frontiers of the Far West, 1848–1880.* New York: Holt, Reinhart, and Winston,1963.

Pearson, Edmund. *Dime Novels; or, Following an Old Trail in Popular Literature.* Boston: Little Brown, 1929.

Pearson, Jim Berry. *The Maxwell Land Grant.* Norman: University of Oklahoma Press, 1961.

Peavy, Charles D. *Larry McMurtry.* Boston: Twayne, 1977.

Peterson, Jacqueline. "Many Roads to Red River: Metis Genesis in the Great Lakes Region, 1680–1815." In *The New Peoples: Being and Becoming Metis in North America,* eds. Jacqueline Peterson and Jennifer S. H. Brown, 37–71. Lincoln: University of Nebraska Press, 1985.

Phillips, Paul Chrisler. *The Fur Trade.* 2 vols. Norman: University of Oklahoma Press, 1961.

Pomeroy, Earl. *The Pacific Slope: A History of California, Oregon, Washington, Idaho, Utah, and Nevada.* New York: Knopf, 1965.

Prucha, Francis Paul. *Broadax and Bayonet: The Role of the United States Army in the Development of the Northwest, 1815–1860.* Madison: State Historical Society of Wisconsin, 1953.

———. *American Indian Policy in the Formative Years: The Indian Trade and Intercourse Acts, 1790–1834.* Cambridge, MA: Harvard University Press, 1962.

———. *The Sword of the Republic: The United States Army on the Frontier, 1783–1846.* New York: Macmillan, 1969.

———. *The Great Father: The United States Government and the American Indians.* 2 vols. Lincoln: University of Nebraska Press, 1984.

———. *The Indians in American Society.* Berkeley: University of California Press, 1985.

Pyne, Stephen J. *Fire in America: A Cultural History of Wildland and Rural Fire.* Princeton, NJ: Princeton University Press, 1982.

Quaife, Milo Milton. *Chicago and the Old Northwest, 1673–1835.* Chicago: University of Chicago, 1913.

———. "A Diary of the War of 1812." *Mississippi Valley Historical Review* 1 (September 1914): 272–278.

Rafert, Stewart. *The Miami Indians of Indiana: A Persistent People, 1654–1994.* Indianapolis: Indiana Historical Society Press, 1996.

Rankin, Charles, ed. *Legacy: New Perspectives on the Battle of Little Bighorn.* Helena: Montana Historical Society, 1996.

Reagan, Ronald. *Ronald Reagan: An American Life.* New York: Pocket Books, 1990.

Redding, Paul. *Wild West Shows.* Urbana: University of Illinois Press, 1998.

Reid, John Philip. "Certainty of Justice: The Hudson's Bay Company and Retaliation in Kind against Indian Offenders in New Caledonia." *Montana* 43 (Winter 1993): 4–17.

———. "Principles of Vengeance: Fur Trappers, Indians, Retaliation for Homicide in the Transboundary North American West." *Western Historical Quarterly* 24 (February 1993): 21–43.

Reisner, Marc. *Cadillac Desert: The American West and Its Disappearing Water.* New York: Viking Press, 1986.

Remini, Robert V. *Andrew Jackson and the Course of American Democracy, 1833–1845.* New York. Harper and Row, 1984.

———. *Andrew Jackson and the Course of American Empire, 1767–1821.* New York: Harper and Row, 1977.

———. *Andrew Jackson and the Course of American Freedom, 1822–1832.* New York: Harper and Row, 1981.

Rich, E. E. *The History of the Hudson's Bay Company, 1670–1870.* 2 vols. London: Hudson's Bay Record Society, 1858–1859.

Rickey, Don, Jr. *$10 Horse, $40 Saddle*. Lincoln: University of Nebraska Press, 1976.

Ridge, Martin. "The American West: From Frontier to Region." *New Mexico Historical Review* 64 (April 1989): 125–141.

Riley, Glenda. *Women in the West*. Manhattan, KS: Sunflower University Press, 1982.

Rischin, Moses, and John Livingston, eds. *Jews of the American West*. Detroit: Wayne State University Press, 1991.

Robbins, William G. *Colony and Empire: The Capitalist Transformation of the American West*. Lawrence: University Press of Kansas, 1994.

Roberts, Bessie K. *Richardville: Chief of the Miamis*. Fort Wayne, IN: The Public Library of Fort Wayne and Allen County, n.d.

Robinson, Elwyn B. *History of North Dakota*. Lincoln: University of Nebraska Press, 1966.

Rolle, Andrew. *John Charles Fremont: Character as Destiny*. Norman: University of Oklahoma Press, 1991.

Ronda, James P., ed. *Thomas Jefferson and the Changing West*. Albuquerque: University of New Mexico Press, 1997.

Rosa, Joseph G. *Age of the Gunfighter: Men and Weapons on the Frontier, 1840–1900*. Norman: University of Oklahoma Press, 1995.

_____. *Wild Bill Hickock: The Man and His Myth*. Lawrence: University of Kansas Press, 1996.

Rouleau, Sister Mary Celeste, R.S.M. "The Miami Indians Prior to 1700." *Mid-America* 16 (April 1934): 225–234.

Russell, Don. *The Lives and Legends of Buffalo Bill*. Norman: University of Oklahoma Press, 1960.

Schiesl, Martin. "City Planning and the Federal Government in World War II: The Los Angeles Experience." *California History*. 58 (April 1979): 127–143.

Schlesinger, Arthur Jr., ed. *The History of American Presidential Elections*. New York: Chelsea House, 1971.

Schmeckebier, Laurence F. *Office of Indian Affairs; Its History, Activities, and Organization*. Baltimore: Johns Hopkins Press, 1927.

Schoolcraft, Henry R. *Information Respecting the History Conditions and Prospects of the Indian Tribes of the United States*. vol. 5. 6 vols. Philadelphia: J. B. Lippincott, 1856.

Schwartz, E.A. *The Rogue River Indian War and Its Aftermath, 1850–1980*. Norman: University of Oklahoma Press, 1997.

Schweikart, Larry. "Abraham Lincoln and the Growth of Government in the Civil War Era." *Continuity* 21 (Spring 1997): 25–42.

_____. *The Entrepreneurial Adventure: A History of Business in the United States.* Ft. Worth, TX: Harcourt, 2000.

_____. *A History of Banking in Arizona.* Tucson: University of Arizona Press, 1982.

_____, ed. *The Encyclopedia of American Business History and Biography: Banking and Finance to 1913.* New York: Facts on File, 1990.

_____, ed. *The Encyclopedia of American Business History and Biography: Banking and Finance, 1913–1989.* New York: Facts on File, 1990.

Settle, Raymond W., and Mary L. Settle. *War Drums and Wagon Wheels: The Story of Russell, Majors, and Waddell.* Lincoln: University of Nebraska Press, 1966.

Settle, William A. *Jesse James Was His Name.* Columbia: University of Missouri Press, 1966.

Shea, John Gilmary. "Indian Tribes of Wisconsin." *Wisconsin Historical Collections* 3 (1857).

Sheehan, Bernard. "Jefferson and the West." *Virginia Quarterly Review* 58 (1982): 345–352.

Sheehan, Bernard W. "Indian-White Relations in Early America: A Review Essay." *William & Mary Quarterly* 26 (April 1969): 267–286.

_____. "Paradise and the Noble Savage in Jeffersonian Thought." *William & Mary Quarterly* 26 (July 1969): 327–359.

_____. *Seeds of Extinction: Jeffersonian Philanthropy and the American Indian.* New York: W. W. Norton, 1973.

_____. "The American Indian as Victim." *The Alternative: An American Spectator* (January 1975).

_____. "Looking Back: Parkman's Pontiac." *Indiana Magazine of History* 92 (March 1996): 56–66.

_____. *The Ohio Country between the Years 1783 and 1815: Including Military Operations That Twice Saved to the United States the Country West of the Allegheny Mountains after the Revolutionary War.* New York: G. P. Putnam's Sons, 1910.

Simmons, Marc. *New Mexico: An Interpretative History.* Albuquerque: University of New Mexico Press, 1994.

Smelser, Marshall. *The Democratic Republic, 1801–1815.* New York: Harper and Row, 1968.

Smith, Dwight L. "Indian Land Cessions in the Old Northwest, 1795–1809." Dissertation, Indiana University, 1949.

Smith, Fay J., John Kessell, and F. J. Fox. *Father Kino in Arizona*. Phoenix: Arizona Historical Society, 1966.

Smith, Henry Nash. *Virgin Land: The American West as Symbol and Myth*. Cambridge, MA: Harvard University Press, 1950.

Smith, William Henry, ed. *The St. Clair Papers: The Life and Public Services of Arthur St. Clair*, vol. 2. Cincinnati: Robert Clarke, 1882.

Sonnichsen, C. L. *Roy Bean: Law West of the Pecos*. Albuquerque: University of New Mexico Press, 1986.

"St. Clair's Campaign." *Western Review and Miscellany Magazine*, (August 1820), 58–61.

Stewart, George R. *Ordeal by Hunger: The Story of the Donner Party*. New York: Henry Holt, 1936.

Stoll, Mark. *Protestantism, Capitalism, and Nature in America*. Albuquerque: University of New Mexico, 1997.

Sword, Wiley. *President Washington's Indian War: The Struggle for the Old Northwest, 1790–1795*. Norman: University of Oklahoma Press, 1985.

Taylor, Quintard. *In Search of the Racial Frontier: African Americans in the American West, 1528–1990*. New York: W. W. Norton, 1997.

Tefertiller, Casey. *Wyatt Earp: The Life Behind the Legend*. New York: John Wiley & Sons, 1997.

Temin, Peter. "Free Land and Federalism: A Synoptic View of American Economic History." *Journal of Interdisciplinary History* 21 (Winter 1991): 371–389.

Thomas, Robert. *Walt Disney: An American Original*. New York: Simon and Schuster, 1976.

Thompson, Charles N. *Sons of the Wilderness: John and William Conner*. Indianapolis: Indiana Historical Society, 1937.

Thompson, Leonard, and Howard Lamar, eds. *The Frontier in History: North America and Southern Africa Compared*. New Haven: Yale University Press, 1981.

Traub, Stuart H. "Rewards, Bounty Hunting, and Criminal Justice in the West, 1865–1900." *Western Historical Quarterly* 19 (August 1988): 387–301.

Trennert, Robert. *Alternative to Extinction: Federal Indian Policy and the Beginnings of a Reservation System, 1846–51*. Philadelphia: Temple University Press, 1975.

Turner, Frederick Jackson. *The Character and Influence of the Indian Trade in Wisconsin*. Baltimore, 1891.

_____. "The Diplomatic Contest for the Mississippi Valley." *Atlantic Monthly* (1904), 676–691, 807–817.

_____. *History, Frontier, and Section: Three Essays*. Martin Ridge, ed. Albuquerque: University of New Mexico Press, 1993.

Twohig, Dorothy, ed. *The Papers of George Washington*. Charlottesville: University of Virginia Press, 1987.

Unrau, William E. *Mixed-Bloods and Tribal Dissolution: Charles Curtis and the Quest for Indian Identity*. Lawrence: University of Kansas Press, 1989.

Unruh, John D., Jr. *The Plains Across: The Overland Emigrants and the Trans-Mississippi West, 1840–60*. Urbana: University of Illinois Press, 1979.

Utley, Robert M. *Billy the Kid: A Short and Violent Life*. Lincoln: University of Nebraska Press, 1989.

_____. *Cavalier in Buckskin: George Armstrong Custer and the Western Military Frontier*. Norman: University of Oklahoma Press, 1988.

_____. *High Noon in Lincoln: Violence on the Western Frontier*. Albuquerque: University of New Mexico Press, 1987.

_____. *Frontier Regulars: The United States Army and the Indian, 1848–1865*. New York: Macmillan, 1967.

_____. *The Lance and the Shield: The Life and Times of Sitting Bull*. New York: Henry Holt, 1993.

_____. *The Indian Frontier of the American West, 1846–1890*. Albuquerque: University of New Mexico Press, 1984.

van West, Carol. *Capitalism on the Frontier: Billings and Yellowstone Valley in the Nineteenth Century*. Lincoln: University of Nebraska Press, 1993.

Vaughan, Alden T. "From White Man to Redskin: Changing Anglo-American Perceptions of the American Indian." *American Historical Review* 87 (October 1982): 917–953.

Wagner, Henry R. *Spanish Voyages to the Northwest Coast of America in the Sixteenth Century*. San Francisco: California Historical Society, 1929.

Wallace, Anthony F. C. "Political Organization and Land Tenure among the Northeastern Indians, 1600–1830." *Southwestern Journal of Anthropology* 13 (1957): 301–321.

Wallace, Paul A. W., ed. *Thirty Thousand Miles with John Heckewelder*. Pittsburgh: University of Pittsburgh Press, 1958.

Walsh, Margaret, ed. *The American Frontier Revisited*. London: Macmillan, 1981.

Way, Royal B. "The United States Factory System for Trading with the Indians, 1796–1822." *Mississippi Valley Historical Review* 6 (September 1919): 220–35.

Webb, Walter Prescott. *The Great Plains*. Lincoln: University of Nebraska Press, 1981.

Weber, David J. *The Mexican Frontier, 1821–1846: The American Southwest under Mexico*. Albuquerque: University of New Mexico Press, 1982.

_____. *Myth and History of the Hispanic Southwest*. Albuquerque: University of New Mexico Press, 1988.

_____. *The Spanish Frontier in North America*. New Haven: Yale University Press, 1992.

Weigley, Russell. *A History of the United States Army*. Bloomington: Indiana University Press, 1984.

Wells, William. "Indian Manner and Customs." *Western Review and Miscellany Magazine* (February, March, April, May 1820): 45–49, 110–112, 160–163, 201–204.

Wesley, Edgar B. "The Government Factory System among the Indians, 1795–1822." *Journal of Economic and Business History* 4 (1931–1932): 487–511.

West, Elliott. *Growing up with the Country: Childhood on the Far Western Frontier*. Albuquerque: University of New Mexico Press, 1989.

_____. *The Way to the West: Essays on the Central Plains*. Albuquerque: University of New Mexico Press, 1995.

_____. *The Contested Plains: Indians, Goldseekers, and the Rush to Colorado*. Lawrence: University Press of Kansas, 1998.

Wexler, Alan. *Atlas of Westward Expansion*. New York: Facts on File, 1995.

White, Richard. *"It's Your Misfortunate and None of My Own": A New History of the American West*. Norman: University of Oklahoma Press, 1991.

_____. *The Middle Ground: Indians, Empires, and Republics in the Great Lakes Region, 1650–1815*. New York: Cambridge University Press, 1991.

_____. *The Roots of Dependency: Subsistence, Environment, and Social Change among the Choctaw, Pawnees, and Navajos*. Lincoln: University of Nebraska Press, 1983.

Williams, Michael. *Americans and Their Forests: A Historical Geography*. Cambridge: Cambridge University Press, 1989.

Wilson, Terry P. *The Underground Reservation: Osage Oil*. Lincoln: University of Nebraska Press, 1985.

Winger, Otho. *The Last of the Miamis.* North Manchester, IN, 1935.

Woehrman, Paul. *At the Headwaters of the Maumee: A History of the Forts of Fort Wayne.* Indianapolis: Indiana Historical Society, 1971.

Worster, Donald. *Dust Bowl: Rivers of Empire: Water, Aridity, and the Growth of the American West.* New York: Pantheon Books, 1985.

_____. *The Southern Plains in the 1930s.* New York: Oxford University Press, 1979.

_____. *Under Western Skies: Nature and History in the American West.* New York: Oxford University Press, 1992.

Worster, Donald, et al. "The Legacy of Conquest, by Patricia Nelson Limerick: A Panel of Appraisal." *Western Historical Quarterly* (August 1989): 303–322.

Wunder, John. *Historians of the American Frontier: a Bio-Bibliographical Sourcebook.* New York: Greenwork, 1988.

Yee, Paul. "A Chinese Business in Early Vancouver." *BC Studies* (Spring–Summer 1986).

Young, Mary. "The Cherokee Nation: Mirror of the Republic." *American Quarterly* 33 (Winter 1981): 502–525.

Young, Mary E. "The Dark and Bloody but Endless Inventive Middle Ground of Indian Frontier Historiography." *Journal of the Early Republic* 13 (Summer 1993): 193–205.